THE NEW ANATOMY OF BRITAIN

ANTHONY SAMPSON

THE NEW ANATOMY OF BRITAIN

STEIN AND DAY/*Publishers*/New York

First published in the United States of America by
Stein and Day / *Publishers* 1972
Copyright © 1971 by Anthony Sampson
Diagrams © 1971 by Hodder and Stoughton
Library of Congress Catalog Card No. 78-186150
All rights reserved
Printed in the United States of America
Stein and Day / *Publishers* / 7 East 48 Street, New York, N.Y. 10017
ISBN 8128-1456-8

Heirs to a society which had over-invested in an empire, and surrounded by the increasingly shabby remnants of a dwindling inheritance, they could not bring themselves at a moment of crisis to surrender their memories and alter the antique pattern of their lives. At a time when the face of Europe was altering more rapidly than ever before, the country that had once been its leading power proved to be lacking the essential ingredient for survival—the willingness to change.

J. H. Elliott: *Imperial Spain*,
p. 378.

Contents

———

PART

TWO

BACKGROUNDS

Contents

PART

FOUR

COMMUNICATIONS

PART

FIVE

FINANCE

Contents

PART
SIX

INDUSTRY

Diagrams

[1] MICHAEL McGUINNESS
[2] NEWSOM REPORT

xiii

Introduction

THIS is the third *Anatomy of Britain*. The first was in 1962, in the middle of the age of Macmillan; the second was in 1965, at the beginning of the Wilson era; and this book has been written during the first year of Heath's government. I have been planning it for the past three years, but I have waited for a new prime minister— with all the scene-changing that it entails—to put it into shape. It has turned out in the end to be really a completely new book, with (as far as I can calculate) only about one sixth left of the original—the unchanging relics of earlier ages, including bits of the Palace, the House of Lords, the City, and Sir Alec Douglas-Home who is once again foreign secretary. For the rest, the new scene has required complete re-writing, with a new perspective. How far it is Britain that has changed, how far it is myself, I can never be sure: I am conscious that, being now the same age as many of the people I write about, my approach may be less romantic, and more sceptical. (It is difficult to take altogether seriously someone one has been at school with.) But there are certainly great changes and the style of Heath's Britain seems different enough for the Age of Macmillan to be now the subject of nostalgia. There is a saying in Whitehall that 'only the names have changed'; but many of the new figures in British life are symbolic (I believe) of a real change of attitude. Such people as Sir William Armstrong, Jim Slater, Anthony Barber, Richard Marsh, Lord Goodman, Peter Walker, Rupert Murdoch, had hardly appeared over the horizon at the beginning of the sixties. More important than new faces are new perspectives; at the beginning of the sixties such words as environment, consumers, ecology, participation, permissiveness, feedback—let alone the four-letter words—were hardly muttered in polite society. Now the environment has its own department, every one is a consumer, and participation is the small change of politicians' weekend speeches. The white-hot technological revolution has come and gone, and the phrase, 'the Rolls-Royce of . . .' has acquired an ominous second meaning.

I aim, as before, to take the reader on a guided tour of the galleries of power, with digressions and interludes on the way, in search of the answers to the question: who runs Britain? But I have felt it necessary to alter the order of the tour: I now begin, not with the aristocrats and the palace, but in the central lobby of parliament, trying to observe Britain from the point of view of the ordinary constituents and the ordinary MP; from there I follow the trail of power up the political ladder, to the prime minister and the new Tory party. In Part 2 I pass to the changing backgrounds of the elites, in education and upbringing, with a long chapter on the universities, the changing-rooms of ambitious careers. In Part 3 I resume the search for power through the intricate world of the bureaucracies—trying (like many MPs) to perceive ways of countering their secrecy and power, and inspecting the fragile relationship between the government and ordinary citizen—a relationship which reaches a critical point with the police, to which I devote a special chapter.

The bureaucracies are followed by their traditional enemies (or should-be enemies) the media of communications. I give them now greater attention, both because they interest me personally, and because (I believe) their role and their own structure becomes more important as other institutions become more vulnerable to them; in the sixties all institutions—except perhaps the legal profession—have become more exposed to the public gaze, more concerned to establish themselves, like the army and the police, as 'a social service'. I devote more space to the influence of advertising, exploiting my advantage of writing in a medium which does not depend on it; I also add a new chapter on the Arts and Leisure, because the arts and the 'quality of life' are increasingly involved with party policies.

In the last parts I move to the interlocking worlds of finance and industry (themselves increasingly involved with government), searching for the connections between ownership and control, and for whom to blame for Britain's poor economic performance; and concluding with the workers on whom the economy ultimately depends—following the trails of power where they disappear out of sight among the tens of thousands of shop-stewards and shop-floors.

Throughout the book I try to develop themes which are common to several institutions and chapters. Many of the themes that seemed most prominent in 1962—the battles between amateurs and professionals, the dominance of Oxbridge or public schools, the gap between prestige and power—seem now less dominating, or at least less clear-cut. Others now seem more pressing: the growing resentments of We against Them, of ordinary citizens against centralised bureaucracies; the difficulties of counterbalancing commercial values, and the search for an alternative society among a new generation; the conflict between the aggressive agents of economic growth, and the defenders of the environment; the coming together of government and industry and the return to mercantilism; and above all the increasing interdependence of Britain with the rest of Europe, and the effect on her institutions. All through the book I have tried to place Britain in a European perspective, making use of the experience in writing my previous book, *The New Europeans*. In the last chapter (which some may prefer to read first) I try to pull together the recurring themes, to assess Britain's position compared to her European neighbours, and to sum up my findings about the structure of power.

This book, of its nature, is concerned with the centralised regions of power; and though I try to indicate where decisions, as it were, go off the map, I cannot pursue them there, for in each geographical area the problems are different. I have thus not felt able to look at the huge problems of regionalism, and particularly of Northern Ireland; or the whole territory of local government, justices of the peace, parish councils or community development. The limitations of this kind of survey will be evident; I have tried to catch a moment of contemporary history on a very large canvas. In my first edition I described the task as being like painting the

Forth Bridge; if I had spent longer on it, the beginning would have become rusty by the time I reached the other end; now the bridge seems longer, and the painter perhaps slower. But I hope the result will be useful to those who (like myself), find themselves both bewildered and fascinated by the examination of power and its practitioners.

My debts, as before, have been very great; I have picked brains remorselessly. Inside many of the centres of power, I have made much use of correspondents who will prefer to remain anonymous, who have provided their own critiques, which I have often incorporated into the book. I have tried to convey the character of several institutions in terms of their style and particularly their language, what might be called 'the linguistics of power'; I am specially grateful to Sir William Armstrong, the Head of the civil service, for arranging for me to spend a week working inside the Civil Service Department, overhearing committees and meetings as a licensed spy.

For specific research, I am grateful to Elizabeth Cohen for arduous work on facts and figures, particularly on schools, universities and trades unions; to Mrs Bridget Cash for research on agriculture; to Mrs Carol Howard for research on honours. For seeing the book through the press, I owe a great debt to Jane Osborn of Hodder and Stoughton, for her patience and speed in deciphering the palimpsests of corrections and last-minute changes. For advice and corrections all through the book, I have leant heavily on my friend and colleague Ivan Yates, with his massive knowledge of the details of the power structure; and also on Virginia Makins, who since helping with the first *Anatomy* has shown a practised eye for detecting nonsense. My publisher Robin Denniston, as with all my previous books, has given invaluable advice. Robert Urwin, who indexed the previous *Anatomies* has again produced a comprehensive index in very short time. Michael McGuinness has transformed facts and statistics into diagrams, and re-designed the end-papers. Most of all I am grateful to my assistant Alexa Wilson, for seeing the book through every stage from scribbles to proofs, for research, checking and advice, and for miraculously producing order out of chaos.

We have taken pains to corroborate facts. But I am conscious that mistakes still creep in, and I will be grateful, as with the earlier books, to anyone who points them out, however angrily, for correction in later editions.

PART

ONE

———

Politics

I

Parliament

The ordinary man in Great Britain has been spending his life for the last couple of generations in this will o' the wisp pursuit of power, trying to get his hands on the levers of big policy, and trying to find out where it is, and how it was that his life was shaped for him by somebody else.

Aneurin Bevan (attacking Eden over the Cairo Conference),
December 1943.

You have not a perception of the first elements in this matter till you know that government by a *club* is a standing wonder.

Walter Bagehot, 1872.

THE most significant frontier of the House of Commons is not the debating chamber, where the parties play their games without reference to the world outside. It is that high gothic hall called the central lobby where the ordinary public—the schoolchildren, the old couples up from the country, the delegations, the tourists— wait to visit their members of parliament, to bring complaints or worries, to find a seat in the gallery, or to see for themselves the heart of democracy. It is here that the representatives meet with the represented, across the gap between the great inside and the great outside.

The setting is heavy with atmosphere: history is pressed down on the visitor as he walks up the long passage past marble prime ministers and painted scenes of the monarchs, until he comes into the vaulted hall itself with mosaics of the four saints of the United Kingdom looking down on him, and sculpted kings, crowns and coats-of-arms crammed into every niche. An ornate ecclesiastical chandelier hangs from the centre, establishing an atmosphere of reverence, like a cathedral. Policemen in helmets guard the four corners of the hall, and messengers in white ties scurry to and fro. To the right the lobby leads to the House of Lords; to the left to the members' lobby and the Commons; and straight on,

3

into the committee rooms, the dining-rooms and the terrace. The awed visitors fill in their green application cards with the policeman, and sit round the edges of the hall, waiting for their members, watching the flow of peers, MPs, officials and tourists through this eccentric cross-roads.

Then the member comes in sight, ambling out from the House of Commons with the loose lope of people accustomed to walk long distances on stone floors; he chats with the policeman, the name of the visitor is called, and the member strides up to him with a sudden transformation of expression—arm outstretched, face beaming to welcome this single voter, this sixty-thousandth part of his electorate. There is perhaps a great pumping hand-shake, a joke, a quick laugh, a how-good-of-you-to-come, a what-can-I-do-for-you, a what-about-some-tea; and the visitor is steered into the hallowed regions, past still more policemen, marble prime ministers and venerable paintings, into the tea-room, the bar, or the gallery of the chamber itself. The business is dealt with, the complaint taken note of, the splendours of parliament explained; then a division bell rings, or a new name is announced on the television screen, or another MP hoves in sight; the member must go and listen, or vote, or go into com-mittee. Another quick handshake, a can-you-find-your-way-out-of-this-maze, and the member lopes off again, back into the recesses of his gothic club.

The architecture and the image of democracy are both Vic-torian; both date back to that golden age of parliament, in the eighteen-fifties and sixties, when the debating chamber was at its most dramatic, when members had the wealth and independence to say and vote as they thought, when they could make and break governments, in the brief interim between the decline of the monarchs and the rise of the parties. Parliaments did not then have to compete with mass newspapers or television, and the notion of parliament as a club, taking over the role of the monarch, seemed itself a sufficient triumph of democracy. In the following century, the Victorian structure survived with apparent resilience the inroads of mass voters, mass parties, mass media. Parliament has not been visibly threatened or undermined by them: it has gone on confidently talking, debating, voting and legislating. What threatens it (and other institutions) is not outright hostility or showdown; but the gradual erosion of its relevance and its position at the centre of events and debate.

Q. Why?

4

Once inside the chamber the visitor, looking down from the gallery, sees his MP in his own habitat, as if coming suddenly upon a pride of lions in their own lair, overheard as if no one were watching. It is like a big club drawing-room with the ceiling removed, so that outsiders can peer down. The smallness of the room—only sixty-eight feet long—is its most astonishing feature: on a crowded day the members squeeze up against each other on the long green benches as if in overcrowded railway carriages. The scene is miraculously insulated from the bustle outside it; like a compounding of all those remote half-forgotten rituals—of school chapels, college dining halls, law courts or funerals—where men defy their workaday surroundings. On a hot summer afternoon only a few shafts of daylight come through from the narrow windows.

More than anything the chamber evokes memories of a school— an eccentric superannuated school whose ageing members have never quite been able to leave. As they stroll in through the swing-doors from the lobby, bowing gravely to the Speaker, standing chatting to the sergeant-at-arms, then lolling on the benches with their legs intertwined, they seem to have kept intact the mannerisms of school prefects who have been given their own study. As they bob up at the end of a speech to catch the Speaker's eye, as if to say '*please*, sir'; as they bay and wave order-papers, shout 'shame' or 'hear, hear', it is hard to remember that a few years ago—or even that same morning—these people were accountants, company directors or even trade unionists, working in ordinary offices outside in the city. The young-old faces and expressions of the most pompous of them seem uncannily reminiscent of those school bores whom everyone once teased. (Isn't that—it can't be—yes it *is*—it's old Smuggins!) On its dullest days the house sounds like a federation of bores who, having been ignored and blackballed by the world outside, have finally found their resting place in a club which has a tacit bargain: if I listen to you, you must listen to me.

Talk is their business, and how they talk! They talk apparently to no one. They address this house, or the right honourable member, or Mr. Speaker, Sir; but Mr. Speaker is chatting to a passing member, the right honourable member left half an hour ago, and this house has just realised it's time for a drink, and is emptying quickly through the swing-doors. But never mind, the words still roll out; and the dedicated parliamentarians seem able

5

to subsist on a diet of motions, amendments and words—resounding and reassuring words, unsullied by ordinary usage; we are seeking, striving, asserting, deeming, deliberating, not shrinking from, taking cognisance of, not gainsaying; we are dealing not merely with taxes and subsidies, but imposts and subventions. The words roll on through the long afternoon—forty thousand of them perhaps in a day, enough for two long plays. The Speaker sits under his canopy, while his name is taken in vain, looking at his papers, his long wig flapping like the ears of an elderly bloodhound.

Meanwhile on the government front bench, chatting or reclining with their feet up on the table, can sometimes be seen the men to whom the talk is really addressed—the heads of the departments of state, who alone can change policy. The visitor soon becomes aware that there is not only a wide gap between himself and the members: there is a gap almost as wide between the ordinary members and the government. Every afternoon, except Fridays, from 2.30 to 3.30 a few of the ministers answer questions. Is the right honourable member aware that? Is he further aware? Does he realise? Does he not comprehend? Will he say what action is being taken? Will he make a statement? Is he satisfied? Yes, says the minister, reading his civil servants' answers from his folder; he *is* aware, he *does* realise, he *has* taken action, assessed the figures, borne in mind the consequences, balanced the forces. The honourable member will appreciate, this house will be kept fully informed, Her Majesty's government is deeply concerned.

The member has done his bit. His question and answer will be reported back to his constituents. But does the minister *really* comprehend, will he *really* take action? Can one man, the sole connection between the elected representatives and their government, be relied on to translate words into actions? Can one man, who was only recently an ordinary member of parliament, know and care so much about such a vast range of questions? And can all that hot air be transformed, as if in a steam engine, into pistons and levers which actually turn wheels?

In setting off for this will o' the wisp pursuit of power, there can be no better starting point than the House of Commons. The member of parliament, however much he may be aware of his unimportance, still tries to place himself in the centre of some kind of web. From parliament he can survey, if he cannot control, the criss-cross threads of British power and institutions which make up the matter of this book.

It has become a commonplace that parliament has lost its power; but the very word power raises questions of definition which recur through this tour. Does it mean the ability to impose conditions, to dominate other institutions, to reflect and magnify opinion, or to create an atmosphere in which other men can reach decisions? There is much debate as to how far the British parliament *ever* had the kind of powers which are now expected of it: 'If those who complain that parliament is losing its authority and influence would take the pains to enquire,' wrote Enoch Powell, 'they would find that at no time for which there are records has that complaint not been heard.'[1] The contemporary laments are often mixed with nostalgia for the most glamorous period in the mid-nineteenth century.[2]

But in the course of this century, with two world wars, the multiplication of the civil service and the strengthening hold of the political parties, the influence and standing of parliament have seemed to most members to be more seriously threatened. The worry was summed up in September 1966 by Richard Crossman, then Leader of the House of Commons, who tried (with very limited success) to reform it:

> The authority of the house has declined, is declining, and will continue to decline unless we take active steps to stop it . . . Procedurally we still behave as though we were still a sovereign body which really shares control of the legislative programme with the government. . . . The ordinary elector is completely baffled by the gap between the way the parliamentary system is supposed to work and the way it actually works. It is that gap which is largely responsible for the decline in the prestige of the house.

In theory and in law the six hundred and thirty members have absolute sovereignty. They can cross-examine civil servants, imprison editors, ordain that black is white. The judges are waiting to interpret their laws, the civil servants to administer them. But

[1] Enoch Powell: Essay in *Rebirth of Britain*, 1964, p. 258.

[2] For contemporary assessments of this 'golden age of parliament', see R. H. S. Crossman: *Introduction to Bagehot's English Constitution* (Fontana edition), p. 97. Ronald Butt, in his book *The Power of Parliament* (Chapter 2), suggests that parliament was less powerful in this period than it looks. But John Mackintosh, in his *British Cabinet* (2nd edition, p. 613), confirms Crossman's picture: 'In that half century, the House of Commons sacked cabinets, it removed individual ministers, it forced the government to disclose information, it set up select committees to carry out investigations and frame Bills and it rewrote government Bills on the floor of the House.'

in practice the sovereignty of parliament gets lost in the intricate labyrinths of power that surround it: and the ordinary citizen, trying to find 'how his life is shaped for him by someone else', finds himself like the member of parliament, in the midst of a maze with no centre.

MEMBERS OF PARLIAMENT

For several centuries the dream of English youth and manhood of the nation-forming class has remained unchanged; it has been fixed and focused on the House of Commons, a modified, socialised arena for battle, drive and dominion.

Sir Lewis Namier, 1928.[1]

The member of parliament is still the critical single link in the democratic chain between the constituency and the country, between the rulers and the ruled. He is a frail link. By the nature of his job the member is the personification of the amateur principle, which runs so persistently through the fabric of English life. He is the chosen representative of ordinary men; he should be able to react as his electors do, to sense their own problems and speak their language. Yet at the same time, he is expected to grapple with all the complex problems of politics and government, technology and economics, to understand anything. The House of Commons includes both extremes—men who can master highly specialised subjects (like Anthony Crosland) but with little common touch; and men who typify the plain man's view (like Sir Gerald Nabarro) but are bored by the technicalities of government. Corporately the House of Commons cannot escape from the tension at the heart of any democracy: six hundred men must be the links between the ignorance of the electors and the specialisation of government.

The amateur principle still governs the organisation of the house. It operates for only about thirty-two weeks a year, with a break for twelve weeks from August till mid-October—longer holidays than any other profession except dons. The chamber sits from 2.30 to 10.30 p.m. (or later) from Mondays to Thursdays, and from 11 a.m. to 4.30 p.m. on Fridays, which can often be cut: the morning is kept for committees, which many members do not bother with. Much of its life is nocturnal, a fact which contributes to the oddity of MPs. Often at 9.45 p.m., a frequent time for

[1] *The Structure of Politics at the Accession of George III*, Macmillan, p. 1.

8

divisions, MPs have to rush from their dinner parties to vote in the house. (Wealthier members favour houses in the 'division bell district', within five minutes' fast driving from the Commons.)

And the amateur principle until recently guided MPs' attitude to their own salaries. It was not until 1911, when Lloyd George proposed £400 a year, that members were paid at all: the wage went up to £600 in 1937, to £1,000 in 1945, and to £1,750 in 1957. Then in 1963 a committee was appointed under Sir Geoffrey Lawrence which reported that members without other incomes were 'forced to endure the discomfort, in spite of tax relief, of cheap and shabby lodgings in London; they cannot afford to use the members' dining-room; they have to submit to the humiliation of not being able to return hospitality even at the most modest level of entertainment'. The government agreed in 1964 that members should be paid £3,250, with £1,250 of it allowable as expenses—a salary which (unlike any other) has not been increased since. In addition, members are given an allowance of £500 a year for secretarial expenses, and are allowed such perks as free telephone calls to the rest of London; free first-class travel to their constituency; a car allowance; and free House of Commons writing paper.

The new salaries implied that members should nowadays be regarded as full-time employees, not as half-time amateurs with proper jobs outside. But the House of Commons still has a fundamental confusion—a very understandable one—as to whether it should consist of amateurs or professionals, or a mixture of both. The accommodation for members is slightly less primitive than it was ten years ago: but it is still operated on the assumption that members should not base themselves on the building. They have to share tiny offices with other members, many of them right outside the palace, in a ramshackle building above the tube station, or down Whitehall. In the palace of Westminster itself most of the eight hundred and fifty offices are occupied by the ministers, officials, law officers, clerks, or the minions of the sergeant-at-arms. The more fortunate MPs have been found rooms in towers or cloisters, up side staircases and down draughty passages, as if they were junior vergers in this rambling cathedral: their secretaries type wherever they can, and try vainly to get numbers on the overloaded telephone exchange.

The House of Commons periodically debates whether the palace should be extended or rebuilt to provide proper offices: the current scheme is for a six-storey building to go up opposite the palace, across from Big Ben, to double the available office space. The argument involves much more than costs and traditions; it is about two opposite methods of living and working. On the one hand is the club-like, collegiate life, with members jostling against each other, creating a palpable atmosphere, where moods can loom and disperse like clouds, where no one can come or go without sensing the 'feeling of the house'; on the other hand is the cellular, atomised organisation of offices, secretaries and telephones, which deals with memoranda and messages instead of talk. No one can doubt that the Palace of Westminster is archaic, incompetent and overcrowded. But the modern office-type alternatives, like the bleak new Bundeshaus in Bonn, can easily replace one kind of inefficiency with a worse one. Democratic politics needs the pressure of propinquity.

And behind this debate, the question remains unresolved: Does parliament *want* its members to be full-time professionals? In the last few years many more members have begun to use the house as an office in the mornings, sitting on committees or answering letters. Fewer members use the dining-room, which serves meals at hotel hours, and more take a bite when they can in the cafeteria and tea-room, which are always open during debates. The House of Commons has become a more serious and studious place: younger members are eager-beavering away in their offices, reading white papers, green papers, blue books, researching in the library (which has much improved, with intelligent graduate girls as researchers). The debates themselves are much better informed, with formidable arguments on both sides. But many members are very unsure how far this has really improved the democratic process. As one Tory backbencher, Richard Hornby, put it to me:

> Members have certainly become better informed and more specialised in the last ten years. But at the same time I think the house has declined as a market-place; the smoking-room is emptier, there's less chatting and standing about; so that it's harder now to organise a faction, or for the whips to sound out opinion. Since 1964 the Labour benches have become more intellectual, and the Tories have become more executive; but they miss the old anchor-men, who knew their own area and their duty, and had real roots in the country; there was a lot that they knew nothing about, but what they knew in their bloodstream they knew very well. The dialogue nowadays is more sophisticated and knowledgeable about the contemporary problems,

but I think the dialogue between the representative and the represented is thinner. The house seems to be becoming more remote from
ordinary people, and the electorate at the same time are becoming
more unpredictable. I think the remoteness is a factor, for instance, in
people's suspicions of Brussels, or of local government reforms.

The cut-offness of parliament from its electorate is not helped
by the oddity of its membership. Parliamentarians often boast that
they are a kind of microcosm of Britain, with experts on any
subject; the members include one duke's son, twenty mine-
workers, ten doctors, and five railway workers. In theory anyone
can become a member except for aliens, minors, non-dissenting
clergy, lunatics, judges, civil servants, peers, bankrupts, felons and
candidates caught cheating at elections. But parliament has never
contained anything like a cross-section of the population, and by
the mysterious distillations of democracy the representative
system throws up very non-representative people—barristers,
teachers, communicators, company directors. These were the
leading occupations of members in 1970 and 1964:[1]

		1970	*1964*
Conservatives:	Company directors	107	83
	Barristers	56	64
	Farmers and landowners	40	43
	Journalists, writers and broadcasters	35	31
	Regular forces	—	16
Labour:	Teachers and lecturers	56	46
	Trade union officials	34	43
	Journalists, writers and broadcasters	25	40
	Barristers	34	32
	Colliery workers	20	21

Many barristers have long ceased to practise, and a farmer can
mean anyone from a large landowner to a retired businessman
living on a few acres. But the figures show a massive lopsidedness
in the house. Ninety-three of the 630 members (including Liberals)
are barristers, and 110 are company directors. There are sixty
journalists and broadcasters, but only twenty-two engineers and
seven accountants.

The educational background is equally unbalanced. It is true
that there are now only 65 Etonians (a tenth of the house)
compared to 68 in 1964, and nine Harrovians instead of 17. There
are many fewer public-school men in the house (191 compared to
285) and a few more grammar-school men (145 compared to 135).

[1] From *The Times* Guide to the House of Commons, 1964 and 1970.

But the number of Oxbridge graduates has increased from 228 in 1964 to 250 in 1970, and two-thirds of the house are now graduates.

The most striking change has been in the number of teachers, from 52 in 1964 to 65 in the 1970 election—nearly all of them Labour. 'This has happened through a combination of solid change and political cunning,' commented the parliament-watcher Andrew Roth: 'The educational ladder into teaching is the most readily available for the bright boy from the working-class. Once in the profession he makes an excellent candidate for a marginal seat; he can appeal both to the working-class of his parents and the white-collar professional class into which he has graduated.'[1] There was also an in-rush of university academics after the 1966 election, which had a special interest; dons transformed into back-benchers could observe the contrast between the theory and practice of government, and they did so with loud disillusion. Having studied the making and breaking of governments, they found themselves sitting on the benches, traipsing through the division lobby without anyone apparently wanting more than their unthinking support for the party. But the complaints of 'the professors' have not been sympathetically heard by the seasoned members, who maintain that parliament has more subtle and tribal functions than to provide a useful job of work, and that politics is not a science but an art.

SPEAKER AND RITUAL

The mystique of parliament is deliberately maintained by what Sir Ivor Jennings called 'The Importance of Being Ancient'. The emphasis on tradition and formality may give it stability, and soften the conflicts between the parties, like tennis-players shaking hands after losing. But it can also bolster the impression that parliament has a meaning quite apart from its functions and powers. There is always something unconvincing about members of parliament themselves being unable to modernise their own procedures, yet urging the modernisation of Britain. In the words of William Hamilton, MP, after one state opening of parliament:

> We must resolve that never again must we tolerate the pantomime, the irrelevant time-wasting slap-stick of the last few days, the time for the fancy dress, for the walking backwards, for the ridiculous ritual dances that we experienced last week. The time for all that has gone.

[1] Andrew Roth: *The MPs Chart, Parliamentary Profiles 1966–7.*

The silly parading of black rods, gold sticks, red dragons, and purple robes—all this nonsense must go. How can we seriously ask the unions and managements to modernise, get rid of restrictive practices, and increase productivity if we continue to work to feudal rules and go-slow and stop productivity as we did for most of last week?

The focus of ritual is the Speaker, and the day begins at 2.30 p.m. with the words 'Speaker in the Chair' being shouted through the lobbies; whereupon the Speaker walks in wearing a full-bottomed wig and sits down on the throne (made in Australia). He is the symbol of parliament's independence since 1694, when members were first able to elect their own Speaker, and since 1839, when Speaker Shaw-Lefevre was elected, he has been aloof from any political involvement. He is chosen primarily as a man trusted and liked by his colleagues: 'All Speakers are highly successful,' wrote Lord Rosebery; 'All Speakers are deeply regretted and are generally announced to be irreplaceable. But a Speaker is soon found, and found, almost invariably, among the mediocrities of the House.' Having been chosen, he is carefully segregated: he lives in a big gothic house inside the Palace of Westminster, earns £8,500 a year, and retires with a peerage and a pension. He is the 'first Commoner', the only subject who can hold his own levees, and can insist on court dress. It is a job which requires a special temperament—phlegmatic but firm. The last Speaker, Horace King, when he was elected in 1965 recalled that nine Speakers had been executed, two of them on the same day: 'I know that in the chequered history of the Speakership there were knavish figures like Trevor and Empson, odd ones like Hanmer, who was the worst editor Shakespeare ever had, and Fletcher Norton, who sent for a pint of porter from time to time as he sat on the chair.' Many Speakers since have been driven to drink.

In January 1971, when Horace King retired, the favoured candidate was Selwyn Lloyd, who had been Foreign Secretary and Chancellor of the Exchequer in Macmillan's government; Macmillan purged him in 1962, when he retired to the back-benches and loyally worked as a 'good House of Commons man', until Sir Alec Douglas-Home brought him back for a year into the cabinet. Some controversy greeted the nomination of an ex-minister who had been involved in Suez and the pay-pause: William Hamilton complained that 'the house is going through the farce of electing a Speaker, but whatever the theory, the fact is that this has been fixed and decided on by the front benches'. But Lloyd was elected by 294 votes to 55, and he duly according to protocol presented himself to the House of Lords with all humility for Her Majesty's gracious approbation, which Her Majesty was pleased to grant. The familiar features of the once much-mocked Foreign Secretary—the beak-nose, the overlapping lip and the high forehead—are now disguised by the full-bottomed wig, the badge of judicial impartiality.

It is the Speaker's main job to keep fair play between the parties and between back benches and front benches, and to protect the house from outside influences: and this can justify much of the pomp. He insists that MPs call each other 'honourable members',[1] bow to him on entering and leaving, and address all their speeches to him. But all too often the Speaker's role degenerates into having to control childish squabbles. The House of Commons is always more likely to become passionate and over-excited when discussing its own rules and behaviour. The question of parliamentary language can waste a great deal of time. The Speaker has to forbid 'grossly insulting language'; past Speakers have disallowed the words villain, hypocrite, murderer, insulting dog, swine, pecksniffian cant, cheat, stool-pigeon, and bastard. The current record-holder for parliamentary misbehaviour is Andrew Faulds, the Labour member for Smethwick. In 1968 he was ordered to contain himself six times, to control himself three times, to learn to behave twice, to allow others to express opinions once; and his abuse included 'shoddy little man', 'whited sepulchre', 'shocking little man' and 'little giggler, go back to Roedean'.[2]

LOBBYING

Whom exactly does a member of parliament represent? He is elected by his constituency as 'their member', but once in parliament his loyalties soon become divided between his constituency, his party, and very often also some sectional interest which is his

---

[1] Any accomplished parliamentarian knows that the word 'honourable' can add edge to insults, as in Aneurin Bevan's remark about Neville Chamberlain: 'The worst thing I can say about democracy is that it has tolerated the right honourable gentleman for four and a half years.'

[2] For an anthology of recent parliamentary bad language, see E. S. Turner: *Punch*, December 18, 1968.

special concern. Some members owe their election to parliament to a trade union; others accept paid positions to become spokesmen for interest groups, as James Callaghan was once the paid spokesman of the police federation.

'Pressure group' used to be a bogy-phrase, and the ideal member was assumed to be insulated from pressures except those of his conscience and his party. But as lobbying has increased and come into the open, so the pressure groups have become accepted and sometimes even welcomed as a legitimate part of parliamentary democracy. (The changed attitude is apparent elsewhere too: in the post-war Federal Constitution in West Germany, pressure groups were deliberately brought into the process of consultation before legislation.) Lobbyists and public relations men have become part of the network of Westminster, closely studied and assessed by political scientists. 'Their day-to-day activities,' wrote Professor Finer, a pioneer lobby-watcher, 'pervade every sphere of domestic policy, every day, every way, at every nook and cranny of government.'[1] 'In no other country,' wrote Robert McKenzie, 'are the great sectional interests . . . brought more intimately into consultation in the process of decision-making in government and political parties.'[2] Pressure groups have come to be regarded as a respectable and even necessary instrument of democracy, so that 'if an organised group does not exist, the government helps to invent it'.[3]

The effectiveness of pressure groups can often be exaggerated. After Edward Heath had announced his intention to abolish Resale Price Maintenance early in 1963, all the interests that dreaded it—the brewers, the chemists, the motor trade, the small shopkeepers—co-ordinated their protests, supplied pamphlets and arguments, lobbied MPs and organised bombardments of handwritten letters from constituents. The Bill cut across an important sector of traditional Tory support, industry and the small shopkeepers. Yet it went through under a Tory administration without much obvious damage to their cause. For the real beneficiaries of the Bill were the millions of consumers, whose votes were worth far more than the sectional interests. As consumers become more demanding and vocal, so both parties try to emerge as the champions of the housewife.

[1] S. E. Finer: *Anonymous Empire*, Pall Mall, 1958.
[2] 'Politics of Pressure', *The Observer*, May 14, 1961.
[3] Allen Potter: *Organised Groups in British National Politics*, 1961, p. 32.

There is still a large body of MPs with business axes to grind: in the new parliament of July 1970 *The Times* found that 218 members had clearly identifiable business interests, including no fewer than 46 members of Lloyd's, 23 in investment and unit trusts, 21 in property: many members covered a wide range, like Sir John Foster with 20 directorships, and Sir Arthur Vere Harvey and Sir Robert Cary with eleven each. Industries which are 'politically sensitive' are not surprisingly very well represented: there are 18 MPs who held directorships in construction companies (before the government was formed), 14 came from textiles, and six from pharmaceuticals.[1]

But most of the very biggest business interests do not bother much about parliament, and few of the big corporations now maintain their own members in the house. They have seen where decisive power lies, and so they now deal directly with cabinet ministers or civil servants; even the trade unions, with their considerable representation in the Commons, often prefer to deal direct with Whitehall. Parliamentary lobbying can hinder, not help, this pressure on the government; and it is typical of Britain, compared to America, that much important lobbying is done over lunches or drinks in clubs or homes. 'It's so much easier here,' a senior manager in one big corporation once told me: 'We don't have to organise great formal expeditions as in Washington. Whitehall is only two tube stations away: we have a permanent secretary to lunch from time to time.' The chairmen of big companies do not need to stir up members of parliament; they are on speaking terms with people in the cabinet and senior civil servants, and can urge their views there. The more civil servants who go into industry, the closer the industry, the easier such informal pressure becomes: pressure to make someone do something they don't want to do becomes in the end a sort of like-mindedness in which it may not be clear who is the persuader and who the persuaded. The really important lobbying—about tax concessions, locations of industries, trade agreements or subsidies—takes place in the recesses of Whitehall long before any Bill reaches parliament. The member of parliament, however much he may resent—or be flattered by—the persistent attentions of the lobbyists, has the uneasy feeling that the real pressures are being exerted elsewhere.

But the respectability and acceptance of modern pressure-

[1] Richard Spiegelberg: 'Parliamentary business', *The Times*, July 3, 1970.

groups, their infiltration beyond Westminster into Whitehall, should not be allowed to obscure the central fact that effective pressure nearly always requires money, that the most effective groups are the richest, and that it is difficult for interests without money to stand up against those with it. A wealthy and determined lobby, with only a handful of people behind it, can still have a spectacular success: the Commercial TV lobby (see Chapter 24) was the classic post-war example: and the Commercial Radio lobby has had almost as remarkable a success. The chief organiser of that lobby, John Gorst, who came into parliament in 1970, is probably the most successful pressure-group organiser: he is a master propagandist (great-grandson of Disraeli's Tory Party organiser) who knows all the tricks of mobilising public opinion. He advised the BOAC pilots in their strike in 1968; he set up the Telephone Users' Association, advocating the injection of private capital into the telephone service; the independent medical services, to encourage private medical care; the Enterprise Association, to campaign against all kinds of nationalisation. He formed the Local Radio Association in the unpromising days of 1964, pressurised the Tory Party to support it in 1966, and worked with the various vested interests to ensure that the Bill would be introduced. All this with no real evidence of public opinion that anyone was likely to benefit, except the investors in it.

PARLIAMENT, PRESS AND TELEVISION

A broader, less tangible, threat to the primacy of parliament has been the emergence of new communications and mass media to threaten its position as the central forum of public opinion, the 'arena for battle, drive and dominion'. Up till the eighteenth century the Press was barred from debates; and to publish them was considered in 1738 'a high indignity and notorious breach of privilege': the *Gentleman's Magazine*—the first to report parliament —employed a memory-man, Guthrie, who memorised speeches and then had them put into classical English by Dr. Samuel Johnson. But today the reporting of parliament affects parliament itself. Official reports are now a hallowed operation: four fast shorthand reporters, working in twenty-minute shifts, take down the debates (they allow members to improve their grammar on the typescript, sometimes too generously: in June 1966 the Chancellor of the Exchequer, James Callaghan, was caught removing a rude reference to farmers from the record.) The reports are rushed to the parliamentary presses across the river, which print 2,300 copies in time to be delivered to MPs for breakfast. But what matters to members is not what gets into *Hansard*, but what gets into the newspapers. Publicity, once scorned, is now courted: big speeches are made early in the day in order to get into the papers, and many theatrically-minded members make scenes with a wary eye on the Press.

Television has now taken over the role of intruder, and televising parliament provokes the same kind of arguments as were levelled against the Press two hundred years ago. 'Parliament should not be as blind and stubborn towards television as it was in its unhappy struggle with the Press,' wrote Robin Day, the chief propagandist for a televised parliament, in a letter to *The Times* in 1969: but parliament has been almost as blind. Members of parliament have already become uncomfortably aware that television has, through its own debates and question times, stolen a great deal of their thunder. In 1963, during Parliament's two-and-a-half month recess, the Profumo affair and the Conservative leadership crisis were played out on television. Angry new issues, like immigration or the students' revolt, are often more likely to be properly debated on television than in parliament. And since Macmillan all prime ministers have been tempted to by-pass parliament (and the Press), appealing to the public directly through the screen.

Parliament is jealously aware of the competition, and is reluctant to come to terms with it. The older MPs are fearful that, once they let cameras into the chamber, the intimacy and rituals of the debates would be wrecked: the public could see members yawning or snoring, and Sir Gerald Nabarro would become even more exhibitionist. But many of the younger MPs are in favour of being televised, and in 1966 a proposal for experimental closed-circuit TV was defeated by only one vote. Certainly the conjunction of the two media, the oldest and the newest, would be a drastic one: the televising of parliament *would* have a great effect on its procedures—much more than the Press has done—and the editing and selection of programmes would need careful control. But television could do more than any other innovation to bring Westminster closer to its electorate, and to improve the 'educative function' (as Bagehot called it) which should be one of the main purposes of parliament. It is the tendency of parliament to talk to

18

itself, to turn inward away from the people it is supposed to represent, which is its most maddening and decadent feature: and for this self-enclosement, TV can provide a drastic shock-treatment.

BACKBENCHERS

One of the most discomforting features of the 1960s was the sudden growth of active disbelief, especially among the younger generation, in the efficacy of our parliamentary democracy.

Richard Crossman, January 1971.

New members of parliament, if they did not know it before, soon realise the limitations of their job. Their most obvious restraint is their party: they are kept firmly in check by the whips —the party policemen, with their mixture of jolliness and toughness; the hot and cold treatment. The government chief whip has a special lash, for he is also patronage secretary, with the prime minister's ear, and can thus fix up promotion and honours: it can be a devastating weapon against a government backbencher. The chief whip lives at No. 12 Downing Street, just round the corner from No. 10, with intercommunicating doors: he sees the prime minister every day, and can slip in at any time unobserved. Ted Heath, having been chief whip himself, knows well enough how to make full use of his own chief whip, Francis Pym. He is helped by a dozen other whips, each of whom keeps in touch with thirty or forty members: as one former Tory chief whip, Lord Redmayne, described it: 'His business is to keep contact with them, and not merely to keep contact with them but to know them so well that he may in an emergency be able to give a judgment as to what their opinion will be without even asking them.'

A small government majority gives the whips stronger arguments: Redmayne maintained that 'the greater the majority, the greater the power of the opinion of the back-benchers. . . . When you have a government with a small majority of eighteen, even the most junior whip could use the argument: "Well, old boy, you mustn't rock the boat." It isn't much use using that argument when you have a majority of a hundred because the boat takes a good deal more rocking.'[1] In the first eighteen months of the Labour government, with a majority of five, Harold Wilson had little trouble from backbenchers, except from habitual

[1] Interview with Dr. Norman Hunt: *The Listener*, December 19, 1963.

rebels like Woodrow Wyatt or Ian Mikardo (in any case, though
the government appeared to be walking a dangerous tight-rope,
there was really a safety-net below—for the Conservatives, in their
shaky condition, did not *want* to bring the government down).
After the 1966 election, with a Labour majority of a hundred, the
back-benchers were much more restless and noisy, and there were
suggestions that the whips were beginning to lose their sting.
Wilson continued to treat his backbenchers with a good deal of
contempt, and threatened to take away their 'dog licences': but
on two important occasions they stopped him doing what he
wanted—reforming the House of Lords and legislating against the
trade unions.

The party discipline is still discouraging to new MPs who
arrive in the house expecting their views at least to be taken note
of. This is how one Labour MP, Michael Barnes, described it to
me:

> What worries me most is the lack of sense of involvement. If an issue
> comes to the boil it's exciting. But for the rest of the time I find very
> little job satisfaction—less and less: I often envy my contemporaries
> who have proper jobs, working closely with other people. The
> chamber is like a football game, but the trouble is you rarely get the
> ball passed to you. I think the people who enjoy it most are the real
> parliamentarians, who love the chamber itself and hate the commit-
> tees; they really believe in the talking and debating. I hate the way
> the whips drag you down to the lowest common denominator of the
> party: it makes me feel like a private, back in the barrack-room, being
> ordered about by lance-corporals. It's degrading.

In one direction the member is faced with the disciplines of the
party machine; in another, by the closed doors of the Whitehall
bureaucracies. Listening to debates and reading white papers, he
finds himself faced with pre-arranged arguments, which have been
thrashed out in detail with the ministries. In theory the parliamentarians, like the shareholders in a company, are the *owners* of
the vast apparatus of government departments and industry,
which controls, among other things, nearly half British investment.
In theory (according to Erskine May, the rule-book of parliament),
'the constitution has assigned no limits to the authority of parliament over matters and persons within its jurisdiction'. But in
practice the member (like the shareholder) finds he cannot get
hold of an issue until it becomes a *fait accompli*, and that the real
battles for power are taking place away from his purview. The

persons within his jurisdiction are too many and too secret to be known, let alone controlled.

In the last few years, under both Labour and Tory governments, MPs have tried to penetrate further into the workings of the bureaucracies, and the 'select committees' of MPs, who can question or subpoena anyone they want, have managed to get occasional glimpses of how decisions are reached (see Chapter 20): the new select committee on expenditure, which has the help of expert advisers, may go further in uncovering the mysteries of the Treasury. But the members are up against the simple fact that neither the government nor the civil servants *want* them to find out what is happening. As one committee-member put it: 'They're playing a poker game, and the fewer people watching them, the better.' And the members lack the will, the knowledge or the time to press home their investigation. The amateur ideal of the MP finally evaporates in the face of the real experts in the committee-room; as another put it, 'we don't do our homework properly; we can never really be a match for the specialist civil servants'. Many MPs, moreover, are uncertain whether it is really their *job* to criticise civil servants; should they not be busy criticising the other party, and thus furthering their career? As the Labout MP John Mackintosh put it in 1971:

> The vast majority of MPs regard parliament as an extension of the political battle between the parties, as a kind of continuation of general elections; they don't *want* to set themselves up against the executive, the civil servants. They think their job is to be anti-Tory, or anti-Labour: why should they co-operate with the other side in a select committee to question civil servants? And if they're on the government side, why should they embarrass their own government? The professionalisation of politics has only made it worse; the more people spend their time in this building, the more they realise that their only chance of real power lies with getting a job in the government, and that the only way to do that is to side with the leadership. There are masses of MPs wandering about this building who have been used to having a proper job, who don't know what they ought to be doing, whether to make speeches, join committees, become specialists; there's no real job satisfaction. If they're not in the government or the shadow government, they feel they're a failure; the day that the prime minister or the leader of the opposition calls for them and says: 'Charlie, I'd like you to be under-under-under-under secretary in charge of tomatoes'—that's the day that he feels his career has really begun.

HOUSE OF LORDS

> I am dead: dead, but in the Elysian fields.
>
> *Disraeli (on being asked how he found*
> *being in the House of Lords).*

The most obviously irrelevant and anachronistic part of parliament is its astonishing second chamber, the House of Lords. If you turn right from the central lobby, instead of left, you come into a world even more peculiar and rarefied, which yet has a charm which few people—least of all radicals—seem able to resist. You walk through a series of high dark rooms, embellished with gothic woodwork and carved ceilings: the dominating architecture, even more than that of the House of Commons, gives an atmosphere of peace and timelessness, like an eccentric but well-run country house. A life-size white marble statue of the young Queen Victoria, sitting on the coronation chair and crowned with laurels, looks down on elderly peers sitting at hexagonal tables, writing letters on gothic writing-paper. Doors lead off to long dining-rooms—one for guests, another for peers only—and to a large bar looking over the river, which serves drinks all day and sells special 'House of Lords' cigarettes. In the ante-room and passages, soft-footed attendants take messages, escort visitors, and address all peers as 'My Lord'. In the dining-rooms a momentary sense of reality breaks in: cosy aproned waitresses are apt to talk about the telly, to call peeresses 'my dear', and serve meals of roast beef and two veg.

There is an aura of contented old age—older than the oldest men's club. The rooms are full of half-remembered faces of famous men, or politicians who dropped suddenly out of public life twenty years ago, who—how shall one put it?—one had forgotten were still around. There is banter between left-wing peers and right-wing peers, and a great deal of talk about operations and ailments and nursing homes. 'You see this is a kind of hospital,' one earl explained to me, after two peers had come up to talk about their recent illnesses: 'You have to be something of an expert on operations.' Occasionally a young man appears among the old faces; there are a few young life peers, like Lord Beaumont or Lady Masham, but most of them are elevated near the ends of their careers.

Leading off the main ante-room is the chamber itself—the fine flower of Pugin's Victorian romantic style. Stained-glass windows shed a dark-red light, and the barons of Magna Carta, looking misleadingly like saints, look down from the walls: it all looks like some eccentric private chapel. The difference from the House of Commons is (as one observer remarked) like the difference between a first-class and second-class railway carriage. On either side of the chamber are long red-leather sofas, facing each other across the gangway with dark wood choir-stalls at the back. Between the two sides is something which looks like a huge red pouf, with a back-rest in the middle of it: this is 'the Woolsack', wool from twelve parts of the commonwealth. Facing the Woolsack are three men in wigs, sitting at a large old desk, full of bits of writing-paper, glue, inkpots, paper clips and an hour-glass. And on the Woolsack itself sits—for the first part of the afternoon —a restless and muttering figure encased in a wig, who turns out to be Lord Hailsham, Lord High Chancellor of England.

Sitting on the red-leather sofas, facing each other, leaning back, whispering, putting their feet up, fumbling with papers, making notes, putting a deaf-aid (supplied by the attendants) to their ear, or simply sleeping, are the peers. The speaker addresses them undeterred with such phrases as 'My Lords', 'Your Lordships' House', 'The Noble Earl'.

The hours are not strenuous: the peers often sit for only three hours at a time, and hardly ever on Fridays. Occasionally there is a marathon session, as in February 1968, when they sat till ten the next morning discussing the Kenya Asians, or in May 1971, when they sat for $17\frac{1}{2}$ hours debating the Industrial Relations Bill. Attendances are better than they were, and in the last decade the average numbers have doubled: since peers can claim six and-a-half guineas expenses a day for attending, more of them have taken to looking in after work, for a sit-down and a drink. But out of a thousand peers there are often only ten in the chamber, and only three peers are needed for a quorum: the House of Lords, in the words of William Hamilton, is 'the only institution in the world which can function only by mass absenteeism'. The record number to have voted since the war is 394, for the debate on the death penalty in 1969, which to many people's surprise resulted in a majority of forty-six in favour of abolition.

It is odd to recall that this magnificent edifice was built by the Victorians in 1847, after the first Reform Act had been passed which began the eclipse of its power. The most that the Lords can do now is to delay a Bill by one year, and any 'money Bill' they can delay only for a month; in fact they dare not delay a Bill at all, knowing that that would create a constitutional crisis. The impotence of the Lords derives ultimately from the discomforting fact that the prime minister can create as many peers as he wants to, and so flood the chamber with his supporters. Ever since 1712, when the Tories created twelve new peers to pass the Treaty of Utrecht, the threat has been in the background. The threat was used to pass the Reform Bill of 1832 and the Parliament Bill of 1911—when the powers of the Lords were curbed after they had thrown out Lloyd George's budget of 1909. Actually to *carry out* the threat nowadays would be embarrassing: but the nightmare is real enough to bring the peers to heel.

There are aspects of the Lords which are delightful—the kindliness, the clubbiness, the eccentric and often very humane discussions—about prostitutes, forestry, homosexuals or deer. The Lords often show a tolerance and curiosity which the Commons have no time for, and they include some unexpected experts, such as Lord Arran, the authority on sexual questions, or Lord Milford, the only Communist peer: 'This country has many anomalies,' said Lord Attlee, welcoming him to the house in 1963, 'One curious one is that the voice of the Communist Party can only be heard in this house. That is the advantage of hereditary representation.' But the House of Lords is still something of an embarrassment to both parties. As a second chamber it is hopelessly unrepresentative and still overwhelmingly Conservative, more conservative than the Tory Party; it has not defeated a Conservative motion since 1832. The Labour Party in opposition like to use it as a symbol of Tory fuddy-duddyness; but when in power they are soon confused as to whether they want to reform it, let it wither away, or continue to use it both as a scapegoat and a useful upstairs, to which to kick their own veterans.

One hopeful reform came in 1958, under Macmillan's government, with the creation of Life Peerages; since Wilson came to power in 1964 no more hereditary peers have been created, and as more life peers are created and the peerages slowly die out, the balance in the Lords is gradually being changed. The prestige of hereditary peers was further diminished in 1963, when they were allowed to renounce their titles and sit in the Commons: Lord Home became Sir Alec Douglas-Home, Lord Stansgate became Anthony Wedgwood Benn, Lord Hailsham became Quintin Hogg (only to come back as Lord Hailsham again in 1970, as life peer and

Lord Chancellor). By the end of 1970 there were 173 life peers, of whom 125 (or twelve per cent of the house) were created by Harold Wilson (see Chapter 13). The life peers certainly cover a wider cross-section; in 1970 the 173 included fifteen industrialists, fourteen academics, fourteen public servants, and eleven trade unionists; they included an accountant (Lord Hirshfield) a West Indian (Lord Constantine), a mountaineer (Lord Hunt), a *Daily Mirror* man (Lord Ardwick), an actor (Lord Olivier) and a Methodist preacher (Lord Soper). But by far the biggest category remains the political peers—66 out of the 173, 48 of them Labour. The *Daily Mirror* complained back in 1955 that the upper house was becoming a 'parking lot for old vehicles that had had their day': Wilson has parked many more old jalopies—with the excuse that he was only redressing the political balance. The House of Lords has become more than ever a kind of politicians' after-life, and the sense of transubstantiation is enhanced by many of them changing their names; so that Nigel Birch becomes Lord Rhyl, Julian Snow becomes Lord Burntwood, Sir William Anstruther-Gray becomes Lord Kilmany, Sir John Vaughan-Morgan becomes Lord Reigate, Alun Gwynne-Jones becomes Lord Chalfont, Thomas Taylor of the Scottish Co-op becomes Lord Taylor of Gryfe. Charles Smith of the Post Office Engineering Union wanted to call himself Lord Windsor after his home town, but was told by the heralds this would be *lèse-majesté*; so he had to tack on an ancestor's name and become Lord Delacourt-Smith.

The industrial or professional life peers have lent the House of Lords a more relevant look: but their performance in debates has been disappointing. A few have been vocal and influential—like Lord Fulton, from the University of Sussex; Lord Holford the architect; Lord Redcliffe-Maud, the former don and ambassador; or Lord Brown, the self-made industrialist. But most of the businessmen, like Lord Sieff, Lord Campbell or Lord Kings Norton (formerly Roxbee-Cox of Metal Box) have added little to the public knowledge of industry; and the idea that the Lords should become an educative forum about industrial affairs has flopped.

In 1968 Harold Wilson, in cahoots with Ted Heath as leader of the opposition, was determined to reform the Lords further. There were long talks between the parties, which Wilson angrily broke off when the Lords rejected the extension of Rhodesian sanctions, but the scheme still went ahead. In February 1969 the

Commons debated the preamble to a new Parliament Bill, which would introduce a 'two-tier' system in the Lords, drastically reducing the number of hereditary peers who were allowed to vote, from 737 to 77, and turning the Lords basically into a house of nominated life peers, with a careful balance to ensure that the opposition and the cross-benchers could outnumber the government. The Bill (which was badly fumbled) provoked furious opposition from an amazing alliance of back-benchers from the far left and the far right. The left thought that the Bill was taking the Lords too seriously, and the right thought it was not taking it seriously enough; but both sides revealed a nostalgic attachment to the traditional House. Michael Foot, the main opponent on the left, protested:

> If one wipes away the hereditary varnish from the rest of the Bill, all one is left with is a Bill establishing a crude, vulgar, nominated chamber which might even be thrown out in the House of Lords . . . Under the government's proposals we are to surrender our obligations, a thousand years of history, into these quivering hands—the Cromers, the Cobbolds, the Caccias, the Brookes, the Bridges, the Hankeys and the Pankeys . . . What we are doing in this Bill is to ensure that for the next twenty, thirty or forty years hence, the constitution's balance will be heavily weighted in favour of reaction, the elderly, the establishment, and those who have exhausted in the main the contribution they can make to the political life of the country . . .

Enoch Powell (himself a historian of the Lords) led the attack from the right, concentrating on the more mystical aspects of the chamber:

> It will be a disgrace to the Commons if it calls into existence of its own volition such an abortion as the two-tier chamber. No member of the Lords, nor the Lords collectively, had the right to sell out valuable elements of the constitution for the sake of advantages which they might hope personally to enjoy during their lifetime. The British constitution is not the personal property of any generation of members of either of the Houses of Parliament.

The backbench rebels were united in their dislike not only of the Bill but of the alliance between the party leaders: 'this Heath-Wilson contraption along the corridor' (William Hamilton); 'this band of brothers between the two front benches, this Cosa Nostra' (Hugh Fraser). Eventually, after angry debates, diversions and ingenious time-wasting, Wilson finally removed the Bill from the government's programme. The rebels' success not only showed the great obstacles in the way of reforming the Lords (for they would have opposed the Bill even if it had been better thought out). It also—perhaps more importantly—disproved current theories about the powerlessness of backbenchers in the Commons; it showed that in the rare event of the two extremes coming together (as they do also in opposing the Common Market) they can defy an alliance of leaderships. The demonstration would have been more reassuring if the alliance and the arguments had been less absurd.

The comic and nostalgic atmosphere of the House of Lords, and the many petty details involved in its reform, tend to obscure the real arguments for and against a serious second chamber. Its anomalies and snobberies could still be justified in the 1970s if it could be turned into a more representative body, able to reconsider and humanise the hectic legislation from the Commons, and to add its more detached expertise. As the proportion of life peers grows, the House of Lords will look less anachronistic and be better able to justify its role as a kind of long-stop in the parliamentary cricket-game. But the corporate function of the Lords and its representation will remain an absurd hybrid—between the old notion of aristocracy, the new notion of 'all walks of life', and the whims and calculations of the prime minister's personal patronage. For this is a worrying side-effect of the life peerage: that the ability to create peers in larger numbers adds still further to the patronage of the prime minister.

TALK AND POLITICS

For any visitor or member who comes to either of the two Houses of Parliament in search of the keys to the labyrinth of power, the disappointment must be great. It *will* be a pursuit of the will o' the wisp. For it is as clear as the Emperor's Clothes that all that most members do about power is to talk about it. The House is like a steam-engine, hissing steam, puffing and whistling, which is secretly powered by electricity. The noble lords go on addressing the noble lords, the honourable members continue to address the honourable, gallant, or right honourable members; but unless there is a temporary and zany alliance of backbenchers the vote always goes with the government. The talk is not only ineffective but often quite irrelevant; and very little of it is eloquent or inspiring. Rhetoric is at a discount in both houses, and only a handful of rather eccentric speakers (such as Foot, Powell, Hailsham, Shinwell) can convey or generate real emotion. The new Tory government is anti-rhetorical, and Heath and Maudling are both masters of bathos.

But the power of talk, however dull it may sound, is not easy to measure or write off. For those who say that parliament is nothing but a talking-shop, it can be replied that that is what the word parliament means. Parliament has always shown a preference for talk over action, and a reluctance—even in its great battles with the monarchy—to press home its powers. When Attlee was asked how Winston Churchill won the war, he replied simply: 'He talked about it'; the greatest tribute that Wilson could pay to Churchill when he died was that he 'was a good House of Commons man'. An observer who inspects parliament in mechanical terms, as if it were an engine with levers and pistons, is bound to conclude that it is subservient; thus Maurice Duverger, the French constitutional expert, concludes that in Britain 'parliament and government are like two machines driven by the same motor—the party'. But many political scientists are now inclined to see parliament more in organic than mechanical terms, as the central nervous system of the body politic: Professor Beer of Harvard sees the real function of parliament not as control, but as 'mobilising consent'. To many MPs, like Anthony Wedgwood Benn and Enoch Powell, talk has a special mystique: as Benn puts it, 'through talk we tamed kings, restrained tyrants, averted revolution'.[1] Professor Crick of Sheffield, though one of the most vigorous advocates of parliamentary reform, admits: 'Perhaps, indeed, it is a general truth that all legislatures are primarily devices to mobilize and organise consent, and are communication centres between governments and populations, far more than they are devices to choose and destroy governments.'[2]

There is always a temptation to expect parliament to be more forceful and decisive than the country at large—to generate issues, to bring new life to politics, to reinvigorate Britain. But by its nature, it can only reflect, obliquely and dimly, the feelings and opinions of the nation. When the nation is united in a sense of purpose it can, as in 1940, serve as an instrument for mobilising that purpose more effectively than a totalitarian regime. When

[1] See also Chapter 24 on TV.
[2] Bernard Crick: *The Reform of Parliament* (2nd edition Weidenfeld & Nicolson) 1968. p. 269.

the nation is exhausted, bewildered, without purpose, it can serve only to reveal that bewilderment. Parliament has many manifest faults of its own; but it is not useful to blame it for the faults of the nation.

2

The Swing

The English people believes itself to be free; it is gravely mistaken;
it is free only during election of members of parliament; as soon as the
members are elected, the people is enslaved; it is nothing. In the brief
moment of its freedom, the English people makes such a use of that
freedom that it deserves to lose it.

Jean-Jacques Rousseau.
The Social Contract, 1743. Book III, Chapter 15.

A GREAT deal of the theory of British democracy depends on what
the Victorian Lord Salisbury called 'the great law of the pendulum'—the expectation that the British electorate would decide at
a general election that it was tired of one party and wanted
another. The whole British system of representation rests on the
hectic three-weeks of electioneering, once every five years or less,
when members and ministers present themselves to their electors
and ask for their support. Then the new parliament is elected, the
new government is constituted, the voters are once again ignored,
and the frenzy dies down as quickly as it came up.

Many foreign observers since Rousseau—particularly the
Americans with their year-long election and their far more
elaborate checks within their constitution—have been amazed by
the suddenness and brevity of this moment of choice, and the
frailty of a system which rests on so precarious a base; and because
the pendulum is such an essential part of the democratic concept,
much time has been devoted by political scientists to wondering
whether it will continue. 'Many of our traditional liberties have
been held to depend on the alternation of the parties,' wrote
Professor Crick in 1968; 'To many "liberty" could be defined (in
minimum if not complete terms) as those rights and conditions

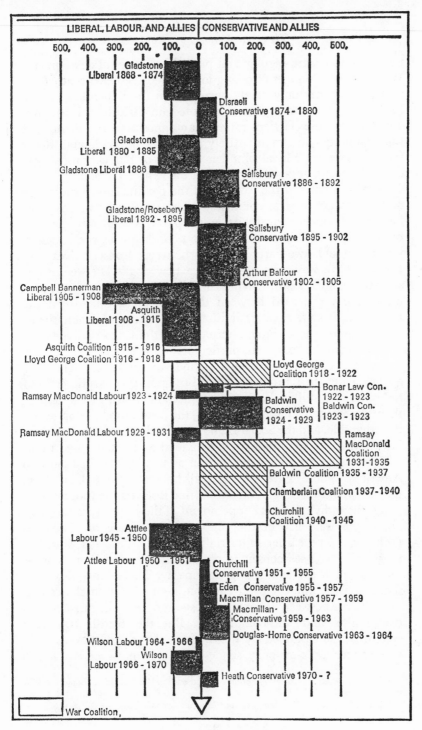

The swing of the pendulum

necessary to ensure regular and peaceful changes of government. We are now in danger of taking for granted the beneficent effects of a process that only rarely occurs.'[1] 'In the mid-1960s,' wrote Professor Mackintosh, 'it is accepted in British politics that governments lose elections rather than oppositions win them, that the advantages lie almost entirely with those in power and that it requires serious political blunders, ill luck or tactical miscalculation if these advantages do not yield the expected results.'[2]

What has ensured the working of the pendulum in Britain—as opposed to continental countries, where it often gets stuck—has been the persistent loyalty to a two-party system over the past hundred years. It showed itself most markedly in the twenties, when the old two-party division between Conservatives and Liberals gave way very quickly to a new duality between Conservatives and Labour, leaving the Liberals within ten years as a minor party squeezed between the two giants. Since then the British left, in spite of angry divisions, have managed to hold themselves together as a viable alternative to the Conservatives. The contrast with the continent, particularly with France and Italy, is striking; even after prolonged periods of centre or right-wing governments, the Latin left failed to bring together its splinters, and has often split still further over the question of how best to oppose them. In Sweden, on the other hand, the pendulum has stopped on the other side, and the Social Democrats for the last thirty-five years have remained victorious over a divided and demoralised right.

There has been much speculation as to why Britain (and also America) should have this special balance; there have been theories about the Anglo-Saxon sporting instincts (de Madariaga), about the individualistic temperament of the Latins (passim), and about the influence of the shape of the House of Commons (Maurois). The earlier industrialisation of Britain left it with a more solid and self-conscious proletariat than the Continent, as the core of a single working-class party. There have also been more divisive influences on the continent—between clerics and anti-clerics, between the monarchists and republicans, between communists and anti-communists. But the British two-party system is also sustained by the method of voting. Britain's insistence on a simple-majority, single-ballot system, which is unfair to

[1] Bernard Crick: *The Reform of Parliament* (2nd edition Weidenfeld & Nicolson 1968), p. 7.
[2] J. P. Mackintosh· *The British Cabinet* (2nd edition Methuen 1968), p. 578.

minority voters, has almost eliminated smaller parties; while the fairer system of proportional representation (PR), followed in most of western Europe, gives much greater scope to runners-up, and thus encourages divisions.

Within Britain there are recurring nightmares that the pendulum has stuck, never to go again. Students of politics were specially anguished after the 1959 election, when the Conservatives won for the third time in a row. It seemed then (as in France, Germany and Italy) that a capitalist government was so successfully harnessing the new consumer prosperity it its political wagon that the opposition could never get rid of it. And in Britain—in contrast to the others—the party in power could declare an election whenever it wanted; so that they could stir up a roaring boom when they wished and then, when public opinion polls indicated the right swing, they could quickly dissolve parliament and declare an election—as Macmillan did in 1959. The ruling party had two instruments which had not existed before the war—the new ability to control the economy, and the advice of opinion polls. They could both stoke up the fire, and measure the heat. How then could an opposition ever unseat them?

After 1959 many post-mortems indicated that Labour could not get back. Since the first Reform Bill there has been a fairly equal swing between left and right: but in the years since 1884—which marked the beginning of universal household suffrage—the right had predominated. 'In the course of the 75 years up to 1959,' wrote Richard Crossman soon after the 1959 defeat, 'there have been only two left-wing governments with outright majorities, the Liberal government elected after the Boer War and the Labour government elected after World War II. Moreover, within five years each of these left-wing governments had lost most of its popular support.'[1]

Behind the Labour Party's distress about the pendulum lay the fundamental question: should they modify their policies to recapture the 'middle ground' on which a majority depended? The argument raged both among trade unionists and intellectuals, with Richard Crossman as chief theorist on the left, and Anthony Crosland on the right. Crossman maintained: 'It seems to be a rule of British democracy that parties of the left can retain their strength and enthusiasm through extended periods of opposition, provided the leadership remains committed to radical

[1] *Labour in the Affluent Society*, Fabian Society, 1960.

33

change. But that strength and enthusiasm rapidly ebbs away if ever the leadership becomes obsessed by electoral considerations and succumbs to the temptation to jettison its radical policies for the sake of office. The study of history, in fact, refutes the theory of the swing of the pendulum . . .'.[1]

But Crosland, Gaitskell and most other Labour leaders maintained that it was the ideological commitment—typified by the Clause Four in the party constitution which demanded wholesale nationalisation—which was preventing Labour getting back; and these revisionists won the day, excising Clause Four and presenting the Labour Party as modern and moderate, appealing to the middle-class as much as to the workers. By 1962, with the collapse of the Tories' common market negotiations, and the dwindling national morale, the pendulum seemed to be swinging again. The Conservatives waited until the last moment; they again stoked up a boom, and very nearly won for a fourth time. But Labour squeezed in by four seats; and then, turning the trick against the Tories, went to the country again eighteen months later, and increased their majority to a hundred.

In spring 1970 the pendulum seemed to have stopped again, this time on the Labour side. The by-elections and opinion polls had for two years shown a massive swing against the Labour government; but that swing had apparently been abruptly reversed by May 1970, when the Labour government had achieved a favourable balance of payments and had been able to relax their incomes policy to allow huge wage rises. During the election campaign nearly all commentators (including myself) believed that Labour would win, and many maintained that they had established themselves as the safe, central party. Thus David Watt, political editor of the *Financial Times* of June 15, 1970:

> The truth is that the Labour government captured the centre in 1964, and instead of trying to deprive them of it, the Conservatives have concentrated on redefining it. This was a brave attempt. Yet all the opinion polls seem to show that we are still in a state of public opinion which approves of the welfare state, which is in favour of some mild redistribution of wealth, and which has no particular wish to be bothered with challenging ideas either from left or right.

The opinion polls differed widely about the margin, but they all concurred in recording a Labour victory, and in showing Harold Wilson to be far more popular personally than Edward Heath. It

[1] *Labour in the Affluent Society*, Fabian Society, 1960.

was commonly believed that, as British prime ministers became more like American presidents, so the personalities of the leaders in elections became more important; on television Wilson was adept and confident, Heath was awkward and seemingly embarrassed. At the campaign press conferences Wilson exuded success and enjoyed cosy repartee with journalists, while Heath stonewalled against constant questionings about Tory Powellism. Conservative commentators as well as Labour ones were already analysing the causes of the Tory defeat, and worrying about the lost sense of identity of the party leaders. For the future, Professor David Butler, the high priest of psephology, had predicted in his massive survey of the electorate[1] that, because children were apt to vote like their parents, there was likely to be a long-term swing towards Labour; and some Tories were preparing themselves for a Swedish future of unending social democracy.

But during the night of June 18th the Conservatives emerged with a majority of 31. The Labour government disappeared through the floor, and with them disappeared the confident theories that had predicted their victory: the opinion polls and the market researchers that produced them; the theories about personalities, television ratings and charisma; the interpretations of the long-term and short-term swings: they all went through the trap-door. The British public had not only swung against Labour, but it had swung with remarkable consistency, from the top of Scotland to the South of England. The swing varied from 6·2 per cent in Lancashire to 2·6 per cent in Clydeside, but in no region was there a swing towards Labour; there *was* a national pattern of disenchantment, if only someone could have deciphered it. Against all the pressures and predictions of the mass media, the people had decided that they wanted a change, and for better or worse they got it. The next morning, with the suddenness characteristic of the British system, the removal vans moved into Downing Street, Harold Wilson's staff went out through the back door, and Edward Heath set off for the palace to become prime minister. The British public (in Rousseau's terms) had exercised its 'brief moment of freedom', and was again enslaved to a new government.

[1] David Butler: *Political Change in Britain 1969*

LEFT AND RIGHT

Do the swings of the pendulum reflect a genuine swing between 'Left' and 'Right', or do they just show the desire for alternative governments, like two rival companies? The definition of what is left and what is right has become harder in the last few years. 'Left' is never easy to define in British terms, for it is essentially a Continental concept dating back to the French Assembly in 1789, when, in the debate on the Royal veto, the different groupings arranged themselves in different parts of the Chamber: the idea of 'left' only became current in Britain early in this century, and could never altogether be equated with the Labour party. There have been many attempts to try to pin down the difference between left and right; these are some of the characteristics that have, from time to time, been implied:

Left	*Right*
Public Ownership	Free Enterprise
Change	Tradition
Egalitarianism	Elitism
Compassion	Toughness
Tolerance	Discipline
Doves	Hawks
Democracy	Aristocracy
Intervention	*Laissez-faire*

None of these definitions stands up to close scrutiny; David Caute in his book *The Left in Europe Since 1789*, after weighing all possible definitions, suggests that the demand for popular sovereignty, rather than the demand for democracy, has been the most consistent central creed of the left:[1] but even this belief is difficult to trace consistently through the history of British Labour politics. A. J. P. Taylor, reviewing Caute's book, insisted that the only real definition of the left is that of Victor Hugo: 'Je suis contre.' This asserts that once a left-wing party is in power, it ceases to be left, and the Labour Party's turnabouts of policy, in and out of office, give some melancholy support to this view.

The six years of Harold Wilson's government generated a good deal more confusion as to what is really meant by left, and further dissociation between the words left and Labour. In the election campaign Harold Wilson seemed to have appropriated many of the characteristics of the right, including a dislike of

[1] David Caute: *The Left in Europe Since 1789*, World University Library, 1966, p. 32ff.

change. He presented himself as a Baldwinesque figure, and said at the opening of the campaign: 'I don't think the people want much change or disturbance'; while Heath tried to present himself as more of a radical, prepared to restructure systems of government and taxation and to shake Britain out of complacency.

The terms have become much more inadequate now that many of the great ideological battle-cries like anti-colonialism and nationalisation have faded; and many politicians as well as voters regard themselves as belonging to one side on some questions and to another side on others. Some contemporary politicians, like Reginald Maudling (see Chapter 6), had some difficulty in choosing which party to join in the first place. Samuel Brittan, in his rigorous study of left and right,[1] suggests that the categories are now virtually irrelevant to politics and proposes—expanding a device of Professor Eysenck—that attitudes could be plotted along a series of bi-axial graphs, showing different sets of beliefs; egalitarianism against radicalism, inequality and equality, authoritarianism against orthodoxy, etc.

Certainly such charts would define more accurately where the individual politicians stand. But the fact remains that there is very little sign of the two great parties re-grouping their forces; and that most people do not have much difficulty in deciding to which side they belong. The allegiance may often be more like that of a church or a large family, in which specific principles are secondary to a broad sense of belonging. But it is usually very easy to distinguish any Conservative gathering or meeting from a Labour one (perhaps with some exceptions, like gatherings of Labour lawyers or Labour peers): and the Conservative way of life, as opposed to the policies of the right, remains sufficiently distinctive in Britain to make its manifestations very predictable; as seen, for instance, in the *Daily Telegraph*, White's club, or hunt balls. The Conservatives have remained, through all their transformations, associated with the settled, inherited society of the countryside; for anyone who believes that the difference between left and right has become quite confused, or that Britain has fully become 'One Nation', the contrast between the Tory countryside and the Labour industrial cities (as shown on the following two pages) is the most effective contradiction.

There has been recently, however, one issue above all others which has cut across party allegiances; the common market. Both

[1] Samuel Brittan: *Left or Right: The Bogus Dilemma*, Secker & Warburg 1968, p. 83ff.

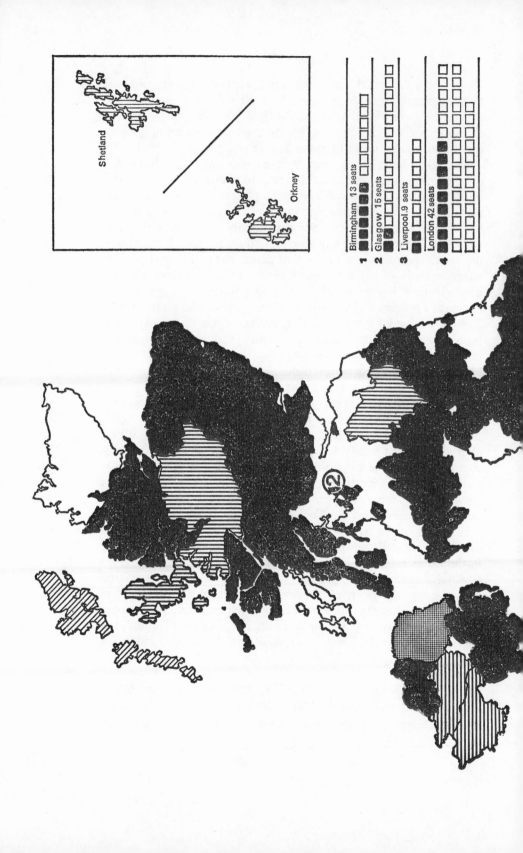

Shetland

Orkney

Birmingham 13 seats

Glasgow 15 seats

Liverpool 9 seats

London 42 seats

1

2

3

4

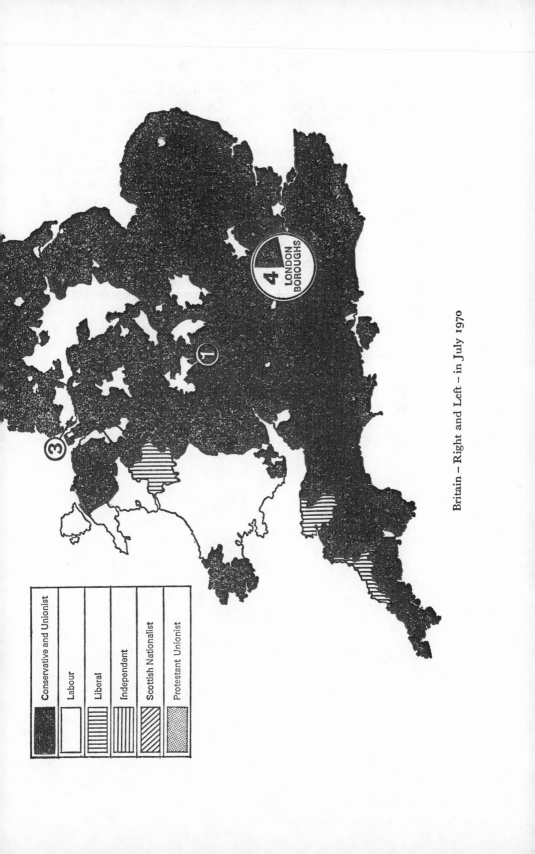

Britain – Right and Left – in July 1970

Conservative and Unionist

Labour

Liberal

Independent

Scottish Nationalist

Protestant Unionist

LONDON
BOROUGHS

parties have been painfully divided about it, which is why the
question hardly emerged during the election campaigns of 1964,
1966 and 1970; and the fiercest opponents tended to belong to the
outside left (like Michael Foot), or to the outside right (like
Anthony Fell), so that the two extremes seem to be meeting round
the back. In some areas it might be possible to equate the pro-
common market factions, particularly amongst the Tories, with a
general sense of liberalism and broad-mindedness: many of the
Conservatives who are bitterly against joining the common
market tend also to be against any immigration and to be for
more 'law and order', including sometimes hanging and flogging.
The 'little Englander' package can often include a general intoler-
ance. On the other hand, the more utopian politicians of the left
feel themselves hindered and corrupted by being included in a
foreign grouping; and a great deal of the idealism of politics,
both on the left and the right, has been associated with the
patriotic context. The common market, by inducing these divisions inside the parties, has faced members of parliament with a
real dilemma, of whom they should represent—their party, their
constituency or themselves, in their view of what is best for the
country. The strains have been painful on both sides, but most in
the Labour Party, which has so quickly moved from its own
attempt to enter Europe, to a position of *je suis contre*.

3

Labour

There is a cracking sound in the political atmosphere: the sound of the consensus breaking up.

Richard Crossman, December 1970.

IT is at the party conferences that the tribal roots of the parties reassert themselves. Every autumn the party delegates assemble at one of three seaside resorts with halls big enough to hold them— Blackpool, Scarborough or Brighton. The end-of-season atmosphere, with empty beaches, yellow leaves and stacked deck-chairs, adds to the sentimentality. The conferences tell you little about the temper of the country; they are gatherings of activists and enthusiasts from the constituencies, reassuring themselves of their party's special mission and the villainy of the others. 'Conference' with a capital C is talked about as if it were a Synod or a Curia; and conference speeches, however boring they may sound to the outsider, have their own secret magic for connoisseurs which can bring the house down.

Television cameras have heightened the intensity: in the last fifteen years they have transformed these tribal occasions into public pageants where (as they cannot in parliament) the leaders and would-be leaders show their paces to the millions. Television is not as dominant as in American conventions. ('The amazing thing about your conferences is that people actually *listen*,' one American observer said to me.) But the TV cameras have become the real audience. The great green vans move up to the side of the conference hall, secreting their intestines of black cables. TV reporters, producers, technicians and secretaries take over a whole section of the hall like an occupation force, and the panjandrums sit in the front of the circle, earphones pressed to their heads, staring at the speakers; while the speakers, bleached by the arclights, look across the delegates to the cameras, pitching their arguments and voices to the unseen masses.

Usually one conference follows the other, only four days apart, in the same hall at the same resort; and it is then that the transformation of faces, decor and language seems oddest. No one *then* can doubt that there is a difference between left and right; the very bars, lounges and foyers seem to have changed their political complexion.

The Labour conference comes first, following a few weeks after the Trades Union Congress, which has prepared some of the more militant motions. The Labour gathering still has something of the atmosphere of a proletarian festival; the delegates seem happiest at Blackpool rather than at bourgeois Brighton or Scarborough. The sedate big hotels are invaded by large men in braces; some bars and lounges are full till late at night with trade unionists gulping beer, others with intellectuals sipping Scotches. The mixed origins of the Labour movement are very evident, and looking round the conference hall you can almost see in the rows of faces the strata of experience, the layers of political geology, that have made up the rock-structure; the non-conformist groups from Wales and the north, with their passionate language of the chapel: the pacifists with their bright eyes and violent convictions; the trade union veterans still dwelling on the memories of the dole and the thirties; the small bands of Marxists, whether the old breed of the twenties, or the new breed of the late sixties; the cranky fringe parties handing out angry pamphlets in the foyer; and the party patricians, the Oxford intellectuals, Labour lawyers or scions of old families, whose mild fruity voices alternate with the rough blasts from dockers or railwaymen, like clarinets after tubas.

The gathering still has a homely splendour about it—the warmth of an in-gathering of the faithful, brought together by their private experiences and backgrounds. The constituencies resent bitterly the compromises of power and the pressures of the central organisation, and the resolutions repeat the theme of discontent with the centre: Bradford West calls for a return to the principles of socialism; Barnet recognises that the Labour Party has not remained sufficiently aware of the changing aspirations and conditions of the people of this country. But they still after seventy years feel themselves part of a 'Movement', and the language of Conference—the references to the Brotherhood of Man, to Comrade Chairman, to Countless Millions Yet Unborn—still reflects the old ideals. And the conference still ends with the singing of the Red Flag:

> The people's flag is deepest red
>   It's shrouded oft our martyrs dead.
> And ere their limbs grew stiff and cold
>   Their hearts' blood dyed its every fold ...

HAROLD WILSON

For the last eight years the history of the Labour Party has been interlocked with the history of Harold Wilson; and it is difficult to recall the time before Gaitskell's death in 1963 when the 'cheeky chappy' of the left was sniping at the Labour leadership and flitting between camps. It was Wilson who must take the credit or the blame for converting the party into a consensus party, whose task was—and still is—to recapture the 'middle ground' from the Conservatives. He is a consummate political manager: and his career thus reflects the changing balances of his party.

Wilson was not at first really committed to the left. He inherited an interest in radical politics from his father, a works chemist in Huddersfield, who was a Liberal: and Harold's first political appearance was at the Oxford University Liberal Club, of which he later became treasurer. He never went through a Communist phase: he looked down on 'the public-school Marxists' who then dominated the Oxford Labour Club and never (he claimed) got past the second page of *Das Kapital*. He was less stirred by the great moral issues of Spain and Nazi Germany than by unemployment; after taking a first in politics, philosophy and economics, he worked with William Beveridge on research into unemployment, at a time when his own father was unemployed. He spent the war in the civil service, where he made a name as an effective but not obviously political administrator. It was then that he met many Labour politicians, and at the end of the war he was asked to stand as Labour candidate for Ormskirk, which he won in 1945.

43

Attlee at once gave him a job as Parliamentary Secretary to the Ministry of Works, and two years later he was President of the Board of Trade—the youngest cabinet minister since Pitt the younger. He was established as a master-technocrat, but not as a politician with any following or recognisable identity.

It was not till four years later in 1951 that Wilson rather suddenly became identified with the left, when Aneurin Bevan resigned in protest against cuts in the Health Service, and Wilson resigned too (though primarily because of defence expenditure). In opposition he became more vocal, attacking American foreign policy and committed to further nationalisation; but he was never closely identified with a group, and when Bevan resigned from the shadow cabinet in 1954 Wilson, to the annoyance of Bevan and the Bevanites, took his place. After 1959, when the Labour Party had lost their third election in a row, he seriously challenged the leadership, in the shape of Hugh Gaitskell. When Gaitskell tried to root out the famous 'Clause Four' of the party's constitution prescribing wholesale nationalisation, Wilson complained 'it was like telling the Salvation Army there was no salvation'. When the left-wing demanded unilateral nuclear disarmament Wilson (though not a unilateralist) attacked Gaitskell's tactics, and stood against him as leader. Gaitskell believed in passionate commitment and in meeting arguments head-on; but Wilson believed in keeping the party together at all costs, in careful ambiguity. He attacked from the left, but he was always seeking the point of balance.

Then in January 1963 Gaitskell died, and the party had to choose between Wilson and George Brown, the mercurial candidate on the right (it is odd to recall how close Brown came to the premiership). Some Labour MPs, including Denis Healey and Michael Stewart, were so appalled by the choice of evils that they nominated a third, James Callaghan. But Wilson emerged as the clear leader and subtly and quickly unified the party, leading it (as Attlee had said it should be led) from left of centre—or so it seemed. But he had begun his march to the middle ground. As the election loomed, he dropped any hint of anti-Americanism and outbid the Tories in his praise of Washington. He proclaimed Britain's world role and supported the British pressure East of Suez. He avoided left-wing noises and made much of the white-hot technological revolution in contrast to Tory amateurism and the Edwardian establishment mentality. He would reorganise government and set up a new department of economic affairs: 10 Downing Street would be not a monastery but a power-house.

When he became prime minister in October 1964 he soon showed himself a master of the consensus, both in the party and in the country. He chose his government with a careful balance; he promoted the then left-wingers, like Barbara Castle, Wedgwood Benn, Crossman and Cousins, into the Cabinet: he was conciliatory to old Gaitskellites like Brown, Jenkins and Crosland. He took three major policy decisions which, though disastrous in their consequences, established him as a patriotic leader in the public mind: he rejected all arguments for devaluation, he stuck to the East of Suez policy, and (in 1965) he proclaimed that he would never use force against the white Rhodesians; and at this last heavy price he achieved the peak of popularity. The Conservatives were dazzled by his showmanship, and depressed by their own leaders—first Douglas-Home, then Heath. By March 1966 Wilson could convincingly present Labour as a natural ruling party—a tremendous personal achievement—and he called and won a general election with a majority of one hundred.

The economic crises of the following four years forced the reversal of most of Wilson's policies. The pound was devalued, the British presence began to be withdrawn from the Far East, deflation caused rising unemployment. The National Plan was *VB* abandoned, the Department of Economic Affairs was closed down. Wilson dropped his old opposition to the Common Market, and in May 1967 applied to enter the Community. He came in conflict with the trade unions, and in 1969 tried unsuccessfully to introduce legislation to control unofficial strikes.

Wilson survived these disasters and reversals with breathtaking bravura and skill in political management. After devaluation, when his promises were discredited, he kept away from television and the party appeared to be ruled by a committee of three. But he soon bounced back. His skills turned out to be almost the opposite of those that were promised before 1964. He was master, not of long-term planning and organisation, but of short-term options and brilliant improvisation: 10 Downing Street, far from being a power house, was a kind of publicity-office, inhabited not by white-hot technocrats but by cosy political friends. As the years passed Wilson became increasingly theatrical. It was partly the Macmillan syndrome—solemn politician transformed into entertainer and gambler. But it seemed even odder in the Labour

45

Party. The Gannex man had become the white-haired showman in the flowery tie.

Few of his colleagues were in a position to complain. Wilson had consistently dominated his cabinet, and his rivals were committed to his policies. When he decided on an election in June 1970, in a mood of euphoria, he had most of his party behind him; so that when he lost there were not many recriminations and no effective rival was in sight. Wilson had apparently converted his party, back in opposition, to recapturing once again the middle ground. The remains of the left wing were humiliated and enraged by his retreat from socialist principles; but Wilson knew, as he puts it, that 'you don't need to worry about the outside left—they've got nowhere else to go: it's the inside left that you must worry about'.

Wilson, at 55, has a unique prestige and experience as the architect of the unified Labour Party, the party of government. But no ex-prime minister can easily revert back to being leader of the opposition. The grandeur of Downing Street, with Whitehall at his command, has shrunk to the gloomy office in Parliament which he left in 1964, with a small ante-room filled with chatting typists, letters, papers and waiting visitors. The huge powers of patronage, which with a stroke of a pen turn enemies into friends or Misters to Lords, has vanished. The old debating tricks that he played on his opposition are now turned against him, to make *him* sound irresponsible, ill-informed. He finds it difficult to stop harking back to past glories, to remind everyone of how much they depended on him, and to justify his mistakes to posterity. Wilson nowadays seems almost mesmerised by his memory, as he recalls the precise moments and words of his triumphs. In the meantime he has been trying to preserve the unity of his party in the face of the divisive issue of the common market; and his sitting on the fence has never been so visible, or so apparently painful. Many Labour MPs insist that they must have a new leader, to restore credibility and to break with the past; but the candidates for the succession are themselves very divided.

WHO RUNS LABOUR?

The fight for the Labour leadership is a very visible battle. The Labour party plays out its rivalries more openly and painfully than the Conservatives; and in its system of elections it is possible to observe something of the fascinating process by which the popular heroes of the masses give way at the summit to the more sophisticated choice of parliamentary colleagues. At the Labour conference each year the party's national executive of twenty-eight is elected from different elements of the party—twelve by trade unions, seven by the constituency parties, one by the professional organisations, and five women elected by the whole party.[1] In addition the leader, deputy leader and treasurer of the party sit on the executive. The constituency votes act as a kind of popularity poll, led by well-known and usually left-wing figures, many of them not associated with government. At the top of the hit parade in 1970 were:

1. Frank Allaun
2. Anthony Wedgwood Benn
3. Barbara Castle
4. Denis Healey
5. Joan Lestor
6. Ian Mikardo
7. Tom Driberg

The executive meets only once a month: its important activities are delegated to committees. The chairmanship of the executive is very part-time and rotates every year, and is thus much less influential than the Tory chairmanship. The most important figure in the party headquarters is hence the full-time senior official, the general secretary who presides over Transport House, the austere block in Smith Square owned and partly occupied by the Transport and General Workers' Union. Transport House has for long been the despair of modern-minded reformers; its dowdy passages, small offices and 'penny-farthing' methods seem in deliberate contrast to the smooth set-up of the Conservative Central Office across the square. There are periodic hopes that a young general secretary will sweep away some of the dust; but Transport House is still the guardian of the austere trade union traditions of the movement, and politicians are wary of trying to reform it for fear of re-opening the whole question of who runs it—the executive, the unions, or the parliamentary party. In the event, the unions are dominant. When the previous secretary, Len Williams, retired in 1968 (to become Sir Leonard Williams, Governor-General of Mauritius), Harold Wilson tried to put forward Anthony

[1] From 1972 the five women's places are expected to be replaced by five more members elected by constituency parties.

Greenwood as his successor; but George Brown and Callaghan wanted to snub Wilson, and persuaded the national executive to choose a 63-year-old veteran trade unionist, Harry Nicholas, the former acting secretary of the Transport and General Workers' Union.

A month or so after the conference (when Labour is in opposition) the parliamentary labour party meets, consisting entirely of Labour MPs. In opposition, they elect their leader (now Harold Wilson), their deputy leader (now Roy Jenkins) and the members of their parliamentary committee, the members of the 'shadow cabinet'. The national executive and the shadow cabinet co-exist painfully. Their conflict arises from the origins of the party, for when it was founded in 1900 the Labour Party was little more than the 'political arm' of the Trades Union Congress, with small prospect of power. But as the movement swelled, grew into a parliamentary party and eventually gained office, so inevitably the actual legislators became the centre of power. In theory the parliamentary party is supposed to be responsible to the annual conference and its executive: in practice the shadow cabinet has its own way. But the wrangling continues; in October 1970 a motion was put forward proposing that conference decisions should be binding on MPs, whether in opposition or government. Harold Wilson warned that the motion raised important constitutional issues and should be remitted or defeated: he quoted the party constitution which says only that the parliamentary party must 'give effect as may be practicable to the principles from time to time approved by the party conference'. Wilson lost the vote, with the two biggest unions voting against him; and there was clearly much resentment at the way the Labour government had ignored conference resolutions. But the motion was no more binding than other motions.

The rows between the conference and the shadow cabinet are only part of the basic tension between the parliamentary leaders and the trade unions, whose ultimate power comes from the fact that they pay for the party; in 1969 they contributed £272,145 out of the total party funds of £366,620. The abortive attempt by Wilson's government to reform the trade unions brought the relationship once again to a head, and raised new doubts about the connection. As Lord George-Brown put it in his memoirs:[1]

[1] George Brown: *In My Way*. Gollancz 1971, p. 17.

It has always been said that the great strength of the British Labour movement is its special relationship with, special dependence upon, the British trade unions. And of course pretty well all our money comes from that source. I wonder whether this is necessarily the right way for us to continue; whether we shouldn't now consider ourselves as a much more broadly-based party, raise our finances in other ways, and not rely upon, or depend upon, this special close attachment to trade unions who can, let us face it, be led by people who have no special attachment to the Labour Party, or can be actively hostile to it.

But there is little immediate prospect of the Labour Party finding an alternative source of large funds; and their contorted relationship with the trade unions is likely to continue. The trade unionists, on their side, know that however contemptuously the shadow cabinet may treat them, they have no other party to go to; and that even though they may be publicly ignored, they have ways of quietly getting their own way on some issues.

SHADOW CABINET

The elections for the shadow cabinet reveal a very different hit-parade from the national executive, with more conservative and responsible-looking men at the top. These were the 'twelve apostles' elected in July 1970, with their votes:

1.	J. Callaghan	178
2.	D. Healey	165
3.	A. Crosland	157
4.	D. Houghton	150
5.	A. Wedgwood Benn	133
6.	M. Foot	124
7.	S. Williams	122
8.	H. Lever	115
9.	E. Short	114
10.	F. Peart	110
11.	G. Thomson	107
12.	B. Castle	98

The list shows how the Labour MPs' ideas of excellence differ from those of the constituency delegates. But this shadow cabinet does not necessarily correspond closely to the actual cabinet-to-be or to the cabinet that has been: in 1970 two ex-ministers came very close to the bottom of the list—John Stonehouse with only fourteen votes and Judith Hart with only twenty-four. The leader is normally expected to give shadow jobs to all the 'twelve apostles'; but he has more than twelve posts, which gives him some latitude. Harold Wilson's full shadow cabinet in July 1970, after the election defeat, with their ages, schools and universities is shown on the page opposite.

Their characteristics show the rarefication of the Labour leadership. Nine of them have been to Oxford, two to Durham University, two to Aberystwyth; only two (James Callaghan and George Thomson) have not been to university. Only one (Roy Mason, an ex-miner) has been a real worker. One (Harold Lever) is a millionaire, four have been schoolmasters and two others university dons. The lack of close links with the workers and trade unionists, particularly in the top rungs of the cabinet, became more marked after the departure of two exuberant ex-trade unionists, Ray Gunter and George Brown; Gunter made the point bitterly when he resigned at his demotion in 1968, that he wanted to return to the folk 'from whence I came'. It is absurd closely to correlate social background with political attitudes; but the abstracted academic background of so many of the shadow cabinet, sharing the same assumptions, reflexes and social milieu, makes the relations between the leadership and the rank-and-file specially spiky. The cabinet's misjudgment in 1969, over their ability to control the trade unions, must be partly ascribed to their lack of colleagues (apart from Callaghan) who could tell them what the workers—and even their parliamentary colleagues— would not stand.

ROY JENKINS

In the shadow cabinet there are three men—Jenkins, Healey and Callaghan—who stand out as possible contenders for the leadership. But all of them are around Wilson's age. Roy Jenkins, at fifty, is the youngest. At first sight he is the most improbable leader of a workers' party. With his big, smooth head he looks like an aristocratic egghead, like a bespectacled Humpty-Dumpty. He talks fastidiously with a lisp, with elaborate qualifications and parentheses, and careful non-enthusiasm: 'I wouldn't be *altogether* excited by that idea ... perhaps not the *most* popular person ... it would be just a *shade* flat-footed.' On television (where he can be very effective) he has developed a habit of wobbling his big head like a goldfish, conveying infinite scepticism. He invites

Harold Wilson (54)	Leader of the Opposition	Wirral Grammar; Jesus, Oxford.
Roy Jenkins (50)	Deputy Leader and Shadow Chancellor	Abersychan Grammar; Balliol, Oxford.
Fred Peart (56)	House of Commons Affairs	Wolsingham Grammar; Bede College, Durham.
Denis Healey (53)	Foreign Affairs	Bradford Grammar; Balliol, Oxford.
Harold Lever (56)	European Affairs	Manchester Grammar; Manchester University.
George Thomson (49)	Defence	Grove Academy, Dundee.
James Callaghan (58)	Home Affairs	Portsmouth Northern Secondary.
Anthony Crosland (52)	Regional Planning, Housing and Local Government and the Environment	Highgate; Trinity, Oxford.
Anthony Wedgwood Benn (45)	Industry and Technology	Westminster; New College, Oxford.
Michael Foot (57)	Fuel and Power	Leighton Park; Wadham, Oxford.
Barbara Castle (59)	Employment and Productivity	Bradford Girls' Grammar; St Hugh's, Oxford.
Shirley Williams (40)	Health and Social Services	St Paul's Girls; Somerville, Oxford; Columbia University, New York.
Edward Short (58)	Education and Science	Bede College, Durham.
Cledwyn Hughes (54)	Agriculture	Holyhead Grammar; University of Wales (Aberystwyth).
William Ross (59)	Scotland	Ayr Academy; Glasgow University.
George Thomas (62)	Wales	Tonypandy Secondary; Southampton University.
Roy Mason (46)	Board of Trade	Royston Senior; London School of Economics.
Lord Shackleton (59)	Opposition Leader in the Lords	Radley; Magdalen, Oxford.
Sir Elwyn Jones (61)	Law Officer	Llanelly Grammar; University of Wales; Gonville and Caius, Cambridge.

comparison with Asquith, the Liberal Prime Minister whose biography he has written: he likes to visit Asquith's grave, one of his closest friends is Asquith's grandson Mark Bonham Carter, and he seems to belong to the Liberal tradition of civilised paternalism. Nothing in his style, except perhaps its tension, could suggest that he was a Welsh miner's son from Pontypool: he never makes reference to his roots. He has risen to be deputy-leader with little intrigue and no demagogy.

His turning away from his roots was emphatic, at the point when he went from Abersychan School (via Cardiff University) to Balliol, where he acquired an owlish manner, long 'mmm's' and a teddy-bear overcoat: he became librarian of the Oxford Union and took a first in PPE. Ever since Balliol he has felt free to pursue his own social and cultural preferences, without bothering too much about his political image. But he had no doubts about his allegiance; he was emphatically not a Tory. He spent part of the war in the Artillery—an experience which left little mark on him—and in 1948 went into parliament. He campaigned for Britain in Europe, and became a close friend of Hugh Gaitskell (he has never been close to Wilson). He often seemed more interested in journalism and authorship than in parliament: but he turned down the editorship of *The Economist*, and when Labour came back into power in 1964 he became Minister of Aviation. His public personality was still rather nervous and forbidding, and he seemed specially ill-at-ease with trade unionists.

His rise in the government was spectacular. By the following year Wilson, forgiving the old enmity, had brought him into the cabinet as Home Secretary, where he managed both to set up the Race Relations Board and to acquire the confidence of the police. In 1967 he took over the Treasury after the disastrous regime of Callaghan; after devaluation he introduced a severe budget which at last cut down on very rich incomes, until Anthony Barber gave it all back. The severity sat well on him, and he looked like Wilson's bank manager, maintaining stern but reasonable discipline behind his leader's showmanship. After Labour's fall from power he left no doubt that he wanted eventually to be leader: he stood for the deputy leadership in July 1970, and easily beat his rivals, Fred Peart and Michael Foot.

Jenkins remains in his style more like a Liberal than a Labour leader: he seems most convincing, most himself, when talking about 'the civilised society' and tolerant values, and in this field his achievement is notable. It is harder to imagine him coping with militant trade unionists; and like Wilson he seriously miscalculated the practicability of legislating against the unions in 1969. He has lost much of his earlier interest in egalitarianism ('when there is no egalitarianism there is no socialism': 1952); watching his patrician style, one might wonder if the Labour revolution of Attlee, Bevin and Morrison had ever really happened—he seems so directly in the tradition of Asquith. But in this high-minded tradition he has carried many younger Labour members with him, and has established a school of Jenkinsites—such as Bill Rodgers, Tom Bradley, Brian Walden, Roy Hattersley, David Marquand, Dick Taverne—to whom he is the guardian of the decent and intelligent principles of the party. And he has remained remarkably steadfast on the issue which has for him been most perilous—the common market. In July 1971 he said he would have accepted the Tories' terms for joining the Six, and thus emerged in angry and open conflict with Harold Wilson.

DENIS HEALEY

Denis Healey is a less evidently complicated and more extrovert character than Jenkins. He has a big frame, a tough face and menacing eyebrows which nearly meet in the middle. He loves fighting, and can be rude and bullying to anyone he thinks weaker: he is a witty and relentless talker, and likes to lay down the law not only about all aspects of politics, but about culture too. His father ran a technical school in Yorkshire, and he went from Bradford Grammar School to Balliol—three years before Jenkins, and at the same time as Heath. He moved sharply left and joined the Communist Party at Oxford for two years. After the war Major Healey was still fiercely radical, and at a famous speech in the 1945 Party Conference he said: 'The upper classes in every country are selfish, depraved, dissolute and decadent'; but he became very anti-Communist. He joined the staff at Labour Party headquarters, became an expert on foreign affairs and got into Parliament in 1952. He kept aloof from the party feuds (though basically Gaitskellite) and was wittily sceptical about everyone; others in turn regarded him as a technocrat—a label he loathes.

In 1964 Wilson made Healey Minister of Defence, where he stayed for the whole five-and-a-half years—a record term. He began as the defender of Far Eastern bases and F 111 planes; he ended by pulling out from the Far East and cancelling the F 111. He was the strong-arm man of the government, showing that the left could be as tough as the right—both with the Russians and with his own generals. In 1967 he was ready to sell arms to South Africa, and he liked to talk bloodcurdlingly about (for instance) blowing up the Russian Fleet in the Mediterranean. Politically, he has never built up a following or school: there are no perceptible Healeyites.

Back in opposition, Healey quickly set about wooing the left-wing of the party, and he achieved second place in the elections for the shadow cabinet. He paid a visit to South Africa, and outspokenly attacked the decision to sell arms, which he had been in favour of three years before. He now admits that he was wrong in 1967, and that in the row about arms he became too preoccupied with his battle against Wilson's methods of government. But the issue raises the crucial question of whether Healey's compassion and sense of justice are too easily overwhelmed by his preoccupations with power.

The rivalry between Healey and Jenkins, the two Balliol socialists, will certainly loom larger. Jenkins has a greater following, and a more liberal appeal; but Healey is more obviously a strong man, more ruthless and not afraid to strike.

JAMES CALLAGHAN

Alone of the top four, Leonard James Callaghan was not at Oxford, and he still has the look and sound of the natural leader who has pushed his way up. 'Big Jim' has a warm presence, like a cuddly bear, and he generates boyish enthusiasm, with expressions like 'Oh boy!' and 'My goodness!', and old-fashioned back-slapping and finger-wagging. He was brought up in Portsmouth; his grandfather was a ship's captain, his father became a chief petty officer, and he himself was a wartime lieutenant on the battleship *Queen Elizabeth*: he still has something of a quarterdeck swing. His first job, at seventeen, was as a tax officer. After the war he went into Parliament and soon got junior jobs in transport and the Admiralty. His was not a great intellect, but once he did understand something he could often expound it more comprehensibly than his intellectual colleagues. In 1964 Wilson rashly made him Chancellor; he never really mastered the Treasury and almost lost control of public expenditure. Eventually, three years later, he was shifted to the Home Office, where he recovered his reputation: in crises like student demonstrations he was able to generate calm, and the Ulster crisis showed him at his Irish best, both tough and understanding.

Callaghan makes no bones about bidding for the leadership. In 1969 he sided with the trade unionists against Wilson, and won: any future rift in the party between workers and intellectuals would probably help his prospects. Since the departure of George Brown, he is the nearest thing to a man of the people. Now, as treasurer of the party, he has a strong base in the Labour machine. But he is four years older than his leader.

ANTHONY CROSLAND

The dark horse in the race is the most outspoken of the Labour leaders, Anthony Crosland, who has been, since he wrote his book *The Future of Socialism* in 1956, the chief theorist of the revisionists in the Party. He has often been bracketed with Jenkins: they were at Oxford together (Crosland is two years older), they were both close friends of Gaitskell, and they were rivals in Wilson's cabinet: Crosland became Minister of Education, then President of the Board of Trade. But Crosland is a more uncompromising figure, a persistent egalitarian; he comes from a family of Plymouth Brethren, his father was a senior civil servant who refused his knighthood, and Crosland himself is a fascinatingly complex personality, who often seems to be lacerating himself as well as everyone else. At parties he is to be seen, a rumpled but still boyish presence, with cigar-end drooping from his mouth, scowling and exploding with his celebrated rudeness, with such phrases as 'if you *really* think that, you must be even stupider than I thought'. He has never found it easy to establish easy relationships with plain men, like his electors at Grimsby, and on television, too, he projects his bad-tempered and petulant style. But in the reaction against the Wilson technique of all-things-to-all-men, Crosland's anti-cosy style has its advantages, as a kind of answer to Heath, and his attacks on the Tories have a cutting edge which makes them more convincing than his rivals' more ambiguous sallies and self-justifications. He remains convinced of the need to increase taxation and public spending, to push ahead with comprehensive education; and in spite of his disdainful attitudes and his own enjoyment of good living, he identifies himself indignantly with the ordinary Labour voter. In November 1970 he gave an impressive lecture to the Fabian Society (the intellectual shock-troops of the party, of which he has been chairman)—setting out his manifesto for 'a social democratic Britain'.

> I have always looked forward, in everything which I have written, to the day when we could stop fussing about growth and the allocation of resources, and turn our attention to more fruitful and cultural pursuits. But that day is not here yet. The basic issues of poverty, inequality, an inadequate social sector and a drab environment are still the overriding ones; and questions of growth, taxation, expenditure and social control remain incomparably more urgent than alienation or student revolt or the mass media. And that is not to mention the impoverished condition of the developing countries. If there were some who doubted this on June 18th, they surely cannot do now. The new Conservative Government is showing itself the most ideological and reactionary right-wing government that Europe has seen in two decades ... Its commitment to lower public spending and its ideology of laissez-faire will mean more poverty, more inequality, a meaner social sector and a worse environment.

POST-WAR SOCIALISTS

Beyond these men in their fifties are the large generation of younger members who came into the party after the war, who can look ahead to the 1980s for their opportunities. Two, perhaps, stand out with special prospects. Anthony Wedgwood Benn, still only 45, has always claimed a special mastery of the future—the man of TV, computers, and all forms of magic communication. As a young socialist he was a keen anti-colonialist and vaguely left-wing: but in power he became immersed in the Ministry of Technology, which he ran for three years. With his science-fiction speeches and his enjoyment of publicity, Benn is subject to some scepticism from his colleagues; but he has a rare capacity for salesmanship, for enthusing others, and placating awkward trade unionists: he is thought to be Wilson's choice as eventual successor.

Intellectually more powerful, but politically less prominent is Shirley Williams, a likely successor to Barbara Castle as the keeper of the party's conscience; she preserves a natural humanity and honesty in the midst of party politics. A Catholic Fabian, she has been concerned both with the third world and with Europe; she sticks to her support of the common market. She has survived her time as the darling of the Labour Party, the praise of Tories and *The Times*, and from time to time she is talked of as the first woman prime minister.

The separate roots of the party, the intellectuals and the workers, are still very evident. At one end is a clutch of young dons, much swelled since the 1964 election, equipped with expertise about economics or political science: like Professor Mackintosh, David Marquand, Brian Walden. On the other side are young trade unionists who have worked their way up through the branches; like the ex-miner Roy Mason; Bob Mellish, the dockers' MP in Bermondsey and present Chief Whip; or Reg Prentice, a former official of the Transport and General Workers' Union. The social contrast is less extreme than it was; several trade unionists (like Prentice) have gone on later to university; and there is a new crop of sons of trade unionists who have partly taken over from the sons of lay preachers (as Harold Wilson calls them) who came in in the 1945 generation. But the cross-purposes can still be considerable; and there are few who have the magnitude to inspire both sides of the party.

OLD LEFT AND NEW

Every year at the Labour conference one evening is booked for the 'Tribune Rally', whose camaraderie is like a wartime reunion: it raises money for the weekly left-wing paper *Tribune* (founded by Sir Stafford Cripps), but it also provides an emotional letting-off-steam for the old radicals, or a stoking-up of their anger against the leadership. The speakers are war-horses like Lord (Fenner) Brockway, the 83-year-old anti-colonialist, or Ian Mikardo, the hefty trade unionist with square glasses and a gargly voice: they are greeted with cries of Mik! or Fenner! like old comedians. The greatest applause is for the most explosive of them, Michael Foot, who inherits the left-wing mantle and the seat (Ebbw Vale) of Aneurin Bevan. Foot orates more brilliantly than any other politician, his long hair flying, his arms flailing, his voice cracking, as if in the last paroxysms of hysteria; while off-stage he has a delightful presence, kind, cultivated and funny. He is the youngest and fiercest of the five Foot brothers, the sons of a West Country Liberal who all but one turned to the Labour Party; Michael first rose as a journalist, and edited *Tribune* for nine years. He laid into Wilson's government for selling out to bankers, Rhodesians and Americans. In parliament he is sometimes in danger of being the licensed jester, the man everyone can afford to love because he keeps to the parliamentary game. But he may still find his way into the cabinet: in 1970 he was voted into the shadow cabinet where he sits rather improbably as shadow minister of power, the lone voice of the left.

The weakness of this old left has been that, though their attacks on Wilson's leadership sounded deadly, they have not been able convincingly to describe how pure British socialism can be workable in the midst of a western world which is basically capitalist. Many of the old radicals, like Michael Foot, appear little Englanders at heart, with their nostalgic picture of Britain finding her Utopia alone; it was ironic that the most striking success of the left was in alliance with the Tory right-wing (though for very different reasons) to defeat Wilson's plans to reform the House of Lords. In their dislike of the common market and Americans the left-wing of the Labour Party can often find themselves joining with the right-wing of the Tory Party, as old-fashioned patriots determined that Britain, in whatever direction, should go it alone.

Outside parliament there are all kinds of groups, old and new, of socialists who were disillusioned (or confirmed in their disillusion) by Wilson's coming-to-terms with international capitalism. Many socialist students in the fifties took as their bible Anthony Crosland's *The Future of Socialism*, with its central message that capitalism can be tamed and modified, to achieve socialist objectives including equality and the abolition of poverty. But the new student generations of the sixties, surveying the neglect of the third world, the Vietnam war, and the continuing poverty in Britain, were much less convinced by revisionist arguments, and a whole cluster of radical magazines and groups have grown up—still more since the student revolts in the late sixties. Many are engaged in local activities, trying to improve housing, social welfare or education among immigrants or the poor—retreating from the national scene, but advancing into more immediate practical action.

And at any Labour or TUC conference demonstration can be seen the ragged ranks of the fringe bodies of the left, the thick-bearded men and patched-jeans girls, the groups loosely known as the Trots and Commies, who have long ago given up parliament as a means of achieving their goals. The extra-parliamentary left in Britain is much weaker than its equivalent in France, Italy or even Germany, but in the last few years it has again shown stirrings; intellectually, if not practically, the old mole of revolution is still burrowing away. The six years of the Wilson government, with the broken promises, turnabouts and debts to international bankers, strengthened their case and their numbers; and the wave of student revolts in 1968 scooped up new young followers.

The oldest and still the biggest of them, the Communist Party itself, is extra-parliamentary by necessity rather than design; it put up fifty-eight candidates in the 1970 election, but between them they achieved only 38,000 votes in the whole country (the only communist representative in parliament is Lord Milford in the House of Lords, a veteran crusader from a Welsh ship-owning family, married to the widow of a former editor of the *Daily Worker*). The CP is not what it was; the party lost about 10,000 members after it had supported the invasion of Hungary in 1956; it now has only about 30,000 members, half its post-war strength: its newspaper the *Morning Star* (formerly the *Daily Worker*) sells about 50,000 copies a day. In the last few years the party has come round to a more independent, Titoist line: and after the invasion of Czechoslovakia in 1968 the national executive condemned the intervention. There were angry protests from veteran Communists including Palme Dutt against this disloyalty to Moscow, but the Congress in 1969 endorsed the condemnation by 295 votes to 118.

The Communists' role in the trade union movement (see Chapter 36) remains very active; the miners' secretary, Lawrence Daly, has been a member of the party; the engineers' secretary, Hugh Scanlon, was a member until 1955. The Communist Party still provides the political education and the old-boy network for hundreds of shop stewards, as Eton provides it for Tory politicians; they are both, as Harold Wilson described the organisers of the seamen's strike in 1966, 'tightly-knit groups of politically-motivated men'. But since the mid-fifties, after Khrushchev's denunciation of Stalin and the invasion of Hungary, the Communist Party has lost most of its appeal for intellectuals. In its place emerged the 'new left' which was born out of the conjunction of Hungary and Suez, and which defined itself as a simultaneous rejection of Stalinism and Social Democracy; its mouthpiece was the *New Left Review*, a merger of the *New Reasoner* with the *Universities and Left Review*. The 'new left' soon gained popular appeal from the Campaign for Nuclear Disarmament, but did not retain it; as the editor of the *NLR*, Perry Anderson (a highly articulate Old Etonian), described its problem in 1965:

> The New Left had begun as a handful of intellectuals: it gained a certain minority-middle-class audience: it never touched any sector of the working-class. Once it had ceased to be a purely intellectual grouping, the hope of becoming a major political movement haunted it, and ended by dissipating its initial assets. The pressure of circumstances was partly responsible for this change. The existence, in CND, of a genuine mass movement with a comparable base, but without any articulated ideology, seemed to offer a vacuum designed for the New Left to fill. It tried to do so, in 1960–61, and paid the price—of being at the mercy of a conjunctural fluctuation. When the tide of unilateralism ebbed after the Scarborough Conference of 1961, its strength seeped away as well. It had lost the virtues of intellectual energy without gaining those of political efficacy.

The *New Left Review* continues to be the main forum of intellectual Marxists, with important contributions from scholars like Eric Hobsbawm, John Rex, or R. D. Laing; but it remains more theoretical than practical, based on the universities, and in the meantime other groups have grown up, more ambitious for action, agitation and contact with the workers. The list opposite shows some of them, as they stood in April 1971, with their policies and leaders, as far as I can detect them.

The Trotskyists, following Trotsky's belief in world revolution as opposed to a purely Russian revolution, gained new support from the anti-Soviet mood of the late sixties. Their members remain predominantly middle-class intellectuals and students; but two groups, the Socialist Labour League (SLL) and the International Socialists (IS), have had some success in penetrating the factories, and have been involved in some of the strikes and protests—at Pilkington's, Ford's and the GEC factories on Merseyside: the Conservative Industrial Relations Bill gave a new chance for them to show their solidarity with the workers, and they were prominent in protests to 'kill the Bill'. The first success of the 1968 revolt in France (which owed much to French Trotskyists) gave encouragement to their British equivalents, and led to the short-lived Radical Socialist Students' Federation (RSSF) (see Chapter 8) and new magazines, including *Black Dwarf* and *Red Mole* (see Chapter 21). The trend against centralised authority, whether among students or workers, has given a boost to anarchist movements. But there remains the awkward problem of how to build an anti-authoritarian movement which

Group	Members	Founded	Prominent Members	Papers	Policy, etc.
Communist Party of Great Britain	30,000	1920	John Gollan (Secretary), Bert Ramelson (Industrial Organiser)	*Morning Star* (Daily)	Pro-Moscow, veering towards Titoist
Communist Party of Great Britain (Marxist-Leninist)	250(?)	1968	Reg Birch	*The Marxist*	Maoist. Based on North London Engineers.
International Socialists	1500	1950	Tony Cliff (founder), John Palmer, Paul Foot	*International Socialism*, *Socialist Worker*	Trotskyist ($\frac{2}{3}$ manual workers, $\frac{1}{3}$ white collar).
Socialist Labour League	300(?) (large periphery)	1958	Gerry Healy, Cliff Slaughter	*Workers' Press*, Fourth International	Trotskyist Apocalyptic. Mostly working-class. Non-collaborating.
International Marxist Group	350(?)	1964	Pat Jordan (Secretary), Tariq Ali	*Red Mole*, *International*	Trotskyist. Mostly Universities. Pro-Guevara.
Revolutionary Socialist League	100(?)	1950s	Ted Grant	*The Militant*	Trotskyist (pro-Labour Party.)
Spartacus League	(?)	1970	Peter McGowan	—	Youth group of IMG.
Solidarists	(?)	1961	Chris Pallas	*Solidarity*	Anarcho-Marxist.

itself has enough authority to retain its own following; anarchist movements, by definition, cannot be mobilised or centralised beyond a certain point.

Ever since its beginnings the Labour party has been torn between being a party of protest and a party of government; and in the fifties the conflict came near to breaking it, when the battle raged between those who insisted that Labour must not give up its principles and those who argued that it must regain the middle ground. After the 1970 election there was much greater agreement on the need to recapture the centre, but argument soon broke out again. On the one hand Richard Crossman, fresh from the compromises of government, established his *New Statesman* as the keeper of the Holy Grail, arguing that the consensus had at last broken up, and that Labour must re-establish a firm position on the left. The Tory Industrial Relations Bill, the budget, the common market negotiations and the Tory Immigration Bill all generated a burst of left-wing opposition, including quick turnrounds from ex-ministers like Barbara Castle. But the leaders of the party were determined not to let Labour slip away from its position as a convincing and moderate alternative party: and Wilson saw as his main achievement that he had made his party into the 'party of government', the equivalent of the Democrats in America.

In the twenty-five years since 1945 the Labour Party had now had eleven years in power, the Conservatives thirteen; the Tories were no longer the obvious natural rulers or the Socialists the natural opposers. The Labour Party looked much more confident and respectable: but on the other hand it was much less clearly defined as the party of radical change, and Heath's Conservative government often looked more radical than Wilson's. 'We must not expect a full-scale peaceful revolution every time a Labour government is elected,' said Roy Jenkins at the party conference in October 1970. 'If we do, I think the occasions on which we are elected will not be as frequent as we should wish to expect. We must keep our radical cutting edge. But we should now see our role as being able to make substantial progress at frequent intervals rather than cataclysmic jumps forward at extremely infrequent intervals.'

After its seventy years history, the Labour Party has almost completely ousted the Liberal Party as the alternative to the Tories; and in the process has taken on many Liberal characteristics. Men like Roy Jenkins, Anthony Crosland or Harold Lever have appeared increasingly interested in questions of individual freedom, rights and privacy, and many of the great achievements of the Labour government—the Family Planning Act, the Divorce Act, the Equal Pay Act, the Abortion Act, the extension of the Arts Council—belonged to the Liberal tradition. As for the Liberal Party itself, it was now very despondent. In the sixties it appeared to be experiencing some upturn after its long downward slope; the regional discontent on the Celtic fringe and the impatience with Macmillan's Tory Party had helped to give them three million votes and nine MPs at the 1964 election, and in 1966 they returned twelve members. The enthusiastic young Liberal speakers, with great freedom to criticise, had captured plenty of headlines; their leader, Jo Grimond (married to Asquith's grand-daughter) was a brilliant mass-orator who offered a gay, classless new Britain freed from the giant party machines; and in 1967 he was succeeded by another showman, Jeremy Thorpe, a theatrical crowd-pleaser who toured the country in a helicopter. The Liberal conferences had a special charm, with rich Whiggish sentiments occasionally interrupted by young angries attacking the rich. Their high command included great individualists: Lord Beaumont, a florid millionaire clergyman; Eric Lubbock, the victor of Orpington; and David Steel, an outspoken young campaigner for abortion and against apartheid. The young Liberals have a special panache and attraction for the radical left—much more than the Young Socialists—and in 1971 they elected a dynamic chairman Peter Hain, an ex-South African of only 22, who had led the boycott of South African cricketers. But in the 1970 election the Liberals were not able to provide a convincing alternative between the two giant parties, and in the regions where they had been strongest, nationalist candidates were now challenging their members. At the election they lost six members—including Lubbock at Orpington—and were back to where they were in 1959. The Labour Party had little need to take note of them.

But Labour's taking-over of some of the Liberal clothes and its preoccupation with 'civilised' issues put the party in danger of alienating some of the working-class support on which its future depended. A Fabian pamphlet published in March 1971 made the case that the element of 'Labourist populism' in the party was becoming too much overlaid by the element of 'liberal progressivism';[1] and that this was one factor in losing working-class support in the 1970 election. The Labour government's 'concern for permissive legislation, the arts, higher education and technological efficiency could not mask its failure to deal adequately with housing, unemployment and the cost of living'. The criticism was taken up by Anthony Crosland, who wrote in the *Sunday Times* (April 4, 1971):

> I have long been locked in conflict with a middle-class element on the left which seems to me to show an elitist and even condescending attitude to the wants and aspirations of ordinary people. (This elitism is notably strong among violently 'radical' students in the universities.) Incredible as it may seem, I and others have had to defend the affluent society and the right of workers to own motor cars and to take packaged holidays. I have recently had to criticise some of my natural friends in the environmental lobby for not realising that eighty per cent of our people live an urban life ... The need for a populist streak in our thinking becomes greater as the social composition of the Parliamentary Labour Party changes and college graduates (often lecturers) increasingly outnumber trade union MPs. The temptation becomes ever-stronger to seek the esteem of the Liberal audience of columnists and television commentators; college graduates also, with essentially middle-class values, who since childhood have seldom ventured out of the introverted world of central London into the rougher provincial world where most Labour voters live.

In the meantime the overwhelming issue of the common market has put old conflicts into a new perspective, and made a deep crack in the Labour Party. The resistance to Britain's entry provides a new rallying cry to unite the trade unionists (like Scanlon and Jones), the far left (like Michael Foot and Ian Mikardo) and the inside left (like Crossman and Benn), together with some men from the Labour right (like Douglas Jay). The entry into Europe had always threatened to divide Labour, for most of the left-wing and the unions have seen the common market as a threat to British ideals of socialism and working-class standards of living; and in 1962 Gaitskell himself, much concerned about the commonwealth, swung against Europe. Harold Wilson managed to persuade his cabinet in 1967 (apart from Douglas Jay, whom he dropped) to reapply for entry; but the terms of their approval were qualified and ambiguous, and

[1] John Gyford and Stephen Haseler: *Social Democracy: Beyond Revisionism*. Fabian Research Series, March 1971.

the Tory negotiations, with public opinion clearly against them, gave a pretext for Labour MPs to swing back again. The Labour Party has always been prone to the illusion that Britain can build her own kind of socialism, independently of the rest of Europe; an illusion which (I believe) threatens to cut them off from the realities of contemporary power. Wilson's years in power showed clearly enough how little room for manoeuvre was left for a Labour Government in debt to foreign banks, dependent on foreign markets and foreign alliances; and the strongest argument of the pro-marketeers is that by entering Europe they will increase rather than diminish Britain's freedom of action. As Roy Jenkins put it, in his speech to New York bankers in December 1970:

> The principal political case for membership . . . is that it enlarges the nation's ability to play an effective role in determining its own destiny. To pretend to exercise a sovereignty which has ceased to be effective is in fact to restrict and not to preserve national freedom. For almost any country, certainly for any power of the second or third rank, to attempt to provide exclusively for its own defence today would mean either that it was dependent on the whims of its neighbours to attack or defend it as they chose, or that it accepted a crippling (and still probably ineffective) burden which in turn greatly reduced its freedom to do other things, including the raising of the standard of living of its population. Equally, in the economic field, to be shut out of the main groups which determine the world's economic climate does not mean exemption from the influence of that climate—you are only too likely to be buffeted about by it—but merely a loss of influence in determining it and less strength with which to withstand its rigours. For any medium rank power today a willingness to pool sovereignty is thus an essential pre-requisite for both influence and, in a paradoxical but real sense, national freedom.

4

Cabinet

IN the pursuit of power, members of parliament enjoy one
over-riding advantage over other professions: only they can be
appointed to the government. Unlike other legislatures—notably
the American and French—the British parliament has a virtual
monopoly of governmental jobs. In recent years only one man,
Percy Mills in 1956, has been brought directly into the government
from outside Westminster (he was immediately created Baron
Mills, and put into the House of Lords): a few others, like John
Davies in Heath's government and Frank Cousins in Wilson's,
have been found seats in the Commons, to get them into the
cabinet. But, in general, the government is reserved for MPs: and
however powerless a backbench member of parliament may feel
himself, he can always hope eventually for a position in Whitehall.
When an MP reaches the higher levels of government, he is
enveloped in the secret self-contained world of state affairs. The
post office engineers arrive at his home to install a green 'scram-
bler' telephone, which can only be unscrambled by other ministers and senior civil servants. He moves around with a big red
leather-covered box with a royal crest and 'ER' on top, to carry
state papers. He has a car and a green chauffeuse to wait for
him wherever he is, to relieve him of all difficulties of transport

66

and topography—a benefit which looms quite extraordinarily large in the attractions of the job.

A government consists altogether of about a hundred politicians —about a sixth of the members of parliament—including such unlikely people as the Solicitor-General for Scotland and the Captain of the Yeomen of the Guard; and on top of these hundred there are thirty to forty 'parliamentary private secretaries' who are unpaid, but who are expected to be loyal to their ministers. Harold Wilson's government had a record number of members; in 1968 there were 128 MPs and peers in the government, including twenty-one cabinet ministers, thirty-two ministers not in the cabinet, thirty-five junior ministers. Edward Heath's government was appreciably smaller, with eighteen in the cabinet, twenty-four ministers not in the cabinet, and thirty-two junior ministers.

A job in the government, after the job of an ordinary MP, marks the entry into the world of People Who Know; even parliamentary secretaries convey that special air of importance, of obtrusive discretion and elaborate busy-ness, which suggests the beginnings of a character-change. But the real goal of most members is to become a cabinet minister. The cabinet is the core, not only of power, but of what can be almost as satisfying to the ego—secrecy. All government is shrouded in the folds of secrecy, but there is no secret like a cabinet secret.

The mystique of secrecy and power surrounding the inner sanctum of government is so exciting to politicians that they easily become bemused by it. Lord Hill described in his memoirs how: 'I never quite got used to the idea that I was a member of the cabinet. For me, every meeting throughout the five and a half years I was a cabinet minister was something of an occasion. I could not get over my surprise that I was there at all . . . Most important to me, *I* was there.'[1]

It is in the cabinet that all the political argy-bargy of parliament, all the high-flown speech-making, attitude-taking, play-acting, comes face to face with the cold facts of government. The cabinet minister is supposed to combine three different personalities. He should like any MP represent his constituency, glad-hand and jolly along with the rest; he should also be the parliamentarian, taking up partisan positions on any issue that requires it; but he must also spend most of his time immersed in

[1] Lord Hill: *Both Sides of the Hill,* 1964, p. 235.

his own office, running 'a great department of state', caught up in the intricate machinery of bureaucracy. The mixture of roles is bizarre. It is not surprising that not many can effectively combine all three, or that cabinet ministers are apt to appear unusually split personalities.

The cabinet meets in a long white room at the back of 10 Downing Street, with awkward pillars in the middle, looking out on to a garden. Ministers leave their hats and coats on a rack outside, labelled 'Lord Chancellor', 'Paymaster General', etc., and sit down in front of green baize, pens and paper, on a long curved table, the shape of an aeroplane wing, designed so that the prime minister can see everyone. The prime minister—who also often uses the room as his office—sits in the middle, facing the Horse Guards. The prime minister opens the meeting, and ministers address their remarks to him, referring with careful impersonality to their colleagues: 'I can't quite agree with the Lord Privy Seal . . .' 'What do you think, Minister of Transport?' This strange diction has the advantage, not only of depersonalising the meeting, but of reminding the members that their presence depends on the title which the prime minister has conferred on them.

Patrick Gordon Walker, who was a cabinet minister under Attlee and Wilson, has described in his short book on the cabinet some of the intimate details of its meetings:

> Members speak as called by the prime minister. The usual way of indicating a desire to speak is to say 'Prime Minister' when the previous speaker has finished—or sometimes before. If several members do this together, the prime minister will call one of them, saying, for instance, 'Secretary of State for Wales'. Whilst someone is speaking a member may indicate his desire to speak, perhaps by waving a pencil or slightly raising his hand. Mr Harold Wilson would often indicate by gesture the order in which he intended to call the next two or three to speak. Speeches are brief and almost always matter of fact: though sometimes passion and even anger can enter in. In 1894 Gladstone was so angry with Harcourt for not backing him on the reduction of the estimates that he moved his chair round and turned his back on him. I have known quick and angry exchanges, sometimes as part of a discussion, sometimes cutting into it or said quietly enough not to be generally heard. At times such as these 'You' rather than the ministerial title tends to be used.[1]

The job of being a cabinet minister is badly paid compared to

[1] Patrick Gordon Walker: *The Cabinet*, Jonathan Cape 1970, p. 106–7.

top jobs in industry, and demands far harder work. It is constantly subject to public criticism. It leaves little time for the normal pleasures of life. It is insecure, and it carries no pension. Yet very few willingly give it up. What keeps them there seems to be not so much the love of power—many are unclear what to do with it—but the love of being at the heart of information and events. As Iain Macleod put it:

> I think the main attraction for me at least, and I believe this would be true of most politicians, is of being at the centre of the web, not just of having power, although I think that is part of the make-up of most politicians, but in the end, in every decision of importance that affects this country, the threads of those decisions run into the cabinet room.[1]

Perhaps only four or five of them have serious ambitions to be prime minister. With many of the others the fear of losing power is probably as great a motive force as the desire to gain it, and it is this which helps to make resigning so difficult, and rare. Inside the cabinet room a minister is caught up in the stream of events, sure of his importance as part of a team, and linked to the network of reassuring officials. Outside, he is alone: and the loneliness of a would-be resigner is terrible. However exhausting or compromising the job, having it is less agonising than losing it, and everyone in power knows that—such is the power of the prime minister and the commitment of his colleagues—any man who resigns does so either too early or too late. As George Brown put it to parliament after he resigned the Foreign Secretaryship, in March 1968:

> To those who say I did it on the wrong issue and at the wrong time and in the wrong temper, let me just say this. There never could be a wholly right time, as those who have walked this unhappy road and spoken from this seat before me can no doubt testify, and if one waited for the cold, calculating consideration of all personal and other consequences, one would probably never move at all.

CABINET NETWORK

Behind the full meetings of cabinet, which only occupy about four hours a week, lies the elaborate information network centring on the cabinet office. The office was established by Lloyd George in 1916, to provide a secretariat for cabinet meetings: before then

[1] Interview with Malcolm Muggeridge. Granada TV, October 16, 1961.

no record was kept, and two ministers would often embarrassingly interpret the same decision in opposite ways. Lord Hartington's private secretary wrote to Gladstone's PS in 1882: 'My chief has told me to ask you what the devil was decided, for he be damned if he knows.'[1] After the war the cabinet office became permanent, under Sir Maurice Hankey (later Lord Hankey), who was its secretary for twenty-two years—under Lloyd George, Bonar Law, MacDonald, Baldwin and Chamberlain—before he joined Chamberlain's war cabinet itself. In its first fifty years the cabinet office grew from Hankey's small base of four assistant secretaries, with a few clerks and typists, into a major department with a staff of 422.

There have only been four secretaries of the cabinet—Hankey, Bridges, Brook and Trend. Sir Norman Brook (later Lord Normanbrook), who retired in 1963, combined the positions of Head of the Home Civil Service with Secretary to the Cabinet; but after his retirement the jobs were separated, with Sir Burke Trend as Secretary to the Cabinet, and Sir Laurence Helsby as Head of the Civil Service. The separation diminished the pressure on a single man, but the cabinet secretary still carries a great load. 'The problem is how to maintain the focus,' as one man in the cabinet office said to me: 'without overloading the system ... the greatest threat to orderly government is the sheer pressure of business.'

The Secretary to the Cabinet is at the centre of the focus, responsible for the organisational nexus behind cabinet decisions. 'Cabinet papers' are kept circulating by messengers with red boxes, giving details of matters which one minister wants to bring up, and providing the secret newspaper for Whitehall (a box goes each day to the Queen). From the cabinet papers the prime minister, with the help of the cabinet secretary, compiles the cabinet agenda—which is itself (like all agendas) an important instrument of policy, playing up some issues and ignoring others.

Sir Burke Trend, the present Secretary to the Cabinet, is well qualified to be the discreet spider in the middle of the web, and for years he has had the reputation of having one of the smoothest minds in the civil service. He came from a minor public school, Whitgift, took a scholarship to Oxford and a classical double first. He moved up through the Treasury, and

[1] Lord Hankey: *Diplomacy by Conference*, pp. 53–67. 1946.

reached the critical job of Principal Private Secretary to the Chancellor of the Exchequer (first Dalton, then Cripps) which nearly always leads to swift promotion, teaching all the arts and tricks of the Whitehall machine. By 1956 he was Deputy-Head of the Civil Service and for the following fifteen years has been continuously at the hub.

Like his predecessor, Trend has a passion for non-disclosure. He leads a very secluded and well-insulated life; he *has* been observed lunching in Soho, but usually he lunches very late in a special corner table in the cabinet office mess. He is the guardian of all information that might embarrass the government; when George Brown wanted to reveal his rows with Wilson, it was Trend who had to approve it; when Jeremy Bray, one of Wilson's junior ministers, wanted to publish a book about Whitehall, *Decision in Government*, it was Trend who advised that Bray should leave the government. The extent of Trend's influence on government policy is one of the best-kept of all cabinet secrets. He is a less formidable and aloof personality than Brook, but therefore more likely to be consulted; his influence over Harold Wilson was considerable—particularly in encouraging his East of Suez policy, and in the regrettable affair of the security 'D' notices. Trend's central position, his shrewdness and clarity, and his quick translations of talk into action, can give him more influence on events than many cabinet ministers.

The cabinet office is augmented from time to time by individual prime ministers, with special advisors and units: Lloyd George had his 'garden suburb' of experts, Churchill had his eccentric private empire, Wilson had Sir Solly Zuckerman (now Lord Zuckerman) and Lord Balogh as advisers on scientific and economic policy. Heath in November 1970 set up a unit called the Central Policy Review Staff, which was meant to provide long-term advice and expertise on the whole range of economic, scientific and administrative problems; at the head of it is the most surprising of Heath's appointees, the sixty-year-old Lord Rothschild—Labour peer, FRS, authority on spermatozoa, just retired from Shell. Rothschild is unlikely to fit in smoothly into a Whitehall department—he rumbles with complaints, like a smouldering volcano—but he is well qualified to provide disinterested and original scientific advice. He and his unit of gilded young Oxford men are supposed to be advising any cabinet minister that needs them; and Rothschild insists that he will not be Heath's personal adviser. But any strengthening of the cabinet office in the past has tended to strengthen the prime minister, who is just through the door and who is not bogged down in a great department.

The summoning and briefing of all the committees falls on the cabinet secretariat. In contrast to the rest of the bureaucracy it is a machine of legendary speed, a kind of flywheel for the engine of government. It operates from the most beautiful building in Whitehall, the 'Old Treasury Building' by William Kent, at the corner of Downing Street, with a connecting door into Number Ten. Many politicians complain that the cabinet office has become too much the apex of all information, giving too much power to civil servants. Its occupants protest that all they do is to co-ordinate the departments: 'All we do,' said one, 'is to try to collect together people to get things *done*. Somebody's got to do it.' But in the modern pattern of government co-ordination is a large part of power.

Their central task is the translation of cabinet decisions into actions. Trend or his deputy sit at every cabinet meeting, and it is their cabinet minutes which are the frail paperchain between the green table and the departments of state. 'I used to check up to make sure that cabinet decisions were carried out,' Lord Butler once said to me: 'but I soon realised it wasn't necessary. The civil servants come out of their caves like hungry animals and gobble them up.' The cabinet secretary transmutes the rambling arguments into a neat summary of de-personalised conclusions. First-person speeches are changed into oratio obliqua, emotional arguments are transformed into reasoned objections, doubt and muddle become dignified imponderables: and two hours of disjointed discussion is boiled down to a few coherent paragraphs, making it look like a rational argument, with thesis, antithesis and synthesis, with impersonal passive-tense phrases: 'It was held that . . . it was rejoined . . . it was agreed . . .' It is not thought that Trend's accounts of cabinets in the sixties, when they emerge from the Public Records Office in thirty years' time, will provide much excitement for the waiting historians.

The cabinet minutes are the process by which the arguments of twenty men with twenty views are distilled into an apparently unanimous policy of 'cabinet decisions'. The cabinet secretary sees himself (as one incumbent put it to me) as the guardian of the principle of collective authority: and if (as can happen) the prime minister tries to push through a personal decision, it is his job to say: 'But shouldn't you consult your colleagues?'

COLLECTIVE RESPONSIBILITY

In neat theories about the structure of government the cabinet is depicted as the place where the threads of government come together, and the institutions of democracy converge—parliament, the political parties, and the civil service. In the words of Bagehot, who first fully analysed the importance of the cabinet:

> The efficient secret of the English constitution may be described as the close union, the nearly complete fusion, of the executive and legislative powers. . . . A cabinet is a combining committee—a hyphen which joins, a buckle which fastens, the legislative part of the state to the executive part of the state. In its origins it belongs to the one, in its functions it belongs to the other.

The theory of the buckle was always too neat to be entirely true. It is hard enough at any time to co-ordinate a single office, let alone an entire government. In Bagehot's time, when parliament had no hand in industry, the cabinet *could* have collective discussions about prisons, post offices or foreign policies. But since the first world war its responsibilities have increased to the point when the government has a finger in nearly every industry, and controls massive social services. As a result of the pressure, as early as 1931 Sir Maurice Hankey drafted a memorandum, saying that ministers should only bring points out to the cabinet after they had been thrashed out with the departments concerned: and since then the cabinet has become more involved in particular disputes and less in general problems. 'I think the difficulty which most cabinets find,' said Edward Heath in 1965, 'is in arranging cabinet meetings in which they can range over a wide field and really co-ordinate a number of broad issues of policy. The danger is that items get into particular watertight compartments.'[1] And Heath's own compartments, with specialised ministers in super-ministries, appear specially water-tight (though not quite without leaks).

The minister himself, rushing between parliament, department and cabinet, is a kind of living 'buckle' with all the strain that it implies. There has always been a British prejudice against having ministers detached from departments, against what Churchill

[1] Interview with Norman Hunt. BBC Television, 1965.

called 'exalted brooding over the work done by others';[1] a cabinet minister (like an advisory director in industry) is apt to lack influence if he is detached from a department. But the pressure on ministers who have to be 'buckles', and who do their job properly, is intense. The solution of 'double-banking' in the heaviest ministries—the Foreign Office or the Treasury—helps to relieve the burden, but increases the scope for friction and muddle. When a problem falls between two or three departments —as most serious problems do—its discussion often goes by default: and some of the most disastrous cabinet decisions have arisen as much from lack of discussion as from positive folly.

The cabinet, like all the committees which spread out from it, is dedicated to the principle of 'collective responsibility': and this insistence on solidarity distinguishes it from the American government—in spite of the fact that American ministers are not always elected representatives. From the outside the appearance of unanimity is quite well kept up, with the help of the cabinet office and its rigid security. But collective responsibility has always been (as Lord Salisbury described it in 1880) a 'constitutional fiction', and the idea of twenty very ambitious rival politicians agreeing twice a week on a whole range of policies is inherently improbable. Gordon Walker maintains that the 'unattributable leak' has become an essential concomitant of collective responsibility—'the mechanism by which the doctrine of collective responsibility is reconciled with political reality'.[2] Quite often in recent years cabinet ministers have aired their disagreements quite openly, without resigning; Callaghan in 1969 left no doubt about his opposition to the Industrial Relations Bill.

The disunity of cabinets is made more likely by the extreme reluctance of ministers to resign on points of principle; they will disagree privately, within the confines of the cabinet, but will avoid clashes in open debates in parliament.[3] This is the most disagreeable aspect of the constitutional fiction—that it prevents the great issues from being aired, and ensures that the chief figures in the party are nobbled by their membership of the

---

[1] *The Gathering Storm*, p. 320, quoted by Ian Gilmour, *The Body Politic*, Hutchinson 1969, p. 237 (which contains an interesting discussion of the problems of separating decision from execution).
[2] Gordon Walker, *op. cit.*, p. 34.
[3] Mackintosh. *op. cit.*, p. 524.

cabinet, to maintain silence. Once a cabinet resigns and dis-
perses—like the Labour cabinet in 1970—they soon reveal how
disparate their views *really* were.

The strains and suppressions in the name of collective responsibility are visible not only in parliament but also (see Chapter
16) all through the labyrinth of the civil service, where hundreds
of inter-departmental committees try to keep policies in line
and where the contorted prose of white papers tries to conceal the
cracks in cabinet policy. Most of the weaknesses of Treasury
control can be traced back to the inability of cabinets to work
together. The hypocrisy and deceit of collective responsibility is
a disagreeable aspect of British government, which helps to
make politicians appear more dishonest to the public and parliament. There are strong arguments for allowing disagreements to
become more open and breaking down the secrecy of the cabinet
office. But the basic strain between the cabinet and the departments, between the centre and the periphery, is part of the inevitable strain of any democratic system.

CABINET AND PRIME MINISTER

The prime minister in cabinet is officially, as his name implies,
no more than 'primus inter pares'—just one member of a committee. But in fact he has a powerful hand. He is chairman of the
committee: he appoints it, summons it, guides it, and can at a
pinch dissolve it. The scope for cabinet-making might not be as
great as it appears from outside: political rivals cannot easily
be demoted, discontented followers must be pacified, left and
right must be balanced, the heads of the most important departments cannot be constantly changed, and the number of first-
class men in parliament does not give unlimited choice. But a
cabinet remains very much the expression of a prime minister's
personality. He can bring in his own protégés, make or break their
careers, turn them into peers, or banish them into darkness. And
Ted Heath's team, more than most previous cabinets, is full of
men who owe their promotion to the prime minister.

Inside any cabinet there usually develops a small group of the
prime minister's confidants who are consulted beforehand, and
who can often fix policy without proper reference to the others.
An 'inner cabinet' is by its nature difficult to define and delineate.
Churchill had an obvious and open group of cronies, like a court;

75

Attlee (in his first years) mediated between Bevin, Cripps and Morrison. Eden had one of the most celebrated inner cabinets at the time of the Suez affair, when Macmillan, Lloyd, Hailsham and Antony Head made the secret plans for the invasion. Macmillan had a fluctuating group of confidants, though he was never very close to his Chancellors of the Exchequer. Wilson frequently made arrangements with a few colleagues, and in 1968 he precipitated the resignation of George Brown by deciding to declare a bank holiday without consulting him: 'Power can very easily pass,' complained Brown, in his statement on his resignation, 'not merely from cabinet to one or two ministers, but effectively to sources quite outside political control altogether.' Heath, a more solitary and self-sufficient man than Wilson, has shown less sign of close relations with any colleagues; but he clearly relies quite heavily on the advice of his two old allies, Lord Carrington and William Whitelaw, and keeps other senior men, like Maudling and Hailsham, at a distance.

In any time of crisis and disagreement the formal structure of the cabinet can become meaningless and the prime minister can easily resort to separate consultations to get his own way. He can neglect to consult the foreign secretary, as Wilson neglected Brown, or he can ignore the advice of the Chancellor of the Exchequer, as Macmillan ignored Thorneycroft. Underneath its rigmarole of titles and meetings the cabinet remains, as it was in the eighteenth century, a secret and variable committee which revolved first round the monarch, then round the prime minister.

The prime minister's hand can also be strengthened by his appointment of 'cabinet committees' which, although they do not necessarily include him, can weaken his colleagues. The committees are so secret that no one is supposed to know which are sitting, when or why; they include the Overseas and Defence Policy Committee, the Home Affairs Committee, the Future Legislation Committee and a mass of miscellaneous committees, set up for special crises, like Wilson's Winter Emergencies Committee. They have the same powers as the cabinet itself, provided they are unanimous; unresolved arguments are passed to the full cabinet (though in 1967 Harold Wilson decreed that the chairman of a committee must agree before a matter is passed to the full cabinet). Wilson made more use of cabinet committees than his predecessors, and it can be argued, as Gordon Walker does, that this gave more scope for ministers. 'The committee system not only enables ministers not in the cabinet to join in the settlement of policies on issues that relate to their departments; it also allows junior ministers, in a way that was not possible before, to learn something about the working of the cabinet system.'[1]

But the growth of cabinet committees is very likely to increase the power of the prime minister: the skilful deployment of these smaller groups can be used by him to by-pass obstacles, and to separate his colleagues as he could not when confronted by a full cabinet. Small committees have a habit of superseding larger ones. Richard Crossman blames the committees for contributing to the passing of cabinet government, from Churchill and Attlee onwards: 'The point of decision, which in the 1930s still rested inside the cabinet, was now permanently transferred either downwards to these powerful cabinet committees, or upwards to the prime minister himself.'[2] Professor Mackintosh has explained convincingly how 'the role of the cabinet and the way decisions are taken have changed, and changed in a manner which leaves more influence and power of initiative with the prime minister'.[3]

Many political scientists, like Mackintosh, believe that cabinet government has given way in the last decades to 'prime ministerial government', and that it is virtually impossible for colleagues to dislodge a sitting premier: 'Even at times when the record and capacities of a prime minister are under the maximum criticism . . . the only way out of the impasse is a recovery of the authority of the prime minister'[4] (though Mackintosh himself was involved in trying to dislodge Harold Wilson in 1969). Several factors have conspired to raise the prime minister to a level quite different from the rest of the cabinet. Television, the Press and universal suffrage have encouraged the presentation of the party leader as the embodiment of his party's policy and character, so that the fortunes of his colleagues rise and fall with his. The government machine has become increasingly intricate, and Number Ten thus becomes the single ganglion of the nervous system, the apex of the pyramid, the only office which really knows everything that is going on. The quickening of international communications, through jet planes and telephones, has made foreign affairs more a question of exchanges between

[1] Gordon Walker: *op. cit.*, p. 48.
[2] R. H. S. Crossman: Introduction to Bagehot's *The English Constitution*, Fontana 1963. p. 49.
[3] John Mackintosh: *The British Cabinet* (second edition, Methuen, 1968), p. 624.
[4] Mackintosh: *op. cit.* p. 435.

chief executives, rather than between foreign secretaries and ambassadors; however much Ted Heath may talk about delegation, it is he who must go to talk to President Nixon, Chancellor Brandt or President Pompidou.

And perhaps most important, the prime minister has overwhelming influence over the whole machinery of patronage—not only promotions inside the government, but appointments to nationalised boards, royal commissions, regius professorships, bishoprics, the conferment of honours and the creation of peers; so that he is able, not merely to reward his friends and hold out hopes for the ambitious, but to influence the whole social atmosphere around him. The innovation of life peers has increased the area of bounty, and the fact that all honours are theoretically bestowed in the name of the Queen (see Chapter 13) makes it all the easier for the prime minister, who is nowadays the real 'fount of honour', to exploit his patronage without being attacked for it. Harold Wilson was able to ennoble a hundred and twenty men in his five-and-a-half years; and although his creations were influenced by political balances, the fact that they were channelled through him enhanced still further the aura of Downing Street. Only when a prime minister loses an election does it become clear how much of his prestige he owed to his control of patronage.

All these factors have helped to separate the prime minister still further from his colleagues, and to make Ten Downing Street the focus of all hopes and fears for his party, and for the nation. A prime minister—even the least theatrical of them, Ted Heath—sets the scenery and style for the whole government; and, however over-simplified, the conception of the Age of Macmillan or the Era of Wilson has the same kind of validity as the Age of Queen Anne or of Charles II.

5

Prime Minister

We were returned to office to change the course of history of this
nation—nothing less.

Edward Heath, October 1970.

ANY untried leader of the opposition is difficult to imagine as
prime minister, before the footlights, the scenery and the new cast
of characters have formed themselves round him. The entry of
Edward Heath on the stage was specially unimaginable. Before
the election the Tories themselves were fostering the idea of
Heath as a failure; and from the time of his election as leader in
1965, Heath had often seemed to be playing out some atavistic role
as scapegoat for a party in the throes of a painful transition. The
great revolving stage of the general election, suddenly presenting
the failure as the leader, demanded an abrupt readjustment—by
his own party as much as by the new opposition.

Since then, power has already begun to change him, at least in
his outward style. He is more relaxed, rather fatter; he wears
very good and quite trendy clothes, which very easily rumple. His
hair is much longer, coming down thickly at the back, and his
sideburns are much more evident; he might even be mistaken for
a musician. Number Ten, which always encourages monarchic
and eccentric tendencies, has had some effect. 'When I was
summoned there,' said one permanent secretary, 'I said to
myself, My God, it's happening all over again! He was talking
just as if he was Harold Wilson.' 'What really struck me,' said

79

one old friend, 'is that he no longer worries about switching off the lights.'

He enjoys the scope of Number Ten, and still more of Chequers —the scope to set the stage as he wishes it. He has no theatrical style himself, but he likes to have players round him. He likes to maintain continuity with his past by entertaining ex-colleagues and Tory dignitaries; he has given parties for his ex-private secretaries, for Macmillan, for Lord Avon, for Lord Butler. He has been at pains to exclude the old guard from his cabinet, but he likes to see himself as part of the great Tory pageant; and it is at these special occasions that he seems most in his element. He has quickly impressed his own tastes on the building: he is much more interested in his surroundings and more aesthetically aware than his predecessors (though that is not saying much), and Number Ten is his only real home. He brought over his modern furniture from Albany—black leather chairs, marble tables, oriental carpets—and chose a new decor of masculine colours for the flat, in place of the chintz of the Macmillans and Wilsons; he hung his Churchill paintings and set out his collection of old porcelain and modern silver.

He runs Downing Street quietly and quickly, delegating firmly through his team of well-polished private secretaries (the first two are old Etonians). Robert Armstrong, his principal private secretary, is a custom-built Treasury man—classical scholar, musician, politically detached, and professionally loyal: in a fine Italianate hand, he translates Heath's wishes and philosophy into practical minutes. Douglas Hurd, the political secretary (though he has written political thrillers) is a thoroughly reliable Tory, tall, grave and decorous; he is the son of a former Tory MP, himself hoping to get into parliament. Donald Maitland, the press secretary, worked for Heath in the previous common market negotiations; a small, precise Scotsman who knows exactly how to handle the Whitehall machine. Heath's brisk relationship with his staff can be disconcerting, but he depends closely on them; in the evenings he likes to talk with them together or listen to them talk while he picks up ideas, views or reactions. 'He's just the same in private as in public,' said one of them; 'he starts business straight away, without any personal chat; it's worrying at first, but you soon know where you are.' 'When he asks you a question,' says another, 'you give an answer, and then there's a deathly silence, while he wears what I call his Easter Island expression. You don't know whether to go on talking or to wait for him to talk. Then after a minute or so, he comes out with his decision, and that's it.' This is the most characteristic signal from the new Downing Street, in place of the reflective discussions of Macmillan, or the quick-fire talk of Wilson: the silence of Heath making a decision, alone.

Part of Heath's style is, of course, a deliberate political reversal, like Nixon after Johnson, or Bonar Law after Lloyd George, to show that action is more important than words, that intervention is discredited, that the prime minister will henceforth delegate. But Heath's contrast with Wilson also marks a huge contrast of personalities. Wilson loves talking; Heath prefers silences. Wilson naturally avoids decisions; Heath *likes* taking them. Wilson enjoys television appearances; Heath dreads them. Wilson encouraged a certain vagueness; Heath likes precision. Wilson wants to be liked; Heath does not seem to mind. To the rest of Whitehall Heath sends out brisk minutes with a Churchillian brevity, though without the eloquence. He likes to disconcert ministers or civil servants with challenges: 'I see no intellectual justification for this . . .' 'What are your reasons? . . .' 'Is this really necessary?' He is determined never to be put upon, not to let them get away with it, and to be like Churchill (his first and lasting hero), the awkward customer in the middle of the machine. To his own staff he is loyal and quite encouraging; he inspires their trust if not their affection. But to other politicians and civil servants, even to close allies like Barber, he can appear very ungrateful.

His speeches, like his minutes, are uncompromising and bare. He has two speech-writers, Douglas Hurd and Michael Woolf, the ex-journalist who inhabits the Lord Privy Seal's office; but he has always been wary of other people's colourful phrases, and most of his speeches still have the authentic Heath touch—what his biographer, George Hutchinson,[1] calls his 'laundry list style'. He likes to make his points in a repetitive, incantatory style— like this one in Cardiff in March 1971:

> Your government, Mr. Chairman, will not fail; we will succeed.
> The people will not lose; the people will win.
> The nation will not be dragged down; the nation will emerge triumphant.

His memories of his past setbacks have strengthened his

[1] George Hutchinson: *Edward Heath, A Personal and Political Biography*, Longmans, 1970.

conviction that it was he all the time who was the one in step. When someone refers to an earlier setback, he likes to make some remark like: 'Ah, that was one more step towards my political ruin.' In speeches he likes to invoke an imaginary *they* like the *they* of Lear's limericks—*they* say, *they* seem to imagine, *they* always complain—and then to dismiss them, looking up with his mouth open, wrinkling his forehead and shrugging his big shoulders, as if to say how can *they* be so stupid; then shutting his mouth firmly, his lips doggedly together.

Heath's public personality has taken a more definite shape since he became prime minister. His bland face and his bare phrases proclaim that here is a man who says what he means, and who does what he says he will do. It is the opposite of those hooded, ironic faces that had become so much part of the British political scenery—the languid Macmillan, the drooping Butler, Home looking down his half-spectacles, Wilson with his darting, half-shut eyes, Jenkins with his clever grin and enormous glasses. Heath's eyes are big and open, without winks or flickers, like sodium street-lights: they advertise a public man without private contradictions. It is all very worrying to the old school of politicians: 'In the old days,' one of the Tory old guard explained to me, 'it was very simple to find out what Macmillan was up to; you only had to listen to what he was saying up and down the country and you could be quite *sure* that he was doing the opposite. Now Ted insists on doing what he said he'd do. It's very confusing. It's like Hitler or Karl Marx—it never occurred to people to actually *read* what they said they'd do.'

But his private personality is more than ever an enigma. In any professional situation he seems quite at ease, but once in a private context, without a defined relationship, he can quickly seem gauche and defensive. Visitors compete in their accounts of his astonishing unawareness of people (even more than other politicians'); when a woman journalist came to see him, tea arrived for one person, which he poured out for himself. His old friends know that it is useless to wait for a drink; you must help yourself. Anyone who tries to probe his emotions, his motivations or hidden resources returns baffled and defeated, and his colleagues have found him more impenetrable in the last few years.

Heath's thick carapace shows no outward signs of having been dented or pierced; and his self-containment and self-confidence go back early into his childhood. Outwardly his battle to the top has been a hard and heroic one—single-minded, hard-working, dedicated. But he has never appeared to be tormented by doubts, guilts or deep personal involvements; he has moved up as if in a space-suit, protected from atmospheres and pressures around him.

During Heath's childhood his family was, if anything, rather poorer than Wilson's. His father is often described as a master-builder, but as a young man he was a jobbing carpenter (*his* father had been a railway-porter). Heath's mother, a gardener's daughter, had been a lady's maid to a Hampstead family who used to come to Broadstairs, where she met Heath's father. At first the Heaths lived on the ground floor of a tiny semi-detached house alongside the railway, where Edward was born in the front room in 1916. Later they moved into a slightly bigger house, where Mrs. Heath took in lodgers for the summer season; it was very cramped, the piano had to be moved round from room to room, and Teddy and his young brother John often had to share a room. But in these constricted surroundings the young Teddy very soon acquired an Olympian isolation, an ability to cut himself off, which he has kept ever since, inhabiting a private world of books, music and knowledge. His mother was determined to keep up standards, to keep her boys well-dressed, and the house spotless; and Teddy had a place of special privilege in the house, not expected to do the washing up, or to interrupt his reading or his deep silences when visitors came.

Broadstairs was very different from the industrial Huddersfield of Harold Wilson's boyhood; it was 'bourgeois Broadstairs', a pretty seaside town catering for holidaymakers in the short summer season: it was more fashionable then than now, when the same families prefer to go abroad. It was, of course, a Conservative stronghold, a kind of junior Bournemouth, with a huge Tory majority: Broadstairs produced Conservatives as naturally as fish. There were plenty of humble families like the Heaths; but there were few factories, and though times were hard in the twenties and thirties, there was not mass unemployment as there was in the north: 'Things were not particularly easy,' Heath has said, 'but we were luckier than most.'

'I have always had a hidden wish, a frustrated desire, to run a hotel,' he once revealed (celebrating a hotel exhibition at Olympia), in a rare glimpse of his fantasy-life. Broadstairs was a town of hotels—many now decaying—and Teddy was very friendly with the people who ran one of them, the Castlemere, which still

stands. Mrs. Heath herself gave bed and breakfast to lodgers. The
fascination with hotel life and with his mother's punctilious housekeeping may have contributed to Heath's passion for efficiency
and punctuality. (Has he, one wonders, now partly achieved his
ambition by taking over the Hotel Great Britain, with Barber as
the new chief cashier, Walker the catering manager, Whitelaw
as the amiable maître d'hôtel, and Sir Alec as the old head
waiter?)

In this world of seaside conservatism Heath's father stood out as
a living advertisement for the virtues of self-help and self-
improvement. William Heath still lives in Broadstairs, now
eighty-three with his third wife, in a comfortable mock-Tudor
house with an orchard at the back. He is a sprightly, stocky man
with his son's protuberant long nose; but the contrasts are more
striking than the resemblances. Old Mr. Heath is humorous and
talkative, still with a twinkle in his sharp eyes; his face is etched
with the lines of experience, very different from his son's blanc-
mange features. In Broadstairs as a young man Billy Heath was
very popular with the girls; his present wife (his first two both
died of cancer) is a striking north country woman. He loves
talking about his son; in the drawing-room there is a framed copy
of the ballot result of 1965, which made Heath leader of the
party, and a big picture of father and son alongside each other.
But he is clearly not overwhelmed by the prime minister; and he
finds much about him that he does not understand.

Old Mr. Heath has reason to be proud of his own career. He
worked hard enough as a carpenter eventually to buy up his own
building-and-decorating business; he worked sixteen hours a day,
from a small office in the house, eventually with six full-time
workers and sometimes twenty casual workers. It was a straightforward success-story, showing that connection between cause and
effect which the prime minister is now so anxious to instil into the
country. William Heath had no very firm political views; he was
originally a *News Chronicle* Liberal, and only later regarded himself
as a Conservative; but he told me: 'I was never Labour—I had
too much to do with labour to vote Labour.' He insists that 'the
government must be run like a business—if it doesn't make a
profit, it must get out'. He despises Labour men not only for their
socialism, but also (with the exception of George Brown) for not
saying what they mean. He is generally distrustful of politics—'my
son's too honest to be a politician'. He never talks politics with his

son, he says; but the old man clearly had much to do with Heath's preoccupation with self-help.

Young Teddy Heath grew up, his father says, a natural Conservative. He was very serious. He had no real friends of his own age, and preferred older people because they knew more: they in turn found him a model child, always listening, polite and modest, never going after girls, drinking or swearing. At eleven Teddy went to the local grammar school, Chatham House, founded at the beginning of the century with plenty of public-school traditions—boaters, debating, houses (there is now a Heath house, but the boys are rather left-wing). Teddy was good at most things except sport and languages (he remains clumsy and his French is still painful). Lord Goodman, who met him when he was a sixth-former, with a solicitor friend, Royalton Kisch, found him already a very political boy—opinionated, polite, unshy and sure of himself, apparently quite detached from class roots. Teddy first became openly political at sixteen, when he was a keen school debater; he opposed the motion that had just been passed at the Oxford Union, 'That this House will in no circumstances fight for its King and country.' He became a model school prefect, very tough with sloppy boys who put their hands in their pockets. He determined to go to Oxford, and chose Balliol because it was a hard-working college. The family could just scrape up enough money (he later won the organ scholarship, which made it easier).

Heath's fortifications were reinforced by his absorption in music. At the age of seven he first began playing the family piano; and up till leaving Oxford, he seriously considered being a professional conductor (though that may have had some connection with his interest in power). He can be deeply moved by listening to music, even to the Last Post, and music seems to give him an outlet for passionate emotion without relationships. His favourite composers—including Mahler, Bruckner, Strauss and (more recently) Wagner—have a mystical romanticism which suggests a need to escape from constraints. He has said that his favourite opera is *Fidelio* and that its theme of liberation fits in with his political ideals. He can identify quite closely with operatic emotions: as one friend put it, 'He could never really enjoy an opera like *Poppea*, where the lovers get away with it.' All his friends agree that he could not survive the strains of politics *without* music. But his musical world and political life are totally compartmentalised.

He does not, like Lloyd George, bring his love of music into the cadences of his speeches, and there is no trace of resonance or romanticism in his style of talk, which is strikingly dissonant, with no trace of 'universal harmony'. He seems to distrust music in his speeches, as much as he loves it in his piano-playing.

Teddy Heath came from Broadstairs to Oxford in 1936, a serious, rather priggish boy, moving into a world of passionate politics and high frivolity; there were plenty of arrogant Tories and public-school Marxists, popping champagne corks at passers-by to make them class-conscious. But Balliol, under its egalitarian Master, A. D. Lindsay, was a relatively classless college: it included during Heath's time Roy Jenkins, the miner's son, and Denis Healey, then a Communist. Balliol set Heath on the road to power, and encouraged him to think that there was nothing he could not do. He remained a convinced Tory (Wilson—whom he never met at Oxford—was then a member of the Liberal Party) : he became President of the Union and of the Conservative Association. But he was impressively independent of Chamberlain's Conservatism: on the crucial issues on appeasement and the Spanish civil war he accused Chamberlain's government of organised hypocrisy, 'composed of Conservatives with nothing to conserve and Liberals with a hatred of liberty'.

Everyone seemed to know Teddy. He was on all kinds of committees, restored the Balliol organ, founded the Balliol choir, wrote music for OUDS plays, became President of the Junior Common Room. His social life revolved round politics, tea parties and the union, and his world (like that of most Oxford politicians) was almost exclusively male. To the more flamboyant political undergraduates he seemed well-meaning, humble, and a bit dim—the 'Widmerpool of British politics,' as his enemies in Parliament now call him, after the dogged character always getting ahead in Anthony Powell's novels. He took only an average second-class degree in politics, philosophy and economics (Wilson took a spectacular first). He was very busy with other things: and his brain has never shown the glitter and quickness of Wilson's (though his memory is almost as good). But he left Oxford with extra self-confidence, already equipped with his formal voice and his curious vowels (a mixture, as his ex-sister-in-law described it, of 'rural Kent and Wodehousian Oxford'). Heath emerged with no visible chip on his shoulder, with an almost Australian detachment from class; and (like Nixon) he is difficult to connect with

any special territory or background. At about this time Teddy
gave way to Ted.

War broke out that autumn. After the outbreak of war he went
on a debating tour of America, and was called up in 1940, into
the Royal Artillery. His war career was conscientious but un-
spectacular. He spent all his time in England until the Normandy
landings; he impressed his commanding officers, as he had impressed schoolteachers and elders at Broadstairs. He rose to be
Lieutenant-Colonel, MBE, mentioned in despatches, and emerged
in 1945 as a Territorial in the Honourable Artillery Company, a
rather grand kind of club which guards the Tower of London and
has august premises in the city. The war increased his confidence
in his leadership, and he liked the discipline and defined relationships of the army: he now has military prints in his drawing-room,
and porcelain soldiers on horseback. But the army did not bring
out any romantic or dashing streak—as it did for such men as
Powell, Macleod or Macmillan.

Demobilised in 1946, Heath determined to get into parliament
in spite of the massive Labour landslide; but in the meantime he
joined the civil service—passing out top in the examination—to
find out more about administration. He worked in Civil Aviation
under Peter Masefield (now head of the British Airports Authority); old Oxford friends were astonished how much he took on
the colouring of a civil servant. He went back at week-ends to his
family in Broadstairs, and Marian Evans, who married his
brother John in 1947, provides glimpses of her brother-in-law at
this time in her revealing book on the Heath family[1] and in
conversation. He was thirty but looked much older; he wore a
long college scarf and was neat, precise and unsmiling. The piano
was covered with photographs of Teddy at various ages, and
Teddy would sit listening to loud music while his mother knitted
socks: he would walk in and out of rooms without apparently
seeing anyone, and went for long walks along the cliffs. Teddy was
aloof but very family-minded, organising outings and picnics,
driving fast with intense concentration, overtaking traffic and
muttering under his breath at other drivers—'dear Sir, dear
Madam . . .' Often the outings were joined by Teddy's long-
standing girl-friend, Kay Raven, who was secretary of his carol
party. Teddy was never very attentive, but Kay didn't seem to
mind: eventually she married a farmer. Teddy's mother was very

[1] Marian Evans: *Ted Heath, a Family Portrait.* William Kimber, 1970.

upset, but Teddy seemed quite unaffected. His mother (who died when he was 35) was keen for him to marry, but his father always said that he was married to politics. At his brother's wedding, Teddy was best man: he made a humorous speech about not being committed because there were no bridesmaids; and he didn't kiss the bride.

As a civil servant he was all the time waiting to get into parliament. In 1947 he was interviewed for three constituencies—Ashford, East Fulham and Sevenoaks—and each time was turned down. Then he was interviewed for Bexley, a London suburb with a small Labour majority—a lower-middle class constituency where Heath's background seemed appropriate. He was selected, and as a prospective candidate he had to leave the civil service. For the next two years he worked on the *Church Times* as News Editor—an extraordinarily unsuitable appointment: he was not really religious; the editor, a keen Anglo-Catholic, didn't like him; he didn't like journalism or journalists, and never wrote for the paper[1]. After two years of it he decided to get some experience of finance, and joined the merchant bank Brown, Shipley, as a somewhat superannuated trainee, paid only £200 a year. At last in 1950 came the general election, and the moment he had waited for. His campaign was well-organised, supported by fellow-officers and bankers; and he scraped in with a majority of 133. Labour was still in power, but the following year Attlee went to the country again. Heath increased his majority to 1,639, and the Conservatives came back into power. At the age of thirty-five Heath's first great political moment had come.

Heath came to Westminster as a rare and politically valuable commodity in the post-war parliament—a Tory with a working-class background, a convincing champion of Tory democracy to set against Attlee's socialism. He was taken up by Churchill, invited to Chartwell, encouraged by the grandees. But Heath himself never made any play with his working-class roots, and he was never self-consciously a Tory man of the people, like Charles Hill or Ernest Marples. He had moved upwards from Broadstairs to Balliol to Westminster with his insulation apparently unbroken, a floating capsule in the Tory atmosphere.

The Tory Party in the early fifties embraced an uneasy mixture of generations. It was still dominated by Churchill, but with a big contingent of young ex-officers with varying degrees of

[1] See Hutchinson, *op. cit.*, p. 62.

radicalism—including Major Macleod, Brigadier Powell, Major Maude, Colonel Alport and Colonel Heath, all of whom joined the One Nation Group, dedicated to improving social conditions, with evocations of Disraeli. Butler was Chancellor, and the age of Butskellism was beginning. Heath showed no sign then of any desire to break up the consensus, or to criticise the welfare state.

The hard-working new bachelor member for Bexley was just the man for the whips' office—the police station of the party system. He became an assistant whip only a year after entering parliament, and he stayed as a whip for the next *eight* years, becoming chief whip when Eden took over in 1955. It was in the whips' office that he made his name: and he was the first chief whip ever to become prime minister (the chief whip used to be regarded as a kind of superior sergeant-major, to keep the troops in order without being concerned with high policy). Heath's long stint in the whips' office, through a succession of crises—first the small majority, then the easing-out of Churchill, then the Suez crisis, then Macmillan's rallying of the party—gave him an unrivalled experience of the machinery and psychology of politicians: how to alternate carrot and stick, hot and cold, how and when to hold out prospects of promotion or honours (the chief whip is also patronage secretary). Heath studied the house like a chess-game; he can always hold his own in discussions with political scientists. His performance through Suez (which he did not really believe in) was a triumph of discipline, and Tory MPs remember with bitterness or admiration his endless chivvying and cajoling, seemingly never letting up or going home. The whips' view is a kind of worm's eye view, and probably contributed to Heath's pessimistic view of his fellow-Tories; as he said later (in June 1962): 'No one knows better than a former patronage secretary the limitations of the human mind and the human spirit.' The remark is in itself dispiriting: but in the bleak years ahead he could remind himself of the frailty of his colleagues.

It was as chief whip that Heath first served Macmillan, after the storms of Suez. They had a famous dinner of game pie and champagne after Macmillan's election, and so began the long and ambivalent relationship, between two men with such different ideas about Conservatism. It seemed a clear contrast; Macmillan the hooded and theatrical Edwardian, Heath the blunt and eager new technocrat. Yet in some ways they exchanged roles: it was

Heath who harked back to the Edwardian days of free-enterprise
and national independence. They each needed the other.
Macmillan appreciated the man who had held the party together,
and who reported faithfully every morning the moods of the
house; Heath knew that his future lay with Macmillan, and
admired his leader's resilience and intellect. He had first met him
twenty years before at Oxford, at a Balliol dinner, when Heath
was an admirer of Macmillan's 'Middle Way'. But now Macmillan's histrionics, his insistence on doing the opposite of what
he was saying, became increasingly repugnant to him.

Macmillan rewarded Heath after the 1959 election with a seat
in the cabinet, as Minister of Labour. It was not an inspired
appointment, for Heath was irritated by the emotionalism of
trade unionists as he was by the emotionalism of Africans or
women. But it was an important experience for him of the limitations of both workers and employers. He was much more impatient
with trade unionists than his predecessors, Iain Macleod and
Walter Monckton, or his aristocratic successor John Hare: perhaps it needed the son of a worker to get tough with the workers.
But the job only lasted nine months, until July 1960, when Heath
was given the job which nearly made him, and then nearly broke
him—as minister in charge of the common market negotiations.
Heath had for long been committed to Europe, though he has
never given a very clear picture of what kind of Europe. He had
first travelled as a schoolboy, and visited Germany just before the
war, with his Jewish friend Madron Seligman (thirty years later
he told Willy Brandt and his guests how he first came to Dusseldorf
as a student, sitting and drinking on the Koenigsallee, and then
came back in the army to find Dusseldorf destroyed). His maiden
speech in the Commons had criticised the Labour government in
1950 for not joining the Coal and Steel Community—the first
step towards the common market.

The European negotiations involved most of Heath's energies
and emotions for two-and-half years. With hindsight, it has been
said that he was too stubborn and too slow to give way on the
'comparable outlets', thus making it easier for De Gaulle to veto;
but the political situation in Westminster was very delicate, and
Macmillan and his cabinet must take much of the blame. When
the collapse came in January 1963 Heath faced it with astonishing
sang-froid; I listened to him at his final press conference coolly
expounding the British case, first off-the-record, then on-the-

record, with a lucidity that amazed foreign journalists. But in the following months he was close to the end of his tether. He was more irritable with his colleagues, but he never broke out: they often wished that he had. He was far less flappable than his unflappable master.

In early 1963 his career seemed in ruins. He was no longer 'Mr. Europe', but just second minister in the Foreign Office. Macmillan, having first pushed him up, had now dropped him. Maudling became Chancellor, Macleod became chairman of the party and Hogg was asked to sign the test-ban treaty; but Heath was out in the cold. He was anyway becoming disillusioned with his leader. When Macmillan triumphantly won the 1959 election, Heath like other young Tories thought that at last the day of dynamic Conservatism had come, after all the compromises of the fifties. But nothing happened. Macmillan became more languid and more cryptic, and after the collapse, first of the summit, then of the common market negotiations, he had no recognisable policy. And Heath became more aware of the growing insularity of Britain; as he told me in March 1971:

> I don't think we realised at the time how far De Gaulle's veto in 1963 turned this country in on itself. I didn't realise it fully until October 1964, when I went canvassing in Bexley. It was then I realised the change from the confidence during the last election in 1959. There used to be a sense of young executives excited and confident at the thought of getting into Europe: but later, after years of lessening profitability, there was much less confidence.

Heath was indignant at Macmillan's purge of 1962, and appalled by the way Macmillan and his new chief whip, Redmayne, handled the Profumo affair (though Heath himself had been one of the last to believe the rumours and had to have the details spelt out to him). When at last Macmillan *did* resign in 1963, before the chaotic Blackpool conference, Heath was in the shadows. He was not one of the four contenders, and in the contest he supported Sir Alec, partly perhaps because he would keep out Maudling and Macleod, and might not stay long: but he and Sir Alec, after their time at the Foreign Office, seemed natural allies. Under Sir Alec's premiership Heath took over the enlarged Board of Trade, and showed a foretaste of his toughness by abolishing

Resale Price Maintenance against heavy opposition from his own party. It was not, as it turned out, as effective in inducing competition as appeared; but it showed younger members of the party that here was someone who was prepared to push through *some* kind of new policy in the prevailing apathy; and the fight was good for Heath's standing.

It was the defeat in 1964 that really gave Heath his chance, for in opposition he soon showed the dogged persistence which most others lacked. The shadow cabinet was very shadowy; Hogg went back to the bar, Maudling went into the city, Macleod was unwell, Powell went wild. Heath, too, took a job in the city (as director of his old bank, Brown, Shipley) where he made a good deal of money. But he also became shadow chancellor, and threw himself into attacking the Labour budget of 1965, which introduced capital gains and the corporation tax. It was at this time that he began planning the new Tory fiscal policies which were to bear fruit six years later. As the Tories became more embarrassed by Sir Alec's fumbling performance against Wilson and his old match-sticks image, so Heath became a more credible leader. A Heath faction began to form itself in the house, led by Peter Walker and not discouraged by Heath (though he kept in the shadows, to avoid the role of Brutus). The old guard of the party had lost their charisma with amazing speed after only nine months; and in the meantime many younger Tory MPs were pressing for a return to 'proper' Conservatism, without the 'pink' policies of Macmillan.

When Sir Alec announced he would stand down in July 1965, three candidates were expected—Heath, Maudling and Macleod; but Macleod quickly stood down (thus, as it turned out, ensuring Heath's election) and Enoch Powell unexpectedly entered the lists. Maudling's campaign was very casual, but Heath's was organised by Walker with mechanical efficiency, and Heath won with 150 votes to Maudling's 133. It was the most sudden emergence since Baldwin; Heath took over the leadership of the party for which, two years before, he had not even been considered a candidate. The one person to thank above all for his fortune was his opponent Harold Wilson; for it was Wilson, at that time riding so high, who had demoralised the Tory Party still further in its post-Macmillan confusion: and who persuaded them that only a Wilson-type leader could rescue the party from its ignominy. It was thus that, for the first time in its history, the Tory Party chose a leader with a working-class background.

It was hardly surprising that the party should have then considered Heath as the right match for Wilson, for at the time they both seemed a new breed of men; both the same age, both sons of lower-middle-class fathers (both still alive); both grammar-school boys who went to study economics at Oxford; both ex-civil servants, talking much about administration; both grey, professional men. When Wilson talked about the technological revolution, Heath seemed the right counter-computer; few people then realised that Wilson's real merits and defects were almost opposite from Heath's.

The real Heath revolution in opposition was at first hidden by the surface continuity, by the adherence of Sir Alec, and by his colleagues' boredom with opposition. Heath went into the March 1966 election with most of the old team, and it was only after that that the Tory Party, more deeply in the wilderness, began quietly to be transformed. Loyal Heath men—Whitelaw, Carrington, Prior, Walker—became more important; Maudling and Hogg retreated, Soames went off to Paris. The party chairman Edward du Cann had a row with Heath and was replaced by a loyal Heath-man, Anthony Barber. Enoch Powell became increasingly provocative, and then made his racial outburst about 'rivers of blood'. Heath was personally disgusted by the speech, and also felt his own position threatened; he quickly sacked Powell from his shadow cabinet. It has since been argued that Powell would have been less dangerous inside the fold; certainly from the time of Powell's ejection, Heath became more concerned with the right-wing of his party than with the left. But if Heath had kept Powell in his team, he would certainly have lost Macleod and Boyle.

Heath's task was lonely and thankless. In parliament he turned out *not* to be the match for Wilson: and though Wilson's glamour soon began to dim, Heath's personal appeal did not turn up, and the polls showed him in the humiliating position of an unpopular leader of a popular party. Many Tories hankered after a more romantic leadership, and Heath's old master Harold Macmillan, still flitting in the shadows, did not make it easier. Macmillan *sounded* loyal enough, but he was suffering (as Churchill suffered) from a familiar illusion of ex-prime ministers: he just couldn't quite believe that the country could survive without him. In the 1966 campaign Macmillan recorded a television interview in which he was asked what would happen if there was a deadlock between the parties; his hooded eyelids suddenly lifted: 'I suppose they *might* have to call me back' (it was quickly re-recorded). In 1967 there was talk of a coalition cabinet, and Macmillan made it known that he would be prepared to lead it.

This was the most testing time of Heath's career. He was under attack from all sides. The old guard who had helped to put him in decided they had backed a loser. There were jokes about his humourlessness and gaucheness at Tory country-houses. The right-wing attacked him for his support of Rhodesian sanctions, and of liberal issues, like abolition of hanging. The image of the New Leader faded as the years of opposition rolled on. It is difficult to visualise the ordeal of this isolated bachelor, surrounded by enemies, at that time. He seemed personally grimmer and more withdrawn; but politically he never lost his head. He needed a fight—as his father always said—to keep him going, and he did not easily relax socially. In private conversation he never enjoyed the kind of casual discursive talk that Macmillan and so many politicians indulge in; even close friends found that he only really came to life when challenged or provoked.

It was at the nadir of opposition, when he was fifty, that he took up sailing—very much as a competitive sport, not for the sake of 'messing about in boats'. He worked out his races like political campaigns, taking into account every factor of wind, tide and crew. His sailing certainly added to his confidence in opposition after the Sydney-Hobart race; as one of his crew put it to me, 'He suddenly felt he was a winner.' His crew treat him with respect as the best skipper they've known, completely cool in a crisis: but they keep their distance, and only one of them can really tease him: 'You laugh at his jokes,' said another of them, 'he doesn't laugh at yours; but he's beginning to be easier.' The crack member of his crew is a huge Essex farmer called Anthony Sampson who assures me: 'When we've had him on board a bit, he begins to relax; after a week he's a lot more human'. Heath clearly feels extended by the physical challenge of sailing; and he has enjoyed comparing his own manly sport with Harold Wilson, sitting on the beach in the Scillies, 'just watching boats go by'.

The election campaign of 1970 brought out all Heath's public limitations. Wilson rushed round the country like a TV magician, solving strikes, exchanging repartee. Enoch Powell made angry outbursts, reported in dramatic detail. Caught between the two actors, Heath's expressionless face appeared every night in fiont of the blue party symbol, making stone-walling replies to awkward questions. Yet, with hindsight, Heath's very awkwardness may well have been an asset in the reaction against slick politics. While Wilson performed his amazing acrobatics, Heath reiterated monotonously his views; this is where I stand; this is my position. Heath's eventual triumph came not because he was so like Wilson, but because he was so different. Very few of his Tory colleagues thought that Heath could win, and some were openly discussing how to get rid of him afterwards. ('The Tories don't like failures ... they're bad losers.') There was a feeling that they had put in the wrong man, that he had been given his chance, that now the party must return to its real roots. So when Heath won, it took some time for the fact to sink in that Heath now *was* the Tory party.

After this lone battle Heath moved into Downing Street in a stronger personal position than any prime minister since Churchill. He felt no need to balance his cabinet delicately, as Wilson or Macmillan had done, and he could put his own men, like Walker, Davies and later Barber (who would have been nothing without him) into key jobs. Inside the cabinet there were no serious challengers; Maudling and Hogg were cast as elder statesmen, and most ministers stuck dutifully to their own departmental subjects. Lord Carrington and William Whitelaw had wide-ranging and vigorous views; but they had been Heath's loyalest allies in opposition, and they were unlikely (at least for a time) to emerge as real rivals.

I asked him, when I interviewed him in March, 1971, how he had tried to change the job of prime minister:

I was determined to have a smaller cabinet, to give time to discuss broad strategy and not to be cluttered up by papers. We've got that—seventeen is the smallest cabinet for a long time. We have managed to integrate departments further than ever before, so that we have all the essential fields represented in the cabinet except for aviation and the post office. I have always thought the more ministers you have in a department, the more work you create. We have cut down to one cabinet a week and changed the cabinet committees, which saves a good deal of time. Of course machinery is not an end in itself; what matters is the decisions that come out of it. I said in my party conference speech that we were determined to get more room for manoeuvre, but of course that will take time. Being prime

95

minister is not a more difficult job than I thought; I have always known it was difficult. I've been quite close to four prime ministers—three of them I used to see in this house—so I knew a good deal about the machinery of government before I moved in.

You've said before that government needs to have the right balance between action and words: do you think your government is open enough?

Open government doesn't mean having press people sitting in the room all the time: it means the government telling the nation what it's doing and providing the facts on which it takes decisions. That's what we have tried to do with Rolls-Royce, local government reform and so on. I am not a great believer in exhortation; I don't think you can get people to change their minds by exhorting them. But I accept that at the moment we are in a transition period, when industrialists have been used to the reverse philosophy to our present one; and we need to explain to them how to get through it.

The change in the party looked abrupt to the public who had last seen it in 1964; but it had been happening under the surface over the years of opposition. Many Tories traced it back to Macmillan's Great Purge of 1962, which first shattered the old loyalties of the party. From that time onwards the party was waiting to group itself round a new leader, and new policies; but it was not till eight years later that they realised quite what they had done. Even after the election many Tories were as surprised as the Labour Party to find that Heath actually intended to carry out his election manifesto and his statements of the preceding five years. At the party conference in October, Heath talked about changing the course of history, and embarking on 'a change so radical, a revolution so quiet and yet so total that it will go far beyond the programme for a Parliament'. But not many people believed it; it was not till the Industrial Relations Bill and the bankrupting of Rolls-Royce that the message began to register.

What had produced the new Tory toughness and confrontation with the workers? Most of the economic difficulties were already evident under Macmillan, who himself talked a good deal about the need for more competition, and for the common market to provide the necessary 'cold shower' for industry. But

Macmillan was held back from any drastic deflationary policies by what was called his 'Stockton-on-Tees complex'; his experiences of unemployment, and of the Somme, had left him with a sense of involvement or guilt towards the workers, a desire to show (as he said after the 1959 election), 'that the class war is obsolete'. The basis of his home policy was a close relationship with the trade unions, which reached its climax in 1962, with Neddy and Nicky. But Heath (and many of his contemporaries) had no such inhibitions. His experience of the slump years in Broadstairs had not been traumatic, and he had no cause, as a worker's son, to feel guilt about the workers. He thought that the workers needed to be taught the connection between cause and effect. The party was no longer held back by 'upper-class guilt', or by the conflicts and ambiguities in Macmillan's mind. There may have been four Macmillans; but there was only one Heath.

Once in Downing Street Heath soon established the style of a strong, silent man—a species that had seemed extinct since Attlee. But neither his strength nor his silence is quite what it looks. The idea of 'action not words', which was the title of his 1966 manifesto and was much plugged since, is not quite so simple. There is showmanship in anti-showmanship—and gimmickry in anti-gimmickry; Heath spends a good deal of time talking about not talking, intervening to say he is not intervening. No politicians can survive without words, which in the end are his only weapons; and in some ways Heath has said more about what he is actually trying to do than Wilson ever did: 'What Heath's already managed is to change the area of debate,' complained one Labour ex-cabinet minister; 'Harold never liked to talk about Socialism, in the way that Heath talks about Conservatism. I wish he had done.'

Heath repeated his message with little variation, summed up in the words 'stand on your own feet'. His conviction about the virtues of self-help stems partly no doubt from his own and his father's careers; but he presents it, too, in historical terms, as a turning away from the collectivist attitudes that Britain has moved progressively towards over the last fifty years. In foreign policy Heath's 'philosophy' is equally simple: as he told the Lord Mayor at his 1970 banquet, 'The time has come to establish clearly and unmistakably that British policies are determined by British interests.' It may be significant that he began his essay on 'Realism in British Foreign Policy', written for the American journal

Foreign Affairs in 1969 with *two* quotations from Palmerston, one of which said: 'We have no eternal allies and no perpetual enemie . Our interests are external and perpetual and those interests it is our duty to follow.' Britain will not be pushed around, whether by the commonwealth, the common market, or the United States. With America he is the least emotionally involved of all the post-war prime ministers—with no American mother like Macmillan or Churchill, and no wartime friendships. Like other Tories of his generation, he feels that Britain has lost out from the special relationship, 'which' (he said in *Foreign Affairs*) 'will continue to the extent, and only to the extent, that each country contributes effectively to the furthering of those common interests.' It is towards Europe that he has looked most consistently: he does not have the same split mind as Macmillan had, between Washington and Brussels, and in his Godkin lectures in 1967 he has complained about 'the instinctive tendency among some British officials . . . to ask first and foremost what the United States will think and how it will act'. A good deal of Gaullism has brushed off on him, as on other European leaders; his vein of nationalism is quite in keeping with the present mood of the common market, which has stimulated national competitiveness rather than (as Monnet hoped) dissolving or by-passing it. It remains to be seen whether, if Europe develops into a more federal structure, Heath would be able to transmute his British patriotism into a European patriotism; but that problem is a long way off—as it is for Pompidou and Brandt.

Heath's picture of self-reliance, whether for individuals or for the nation, is emphasised by his style: this is where I stand, this is my position. In politics as in personal encounters, he insists on confrontation and argument; he likes to meet issues head-on, and in this (as Iain Macleod once said) he had some resemblance to Gaitskell. But his plain speaking is not quite as it looks: he may, as his father says, be too honest to be a politician, but he is also too much a politician to be entirely honest. He is not above such tricks as promising to stop prices rising 'at a stroke', and behind his dogmatic statements he can be very pragmatic. After having his showdown, as with Rolls-Royce, he is quite capable, after making the point, of climbing down and coming to terms with necessity. His dogmatic style is partly a personal habit; but it is also a political front, to keep his right-wing happy. His showdowns, whether with the trade unions or the black commonwealth, show that he, like the nation, will not be pushed around; and his own mood probably chimed quite well with the national mood. He will not, like Powell, pursue his dogma to the bitter end.

But in some of his confrontations he shows a personal stubbornness and emotionalism which worries his colleagues; and it showed itself most openly in his reaction to the black commonwealth over the selling of arms to South Africa. He has never been deeply involved in African questions: he disliked white South Africa when he went there, but he believes black Africa is much less important than Asia. African emotionalism, however, very easily gets on his nerves; he was acutely irritated by Kaunda's frenzied gestures and Nyerere's philosophising, and reacted as if he was personally threatened, with none of the traditional fatherly patience towards the commonwealth. The atmosphere of the commonwealth and the UN annoys him: 'We want to avoid the danger of being swept along by emotional pressure generated within these international organisations,' he said in October 1970. But at Singapore it was Heath himself who generated much of the emotion: he escalated the argument into a dogmatic statement of principle, even though in private he was moderating his policies—the reverse of normal diplomacy.

It is emotional pressure that Heath finds most difficult to cope with, and which provokes his own emotional reactions. When he feels put upon or pressured, he seems to feel vulnerable and even perhaps insecure: it is as if opera had suddenly broken through into his political life, and knocked down the neat compartments between emotion and reason. The abhorrence of emotionalism may prove in the end his most serious limitation, not only in diplomacy but in his national leadership. It can be argued that Britain needs some harsh realism, and even some sense of fear, to face up to her current problems; and for this confrontation Heath is well suited. But in the end every country needs also reassurance and hope with which to face a difficult future. That role (the role of the family doctor, as Wilson describes it) is one that Heath finds difficult to play; and though he speaks convincingly about the need for freedom—both for the individual and the nation—he has not yet answered the question: freedom to do what?

Was there a particular time, I asked the prime minister, when he decided that the consensus should be broken up?

There never was a consensus in the sense of a deliberate effort of will and thought to create a particular situation: in that sense it certainly didn't exist. The parties never came together in their policies. Even the idea of 'Butskellism' was sloppy and inaccurate; it bore no relation to the facts. It has been said that between 1961 and 1963, when Macmillan and Selwyn Lloyd introduced Neddy and Nicky to provide an incomes policy, that there was some consensus. But Nicky was not accepted by the Labour Party, and it was repudiated by the trade unions. There was some measure of consensus over defence policy: that was broken up by the Labour Party over the Far East.

There had been a kind of consensus about collectivism which really began I suppose with the first world war, and the terrible losses of men. The depression of 1931 and the unemployment all led to a general attitude of letting the state step in and solve people's problems. The Conservatives did manage to do quite a lot between 1951 and 1964: we threw out restraints and rationing; we improved housing, schools and economic growth, but we hadn't succeeded in changing people's attitudes. Now we have to get back to the traditional British attitude of independence from the state, which was so strong in the nineteenth century, when the British were known for their ability to take risks and benefit from the profits from them. It's only relatively recently that we have felt the need to withdraw from overseas affairs and to look to the state. Of course our view is not an extreme one; we accept that there are many fields, like pensions, defence and aviation, where the state must be involved. I am satisfied that already people's attitudes are beginning to change.

Was there a particular moment when the basis of your present policies emerged?

In 1959, when I was Minister of Labour, I began to see more clearly that we wouldn't get an up-to-date industrial system by leaving it to the employers and trade unions to create it. It would have to be done by the government of the day. My feeling was reinforced by my experience of the European negotiations which showed the growth of the European economy and what we would have to do to compete with it. It was reinforced again by what I saw in the Board of Trade, where I realised that we had to have a policy to stimulate competition, to provide incentives for individuals, to provide more effective regional development, etc. When we were out of power in 1965 there was a chance to sit back and work out the policy in detail; by September 1965 all our present policy was already written down in detail in our policy statement.

6

Conservatives

We have created what we promised, a new style of government.

Edward Heath, October 1970.

THE conflict between new Tories and old is a recurring epic—
Disraeli against Peel, Joseph Chamberlain against Balfour,
Baldwin against Curzon. The breaks are never as drastic as they
seem, for the Conservatives have an instinct for self-preservation;
they continue to woo the same voters, to balance the same forces,
and when election-time approaches, to search again for the middle
ground. Often the break is papered-over by apparent agreement;
as when, in July 1965, Sir Alec Douglas-Home resigned and was
succeeded by Edward Heath. But that change was, in fact, a real
climacteric in Tory history—though it did not become apparent
till five years later. It was the delayed end of the Macmillan era, of
the dominating influence of the man who had restored and united
the party after the crises of Suez in 1956.

The end of the Macmillan era and the beginning of opposition
left the Tories confused about their identity and purpose. It would
be rash to attribute this too directly to Macmillan's neglect, or to
his messy inheritance, for he himself in his time had restored
confidence after the ditherings of Eden. Much Tory confidence
has always depended on being 'born to rule', and the restoration of
this confidence after the fiasco of Suez was Macmillan's achievement. He was able, by brilliant sleight-of-hand and a good deal of

double-talk, to combine his own intellectual approach with presenting the party as part of the natural order with natural rulers, set against the alien doctrines and unreliable men on the left: and he was able to disguise—at least for four years—his own desire for a modern consensus and a pact with the trade unions under the camouflage of his Edwardian manner.

The hasty exit of Sir Alec and the brisk entry of Heath marked an abrupt scene-change, not only because the Magic Circle had gone up in smoke, or because Heath came from a new class—not very different from Wilson's class; but because with Heath there emerged too a more aggressive element in the party, who had felt suppressed under the rule of the politicians: like Heath, they had little class-guilt, and were prepared for a showdown with the trades unions.

There were few bridges between the two styles: as one of the most romantic Tory apologists, Peregrine Worsthorne, described it in April 1970: 'The Mr Efficiencies hark forward to a new ideal of technical expertise that leaves the public not only cold but shivering, while the old guard hark back to a style of leadership that seems old-fashioned to the point of caricature.' The Tories have always concocted mixtures of very different ingredients; defensive and aggressive, old rich and new rich, old metropolitan and new colonial or provincial. Much energy and radicalism has come from its periodic bombardments by foreign particles—Disraelis, Chamberlains, Bonar Laws. But in the midst of these intrusions and dilutions, the Conservatives have needed to retain a picture of themselves as a tribal, atavistic gathering, representing a special kind of robust and manly England; Conservatives often like to talk about their own party with a kind of awed fascination, half admiring, half dreading, as if they were talking about a Tudor court; 'The Tories don't like failures' (Anon); 'Loyalty is the Tories' secret weapon' (Kilmuir); 'The Tories are bad losers' (Macmillan); 'Tories don't like cripples' (Anon). Even such phrases as the Magic Circle (Macleod) or the Night of the Long Knives convey fascinated awe, depicting the Tories as more like a Turkish regiment or an initiation school, than as the federation of interests that it is. This self-portraiture has clearly been important to them, helping to make the dull seem exciting, the suburban seem imperial, and the new seem old. But the cultivation of this kind of romanticism is no part of Heath's style; and the men who emerged as the party leaders in the Tory government—

Barber, Joseph, Rippon or Walker—are not men who were either equipped with, or inclined to, the rhetoric of the regiment.

Macmillan, moreover, left the party without any plausible moral purpose, with only the bitter echoes of 'you've never had it so good'. In a famous phrase Macmillan had complained: 'If people want a sense of purpose they should get it from their archbishop.' This abdication may have suited his own premiership, basically an age of retreat, but it left an uncomfortable vacuum in an age when moral issues were coming back to the forefront—filled erratically, either by the windy rhetoric of Hogg, or the manic outbursts of Powell. Even the easy-going Reginald Maudling has insisted that the moral problems of the future cannot be left to the archbishops: 'Politicians must not flinch from their responsibility,' he said in October 1970, 'nor can the churches achieve for politicians what they themselves fail to do.' But the infusion of moral leadership, or even rhetoric, was again not in keeping with the style of the Heath conservatives.

Heath's cabinet (see opposite) might well appear to be a natural progression from the previous Tory cabinets of Douglas-Home or Macmillan. Nine of them had been cabinet ministers under Macmillan. Sir Alec was once again Foreign Secretary, which he had been ten years before—a living guarantee of Tory continuity, always ready to be wheeled on at awkward moments of party conferences, to counteract Enoch Powell or to combat anti-Europeanism. Several of the most important new men, like Rippon, Joseph, Barber and Heath himself, owed their promotion to Macmillan; Heath as prime minister still asks Macmillan for advice. The dynastic continuity of the Tory party was looked after. Macmillan's son Maurice was now Chief Secretary at the Treasury, and his son-in-law Julian Amery was Minister of Housing; Churchill's son-in-law Christopher Soames was ambassador to Paris, and his grandson Winston Churchill was befriended by Heath. Even Lord Avon had a nephew in the government—Sir John Eden, the Minister for Industry under John Davies. There were still debonair peers in the cabinet, Jellicoe and Carrington, in the Macmillan tradition; there were still rich landowners from Scotland or the borders—Douglas-Home, Whitelaw, and Campbell—to keep up the grouse-moor image.

But the continuity concealed a revolution. The young 'technocrats' that Macmillan had brought in to run the more industrial ministries were now in the key positions in government—still

Ages as at 31 December 1970.

Edward Heath (54)	Prime Minister	Chatham House, Ramsgate; Balliol, Oxford.
Reginald Maudling (53)	Home Secretary	Merchant Taylors'; Merton, Oxford.
Sir Alec Douglas-Home (67)	Foreign Secretary	Eton; Christ Church, Oxford.
Anthony Barber (50)	Chancellor of the Exchequer	Oriel, Oxford.
Lord Hailsham (63)	Lord Chancellor	Eton; Christ Church, Oxford.
William Whitelaw (52)	Lord President of the Council and Leader of the Commons	Winchester; Trinity, Cambridge.
Lord Carrington (51)	Secretary of State for Defence	Eton; Sandhurst.
Sir Keith Joseph (52)	Secretary of State for Social Services	Harrow; Magdalen, Oxford.
John Davies (54)	Secretary of State for Trade and Industry	St Edward's School, Oxford.
Geoffrey Rippon (46)	Chancellor of the Duchy of Lancaster	King's College, Taunton; Brasenose, Oxford.
Robert Carr (54)	Secretary of State for Employment	Westminster; Gonville and Caius, Cambridge.
Margaret Thatcher (45)	Secretary of State for Education and Science	Kesteven and Grantham Girls' School; Somerville, Oxford.
Gordon Campbell (49)	Secretary of State for Scotland	Wellington.
Earl Jellicoe (52)	Lord Privy Seal	Winchester; Trinity College, Cambridge.
Peter Walker (38)	Secretary of State for the Environment	Latymer Upper.
Peter Thomas (50)	Secretary of State for Wales	Epworth College, Rhyl; Jesus, Oxford.
James Prior (43)	Minister of Agriculture	Charterhouse; Pembroke, Cambridge.

more so after the death of Iain Macleod a month after the election, and his succession as chancellor by Anthony Barber. The new cabinet had closer links with industry than any since the war; Joseph and Rippon had both been chairmen of construction companies (Bovis and Cubbitts); Peter Walker had made his fortune in insurance and unit trusts; John Davies had moved from Shell to be Director-General of the Confederation of British Industries, and after only three months in Parliament went straight to the cabinet. James Prior had been a farm manager before he bought his own farm; Robert Carr was once a shift foreman in John Dale, the engineering firm which his great-grandfather founded; later he became chief metallurgist, and eventually chairman.

Macmillan (in his later years) and Churchill before him had regarded industry as boring and secondary to the great questions of diplomacy, to be left to accountants in back rooms; *their* idea of a proper industrialist was Lord Chandos; or, as a cheeky exception, Ernie Marples. Now for the first time since before the war a Tory government was dominated by men who sounded actually interested in industry; and who were dedicated to making the capitalist system work, with tougher competition, greater incentives and the injection of eager management methods into government. There is a sense of boyish zeal and certainty in the new Tory cabinet, a hint of which might be found in their looks. When they are lined up together on the front bench or at a party conference, they have—much more than their predecessors—the look of a superannuated schoolboy team, as if Greyfriars had finally conquered Westminster. There are the Owls of the Remove—Whitelaw and Maudling; there is Rippon, the Bounder; Douglas-Home and Carrington the Swells; Joseph and Barber, the school swots; Walker the school prefect, and Heath the head boy who will not tolerate slacking or sloppiness.

The break with the aristocracy should not be exaggerated. There were still three Etonians in Heath's 1971 cabinet (compared with six in Macmillan's 1962 cabinet)—the Lord Chancellor, the Foreign Secretary and the Minister of Defence. Heath's two closest allies in opposition had been Lord Carrington and William Whitelaw, both aristocrats with an extrovert style quite unlike Heath's own. Both of them are vocal in cabinet, and indispensible to the party. In Heath's whole government, twenty-two per cent are Old Etonians, including such feudal figures as Lord Balniel, son of the 28th Earl of Crawford and Balcarres, and Lord Lambton, who renounced the Earldom of Durham (while insisting on still being called Lord). But broadly, and with notable exceptions, it was now the Etonians who were in the junior positions, with the new men above them. It can be very misleading to identify backgrounds with attitudes: there is the technocratic Old Etonian, David Howell, the minister for the civil service, who looks lanky and effete; or there is the ex-mayor of Surbiton, Geoffrey Rippon, who cultivates a casual style. But it is still very relevant that many of Heath's government are men who see politics, not as an extension of an estate, a family or a regiment, but as an extension of business.

After the election victory, Heath's domination of his party was so accepted that it was hard to visualise challengers or contenders. Heath could construct his government without bothering about balances between Maudlingites, Hoggites or Powellites; it was Heath's victory, and it was Heath's government. The top positions were occupied by men who were unlikely to challenge him: the Foreign Secretary, because he was too old, and had already been discarded as prime minister, the Home Secretary (see below) because he had already been beaten by Heath, the Chancellor because he was politically dependent on Heath. Many of the New Tories were too preoccupied with running their complicated ministries to argue about more general issues in the cabinet. But the cabinet is still a kind of miniature history of the Tory Party, ranging from Sir Alec, at sixty-seven, to Peter Walker at thirty-eight; and it embraces very different species of New Tory, of which these are three examples.

REGINALD MAUDLING

A thorough contrast to Heath, as a kind of relic of the consensus, is found in the shape of the Home Secretary and Deputy Leader, Reginald Maudling, who for the last fifteen years has been very much part of the Tory furniture (a deep club armchair, compared to Heath's straightback, or Hogg's baroque throne). His is a reassuring presence, with his amiable smile, his reasonable voice and his appropriate-sounding name. He was the son of an actuary, took a first at Oxford, married an actress, spent the war in the air force; there is still a touch of the RAF about him. He decided with some difficulty that he was a Tory and not a Socialist. He only went into parliament in 1950, and never spoke stirringly; but three years later he was made Economic Secretary to the Treasury. He moved up steadily, making few enemies, until in 1962 Macmillan made him Chancellor. At the Treasury he was a bold expansionist, and faced with an imbalance of payments tried to break out of the vicious circle of 'stop-go' by spending, producing the great Maudling boom of 1964—which left the Labour government with the notorious £800 million deficit. When Labour blamed the mess on their predecessor, Maudling with characteristic honesty agreed.

Maudling is not a militant Tory, and his attitudes are not easy to distinguish from those of (say) Roy Jenkins; he is humane, tolerant, anti-Puritan, though now showing some worries about the permissive society. He enjoys good living and café society; he is one of the few top Tories who feels at ease in frivolous company. He opts out of much Conservative dogma ('I am a little sceptical about some of the things that are said about the need for incentives,' he said back in 1967), and he has some difficulty in hating Socialists, which makes him distrusted by his committed colleagues. He expects people to realise his excellence without his having to push it at them. His speeches are boring, and he is a master of bathos, which touched bottom in October 1963, after Harold Macmillan announced his resignation: Maudling had a good chance of the premiership, but the following day he made a speech that was so anti-climactic that it put off many of his supporters. In 1965 he had another chance of the leadership; but he was just as reluctant to organise himself against Heath. His defeat by Heath, though he concealed his disappointment, was a great blow to him, and thereafter he lost some of his zest for politics. He also became more interested in making money; he already had some lucrative directorships, including a seat on the board of Kleinwort Benson's bank; but in 1969 he agreed to become President of an offshore fund, called the Real Estate Fund of America, run by an American financier Jerome Hoffman, who had been banned from dealing with securities in New York. Maudling's support for the fund, together with that of men like Robert Wagner, Paul-Henri Spaak and Lord Brentford, gave great respectability to the fund, and helped to make Hoffman's fortune; its collapse the following year, leaving vast debts and revealing the basic dishonesty of Hoffman's enterprise, caused much criticism of Maudling's judgement.[1] When he came back into office as Home Secretary, he appeared to have lost much of his energy and decisiveness; surrounded by tougher and more single-minded Tories, he seemed to belong to a vanished era of easy-going conservatism.

PETER WALKER

The most obvious prodigy of the New Toryism is Peter Walker, the self-made millionaire who in 1970 became Minister for the

[1] For an account of the Hoffman affair, see *Do You Sincerely Want to be Rich?* by Charles Raw, Bruce Page and Godfrey Hodgson: Andre Deutsch, 1971, pp. 305–6.

Environment at the age of only thirty-eight. He looks (much more nowadays than Heath) the model of virtue rewarded, tall, upstanding, clean-limbed, with his brisk school-prefect manner; he stands with his arms folded, looks at you with hard, straight eyes, smiles with a confident smile from his long horsy mouth. His style suggests that everything when understood is really very simple: 'Jolly good,' he says after a brisk talk on the telephone.

He loves to retell his remarkable success-story: brought up in Gloucester, the son of a small grocer; went to Latymer Upper school, where, after a debate, he met old Leo Amery, the Tory idealist, who encouraged him to go into politics, but advised him to make money first. Left school at sixteen, went into insurance because the only man in his street with a car was in insurance. Joined the General Accident company in Gloucester as a stamp-licker. After national service, joined up with an accountant, David Moate, to form an insurance broking firm, Walker Moate, which was his first gold-mine. He realised the tremendous potential of new savings and new kinds of investment, and knew how to get at the consumer; expanded into unit trusts, property and banking; met Jim Slater—the other great city success story of the sixties (see Chapter 26)—and with him set up Slater Walker Securities. The two young men got rich together. In the meantime he had been preparing his political path: at fourteen he joined the West Harrow Conservatives; in his teens he was speaking round the country, and studying American elections; at twenty-nine he was elected as MP for Worcester, and by 1963 he was Selwyn Lloyd's parliamentary private secretary. In opposition he firmly linked his fortunes with Heath's: in 1965 he organised his campaign for the leadership, and supported him through the barren years, with his high-powered secretariat.

Walker is not very popular with his own party, and to the left he is a useful bogy; his style and his career stamp him indelibly as a technocrat. He is a dull speaker, and his political philosophy is unexciting. He looks like a new manifestation of the manager-minister (like old Marples) who runs a department as if it were a giant corporation. But in the department he has been spectacularly efficient—much more so than the other super-minister, John Davies—delegating smoothly, resolving conflicts, reorganising committees and communications.

Walker is unlikely to acquire the kind of political appeal that could make him prime minister (though this was often said of

Heath). But he is not as mechanical and inhuman as he looks. He sees himself as a patriot, in the enlightened mould of Amery or Milner: 'Pride in our country, which must make us loathe the spectacle of the degrading conditions in which so many of its people are still condemned to live.' (Milner). He insists that he is on the left of his party, divided by a generation gap from Heath and the pre-war men. Abroad he is much more interested in the black commonwealth than Heath—he was originally against the common market partly on those grounds—and at home he has never accepted that housing can ever be left to free-market forces. He may well do more to improve the worst housing conditions than his Labour predecessor, Greenwood; he is adept at pressurising local councils and exploiting the media to get poorer people to use the grants. ('It's no use legislating without telling people about their rights' is one of his refrains.)

SIR KEITH JOSEPH

Intellectually more interesting as an exponent of New Conservatism, and a more complex character than Walker, is Sir Keith Joseph, now Minister for Social Services. His style is rather forbidding; he has a grave stony face, cold eyes and a white-rabbit intensity: a favourite phrase is 'dear me'. His shiny hair, dark suits and precise politeness all suggest that he belongs to the aldermanic school of Conservatives, and he was indeed an alderman, the son of a mayor. At the same time he has an intense, very earnest social conscience. He expounds with great fervour the case for all kinds of underdog—homeless, alcoholics, addicts, mental patients, all of them—and he is specially concerned with the cause of spinsters (he wants them all to be called Mrs as in Sweden).

Joseph's career was golden; he inherited from his father a baronetcy, plenty of money, and an interest in a building company, Bovis. After Harrow, Oxford and a good war he became a barrister and Fellow of All Souls. He married an attractive American sculptress and went into Bovis, and then into parliament. Under Macmillan he became one of the 'eager beavers', and eventually came into the cabinet as Minister of Housing. In opposition he became one of the party's chief theorists about industry, and talked with great clarity about the new policy: 'We have declared our intention to pursue a policy of civilised capitalism,' he said in

March 1970, 'based on competitive free enterprise in a content of humane laws and institutions.' He was determined to make capitalism work, to break up cartels, to mobilise shareholders, to disclose true company profits, to use government to maintain competition because, 'left to themselves most businessmen would share the market and keep newcomers out'. He sometimes sounded like Enoch Powell, but he has much more compassion and vulnerability than Powell, and he insists (for instance) that regional subsidies are essential to avoid the 'obscene' consequences of overcrowding in the South-East. His fiercely rational approach to industry frightened industrialists as well as trade unionists—which may be why Heath put him in charge, not of industry, but of social services. He is a figure of formidable integrity, and he is quite capable of standing up to Heath. But he has always lacked political sex-appeal, and there has so far been a large gap between his grand designs for reform and his actual achievement.

ENOCH POWELL

A politician crystallises what most people mean, even if they don't know it.

Enoch Powell.

In the meantime, the Conservative leaders continue to be uncomfortably conscious of the presence of Enoch Powell, right outside the government, appealing both through parliament and direct to the electorate, projecting a more exciting and romantic brand of conservatism than the government's. Powell has become one of that special class of politicians like Goldwater or Poujade, who claim to represent the dark, secret heart of the nation.

As an orator Powell reveals the limitations of the others: in full flight, with arms waving, body crouching, eyes burning, voice hissing, he is one of the great sights of contemporary Britain; his body and mind seem united in animal intensity. But he is not a demagogue in the sense of making blatant concessions to the masses. His high emotion is that of a philosopher who has triumphantly discovered the truth; he constructs theories step by step, clause by clause, developing arguments to logical but often absurd conclusions. His speeches are frequently intellectually interesting, and it is his union of careful reasoning with intense romanticism which gives him his special hold on younger members of the party.

That union was the key to his intellectual development: after winning classical prizes at Cambridge (which he found suffocating) he fell in love with German philosophy, specially Nietzsche 'like some traveller who, in the moonlit clearing of a forest, comes upon another human being pursuing the same journey'.[1] He was enthralled by the Germans' intellectual precision combined with the romantic sense of infinitude in their poetry. He became professor of Greek in Australia at twenty-five (a year older, he laments, than Nietzsche arriving in Basle) and read Schopenhauer on the Sydney tramcars. He came back to England to join up in 1939, and rose from private to brigadier. He ended up reporting on the post-war Indian Army, filled with admiration for the Raj: a year after ¦Indian independence he amazed Churchill by proposing to *recapture* India. After imperialism was a lost cause, when Churchill gave up the Suez Canal base, he switched abruptly to being a Little Englander, dedicated to High Toryism and the free market, which he now invested with the same kind of mystic splendour that he had given to the British Raj: his model was now the German 'free-market economy' of Erhard and Adenauer.

His extreme theories did not keep him out of office; Macmillan made him Financial Secretary to the Treasury, but he resigned with his Chancellor, Thorneycroft, in protest against Macmillan's inflationary policies. He came back a few years later as Minister of Health, (where he massively increased public spending on hospitals) but resigned again when Sir Alec became premier, and then began to expound his doctrines more boldly. In 1966 Heath included him for a time in his shadow cabinet; but when Powell made his first racial outburst, about 'rivers of blood', Heath sacked him, and he has been in the wilderness ever since.

Powell's attacks on immigrants were the outbursts of an opportunist more than a racialist. Up till 1966, though his constituency of Wolverhampton was multicoloured, he scarcely mentioned the subject; but by the next year he saw immigration as his chance. Somewhat like Churchill in the early thirties, Powell was searching around for a popular cause; and immigration was the more effective because both parties and all the mass media had tried to sweep it under the carpet. Powell could present himself as the people's champion against parliament's conspiracy of silence, which suited his mystic picture of Toryism: 'I've been heard, heard as no man in this country has been heard in thirty

[1] See *The Listener*, June 25, 1970.

years.' Later Powell turned his guns onto the common market. He had begun as an advocate of Britain's joining this great new free market, but in the late sixties he decided that Britain should go it alone, which fitted better his High Tory patriotism: like Disraeli, in 1846, he doubtless saw protection as an issue through which he could first split, and then rule, his party.

Powell's frenetic election campaign in 1970, culminating in his attack on the 'enemies of state' inside Whitehall and in a bid for the leadership, was evidently based on the expectation that Heath would lose; the party, having lost its way, would turn to him as the embodiment of an ancient, mystical Toryism. After Heath inconveniently won, Powell soon proclaimed that he no longer had ambitions for office. But his position was still formidable; he had a power-base in the Midlands, a group of Powellites in parliament, and he could and did boast that without his support, the Tories would not have won the election.

BOW GROUP

Below the level of the leadership there are various Tory stables which train the runners of the future. The most influential of them has been the Bow Group, founded in 1951 (when it held its first meetings in Bow), representing the more intellectual and questioning younger conservatives, a kind of Fabian Society of the right. After the 1970 election the Bow Group held a party at the House of Commons to celebrate their special victory, with thirty-eight members in parliament (compared to only seventeen before) It was a subdued occasion. Looking round the demure gathering it was hard to detect what was characteristically Tory about it: the dark suits and quiet Oxbridge voices, the devotion to statistics, might as well have come from the Society of Labour Lawyers. In theory, the Bow Group has no corporate policy, and its members include John Biffin, a Powellite, and Piers Dixon of the Monday Club, the far-right son-in-law of Duncan Sandys. But in the past its dominant characteristics have been tolerance and social conscience, with special concern for the welfare state and for Africa. It was founded by a group including James Lemkin, who had some influence in liberalising Macmillan's African policies: Black Africa remains a great concern of the Bow Group, and in July 1970 several of them signed a petition questioning the supply of arms to South Africa. Nowadays the Bow Group is less of a pressure-group than an intellectual ante-room to the chambers of power. Heath brought several Bow Groupers into his government, including Sir Geoffrey Howe, the young solicitor-general, David Howell, minister for the civil service and Christopher Chataway, minister of Posts and Telecommunications. But with this closeness to government, the more militant members have become worried about the orthodoxy of the group; there has been talk of an 'ideological crisis', and by 1971 there was a serious lack of funds.

MONDAY CLUB

A more cohesive and much less intellectual grouping are the right-wing Tories called the Monday Club: they, too, held a stately little party after the 1970 election, to celebrate *their* victories —thirty members of parliament, six members of the government, and a cabinet minister (Geoffrey Rippon). They were confident of a revival not only of conservatism, but of right-wing, romantic, Monday conservatism; believing not only in free enterprise and an independent Britain, but in support for white South Africa and Rhodesia. Their gathering seemed like a flashback, not so much to the Macmillan era, as to the late Churchill era. The room was full of long, eccentric faces, loud, fruity voices, and half-forgotten names. They included Richard Law, Bonar's son, now Lord Coleraine; Lord Hinchingbrooke, now known as Victor Montagu; Julian Amery, now Minister of Housing. The guest of honour was none other then the Marquess of Salisbury, the club's father-figure, now seventy-seven and walking with a stick. The Marquess made a speech with the benign confidence of someone who always knew he was right. He spoke with forgiving tolerance of the left-wing Tories, and reminded members of how the club was first formed; how five worried young Chelsea Tories came to see him ten years before, to ask his blessing for a group to combat the leftish policies of Harold Macmillan, and to keep alive the true blue tradition. Macmillan was then the arch-enemy, the crypto-Socialist. In opposition the Monday Club swelled, and turned their attention to attacking the real Socialists. Now in 1970 they claimed credit for the Tory landslide; and new Monday Club MPs had ousted George Brown and Jennie Lee from the Commons.

There is still a special fervour about many Monday men—the breeziness, the light in the wide eyes, the expansive smile, the slightly zany charm, that used to characterise old settlers in Africa.

Their vocabulary of doom—about anarchy, conspirators, wreckers, chaos, betrayal—casually slips off the tongue; they have a mixture of military and revivalist zeal, like some guards regiment that has had suddenly to resort to guerrilla warfare in an occupied country. White Africa is the common enthusiasm for many of them, and they stride round rooms as if they had just come in from the veldt. But their enthusiasm is not disinterested. Many Monday members derive income from South Africa. They are not so much a club as a lobby.

Alongside the buccaneering Monday men there are people who come from the solid regions of management, computers or local councils, and who perhaps look to the Monday Club to give purpose or glory to their humdrum lives. From the suburbs and local administration the Monday Club draws much of its support, and Surbiton has been a special hive of Monday activity: the one Monday member of the new cabinet, Geoffrey Rippon, was Mayor of Surbiton at the age of twenty-seven. Rippon is an interesting study. He is only forty-six, but he is huge, with a big round head, several chins and a rubber smile—a kind of solemn version of Charles Laughton. His early career was steadily municipal; after Oxford and the Bar, he worked his way up from his Surbiton base through the whole world of munici-palities. He went into parliament in 1955, became an expert on housing, and eventually Macmillan made him Minister of Works. In opposition, he became chairman of the construction company, Cubitts: he became more prosperous, more flamboyant, and moved ponderously to the right; he wrote a crude pamphlet for the Monday Club called *Right Angle*, complaining about the Tide of Moral and Social Decay, the Socialist Curse, and the Steady Erosion of Our Influence in the World. But Rippon is a more formidable figure than he looks and sounds: he played the common market negotiations with studied languor worthy of Macmillan, and like Macmillan he conceals a sharp mind behind his political play-acting.

Heath's strategy with the Monday Club seemed to be: bring them into the government with unromantic hard-working jobs where they couldn't be too much nuisance. Julian Amery went first to the Ministry of Works, and then to Housing; John Peyton went to Transport (Peyton's Place). The Monday men were anxious to stress that they would not be divisive in Heath's govern-ment, as they were in Macmillan's, and to dissociate themselves as a group from Enoch Powell (who has never been a member though he has often addressed them): their policies are often the same, but Powell is playing a more open and dangerous game.

WHO RUNS THE TORIES?

Since the last war, with the professionalisation of politics, the Tory headquarters have strengthened their hold on the party. The Conservative Central Office in Smith Square and its academic offshoot, the Conservative Research Department, have always been far better organised and financed than Transport House, a stone's throw away. Central Office looks like a commercial public relations company, full of eager men and keen county girls; the large hall has room for a full press conference, and there are hand-outs about almost everything. Central Office has to keep up the appearance of unity in the Tory line, and to stir up the waning enthusiasm of party workers. As a monument to its industry is the *Campaign Guide*, a thick blue volume prepared for each election by the Research Department, under Brendan Sewell, which tells candidates how to reply to those awkward questions, and how to spell out the full wickedness of Labour: it is like a creed or a catechism, to rally the faithful:

> They promised to stop the rise in the cost of living –
> and have failed
> They attached great importance to incomes policy –
> and have failed
> They implied that they could deal with the unions –
> and have failed
> They promised to build 500,000 houses a year –
> and have failed.

At the head of Central Office is the full-time chairman of the party, chosen by the leader himself, with the prime task of ensuring that the next election is won. Few jobs have had such a range of occupants, from tycoons like Lord Woolton, Edward du Cann or Lord Poole to peace-keepers like Lord Blakenham. It is hard to find a man with the showmanship to rally his own party, without (like Lord Hailsham) frightening voters away. The present chairman is unlikely to frighten anyone; Peter Thomas is a Welsh barrister with a matinée-idol look: he is a loyal supporter of Heath, who combines the chairmanship with being Secretary for Wales. Nearer an election he may be replaced by a more prominent figure. Much of the organisational work falls on the deputy-chairman, Sir Michael Fraser—the wise old man of Tory politics, with the gravity of a bishop, who for the last quarter-century has been toiling in the Tory bureaucracy, slipping unobtrusively among the flamboyant politicians, with his Aberdonian detachment.

WHO PAYS?

The secret funds of the Tory Party were for long a favourite bogy for Labour, who feel handicapped by their smaller levies from the trade unions (see Chapter 36), and in 1967 the Companies Act required all firms to declare their donations to political bodies. Labour hoped that by revealing these sums they might frighten the directors from giving them. But when the Conservatives appealed for £2 million in 1968 they raised £240,000 more than they asked for; and the first list of donations published in 1969 showed little sign that companies were deterred. It did however provide an insight into Tory links with the city and industry. The Tories depend (it turns out) on relatively few banks or big companies: most of the great corporations, like Shell, Unilever or ICI, gave nothing, but a handful of the next biggest, usually with a strong family tradition or a Tory politician on the board, gave quite large slices. Guest, Keen and Nettlefolds, the Midlands engineering company, gave £41,000 to Tory party and right-wing pressure-groups; Watney Mann gave £24,750. The Rank Organisation gave £25,000 and Dunlop gave £21,000; Rank Hovis MacDougall, the bakers, gave £18,500. The brewers (who have always felt the Tories were more pro-drinking) gave between them £71,000. The Tory strongholds in the city are the merchant banks, and Montagu's, Barings, Brown Shipley, Kleinworts and Hambro's (most of which have had Tory ministers on their boards) each gave over £10,000. Most donations went direct to Central Office, but almost as much went to the curious propaganda organisations which exist to foster free enterprise and to counter socialist or 'communist' principles; these were the total annual donations in 1968:

> Conservative Party: £448,040
> British United Industrialists: £282,952
> Economic League: £58,402
> Aims of Industry: £28,111
> Common Cause: £6,367
> Miscellaneous: £79,638

The right-wing pressure organisations date back to an earlier era of anti-socialist zeal; but they are still strident.[1] British United Industrialists, the biggest of them, is run from Park Lane by an ex-Bengal lancer, Colonel Hobbs, with the help of diehards as Sir Halford Reddish and Lord Renwick, the co-founder of Associated Television, who works next door. The Economic League was established by coal and steelmasters after the first world war, and offers among other things information about subversive elements; its present president, oddly, is Sir David Barran, the chairman of Shell. Aims of Industry was set up in 1942, and organised the 'Mr. Cube' campaign to stop the nationalisation of Tate and Lyle, who still gratefully support it; its council includes such archetypal Tories as Lord Rank and Colonel Whitbread, and its president is Sir Ian Lyle, the current sugar king.

The Labour Party claim that such subventions are anti-democratic: trade unionists *can* contract out of a union's political levy to the Labour Party, but shareholders cannot avoid contributing to the Tories—except by selling their shares in Hambro's, GKN, etc. (this might involve financial self-sacrifice: when *The Economist* tested different selections of shares in 1970, it was a group of Tory-supporting companies that showed the greatest capital appreciation). The Tory Party appear unembarrassed by the disclosure of their funds; though the revelation that half their money comes from twenty companies, and much of it from old die-hards, does not help their image as the party of people's capitalism. They are disappointed that more of the big industrialists do not realise their virtues. In April 1971 Lord Chelmer, the chairman of the Central Board of Finance, revealed that the party was facing a financial deficit of £350,000 in the coming year, with total costs of £1.3 million; he was 'surprised and disappointed' that out of the top hundred companies only forty supported the party, and none of the fourteen biggest. 'At a time when capitalism is under attack from Maoism and Marxism it is surprising that industry recognises so little the effort put into this battle by the one party which supports it.'

Does he who pays the piper, call the tune? Has the right-wing money helped to pull the Tories in a right-wing direction in the last few years? It would be difficult to prove. The interplay between industry and the political parties is now so complex, so

[1] See Paul Ferris: 'The Mysterious Men in their Propaganda Machine'. *The Observer*, October 19, 1969, for further details.

full of paradox, that the donations are only a small part of the equation. A company in difficulties, like Mersey Docks or Rolls-Royce, might have been safer with the Labour Party; if the Conservatives really stimulate competition and pull away props, many companies that have romantically supported 'free enterprise', including the brewers, may find themselves embarrassed by real competition. But there can be little doubt that the right-wing pressure-groups played a part in the revival of interest in free enterprise in the mid-sixties and after, both in such specific Tory campaigns as the crusade for commercial radio (see Chapter 1) and in fostering intellectual discussions like these promoted by the Institute for Economic Affairs (see below). These movements of opinion might have happened anyway: but the backers' money gave them solid shape, respectability and direction, and made bridges from theory into political action.

SWING TO THE RIGHT

The swings of the pendulum have been so incalculable that interpretations are dangerous: but during the late sixties there were signs of a rightward movement, culminating in the 1970 victory for the Conservatives. This was widely presented as a break-up of the consensus, initiated by the Tories; and certainly Heath had abandoned Macmillan's insistence on co-operation with the trade unions, and keeping a low level of unemployment, which had made it hard to distinguish Tory from Labour policy in 1960. But the break-up was not as simple as it seemed; for the Labour Party itself had abandoned at least tacitly some of its tenets. The confrontation with the trade unions was begun not by Heath but by Wilson; and the Labour government had already undergone some dis-enchantment with aspects of the welfare state. As one chronicler of the Labour government, Brian Lapping has put it:[1]

> The traditional view of social policy, developed by social democratic parties in Europe, and largely accepted by conservative parties too until the 1960s, was that the advance of the welfare state was an inevitable and fairly simple process; more education, more health, more housing assistance, more pensions, more social work would be distributed by the state. During the 1960s this view came for the first time to be seriously challenged.

The Labour government found public expenditure on social

[1] Brian Lapping: *The Labour Government 1964–70*, Penguins, 1970. p. 128.

services increasing so alarmingly that some modification began to seem essential—though the crisis was partly alleviated by the cutting-down of defence spending. In the meantime Conservatives were investigating systems of more selective state subsidies, and the Tory theorists of the Institute of Economic Affairs were putting forward plans for introducing the market mechanism into some sectors of the social services. The IEA had at first been regarded simply as propagandists for doctrinaire free-enterprise, but in the mid-sixties they provoked a major debate on the future of the social services. In 1967 an ex-Labour cabinet minister, Douglas Houghton, wrote a pamphlet for the IEA called *Paying for the Social Services*, which opened up the whole argument on selective state spending. The issue of state involvement was most pressing in the field of pensions, where Labour dropped its earlier plans for a national superannuation scheme, and came to terms with the growing number of private pensions schemes; so that Richard Crossman's great pension plan of 1969/70 was a complex compromise between state and private schemes.

Behind the question of state subsidies lay the argument between the Universalists and the Selectivists—between those who believed that the state should not discriminate or impose any kind of means test, and those who insisted that the state should only help those who really needed it. As public expenditure mounted, and as the really poor were still in desperate need for help, so the Labour government began to turn towards selectivity (though the argument was much less simple than that). At the same time the old Labour belief in egalitarianism was also in retreat in the field of taxation and incomes. There was growing discussion as to how far economic growth was linked to 'incentives' for managers; and increasing comparison with the rest of Europe. Even though high-growth countries like Sweden and Germany were more heavily taxed than Britain, their tax on higher incomes was much less, and this (it was argued) helped to stimulate their industrial competitiveness (see Chapter 10). Former egalitarians like Roy Jenkins had come round to the view that some increase in 'incentives' was necessary for Britain to compete with the rest of Europe, and that equality was not in itself a paramount need.

These movements of Labour policy had not come right out into the open, but the problems were building up for after the election: whichever party had been in power in 1971, the budget would have been more favourable to the rich. The Labour leaders, in attacking the budget and the Industrial Relations Bill, were partly attacking themselves and trying to win back the support of the trade unions; if they had still been in power, they would still have had to face the problems of growing public expenditure and mounting industrial strikes. The break-up of the consensus was not so much a break between Conservatives and Labour as between both governments and the trade unions; it was the gap between the rulers and the ruled, more than the gap between the parties, that was widening.

In this limited sense there has been some governmental swing to the right in the late sixties; and at the same time there has been a revival of the intellectual right, which had been so markedly absent in the late fifties and early sixties—when the egghead magazine *Encounter* had to fall back on a tiny stage army of Tory commentators (Peregrine Worsthorne, Henry Fairlie, Robert Conquest, etc). By the late sixties there was much more intellectual activity from the right, whether in the old organs like the *Daily* and *Sunday Telegraph*, or in the IEA, or in the revived *Spectator*, now bristling with Powellite views. And a succession of ageing former 'angry young men' have announced their defection to the Right. John Braine, the Yorkshire author of *Room at The Top* who had now moved from Bradford to Woking, wrote a candid pamphlet in 1968 for the Monday Club, explaining his conversion to capitalism after a visit to America: 'the name of the happiness was freedom'.[1] Kingsley Amis (once briefly a communist) described to *Sunday Telegraph* readers *his* progress to the right:

> Growing older, I have lost the need to be political, which means, in this country, the need to be left. I am driven into grudging toleration of the Conservative Party because it is the party of non-politics, of resistance to politics. I have seen how many of the evils of life— failure, loneliness, fear, boredom, inability to communicate—are ineradicable by political means, and that attempts so to eradicate them are disastrous. The ideal of the brotherhood of man, the building of the Just City, is one that cannot be discarded without lifelong feelings of disappointment and loss. But, if we are to live in the real world, discard it we must. Its very nobility makes the results of its break-down doubly horrifying, and it breaks down, as it always will, not by some external agency but because it cannot work.[2]

John Osborne, the explosive playwright, wrote in to give Amis rather incoherent support: 'The thing about Lefties is simply not to have them or their appalling journals or newspapers in your

---

[1] John Braine: *A Personal Record*, Monday Club, 1968.
[2] *Sunday Telegraph*, July 2, 1967.

house.' John Braine protested that 'the Lefties are almost completely in control of the nation's communications'.

But these intellectual defections were not very inspiring to the Tories, and Colin Welch, the deputy-editor of the *Daily Telegraph*, welcomed them with some misgivings to the fold: 'They come to their new home for the most part reluctantly, not for positive reasons but for negative, not because they "like it here" but because their last abode collapsed about their ears.' Their new world, he warned them, would be far less vivacious and argumentative than their old one: 'To be conservative requires no brains whatsoever. Cabbages, cows and conifers are conservatives, and are so stupid they don't even know it. All that is basically required is acceptance of what exists.'[1]

[1] *Spectator*, July 21, 1967.

PART

TWO

———

Backgrounds

7

Schools

Britain, in common with other European countries, is making a troubled and puzzling journey—the journey from a system of secondary and higher education designed to educate a small elite, to a system in which these kinds of education are to be made available to vastly greater numbers of boys and girls.

Newsom Report, 1968.

The most striking feature which distinguishes this country's schools from those of most of our neighbours and economic competitors is the large proportion of our pupils who abandon full-time education at the earliest opportunity.

Donnison Report, 1970.

EDUCATION has very rapidly become a dominant issue in politics: as military and imperial values have retreated into shadows, so the problems of schooling have taken their place in the foreground. Looking back now on the years between the wars, it seems odd how little the education system was then challenged; the public schools produced rebels and communists, but their class-structure remained little changed; the universities hardly expanded in those twenty years. The intellectual left was too preoccupied with the economic problems of employment, with anti-colonialism, communism and nazism, to think much about the educational ladder up which they had themselves climbed. The war itself produced the most important reform for seventy years—Butler's Education Act of 1944—but it was not till the late fifties, as the empire diminished and British politics turned inward, that education became a national preoccupation. Educational expenditure rose from 3·2 per cent of the GNP to 1954 to 6·5 per cent in 1970. For the first time the nation was spending more on education than on defence.

Educationists have found themselves at the centre of all kinds of national debates—whether about elites, competition, permissiveness, or economic growth—and education has become a red-hot political subject, a dividing-line both between the parties and inside them. It was hardly surprising. Once the national self-examination had |begun, as it had to, teachers more than anyone were involved with the question: what kind of people should the British be? The schools could lay the foundations of new skills, new adaptability, and new values. Changes have been quickened by our understanding more about how children learn. Many primary schools have been turned upside down by the work of Freud, Froebel, Montessori, and Piaget, and the British primary school is now a place of pilgrimage to foreign educationists. But behind all the new opportunities and discoveries, the educationists and politicians are still faced with the unavoidable question, of how far the system should be geared to provide an elite of the cleverest children, how far it should provide equal opportunities for all.

Much of the political debate about education hinges not on the practicability of education policies, but on pictures of an underlying social order. At one end are idealists like Brian Jackson, the Director of the Advisory Centre for Education (ACE), who wants a change in a system which he believes, is based on a 'philosophy of failure'. Enough people succeed to keep the machine going, while the rest are fodder for the industrial machine: the Bradford schoolmaster tests the quality of his boys for 'grammar school material' as his factory-owning neighbour feels his worsteds. At the other end stands the Black Paper lobby, a pessimistic alliance of elitists for whom education has become the focus of all anxiety about Law, Order and Patriotism. ('Are we no longer proud to be British?' asks Dr. Rhodes Boyson, headmaster of Highbury Grove Comprehensive.[1]) 'The new fashionable anarchy flies in the face of human nature,' wrote the group's leaders, C. B. Cox and A. E. Dyson, in their first Black Paper in 1969, 'for it holds that children and students will work from natural inclination rather than desire for rewards.'

At the centre of all the debate is Margaret Thatcher, the Tory Minister of Education. Like the prime minister, she is a triumphant product of the selection system of thirty years ago: she went to the local high school (Grantham) and then on to Somerville, Oxford, where she was expected, but failed, to get a first. She became a research chemist for four years, married a businessman, and went into parliament in 1959. She has a very quick mind, mastering

[1] *The Times*, September 9, 1970.

difficult statistics, and soon made her mark in politics. She speaks firmly and briskly, with a sugary smile and jollying words: 'come, come'. She has brought with her into the ministry all her party's enthusiasm for efficiency and a scientist's interest in teaching machines and aids: she is well able to defend her ministry's interests in cabinet. She has little tolerance of organisations over which she can have no control—a frustrating weakness in her job, for the British distaste for centralised authority has nowhere been more evident (except perhaps in the police) than in the schools system.

Education is run by what are euphemistically called 'the Partners': the Department of Education and Science (who spent £2,036 million in 1969) and the local education authorities (LEAs), who spent £1,699 million. The department controls building expenditure and the number of teachers, but it is the local authorities and their education officers, like Clegg of the West Riding and Mason of Leicestershire, who decide on the shape of education in their counties. Even the London borough of Barnet, which contains Mrs. Thatcher's own solidly Tory constituency of Finchley, is going ahead with comprehensive reorganisation. Others are now muscling in on the dual partnership. The teachers, who have long since controlled what happens inside the schools are now demanding more say in making national policy. Middle-class parents want more influence over their children's schools. The Schools Action Union, organised from grammar and public schools, is campaigning for more student government, co-education, comprehensive reform, etc. Education is becoming a prime battleground for participation. The dispersal of power and balance of forces can produce much confusion; but it guards against the abuses of power that can result from concentration.

THE WASTE

The growing awareness of the wastage of ability among the majority of the population has been one of the decisive changes in post-war Britain. The old notion of a limited 'pool of ability', from which clever boys could be fished out, has given way to all kinds of doubts about the size of the pool, and the meaning of ability. The fact that a few clever boys from poor homes *could* reach the top through scholarships itself threw doubts about the pool: 'It was precisely the introduction of these scholarships which pointed to the pool of potential talent among the working classes and the amount of wastage in the education system.'[1]

Army tests of new recruits, published in the Crowther Report of 1959, showed that over half the ablest children left school as soon as possible after 15; most of them were sons of skilled and unskilled manual workers, with many brothers and sisters. J. W. B. Douglas, in his comprehensive study of every child born in a week in March 1946,[2] showed that fifty-four per cent of the upper middle-class children got places in grammar schools compared with eleven per cent of the working-class ones: they had an advantage over working-class children of *equal intelligence* in the scramble for places and only the top two per cent of the ability range could be sure of getting into grammar schools. Survey after survey, both in Britain and abroad, showed how poor housing could affect a child's progress at school.

The country's children were sorted into carthorses, riding horses and thoroughbred racers. The 1944 Education Act provided for secondary modern schools, grammar schools and technical schools, which were meant to form the 'tripartite' system. As there were only very few technical schools, it was in practice a bipartite system, in which 'the submerged three-quarters' (as the teachers called them) went to jumped-up elementary schools. The 'clever' boys went to grammar schools on what was till recently the standard European pattern: in France and Italy they went to *lycées* and in Germany and Sweden to *gymnasien*. All three kinds of schools in Britain were meant to have 'parity of esteem', which was a flagrant though consoling hypocrisy in a society which pays such respect to academic values.

Many of the three-quarters were sulkily conscious of their failure: Lady Plowden's Report of 1968 showed that many children have lower levels of attainment at age fourteen than they had at eight. Some children stay in their own worlds of feeling, more real to them than the teachers' world of abstract 'cognitive' development. Basil Bernstein, professor at the Institute of Education, has explored the different language 'codes' of children; the middle-class child at home learns the 'elaborated' code which is used in schools; the working-class child learns the 'restricted' code of his particular small community, with allusive pronouns which

---

[1] Julia Evatts: 'Equality of educational opportunity', *British Journal of Sociology*, December 1970.

[2] *The Home and the School*, J. W. B. Douglas, 1964.

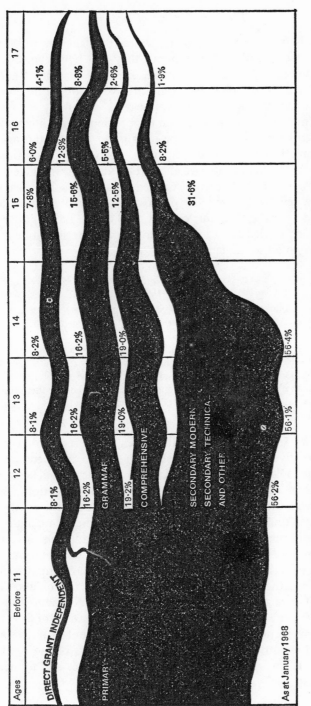

THE STREAMS OF SCHOOLS: Proportions of each age-group in 1968 at different types of school.

everyone is meant to understand. Unless the teachers recognise and accept the world of their pupils they will never be able to educate them. A change of attitude, said the Newsom Report, 'cannot be achieved solely by administrative action. It involves a change of thinking and a change of heart'.

In the meantime, as the chart on the previous page shows, children are still sorted, streamed or channelled around the age of eleven; and just about half—though a dwindling proportion—leave school as soon as they are allowed to, at the age of fifteen. In his 1959 report, Lord Crowther wanted to raise the school-leaving age to sixteen by 1966–9; the proposal was accepted, and then postponed after the economic crisis of 1968 by the Labour government (which caused Lord Longford to resign from the cabinet); it is now proposed to implement it in 1972–3.

PUBLIC SCHOOLS

The public schools are not divisive simply because they are exclusive. An exclusive institution becomes divisive when it arbitrarily confers upon its members advantages and powers over the rest of society. The public schools confer such advantages on an arbitrarily selected membership, which already starts with an advantageous position in life. There is no sign that these divisions will disappear if the schools are left alone. It is time we helped them to change a situation which was not of their own making.

Newsom Report 1968, para. 102.

In a very separate stream of their own, often segregated from the age of five or six, are the children at the independent or 'public' schools which for the past two decades have been the cause of more controversy than any other British institution. Their influence on the present British power structure, as we will see elsewhere in this book, is not quite what it was: the prime minister, the heads of the civil service and the Treasury and the Governor of the Bank of England are now all grammar-school men. But the products of a handful of public schools still crop up through government, the city and the professions; and the balance has not greatly changed since 1967, when the Newsom Report showed (see the chart opposite) that seventy per cent of directors of big firms went to public school, eighty per cent of judges and QCs, and seventy-seven per cent of the directors of the Bank of England. Whatever the future, the public schools still influence the present.

THE PROPORTIONS OF INDEPENDENT AND DIRECT GRANT SCHOOL PUPILS AT VARIOUS STAGES OF EDUCATION COMPARED WITH THE PROPORTIONS FROM THOSE SCHOOLS IN A SELECTION OF PROFESSIONS AND POSITIONS

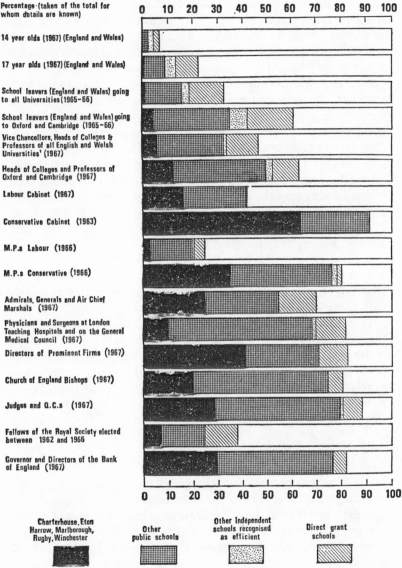

Percentage·(taken of the total for whom details are known)

14 year olds (1967) (England and Wales)

17 year olds (1967) (England and Wales)

School leavers (England and Wales) going to all Universities (1965–66)

School leavers (England and Wales) going to Oxford and Cambridge (1965–66)

Vice Chancellors, Heads of Colleges & Professors of all English and Welsh Universities[1] (1967)

Heads of Colleges and Professors of Oxford and Cambridge (1967)

Labour Cabinet (1967)

Conservative Cabinet (1963)

M.P.s Labour (1966)

M.P.s Conservative (1966)

Admirals, Generals and Air Chief Marshals (1967)

Physicians and Surgeons at London Teaching Hospitals and on the General Medical Council (1967)

Directors of Prominent Firms (1967)

Church of England Bishops (1967)

Judges and Q.C.s (1967)

Fellows of the Royal Society elected between 1962 and 1966

Governor and Directors of the Bank of England (1967)

Charterhouse, Eton Harrow, Marlborough, Rugby, Winchester

Other public schools

Other independent schools recognised as efficient

Direct grant schools

Notes

1. In this and the following professions or positions former pupils of Scottish schools are included. Pupils at Scottish schools have not, however, been included in the totals of those at present receiving education because the categories of school in Scotland do not come within the same definitions as those in England and Wales. Inclusion of Scottish figures would not in any case significantly alter the diagram.

Most public schools were founded in Victorian times, partly to provide recruits for the empire and the army: the Imperial Service College, now merged with Haileybury, fed its old boys to the East India Company. The Victorians used the public schools to remove the sons of tradesmen from the taint of trade: and it is still often true, as G. K. Chesterton put it, that 'the public schools are not for the sons of gentlemen, they're for the fathers of gentlemen'. Most of the boarding schools were set up in the railway age, far from the main centres of population, so that the boys spend eight months a year for five years in the exclusive company of other boys: sometimes this weaning starts at preparatory (prep) schools at the age of seven. The introverted society thus created provided an experience from which many public-school boys never recovered, and the boarding system has been blamed for most of their subsequent failings—their veneration for authority, their obsession with tradition, their frustrated sex-lives. It was by uprooting boys from their parents and forging them into a tough society that imperial leaders were created; a boy could pass from Eton to the Guards to Oxford to the Middle Temple and still remain in the same male world of leather armchairs, teak tables, and nicknames. They never needed to deal closely with other kinds of people, and some still do not.

It is changing. Nowadays mothers are reluctant to part with their children so early, and the numbers of boarding prep schools —the first stage in the separation—has decreased; though more prep schools now take day pupils and the actual numbers of pupils has soared over the last decade—as shown by these figures from the Independent Association of Preparatory Schools:

	1960	*1970*
Schools	506	472
Pupils	55,513	62,354

All age groups, particularly girls, are moving away from boarding education: in the three years from 1965 the number of boarders in Headmasters' Conference schools dropped by three per cent. Some schools like Sebright, have closed down, others have extended their places to day boys or lowered their standards for entries.

The public schools are nowadays less obviously different from the top grammar schools in their ethos and value-system; they are less obsessed by team-spirit and character-building, and more concerned with examinations and universities. But they still give their pupils a very special sense of their mission and confidence. As the Newsom Report put it:

> These schools believe in inculcating certain virtues—service to the community, leadership, initiative and self-reliance. There is nothing exceptional in this. All schools try to develop virtues in their pupils. But what is distinctive about the public schools is their claim that these virtues can be inculcated especially effectively through boarding and by protecting their pupils against malign influences in the outside world (including sometimes those in their families).

A small number of public schools have had a quite disproportionate influence. Below are the nine schools which were singled out by the Clarendon Commission of 1861–4 (itself an interesting example of Victorian state intervention), as 'significant of the position that a few schools had gained in the public eye'. Since then a few old schools have risen in prestige and a few new ones, like Stowe (1923) and Gordonstoun (1934) have become prominent. But the 'Clarendon Schools', a hundred years later, remain among the most important, and in public schools there is still no substitute for antiquity and tradition. These were they in September 1970:

	Fees £	No. of boys	Headmaster	Date of foundation
Charterhouse	750	650	A. O. Van Oss	1611
Eton	765	1,195	M. W. McCrum	1440
Harrow	759	700	R. L. James	1571
Merchant Taylors'	550	660	B. Rees	1561
Rugby	675	710	J. S. Woodhouse	1567
St. Paul's	567	780	T. E. B. Howarth	1509
Shrewsbury	675	580	A. R. D. Wright	1552
Westminster	780	461	J. M. Rae	1560
Winchester	762	530	J. L. Thorn	1382

ETON AND WINCHESTER

In spite of everything that has happened in the last six hundred years, the two oldest medieval foundations, Eton and Winchester, still retain a greater influence on the British power-structure than any other single school.[1] These two elites have in many ways opposite characters; but what the schools have in common is

---

[1] They are not *the* oldest: King's School, Canterbury, was founded in 600, followed by King's School, Rochester in 604.

antiquity, wealth, and a capacity to generate exceptional confidence and ambition in their boys.

Eton, ever since its foundation by King Henry VI in 1440, has had a special closeness to the crown, which has added to its authority. The provost—a kind of resident chairman of the governors—is appointed by the crown (the current provost is Lord Caccia, former head of the Foreign Office) and other governors are elected by Oxford, Cambridge, the Royal Society and the Lord Chief Justice. They elect the headmaster who, with the establishment thus looking over his shoulder, is in an uneasy position. The headmastership of Eton is still regarded as some kind of peak of the teaching profession; but more than any other headship it combines the duties of bishop, diplomat, and company chairman. It is not an easy job to fill, and headmasters soon come under fire from influential parents; Robert Birley, the outstanding headmaster who retired in 1963, to become an anti-apartheid professor in South Africa, was known as 'Red Robert'. He was succeeded by Anthony Chenevix-Trench, a classicist and strict disciplinarian, who left six years later. Trench was replaced by Michael McCrum, from Tonbridge School, a devout Christian, the son and brother of naval captains and son-in-law of a headmaster (Sir Arthur fforde of Rugby); but a more easy-going man than Chenevix-Trench. McCrum has carefully played down his role: 'I think headmasters tended to be thought of as witches, armed with a broom,' he said on his appointment. 'I see my role more as that of a learner-driver.' 'I think that the function of a headmaster,' he said later, 'is to inject a little order and rationality into confused lives.'

The influence of Eton does not rest primarily on its intellectual achievement, which is relatively low (see below). The scholars are kept in a separate hot-house (as at Winchester and Westminster), and have included such varied brains as George Orwell, Cyril Connolly, Harold Macmillan, Lord Hailsham and Lord Keynes. But Eton scholars are still apt to be looked down on by the others, the 'oppidans': of the eighteen British prime ministers who went to Eton, only two (Walpole and Macmillan) were scholars. The main attribute of Eton has been its political influence and its wealth; about a third of its income still comes from its endowments, which include valuable urban land; and on the rents and investments, much augmented by the very high fees (£765 a year in 1970), it can afford more and better teachers, more accommodation (a room for each boy) and more personal attention than other schools. Etonians like to refer to their school as the first of the comprehensives, which is true in that it includes all kinds of boys—stupid, clever, lazy, ambitious, creative or dull. But their parents are nearly all rich.

It is not easy to disentangle the influence of the school from the influence of parents; two thirds of Etonians are sons of old Etonians, which makes it more than any other school a hereditary club for the rich and influential. Political parents and the school's own traditions combine to give Eton a great awareness of politics; the twenty members of the school's club 'Pop' are a kind of teenage cabinet, the youngest of many self-perpetuating oligarchies which crop up in this book, whose past members include Sir Alec Douglas-Home, Lord Hailsham, John Grigg and Peter Fleming. In the outside world, the political influence of Eton is not what it was in the age of Macmillan, who boasted six old Etonians in his cabinet: Harold Wilson could make do without any in his cabinet (after the resignation of Lord Longford) and Edward Heath has only three. Old Etonians nowadays like to speak of themselves as a persecuted minority, whose school is an obstacle to their career. But 22 per cent of the members of the government are old Etonians, and there are still 65 in parliament, far more than any other school, including two Labour MPs, Reginald Paget and Tam Dalyell. Many Labour parents, including Canon Collins, Lord Snow, Sir Frederick Ayer and Professor John Vaizey, insist on sending their children to Eton.

Winchester produces a much more rigorous schooling, preoccupied not with politics or all-round confidence, but with intellectual performance. Its products are more homogeneous and branded, less charming than Eton's; and Wykehamists (as they are called from their founder, William of Wykeham) tend with remarkable uniformity to be tense, ambitious, intellectually highly developed and emotionally under-developed. In their owlishness and their capacity to reduce everything to 'sound judgement', they have something in common with the products of the top French *lycées* or the *Polytechnique*, and they have a similar success in the fields of power, finance and academia; prominent Old Wykehamists include Sir David Barran, the chairman of Shell; Sir Michael Carver, Chief of the General Staff; Lord Wilberforce, the Law Lord; John Sparrow, the Warden of

All Souls, Oxford; Sir William Hayter, the Warden of New College (Winchester's sister-foundation); Lord Sherfield, the ex-ambassador to Washington; Cecil King, the ex-chairman of the *Daily Mirror*; Jeremy Morse, the youngest and cleverest of the Directors of the Bank of England. In politics Wykehamists are less prominent than Etonians, with thirteen members of parliament, and the Wykehamists among Heath's senior ministers are both very untypical—William Whitelaw and Lord Eccles. But Winchester has played a large role in the Labour Party: Hugh Gaitskell and Richard Crossman, who were rivals at school, became rivals in re-thinking party policy in the late fifties; Crossman and Douglas Jay (the former cabinet minister) and his son Peter (economics correspondent of *The Times*) are all now intransigent opponents of the common market. Winchester represents in an extreme form the old puritan ethic of the intellectual public schools—defying the emotional turmoils and distractions of adolescence by a regime of intellectual discipline and monastic enclosure. In an age of certainty and imperial service the Winchester training appeared part of the splendour of the British way of life—stiff upper-lip, incorrupt-ible, and forbiddingly clever; but in an age concerned with self-discovery, both national and individual, the austere Wykehamist seems like a Roundhead after the Restoration.

PUBLIC SCHOOL REFORM

We have learnt to become marvellous pachyderms these days, almost rivalling in our insensitivity to criticism the rhinoceroses of the intellectual left.

Tom Howarth (Headmaster of St. Paul's), 1969.

Under the Labour government the independent schools, with their revered traditions, were large stumbling blocks on the path to egalitarianism. In 1965 Anthony Crosland, then Minister of Education, asked Sir John Newsom to head a commission to find ways to integrate into the state system the independent boarding schools which (as Newsom put it) 'have so much to give and so much to learn'. Newsom recommended that local authorities should assist half the total pupils at the public schools; but most authorities felt they had more pressing uses for their limited money. The state in fact already assists some 40,000 children at independent schools—about ten per cent of the total, including sons of soldiers, sailors, airmen or diplomats (who get £500 a year to educate each child while they are abroad). The Newsom Commission wanted the assisted boys to be selected on the grounds of their 'need' for boarding education—not for their social acceptability or academic ability; but most headmasters wanted to select their kind of boy who couldn't pay their kind of fees. 'That's one-way traffic, not integration,' said Royston Lambert (now Headmaster of Dartington Hall) who did the commission's research, which showed what everyone knew anyway—that the ethos of the public school reflects and is intimately connected with the middle class.

Much of the public-school's capacity or willingness to change depends on the headmasters, who enjoy a personal power only equalled perhaps by surgeons and judges. They are awesome and formidable men whom few ex-public-school boys can recollect in tranquillity: the film *If* gives one indication of the traumatic memories they conjure up. They can still maintain exact if sometimes irrelevant standards: they are figures of massive integrity and moral uprightness, and a divorced headmaster is almost unimaginable (in 1971 one public-school headmaster *did* get divorced, and had to leave). Most of the major headmasters are still firmly Anglican: Fisher of Wellington is the son of the former archbishop, Woodhouse of Rugby the son of a bishop. But a few headmasters have even abandoned the whole idea that boys' characters need to be *moulded*: Royston Lambert at Dartington hopes to become 'the first non-head of the first anti-school in the country—the first of many': the Dartington faith is 'the development of personality through the greatest freedom of choice'.

The Headmasters' Conference, the club of two hundred heads which was founded a hundred years ago under the aegis of the great Thring of Uppingham, still conveys some of the old confidence; their magazine *Conference*, set up in 1963 to combat the damaging impressions given in *Anatomy of Britain* and elsewhere, conjures up that mixture of authority and uncertainty that makes the modern headmaster: on the one hand advertisements for gowns, for Gabbitas and Thring, for commissions in the army, attacks on the Donnison Report; and on the other hand articles about fund-raising and escalating fees, and hints on how to plan a prospectus or cut catering costs. Since 1964 the HMC has employed a public relations firm to improve the headmasters' image: 'There are slow and subtle changes in the public schools,' said the secretary of the HMC, 'from being rather inward-looking and exclusive, they now want to identify themselves with other happenings in the education world.'

The public schools have certainly, in the last decade, become much less isolated. Some are even going co-educational: King's School, Ely, and Marlborough both allow girls into the sixth form. Most schools have abolished fagging and flogging of younger boys by older ones. The most assured schools are not now fussy over long hair, wild clothes or voices—many public schoolboys now deliberately react against the 'public-school accent' which used to be one of their chief weapons in the outside world. 'I don't think this striving for a classless appearance is anything but good,' said Oliver Van Oss of Charterhouse at the 1969 Headmasters' Conference at York, 'except for the lack of confidence it betrays and which I hope it will survive.' 'I am prepared to give the boys more liberties,' said McCrum of Eton, 'provided they do not take them.' The public schools have become less philistine and less classical. Art is no longer regarded as pansy, and schools like Merchant Taylors', Sevenoaks and Highgate have set up expensive art centres. Many public schools have greatly expanded their science sides—helped by special investment funds from big companies. Business has become respectable, and some boys play the chartered accountants' business game with computers, against other schools.

These innovations are paying off in worldly terms, and the public schools have adjusted themselves to the end of the empire. A survey in 1968 by the Public Schools Appointment Bureau showed these top ten careers chosen by the boys in that year[1] (18·2 per cent were 'undecided', many of whom went on to higher education):

		per cent
1.	Engineering	10·5
2.	Science	7·3
3.	Commerce or industry (admin. or sales)	7·0
4.	Medicine, Dentistry or Veterinary Science	5·3
5.	Law	5·3
6.	Chartered Accountancy	3·6
7.	Agriculture, Forestry or Horticulture	2·9
8.	Teaching	2·4
9.	Banking	2·3
10.	Services	2·1

[1] Public Schools Appointments Bureau: *News Bulletin*, February 1969.

Many British institutions still have great admiration for the public-school values: the BBC, in its evidence to the Newsom Commission, was lyrical: 'It would seem safe to say that that part of the public-school education which instils a sense of self-discipline, a sense of being part of a community and having to come to terms with it and a sense of public service, has found and produced strong echoes in an organisation which is itself geared to public service and to reflecting and serving the community within which it exists.' But the future is much less assured: 'The public-school boys' favoured position has long since been whittling away,' the Cambridge Appointments Board said in its evidence to Newsom, 'because of the larger number of graduates from other schools. Nebulous changes in the climate of opinion have occurred ... and there is the feeling that since the national power has declined under public-school leadership, it was because the leaders were from public schools that they failed.'

Whether the public schools will be able to maintain their confident position in the power-structure of the nineteen-eighties must be very doubtful. As the universities become more important as the testing-ground, so the public schools become more vulnerable; in 1967–8 they still accounted for thirty-eight per cent of the entrants to Oxbridge, but for only sixteen per cent of all university entrants. As the big grammar schools step up the pressure, so public schools find it harder to beat them in the quality of their teaching, which pushes the fees higher and higher. All but the top public schools have found it harder to fill their places, and many have had to lower their standards. Some have had to admit girls— or still more dangerous—American boys, who are sent over to British schools because they are often better and cheaper than schools on the Eastern seaboard; but the boys may bring with them what headmasters most dread—pot. For pot, spreading through the closed society of a school, can undermine the whole hard-working, self-denying ethos of the public-school tradition.

GRAMMAR SCHOOLS

We are agreed that the conventional grammar school, selecting about twenty per cent of children at about the age of eleven, will not provide what the country or its most gifted children need.
Donnison Report (para. 27), 1970.

In the last twenty years the public schools and the most

successful grammar schools have—as competitors so often do—
become increasingly alike; and the increasing movement towards
comprehensive schools, which threatens both of them, has forced
them into a friendly alliance. The public schools have become
more concerned with intellectual training, less with character-
building; the big grammar schools—or some of them—have
become more broad-minded in their view of education; and both
kinds of school have become more preoccupied with getting their
pupils to university, and particularly to Oxbridge. Since the end
of the first world war, the trickle of grammar-school boys to
Oxbridge has turned into a flood: most of them, without strong
family connections or wealth, have known that their career
depends on a university place, and both in intelligence and
ambition they compete strongly with the public-school boys. In
1967–8, forty-eight per cent of the direct-grant grammar-school
boys went on to university, and twenty-six per cent of the maintained grammar-school boys, compared to thirty per cent of boys
from independent schools 'recognised as efficient'.[1] Once at
university, the confidence gap between the public-school and
grammar-school boys has visibly diminished, and clothes and
accent no longer distinguish the public-school undergraduate:
in later life men like Roy Jenkins, Denis Healey or Anthony
Barber show no signs of lack of confidence behind their
ambition.

Most of the oldest, largest and most famous grammar schools
are not state schools at all, but semi-independent ones. These are
the 178 'direct-grant' grammar schools, financed partly by fees
and funds, partly by the Department of Education (the direct
grant). They earn the grant by taking not less than a quarter and
now as many as sixty per cent of their pupils from the state system:
the rest are fee-paying. They must have local government people
on their boards of governors, but the local authorities cannot really
interfere as they do with ordinary grammar schools. Some
direct-grant schools are just small denominational schools (nearly
a third are Roman Catholic) but the most successful are big and
fairly secular: Bradford, Bristol, Manchester, Birkenhead;
Haberdashers' Aske's and Latymer Upper, in London; the Royal
Grammar School, Newcastle; King Edward's, Birmingham. They
rival the top public schools with their traditions, huge sixth forms,
and entries into university. In comparison with the 1,098 other

[1] Donnison Report, 1970, table 12, p. 69.

grammar schools, 'maintained' (and often interfered with) by the local authorities, they are privileged schools. In 1968 thirty-one per cent of boys and girls from direct-grant grammar schools went to university compared with 19.6 per cent from maintained ones. Their reputations help them to go on attracting the best teachers; they benefit too from the big city 'catchment areas' as their recruiting territory is gruesomely called. The competition for entry in some cities is as much as ten for each place.

The direct-grant schools are, as the Donnison Report of 1970 (para 115) said: 'Predominantly middle-class institutions ... Three out of four pupils come from the homes of white-collar workers: three out of five have fathers in professional or managerial occupations. Only one out of thirteen comes from a semi-skilled or unskilled worker's family.' Many of the 178 schools are in the north: there are forty-six in Lancashire alone, nineteen in Yorkshire, seven in Bristol, and only twenty in Greater London. In some ways the direct-grant schools are the northern equivalent of the public schools, which recruit their boys predominantly from the south-east. The fact that many of the parents pay fees is thought by many to preserve the school's independence and to encourage the interest of parents: 'Here in Yorkshire they only pay for what they value,' one headmaster told the Donnison Commission (para 166): 'And after demonstrating their interest not only in words but cash, they watch their investments carefully.'

In this situation the direct-grant schools and the public schools have become more alike. The major public schools, even Eton, have stiffened their entrance requirements to throw out the stupider boys, in their efforts to retain their supremacy. The direct-grant schools have increased both their numbers of pupils and their success at universities. Public-school headmasters rally to the defence of the direct-grant schools: 'Here is a system,' wrote Tom Howarth in *Conference* in February 1970, 'where private enterprise and public provision have worked and do work happily together. To throw away a national birthright like this for a mess of doctorial pottage would be so incredible that one can hardly imagine that it is likely to be proposed in tones of ringing conviction and rational plausibility.'

The actual definition of a public school is increasingly difficult: usually a 'public' school is taken to mean any independently financed one; but, strictly speaking, it is a school whose headmaster belongs to the group of about two hundred members of the

Headmasters' Conference which included (in 1967) fifty-nine direct-grant grammar schools, and twelve ordinary grammar schools. The HMC used to select members by success in the Oxbridge entrance competition; but since 1964 they have realised that some of the best students may go to other universities or even to polytechnics, so they now select according to the number of A levels: schools that are not up to scratch may (in theory) be rejected when a new headmaster is appointed (rather as French restaurants in the *Guide Michelin* may lose their star when the chef changes).

The public and grammar schools still jostle each other in the traditional league-table of academic success—the numbers of awards to Oxbridge. The publication of this list is itself much criticised, as encouraging a rat-race, and the comparisons are not always straightforward, since some schools have their own closed awards. But opposite, for what it is worth, are the schools which won most awards (including closed awards) during the four years 1967–70 in proportion to their numbers, with the average size of their sixth form, and the proportion of annual awards to the sixth form:[1]

A broader indication of the schools' success comes from the total numbers of boys going to all universities, with or without awards. These were the schools sending the largest proportions of boys to full-time university courses in 1968 (according to the Public Schools' Appointments Board Survey):

		per cent
1.	Winchester	87·2
2.	Manchester Grammar	77·0
3.	Glasgow Academy	76·6
4.	George Watson's College, Edinburgh	68·9
5.	Haileybury	68·2
6.	Edinburgh Academy	66·6
7.	Marlborough ⎫ Rugby ⎭	66·4
9.	Royal Grammar, Newcastle	66·0
10.	Fettes	65·9

The top grammar schools do not yet have the same close association with the world of power as the big public schools; most of their boys go unobtrusively into the professions, industry or engineering; but a few direct-grant schools have acquired a

[1] Collated from *The Times Educational Supplement*, 1967–70.

League Table of Success

School	Average sixth form	Total awards 1967–70	Percentage of sixth formers taking awards
Newcastle Royal Grammar	227	65	7·1
Dulwich	436	115	6·6
St. Paul's	359	95	6·6
Westminster	317	79	6·2
Winchester	366	88	6·0
Nottingham High	218	52	5·9
Christ's Hospital	272	61	5·6
Magdalen College School, Oxford	147	32	5·4
King Edward's, Birmingham	251	50	5·0
King's, Canterbury	357	70	4·9
Merchant Taylors', Northwood	278	55	4·9
King's College, Wimbledon	285	55	4·8
Manchester Grammar	537	101	4·7
St. Albans	193	36	4·7
Bradford Grammar	338	59	4·5
The Perse	122	21	4·3
City of London	252	42	4·2
Downside	285	47	4·1
Haberdashers' Aske's	283	47	4·1
Latymer Upper	311	49	4·0
Harrow	353	55	3·9
Clifton	352	47	3·8
Eltham College	143	22	3·8
University College, Hampstead	211	32	3·8
Highgate	237	35	3·7
Tiffin	241	36	3·7
Sherborne	305	44	3·6
Tonbridge	279	39	3·5
Rugby	415	56	3·4
Wyggeston	226	31	3·4
Eton	539	71	3·3
Sedbergh	199	25	3·1

special reputation. The most famous of them is Manchester Grammar School (MGS), with 1,400 boys in a low, brick building outside the city, which has become a legendary stronghold of the 'meritocracy'. For sixteen years the High Master of MGS was Eric James, now Lord James, Vice-Chancellor of York, who regarded the school as the 'spearhead of social mobility'. He was succeeded by Peter Mason, himself from King Edward's School, Birmingham, who has taken over the role of champion of the grammar-school elite: attacking the Donnison Report in *The*

Times in March 1970 he explained how the Labour Party's policy 'will at the end of the day break down the bridge between the private and maintained sectors and separate them more sharply than before. Is this for some people a consummation only less devoutly to be wished than the abolition of freedom to buy education at all, or is it just one more proof that nothing but a nonsense can result from so prejudiced an enquiry?' A large proportion of Old Mancunians are scientists, many go into business, and many into the civil service; there are one permanent secretary, Sir Geoffrey Wilson, and three MPs—Harold Lever, Frank Allaun and Tom Normanton. Their most famous products are the ruling families of Marks and Spencer; the first Lord Marks was there at the same time as his future brother-in-law, now Lord Sieff; and other Sieffs have followed; Marks and Spencer have given a large donation to the current MGS appeal to raise £500,000 for new buildings.

A rival to MGS in the league tables is Latymer Upper, the Hammersmith school which straddles the Great West Road; the school was founded in 1895 (based on a seventeenth-century foundation) and in the last decades has built up strong university connections, particularly with Cambridge; between 1967 and 1969 they sent fifty-nine boys to Cambridge, twenty-eight to London, eleven to Oxford: at the entrance to the school is a high gloomy hall adorned with the gold-painted names of Oxbridge scholars. Latymer is locked in combat with the Hammersmith public school, St. Paul's, run by the high priest of independent schools, Tom Howarth, and the two schools, competing for the same Oxbridge prizes, become more alike. Latymer has six members in the present parliament, more than any other grammar school: five of them are Tory, including Peter Walker, the Minister of the Environment, and Roger Moate, the right-wing insurance broker.

The grammar schoolboys are making deeper marks on the British power-structure. It is sometimes claimed that the direct-grant schools are forcing grounds whose products soon fizzle out, at university or later; but there is no evidence for this. The Donnison Report showed that they get more firsts and seconds than the average; and one teacher at Manchester Grammar School, Dr. Copley, showed that of the boys who graduated at Oxford in 1964, fifteen per cent got firsts. The grammar schools appear to be less prone to drop-outs, pot-smokers and general *ennui* than the public schools; without boarders, they have a less highly-charged atmosphere; and with fewer boys from rich homes, there is a more straightforward ambition for success. The idea of *noblesse oblige*, which the public schools have liked to think of as their special ethos, has been taken over by the major grammar schools; but the ideals of self-help and self-improvement rank higher in practice; and in the Tory cabinet Heath, Barber, Walker and Thatcher are appropriate symbols of this ambition. In the Labour Party there are fewer public-school men and many more grammar school men among the younger generation of MPs: one school (Quarry Bank, Liverpool) has produced two prominent ex-ministers, Bill Rodgers and Peter Shore, (one ardently for, one against, the common market) and a trades unionist, David Basnett.

All the grammar schools are blocks on the road to comprehensives; but the direct-grant schools, with their fee-paying pupils, are doubly in the way. Like the public schools, they give an advantage to better-off children, and, like the other grammar schools, they are based on early selection. In 1970 the Public Schools Commission—with Professor Donnison taking over from John Newsom—published its second report for the Labour government, this time concentrating on direct-grant schools. The commission concluded, sadly but firmly, that (para 259): 'Grammar schools of the traditional kind cannot be combined with a comprehensive system of education: we must choose what we want. Fee-paying is not compatible with comprehensive education.' They recommended that schools receiving grants must work out schemes with their local authorities to participate in comprehensive reorganisation, while admitting that the process would be a slow one: and that if they would not, they were free to become independent schools, with their direct-grant gradually withdrawn—an option that several big schools quickly decided to take, if they had to. But the report was never accepted by government, and soon afterwards the Conservatives came to power, so the whole problem of the grammar schools was shelved, and the big direct-grant schools remained intact, the second obstacle on the way to a democratic system of education.

COMPREHENSIVES

For six years up to 1970 the expansion of comprehensive schools and the gradual weakening of the grammar schools was widely associated with Labour Party policy, at odds with Conservative opinion. But in fact the movement began long before Labour came into power, and continued afterwards: it was part of a tendency shared by other parts of Europe, away from the ruthless sorting-out of pupils at the age of eleven—which was first emphatically rejected in Britain by the Crowther Report of 1959. The pressure for 'comprehensivisation' often came more from the local authorities, themselves responding to the pressure from parents, than from the Department of Education; and the Labour government was very cautious—many people believe excessively cautious—in not laying down instructions or legislation for comprehensive schools. The famous circular 10/65, issued by Anthony Crosland as Minister for Education, only *requested* local authorities to submit plans for comprehensive reorganisation, and did not try to enforce them. The circular the following year, 10/66, tried to bring pressure by refusing to allocate building grants to schools which were not reorganising; but some authorities did not need new buildings, and others could obtain money without reorganising. The Labour government, by discreet pressure, tried to avoid an open clash between the 'partners' of the educational system; and a great deal of the initiative, and of the resistance, came from the local councils who produced amazingly different systems throughout the country.

The local pressure against the 'eleven-plus' has become much fiercer, and in the last decade the number of comprehensives of some kind in England and Wales has multiplied ninefold; these figures show the growth since 1950:[1]

Year	*1950*	*1955*	*1960*	*1965*	*1968*	*1971* (est.)
Schools	10	16	130	262	745	1,275
Percentage of total secondary-school population in comprehensive schools	13	16	4·7	8·5	20·9	35

But the word 'comprehensive' can have many different meanings, and Caroline Benn in 1970 estimated that only twelve per cent of the schools were 'operating in anything like "fully comprehensive" circumstances'.[2] The others are unhappily co-existing

[1] From Benn and Simon: *Half Way There*, 1968.
[2] Caroline Benn: *1971 Survey of Comprehensive Reorganisation.*

with the grammar schools which separate many of the cleverest; and in large towns only a fraction of the cleverest pupils are in comprehensive schools. The co-existence, and the awkward mergers, have produced a great range of different kinds of re-organisation bewildering to the lay parent, and often to the teacher: impending reorganisation is often an excuse for inaction. There are all-through comprehensives 11–18; tiered schools where all children transfer from the lower to the upper tier; 'parallel' tiered schools where only some pupils choose or are *selected* to transfer; 11–16 schools, co-existing with 11–18 schools co-existing with grammar schools. And then there are middle schools of 9–13 and 8–12 which straddle the old transfer age of 11. Some lead to comprehensive upper tier schools, but others to a divided system of 'long course' and 'short course' upper schools.[1] The ways in which schools may recruit their pupils are almost equally confusing: there are geographical catchment areas, zoned catchment areas, feeder schools, balanced ability (a distributive selection), and choice; there are basically two types of choice —'free' and 'guided'.

It is impossible to generalise about comprehensives because of the variety of schemes and attitudes of the local authorities, and the influences of parents and communities. Many of the schools are still too young to have acquired distinct characters. But strong headmasters or headmistresses, and dedicated teachers, have already stamped some of them with their personalities and theories. Dame Mary Green, headmistress of Kidbrooke since 1954, built up one of the first of the specially designed comprehensives—a spectacular place at Blackheath, with two thousand girls all in grey skirts. David Lister school in Hull is run by one of the great apostles of 'unstreaming', Albert Rowe. Banbury school is run by Harry Judge, who sat on the Public Schools Commission. Cyril Posner first set up Lawrence Weston school, near Bristol, as a pioneer community school (with the public library inside it), and has now started a new community school in Stepney. Holland Park Comprehensive, on a superb site on the top of Campden Hill in London, is sometimes (absurdly) called the 'Socialist Eton': Caroline Benn, whose husband was Minister of Technology, is chairman of the governors, and their four children went to school there. It has a large sixth form, swelled by

[1] For a thorough rundown of the present state of play in comprehensives, see *Half Way There*; Caroline Benn and Brian Simon, McGraw-Hill 1970.

refugees from the public schools; but it is far from being a middle-class school, and it includes thirty-five nationalities, with many West Indians and several skinheads from the Notting Hill slums.

Because of the huge numbers in the big comprehensives, often more than 1,500, there is much argument about the division of the pupils, which can affect the whole character of the school. Highbury Grove Comprehensive, under its controversial head-master, Rhodes Boyson (one of the Black Paper writers) has established house rooms, to provide a kind of home for each boy, like a public school. But Margaret Miles at Mayfield believes that the house system encourages an immature competitive spirit, and instead (like many other comprehensives) divides pupils by years with a special 'year mistress' who remains with her pupils as they go up the school.

Some counties are much more experimental in their conception of comprehensives than others. The most famous is Leicestershire, which for much of this century has been known for its educational innovations: their present Chief Education Officer, Stewart Mason, only the second since 1903, was the architect of the Leicestershire two-tier plan for secondary education. The most daring school in the county is the brand-new Countesthorpe, just outside Leicester city, which deserves brief inspection as the most avant-garde of them all: it has already become the prototype for others, including one in London. At present it is a junior high school, for 11–14, but eventually it will become a proper (though quite untypical) comprehensive. Countesthorpe College rises from a sea of mud in the midst of a middle-class housing estate, and two miles from a working-class estate: the two form the main catch-ment area. Local adults can use the school's facilities, and their community association is part of the buildings. The school is built in the shape of a big circle, of one storey only; the grey brick and stained woods, the curved walls, and the skylights dispersing soft light give a background of peaceful relaxation, and the windows look out on to greenhouses and fishponds. The school is made up not of rooms but of spaces and recesses—essential for the 'project work' on which the teaching is based. There are dramatic gyms, a huge art space, a black cube-shaped theatre workshop, and a stage. The lessons are equally unconventional: the courses have elaborate titles like 'Creative Expression in Two and Three Dimensions' or 'The Individual and the Group', reflecting the inter-disciplinary

approach as in new universities. The children are only streamed
for learning languages; the rest of the learning is through project
work. There are special sessions for 'non-involved' children who go
into a remedial group to work on motorbikes to satisfy their
aggression. The children are encouraged to express themselves by
using tape recorders: 'The spoken word is more important for most
than the written word.'

There is no headmaster at Countesthorpe, only a 'warden'
called Tim: he has no proper office, but moves around, in a
springy and speculative walk, from recess to recess. Tim McMullen
is a genuine 'anti-head': he is a slim, complex man, whose own
shape and style seem experimental. He came from a public
school, and hates the public-school system. He is a temperamental innovator whose history is part of the history of the
growth of comprehensive education in this country. He was
deputy head of Forest Hill, a London comprehensive, and then
head of the Thomas Bennett School in Crawley; then went to the
Coventry college of education, and then to the Nuffield project
on Resources for Learning: he had just finished a year's working
for OECD in Paris before he came to Countesthorpe. Experiments
can't do worse than the existing schools, he maintains. As warden
he wants each of the forty-five teachers to decide what and how
they teach: though his friends know him as an authoritarian
democrat, the Countesthorpe teachers were all drawn by the
experiment, and they spend hours discussing methods in their
'moots' (meetings). Most parents appear pleased because their
children enjoy school, though some are withholding judgment until
they see the academic results; a small but angry minority resent
their children being guinea-pigs. McMullen admits that his life is
made easier by the existence of independent schools, who take the
children whose parents are most likely to be critical.

Countesthorpe is an extreme case of experiment; most comprehensives are much more conservative, and some are more like
bilateral schools, divided into 'grammar' and 'modern' sides, with
streams of less clever children kept very separate. As more schools
go comprehensive, so the arguments between 'streaming and 'non-
streaming' take the place of the old arguments between grammar
schools and comprehensives. But increasingly comprehensives are
going over to different forms of non-streaming—combinations of
'banding' (wide ability streams); 'setting' (with or without special
remedial groups) and complete 'mixed ability' groups. As the late

Derek Morrell,[1] the first secretary of the Schools Council, put it:

> To understand what is really going on in school we have to come
> to grips with extremely complex, constantly changing, and immensely
> particular systems of personal inter-action, involving complex
> relationships between the experience, language and values which the
> pupils bring into their schools from their neighbourhoods, and those
> which are imparted by the teacher.

TEACHERS

He who can, does. He who cannot, teaches.
He who cannot teach, teaches teachers.
Bernard Shaw (amended).

The more complex and far-reaching the 'comprehensive
revolution', the more important becomes the selection of training
for teaching: 'A commitment to a comprehensive system,' say
Benn and Simon, 'requires a complete reconsideration of the
content and method of teacher training.' There are now for the
first time more teachers in Britain (352,000 of them) than members
of the armed forces; and Britain's survival is likely to depend more
on her schools than on her military strength. But the status of
teachers has always been lower in England than in France or
Germany: there is still a slight hangover from the time when
tutors or ushers were regarded as the underpaid servants of rich
parents, rather than (as in France) the guardians of national
culture and enlightenment. The new national priorities, which
make headmasters obviously more important than admirals, are
not yet so visible in status. The standing of teachers is partly
reflected in their salary scales; the basic scale in 1971 was still only
£930 rising to £1,720 after fourteen years; responsibility scales
are loaded in favour of secondary schools with large sixth forms:
children under thirteen count for one and a half units but a
seventeen-year-old counts for ten. All teacher graduates have an
allowance of £105, and good honours graduates (firsts and
seconds) have an extra £125 a year which can be payable even
after twenty years of incompetent teaching.

The main 'teacher crisis' is still one of shortage; in 1970 it was
estimated that there were 40,000 too few. But the figures are not
compiled by the people who have to deploy the teachers. In 1968

[1] See also Chapter 11.

30·2 per cent of children were still in classes over the prescribed secondary limit of thirty. The independent and direct-grant schools still have many more teachers per pupil: teacher-pupil ratios in 1968 were 21–1 in maintained grammar schools; 16–1 in direct-grant schools, and 13–1 in independent schools. In primary schools if the average number of children in a class were dropped from forty (where it now is) to thirty as the National Union of Teachers wish, an extra 60,000 teachers would be needed. There is a great deal of waste from the colleges and university departments of education: in 1966–7 24,900 women entered training but 21,800 women left in the same year.

Even if the recruits come forward, numbers alone are no answer to the problem; teaching needs to attract the right people, who are not necessarily those with the minimum qualification. A survey[1] of third-year students at colleges of education showed that half of them entered training college reluctantly and many of them would have preferred to be entering the more highly paid and higher status professions of law and medicine; those who had failed to get into university wanted a general, not a vocational education.

Teacher Training Colleges are expanding their capacities fast, but there has been no drastic re-thinking. Some married women have come back to teaching, which serves as a stop gap, but does not help to build up a teaching force balanced in age, sex or career ambition. The golden age of teacher recruitment was in the slump of the thirties, which (as with the civil service) induced a high proportion of first-class minds to go into teaching: teaching then was also the chief way up the social ladder for a bright working-class boy. But when the grammar schools and universities widened their gates, and the competition for graduates from industry became stronger, teacher recruitment passed (in Lord Crowther's phrase) into 'an ice age'. Only a fifth of teachers are university graduates: the rest of them are trained in the 164 colleges of education, often isolated and rather cloistered, run by the local authorities. The Robbins Report recommended integrating the colleges of education with the universities, and the National Union of Teachers still want a 'Comprehensive University', incorporating their training colleges: but that has so far been strangled by the vested interests—including the local authorities jealous of their control. In 1970 a new commission was set up, under

[1] *New Society:* Smithers and Carlisle, 'The Reluctant Teachers', March 5, 1970.

Lord James, to investigate teacher-training: the National Union of Teachers in its evidence asked that the training colleges should be virtually abolished and absorbed into the higher education system, so that teaching would eventually become an all-graduate profession.

Teachers, like other trade unionists, can be maddening in their demarcations and restrictive practices; they guard their classrooms jealously from intrusion by those outside their union, and refuse to consent to briefly-trained 'teaching auxiliaries' to make up for the shortage. But their situation is a difficult one—underpaid, taken for granted, yet required to be the main agents of the great character-change of the British people. To some teachers the change is a demoralising retreat from authority and discipline; to others it is an opening-up of the minds and imaginations which gives them far greater fulfilment.

The second group have an official base—the Schools Council for Curriculum and Examinations, set up in 1964 with an unwieldy system of control by all the groups involved in education: the Department, the local authorities, the teachers' organisations. The teachers slowly overcame their suspicions as they realised that their representatives really could run the council, and the last official tie with the Department was severed in 1970. The schools council covers all levels of school education, from infants to sixth form. Its curriculum projects cover an enormous and often contradictory range: while one group may be trying to improve classical subject teaching, another will be trying to break down subject barriers and promote team teaching or interdisciplinary stuff. But they have been a forum for new ideas and practice, producing materials and running courses for teachers. At the local level they have sponsored teachers' centres—there are now over 500—to break down the isolation of teachers in their classrooms and provide a place for them to swap ideas (and grumbles).

But new curriculum ideas are useless if they bump up against old exams. The Certificate of Secondary Education was started for less clever children who couldn't do GCE O-level. It has pioneered a lot of new techniques in examining—letting teachers set their own syllabuses and papers, and allowing everyday school work to count in the final result. Now it is almost certain that the CSE will swallow up GCE O-level. But the sixth form syllabus, bound in the straightjacket of A-levels, is proving harder to reform. It is the A-levels which sort out who gets university places; and the universities and schools blame each other for the effects of A-levels, which cause children to specialise too young in narrowly academic courses. A child may be forced to decide between arts and science at 14, and afterwards he will study very little but sciences (divided into rigid compartments—physics, chemistry, biology) and maths. The Schools Council set up two committees to look at the sixth form curricula. Buffeted between the universities and the schoolmasters, between the scientists who want change and the others who do not, they produced a compromise idea that there should be two higher exams, one for 17 year olds covering a broad range of subjects, and a more specialised university entrance one. (Their case wasn't helped by adding more initials to British education's alphabet soup—the exams were to be called Q and F levels). The proposal was howled down by radicals and conservatives alike, and the committees were sent back to think again. But something like their solution is likely to eventually be adopted.

The openings between schools and the outside world—whether universities, further education, or just jobs—are gradually being widened, examined and explained, and teachers and pupils are beginning to feel themselves part of a larger world. 'Vocational Guidance' is beginning to be a separate sub-profession. One pioneer organisation, called CRAC (the Careers and Advisory Centre) set up by an enterprising Old Etonian, Adrian Bridgewater, now provides courses, booklets and detailed information to explain to teachers the range of opportunities. As with so many other fields of reform (like housing or the health service) communications can be almost as important as legislation in breaking down the barriers; but the beating of new trails, the building of bridges and the dispelling of the fogs of ignorance will not be accomplished in one generation.

The movement to democratise education, to provide real opportunities for all clever children, and to rescue the near-illiterate failures, has become a national priority accepted by all parties. But as the process goes slowly forward so the problem becomes more complicated than it first seemed; for it turns out to be bound up with the deeper problems of society—of upbringing, housing and local environment. Each stage of reform, like the skins of an onion, reveals a new stage underneath it. As the public schools begin to lose their unquestioned supremacy, so the grammar schools have emerged as a new kind of middle-class

elite, in some ways more determinedly separate. As the comprehensives push ahead, so the schools in the middle-class areas,
pressed by attentive parents and with a core of like-minded
pupils, become new centres of privilege, with big sixth forms
prepared and geared for university entrance; and the top streams
take the place of the old grammar-school selection.

Parents become increasingly important as pressure-groups for
improvement: the grown-up children of parents who used to send
them without great doubts to a boarding public school, leaving
the headmaster firmly *in loco parentis*, may now, with *their* children,
interest themselves in detail in the running of the school. But this
interplay of schools with their local communities helps to increase
(as in America) the geographical segregation of big cities, leaving
schools in working-class areas without the incentives to compete.
It is more evident in education than anywhere—whether in the
health service, in housing grants, or tax relief—that the middle
classes have been able to bend the welfare state to their own
advantage. The institutions which have upheld the class structure
of Britain, are beginning to be opened up; but as the first roots of
the old system are unearthed and cut down, so much longer and
thicker roots are revealed, deep underground. And in the meantime the British can still astonish other Europeans by their
assumptions of deference and leadership.

8

Universities

The one thing that is certain is that either party will form a cabinet almost exclusively influenced by the values of 50-year-old Oxford men, advised by senior civil servants who were up at Oxford at the same time.

The Times, June 6 1970.

THE sixties in Britain were the decade of the degree; at the end of it there were twice as many students as at the beginning. In the last ten years, whether in industry, in administration or even in the city and the army, the BA or MA has become the password to promotion, and a main instrument of social change—the most important rung in the ladder of self-improvement.

The real value of a degree to employers might be greatly doubted; many businessmen maintain that for the jobs which need drive, decisiveness and enthusiasm, university experience is dulling and confusing, teaching people reasons for *not* doing things. Many tycoons like to explain that *their* experience came not from the university but from the 'Adversity' or (as the first Lord Lever-hulme put it) 'from the University of Hard Knocks'. There are still many interesting top people who crop up in this book who did *not* go to university, including the governor and deputy governor of the Bank of England; the industrialists Lord Stokes, Lord Robens, Lord Cole; the scientist John Adams, the director of CERN; three important cabinet ministers, Peter Walker, John Davies and Lord Carrington; a permanent secretary, Sir Arnold France; a law lord, Lord Donovan; Princess Anne; and most trades union secretaries and property developers.

But the wider the universities have thrown their nets, the fewer clever boys have escaped them; and bosses have been more likely to assume—rightly or wrongly—that if a man is not a graduate, he is not very clever. Boardrooms which in the fifties would have scoffed at degrees, began sending their recruiting officers each year on 'the milk round' to scour the universities for talent. Businessmen liked to adopt the language of academia, and any conference of second-rate salesmen is now liable to be called a seminar, any old chat a study-group, and any report a thesis. The huge new flow of graduates going into industry had an inevitable setback with the first impact of a recession. In 1970 the 44 British universities produced about 47,000 new graduates, an increase of 6 per cent over the previous year; but industry had drastically reduced its demand, and six months after taking their degree at least 2,500 of them were still looking for work: the public investment in the higher education of those unemployed (the *Financial Times* ruefully point out) totalled about £10 million.

In a man's social advancement (though not a girl's) the universities have become the clearing houses, the changing rooms of their careers: a man like Ted Heath can enter as a carpenter's son and emerge three years later as a Balliol intellectual, with only a few hints of his background. The ability to lead on to the best universities is now the most important criterion of schools; Eton or Rugby are no longer sufficient qualifications in themselves. At the other end, when a man leaves university he is at the threshold of deciding what kind of person he is. He has to cross over from the questioning theoretical university world into the regimented and practical world of corporations and organograms, the self-contained citadels of big organisations, which can each condition their members almost as effectively as families or countries. The question, who runs Britain, leads on unavoidably to the question of who are the graduates.

The new prestige of the British graduate is the more spectacular because in the past Britain has been much less interested in universities and degrees than other advanced countries—or even some backward ones. In 1901 Ramsay Muir observed that Britain had fewer universities per head than any other civilised country in Europe except Turkey. A UNESCO survey in 1967 showed Britain still close to the bottom in Europe, in terms of the proportion of the age-group from twenty to twenty-four who were enrolled in higher education. Most continental countries in the last decade have expanded their higher education faster than Britain. University statistics are notoriously difficult to compare, because of the different implications of the word 'student'; in most continental countries any one who passes his final school exam—the *baccalauréat* or *abitur*—is entitled to go into the university on the principle of 'laissez-passer', but he has no guarantees of tuition or personal attention. Partly as a result there are far more drop-outs and 'ghost students'; in France half the students never become graduates. A comparison of graduates, as opposed to students, shows Britain in a more favourable light, for most British students take a degree. But even in terms of graduates, Britain is still low in the Europe league.

Going to university is a much more solid ambition among the sons of the bourgeoisie in France or Germany than in Britain; many of the British middle-classes—particularly the shopkeepers and small-business men—have tended to be sceptical, if not actually hostile, to university education for their children, and there are still rich and quite intelligent parents who will prefer their children to go straight from school into the city, to the army or to farming. But the attractions of a BA or an MA have penetrated into areas, both among the rich and the poor, where they would not have been felt twenty years ago; and there are far-reaching social repercussions in the high proportion of students who are first-generation undergraduates, who come from homes without a university tradition. Here, too, Britain is in marked contrast to the continent: the UNESCO survey of 1967 showed Britain with a much higher proportion of working-class students (a quarter) than any other Western European country.[1]

The wave of rapid British expansion dates back to the late fifties, when the University Grants Committee realised rather suddenly that more children were getting A-levels than the universities could cope with. It was then—under Macmillan's government—that plans were made for building seven new universities. The need for expansion was enshrined in that historic document of 1963, the Report of the Robbins Committee on Higher Education. Lord Robbins, with his colleagues, after producing some devastating statistics, proposed that students in full-time education (including teacher training colleges) should go up to 390,000 by 1973–4 and to 560,000 in 1980–1. The predictions nearly all turned out to be under-estimates; in 1970

[1] UNESCO: *Access to Higher Education*, vol. 4, p. 28, Vienna, November 1967.

the Report on Student Numbers in Higher Education (basing itself on rather rigid assumptions) estimated that the students in full-time higher education could reach 835,000 by 1981, having doubled their number in a decade. The late seventies will show a sharp increase in demand for university places, if only because of the 'bulge' in the birth-rate, which will send up the numbers of eighteen-year olds from 750,000 to 900,000. The bill for this huge extra education, growing much faster than the national income, has forced governments to look at ways of economising, and of fitting more students into the same buildings and classes. The spaciousness of the more privileged universities, the fact that they are only used for half the year, and the high teacher-student ratio (one teacher to eight or nine students, a far higher proportion than on the continent), all begin to look very extravagant.

At the same time the universities, like the schools, have found themselves more exposed to the influences and criticisms of society as a whole. Britain's new introspection, the speeding-up of communications and the parents' concern with education, have all helped to breach the high university walls, and to bring students into the arena of national debate.

OXBRIDGE

Nowhere has this been more marked than in the two universities which for seven hundred years have dominated British education, and which have preserved an antique way of life in the midst of the twentieth century. Their prestige and wealth is perpetuated by the large numbers of their alumni who themselves control corporate wealth. They still hold their own in centres of power. Oxford and Cambridge in 1970 still provided twenty-six of the thirty permanent secretaries, 250 of the 630 members of parliament. Ten members of Harold Wilson's cabinet were at Oxford and fourteen members of Ted Heath's 1971 cabinet of seventeeen were at Oxford or Cambridge. In the world of communications— particularly in serious newspapers, television current affairs and satire—Oxbridge men have a special hold,[1] and all kinds of in-groups love to write about each other. The eighteen thousand students of Oxbridge make up, as viewed from the outside, one of the most elite elites in the world.

Oxford is older than Cambridge, more worldly, more philo-

[1] See the run-down by Christopher Booker in *The Neophiliacs*, 1969, p. 340-1.

sophical, classical and theological (eight professors of theology to two of engineering), and with a special flair for self-congratulation and public relations. Cambridge is more isolated, more theatrical, more scientific. Cambridge has a more self-contained intellectual class, fortified by the tradition of intermarried Darwins, Keyneses, Wedgwoods, and more cut off from London; it is also much more radical and critical (with King's College now a left-wing stronghold), and has had much more student trouble. But compared with the others, these two stone cities, with their quadrangles, cloisters, damp staircases and punts, look very alike. Much of their attraction depends on the individual tutors, the peculiar range of lecturers, the sense of being an international centre, exposed to some of the best minds in the world. But much, too, depends on the social climate—the unchanging calendar of boat races, college balls and summer frolics. From outside, Oxbridge might appear as a citadel which can only be stormed by the cleverest invaders; but from inside it looks curiously as it always has, with its surface of pageantry, idleness and sport.

Oxford and Cambridge are now less firmly controlled by their individual colleges. But they still, like Inns of Court or regiments, foster eccentric muddle, and retain a jealous autonomy, which makes them as different as Southend from Bournemouth. They constitute in themselves a miniature social history of Britain, beginning with University College, Oxford, in 1249 and reaching the new Wolfson College, Oxford, in 1965. They range from wealthy old colleges with loud, rich undergraduates to poor new colleges, with no endowments and quiet grammar-school boys.

The traditional nursery of Tory politicians is Christ Church, Oxford, founded in 1546 by King Henry VIII, with endowments which bring in more than £100,000 a year. It has educated thirteen out of forty-seven prime ministers, and the road from Eton to Christ Church to politics has been well travelled for two hundred years; but its success has never had much to do with intellectual achievement, and in 1970 it still had one of the lowest proportions of first and second-class degrees of any Oxford college. No Christ Church man can write altogether objectively about his own college, which generates love-hate relationships. It contains all kinds of divisions—between canons and anti-clerical dons, between classicists and scientists, or between the four quadrangles with their social labels. But the socially dominant group is still (I am assured) made up of beagles, sports-car drivers

159

and champagne party-givers. The annual newsletter records cabinet changes, ambassadorships and honours as if the whole world existed as after-care treatment for Christ Church men, though recently a more defensive tone has crept in: thus in 1969—

> Sociological commentators will, no doubt, draw grave conclusions of social divisiveness and reaction within the House from the news that the number of Schools supplying our total body fell from 168 to 162 and that our graduates represented only 30 universities and technical colleges as against 35 in 1968. Further head-shaking may greet the confession that though the Westminster, Harrow and Charterhouse contingents fell by one each to 36, 11, and 8 respectively, Eton increased for the second year running to reach 30 for the first time since 1965. Two other schools 'returned to the charts', as the commercial calculators of the ephemeral appeal of 'Pop' records phrase it, Dulwich with 9 and Winchester with 7.

For worldly success, the most formidable college is *still* Balliol, Oxford. Ever since Benjamin Jowett was Master, from 1870 to 1893, Balliol has been preoccupied not so much with scholarship as with success, producing with considerable effort 'a sense of effortless superiority': in 1970 they had the third highest proportion of first-class degrees (17·3 per cent) of any Oxford college. Even though they now have a Marxist master, Christopher Hill, they remain intensely ambitious for conventional success: 'Life is one Balliol man after another,' the late Lord Samuel said, and it still is. They include:

Harold Macmillan (plus son and grandson)

Ted Heath	Sir Denis Brogan
Roy Jenkins	Arnold Toynbee
Denis Healey	Ivor Brown
Lord Fulton	Cyril Connolly
Lord (Henry) Brooke	Graham Greene
William Rees-Mogg	Sir Julian Huxley
Julian Amery	Raymond Mortimer
Sir Dingle Foot	Beverley Nichols
Hugh Fraser	Lord Greenwood
Lord Stow Hill	Mark Bonham Carter

Balliol (like Winchester) gives the impression of being more a cult than a college; and Balliol men love encouraging each other. In 1957 they held a special dinner in the city to celebrate the fact that, for the first time since Asquith's government in 1908, the Prime Minister and Lord Chancellor were both Balliol men. In

1963 they successfully appealed for a million pounds for their 700th anniversary. The future political battles may well be between two Balliol men, Heath and Healey, or Heath and Jenkins, described by the Balliol editor of *The Times* as 'those two pillars of High Balliol seriousness'.

In the early 1960s the outside world began battering on the old Oxbridge college doors. The Robbins Report of 1963 complained that their anomalies were incompatible with their dependence on public funds, and threatened that they might be the subject of independent enquiry. The wave of anti-Oxbridge feeling was swollen by a succession of attacks; and the new universities, which took some of their cleverest young dons, provided a kind of bloodletting. In 1964 Oxford at last reacted, and set up a commission of almost royal scale, under Lord Franks, the fashionable committeeman of the time. Franks recommended quite drastic changes, many of which—like the Council of Colleges and the Super-faculty boards—were turned down by the university parliament, 'Congregation'. But they agreed on a stronger and more centralised administration, under the Registrar, and on a full-time vice-chancellor to be appointed for a four-year term. The new vice-chancellor, Alan Bullock, biographer of Hitler and Bevin, with his down-to-earth Yorkshire accent and his businessman's approach, is the symbol of Oxford's coming-to-terms—or appearing to—with the rest of society.

The hold of Oxbridge on British public life may not be quite so strangling in the future. The civil service, a kind of bell-wether for other recruiters, has spectacularly diminished its proportion of Oxbridge entrants,[1] though it is still too early to say whether the newcomers will break into the top jobs, and invade the Oxbridge circle of permanent secretaries. The Oxford accent can no longer in itself demoralise earthier voices. The range of subjects in many new universities, with their inter-disciplinary scope, makes them more attractive to the more adventurous schoolboys. Statistics even suggest at first sight that competition is much greater to get into some other universities like Sussex (which has twelve applicants to every place) than to enter the ancient universities where the ratio is only two to one. But such figures are misleading; for the sad fact is that many clever undergraduates are discouraged from applying to Oxbridge by their awe of the place, and by the old

[1] See Chapter 12.

tribal patterns which guide boys from traditional schools to traditional universities. Candidates to Oxford and Cambridge are largely self-selected, much influenced by parents, school-friends and family backgrounds. But the narrowness of the choice does not apparently lower the standards, and judging by the numbers of A-levels (a very inadequate measure, but the only one we have got), the standards at Oxbridge are still much higher than elsewhere.

THE UNIONS

Debating is likely to lead young men to form premature ideas.
Cardinal Manning.

For the last century, the ancient universities' links with national politics have been strengthened by their debating societies, the Oxford and Cambridge Unions. In the other universities a union is simply the student centre, with its own premises, restaurant, bars and offices. But in Oxford and Cambridge the union has been a quite expensive club, revolving round a debating society with its own rituals and values, which has come to be regarded as an anteroom to parliament. The elected union officials show the traits of politicians in embryo; they talk loudly; they read a lot of Victorian biography; they are often more at ease in public than in private; a large proportion marry late; and most go into very public professions—the bar, journalism or television, and specially politics. The egocentric accents of the union manner, the modulated phrases, the postures, the narcissistic rhetoric, resound through the extrovert areas of the British power-structure.

The Cambridge Union, founded in 1815 by Augustus Hare, has contributed an odd mix-up of contemporary politicians and publicists, including Lord Devlin, Lord Caradon, Humphry Berkeley, Sir Geoffrey de Freitas, Sir Elwyn Jones, the Archbishop of Canterbury, Philip Noel-Baker, Lord Crowther and Norman St. John Stevas, and now an active batch of young Tory MPs. But it is the Oxford Union which has most influenced parliament. It was founded in 1823, as an aristocratic club with 'no pretence of democracy';[1] and its gloomy debating hall, now adorned with busts of ex-union prime ministers (Gladstone, Asquith, Salisbury and Macmillan) sets the atmosphere of

[1] Christopher Hollis: *The Oxford Union*, 1965.

pomp and nostalgia. But the expense of maintaining a privileged club in the midst of a supposedly democratic university is increasingly heavy; and in 1970 the union proposed to open up its buildings to a much larger membership and to hive off the debating part into a separate club—much, in fact, as it had begun

During the sixties, the unions have declined in their influence and attraction, but they have left a deep mark on British politics. Among union officers who failed to become president were Harold Macmillan, Roy Jenkins (a great disappointment to him) and Geoffrey Rippon, and among living ex-presidents are (in order of election):

Beverley Nichols	Anthony Crosland
Kenneth Lindsay	Anthony Wedgwood Benn
Christopher Hollis	Lord Boyle
Lord Gardiner	Peter Kirk
Lord Molson	Uwe Kitzinger
Lord Boyd	Robin Day
Roger Fulford	Godfrey Smith
Sir Dingle Foot	Jeremy Thorpe
Lord Hailsham	William Rees-Mogg
Michael Stewart	Ivan Yates
Edgar Lustgarten	Bryan Magee
J. P. W. Mallalieu	Tyrrell Burgess
John Boyd-Carpenter	Michael Heseltine
Lord Foot	Jeremy Isaacs
Lord Greenwood	Anthony Howard
Michael Foot	Brian Walden
Christopher Mayhew	Peter Jay
Philip Toynbee	Phillip Whitehead
Edward Heath	Paul Foot
Hugh Fraser	Tariq Ali
Nicholas Henderson	Gyles Brandreth

OLD AND NEW UNIVERSITIES

The other English universities had very separate origins, and only in the last decade have the old and new begun to converge and to crossfertilise each other. When Oxford and Cambridge were exclusively Anglican, nineteenth century universities were built to provide a liberal education for the poorer boys and dissenters of the provinces—and to give technological training. They grew up outside the old aristocratic pattern, and were thus associated with austere self-improvement and nonconformity.

Oxford and Cambridge graduates scorned them, and London University, which was founded in 1836, was referred to as 'that joint stock company in Gower Street'. The Scottish universities on the other hand, like their schools, avoided the rift of class which divided the English. Even in the fifteenth century there were three Scots universities, and the Scots, being poorer and more ambitious, were long ago more convinced of the necessity of education than the English.

The word 'Redbrick' summed up the old Oxbridge assumption that all other universities were alike in their gloomy practicality. In fact, even in architecture they varied from the granite fastness of Aberdeen to the daring new buildings of Southampton. British universities are much more diverse in their origins and characters than those of France or Germany: an idea of their range can be glimpsed from the inset pages. Several, like Birmingham or Leeds, are in origin 'civic' universities, founded by the mayors and corporations as the symbols of local pride; many of them still maintain a town-hall attitude, regarding students' frolics as an affront to civic dignity. Then there are the big, impersonal city universities like Manchester, Liverpool or Leeds, where most students live in digs on the outskirts and commute like office workers. There are the superior provincials, like Nottingham or Bristol, which have cleaner air and a tradition of undergraduate spirit. And there is London, in an extraordinary shapeless class of its own, with three times as many undergraduates as any other university, five hundred professors, and including four colleges which are each virtually universities in themselves—University College in Gower Street, King's College in the Strand, the London School of Economics behind Kingsway, and the Imperial College of Science and Technology. The most scattered university is Wales, with components at Cardiff, Swansea, Aberystwyth and Bangor.

The sudden gush of government spending in the sixties changed the face of many of the dingier Victorian universities, and the contrast with the facilities of Oxbridge became less extreme: there are now more individual tutors, more halls of residences, better libraries. Birmingham for instance has expanded from its blackened buildings and Victorian Chamberlain tower to a central campus with shops, restaurants, a skyscraper and halls of residence grouped round a lake. Manchester has a huge university complex built on land freed by slum clearance.

In the late fifties the very idea of a new university was new; for in the past it was felt that you could no more invent a university than you could invent a child. The 'university colleges' that were built in the early twentieth century, at Leicester, Exeter, etc., were regarded as the children of London University, like colonial colleges, taking London exams and supervised by London dons—a tutelage which added to their inferiority complex. A first breakthrough was made after the war, when the university of Keele was set up in 1949 to provide a quite new kind of four-year course, with its own degrees. But Keele was small, poor and rather resented by the local worthies. Twenty years later it still had only 1,800 students, and had to abandon an appeal for funds.

As the older universities began to split at the seams in the fifties, and Britain at last became worried about the lack of higher education, so the idea gathered weight of building new ones, with real independence: like comprehensive schools or commercial television, they were rare British examples of institutions being imposed, quite suddenly, where before things had 'just growed'. At first they looked naked and raw, like saplings in a park of old oaks. But already, after ten years, they have become part of the landscape, and the new universities have more contact with the old ones than with each other.

The first and most famous was Sussex, now the most evident rival for the prestige of Oxford and Cambridge. It began with natural advantages, and a beautiful site, four miles from Brighton and an hour from London. It was set up with an elitist emphesis, influenced by Balliol through its first vice-chancellor, John Fulton (now Lord Fulton): it has only 4,000 students, and does not want to get big. Its main buildings, grandiose and grim like a cross between a viaduct and a cathedral, were designed by the austerely passionate architect, Sir Basil Spence 'Saint Basil'. Sussex soon enjoyed special publicity as a kind of glamorous Brighton finishing-school full of pretty girls and avant-garde intellectuals—an image which for all its absurdity helped to establish the university's existence in the public mind.

Sussex in fact had from the start a high seriousness encouraged by a group of adventurous professors from Oxbridge, who were prepared to work as a team. After Fulton left in 1967 he was succeeded as vice-chancellor by Asa Briggs, the Victorian historian and chronicler of the BBC, who was committed to 'redrawing the maps of learning' through interdisciplinary studies, to allow students to escape from the old rigid faculties. Sussex was bent on change, sometimes to the point of fetish (as one new lecturer complained: 'Nothing in Sussex has an ordinary name; the school of education is the School for Cultural and Community Studies). It has its own system for caring for its students, with sub-deans, personal tutors and a remarkable psychiatric health service. This can lead to a self-conscious having-to-be-different complex, sometimes to controversial innovations—like the change from examinations to marking by assessment, which came into force in 1971. The interplay of ideologies and interest groups keeps Sussex always in flux. But the 'questioning vortex', and the insistence of having nothing in common with anyone, can be a strain on students.

Other new universities followed fast. Outside Norwich, the rich smug old capital of East Anglia, bold white-terraced buildings began to grow up (at first designed by Denys Lasdun) alongside an old Jacobean mansion. The vice-chancellor, Frank Thistlethwaite, is a Cambridge historian much influenced by America, and he grafted Cambridge traditions and dons on to Norwich. He followed some areas of Brighton's new map, and added more American regions: he also made use of the engaging East Anglian cultural worthies, Benjamin Britten and Angus Wilson. York University, opened in 1963, is more staid and conventional, with degrees more like Oxbridge ones. Its vice-chancellor, Lord James, was for fifteen years High Master of Manchester Grammar School, and prophet of the meritocracy. The university of Essex at Colchester, opened in 1964, has an idealistic vice-chancellor from Liverpool, Albert Sloman, and the heaviest concentration on social sciences, including a radical sociologist, Peter Townsend (a campaigner on the Child Poverty Action Group). Essex wanted to be a huge university, but still has only 1,400 students. The university of Lancaster has an industrial economist at its head, Charles Carter, and offers such up-to-date subjects as Operational Research and Environmental Studies. The university of Kent at Canterbury is the most conservative and paternalistic. It is run by a medieval historian from Birmingham, Geoffrey Templeman; and it seems over-obsessed by the cathedral—the dining-halls have it framed in their windows.

These varied arrivals, with the government and industrialists looking over their shoulders, soon raised further the awkward question: 'What is a university *for*?' Should they equip modern managers, should they give an enriching cultural background, or should they pursue fine scholarship? If they should do all these things, where should the balance rest? The arguments between the cartographers of learning were fierce, and soon spread to the students: they will reverberate through this chapter.

While these bright and extravagant new places were popping up in the early sixties, the thinking that brought them into being was being overtaken by the need for more drastic expansion. By 1970 the seven new universities—the 'Shakespearian Seven' as they were called from their ducal-sounding names—accounted for only 16,300 students, while during the decade the student population had expanded by 122,000, and expansion was transforming the university perspective. Building new universities was not as expensive as expanding some old ones, because their land was cheap and sometimes given free: but the grandiose arched buildings, high-roofed refectories and echoing common rooms looked oddly out of keeping with a time when all universities were scrabbling for money to cope with armies of new students. The Labour Party's report by Lord Taylor, published in 1964, complained that they were too cut off, in their sleepy cathedral cities; and Sir Edward Boyle—now Lord Boyle, vice-chancellor of Leeds—decided that his party might have been mistaken in founding so many new universities. It is one measure of the change in a decade that these new campuses, which seemed so innovatory and democratic in 1960, now began to look elitist and extravagant. They had breached the old walls between Oxbridge and the rest; they had considerable social effects by (for instance) mixing up upper-middle-class girls with working-class men; and they had established their new interdisciplinary courses as respectable. But the major expansion of higher education is now happening in less glamorous and privileged surroundings—in the enlarged Redbrick universities, like Manchester and Leeds, in the technological universities, and in the promoted polytechnics.

TECHNOLOGY

The most sudden expansion has been in the technical colleges, which had grown up in the last century doubly separated from the traditional world of power and politics. The industrial revolution had very little to do with the universities. In the early nineteenth century Oxford and Cambridge took little interest in the new sciences. The technologists like Watt, Boulton or New-comen came from the factories and workshops, while the great pioneer scientists—Priestley, Dalton or Joule—taught in dissenters' academies, many of them Quaker, in the north: so that the rift between science and the humanities was widened by the rift between Anglicans and nonconformists. It was only after France and Germany had founded their *polytechniques* and *hochschulen* for technomanagers that Britain gradually felt the need to adapt their universities to technical education and set up the new scientifically-minded universities of the 1870s, planted in the middle of the industrial cities of the north and midlands. They were designed not, like the continental schools, to produce a separate scientific culture, but to bring the new world of technology into the old world of liberal education.[1] In the last two decades, laboratories and workshops have crept up on the libraries and lecture halls—not only in the new universities but in the old ones. In North Oxford and East Cambridge new scientific cities have grown up beyond the colleges, with government endowments far larger than those of the ancient foundations. But just as the universities preferred mandarin to modern Chinese, they preferred science to technology, which was only developed grudgingly as a second-class subject.

There were three important exceptions—the three great 'techs' in Glasgow, Manchester and London, which have for a long time been virtually independent, and are now major universities. The Royal College of Science and Technology in Glasgow began in 1796, under the will of the professor of natural philosophy, John Anderson, and became the pride of Scottish engineering; one of its distinguished alumni was Lord Reith, who described his 'years of intellectual and social frustration' there, doing evening classes from 7 to 10 p.m, before the first world war. In 1964 it became the first technological university, with the romantic new name of Strathclyde, with some confusion of identity between its old and new character: 'Can the Glasgow "Tech" become a university without losing its craggy identity?', asked Stuart Maclure, editor of *The Times Educational Supplement*,:[2] 'Must joining the university club rub off the old corners? Must it mean contempt for the world of work?'

Manchester 'Tech' has spread itself through old slum areas of

[1] See Sir Eric Ashby's terse and brilliant study: *Technology and the Academics*, Macmillan 1958.
[2] *The Listener*, June 10, 1965.

the city, alongside the University: it now calls itself UMIST, the University of Manchester Institute of Science and Technology, but it is really a university of its own. It is run by one of the master-publicists in British education, Lord Bowden, an ex-computer salesman who became in the sixties the chief spokesman of technocracy's interests against the amateurism of the arts men; he even for a short time joined the Labour government as one of the white-hot men, but his enthusiasm for national politics went cold. Imperial College in London was founded in 1907 by a merger of three London Colleges, and although it was always part of London University, by the 1930s it was already virtually a university of its own, with its world-wide reputation. In the fifties modern green shoeboxes rose up to replace the old Edwardian buildings, with only one Byzantine old tower left, and by the mid-sixties South Kensington was hailed as the shining scientific capital of the New Britain; Lord Penney, the nuclear physicist, is now its rector. Student numbers were increased from 1,600 in 1953 to 4,000 in 1970—almost half of them post-graduate: Imperial College has the highest professor-student ratio in the country.

Apart from these great technological centres, there grew up from the early nineteenth century onwards all kinds of modest colleges in industrial centres, to provide practical training for local boys paid for by local councils and local industrialists. While the old universities developed from monastic origins, abstracting young people from their communities, these places were firmly accountable to local needs. The hundreds of technical schools were disconnected and uncounted—the 'uncharted territories of English education', as Eric Robinson calls them; it came as a shock when the Robbins Report revealed that forty per cent of all people in higher education were outside the universities. But from their humble beginnings, many of them grew up into important establishments, 'techs', polys or mechanics' institutes, providing the all-important expertise for industrial expansion. As governments became more conscious of their dependence on technology, so they began to take them much more seriously.

In the mid-fifties the Ministry of Education, pushed by David Eccles and Antony Part, turned to the neglected world of the 'techs', and singled out a few colleges to develop them for advanced work; they were landed with the unfortunate name of Colleges of Advanced Technology (CATS) and their muffled launching in

1962 was in great contrast to the fanfare that accompanied the seven new universities. But the Robbins Report the following year recommended that the CATS should become full universities, with self-governing status, awarding their own degrees. The CATS jumped quickly on to their rooftops, acquired new names and new ambitions and developed very separate characters. Bristol CAT acquired a beautiful site, and became the University of Bath; Battersea did a deal with Guildford; Brunel CAT, which used to be Acton Tech., became Brunel University, named after the great engineer whose Great Western Railway passes through Acton.

The development of sandwich students, bridging the world of universities and the world of industry, was the special contribution of these technological universities. But the part-time students—who accounted for most of the working-class element—were quickly shed; and in the process of becoming universities the CATS became much more middle-class, more conscious of their respectability. There was some doubt as to how far the change had helped the cause of technology, and in fact most of the additional advanced study was taking place outside the CATS. 'In the ten years of their development,' wrote a formidable critic, Tyrrell Burgess, 'the colleges of advanced technology turned their backs on their technical college tradition and embraced that of the universities. In part this was intended; they were meant to become less comprehensive by dropping lower-level work. But in the main they were chosen for development because they represented an alternative to the existing universities, and one that was to be encouraged. By the end, only in their adherence to sandwich courses, in the continued intimacy of their links with industry, and perhaps in their continuing acceptance of ONC (Ordinary National Certificate) entrants, did the CATS retain a recognisedly technical college outlook and a link with social or industrial need. Despite all the lip-service, no serious effort was made to prevent the change.'[1]

POLYTECHNICS

As the demand for higher education still increased, and as some technical colleges were up-graded first into CATS, then into

[1] Tyrrell Burgess and John Pratt: *Policy and Practice* (LSE Studies in Education), Penguin Press, 1970, p. 172–3.

universities, so 'other' colleges, the tail-end-charlies, in turn became more involved in the national pattern, and more interesting to politicians and planners. Many of them were loosely described as polytechnics—a word with less grand connotations than the continental *polytechniques*, with their associations of high technocracy. The first 'polytechnic' was set up in 1838 in Regent Street and was revived and enlarged in 1881 by Quintin Hogg, grandfather of the present Lord Chancellor; the name spread through the country, in the wake of new industries and technologies. Many of the 'other' colleges had very direct connections with the workplace, like Glamorgan College of Technology, started by Welsh coal-owners in 1913 to train their working force. In 1966 the polys came suddenly into the political forefront when the minister of education, the stormy reformer Anthony Crosland, announced plans to turn an odd jumble of sixty colleges of technology, commerce and art, into thirty 'New Polytechnics', which would cater for students 'who cannot on entry show that they are of university calibre'; many of them would be part-time students, but some would be able to take on a full-time degree course. The New Polys could not award their own degrees; but some of their courses could be accepted for degrees by the watchdog-body, the Council for National Academic Awards. The CNAA thus became an important arbiter of status, made up of twenty-four engineers, academics and industrialists, who in 1969 awarded 2,100 degrees, nearly all BSc's. (They also fulsomely honour each other; at their first ceremony, their chairman, Lord King's Norton, gave a doctorate of laws to their president, Prince Philip, and the Prince gave a doctorate to their chairman.)

In creating the New Polys, Crosland also rashly proclaimed a 'binary' policy, by which the Polys were to be kept separate from the universities, under more direct control from government and local authorities: a policy opposite to that of the Robbins Report. The 'other' colleges had always in fact been very separate, and of their nature they were more sensitive to outside pressures, whether from mayors, factory-owners or governments; but Crosland elevated their separateness into a principle, which has become one of the great debates of education. By some it was welcomed as a championing of these local institutions: by others it was attacked as an imposition of the dogma of the department's theoreticians (notably Toby Weaver, the deputy-under-secretary). In a speech in January 1967 Crosland explained:

No doubt the distinction between the universities and other colleges
will lessen as on the one hand we seek to give more academic freedom
to the latter, and on the other hand the universities come under
growing though friendly scrutiny from the UGC[1] and public and
parliamentary opinion. But I feel clear that side by side with an
autonomous sector of higher education we must also have a public or
social sector.

Most of the New Polys are still just old places with new names,
or awkward mergers of scattered municipal colleges, each with its
own speciality. The South Bank Polytechnic is a wonderful mixture
of the City of Westminster College of Commerce, the Borough
Polytechnic, the Brixton School of Building, and the National
College for Heating, Ventilation, Refrigeration and Fan Engineering. The bringing together of these workaday components into a
serious campus will take many years, and much new building; and
in all the polytechnics there are signs of a split personality, pulled
between local communities and trades and the ambition to become
autonomous quasi-universities.

Probably the closest to actually *becoming* a university is the
North-East London Polytechnic (NELP), in the East End of
London, which deserves special notice. It is made up of three old
'techs', at Barking, Waltham Forest and West Ham, miles apart,
cutting across public transport lines. The New Poly still has the
gloomy aura of Victorian self-help: the headquarters building is
the 'West Ham Precinct', ten minutes muddy walk from Stratford
station, along the grey suburban high street: it is a red-brick
building next to the public library, built in Victorian Renaissance style, with a frieze of stucco cherubs and topped by a
weather vane. Inside the bleak corridors, painted in institutional
brown, green and cream, are echoing with student sounds—from
turbaned Sikhs, Africans, Pakistanis, Arabs and English. The
notice-board proclaims the beginning of a sense of unity—
demands for student participation on the governing body, and
student activities in which the crucial words are 'transport provided'. The proud Victorian decorations are almost lost in the
impedimenta of expansion—metal lockers in the passages, and
high scaffolding for extra books in the library. There are a few
gestures to 'culture', like a reproduction of Picasso's Guernica in
the refectory; but the prevailing atmosphere of the building is
hectically practical, like a public library near closing-time.
At one end of the main corridor is an office with walls of black

[1] See p. 184.

cork, black-and-white furniture, acid green curtains, and the director, George Brosan, is one of the dynamos of the New Polys: a Dickensian ex-businessman, an autodidact with a big round head on a round body, and a rich voice which resounds with confidence and improvement. He wears a sleek dark suit, a bold tie and carries an ivory-handled umbrella; a chauffeur drives him in from the station. He is determined to Get Things Moving, and to defy municipal meanness: 'Who's the director; you or me?' He moved in in 1970 from Enfield—one of the most reactionary local authorities—and brought with him Eric Robinson, one of the champions of polytechnics as local institutions, who wrote a book about it; and he also invited in the Centre for Institutional Studies run by Tyrrell Burgess, another Poly enthusiast.

In the old days the Polys depended on London University—as the provincial universities did—to award their degrees; and their breaking-away from London is a coming-of-age, which forces them to think out problems for themselves, and to argue with the CNAA about degree subjects. Some of the goulash of Poly courses is rather absurd ('you can study religion, philosophy and woodwork—that's for an undertaker!') and NELP has an astonishing department of 'applied philosophy': no-one is quite sure what it means. But combining practical and academic subjects can be a challenge for teachers, and the Polys now have to work out their identity for themselves—as the new universities had to in the early sixties.

Brosan and his colleagues insist that the polytechnics must keep their connections with the town halls and the community. 'If we broke away from the local authorities,' Brosan said to me, 'it would be a disaster. The danger is that the Poly directors will sell out to the universities, because they're fed up with the nonsense of the local education authorities, without realising that the universities are an even greater nonsense.' If the Polys aspire to become like universities, they will drop off their part-time students—who make up half of NELP's students—in favour of full-time degree-chasers. As first the CATS then the Polys move away from their local roots, so it is the part-timers who suffer, bumping along at the bottom of the moving staircase. The tension between Polys and universities is part of the tension stretching through many British institutions—schools, hospitals, political parties—between the centre and the circumference, between parts that have grown up from the ground, and parts imposed from above.

OPEN UNIVERSITY

In the meantime a new kind of university has appeared on the
scene, which may in the end revolutionise the techniques of all
higher education; and which draws on the experience of universities, techs *and* polys. The Open University has its headquarters in
a plain Georgian house in the Midlands, with a few functional
brick buildings round it. It looks like a ghost university. There
are dons to be seen, textbooks, charts, addressing machines, time-
tables, computer print-outs, TV devices. But there are no students.
It could be a science-fiction establishment (like a setting for
The Avengers), and the setting is appropriately creepy; it is a mile
away from exit 14 of the M1, in the middle of flat pastures which
will eventually become the new city of Milton Keynes. As Lord
Crowther, the chancellor of the university, described it, in a mood
of rare rhapsody:

> The university has no cloisters—a word meaning closed. Hardly
> even shall we have a campus. By a very happy chance, our only local
> habitation will be in the new city that is to bear two of the widest-
> ranging names in the history of English thought—Milton Keynes. But
> this is only where the tip of our toe touches ground. The rest of the
> university will be disembodied and airborne . . .

The university is an ironic monument to the Labour government; for it was proposed before Labour came in, and began
functioning after they lost. It was first announced by Harold
Wilson in 1963, as part of that forthcoming 'white-hot technological revolution'; as the 'University of the Air' it became the
special protégé of Jennie Lee, who protected it from all economic
crises. She appointed a committee of academics to plan it, led by
Sir Peter Venables of Aston, the respected technological ex-vice-
chancellor of Aston. They changed its name to the Open University, and aimed to use television more as an adjunct than as a
basis; they appointed as vice-chancellor a bald Scots pharma-
cologist from Edinburgh, Walter Perry—who, though enthusiastic
and wryly humorous, could not be accused of wildness. When the
Conservatives came back in 1970 there were fears that Mrs
Thatcher would cut it down. But a correspondence course can
provide degrees much more cheaply than conventional universities,
even allowing for a huge rate of drop-outs. It educates 25,000
students for about £5 million a year, and is thus the ideal let-out for
a government that wants to cut down costs while increasing students.

The Open University is not quite as odd as it looks. Perry insists that his hundred and fifty dons are chosen like any others, by rigorous academic standards; that they are not special missionaries of workers' education; and that television is secondary. The planning committee and the external examiners should keep the degrees up to other universities' standards. But the teaching, Perry maintains, is likely to be better, because exposed to public gaze; a don, who at Oxford could get by with silent tutorials and mumbled lectures, at the Open University would have to write down his thoughts into textbooks, work out his courses in committees, or even appear on the TV screen. The main instrument of teaching is the correspondence course, a technique already developed in the Commonwealth, augmented by two hundred and sixty 'study centres' set up all over Britain, and by summer schools at other universities; television is only used (so far with limited success) to supplement and stimulate the course. The interaction of the new techniques on all teaching may be far-reaching; already the Open University, with its 25,000 students—more than Oxford and Cambridge together—can produce textbooks and equipment much more cheaply than others; and after thirty-five years of TV its educational scope is at last being explored. There are problems in keeping the attention and persistence of home students; in the first five months of 1971 21 per cent dropped out.

How far will the Open University make education accessible to a new class of students, as its inspirers had hoped? Forty-two thousand applications were made for the twenty-five thousand places, which were selected by a system of quotas to favour the less privileged; but even so, a third of the first students are teachers (who want degrees for professional advancement). These were the percentage of students in the main categories for the 1971 course:

	per cent
Teachers	33·0
Professions and the arts	9·7
Housewives	9·6
Qualified scientists and engineers	9·0
Clerical and office staff	8·0
Administrators and managers	5·4

Perry insists that he is not surprised or disappointed, and that there is bound to be a time-lag before it becomes accessible to working-class students. It is part of the old pattern, of the middle-classes benefiting most from each innovation; and if the Open

University is made available to eighteen-year-olds, as seems likely, the idea of 'the University of the Second Choice' will fade further. But even with its immediate social limitations, the Open University has great implications; as Tony Watts (research office of CRAC) put it: 'It offers a greater prospect than ever before of breaking up the division between "education" and "employment" and of disturbing the relentless programme of students up the educational escalator—or at least of allowing them to step off it without feeling that they are burning their boats irretrievably.'

VICE-CHANCELLORS AND STUDENTS

Every two months in the Senate House in London about eighty men assemble for an all-day meeting; brisk, urbane, white-rabbity, rushing from somewhere to somewhere. Few of them look very academic: one was a general, another a civil servant, another a headmaster; perhaps the most donnish-looking of them (Lord Boyle) was a cabinet minister. Many are massively dull, with that enveloping dullness that makes everything seem less exciting. And perhaps that is necessary; for these vice-chancellors stand on the exposed peaks of British higher education, scapegoats for everyone from students and professors to civil servants and politicians. One of them likened his profession to that of an old colonial governor: 'You seem to be in full control, and you have to make long-term plans for the future: but you can never predict when trouble will suddenly break out.' But the vice-chancellor, unlike the governor, has no troops; and the arrival of the police is the ultimate sign of his failure (the shrewder ones make careful plans to prevent the police being summoned until the last possible moment).

It is not easy nowadays to find scholar-managers; and most vice-chancellors have settled down to a career as administrators. There are eight fellows of the Royal Society (Pitt, Mather, Merrison, Christopherson, Curran, Swann, Smith and Penney); but most have given up research. Professor Dainton, the most remarkable amphibian, gave up the vice-chancellorship of Nottingham in 1970, with evident relief, to become chairman of the Council for Scientific Policy.[1] Some vice-chancellors still pop up in many other roles. Asa Briggs of Sussex, the most inexhaustible, keeps up with Victorian history, is chairman of a committee on

[1] See Chapter 17.

nurses, writes the history of the BBC, and travels continually. Lord Annan at University College, London, is a tireless commissioner, reviewer and party-goer, and one of the planners of Essex and East Anglia. But most vice-chancellors move over from the library or the laboratory to the committee-rooms, and become more fascinated by the world of telephones and money than the world of scholarship. Perhaps the most interesting new vice-chancellor is Sir John Hackett, the former Commander of the British Army of the Rhine who took over King's College, London, in 1968. He looks and is unashamedly military: red-faced, moustached, brisk and small (like most generals), but is enough of a scholar to pass muster, and has been president of the Classical Association. Though an elitist, he regards himself as on the left of most of his vice-chancellorian colleagues. He insists that his military experience makes him understand better than the others the basic problem—how to have good communications with the troops—and he enjoys establishing cosy relations with student leaders. 'People talk about clasping the snake to the bosom: but I think the bosom's the best place for a snake to be.'

The cross-purposes of the vice-chancellors show themselves in their committee; there are so many of them, with such conflicts of interest, ranging from the 'production line' universities to the Ivory Towers, that they cannot agree on issues which involve deciding what universities are *for:* their meetings (one of them complained) are very like the United Nations, with long speech-making and posturing. Most of them are rightly preoccupied with their autonomy, and with keeping the support of their own senate. But they are pressed on all sides to become a more solid bloc: by the government, which needs a single spokesman; by the technicians' trade unions which make national wage-claims; and by the students, with their own national union. It was the confrontation with the students which brought them into the political firing-line. In October 1968 they signed the now famous *concordat* with the National Union of Students, cautiously and ambiguously stating their attitude, and agreeing that 'the form of the academic community and the role of students within it should be correspondingly modified and modernised': they now periodically meet the union officials, with solemn bureaucratic exchanges as if they were the TUC and the CBI. In February 1970, after the great rumpus at Warwick, (see p. 181) the vice-chancellors met the students and issued a statement rejecting the need for political files on students. The Conservatives leapt on it: Iain Macleod said the vice-chancellors were 'letting us down'; Ted Heath said 'they were abdicating their authority and responsibilities'; Enoch Powell compared the British universities to the Chinese ones and protested against 'the cringing public apology'. Sir Roger Stevens, then at Leeds, complained that 'baiting vice-chancellors had become a favourite Conservative weekend sport'.

Behind the 1968 concordat there was much disagreement; as Hackett put it, with a glint in his eye, 'Some of them thought it was a cork in the bottle. Some of us thought it was a corkscrew.' But most of the vice-chancellors realised that they would have to work together increasingly closely with students whether they liked it or not, to plan for the future: the problem of vice-chancellors is not so much when to give in to the students, as how to combine forward planning and investment with proper participation, and how to co-operate closely with each other, without losing the autonomy of universities. A principal reason why student revolts in Britain have been less angry and effective than in France is the fact that British universities are much more autonomous: the students' enemy is not remote and bureaucratic, but local and visible in the shape of the vice-chancellor. The vice-chancellors are a vulnerable bunch, straddling the two worlds, torn between government committees and local professors. But their autonomy is one of the great distinguishing features of the British universities, as against the American or the French. The alternatives, of professional administrators or centralised government control, would provoke much more dangerous encounters.

The 'concordat' was the culmination of a long and chequered relationship between vice-chancellors and students. The National Union of Students was established after the first world war by ex-officer undergraduates, with international idealism; but its main activity soon became its travel service (which still accounts f r a large part of its staff). After the second war the NUS became deeply involved in the intricacies of European student politics, and the subsequent disillusion with fellow-travellers. In the fifties the NUS was dominated by right-wing Labour students, who maintained their position against the left with some 'Tammany Hall politics', made easier by their remarkable system of multiple voting.

From the early fifties the NUS pressed for consultations with the Ministry of Education; eventually David Eccles—the most far-sighted post-war minister—took them seriously and agreed against his officials' advice to see them. By 1959 the University Grants Committee began asking for the union's viewpoint; the 'student estate' was embraced by the establishment, and by 1965 the executive were actually invited to dine with Harold Wilson in Downing Street. From the mid-sixties the union was becoming more interested in ideas of participation in university government, and it successfully demanded consultation in the new charters of the new technical universities. In September 1966 the Vice-Chancellors' Committee at last agreed to meet the union: 'It is remarkable,' commented Sir Eric Ashby (former vice-chancellor of Cambridge), 'that forty-four years had to pass before two bodies so deeply involved in the welfare of universities met officially to discuss common problems.'[1]

In the late sixties new left-wing groups made themselves felt, angered by the compromises of the Labour government, the escalation of the Vietnam war, and the conservatism of their union's leaders. A Radical Students Alliance was formed in 1966 (later absorbed in the Radical Socialist Students Federation, which disintegrated in 1970 into splinters of 'red bases') which successfully pressed the NUS to make more militant stands. In 1969 a more fiery president, Jack Straw, was elected and re-elected the next year. Straw is a very political campaigner from Leeds University, with a black thatch of hair, the son of a conscientious objector and the grandson of a shop steward. He soon became a bogy to right-wing politicians, but in fact he was always in danger of being undermined by his left-wing: he will be succeeded by Digby Jacks, a communist founder-member of the Radical Students Alliance. The National Union, like the TUC, is not able to control its members—four hundred thousand of them, scattered over forty universities. It has its own large bureaucracy, in two crowded houses in Bloomsbury, revelling in elaborate and formalised correspondence with the ministry, the vice-chancellors or the UGC; but like any other union, it is always being harassed from the shop-floor, and it can never predict—let alone organise—where trouble will break out next.

[1] Sir Eric Ashby and Mary Anderson: *The Student Estate*, Macmillan 1970, p. 213. This book is an important source for the union's history.

LSE AND WARWICK

The student revolts first hit the headlines in 1966, in the traditional nursery of the left, the London School of Economics. The LSE had been founded by the first Fabian, Sidney Webb, and later administered by William Beveridge; but since then its teachers, if not its students, have become much more conservative. The LSE in 1966 contained many explosive ingredients: a mixture of restless cosmopolitan students, including very vocal Americans; preoccupation with the social sciences, which always provide the most rebels; gloomy overcrowded premises for the four thousand students, jammed into libraries and lecture-halls in a bleak street behind the Aldwych; right-wing academics and insensitive rulers cut off from student opinion. The 'Court of Governors' had eighty members, rather like the board of an insurance company; but the real power was firmly held by the chairman, Lord Robbins, a useful hate-figure for the left, on the frontiers of academia and big business, who was also chairman of the *Financial Times*.

In 1966 Lord Robbins appointed Walter Adams, from the university of Salisbury in Rhodesia, to be the new director, and that lit the fuse. Adams was unfairly accused of supporting apartheid; what was more relevant was that he was not a strong administrator or a great scholar, and was unprepared for troubles. Over the next two years there were sit-ins, demos, slogans and muck-raking; the fires were stoked up further by the continental student leaders in the summer of 1968—though the British students were sceptical of the Marxist rhetoric. The chairman and director repeatedly played into the revolutionaries' hands. In January 1969 they put up new steel gates to protect the college; the gates were torn down, and the college was closed. Compared to the troubles in France, Germany or America, the disturbances were tiny; but in the relative calm of the British scene they made the LSE a by-word for student chaos.

The LSE troubles were followed by lesser outbursts elsewhere—including Birmingham, Manchester, Edinburgh, Bristol and Essex. But the most spectacular flare-up, in February 1970, was at Warwick—which had become the symbol of the 'business university', and was an appropriate battleground for the war between radicals and capitalists.

Warwick was the most ambitious of the seven new universities: it was designed from the first to be a kind of British version of the

Massachusetts Institute of Technology—a giant university to serve the industries of the midlands, aiming to have twenty thousand students. The chairman of the original promotion committee was Lord Rootes (who died in 1964), a tough old motor pioneer who quickly raised a million pounds from his industrialist friends; and the vice-chancellor, 'Jolly Jack' Butterworth, was the former bursar of New College, Oxford, well-connected with businessmen, a lawyer and man of the world. The first chancellor was Lord Rootes himself, but after he died his post was taken by Lord Radcliffe, a much more sophisticated symbol of order—the fine flower of the legal profession, a fastidious and brilliant ex-judge with an intense dislike of mass media, egalitarianism and politicians, who had been in and out of the Establishment for the past thirty years: 'Let a fairy grant me my three wishes,' he said in his Rede Lecture in 1961, 'I would gladly use them all in one prayer only, that never again should anyone using pen or typewriter be permitted to employ that inane cliché "Establishment".' The fairy failed him.

The Council of the University was headed by the new Lord Rootes, and included the boffin-tycoon Sir Arnold Hall, then running Bristol Siddeley; Gilbert Hunt of Rootes; Lord Iliffe of Coventry Newspapers; A. F. Tuke of Barclays Bank; and Sir William Lyons, of Jaguar Cars. Many big companies chipped in to provide buildings and professorships; there was a Pressed Steel Professor of Industrial Relations, a Barclays Bank Professor of Management Information Systems, an Institute of Directors Professor of Business Studies and a Volkswagen Professor of German. Academics and politicians were excited by this new cornucopia of university finance. In fact, the capital that came from industry was only an eighth of the total, and the real benefactor—as with all other universities—was the University Grants Committee. And when the university opened up, many more students were studying arts and social studies than scientific subjects (partly because arts equipment is cheaper), and the most distinguished dons had no links with industry, including Professor Zeeman the mathematician, Professor John Hale the Renaissance historian, and—an appointment fraught with consequences —Edward Thompson, the tousle-haired historian of the British working classes. Thompson had a special following among left-wing students; he was a former member of the Communist Party, and an ex-editor of the *New Left Review*, and he soon became a thorn in Butterworth's flesh; though his very presence at Warwick contradicted the suspicions that here was a university exclusively dominated by right-wing tycoons.

By 1969 the university had fifteen hundred students, isolated and frustrated in their half-empty site, and becoming gradually politically active; they heckled Major Patrick Wall, the pro-South African MP, and staged a sit-in in support of the LSE students. But the explosion came from a self-centred issue. The students were impatient about a new social building—a smouldering issue since the university began—which they wanted to run themselves, and they staged a sit-in in the registry building. While they were occupying it one student found a file called 'Student-University Relations', which revealed how a Mr Catchpole, the legal expert of Rootes, had been sent to listen to a visiting historian at Warwick, David Montgomery, to see if he might be prosecuted under the Aliens Restrictions Act. The letter was read out to the excited students, who then searched all the files and found other examples of interference from industrial backers, and a letter from a headmaster explaining the political record of an applicant, with a note from Butterworth saying REJECT THIS MAN. The next day the students held a mass meeting to read out the documents, and Edward Thompson appealed to his fellow dons to protest. The university replied by reading an injunction over the loud-hailer, forbidding publication of the documents: but the *Birmingham Post* published them, and the case quickly became a national one. The question of 'political files' spread from university to university; at Manchester hundreds of students occupied the admissions block, and a wall was scrawled with 'FOR A DEMOCRATIC UNIVERSITY—NO DOSSIERS!' At Oxford police guarded the proctors' files. A fortnight after the Warwick disclosures the Committee of Vice-Chancellors felt impelled to give their formal pledge that no political files would be kept.

In the meantime back at Warwick Lord Radcliffe, the chancellor, had stepped in and asked everyone to submit evidence about political files. In his report he was satisfied that no political files were kept or had ever been kept at Warwick; but he recommended that the vice-chancellor should no longer be allowed to veto the admission of a student without giving reasons, that convictions should no longer be recorded in students' personal files, but defended the vice-chancellor's right to keep his eye on the preservation of order: 'There is no rule either of equity or of common sense that one ought to wait to be blown up by an explosion before trying to detect the likelihood of its occurrence.'

Edward Thompson wrote his own 'Report on Lord Radcliffe' a month later, which summed up their difference of backgrounds:

> He belongs securely to—and has been a distinguished member of—a governing class. He is not ashamed of that, he shares its *esprit de corps*, and he has an unusual sense of its difficulties and duties. And I belong—much as I may try to disguise the fact even from myself—to a kind of shabby sub-Establishment, part literary, part academic, part Dissent, part (perhaps?) poaching for some hundreds of year, resisting its pretensions, throwing back its encroachments, but never, finally, challenging its power. . . . His convictions as to what is necessary for the government of an academic institution are, without doubt, sincere, and so are the convictions of those who find scrutiny opprobrious and who are attempting to develop new modes of self-government. The report does not even serve as a hyphen between them. We (the governed) are here and he (the gov.rnor) is there.[1]

Warwick was never the same again. Even before the furore, the registrar and deputy registrar had resigned; after it many arts dons left, and Edward Thompson retreated to the West Country to write books (though followed at Warwick by an equally left-wing don, John Rex). The dream of a great midlands 'MIT' was already dimmed, and the University Grants Committee had lost its enthusiasm. By American or continental standards the Warwick troubles were minuscule (at the university of Vincennes, where I was lecturing at that time, there was a disturbance on that scale about once a fortnight.) But in the British context, the Warwick affair had a significance which has repercussed since; for it revealed the vulnerability of a university to industrial pressures, and it showed a dangerous confusion of academic and commercial values. When Warwick was planned, most people saw little wrong in this coming-together of big business and academia; it was a left-wing politician, Richard Crossman, who was credited with the idea of a midlands 'MIT'. But in the intervening decade the whole political climate in the universities had changed, and the students' worry and anger about a 'business university' had escalated. This is how the Warwick rebels depict it in *their* account of the conflict:[2]

[1] *New Society*, April 30, 1970.
[2] *Warwick University Ltd.* (edited by E. P. Thompson), Penguin, 1970, p. 17.

It is sobering to realise that the mid-Atlantic of the Midlands Motor and Aircraft Industry offers one possible model of a British future. It is a febrile, wasteful, publicity-conscious world, whose prosperity floats upon hire-purchase and the shifting moods of the status-conscious consumer; a brash, amoral, pushful world of expense-account living, lavish salesmanship, cocktail bars in restored sixteenth-century inglenooks, and of refined managerial techniques and measured day-work; a world of mergers and takeovers, of the unregenerate, uninhibited Mammon of the Sunday business supplements.

WHO RUNS THEM, AND WHY?

In every advanced industrial country, the question of who should control the universities is now far-reaching, for it affects the character and perhaps the stability of the future society. Many estates have an interest in expanding and influencing them with different and sometimes opposite motives; the industrialists, to provide their future managers and technicians; the students, to develop their own interests and personalities; the dons, to perpetuate scholarship and to recreate their own species; the government, to placate the opposing groups, or to maintain the country's prestige in the world. Each sector has its own answers to the question: What is a university *for*? Their interests cannot be convergent, the universities can never be subject to a consensus. A measure of conflict is inevitable in the relationship between universities and society.

The British long ago found their 'characteristically British solution' to the allocation of money. The vast majority of it—about eighty-five per cent—now comes from the government, and no university need be dependent on industry or private benefaction. The first grant of government money was £15,000 distributed to universities in 1880; since then the sum has multiplied by 16,000, and in 1970 came to £242 million. But this sum is allocated not by the Treasury or the Department of Education, but by the twenty-one members of the University Grants Committee, on the time-honoured principle (as with research councils or the Arts Council) of leaving the carve-up to the profession concerned—a kind of indirect rule. The only full-time member of the committee, with a salary of £8,300 a year, is the Chairman. The last two incumbents, Sir John Wolfenden and Sir Keith Murray, came direct from academia; but the present chairman, Sir Kenneth Berrill, came from the Treasury, where he had been special adviser on education—a translation which some suspected would imply a stricter government surveillance. In fact Berrill is very much an academic (he was lecturer in economics at Cambridge for twenty years) and is determined to be detached from government attitudes; but he is very much a realist, acutely conscious of the quantitative problems. The UGC, facing crises of costs, is having to work more closely with government, and to become involved in *dirigiste* policies: however academic the UGC may be, it is sensitive to the government's wishes. The government may not control the break-down; but it controls the total. 'National apathy about universities had accompanied the great days of the UGC; when governments actually evolve policies for them or Public Accounts Committees, Select Committees and Prices and Incomes Boards begin to pry, there is nothing in the UGC arrangements to stop them.'[1]

The UGC is still able to act as some kind of buffer-state between the interests of government and industry, and the needs of academics; British universities have been much less influenced by big business than American ones, much less directed by government than (till recently) French ones. The indirect rule and the proud autonomies have succeeded in insulating higher education from the most utilitarian pressures. But there must be a continuing conflict between the view of higher education as an economic necessity, as a part of the human investment of a modern managerial state, and the view of it as part of each individual's right to self-fulfilment. Universities have to defend values and ambitions which are essentially uncommercial and materially unproductive. Their insistence on 'academic freedom' can, in the extreme, lead to abuses and self-aggrandisement by professors; but the relinquishment of it can lead to a commercialised society without countervailing values—against which future generations of students will react far more fiercely than those of the LSE and Warwick.

[1] Tyrrell Burgess: *Policy and Practice*, 1970, p. 175–6.

9

Churches

I believe that the national recognition of the Church of England
gives the impression that England is more Christian than it really is,
and encourages delusions of grandeur within the Church itself... I
believe also that the special status accorded to the Church inhibits us
from accepting the truth that we are a minority group.

Peter Cornwell.

FOR many people the Churches are no longer regarded as forming
part of Britain's power structure, or as being a significant factor in
the background of her young generation. Yet a hundred and
twenty years ago the Church of England ran the nation's education—which is one reason why the apparently pointless question
of religious instruction in schools can still provoke emotion. The
chief means the Churches have always found for perpetuating and
increasing their strength is to indoctrinate the young. Gradually
since the 1944 Education Act the primacy of religious knowlege
has been eroded. There are still church schools, but the Church
has decided to put more of its resources into teacher-training
colleges to produce Anglican-minded teachers. The task of in-
doctrinating the children at this stage is clearly beyond its powers
and is fiercely opposed by a vocal ministry of rationalists, led by the
National Secular Society. There is still religious instruction of a sort
in all schools but it is far from being the Bible-reading affair it used to
be. The foundations of belief have sunk nearly out of sight. But the
moral authority that the Bible gives to codes of social conduct is
rather missed by many who do not actually believe in God: and
nothing has yet appeared to take its place.

The Christian religion is so deeply embedded in the history of the British people that though it has lost its power over people's lives and morals, it is still to be found attached to the state by law, and heavily involved in most charitable work not taken over by state welfare. The Church's relations with the state is still a pressing question, with wide repercussions and historical resonance: the Church hierarchy has only recently lost its public power and affluence. At the turn of the eighteenth century bishops were paid £40,000 a year. Even in 1906 the archbishops received an income of £15,000 p.a.—one hundred times more than the average parson. To a generation that is unconscious of any relation between spiri. al and temporal power, the sight of bishops in their antique finery can be comic or offensive; but in the eighteenth century the Anglican Church, created to save the nation from self-destruction, complacently ran the less political aspects of national endeavour. Later the Evangelical or Low Church movement came to see in the Church-State relationship a form of insurance against the catholicism of the Oxford Movement which, begun in 1833, sought to re-discover and re-enact the liturgy and ceremonial of the early Church. These two movements, high and low, have dominated church politics since that time, and their rivalry has maintained the Church-State relationship—as if parliament were an elder brother brought in by two perpetually quarrelling younger brothers. In the mid nineteenth century the High Church movement was in the ascendant, as it was again around the turn of the century. Many new churches were built in neo-Gothic style. Monasticism was reintroduced. Vestments and incense crept in. Against this the Evangelicals fought hard and with success. Their puritan pietism made common cause with any government interested in keeping people quiet, in their proper stations. The establishment has always tended to be Low Church for this reason. High Church has tended to be more radical and more subversive, less interested in this-worldly virtues, a bit racier.

Seventy years and two wars later the situation is still broadly similar, except that many fewer people go to church now. The High Church faction—Anglo-Catholicism—has seen its great days fade away, and it no longer represents a Romeward tendency. It has fed some ideas fruitfully into central Church thinking; like the liturgical movement which has led to the parish communion and the new experimental Series 2 Communion service. But the Evangelicals are nowadays much stronger. The strength of their conviction that they alone carry the gospel of Christ to the people, prevents them playing a full part in church life. An Indian evangelical recently and powerfully criticised the apartheid nature of evangelical congregations in this country. He was also startled to find how the whole religious edifice was limited by an obsessive concern with the biographical details of its Founder. But a new movement amongst evangelicals is leading this wing further towards playing a full part in Church politics.

CHURCH AND STATE

The culmination of years of arguing about Anglican Church government came on September 28, 1970, when elections took place for representatives to the new General Synod. For centuries the Church has been ruled by its convocations, which excluded the laity. So the Church Assembly was invented in 1919, which included a house of laity as well as the existing convocations of bishops and clergy, meeting three times a year—a peculiarly futile body, whose proceedings were often dominated by cranks and fanatics. In its place now come the Deanery, Diocesan and General Synods. The position is not all that different. The House of Bishops still has all the forty-three diocesan bishops, the House of Clergy consists of not more than 258 members, many fewer than before, omitting numbers of *ex officio* Church dignitaries. The House of Laity consists of about 260 members, only thirteen of whom are not elected by the voters in the dioceses. The new General Synod is meant really to run Anglican Church affairs, besides being the arbiter of matters of faith and doctrine; parliament's functions in these respects would in due course lapse. The laity would thus play a far greater part than ever before. The trouble is that Church laypeople can be more churchy even than the clergy, and much more stick-in-the-mud.

The first full session of the synod in February 1971 was faced with depressing evidence of the financial difficulties of the Church; six of the forty-three dioceses could not pay their share of the central budget, and the bishops had to propose the closure of four of the twenty-one theological colleges—partly for financial reasons, partly for lack of ordinands. The main income of the Church, apart from the offerings of the faithful, comes from its own land and capital, which are independent of the state. The Church is one of the biggest proprietors and landowners in the country, with an income in 1969–70 of £24.5 million; it owns about 200,000 acres of land, third only to the Forestry Commission and the Crown. In the past few years the team of commissioners who administer the funds, now headed by Sir Ronald Harris (a vicar's son who came up through the Treasury), have succeeded in stepping up the income by shrewd investments, including big joint developments with property tycoons on their valuable London estates (see chapter 29): and at the same time more money has been raised from worshippers through 'stewardship' campaigns. These increases have given some benefit to the 9,600 rectors and vicars—though in 1970 three-quarters of them were still receiving less than £1,500 a year (plus a free house). But the Church has huge commitments, including the upkeep of the cathedrals and Church schools all over the country; and the financial crisis is likely to limit its scope in international organisations, like the World Council of Churches.

The importance of the General Synod would be greatly increased if and when the Church of England were to be disestablished, and thus lose all control by the state. The pros and cons of disestablishment have been a recurring argument, and in December 1970, after a leisurely four-year deliberation, the Chadwick Commission reported to the Archbishops. The previous team, under Lord Howick (the former Governor of Kenya), had produced a report to which so many people objected that a new group was appointed under Professor Owen Chadwick, an ecclesiastical historian who is Master of Selwyn College, Cambridge, and brother of the Dean of Christ Church, Oxford. In mellifluous Anglican prose half the new Commission decided to take the responsibility for appointing bishops away from the prime minister and hand it over to the new synod, working through an election board. The other half decided to maintain the prime minister's traditional role. It also suggested that the bishops moved over to allow some Free Church dignitaries to sit in the House of Lords, and that parsons should be eligible to sit in the Commons.

The Commission went most of the way to the final jump of disestablishment and there got in a muddle. Some wanted to go all the way, led by Miss Valerie Pitt, an extremely articulate university lecturer. She said: 'The institutions of the Christian past are venerable, beautiful, hallowed in our own experience, but what of that? When the shape, the structure, the colour of English life is changing what we have to ask is: are they apt to present Christ to generations impatient of the appeal to tradition?' No, she said firmly. Others on the Commission included two establishment bishops (Chester and Leicester), two archdeacons, of whom one is a known radical (Edward Carpenter), a baronet, an ex-MP, two ordinary clergymen and William van Straubenzee, now junior minister for Education. The composition of the Commission determined the general trend of the report and the fact that it was far from being an unanimous one. Any appearance of unanimity would have stamped the report as either grossly superficial or the product of one unrepresentative strand of churchly attitude. Chairing an Anglican Commission is like being a coach-driver whose spirited horses galloped madly off in all directions. In the event the report was sound and charitable enough to gain wide acceptance. And disestablishment in the formal sense is likely to take place by 1990. The possibility that by then no one will care has to be noted.

Many diehards wish to see the establishment maintained because they have an ill-defined feeling that the C of E is more than a Church, it is the focus of the religious and moral feelings of people who have no intention of embroiling themselves in the costly sacrifices of becoming a fully paid-up member of an actual Church. Apparently over half the British population calls itself C of E; but only two million fulfil the minimum condition hitherto accepted for Church membership—attendance at Easter Communion. What has happened to the twenty-three million people who are Anglicans only in name? It could be that many regular or intermittent churchgoers, Anglican to their eyebrows, do not accept the Easter Communion definition; it is also true that in the words of the Report on Church and State 'there is a typical age-cycle in which people give up churchgoing in their teens and early twenties, but rejoin in their thirties and forties'. The half of the population who are fitful churchgoers have the curious effect of giving support to the diehards. Other statistics point to the declining influence of the Church. Confirmations and baptisms are going down steadily, but less so in the rural than the urban areas: thus Hereford and Worcester, with Lincolnshire and Norfolk, come out top. Urban areas with a fast-changing population, or where change is a stronger influence, like London, Liverpool and Bradford, show a much bigger decline.

The decline in congregations and the rapid extrusion of the old parish system into bigger but still parochial groupings has brought new types of clergymen and ministry into being. Parsons are coming together in groups to run a whole series of parishes not just in rural but in urban areas. For instance, in Southwark and Stepney the Bishops, Mervyn Stockwood and Trevor Huddleston, have revived the old notion of the priest-workman. Groups of dockers and industrial workers, some ordained and some lay, continue the work of carrying the Church to the people while to all intents and purposes remaining ordinary members of the working community. The development of *ad hoc* Christian groups is most significant. Whether under less radical leadership such new activities would be sanctioned and encouraged it is too early to state with confidence. But that way, it seems, the future lies.

BISHOPS

To the Press, television and much of the public, the most visible part of the Church is its bishops. When, as has happened recently, a bishop gets into trouble, news is made. There is no lack of interesting and unusual clergymen. But the tendency, not reduced during the Ramsey-Coggan regnum, has been to appoint adequate rather than inspiring men as bishops: the two important sees of Oxford and St. Albans both went in 1970 to former heads of theological colleges, Kenneth Woolcombe and Robert Runcie. The new bishop of Birmingham is the old bishop of Warrington. The new bishop of Worcester is the middle-aged dean of Windsor and chaplain to the Queen. These are safe, good and godly men, but they are not doing much to improve the image of the Church. The best recent appointment is Stuart Blanche of Liverpool, a moving spirit in a campaign for a mission to the north, to embrace all denominations including RCs.

Ian Ramsey, Bishop of Durham, is the strongest contender for Dr. Michael Ramsey's throne at Canterbury, which will probably be vacant in the next two or three years (the two men are not related). Ian Ramsey speaks in a northern accent, took three firsts at Cambridge (in mathematics, philosophy, and theology), and has written some important and intensely theological books. He is a political activist who led a deputation to Heath about the plan to sell arms to South Africa, well knowing it might prejudice his later chances of the top job. He seems less likely to be enfolded into the delightful, cosy and slightly absurd aura of the Anglican episcopate than most other putative outsiders. But whether it will be possible for him or anyone to become a national figure like William Temple or even, stretching a point, like Michael Ramsey, is rather doubtful. With his grammar-school background—uncommon among English bishops—and love of detailed planning, he is more like Wilson's or Heath's archbishop than his more lordly predecessors. He is a chairman-figure rather than a charismatic leader.

The present Archbishop of Canterbury, Michael Ramsey, came to Canterbury amidst a lot of muttering on the part of Church politicians and open suspicion in the evangelical ranks. His appearance and style on TV were against him, and he did not seem to stand for anything very contemporary. Many people would have preferred Donald Coggan who, it was felt, both knew the modern world and stood for basic Christianity as well; but he went to York. To some extent the position has reversed in the ensuing ten years. Dr. Ramsey has not, it is true, made any dramatic gestures. His flock continues to dwindle in a way which alarms statisticians more than him. But he has evolved his own style, which is distinctive and successful. It is a theological style. There is no chatting up, which his predecessor, Dr. Geoffrey Fisher (now Lord Fisher of Lambeth) was so good at. He prefers living at Canterbury to Lambeth Palace, and prefers the company of clergy and church-people to that of the more gilded world outside. But he is very alive to all public issues and has travelled a good deal, culminating in a much publicised trip round Southern Africa in November 1970. Many criticised his decision to go, many others felt his views on apartheid were predictable and unhelpful; the congregations he attracted were small by African standards—his last rally being attended by about five thousand people. But it was a courageous visit, which left little doubt as to where Ramsey stood. While not setting out to be a world figure or spokesman, he does represent the mind and spirit of the Church, conscious of its troubled history, conscious of the contrary drives towards worldly power on the one hand and mass evangelism on the other. Dr. Coggan, on the other hand, seems to be dealing with issues which were of real importance twenty years ago, but are now mostly over and done with. A Biblical scholar of great distinction, his most important work has been connected with the New English Bible whose publication in 1970 was a big event.

The archbishop's dilemma in Africa—which contains a large proportion of the worldwide Anglican flock—came to a head in

1970. The British Council of Churches nearly, but not quite, joined with the World Council of Churches to back a resolution supporting freedom fighters in South Africa, with money which could be used to buy arms and explosives. 'Only if the Church is, and is seen to be, on the side of the revolution in Southern Africa, suffering and sharing in the guilt of spilt blood, can the Church then, from within the situation, judge the revolution.' Canterbury was against the decision but put the case very fairly. The emotive presentation of the issue by the opposition at home suggested that pious Church people would be dropping into the plate their shillings which would be immediately employed to blow up harmless South African whites.

The climax to the world role of the archbishop comes when he presides, every ten years, over the Lambeth Conference. The Church of England is pre-eminent but heavily outnumbered—the number of American bishops alone is twice the number of English. The last conference was held in 1968: five hundred bishops gathered at Lambeth, representing nineteen provinces (England has two), with one-sixth of the bishops coming from non-European stock. Fifty observers from other Churches took part in the discussions, which were dealt with in thirty-three sub-committees. What emerged from these discussions seems to have been rather woofly: but the Archbishop of Canterbury, with his remarkable memory for names and faces, chaired the proceedings with great dignity and sense of personal *rapport*.

CHURCH OF SCOTLAND

In remarkable contrast to the Church of England is its neighbour the Church of Scotland: the co-existence of these two disparate bodies is one of the oddest features of the kingdom. When the Queen goes to Edinburgh every year she becomes suddenly Scottish, and attends a Church which is Calvinist, Presbyterian, cool about bishops and unrelentingly hostile to the Pope. Every year the Church of Scotland holds its General Assembly, when about 1,400 commissioners gather to debate Scottish and world affairs. The membership is impressive: 1.2 million Scotsmen are communicant members, out of three and a half million adults—compared to only two million communicants in the Church of England. The Assembly comes near to taking the place of a Scottish parliament, and is often regarded

as the 'Voice of Scotland': the splendour which surrounds
Assembly Week, some Scotsmen suggest, is a substitute for the
gap left by the departure of a Scots king and a Scots parliament. The General Assembly is much more politically outspoken
than the Convocations or Church Assembly in England, and it
does not confine itself to Scottish affairs. Their most angry debates
in recent years have been over Africa—and many Presbyterian
ministers have emerged to champion African rights. The most
persistent of them has been the Rev. Lord Macleod of Fuinary,
a former Moderator who was the founder of the Iona Community.

OTHER CHURCHES

Apart from the erosion of the Church-State relationship, the
most important change in the British Churches in the last two
decades has been the growth of the ecumenical movement, towards unity between the Churches—particularly between the
Anglicans and Methodists. In 1968 proposals for a full merger
were put before the two Churches: the Methodists voted with the
necessary majority in favour, but the Anglican Church Assembly
produced a simple majority in favour, which was not enough.
This may reflect the fact that Methodism is losing members faster
than Anglicans and has an acuter problem over the numbers of
ministers: Methodist membership dwindled from a million in 1960
to 760,000 in 1970 and ordained clergy from 5,003 to 4,344 in the
same period, whereas the full-time Church of England clergy
went up by 25, to 15,778. At Sunday School level Methodism
is declining at an alarming rate, though no more so than the
Church of England; but in universities it is still very active.
Less cumbersome, and less fraught with ancient ties and ancient
hatreds, Methodism is nonetheless considerably split over
whether it ought to be merged in the Church of England, not just
because of organisation and liturgy but because of such sensitive
subjects as teetotalism.

Methodist ministers, like those of other free Churches, are paid
for almost entirely by legacies and by their own congregations.
(If the C of E clergy had to rely on *their* faithful they would be in
pretty poor shape.) Overseas, particularly in America, the
Methodists are a very powerful Church, dwarfing the Anglican
equivalent there—the Episcopalian Church. Methodism is not a
parish system but is based on circuits, linked to districts and

associated with their annual conference. The local minister, with his groups of faithful, is much more at the beck and call of his superior than is the Anglican parson, but the local congregations have more real autonomy than an ordinary parish.

Methodism has had an important influence on British political attitudes: Liberalism, particularly in the north, has strong nonconformist roots, and the Labour Party, as Morgan Phillips once said, owes more to Methodism than Marxism. Many Labour men, including Harold Wilson, come from a nonconformist background; Wilson married in Mansfield College (Congregationalist) chapel; George Thomas, the former Secretary of State for Wales, is the most active Methodist in the Commons. Lord Rank, the president of the Rank Organisation, is the most prominent Methodist in business: the most vocal of the Methodists is Donald Soper, the soap-box orator now elevated to the House of Lords. But there is no strong nonconformist political lobby, and no real Methodist aristocracy: Methodist families, once they become prosperous, have tended to turn to Anglicanism: 'The coach and pair,' says the old Victorian saw, 'does not pass the church door for more than two generations.'

The Presbyterians and Congregationalists are planning their own merger, which is likely to take place without a significant public fanfare. Their deliberations are couched in low-tension prose: 'We would certainly not wish to make unreal claims for our proposed union. It will not of itself make a breakthrough to effective mission.' It will take place in 1972, barring accidents, and will be called 'United Reformed Church': many unions of congregations have already taken place at local levels. The United Reformed Church may put a spoke in the wheel of the ongoing Methodist-Anglican dialogue, because Anglicanism is historically Catholic as well as Protestant and might not easily join an all-Protestant body. Many of its members are more interested in a move towards the Vatican than a humdrum marriage to the girl next door.

Outside any likely merger are the British Baptists, a tiny part of the huge world-wide Baptist Church. They had 274,871 members in 3,264 churches in the British Isles in 1969—showing a gradual decline in numerical strength. Apart from London, their strongest area is Lancashire and Yorkshire. More solid and unmoving than Congregationalists or Presbyterians or Methodists, they are nonetheless a still important social factor, resistant to swift change and extremely anti-permissive. And the Baptists, too, are having doubts about their rigidity: 'This loosely-knit body,' says the annual report of the Baptist Union for 1970, 'can easily be disrupted; but by its very lack of rigidity, by its flexibility, it is perhaps in a better position than many other Church bodies to experiment and to adapt its life and structure to meet the needs of the hour. The Union is an instrument in the hands of God, or it is nothing. It is not as effective an instrument as it might be. Perhaps it has been too conscious of its own identity and too anxious about its own solidarity and too little aware of its divine destiny.'

'Fall out the RCs and Jews,' used to be the cry of the sergeant-major. Roman Catholics have, since the Reformation, been discriminated against and still have the worst of both worlds politically: their priests are unable to stand for parliament but unlike the C of E, none of their hierarchy may sit in the Lords. Now termed Britain's powerful minority they are, in fact, deeply split on religious matters, between the conservatives and the radicals. Cardinal Heenan of Westminster tries to hold the middle and at the same time to defend the Pope's archaic views on birth control in terms which allegedly make theological sense. But some priests, and many laymen, are outspokenly critical. The Mass is now normally said in English which takes away some of the magic. Vocations to the priesthood are falling off. One of the best English theologians, Charles Davis, made news when he married and left the priesthood. Others have followed his example, and the whole picture is an open-ended one. There are still some six million Catholics in the country, and, oddly, there are more radical movements in the Catholic Church than the Church of England; there are even those who believe that women priests will be introduced into Catholicism, that stronghold of male domination, before Anglicanism.

Relations between Catholics and Anglicans are about as cordial and detached as between Britain and America. The Archbishop and the Cardinal meet and have services together, but it is doubtful if they have much in common. Matters were not helped when in the summer of 1970 forty English martyrs of Elizabethan times were canonised by the Pope in St. Peter's. Cardinal John Heenan of Westminster is a strong man, excellent on television, usually good with his clergy, unyielding on doctrine, concerned mainly, and rightly, with the souls of his people. In this concern education plays a very large and increasingly controversial part.

Socially the discrimination against Catholics still continues residually in Scotland, some of whose institutions still feel about Catholics as some golf clubs do about blacks and Jews. But lower down the scale, particularly in the trade unions, the infiltration and assimilation is total. Catholics are well represented in most of the important regions of the British power-structure, particularly in communications (Charles Curran of the BBC, William Rees-Mogg of *The Times*, Paul Johnson, ex-editor of the *New Statesman*). In parliament the Catholics increased their number of members in 1970 from thirty to thirty-seven—the highest total since the Irish Nationalists departed more than half a century ago. Thirteen of them are Conservatives, including three members of the government—Lord Windlesham, David Brand and Sir Peter Rawlinson, whose presence as Attorney-General raises the constitutional question of whether there could be a Catholic Lord Chancellor, to walk on Cranmer's grave. Twenty-two are Labour MPs, including three ex-ministers (Shirley Williams, Maurice Foley and Bob Mellish) and one new member called Stanley Cohen. Catholics are often *said* to be specially keen on Britain joining the common market, and members like St. John Stevas and Shirley Williams are steadfast Europeans; but others, like Hugh Fraser and Anthony Fell, are equally determined opponents. There is no organised Catholic lobby in parliament, and no unanimity of view.

In Ulster, where the horror of Rome is an ancestral memory of startling power, anti-popery slogans can still be believed and acted on in Belfast. The Protestants have gained advantages in housing and status which the Catholics deeply resent. Both sides look to Westminster to back their *ex parte* views. The Ulster upper class and lower middle class make common cause against what is thought to be the fecklessness and foreign orientation of the Catholic minority. It is not a pleasant alliance, which is why Bernadette Devlin initially commanded so much sympathy.

The Jews are a much smaller minority, about one per cent of the British population. In Jewry the same struggle between conservatives and radicals is taking place as in other Churches; most rich and successful Jews tend to be ecclesiastically conservative, but a younger generation of theologians is seeking to remove some of the fundamentalism with so far only modest results. There are now more separate Jewish schools and some very self-contained Jewish communities. But there is a new sense of Jewish integration and security, which may be summed up by the growing number of Jewish members of parliament; thirty-nine, a record number, were elected in 1966, in 1970 there was one fewer, but a striking shift took place towards the Tories, with eight Tory MPs compared to two in the earlier parliament. They included one member of the cabinet, Sir Keith Joseph (the first since Hore-Belisha, and in a much more secure position); one member of the Monday Club, the South African Harold Soref; and the president of the Jewish Board of Deputies, Michael Fidler (the previous president, now Lord Janner, was a Labour MP).

FRINGE RELIGIONS

What the young are obviously telling us is we want beards, we want massive costumes and vestments for everybody. We do not want any of this simple, plain individual stuff.

Marshall McLuhan.

The existing Church institutions all show a significant decline in membership. But if the Churches themselves seem to be in retreat, the general interest in religion is not. In so woolly an area generalisations are deeply suspect: but students and other young people, while they identify organised religion with the legalism and greed of the old, are keenly concerned on the one hand with social injustice and what to do about it, and on the other with the exploration of areas of experience denied or ignored by their empirical elders but cognate to religious experience. In one area anarchic social helpers find themselves working alongside Christian teams, in others (in pop music, pop art or the use or misuse of drugs), there is a common meeting ground which can only be called religious. Some Anglicans are prepared to be hopeful about this movement of the young (if you can't beat 'em, take 'em over): 'It is very evident,' said the anonymous author of *Crockford's* preface (published in March, 1971), 'that the disenchantment with the Church felt by many young people is by no means a repudiation of the Christian religion, and that some of the apparent excesses of the young represent a search for that which Christianity offers. It should be remembered that in the long history of mankind religion and sex have been closely intertwined as forces in human nature and that the present public preoccupation with sex may also be part of a search for God. A great problem for the Church is to discover the right response for these movements. There are still some of the clergy and many more of the laity who dismiss them with impatience and horror, many more who regard them with distressed, uncomprehending bewilderment.'

The whole search for a richer and more meaningful life has a religious tinge to it. It is a long way from the organised religion we know, perhaps too far. It brings to the fore the basic dichotomy of all organised religion—the urge to pietism and conformity on the one hand, and towards experience and exaltation on the other. In recent centuries the first urge has been the conditioning factor in the religious life of Northern Europe. Its partial collapse may open up new opportunities for religion's other aspect. 'Many people resort instantly to the occult, to ESP and every form of hidden awareness,' says Marshall McLuhan, 'in answer to this new surround of electric consciousness. And so we live, in the vulgar sense, in an extremely religious age.'

10

Aristocracies

It is not true that England is governed by an aristocracy in the common acceptation of that term. England is governed by an aristocratic principle. The aristocracy of England absorbs all aristocracies, and receives every man in every order and every class who defers to the principle of our society, which is to aspire and to excel.

Disraeli.

ON the surface at least the old English aristocracy, which has survived so many upheavals, is now at last losing its hold on politics and government, and its privileged place in the educational system. The top men in the Heath government owe less to hereditary advantages than Wilson's team, and far less than the grandees of Macmillan's cabinet. The old aristocratic road to political power, the comfortable path through Eton and Christ Church, up which Sir Alec Douglas-Home and Lord Hailsham both trotted, is now less certain to lead to the top: and in other fields of hereditary privilege—in banking, stockbroking or diplomacy—there have been incursions from proletarians, as we see in later chapters. Aristocrats nowadays like to cultivate an impression of being a persecuted minority, forced out of power by prejudices against loud fruity voices or tall languid shapes. But British aristocrats have always shown a much greater ability to survive and exploit new situations than their continental equivalents; and they have a habit of going underground and popping up again in unexpected places.

They have survived better than most, partly because they have never been very exclusive, and have always been ready to admit outsider sons-in-law, provided only that they were rich. There has never been a nobility as in pre-revolutionary France, where a hundred thousand aristocrats had a separate, privileged life of their own. By continental standards, the English aristocracy is not really aristocratic at all, and its history has been provisional and mercenary. Only two families, the Ardens and the Berkeleys, can be traced with certainty to before the Norman Conquest. A few aristocratic families such as the Giffards and Ferrers came over with William the Conqueror: but a large number of titles—including all the dukedoms—were killed off in the Wars of the Roses. 'Where is Bohun? Where's Mowbray? Where's Mortimer? And nay, which is more, and most of all, where is Plantagenet? They are entombed in the urns and sepulchres of mortality.'[1] A batch of surviving peers stem from the dissolution of the monasteries in 1533, which founded the persistent fortunes of the Dukes of Bedford and Devonshire and the Marquesses of Bath. But the numbers of the peerage were doubled by James I and Charles I, who made seventy-two peers in twenty-six years: King James, needing the money, charged £10,000 for a barony. Another large increase came with the younger Pitt, and the new aristocrats soon became merged with the old. In the nineteenth century scores of politicians, bankers, and merchants became peers, and a vast increase came with Lloyd George, who raised over three million pounds for the Liberal Party by the sale of peerages. Another boom—without the political strings—came after the last war under Attlee, who made ninety-eight in six years, and continued under Macmillan and Douglas-Home. A new spate, of life peers only, came with Harold Wilson's government (see Chapter 1).

While the aristocracy was being broadened through new titles, peers introduced new blood to their families by marrying heiresses. Long before death duties, gambling, drinking and building had reduced many noble fortunes, which could only be revived by marrying money. And the British aristocracy kept itself rich by the ruthless custom of primogeniture, by which the estate and the title passed only to the eldest son, and other sons had to make their own way in the army, the Church or business.

The British aristocracy is in any case far from being synonymous with the peerage, and outside the world of lords and honourables there are thousands of families who have continued for centuries, living prosperously in the country—loosely known as 'the gentry': there are 2,840 pages of them in *Burke's Landed Gentry*. There is also

[1] Lord Justice Crewe, speech to the House of Lords, 1626.

the curious title of baronet—a kind of hereditary knight—invented by King James I to pay for the settlement of Ulster, 'so that the King's wants might be relieved out of the vanities and ambitions of the gentry'. There are now about 1,500—nearly twice the size of the peerage—including no fewer than 12 Tory MPs: but their future seems shaky: the Labour government of 1964–70 stopped making new ones—even Lord Mayors of London, who used to be given baronetcies as of right—and the Conservatives have not revived them.

The tangible advantages of a title are very few. A peer can claim six-and-a-half guineas for every day he signs in at the House of Lords, and receives Hansard free every day: he can let everyone know he is a peer by having a badge on his car saying 'House of Lords Motoring Club'. Some young peers like to claim that a title is a handicap, which leads others to expect them to be very rich, and which labels them as amateurs in a professional age. But for anyone in occupations where social prestige is important, a title properly deployed is still invaluable, particularly in showmanship and salesmanship; the eighth Marquess of Hertford and the fourth Earl of Kimberley each runs a public relations firm, and the rival owners of stately homes—the Duke of Bedford, the Marquess of Bath and Lord Montagu of Beaulieu—have taken over from circus-owners and fairground operators as master-impresarios. In the sixties, with the great Beatle boom and the craze for 'Swinging London', the old aristocratic style of understatement, old clothes and plummy voices seemed to be threatened by the vogue for dandyism and flat Liverpool accents; but the aristocracy proved quite able to adapt itself to that, too, and to produce dandy peers, like the Earls of Snowdon and Lichfield, who could bridge the two worlds. The more confused the social structure in Britain becomes, the more attractive, it seems, is the status-symbol of a title. It is often argued that snobbery—the 'pox Britannica' as it has been called—is most rife when classes are confused. 'Snobbery belongs rather to the situation where one class melts imperceptibly into another,' says Sir Anthony Wagner, the Garter King of Arms, 'and where fairly free movement from one into another is possible.'

Ever since the British aristocracy began to lose its territorial power and extreme wealth, its influence has rested on effective communications and public relations, on a confidence trick based on traditional English snobbery or deference. Much of this it retains. The network of common schools, colleges or regiments, of country-house weekends and dinner parties still provides an effective bush-telegraph, a means of quick brokerage, of mutual support and contacts. Even though the amateur has been in decline and the professional in the ascendant, there is still scope for the people who can bridge the different worlds; indeed in some ways the more specialised the professions, the more scope for shrewd amateurs to operate between them, for the self-made specialists are often narrow in their experience, without contacts in other professions. It is thus that the battle (see Chapter 26) between the old merchant bankers and the new money managers of insurance companies and pension funds has a special inwardness. The new managers are responsible for many more millions, and are beginning to flex their financial muscles: but the old bankers still have their social network, which enables them to find the directors and managers to put on to the boards, and to know through international gossip and social contacts where big deals can be put through. As Britain becomes more involved in European finance, so the cosmopolitan background and foreign languages of the aristocratic bankers provides new secret weapons.

The drawing rooms of 'society' are less vibrant with political gossip than they were in the Macmillan era: Geoffrey Rippon may enjoy dancing at Annabel's, Lord Jellicoe may enjoy a joke at the Weidenfelds', but most of the Heath-type Conservatives are not at ease in frivolous company. Heath, Walker or Joseph are not men for badinage or small-talk, and there has been almost a reversal of the traditional social pattern of Tory and Labour. It is the Labour ex-ministers who (even apart from their new-found leisure) are the drawing-room men, who love long dinners, large parties and weekend invitations. Their donnish repartee fits easily with the old Whiggish tradition: Harold Lever, the millionaire ex-Labour minister, moves comfortably between the worlds of the rich and the clever.

In spite of the austerity of the new Tory regime, the salons and hostesses are not without influence: they keep their links with the world of communications—of the Press, television, books—which are themselves large industries and the source of influence over others. The drawing-rooms of Lady Hartwell, Mrs. Ian Fleming or Fleur Cowles remain meeting-places where left and right, businessmen and intellectuals, politicians and artists converge; the social scope of Lady Antonia Fraser is enhanced by the convergence of two large Catholic families, the Tory Lovats and the Labour Pakenhams, with tentacles in nearly every profession: when fully mobilised, as for the Biafra crusade, they can muster a formidable polemical army. The lavish world of the publisher Sir George Weidenfeld, the most tireless of London hosts, is predominantly left-wing, providing a special solace to Labour ex-ministers; but it cuts a broad swathe, ranging from Marks and Spencer aristocracy to Upper Bohemia, with a few connecting paths to New Tories.

There are of course many other aristocracies in Britain apart from the old nobility; and intellectuals and scientific families have intermarried into their own kind over generations without overlapping with the landed aristocracy. Lord Annan has traced the development of interlocking cousinhoods from the early nineteenth century, when the Clapham evangelicals, the Quakers and the Unitarians were drawn together by philanthropy and liberalism, married each other's daughters, and established a tradition of plain living and high thinking which (though based on inherited wealth) was totally separate from that of the landed aristocracy. They brought up their children in a world of books, competitiveness and social conscience, but without much concern for art: 'Their comfortable ugly houses, in Kensington, Bayswater and North Oxford, rambling untidy, full of glory-holes and massive furnishings and staffed by two or three despairing servants, were dedicated to utility, not beauty.'[1] The influence of such families, centring round Cambridge and Oxford, nearly all connected in some way by marriage, has extended through the twentieth century; Stracheys, Wedgwoods, Trevelyans, Arnolds, Forsters, Keyneses, Stephenses, Vaughans, and Butlers crop up not only as professors and masters of colleges, but as reformers and public servants—particularly in India where the intellectual tradition merged with administration. The endogamy and self-containment has been most evident among scientists, partly no doubt because no one else can understand what they are talking about; Darwins, Huxleys, Hodgkins, Thomsons, Barlows and Haldanes have provided a long line of eminent men, inter-related to each other. The expansion of institutions in the late nineteenth century gave many of these families an opportunity to dominate large areas of administration; and while remaining, for the most

[1] Noel Annan: 'The Intellectual Aristocracy', in *Studies in Social History*, a Tribute to G. M. Trevelyan, Longmans 1955, p. 251.

part, interested in reform, they became very much an establishment of their own. As Annan describes them:

> The influence of these families may partly explain a paradox which has puzzled European and American observers of English life: the paradox of an intelligentsia which appears to conform rather than rebel against the rest of society. The proclivity to criticise, of course, exists; Matthew Arnold flicked Victorian self-confidence with his irony, and in recent years notable members of these families were among the leaders of the ethical revolution which took place in the decades immediately before and after the first world war. But the pro-consular tradition and the English habit of working through established institutions and modifying them to meet social needs only when such needs are proven are traits strongly exhibited by the intelligentsia of this country. Here is an aristocracy, secure, established and, like the rest of English society, accustomed to responsible and judicious utterance and sceptical of iconoclastic speculation.

This close-knit intellectual aristocracy is now much less pervasive; the expansion of education, which they themselves did much to encourage with reforms like the Forster act of 1870 and the Butler act of 1944, has helped to break their monopoly. Oxford and Cambridge are no longer influenced by a handful of families, and it is no longer easy for a dominant don, like A. L. Smith, the Edwardian Master of Balliol, to establish a dynasty by marrying off his daughters to the cleverest undergraduates. The Royal Society is full of self-made men, even though it includes two Huxleys, and its president is a Hodgkin; and science is now a large avenue of social mobility.

The old academic families are now less confidently separate from other worlds. In Macmillan's government there were two notable representatives of the intellectual aristocracy, Macmillan himself and R. A. Butler; but both had married into very different worlds— the Devonshires and the Courtaulds—and adopted some of their values. Wilson's government, a much more academic one, owed something to intellectual families: Anthony Crosland, the son of a low-church senior civil servant; Lord Longford, a mixture of the North Oxford tradition with the Anglo-Irish ascendancy; Lord Kennet (alias Wayland Young) from a family of public servants; Richard Crossman, the son of a judge and a Quaker mother; Shirley Williams, the daughter of Professor Catlin and the novelist Vera Brittain. But Heath's government owes little to academic dynasties; and only among the junior members like Julian Amery and his brother-in-law Maurice Macmillan, (from the old firm), are there relics of the high bookish tradition.

With the decline of its religious basis, the intellectual aristocracy is now less confidently separate, less dedicated to plain living, more inclined to intermarry with the old, or philistine aristocracy (though the frontiers are now much less easy to draw). Intellectual families have come more to terms with the style of the hard-core aristocracy, and this *rapprochement* is indicated by their great reluctance to refuse honours, knighthoods and peerages.

PLUTOCRACY

In terms of sheer wealth, the old aristocracy can still hold its own; most of the dukes are millionaires, and many old families, like the Westminsters, the Derbys and the Devonshires, are among the richest in the country. But in the post-war decades, many huge new fortunes have eclipsed the old ones. The long boom from the mid-fifties gave great scope for new fortunes in share-dealings and take-overs. Charles Clore and Sir Isaac Wolfson made the first big take-over fortunes: each of them must have made over £50 million. The Moore Brothers still control Littlewood Football Pools, a private company whose value is thought to be about £100 million. Sir Jack Cohen, who built up the Tesco supermarkets, has shares—with those of his sons-in-law, Herman Kreitman and Leslie Porter—worth about £40 million. The biggest scope for quick new fortunes has been in property, which had made at least a hundred men millionaires by 1967 (see Chapter 29). Some of them, like Sir Harold Samuel and Sir Max Rayne, have become well-known benefactors; others like Harry Hyams, have hidden in secrecy. The most unobtrusive of all the new multi-millionaires is Sir Godfrey Mitchell, the chairman of Wimpey's construction company, which also has a half-share in Hyams' property company; Sir Godfrey's charitable and family trusts, which control Wimpey's, are worth about £55 million.

In the six years of Harold Wilson's Labour government, there was little sign of the gap narrowing between the very rich and the very poor; and the old radical concern about inequality, which had been so evident in the early part of the century, was lost in the mass of considerations about incentives, international competition, and the safety of sterling. The whole machinery of the welfare state, and the universalist doctrine that lay behind it, seemed to be benefiting the middle-classes more than the poor; and the battles against inflation underlined the different attitudes to the poor and the rich. A demand for £2 a week for a bus-driver was an inflationary menace; while a request for £20 a week for a senior civil servant was an essential incentive.

Incomes in Britain show a large concentration of people in the middle regions; in 1968 more than half the total wage-earning population was earning between £800 and £1,500 a year before tax (whereas eight years before most people were earning between £300 and £600 a year). But at the top end of the scale the numbers of people earning more than £20,000 a year nearly tripled in the eight years since 1960, and the numbers earning more than £5,000 have nearly quadrupled—an increase far ahead of the effects of inflation. The British tax authorities (they assure me) are very discreet about their clients: they do not, as the Americans do, publish the names of the largest salary-earners; nor do they, like the Australians, record the most notable tax-defaulters. But since the new regulations about publishing directors' salaries came into force in 1967, we have had a clearer idea of individual incomes (see Chapter 33). This table from the Inland Revenue shows the distribution of incomes by size, before tax, in the tax year 1967–8.[1]

Annual Income Before Tax	1967—68	1959—60
More than £20,000	6,000	2,200
£10,000—20,000	34,000	10,300
£5,000—10,000	152,000	43,500
£3,000—5,000	367,000	98,000
£2,000—3,000	1,028,000	161,000
£1,500—2,000	2,841,000	235,000
£1,000—1,500	6,475,000	745,000
£800—1,000	3,134,000	1,330,000
£700—800	1,543,000	1,470,000
£600—700	1,517,000	2,140,000
£500—600	1,606,000	2,800,000
£400—500	1,516,000	3,320,000
£300—400	1,312,000	3,280,000
£250—300	272,000	1,061,000
£200—250	—	990,000

It is in the distribution of *capital* that the inequalities of Britain are glaring—more glaring, for instance, than in the United States. There have been many attempts to calculate the ownership

[1] From *Annual Statistics* of the Board of the Inland Revenue, 1970.

of wealth; in 1961 two statisticians, Lydall and Tipping, calculated that the top one per cent of British adults owned 43 per cent
of the total net capital, whereas in America (in 1954) the top one
per cent owned only 24 per cent of personal wealth. In 1968 Oliver
Stutchbury, the Labour fund-raising expert reckoned that less than
half-a-million people owned 60 per cent of investment income.
One estimate of the ownership of wealth is given by the Inland
Revenue statistics (see opposite) based on figures from death
duties; and these—like the figures for incomes—show a large
increase in the top groups. Between 1960 and 1968 the numbers
of people with more than £200,000 went up from 7,000 to 20,000;
in 1968 there were 180,000 people owning more than £50,000,
compared to five million owning less than £1,000.

The measurement of individual wealth remains very difficult
to determine partly because, to avoid taxation, rich men dis-
seminate their capital through their families. Roy Jenkins' 1968
budget, by taxing children's incomes, did something to restrict
this family wealth; but this was reversed by the Barber budget
of 1971, which allowed both children and wives to have their
incomes taxed separately. There always remains the rich man's
greatest friend—which looms so large in the minds of the accountants—the Discretionary Trust. And the wealth of very rich
families can be scattered in 'tax havens', like the Channel Islands,
the Isle of Man or the Bahamas, which are out of reach of the
Inland Revenue. The family has a special fiscal importance as
a unit because it does not die, and therefore its money never
emerges into the open, to be counted, taxed and recorded; the
great family trusts are like underground rivers in barren countryside, the only signs of whose existence are the green fields they
make fertile in unexpected places.

The old rich have long ago acquired the posture of persecution,
however well they are doing, of screaming before they are
touched. Many of them have increased their wealth massively
without any difficulty—simply by sitting on what they already
have; for their favourite commodities—land, old houses, old
masters, furniture, silver—have all shown spectacular increases in
value as their scarcity becomes greater and the market becomes
larger; the big auction-rooms, Christie's and Sotheby's, have
become sophisticated stock exchanges, making the collections of
the old rich easily marketable both as status-symbols and as hedges
against inflation for the new rich.

Estimated Total Net Weath by Size in Great Britain

Wealth	Numbers of People 1968	Total (thousand millions)	Numbers of People 1960	Total (thousand millions)
Over £200,000	20,000	7·8	7,000	3·7
£100,000—200,000	40,000	5·4	20,000	3·0
£50,000—100,000	121,000	8·1	64,000	4·4
£25,000—50,000	326,000	11·2	170,000	5·9
£20,000—25,000	148,000	3·5	87,000	2·0
£15,000—20,000	288,000	5·1	145,000	2·5
£10,000—15,000	598,000	7·4	314,000	3·9
£5,000—10,000	2,191,000	15·6	958,000	7·0
£3,000—5,000	2,918,000	11·4	1,342,000	5·2
£1,000—3,000	5,415,000	9·7	5,817,000	10·1
£0—1,000	5,190,000	2·8	9,003,000	3·9
Under £5,000	13,523,000	23·9	16,162,000	19·2
Over £5,000	3,732,000	64·1	1,765,000	32·4
Total	17,255,000	88·0	17,927,000	51·6

The advantages of large capital or large salaries are of course diminished by taxation; according to the Inland Revenue, in 1967–8 only 1,000 people were earning more than £10,000 a year after tax. Incomes in Britain after tax, even after the Barber budget, are a good deal more evenly distributed than in most continental countries; higher incomes are taxed up to seventy-five per cent, while in France, Germany or Italy they are not taxed beyond fifty-five per cent. But the British figures for top incomes after tax are misleading; for rich men can still greatly benefit from tax relief on mortgages or pensions, from their expense accounts, and above all from capital gains.

The boom in quarter-millionaires and in high incomes after several years of socialist government provoked a good deal of bitter comment: thus Professor John Vaizey, one of the disillusioned, writing in 1969: 'The Labour government, by inflating capital values, by encouraging mergers, by handing out lavish subsidies to private business, by legislation to keep down wages, by making tax laws so complicated that well-paid private lawyers are bound to beat poorly paid civil servants, by eroding welfare benefits through price rises—by all these means (to mention only a few) it has made the rich more secure and the poor less secure.'[1] Many economists now believe that, so long as most property is in private hands, the pressure towards inequality is bound to continue; John Hughes, one left-wing investigator of the effects of Labour's policies, concluded in 1968 that 'although some measures have aided particular low-income groups, the main drive of the system towards inequality has been heavily reinforced'.[2]

ARISTOCRACY AND AMBITION

Nobility of birth commonly abateth industry.
Francis Bacon.

There have always been very separate pockets of rich men who have had little to do with national politics or London society; like the industrial aristocracies of Yorkshire and Lancashire, where sons and grandsons can still remain in the same business without ambition for politics or cosmopolitan fame; or the London Jewish millionaires with mansions in Bishops Avenue or Winnington Road, whose lives overlap very little with the freeholders of Westminster or Kensington. But it has been the special mark of the old British aristocracy that, in the national context, it has maintained the impression of being the *only* aristocracy—keeping its edge over the urban rich or the mercantile rich. The world of *The Tatler*, of hunt balls, deb dances, race meetings and guards officers' weddings still carries on as if nothing else much mattered. It was significant that when Lord Thomson launched a modernised version of *The Tatler*, called *London Life*, to cater for the new café society, it was a complete flop, and simply led to someone else reviving the old *Tatler*. In spite of, or because of, the great social changes of the post-war decades, there was still no real substitute for the aristocratic ideal, with its associations with land ownership, country sports and amateurism.

It can be presented as either a liability or an asset. On the one hand the transformation of a thrusting businessman into a country gentleman, a knight or a peer, can be represented as a stabilising factor in an industrial society, and an important escape route from a purely commercial value-system: the new Sir or Lord becomes part of the traditional landscape, and may even (like Lord

[1] John Vaizey: 'The Mystery of Money', *The Listener*, 5.6.69.
[2] John Hughes: 'Why the Gap between Rich and Poor is Widening', *New Statesman*, November 8, 1968.

Thomson) be persuaded to part with much of his money. The ideal of the gentleman, with its feudal or pre-industrial nostalgia, may be some kind of counterweight to materialism, and it provides a form of ritual for leisure. Self-made millionaires are apt to be a social problem; it is not easy to convert money into prestige or social responsibility, and in America the transition often has to be manipulated by public-relations men, arranging gifts to art galleries or centres of culture. The British aristocratic system (it can be argued) is a simpler and time-honoured machinery for the conversion of money into prestige, through the old ladder of honours, culminating with the House of Lords; the disrupting energy of the new rich is thus channelled into the harmless waters of the peerage. This is one justification for the House of Lords—that it buys off alienation and discontent, and confuses the new rich with the old, to the convenience of both.

But what can serve as a stabiliser for the first generation of money-makers can all too easily serve as a too-comfortable cushion for their children and grandchildren, who are able to enjoy the prestige of acceptable wealth without any sense of involvement with its source. The old lure of the country estate has often been blamed for the decline of British industry over the last century, for the hopelessness of its management and the failure of its technology: the owners and controllers of industry, it is held, lost their interest in competition and innovation, in favour of country sports, aristocratic prestige and a coddled parasitic existence: they moved from the 'furnace to the field'.[1] This aristocratic embrace cannot be held altogether to blame, if only because industrialists in many crucial sectors, in the Midlands or the North, never came into contact with the aristocracy; there are also convincing economic explanations for the decline, and the forsaking of trade may have been as much a consequence of the decline as a cause of it.[2] But the aristocratic ideal as fostered by families and by the public schools, has certainly made it harder for new British middle-class generations to come to terms with the harsh facts of Britain's economic situation. The heritage of great inherited wealth, and the escape-routes it provides, makes it harder to induce realism. Ted Heath and his colleagues in the

[1] See D. H. Aldcroft: 'The Entrepreneur and the British Economy'. *Economic History Review*, August 1964, p. 129.
[2] See Eric Hobsbawm: *Industry and Empire*. Weidenfeld and Nicholson 1968, p. 155.

unaristocratic Tory cabinet have talked a good deal about the need to get back to the more competitive atmosphere of Victorian times, and have used this to justify the tax concessions, as 'incentives' to new managers and entrepreneurs. But most of the pressure for 'incentives' has come from the already rich, who simply want to be richer; and the concessions will favour them far more than they are likely to encourage the newcomers.

PART

THREE

———

Government

11

Monarchy

No one has come up with a better solution.
Prince Philip, November 1969.

In a dictatorship the power and the glory belong to the same person. In England the real power belongs to unprepossessing men in bowler hats: the creature who rides in a gilded coach behind soldiers in steel breast-plates is really a waxwork. It is at any rate possible that while this division of functions exists a Hitler or a Stalin cannot come to power.
George Orwell, 1944.

THE elaborate pretence that the Queen is the real ruler of Britain still decorates the machinery of British government. Every Royal Commission begins with the Queen saying, 'Greeting!' to her trusty well-beloved servants; 'Now Know Ye that We, reposing great trust and confidence in your knowledge and ability . . .'. Every Act begins with the words: 'Be it enacted by the Queen most Excellent Majesty, by and with the advice and consent of the Lords Spiritual and Temporal, and Commons, in this present Parliament assembled . . .'. Politicians, particularly when harassed, like to refer to Her Majesty's government in tones of special reverence, as if it was nothing to do with *them*. The charade reaches its climax in the state opening of parliament each year, when the Queen sits on her throne in the House of Lords, surrounded by her peers, and summons the Commons to hear the Queen's Speech, written by the Prime Minister, in which she solemnly talks about 'my government', as if presenting her own ideas. This grand deception, it is often argued, serves an important psycho-political purpose as a ritual for unification and continuity: after a ferocious general election and a painful change of government, the two leaders are compelled to walk side-by-side down the aisle, followed by the rival ministers and ex-ministers, as loyal subjects of her majesty. But the pretence does nothing to illuminate or explain the processes of a modern democracy.

Much of the intellectual justification of the deception still stems from Walter Bagehot, who analysed British government (1865) at a time when the constitutional monarchy was settling into shape. It was one of his central arguments that government could be divided into the 'dignified' and the 'efficient' parts, and that the monarchy was in the centre of the dignified part. He saw Britain as a 'disguised republic', in which constitutional royalty was a pageant, behind which the real business of government could more easily proceed: 'The apparent rulers of the English nation are like the most imposing personages of a splendid procession; it is by them the mob are influenced: it is they whom the spectators cheer. The real rulers are secreted in second-rate carriages; no one cares for them or asks about them, but they are obeyed implicitly and unconsciously by reason of the splendour of those who eclipsed and preceded them.' Behind Bagehot's notion lay a basic contempt for the political sense of the populace, which made his doctrine particularly attractive to the Victorian middle classes: constitutional royalty, he said, 'enables our real rulers to change without heedless people knowing it. The masses of Englishmen are not fit for an elective government; if they knew how near they were to it, they would be surprised, and almost tremble'.

Bagehot's view of the 'disguised republic' has been reassuring to politicians and administrators over the following hundred years, for it justified their sheltering behind the disguise, and permitted them to enjoy some of the psychological comfort of monarchy, without its constrictions. But since Bagehot's time, the situation has materially changed. The masses of Englishmen have become quite accustomed to elective government, so that few of them can really *still* believe that the Queen is the real ruler. And it has become very uncertain—watching the antics of parliament, or the evasions of civil servants—exactly who is fooling who, for what reason. As Richard Crossman puts it, in his essay of 1963 bringing Bagehot up to date:[1] 'What gives the British monarchy its unique strength is the fact that the court, the aristocracy and the Church— not to mention the middle classes—are just as credulous worshippers of it as the masses.' The pleasure in the pretence is more evident among the rulers themselves than among the ruled.

The fact that the Queen is officially the head of the civil

[1] Introduction to *The English Constitution.* Fontana Edition. 1963, p. 33.

service, and commander-in-chief of all British forces can be regarded as an agreeable make-believe, which means nothing in terms of real policies, appointments or organisations. But monarchy can also be a habit of mind, as much as a piece of machinery. The British executive has evolved from the monarchical system; and though parliament has attacked, tamed and controlled the monarch's prerogative, and can question and cross-examine her servants, the huge areas of the administration and the armed forces have grown up from beginnings very separate from parliament's, with no revolution to proclaim a decisive change. The traditions of autonomy and secrecy in government go back to its own closeness to the monarchy; and modern administration is still, as it has been called, 'the secret garden of the crown'.[1] The almost impregnable position of British prime ministers, and the entrenched power of the executive, which so successfully eludes the attempts of parliament to control it, owe much to the legacy of monarchy. As one recent student of parliament has put it: 'Britain is still a monarchy in the practice of government and not simply because a constitutional monarch occupies the throne, reigning without ruling. It is a monarchy in the sense that the power of the executive is of a monarchical kind. The cabinet is the monarch in commission, with the prime minister as first commissioner.'[2]

MONARCHS AND PREMIERS

As soon as the results of a general election are known the retiring prime minister submits his resignation to the Queen and his successor drives to Buckingham Palace to be invited to form a government. The quick-change act is couched in the language of the court: 'Her Majesty has invited Mr. Wilson to form a government'; but the role of the Queen in the matter is now effectively nil. In theory the Queen has the right both to dissolve parliament and to choose the prime minister. The first power has not been exercised in the past hundred years. In 1951, according to Attlee, the dissolution of the Labour government was influenced by the King's anxiety and ill-health; but the main reason for it was Attlee's own worries about the insecure Labour majority. In 1969 there was some discussion as to whether, if Harold Wilson were to

[1] Quoted by Kenneth Mackenzie. *The English Parliament:* Penguin 1968, p. 199ff.
[2] Ronald Butt. *The Power of Parliament,* p. 403.

have asked for a dissolution against the known wishes of his own party, the Queen could have refused it. (The only recent precedent had been from South Africa, when in 1939 the governor-general, Sir Patrick Duncan, refused a dissolution to the prime minister, Hertzog, and asked Smuts to form a government, thus bringing South Africa into the war.) If Wilson *had* foolishly insisted on a dissolution, the Queen could have followed that precedent; but the question remained a very hypothetical one.

The second royal power, to appoint the prime minister, has only recently become a fiction. Three times in the last twenty-five years has the choice of prime minister been in question. The first was in 1940, when the King made it clear that, if he had been given the choice, he would have chosen Lord Halifax. The second was in 1957, when Sir Anthony Eden resigned: the Queen's choice of Macmillan depended on the sounding-out of the Tory party, the Lords and the cabinet, made by Lord Salisbury and the Lord Chancellor. The third and most controversial occasion was after the announcement of Macmillan's resignation in 1963. Macmillan was anxious that the palace should not be required to settle the choice; he conducted from his sickbed his own elaborate but far from conclusive soundings, and deduced that all sections of the party were in favour of the foreign secretary, the Earl of Home. With what appeared to be unseemly haste, Lord Home was summoned to the palace on the same afternoon, was invited to form a government, and became prime minister next day. The brisk time-table made it seem that the Queen was not intended to have a say in the matter. If the choice had been delayed, R. A. Butler would have stood a good chance of becoming prime minister. It is difficult to see how, in this instance, the Queen could have delayed the decision without provoking a further political crisis; but the Queen's involvement, such as it was, served to reveal the obscure and muddled methods of the Conservative electoral process. The muddle was so apparent that soon after the election the Conservative Party abandoned the 'customary processes', and adopted, at the suggestion of a maverick back-bencher, Humphry Berkeley, a straightforward system of ballot, with a second ballot if necessary to elect the leader by a simple majority—as already practised by the Labour Party. (The ballot had the surprising effect of turning up Edward Heath as leader in 1965, whereas the customary processes might well have produced Reginald Maudling.) Since 1965 both parties have thus been able to present the Queen with their choice of leader, and thus effectively to cut her out of the decision. But this may not be quite the end of her role: a correspondent in the Palace advises that 'though it is some time since we were governed by a coalition, it may be premature to conclude from the present state of affairs that the Queen will never have to choose another prime minister'.

The prime minister, once in office, preserves the appearance of a subservient relationship to the Queen; every Tuesday night, when she is in London, he goes round to Buckingham Palace for a talk with her majesty. The relationship is not quite what it was; when Chatham was Prime Minister, he bowed so low, as one witness put it, that you could see his great nose between his knees. When Gladstone went to see Queen Victoria, he remained standing up. Nowadays, the prime minister is allowed to sit down and even to smoke. There is nothing to stop the monarch trying to influence the prime minister: King George VI claimed to have influenced Attlee to appoint Bevin as foreign secretary in 1945 instead of Dalton, though Attlee denied it. The monarch is well furnished with information, and she is well-placed to be the best informed person in Britain, since she knows the secrets of past governments, as well as the present one. All cabinet minutes and cabinet papers go in red boxes to Buckingham Palace; atomic secrets, correspondence with presidents, Budget plans, all make their way to the Queen, whether at Balmoral, Windsor, or on the royal yacht. To save her having to read the whole of Hansard, a daily report of seven hundred words is written at six o'clock every evening, by a junior member of the government, the Vice-Chamberlain of the Royal Household (at present Jasper More, MP), which is taken round immediately by messenger to the palace.

The present Queen, who has already dealt with six prime ministers, will by the end of her reign have accumulated a formidable quantity of secret information with which to buttress her arguments. But her power to persuade rests only on her personality, and the social power of her surroundings. However much the prime minister may nod, bow and hover, he knows that he is the embodiment of parliament's power, and that in theory (as Bagehot put it) if a Bill were passed for the execution of the Queen, the Queen would have to sign it.

THE QUEEN

In Europe in 1900 there were kings or emperors in every country except France and Switzerland. Now there are only six reigning European monarchs left: the last one to go into exile was King Constantine of Greece, in 1967, but the numbers may be kept up by the elevation of Prince Juan Carlos of Spain, after Franco goes. The survivors are, in order of number of subjects:

> Queen Elizabeth of the United Kingdom
> Queen Juliana of the Netherlands
> King Baudouin of Belgium
> King Gustaf Adolf of Sweden
> King Frederik of Denmark
> King Olaf of Norway

They are a select, endogamous profession: four of them are descendants, or married to descendants, of Queen Victoria, 'the matriarch of Europe'. Both the King of Sweden's wives have been descendants of Queen Victoria: and the King of Denmark married the daughter of the King of Sweden. But the British monarchy is in a class by itself, and in the past fifty years it has become increasingly cut off from the rest. Only in Britain is there still a monarchy on the grand and sanctified scale, supported by religious processions, courtiers, and a titled aristocracy.

At the head of this unique institution is Her Most Excellent Majesty Elizabeth the Second, by the Grace of God, of the United Kingdom of Great Britain and Northern Ireland and of Her other Realms and Territories Queen, Head of the Commonwealth, Defender of the Faith, Sovereign of the British Orders of Knighthood. The Queen is the fortieth monarch since the Norman Conquest, descended among others from Charlemagne, Egbert King of Wessex, Rodrigo the Cid, the Emperor Barbarossa, George Washington and (according to Robert Graves, a fellow-descendant) from Mohammed. Ingenious genealogists can show that the Queen is related to all kinds of useful people. She turns out to be descended not only from William the Conqueror, but also from King Harold;[1] and she is also sixth cousin twice removed from George Washington. ('Few living people', writes the Garter King of Arms, 'can be related much more closely.'[2])

[1] P. W. Montague-Smith: Introduction to *Debrett's Peerage*, 1966.
[2] Sir Anthony Wagner: *New York Genealogical and Biographical Record* (vol. 70, pp. 201–6) 1939. See also *Sunday Times* April 10, 1966.

The Queen's own life remains remarkably well concealed: she has never yet given an interview to a journalist. She is known to be shy, conscientious and painstaking: as an employer she is said to be fair, kind, but exacting. There is no sign that she has difficulty in the central role—being royal. In spite of the intrusion of democracy, the votes of parliament and the pressures of the populace, the world of the palace remains something quite separate from the world of Whitehall or Westminster, and that world revolves firmly round the royal personality. 'You can't separate the private and public functions of the Queen,' said one court official; 'that's the main difference between a monarchy and a republic. In a republic you know that the president's life is arranged by the state, and that eventually he'll retire back to his own home. But what most impresses the visitors to Windsor or the royal yacht is the feeling that they're in a private home—that it's part of a family life.'

The Queen's British calendar has changed very little since her accession, and she preserves the annual routine of a nineteenth century aristocrat in spite of the great changes in her kingdom. But it is clear that the royal family feel strongly about the Commonwealth, as part of their *raison d'être*. Prince Charles has already spoken eloquently about the multi-racial role of the Commonwealth, and the Queen often seems more interested in it than her governments do: she was insistent on going to Ghana in 1961 when her political advisers were against it. She has become more adventurous in her tours, with 'walkabouts' in Australia in place of the traditional formality. Since her accession she has been to Canada six times, Australia, New Zealand and Fiji three times, Jamaica, Tonga and Malta twice—though to India, the largest of them all, she has only been once, for three weeks.

THE DUKE

Dashing in and out of the settled world of the palace, taking off from the garden in a helicopter, is the restless figure of Prince Philip, Duke of Edinburgh, who married Princess Elizabeth in 1947. The Duke, like Prince Albert, has strong ideas about the role of a consort, but less scope for playing it than Albert had. He has been strongly influenced by his formidable uncle, Earl Mountbatten; and he has tried to identify himself with the future rather than the past, and particularly with youth, science, industry and technology. He writes his own speeches, and occasionally appears on television: he enjoys publicity, but dislikes journalists. He has described himself as 'one of the most governed people you could hope to meet', and 'being almost permanently under arrest', but he has managed to establish a place for himself as a free-booting critic, bursting out with occasional pep-talks, in the style of an exasperated housemaster, about the slacking and slovenliness of the nation, and the need to pull socks up—about the hopelessness of British design ('simply drives me up the wall,' November 1968), about the inability to take technological decisions ('I suspect we suffer from a "decision gap," ' March 1968), or about the incompetence of British exporting ('I'm sick and tired of making excuses for Britain,' February 1967). He has set himself up as a kind of bridge between sectors of the nation: 'At the bottom of much of the present student unrest,' he said in July 1969, 'there is the same lack of communication. Once people in any group start using the expression "they" and blaming "them" for their dissatisfactions, you can be certain there is no communication with "them".' Occasionally his pep-talks raise complaints in parliament, and after his 'sick-and-tired' speech, the trades unionist Clive Jenkins said he was the best argument for republicanism since George III. But he is usually careful to avoid political themes, and most of his complaints have no discernible effect; the only criticism that achieved any change (he claimed in March 1969) was about the rear lights of lorries. Recently the Prince's most persistent campaign has been conservation, which he described in March 1970 as 'the first anti-materialist argument for about the last 100 years': and the Prince (like Prince Bernhard of the Netherlands) is at the peak of the aristocratic movement for preserving nature, wildlife and the countryside. He espoused the cause of conservation long before it became fashionable, before words like ecology and environment became rallying-cries for a student generation. But the difficulty about the ducal view of conservation is that it easily becomes associated with the deepest forms of conservatism; and that the public is expected to conserve not simply the flora and fauna, but the aristocrats of the human species too, preserved in their own traditional habitat of great houses and parklands.

THE COURT

Even after the first world war there were still people like Lord
Derby or the Duke of Devonshire who were richer than the
monarch. Buckingham Palace, though the biggest, was only one of
many great town houses, and the dukes and parvenu millionaires
could rival royal entertainment. After two world wars taxation cut
down all the other palaces, and diminished the great country
estates, but the Sovereign's allowance remained exempt from his
tax commissioners, and his land and palaces remained the sole
relic of the old order, with Buckingham Palace at the centre. The
isolation of the palace has transformed the social role of the
monarch. 'Before it was like a pyramid,' explained one courtier,
'now it is more like a bumpy plain, with an island in the middle.'
Sitting on this island, the palace has become much more aware of
being watched and judged: royal lunches and garden parties
acquire a unique significance, and every new guest is interpreted
as a national gesture. Most of the extraordinary collection of
people called the 'Queen's Household'—such as the Master of the
Horse, Gold Stick, the High Almoner, or the Mistress of the
Robes—are not to be seen wandering through the corridors of
Buckingham Palace; they are unpaid, and very part-time, and
normally only emerge from mufti for royal processions or corona-
tions. The full-time household—apart from servants and grooms—
amounts to only seventy people, headed by the Lord Chamberlain,
Lord Cobbold, a former governor of the Bank of England. In
Buckingham Palace, apart from the Queen's own lunch-table,
only about fifteen people—private secretaries, privy purse people,
equerries or press officers—sit down to lunch. Still, the courtiers
are sufficiently formidable to maintain a sense of a court, isolated
from the outside world, and to act as cushions between royalty and
reality. In the last few years there have been more intrusions from
outside professions, like Philip Moore, the assistant private
secretary to the Queen, who came in from the civil service, or
Geoffrey Hardy-Roberts who became Master of the Household
after being a hospital administrator.

The most important job in the palace is the private secretary
to the Queen, for he is the main link between the monarch and
the world outside. Sir Michael Adeane, the present secretary,
might seem the quintessence of the professional courtier: his
grandfather, Lord Stamfordham, was private secretary to Queen

Victoria and King George V, and Adeane himself began his royal service at the age of thirteen, as a page of honour to King George V. He took a first at Cambridge and has been a keen wild-fowler. He is a neat, compact man, with old-fashioned courtesy, who arrives at Buckingham Palace every morning from his flat in St. James's Palace. He is essentially a realist in his approach to the monarchy. He does not, like many courtiers, regard himself as part of the mystery, and privately he talks shrewdly about his problems. In the changes in the monarch's role since the war—particularly in the handling of the Commonwealth—Adeane has played an important part.

The remoteness of the Queen is enhanced by her entourage. Most of her time is spent with people who, from the public's point of view, are in a half-and-half world between royalty and ordinariness. Many of the guests at Windsor or Balmoral have titles, and dukes, particularly racing dukes, make up the foothills to royalty. The monarchy, it is true, is not the undisputed centre of the aristocracy, and since Charles II's time the monarch has ceased to be the acknowledged head of London Society (in so far as that exists). But the monarch and the aristocracy for their prestige are mutually interdependent. The aristocracy would not be the same without a pinnacle and a mystery at the top: and the palace would not have the same mystery if it were surrounded by misters.

THE COST

The total cost of this apparatus is hotly debated, and some even insist that the monarchy makes a profit. This argument assumes that the Queen is the real owner of the Crown Lands of which the revenue, since the time of George III, has been handed over to the state. The Crown is the second biggest landowner in Britain, with 182,313 acres in England, 85,290 in Scotland, and valuable city properties, including Regent's Park, Carlton House Terrace, and chunks of Pall Mall, Piccadilly, Holborn and Kensington. All these properties are run by the Crown Estates Commissioner in Whitehall, under the First Commissioner and Chairman, the Earl of Perth, a former minor Tory minister. Their surplus profits, which after tax and expenses amount to over £3½ million a year, is handed to the Exchequer. This income, it is argued, more than makes up for the Queen's salary. But the Crown Lands must really

be regarded as belonging to the state, and by any sensible calcula-
tion the monarchy is an expensive affair.

The sovereign's salary is fixed by parliament at the beginning
of the reign. Queen Elizabeth's allowance amounts to £475,000 a
year—which has hardly changed since George V's time, and is
now worth only a quarter as much. It is made up by:

	£
Her Majesty's Privy Purse	60,000
Salaries of Household	185,000
Expenses of Household	121,800
Royal Bounty, alms and special services	13,200
Supplementary provision (to allow for inflation, Duchess of Kent, Princess Alexandra, etc.)	95,000
	£475,000

The Prince of Wales is entitled to revenues from the Duchy of
Cornwall, amounting to £200,000, half of which he surrendered to
the nation when he came of age. Separate allowances are voted
by parliament for a few other members of the royal family:

	£
Queen Elizabeth the Queen Mother	70,000
Duke of Edinburgh	40,000
Duke of Gloucester	35,000
Princess Margaret, Countess of Snowdon	15,000
Princess Anne	6,000
	£166,000

The actual upkeep of the official royal palaces is paid for by
that ubiquitous patron, the Department of the Environment:
it spends no less than half a million pounds on maintaining,
heating and lighting Buckingham Palace, St. James's Palace
and Windsor Castle, and it employs two hundred people there
and in Kensington Palace. The cost of the Queen's Flight, which
the royal family (as well as members of the government) now use a
great deal, is paid for by the RAF: there are three Andovers, two
helicopters and a Bassett, all painted fluorescent red and with
140 people to look after them. The cost of royal tours is borne
by the host governments in the Commonwealth countries.

The cost of the royal trains, royal postage, royal telegrams (which have precedence) and telephone calls, all falls on the state. The most obviously extravagant royal perquisite is the yacht *Britannia*, paid for by the navy: it cost £2 million to build, and its upkeep and crew of 250 cost about £500,000 a year. Altogether the cost to the state of the monarchy is probably not less than three million pounds a year —about the same as Ariel and Radiant spend on advertising.

On top of this the Queen has her private fortune, a source of interminable speculation. King George V is said to have left a million pounds to each of his four sons: and Queen Mary left £406,000—though to *whom* it was bequeathed is not known. In addition to her capital, the Queen owns the finest art collection in the world, amassed by Henry VIII, Charles I, George III, George IV and the Prince Consort. The Queen also personally owns Sandringham and Balmoral (when Edward VIII abdicated, George VI had to buy them from him). And there is the royal jewellery, the royal stamp collection, the royal racehorses, which yield a profit, and a great hoard of gold plate. The income from the royal investments (including the profitable Duchy of Lancaster) is secret, and tax-free.

Inflation since 1952 has made large inroads on royal allowances. In November 1969 Prince Philip dropped a calculated bomb in a television interview, when he was asked about the royal finances: 'We go into the red next year,' he said, 'which is not bad housekeeping if you come to think of it. We've in fact kept the thing going on a budget which was based on costs of eighteen years ago . . . Now inevitably if nothing happens we shall either have to—I don't know, we may have to move into smaller premises, who knows? We had a small yacht which we've had to sell and I shall probably have to give up polo fairly soon, things like that . . .' In May 1971 a high-powered select committee was finally appointed to investigate the Queen's budget, for the first time in nineteen years.

THE PRINCE

We must not let in daylight upon magic.
Walter Bagehot.

The coronation of 1953 marked a high tide in enthusiasm for the monarchy: the combination of a young queen, a resurgence of nostalgia and a wave of optimism about a generation of adventurous 'New Elizabethans' coincided with the first televised ceremony, of almost papal proportions. Ten years later most of the enthusiasm had faded; the Queen had settled into middle-age, her sister had married a photographer, and the New Elizabethans proved very unadventurous. The growing-up of a new Prince of Wales, from what leaked out, did not show much promise. Princes of Wales are apt to be an embarrassment to the court; the previous one had nearly brought the monarchy down, and King Edward VII, who was Prince of Wales until the age of 59, was an object of continual alarm to his mother and her courtiers. It was with an eye on him that Bagehot wrote his warning:

> All the world and all the glory of it, whatever is most seductive, has always been offered to the Prince of Wales of the day, and always will be. It is not rational to expect the best virtue where temptation is applied in the most trying form at the frailest time of life.

Prince Charles, being educated under the spartan regime of Gordonstoun, his father's old school, had not yet tasted all that was most seductive; but his gangling shape and weak chin did not suggest strength of character, and stories about drinking cherry-brandy, together with his being sent out to Australia, gave hints of a problem child. By the mid-sixties the monarchy generally seemed to be vulnerable not to any surge of republicanism but to a general withdrawal of interest. The courtiers knew that monarchs, however carefully they pretend to avoid it, depend on publicity as much as film stars; and middle-age is the most difficult time for publicity. But there was the perennial problem of how to maintain or step up publicity without destroying the aura of mystery and fairyland which hangs round the palace.

The obvious opportunity for a re-launch of the monarchy was the investiture of the new Prince of Wales, timed for his twenty-first birthday in 1969. The palace advisers decided on quite a bold opening-up. They knew, as the public did not, that the Prince was livelier than he looked and that he was able to face the public without too great risks. The palace public relations had been strengthened by two businesslike arrivals from outside courtly circles; Bill Heseltine, an Australian schoolmaster's son, had taken over as press secretary from an old stone-waller, Commander Colville; and Prince Charles had his own adviser, Squadron-Leader Checketts, who had been a professional public-relations man in the firm of Neilson McCarthy. They, with other courtiers, decided to let in a good deal of daylight, or arc-light, on to the magic.

Before the actual investiture, Prince Charles did what his mother and grandfather had never done; he gave interviews to journalists on radio and television, and emerged, to general astonishment, as an articulate human being. He appeared as a cheerful, reassuring young man of the kind that might be seen strolling through Harrods' men's department. He gave views which, while unexceptional, sounded like his own; he explained that realising that he was heir to the throne was 'something which dawns on you with the most ghastly inexorable sense'. He said his father had a strong influence on him, and that he thought he was late in developing. He used to think that Charles I was splendid, until he read about Cromwell, whom he now admires. He would prefer to marry somebody 'English, or perhaps Welsh'. Did he feel himself, as his grandfather had described it, to be a member of a firm? 'Yes,' he said, 'a family firm—I think that probably puts it right.'

The climax of the publicity campaign involved the whole family. For a year before, a discreet BBC television team led by Richard Cawston had been following the Queen and her family: the Queen had agreed that, for the first time, the inside of her palaces should be televised—on condition that she had right of veto. The showing of the film 'Royal Family' just before the investiture marked a fusion between these two potent forces, monarchy and television, both naturally attracted to each other. The French president had discovered how conveniently the pageantry of state could be married to television; the British royal family could offer the extra ingredient of family interest. Television could provide what Disraeli or Napoleon III might have dreamt of—the means to connect up the appeal of the monarchy direct with the people.

The film displayed the monarchy in all its confident yet cosy surroundings; so that, while from outside the institution might seem isolated and anachronistic, from inside it appeared as the most natural way of life, with which the rest of the world came quietly to terms. It was not the Queen who had to come awkwardly down to the market-place, but everyone else who had to clamber up to her; the rugged American ambassador, Walter Annenberg, was disclosed waiting anxiously behind double doors for his audience, practising putting his left foot forward; President Nixon came to lunch, buttering-up Prince Charles; Harold Wilson arrived for his

Tuesday chat, properly deferential; on journeys abroad, Lord Chalfont from the Foreign Office danced attendance; and the private secretary, Sir Michael Adeane, kept on popping in and out, bending low in homage. Everyone conspired to give the illusion that the monarch was the centre of the universe. 'Royal Family' was in fact a very political film; and the solemn commentary, written by Antony Jay, stressed the splendours of the British monarchical system, and spelt out the central message (the same message as Orwell's), that the monarchy is a bulwark against dictatorship: 'The strength of the monarchy does not lie in the power it has, but in the power that it denies to others.'

The film was rapturously received; and the reception allayed any fears that as soon as the workings of the palace were revealed, the whole magic of the institution would dissolve. Television, suitably edited, added its own magic, and left enough mystery still unrevealed. But the climax of the royal year, the investiture of the Prince, was still to come, and the decision to hold a full-dress ceremonial at Caernarvon Castle at the cost of about £120,000 was a further venture into political territory. The separatist movements had been building up both in Scotland and Wales; and since the monarchy symbolised among many other things the unity of the United Kingdom, the monarchy was both a tempting target for the nationalists, and a potential weapon against them. A first move in deploying the royal family as a kind of expensive cement had been made earlier in the year when, for the first time, the reigning monarch had appeared at the General Assembly of the Church of Scotland. But Prince Charles's Welsh operation was more tricky, for Welsh terrorists had been seriously threatening; and however much the Prince talked in Welsh about his Welsh blood, and his love of Wales (he had spent a term at Aberystwyth), he was very obviously an English import. The ceremony went ahead, with decor designed by Uncle Tony, Lord Snowdon, who was wearing a special bottle-green uniform for the occasion. The pageantry prevailed, the terrorists only blew up two of their own troops, and Charles was without incident crowned by his mother— the first television prince. There was a burst of emotion from the Press. Peregrine Worsthorne, in *The Sunday Telegraph*, exclaimed: 'How strange and rather wonderful it is that it should be the role of monarchy today not to act out fantasy but to be the one institution that seems able to be natural and normal.'

The blaze of new publicity and the evident confidence of the royals certainly revealed an unsuspected resilience in the institution: the British, it seemed, still needed to be reassured by the existence of this old secure family, and could still identify themselves with it. Yet it would be surprising if there were not some price to be paid for the reassurance. The national habit of mind which enjoys the suspension of disbelief in royal occasions can easily spill over into a suspension of realism towards the workings of the administration.

12

Civil Service

Wise men have always perceived that the execution of political
measures is in reality the essence of them.

Sir Henry Taylor, 1892.

WHEN the political pendulum swings in Britain, the new party
comes into power with a suddenness and cruelty that can amaze
foreign observers. In the United States there is a two-month
interim of awkward caretaking, between the election of a new
President and his coming into office. In Britain the result of the
Thursday election usually becomes clear early on Friday morning.
By the same afternoon the new prime minister is calling at the
Palace and moving into Downing Street. The fact that many cabinet ministers now live 'above the shop' makes the transition more
brutal, for overnight they lose not only their office, but their
house. The chancellor of the exchequer in Downing Street,
Number 11, has only one door, so that the change is visible to any
passers by: out of that door must come the old chancellor, his
family, trunks, packing cases and empty bottles.

The abruptness has obvious advantages compared to the
American system. There is no awkward hiatus, no period with
no one properly in control. It gives to the workings of democracy
the dramatic immediacy of a *coup d'état*, with removal vans in
place of machine-guns. But the combination of sudden change
and smooth continuity reveals that behind this apparent break
there is a heavy fly-wheel that keeps its momentum and survives

any transition: the great machine of the permanent civil service. That moment of change of government is the moment of truth in the relationship between politicians and bureaucrats.

There are many elections, like those of 1959 and 1964, when the balance seems a fine one. But in two elections in this century there have been reversals which took nearly everyone by surprise, when democracy showed itself with all its ruthlessness. The first was in 1945, when Churchill confidently expected to be returned to power. The election period coincided with the Potsdam Conference with Truman and Stalin; and when the results finally emerged Stalin found himself, to his evident astonishment, talking after a few days' delay to a different prime minister. Churchill conveyed vividly the psychological problem, describing his sudden presentiment of the landslide, his vision that 'all the pressure of great events, on and against which I had mentally so long maintained my "flying speed", would cease and I should fall'.

The second great reversal was in 1970 when the election campaign appeared to reveal a certain Labour victory. The civil servants were as surprised as most of the public when the Conservatives were returned; but they had nevertheless made their plans. Before any election there are secret talks between top civil servants and the Opposition, in case they win: there were long talks before Wilson came to power in 1964, and more talks with Heath in the months before June 1970. The civil servants read up the pamphlets and the schemes for reform, and make their 'contingency plans'—civil servants love their contingencies. But the meetings and plans are kept secret until after the election; when the fact emerges that there *have* been talks, as it always does, the betrayal seems all the greater.

The transition in Britain is more poignant, too, because of the relative fewness of the politicians who move out and in. Only about a hundred men change their offices in Whitehall after the election (another forty may become parliamentary private secretaries, with a loose relationship with their office). In the United States thousands change their jobs; and even in France, which has an equally powerful permanent bureaucracy, a new minister can bring with him his own *cabinet* of political friends to help him run his department. But in Britain even the minister's private secretary—his most intimate confidant—will stay to serve his new master, abandoning overnight the loyalties and policies of his predecessor, suddenly acquiring that professional enthusiasm for the ex-enemy which is the special mark of the dedicated civil servant: 'You know, when you get to know him, he's really a very remarkable man.' It is a painful switchover, but in terms of the democratic system an impressive one: as one civil servant wrote to me after the 1970 election:

> I have been astonished to see with what automatic loyalty officials set out at once to apply the new Tory doctrines of freeing the individual from over-much government. Whatever their personal scepticism and reservations, the very fact that the doctrine *was* purely political made it all the more a matter of conscience and duty scrupulously to put it into practical effect. In this sense, our service is less technocratic, less an independent force in politics, than perhaps the French (and of course certainly less so than the Brussels Commission).

When new ministers arrive, the officials are studiously friendly and helpful, telling them most things they want to know, and all the arguments for or against any decision that have been put forward. But they will never tell them the secrets of the previous government's policy decisions, or the personal details of who said what to whom. The filing cabinets remain firmly guarded with combination locks by the civil servants, and on the key questions a new file is opened on the day the government comes to power. If an incoming minister asks to see the files about devaluation or Rhodesia the crucial documents will have been removed. Before the election Treasury and other officials carefully re-draft important papers, with political secrets omitted. This arrangement is by agreement of the incoming prime minister, who always accedes to it, knowing that when he in turn departs he will not want to bequeath his party's secrets; when ministers or advisers complain about files being withheld—as they have done—they are quietly referred to the prime minister.

In the nineteenth century, before the bureaucracy had become so well organised, the embarrassing political discussions were outside the civil servants' purview or control; they were recorded in clubs or private houses in longhand or often not recorded at all. It was only after 1916, with the establishment of the cabinet office, that the civil servants became the guardians of party secrets; and the system was perpetuated after 1922, when Bonar Law took over the cabinet secretariat from Lloyd George. The civil servants are very conscious of the nature of their bargain with the politicians. As one permanent secretary put it to me: 'We say to them, in effect, that their dirty linen is safe with us. If we can't promise them that, then they'll take the dirty linen somewhere else.'

The fact that the top civil servants know so much more than their political masters, and much that they must not disclose, adds a special piquancy to the relationship, like that of a widow who remarries overhastily and is still half in love with her first husband. The civil servants know that the politicians know that the civil servants know more than they; and even if they lean over backwards not to take advantage of it, the politicians are bound to be resentful. 'They regard us,' said a permanent secretary, 'partly like old retainers in a big house which has been let for the holidays; who are always thinking that's not the way the other people did it. And partly, more simply, as jailers in a prison they don't understand.' A special awkwardness is apparent at those occasions, like embassy receptions, where civil servants and politicians of both parties are invited together. The discarded leaders have to watch the men who only a few days ago were their closest colleagues, chatting and smiling with the enemy, looking just as friendly and confidential as ever they were to them.

> O God! A beast, that wants discourse of reason,
> Would have mourn'd longer . . .

ARCHETYPAL BUREAUCRACY

We have already encountered politicians in three different spheres—in parliament, in their party organisations and in cabinet. Now we see them in their most important, but least visible role—running their departments in the midst of Whitehall—and here, for the next chapters, we peer at the opaque regions of the bureaucracies. Nothing in Whitehall is quite what it seems. Policy becomes muddled with execution, politicians with officials. The political masters in Britain can only attend to the broadest principles of policy. The rest of the administration falls on the shoulders of a permanent civil service which likes to depict itself as de-personalised, without opinions or policies. But behind the public façade the bureaucracies are still run by individuals, each with his own views and values.

Many of the most important government departments are now in fact right away from Whitehall, but the tingling centre of the civil service, where the major decisions are taken, remains the half-mile of stone buildings from Trafalgar Square to Westminster Abbey, with high classical façades, tall cupolas, and heavy marble staircases. The propinquity is important: ideas, misgivings, suggestions can brush from one to another in Whitehall as casually and smoothly as dust on to a coat. In a walk through the park you can have a few casual encounters and at once sense the political attitude; so that there is still some sense of the idea of 'Whitehall thinks.'

The man from Whitehall has been a stereotype for so long that he clearly fills an emotional need. He is the universal killjoy, the busybody, the pedant; the personification of 'them', of London against the countryside, of the old against the young, of caution against daring. The time-honoured caricature of the pompous, pale bureaucrat with his umbrella, brief-case and bowler still stalks through films, television serials and anti-Whitehall propaganda; the rural councils, in their campaign against the Maude reforms, conjured him up once again—with his brief-case labelled 'R. E. MOTE'. Behind this barrage of clichés, of saloon-bar jokes and *Daily Express* cartoons, the civil servants themselves are tempted to give up trying to project their true character and to resign themselves to the fact (as Lord Bridges once put it) 'that we shall continue to be grouped with mothers-in-law and Wigan pier as one of the recognised objects of ridicule'. They seem to enjoy conforming to some kind of caricature; one of their trade union magazines is called *Red Tape*, and in Whitehall they still work in high, echoing Victorian offices, guarded by ancient white-haired doormen. Long linoleum corridors lead to anterooms full of homely typists, knitting and brollies; the officials' language still suggests a priestcraft of power, intoning the PM, PUS, HMG, SOS, MOD and the rest. But the accoutrements of the stage civil servant have long since disappeared in the actual Whitehall. The suits are grey, not black; the collars are white, but not stiff; umbrellas are scarce and bowlers are almost non-existent; in a week's stay in Whitehall I saw only one bowler-hat, and gaggles of dolly-girls.

The professional civil service is a Victorian invention—dating back to that dynamic third quarter of the nineteenth century when so many of Britain's institutions took shape. It is the archetypal bureaucracy (though the word 'Civil Servant' dates from the East India Company, the original 'John Company'), and over the last century it has helped to set the pattern for others. The Victorian idea was that administrators should be chosen, not with special experience of government, but as intelligent, well-educated university graduates. This crucial principle was stated by Lord Macaulay, who recommended the reform of the Indian Civil Service in 1854, in a famous and reverberating passage:

> We believe that men who have been engaged, up to twenty-one or twenty-two, in studies which have no immediate connection with the business of any profession, and of which the effect is merely to open, to invigorate, and to enrich the mind, will generally be found in the business of every profession superior to men who have, at eighteen or nineteen, devoted themselves to the special studies of their calling.

The reform of the Indian Civil Service was the model for the reform of the British one: an interesting example of how external developments provoke internal ones (rather as the Victorians first used central heating for their conservatories, then belatedly began using it for their houses). In 1853 Charles Trevelyan (Macaulay's brother-in-law, who had spent fourteen years in India) and Sir Stafford Northcote (who had been at Balliol with Jowett) were asked to report on reorganising the home civil service. They reported that the public service was 'attracting the unambitious, and the indolent or incapable'. They insisted that the public service must become a profession rather than a job to which 'the dregs of all other professions are attracted'. And they proposed recruiting from the universities by open competitive written examination—turning Greek and Latin scholars into a new race of administrators.

This ruthless report provoked uproar, and complaints that it would provide 'picked clever young men from the lower ranks of society'; but the incompetence of the Crimean War brought Whitehall into further disgrace. Eventually, in 1870, Gladstone instituted most of the Northcote-Trevelyan proposals. The reform was decisive. It produced, as it was meant to, a profession as dedicated as doctors or barristers, with a powerful collegiate sense, uncorrupt, clever and versatile. The new civil service became part of the core of the middle class, and it generated its own traditions, with the sons and grandsons of civil servants becoming civil servants. The 'picked clever young men' became— within the limits of Oxbridge—the first great meritocracy. The reformers not only transformed the civil service, but (as they realised) quickened the universities as well—providing a goal beyond the examinations.[1] They had no doubts that examinations were the index to worldly success. 'The general rule is, beyond all doubt,' wrote Macaulay in 1853, 'that the men who were first in the competition of the schools have been first in the competition of the world.'

For the past century, the elite of the civil service, the 'Administrative Class', have been chosen—with a few modifications—in this way. There have been increasing numbers of promotions from junior grades: in 1969 forty per cent of the 3,000 people in the Administrative Grade consisted of promoted men. But the core of the civil service remained the recruits from the universities, highly-educated non-specialists. It was a central tenet that administration was an art, which could be applied to anything.

REFORM

But in the century since 1870 the whole role of the civil service was changing. It increased in size twentyfold; and found itself involved in technical and commercial problems which Macaulay never dreamt of. The old civil service was mainly concerned with regulating people: collecting taxes, running a police force and prisons. What the Victorians wanted was 'a corps of reliable umpires'.[2] The contemporary civil service is occupied in directing industries, allocating vast research programmes, building airports, running social security, planning roads—in fact running half Britain: and the administrators are now entangled in an undergrowth of specialists—engineers, scientists, economists, accountants, agronomists. The conflict between amateurs and professionals, which has run through so many British institutions had its most troubled frontier in the civil service. 'In an age when the importance of science and specialised knowledge has increased so much,' said the Fabian report in 1964, 'the perpetration of this kind of class distinction is indefensible.'[3]

The civil servants themselves reacted to criticisms with sensitivity and pride; this is how one of them—Richard Wilding, who became secretary to the Fulton Commission—described it:

> If you think back to the first half of the sixties, it is undeniable that the civil service had grown a poor image—and that this had communicated itself quite widely throughout society. . . . The belief that

[1] Lord Bridges: *Portrait of a Profession*, p. 9.
[2] Fabian Society: *The Administrators*, 1964.
[3] *The Administrators*, p. 36.

civil service organisation was a gently ossified muddle staffed by intelligent, urbane but managerially innocent mandarins became the accepted wisdom of the day. And to some extent, at least, we let this happen. We fell to that insidious spiritual temptation—the thing that really does mark the mandarin—the feeling that to be misunderstood by the ignorant is inevitable, and that to be traduced as a result is our peculiar badge of honour.[1]

Then, in February 1966, Harold Wilson appointed a committee of twelve people, 'to examine the structure of recruitment and management, including training, of the home civil service', consisting of:

Lord Fulton	Chairman. Then vice-chancellor of Sussex University.
Sir Norman Kipping	Vice-chairman. Former director-general of the Federation of British Industries.
Sir Philip Allen	Permanent under-secretary at the Home Office.
W. C. Anderson	Then secretary of National and Local Government Officers Association (NALGO).
Sir Edward Boyle (now Lord Boyle)	Former minister of education, now vice-chancellor of Leeds.
Sir William Cook	Adviser to the Ministry of Defence on Projects.
Sir James Dunnett	Permanent under-secretary of Ministry of Defence.
Dr. Norman Hunt	Lecturer in politics at Oxford. Representative of the prime minister.
Robert Neild	Director of Peace Institute at Stockholm; former Economic Adviser to Treasury.
Robert Sheldon	Labour MP and member of Public Accounts Committee.
Lord Simey	Professor of Social Science at Liverpool.
John Wall	Deputy-chairman of Post Office Board, formerly of Unilever.

The committee sat for two years, at the cost of £51,854, and in 1968 produced three volumes of evidence and one volume of 'the Fulton Report'. It began with the words:

> The home civil service today is still fundamentally the product of the nineteenth-century philosophy of the Northcote-Trevelyan Report. The tasks it faces are those of the second half of the twentieth century. This is what we have found; it is what we seek to remedy.

It went on to state fairly boldly its criticisms of the service.

[1] 'The Post-Fulton Programme': talk by R. W. L. Wilding, March 9 and 16, 1970.

It was based on the cult of the amateur (or 'generalist' as they preferred to call him), which was obsolete in all parts of the service. It was riddled with compartments and classes—no fewer than fourteen hundred of them—which hampered the service in adapting itself. It did not give proper responsibilities to scientists, engineers and other specialists. It did not have enough skilled managers. And it did not have enough contact with the rest of the community.

The committee's recommendations seemed, at first sight, equally bold, representing a complete break with the Northcote-Trevelyan philosophy. It proposed that all classes should be abolished and replaced by a single, unified grading structure. That a new Civil Service Department should be set up, under the prime minister, to reform and run the service. That there should be a Civil Service College, to provide training and research in management. That specialists should be given more responsibility, and that administrators should be more specialised. And that (among many other charges) there should be more coming-and-going between the civil service and other jobs.

The report, launched with ballyhoo in June 1968, was quite well received, both inside and outside Whitehall; the main recommendations were quickly accepted by the government who had helped to inspire them. But many of the proposals were in fact very vague, and a great deal still depends on how and whether they would be implemented by the civil servants.

CIVIL SERVICE DEPARTMENT

The temple of Fultonism, the repository of its ideals and ambitions, is the Civil Service Department which was set up in 1968. It was made up of the former pay-and-management side of the Treasury, and of the old Civil Service Commission which selects the recruits: but to these were added new men from other departments. The department takes the Fulton Report as its bible, with its own exegetes and prophets; and in the corridors and committee rooms the precepts of Fulton are to be gradually transmuted into action. In September 1970 I spent a week inside the department, overhearing committees and meetings as a fly on the wall, and talking to the main activators, trying to observe the process of reform filtering through the machine.

As always in Britain, the change is not quite what it seems.

The Fulton Report had two basic themes—the need for greater equality, to be rectified by breaking down the class barriers; and the need for greater efficiency, to be rectified by more training and specialisation. The two ambitions cannot necessarily be reconciled. The old aristocracy of the administrative grade is abolished, but it may make way for a new aristocracy of graduates: the department soon decided it needed a hundred extra graduates a year on top of the usual seventy-five or so, so that it may well become harder for the non-graduate to reach top positions. The new system is closer to that of big industrial companies, like ICI or Unilever, who recruit graduates as trainees, without first putting them in a privileged class. There will also, it is true, be a hundred non-graduates from inside the service, each year promoted to be 'administrative trainees' alongside the graduates; but the graduates, with their greater confidence and articulation, are more likely to become 'fliers' (in the romantic jargon) than the non-graduates. The separation of the swans from the geese will be less blatant than the old classification of grades (which, like the army distinction between officers and NCO's, dated back to the more overt rigid class system). But if nearly all the swans turn out to be graduates, it will be more painful for the geese.

Nor is the integration of specialists as straightforward as it seems. Most scientists or engineers are inclined to be instinctively wary of the rarefied world of administrators and policy-makers; they often prefer the attitude (as one engineer-manager put it): 'You get the money and I'll build the bridge.' Administration in the civil service is a more subtle and verbalising process than in industry, and rugged men from laboratories or drawing-boards not surprisingly take fright on observing the intricate word games, the minutes and nuances involved in playing the Whitehall machine. There are still no scientists to be found in the ministers' private offices, where civil servants learn the arts of power.

In the contentious field of recruitment, the civil service had already before the Fulton Report begun to open its ranks. The service is the biggest employer of graduates in the country (except the teaching profession, which is not centralised); and as such, its recruitment policies have been subject to special scrutiny. Since the 1870 reforms, the administrative grade of the civil service has built up a powerful collegiate tradition; it was, in the words of Professor Beer of Harvard, one of the 'forms of corporate social existence which flourish widely in England and the origins of which often ante-date the era of individualism'; or in the words of the Fabian Report of 1964 'as closed and protected as a monastic order'. Not only were the senior civil servants turned in on themselves; they also came from a very limited educational background. Between 1948 and 1956 half the recruits to the administrative class came from Oxford, and thirty per cent from Cambridge, leaving twenty per cent for all other universities; and thus in the higher reaches of the service today it is still the Oxbridge accent, and the Oxbridge style of communication which predominates. This near-monopoly of Oxbridge was a subject of growing attack in the sixties, and by 1964 the civil service was more seriously 'beating the drum' in other universities, encouraging the appointments boards and appointing liaison officers to spread the good news. The propaganda—together with the general increase of students in other universities—stimulated one of the central changes in the pattern of British elites over the last decade. In 1969 a committee of enquiry,[1] under Jack Davies, former head of the Cambridge appointments board, showed that while between 1957 and 1963 Oxford and Cambridge provided eighty-eight per cent of the successful candidates into the administrative grade, by 1968 their proportion had fallen to fifty-nine per cent. Public-school boys had likewise decreased: between 1957 and 1963 the local education authority schools provided only twenty-nine per cent of successful candidates; by 1968 their proportion was forty-one per cent. There was not much increase however in working-class recruits; the proportion of successful candidates from Social Groups I and II (roughly, the middle-class occupations) had only fallen from eighty-seven per cent to eighty-one per cent.

The successful Oxbridge candidates are still quite out of proportion, since Oxbridge only accounts for ten per cent of new graduates. The Davies Committee, gingerly inspecting the evidence in white paper language, deduced that 'many of the factors influencing the vocational choice are deeply rooted in the social structure and the educational system': in other words, people choose jobs because of their teachers, friends and families. Looking at the very high proportion of boys with three A-Levels going up to Oxbridge in the first place, they decided that 'it seems to us almost inescapable that a difference of this order must reflect

[1] Command 4156, 1969.

241

a significant difference in the average quality of the undergraduate populations of Oxford and Cambridge compared with other universities'; in other words, that Oxbridge men were cleverer.[1]

The Oxbridge success is clearly partly due to the phenomenon recurring in this book—the persistence of old social patterns, in which boys select themselves, more than they are selected. Many clever boys would never dream of applying for the civil service. The ravine between the world of the remoter universities, like Exeter or Aberdeen, and the world of Whitehall is still wide. In the future the doubling of the graduate recruits is likely to bring in a larger number of non-Oxbridge men; but there will not necessarily be fewer Oxbridge men at the top of the service. For the higher civil service, as it is constructed, consists of a very subtle kind of communication, with assumptions closely connected to the Oxbridge tradition, with much less in common with the tradition of Loughborough, Stirling or Keele. Non-Oxbridge graduates, and still more the non-graduates from inside the civil service, can easily be awed by this sophisticated style. The problem of the Fulton reformers is not simply to widen the path to the top, but to break down the psychological obstacles and traps on the way.

THE HOUSE OF WORDS

The higher regions of the civil service have an atmosphere quite different from any industrial concern or any other profession. Its practitioners are dedicated not to production, profits or services, but to the delicate operation of translating political decisions into legitimate action; the concept of *legitimacy*, which plays only a small part in companies, in government 'has loomed so large as to have become preponderant'.[2] At the top of the service, behind every committee and minute, everyone must be aware of political decisions and implications. Civil servants talk about politics as a yachtsman might talk of the wind—a wild irrational force, always liable to upset the navigators' calculations, yet having to be calculated for by systems of tacking, reefing or battening down; it is no accident that sea metaphors abound in committee discussions—and that arguments run aground, veer round, are eroded, or taken aboard, as the great ship of policy is battered and

[1] See Chapter 8.
[2] Sir William Armstrong: *Professionals and Professionalism in the Civil Service*. LSE 1970, p. 10.

blown right off course by the political gales. The civil servants' own assessments, of course, have the language of indisputable logic, like a quiet current: arguments flow, follow and repercuss, full of consequences and corollaries; but then the sea is roughened by a new political squall, and the ship has to change course once again.

Civil servants, too, sometimes talk about 'politically sensitive areas' as if they were regions of radioactivity, where geiger-counters frantically oscillate, which can only be entered with a full protection of asbestos suiting and visors. Or they talk about coming into the 'sexy stuff' (one of many examples of sex being sublimated into administration): the quiet logic is overturned by the torrid passions and the writhing embraces; the smouldering desires flare up into sensuous flames; the smooth linen is left a crumpled heap. To cope with the wild world of politics, to tame it and translate it into some kind of sensible action, the civil servants have their special fine armoury of words—words that have been refined, sharpened or carefully blurred over the last few hundred years to express the nuances, doubts and delicately balanced arguments on which the business of administration depends.

The civil service is no longer closely connected with the pure world of literature; gone are the days when writers like Edmund Gosse and Austin Dobson worked at the Board of Trade, when Humbert Wolfe wrote sonnets from Whitehall, or when the head of the civil service (Edward Bridges) was the son of a poet-laureate; the obsession with precise use of language, summed up by Sir Ernest Gowers in his book *Plain Words*, has waned. The 'elegant minute' fashioned as lovingly as a Greek pentameter is somewhat out of fashion in an age of time-and-motion study, of costings, input and output: the American management jargon and the harsh Germanised compound nouns have broken up the literary cadences of Gowers and Bridges. But language remains the basic machinery and product of Whitehall, as oil is to Shell or chemicals to I.C.I., and through its language we can find some insight into this rarefied profession.

The dramatic battles of words are to be observed in the committee—that most British institution which reaches its subtlest form in Whitehall. The committee is the means of consensus and compromise, the discreet battleground in which the concept of 'collective responsibility', of unified government policy, is thrashed out and resolved all the way down from the cabinet to the local authorities. In Whitehall men do not come into committees impatiently or reluctantly, as businessmen might; they stride in, with their agenda firmly under the arm, as knights to the joust; they sit down with their pipes and papers beside them as if establishing a stronghold; and the language of committees, when you have learnt it, has the faint but clear overtones of distant warfare. On the surface, on the polished surface of the table, the scene looks almost totally dispassionate and inert: the pipes puff, the eyes look down, the boyish faces look infinitely patient as Big Ben punctuates the quarter-hours, like a school chapel chiming through prep. The assumption of the committee is that everything can be and will be resolved. People outside may be difficult and stroppy; Buggins has gone skirmishing off into an ad-hoc enquiry, and Boggins and his merry men have been cutting up rough, but here in the committee we are all rational beings, appreciating all the difficulties and sensitivities; we are seized with the arguments of Foggins, we are exercised by the difficulties of Fuggins, the complexities have been borne in on us, and we will weigh up and appraise the problems, give them keen consideration and eventually reach the felt fair point, the point of equity and resolution. We may have our own views and emotions, but we will bow to the general will with a consensus smile—the pained but generous smile of qualified assent.

Above the table, yes, all seems calm and controlled; but under the table can be seen the outward signs of emotion—legs twisting round each other, feet pounding, shoes pressing against each other. Just occasionally a phrase will erupt which betrays signs of anger—'with respect', or worst of all, 'with great respect'—which shows that the battle has become really deadly. The depersonalisation of the committee is its precondition; after a long session one can imagine the arguments and concepts taking off from their proponents, like balloons in comic-strip cartoons labelled 'thinks . . .', battling ferociously with each other above the committee table, while their originators puff at their pipes below.

The conflict between intellect and emotion is concealed, but often acute. Some civil servants, undoubtedly, have an inborn combination of low blood pressure and quick thinking; but others—including many top ones—have learnt with some difficulty to keep their emotions under control; only a vibrating cheek bone, a slight change in complexion, a slight stutter, will show the strain. The enthusiasm and drive must be concealed, but they are there, if you are attuned to the language; and civil servants will sometimes talk about their operations as if the whole building was about to go up under the pressure: 'There's a terrific head of steam ... we're really putting the heat on ... the electricity's buzzing along the wires.'

Whitehall linguistics can also be usefully studied in white papers. They are supposed to proclaim changes of policy to the general public, but they are very often preoccupied with concealing the changes: 'The Treasury is like the Vatican,' one civil servant once explained to me: 'whenever it says something new, it has to pretend that it's really just the same as before.' A *locus classicus* for the obscurantist Whitehall style was the Plowden Report of 1961, which concealed fierce criticism of the current system of Treasury control under a façade of amiable congratulation. In 1962[1] I offered my own translation of some phrases in Lord Plowden's choice kid-glove language: 'We hope that it is fully appreciated that' meant 'you completely fail to realise that', and 'our enquiry seemed to provide a welcome opportunity for discussions of problems of this kind' meant 'no one had thought of that before'; the challenge was taken up by W. J. M. Mackenzie, Professor of Government at Glasgow and a former philologist, who provided a translation of the entire Plowden Report,[2] at a fifth of the original length, beginning thus:

ORIGINAL

1. At our first meeting, in October 1959, we decided to concentrate in full committee on the central problem of public expenditure, which is the determination of policy and the distribution of resources, while studying in smaller groups particular aspects of expenditure control or areas of expenditure. For these studies we co-opted the permanent secretaries of the departments with whose expenditure we were concerned or who had special experience of the general problems under review. In some cases we sought specialist advice from outside the civil service. We decided, however, not to take evidence from outside bodies: our review was primarily concerned with the inner working of the Treasury and the departments, and was necessarily confidential in character, and we decided that the group itself (except on certain specialist matters) provided a sufficient body of outside opinion to bring to bear on this task.

[1] *Anatomy of Britain*, 1962, p. 293.
[2] *The Guardian*, May 25 1963. Reproduced in *Policy Making in Britain*, edited by Richard Rose.

TRANSLATION

1. We proceeded on two principles: no dirty linen in public; outside critics are bores.

2. We did however chat to a great many civil servants, and two years of that is more than enough.

3. Unluckily, it turns out that the real problem is about the nature of government in general, and of British government in particular. This is what we are discussing, but of course we have to wrap it up in mandarin prose.

4. Our general impression is that the civil service is extremely old-fashioned and riven by jealousies: but there is public spirit there, and some of them do try quite hard.

5. This report is just 'key-note' stuff: detailed proposals have been handed in separately.

This obscurantism has deep roots. It comes partly from the instinctive caution of Whitehall, which always likes to disguise instructions as suggestions; departments are never ordered to do anything; they are 'invited to submit proposals'. Learning this kind of language is part of the process of becoming house-trained in Whitehall. In this context, the double negative comes naturally, and sometimes whole reports seem to be marching backwards, retreating from negative to negative, as if crouching in masochistic passivity, with such phrases as 'not intolerable' (ouch!) 'we cannot but be struck by' (thump!) 'it is a matter of regret that' (ow!): and a specially delicate vocabulary is available to explain why things can't be done: 'it would be a sterile exercise to . . .' 'it would be rendering a disservice to . . .'

Civil servants maintain that this process is part of the machinery of government, and that the ambiguities and evasions stem from the chief committee of all—the cabinet. The fogginess of white papers can often be traced back to the politicians. A particularly appalling example was the white paper on the common market in February 1970, which effectively concealed most of the important questions about Europe and resorted to linguistic contortions to avoid reaching any conclusion. The distinguished civil servants who put it together could blame it on the ambiguities of Harold Wilson and his cabinet, and *their* fear of explaining anything to the public. But much of the fogginess has long ceased to be a temporary smokescreen, and has become a permanent and convenient camouflage, which cuts off the bureaucrats from the people they are meant to be serving. It is language which betrays the civil servants' natural clandestine tendencies in their 'secret garden of the crown'.

The consensus of the committee, the reduction of all policy to the common denominator, can result in a terrible dehumanisation and lack of imagination in final decisions. For some bureaucrats themselves, the suppression of individuality enforced by the committee-machinery is a great personal strain; in May 1969 a remarkable civil servant from the Home Office, Derek Morrell (a Catholic reformer who died the following year) made a speech at a meeting of the First Division Association, the trades union of the administrative class, which made a great stir among the other members:

> Speaking personally, I find it yearly more difficult to reconcile personal integrity with a role which requires the deliberate suppression of part of what I am. It is this tension, and not overwork, which brings me, regularly, to the point where I am ready to contemplate leaving a service which I care about very deeply.
>
> But the price which the public has to pay is even heavier. For the part of ourselves which we are asked to suppress is the creative part. There is nothing more individual than an idea. No committee ever has, or ever will, form an idea. It can only adopt one. Ideas are formed by individuals from the depths of their personalities: they have to be felt before they can be brought to consciousness. And they often have to be sustained over a long period, not infrequently with a modicum of passion, before a process of critical appraisal by others defines their realisation as a valid object of public policy.
>
> I reject the many smears to which we are subject. But I accept as valid the charge that creative administration is not our strong point: and I accept the charge, which is really to say the same thing in different words, that we often seem insensitive to the needs and feelings of the governed, valuing the integrity of our own systems more highly than the integrity of those whose needs we exist to meet. I do not however accept that we behave like this because we are personally insensitive or personally lacking in creativity: the nigger in the woodpile is the myth that personal objectivity is attainable.

Morrell's complaints caused a sub-committee of civil servants to report on professional standards, who insisted that they must be responsible to society, as well as to their ministers. One of them, Dr Hugh Phillips, wrote a memorandum in which he said:

> ... We want an end to the suppression of selected facts and figures, and to a promotion system which gives priority to the mealy-mouthed purveyors of prejudice and half-truth rather than to the collectors of fact and the people who call a spade a spade. We do not think that it is part of the function, either of Ministers or of senior officials, to

censor the non-political views of civil servants, to prevent officials seeing ministers, or to suppress the views and/or facts produced by officials—provided that these views and those facts have been properly produced as part of the job of the individual concerned . . . Let 'Committees' become places where qualified persons dispute alternative courses and try to agree on action, rather than places where selected 'front' men with little knowledge 'simper' to an agreed tune, with a view either to delaying action or to saying what it is thought Ministers *want* to hear . . .

'It's a bit too smooth,' Lord Butler once said to me, about the civil service; 'it needs *rubbing up* a bit': and this, I believe, is still true. Many civil servants are conscious of the limitations of the committee, and the civil service department has even experimented with 'think-tanks' and 'brainstorms', borrowed from industry or advertising, to try to stimulate new ideas. The Fulton reforms, by bringing in outsiders, by breaking down the internal classes, and by exposing civil servants to training, may have some effect in rubbing up; scientists have an innate disrespect for formalities. But the great flywheel is so heavy and well-oiled, the machinery so intricate, that it is difficult for outsiders to dent it. The subtlety and implications of the language can easily demoralise rugged men who have come in from laboratories or factories. The aura of Whitehall casts its spell on all who come near it; the most improbable people end up writing in white paper language. The huge shape of government spreads its shadow through the circumference of institutions, councils and outside committees: however supposedly independent, they tend soon to adopt the same emaciated style. Inside many a rip-roaring rebel, there is a pedantic bureaucrat trying to get out.

The need for more straightforward communication is made more urgent by the mounting public hostility to the central bureaucracies, and the insistence on closer participation between governors and governed. The whole confident authority of Whitehall rests in the end on the consent of the millions; and in a questioning and rebellious age their acquiescence cannot so easily be taken for granted. Not long ago a minister, discussing an industrial problem with his permanent secretary, asked him to summon a prominent businessman. The permanent secretary paused for a moment, and the minister asked what was wrong. 'Nothing', he replied: 'but I was just wondering what would happen if he just said "fuck off".' The problem of consent may well face other countries more fiercely—particularly on the continent, where the tradition of bureaucracies is deeper and longer, predating the tradition of parliament. But Britain, too, is facing more bitter resentments, both from the outlying provinces who feel themselves over-ruled by distant officials, and from a new political generation with less sense of involvement with the obfuscations of Whitehall and Westminster government. The alienation makes it more urgent that the civil service should evolve methods and styles which could give it much closer contact with the public, enable it to communicate honestly and informally with its customers, and which could make Whitehall appear, not as a single central bureaucracy but as a collection of separate, different and accessible departments, organised to cope with their special problems and special public. In the past, Britain has been more successful than most countries in evolving a type of government that is both effective and human. It should still be possible for Britain to take the lead in the next steps towards 'democracy with a human face'.

SIR WILLIAM ARMSTRONG

It was an important coincidence that at the time when criticism of the civil service was at last inducing reform there should be a man at the top of it who saw his life-work as a reformer. The personality of Sir William Armstrong may emerge historically as a more important factor than the Fulton commissioners, for no bureaucratic reform is possible without strong support from inside. In 1968 Sir William took over the job of head of the home civil service, including the new civil service department, and committed himself—with publicity unprecedented for a civil servant—to implementing the Fulton reforms. Armstrong's position is not quite as powerful as that of some earlier heads, like Sir Warren Fisher or Sir Norman Brook, who was at the same time secretary of the cabinet; the cabinet job is now separate, under Sir Burke Trend.[1] But Armstrong retains the oversight of all departments, and all senior appointments go through him. His importance is enhanced by his permanence; it is nine years since he first reached the peaks of government as joint permanent secretary to the Treasury, and he is still only fifty-six. To politicians he is the very symbol of the continuity of the civil service, of 'ongoing reality' as

[1] See Chapter 4.

Armstrong calls it. 'Whichever party's in office,' complained one politician, 'it all comes down to Armstrong.'

He seems in many ways a personification of the ideal of a neutral, loyal civil servant, carrying out the wishes of the party in power to the vexation of the opposition. 'The wonderful thing about William,' said one newly-arrived Tory minister in 1970, 'is that he's a real democrat; he really *believes* that his job is to serve his political masters.' 'The trouble with Armstrong,' said one newly-retired Labour minister, 'is that he's always been somebody's secretary.' He is a shortish, rather grey-looking man, with large melancholy eyes, broad shoulders and the burdened look which is observable in many top civil servants, as if they were literally carrying the country's whole weight on their shoulders. His background is amazing for a civil servant. His parents were officers in the Salvation Army, and he spent his childhood travelling round with them through the poor quarters of England, and carrying the banner for the processions—he was not musical enough to play an instrument. His background now hardly shows itself, except in a zeal for democratisation of the service, and perhaps a suppressed fondness for talking. From this austere beginning he was suddenly dropped into pre-war Oxford, with a scholarship to Exeter College. His mind was superbly efficient; he took firsts in Mods and Greats, and acquired an easy mastery of logic. But he was quite uninterested in politics, unmoved by the questions of unemployment or the Spanish civil war, and he has maintained his political neutrality without visible difficulty during his thirty-four years in the public service. In 1938 he went into the Board of Education—probably the only man in the administrative grade who had been through the system of education that they were administering. After the war—when he worked as secretary to Sir Edward Bridges in the war cabinet—he became private secretary to the chancellor of the exchequer, always a key job, and served Cripps, Gaitskell and Butler. By 1958 he was running the very complex Home Finance Department of the Treasury. When in 1961 plans were afoot to reorganise the Treasury, Armstrong submitted his own ideas; many of them were accepted, and he himself was appointed to implement them in 1962. For the next six years, a period of successive economic crises, he was head of the Treasury—an exhausting and dispiriting ordeal. When the Fulton Report was accepted, Armstrong was the obvious man to carry it through, as head of the civil service.

It All Comes Down to Armstrong

Unlike his predecessors, Sir William's name is quite famous. He has appeared on television, made speeches and lectures about civil service reform, and he believes that senior civil servants should be prepared to explain their policies and ideas to the public—itself a revolutionary idea in Whitehall. He openly exhorts his own civil servants. 'We are not in business on our own account, we are not a debating society, a private army or a social club'; he said to a civil servants' conference in 1968, 'we are the instruments through which our fellow countrymen seek to exercise their collective will—for their benefit, and only incidentally for ours.' 'We shall have to do better than private enterprise,' he said to the Institute of Public Administration, 'because we shall have to find ways of getting efficiency without the spur of the market place and the profit motive.' He has even appeared to welcome the invasion of businessmen after the 1970 general election. But he remains very much the head of a proud profession, defending their rights and dignity: 'It is simply not possible for any group of people,' he warned in June 1970, 'whether they come from outside or whether they are styled the top management of the civil service, simply to design new systems of work, new arrangements for recruitment, selection and training and hand them out ready-made to the waiting flock.' He sees the civil service as a stronghold of wisdom and experience, which politicians ignore at their peril: 'The chief danger to which politicians and ministers are open is not, as is often supposed, that obstructive bureaucrats will drag their feet in implementing their schemes, but that their own optimism will carry them into schemes and policies which will subsequently be seen to fail and which attention to the experience and information available from the service might have avoided.'

Armstrong is an enigma to many of his colleagues, not least because, having worked for so long in the centres of power, he has become a subtle master of its techniques. This is how one of his former secretaries, Peter Jay, described his mystery:

> Many of those who have known him well and worked with him closely find it hard to define wherein exactly lies the special magic which makes Sir William almost everyone's first choice for virtually every public appointment of any exceptional difficulty or importance. What is most impressive, perhaps, is the confidence in his ability to get results, to win people round, and to create agreement where nothing but dissension could be discerned by ordinary eyes. This

reputation is all the more striking in someone who at times appears to the casual observer to carry the doctrine of *festina lente* to the point of indecision. There have reportedly been moments when Sir William seems to have dribbled the ball so far back towards his own goal-line for the sake of a better opening that he has looked in danger of scoring against himself. But a more apposite metaphor is to be found from his own favourite hobby—sailing. Sailing boats progress not into the teeth of the elements but obliquely, harnessing their energy to the boat's own purposes; and the best helmsman is he who most accurately judges the shifts and changes of wind and tide. At times he may seem 'no painful inch to gain'; but then, suddenly, when the untutored least expect it, they come 'silent flooding in' to port. Sir William is incomparably the master helmsman of Whitehall.

It is hard not to be impressed by Armstrong's openness, his sensitivity and his preparedness to discuss any aspect of his job. He runs his own department informally, with easy communication; his staff call him William, not permanent secretary. His whole style is a break from his predecessors', and his own candour has helped to open up the service. He combines a penetrating intellect with real imagination—a rare mixture: he tries to visualise how situations might be, and is not stuck in that deadly bureaucratic assumption: 'Things being as they are.' To many young civil servants he is the personification of their hopes and ideals. But his real problems remain all too practical; and there are some who fear that, sitting at the top of his pile of pyramids, he becomes too lost in the higher theories, too engrossed in the far future—as permanent secretaries are apt to be—to be able to grapple with the appalling immediate problems of refashioning the whole bureaucracy. The limitations of his scope are acute; for the civil service is essentially a federal organisation, and the effectiveness of the reforms depends in the end on the ability of the civil service department to cajole, persuade, or bully the hundred departments each of which prides itself on its own character and autonomy. It will be only in twenty or thirty years' time, when a new generation of civil servants have come to power through the new recruitment and training, that the success or failure of Armstrong will really be known.

DEPARTMENTS

To the general public the civil service looks like one great monolith, with the same austere buildings and the same bleak letter-heads, the same messengers and doormen in blue uniforms with crowns on their lapels. But to anyone inside, it is not the civil service but the department which commands his main loyalty; most civil servants spend their whole lives within a single department, and they come to regard other ministries as enemies rather than as allies. The autonomy of the departments is often defended as being an important element of the British democratic tradition, though it is largely the result of the kind of accumulating cross-purposes that affect I.C.I., Shell and any bureaucracy. Before 1870 they had little contact with each other; they were private empires with no common recruitment policy or common salaries; and in spite of all the later enlargements and coordinations, they still preserve their separate characters and philosophies. The hundred departments vary in size from the Ministry of Defence, a kind of microcosm of the whole civil service, to tiny councils and commissions, like the Privy Council office or the Countryside Commission, with only a handful of members. Here are the most important home departments with their permanent secretaries:

Civil Service Department	Sir William Armstrong
Treasury	Sir Douglas Allen
Home Office	Sir Philip Allen
Defence	Sir James Dunnett
(Administration)	Sir Arthur Drew
(Equipment)	Sir Martin Flett
Health and Social Security	Sir Philip Rogers
Employment	Sir Denis Barnes
Education and Science	Sir William Pile
Environment	Sir David Serpell
(Housing and Construction)	Sir Michael Cary
(Local Government and Development)	J. D. Jones
Trade and Industry	Sir Antony Part
(Trade)	Sir Max Brown
(Industry)	R. B. Marshall
Agriculture, Fisheries and Food	Sir Basil Engholm
Scottish Office	Sir Douglas Haddow
Welsh Office	I. V. Pugh
Customs and Excise	Sir Louis Petch
Inland Revenue	Sir Arnold France
Aviation Supply	Sir Ronald Melville

The characters of the departments are much influenced by their history, their role and their clients 'in the outside world'. The oldest department, the Home Office, has a rigid hierarchical

253

structure, and is preoccupied with questions of discipline—prisons, police, or immigration; it is the most daunting of departments and few politicians have made much of a dent in its iron structure. The newer ministries, like Transport and Housing (both now part of the Department of the Environment) have become closely involved in running huge industries and have themselves become more like industrial bureaucracies. Education and Science has taken on some of the headmasterly characteristics of the schools it is trying to control; the Ministry of Agriculture still has a slight whiff of the farmyard (the minister himself is usually a farmer). The intellectual atmosphere of departments ranges from the rigorous exclusiveness of the Treasury, to the flabby pragmatism of the old Board of Trade. In their own social attitudes the departments vary almost as much as countries: in their treatment of women, the Inland Revenue and the Department of Health and Social Security might almost belong to Islam.

The departments are inclined to treat each other more as foreign powers than as part of the same central government: their civil servants will refer to 'the MAFF' (Ministry of Agriculture, Fisheries and Food) or the 'MOD' (Defence) as if they were on the Amazon. To co-ordinate their policies the creaking machinery of interdepartmental committees has grown up, as one of the most characteristic institutions of Whitehall, churning out what Churchill called 'inter-departmental slush'. Representatives from the departments come together as embattled as ambassadors at NATO, to co-ordinate, raise objections and reluctantly compromise; and many of the most maddening characteristics of government—like the prose of white papers—are the result of this interdepartmental process. It astonishes many visitors to Whitehall to realise how many policies are the product not of clear-cut central decisions, but of these slow-motion battles between the separate bureaucracies. Yet it is the inevitable price of the British pattern of democracy; for each minister is responsible to parliament for running his ministry and also collectively responsible for the decisions of the cabinet. The strains of this double role show themselves all the way down the departments; interdepartmental committees are confused miniature reflections of the cabinet trying vainly to produce collective decisions.

As government has become wider in its scope, so departments have overlapped further, and the ministers' separate responsibilities have become more confused on the wide margins of their ministries. This has been an over-riding problem of successive prime ministers; and as Britain's overseas problems have waned, so the machinery of government has become an engrossing subject for politicians. The energy that once went to planning constitutions for Kenya or Nigeria is now devoted to planning new structures for the Ministry of Works or the Board of Trade. In the lack-lustre prose of the Conservative government white paper of October 15, 1970:

> In recent years it has become clear that the structure of inter-departmental committees, each concerned with a separate area of policy, needs to be reinforced by a clear and comprehensive definition of government strategy which can be systematically developed to take account of changing circumstances and can provide a framework within which the government's policies as a whole may be more effectively formulated. For lack of such a clear definition of strategic purpose and under the pressures of the day to day problems immediately before them, governments are always at some risk of losing sight of the need to consider the totality of their current policies in relation to their longer term objectives; and they may pay too little attention to the difficult but critical task of evaluating as objectively as possible the alternative policy options and priorities open to them.

In other words: 'Governments are so busy compromising between departments that they forget what they're trying to do.'

In the last ten years both Macmillan and Wilson took steps towards creating 'monster ministries', such as Defence or Technology, to embrace all the related sections of one activity under the same boss, and thus to escape from interdepartmental muddle. And in 1970 Heath constructed two new monster ministries or 'unified departments'. The new Department of the Environment (a word hardly uttered two years before) was created to merge housing, transport and local government under a single minister, Peter Walker; and the Department of Trade and Industry merged the Board of Trade with the remains of the Ministry of Technology. The aim of both mergers, as the white paper explained, was to resolve conflicts 'within the line of management rather than by interdepartmental compromise'. Ministries which had formerly been proud separate entities, like Transport or Overseas Development (now merged with the Foreign Office) were rudely reduced to 'functional wings'.

These big mergers were difficult for the opposition to attack, for nearly everyone was agreed about the wastage of the inter-departmental conflicts. Nor were super-ministries particularly

new: seven years before, Ted Heath himself had been given an
enlarged Board of Trade, and was grandiloquently described as
'Secretary of State for Industry, Trade and Regional Development and President of the Board of Trade'. But behind the theory
of super-ministries there have always been two snags. First, how
to find super-ministers to run them; and second, how to square
them with the traditional notions of democracy. For the very
fact that conflicts will be resolved in the intestines of huge unified
departments makes it harder for parliament and the public to
observe them; just as the unified Ministry of Defence has successfully concealed the bombardments between the Army and the
Navy,[1] so the new monster ministries will hide the conflicts
between Environment and Industry. Many of the interdepartmental arguments have been absurd, but others are part of the
stuff of democracy. The white paper hopefully explains that 'a
department unifying a group of functions will be less open to the
risk of being parochial and will, therefore, be more answerable
to parliament and the community at large'. One Conservative
minister assures me that: 'far from closing areas the new departments represent the first serious attempt to open out government
and create new centres of authority and sources of policy below the
level of the prime minister and the cabinet ... Government by
lots of small departments guarantees over-centralised and
secretive government.' But the actual accountability takes the
shape of a single cabinet minister at the top who is able—if he
wishes—to conceal a great deal of the argument and misgivings
within his large empire. And the worry is greater since both the
super ministers, Peter Walker and John Davies, have come from
the world of big business, and are not notable 'House of Commons
men'. Parliament's worries appeared to be justified in April 1971,
with the Department of Trade's apparent mishandling of the
collapse of the 'V and G' insurance company (see chapter 28).

To prime ministers these shiftings of ministries take the shape of
simple deployment of political colleagues; but to the civil servants
they seem almost as drastic as moving a county from England to
Wales; and each new reshuffle produces a new wave of worry.
In the last ten years one man doing the same job could have
served in the Ministry of Aviation, in the Ministry of Technology,
and in the new Ministry of Aviation Supply, soon to become part
of the Ministry of Defence. The repercussions on civil servants can

[1] See Chapter 16.

be very demoralising, and the weighing-up of the long-term efficiency of monster ministries with the short-term bewilderment is a difficult equation: not least because a new government may soon, once again, reshuffle the pack.

Every change is supposed to reduce the numbers of civil servants; in the words of the white paper, to produce 'less government and better government, carried out by fewer people'. There are promises that the giant departments will show a reduction; but in earlier mergers the numbers have never actually gone down. The merged ministries, far from getting one man to do the job of three, often prefer to bring in a fourth to co-ordinate the other three. Even computers and new management techniques do not seem to cut down the staff; they need new men to work the computers and techniques, and the most immediate result of the Fulton Report was the ever-growing Civil Service Department. The British bureaucracy, like all other government bureaucracies, has its own imperatives and its own tribal strength which defies all reshuffles: whether in one ministry or another, the same group of men do the same jobs in the same way. The civil servants are more part of the country, more permanent and continuous, than any politician or management consultant; they are not part of the 'machinery of government', as politicians like to describe them, as if they can be dismantled, re-jigged and replaced: they are more like a family or a village community, which can take a generation to change. And behind all the good intentions of governments there is always the conflict within each of the ministers themselves: that while they are a cabinet they are united against extra public spending, but when they are individual ministers they are each determined to spend more.

MINISTERS

Political heads of departments are necessary to tell the civil service what the public will not stand.

Sir William Harcourt.

Ministers can be divided into those who run their departments and those who are run by their departments. I believe parliament finds out jolly quickly into which category ministers fall, and civil servants know within forty-eight hours of the minister putting his foot over the doorstep.

Iain Macleod, January 1964.

The two heads of each department, the minister and the permanent secretary, are from two opposite worlds, and their relationship is the vital joint in Whitehall—the elbow of government, between decision and execution. On the one hand is the minister—famous, extrovert, politically committed. In the waiting-room there is no photograph of the permanent secretary, but a row of photographs of past ministers, from proud bearded Victorians in faded daguerreotypes, gradually changing—with the pressure of universal suffrage—to the beaming and plausible men of the present. The minister embodies the whole public personality of his ministry, and he alone is blamed for its public faults.

He must defend and explain his department to parliament: and this public accountability remains in theory the over-riding difference between a civil service department and private industry. It takes its most obvious form in parliamentary debates and the parliamentary question. The PQ, in theory at least, is the eye of the public, and it certainly affects the character of the ministry: rooms full of filing cabinets, overflowing with trivial correspondence, are preserved for fear of some future awkward question. Many a civil servant will dream of the peaceful opaqueness of Unilever and ICI, where millions can be lost and no questions asked. The traditional caution of civil servants, their dislike of publicity, their obscurantism, all derive from the dread of the public. 'How did the questions go?' asks a permanent secretary, as if awaiting news of a distant battle. The PQ is a much less seeing eye than it used to be: in the bowels of the big departments, enormous incompetence can be perpetrated and never come to light. But a well-informed question can still disrupt a department. The track of questions is time-wasting and can cause colossal delays: but it is a prime example of the inefficiency that is the price of democracy.

It is in their departments that the ministers appear in all their splendour, talking with carefree indiscretion behind their big leather-topped desks, leaning back on their chairs. It is not difficult to understand why they are always reluctant to resign. Compared to the other two parts of his job—parliament and cabinet—a minister is here his own boss, able to do what he likes, with the whole structure of the department built round him, and a private office run by male secretaries next door dedicated to the task of keeping him happy. In parliament every blunder and anxiety is exposed. In the ministry—where he may spend nine-

tenths of his time—the whole staff is there to support and defend
him. This is what some ministers, both Conservative and Labour,
have said to me about their jobs:

> The power a minister's got is amazing! Now I realise why every-
> one's always so keen to set up boards and councils and authorities—
> to put their friends in!
>
> Running a civil service department is like playing an organ—you
> can do almost anything with it. No industrialist gets the same kind
> of service. A minister can ring a bell, ask for a report on anything,
> and get it.
>
> Boy, those people next door are wonderful! I tell you, my speeches
> are going to sound a lot better from now on!
>
> You know, the civil servants have got a wonderful political sense,
> without themselves being political. They can get the feel of your ideas
> very quickly.
>
> They often give you advice based on assumptions of government
> policy which turn out to be quite wrong.
>
> Of course I know their tricks: they fill up your in-tray so that you're
> too busy to make any changes. But I keep a check on things I've asked
> to be done and make sure they've done them. They're wonderful
> people really.
>
> They can ruin a minister if they want to, you know.
>
> Any fool can find the answers to the questions. The difficult thing is
> to find the questions to the answers.

A good deal of the influence of a civil servant on a minister
depends on disguising his influence, making him think that their
idea was *his* idea. In business, as well as in Whitehall, a chairman
may *imagine* he is running a company—like a pianola-player, sitting
on the music-stool, varying the speed and volume, while the tune
is being played by the machine. In the past the minister was held
responsible for things he knew nothing about: Austen Chamberlain resigned over the medical supplies to Mesopotamia, and Sir
Thomas Dugdale resigned over the Crichel Down affair. 'The
one thing a minister must never be able to say,' said Sir Richard
Hopkins, 'is "Why wasn't I told?"' And that angry question
reverberated through the Profumo affair, and through the V and G
affair. But in the more technical and managerial ministries, it is
impossible for the head to know everything: once he started
asking 'Why wasn't I told?' there would be no end to it. Every
minister nowadays finds himself signing minutes he knows nothing
about. Inevitably, like a good chairman, a minister must delegate

to his juniors—and the frontier between politicians and civil servants is lost.

The permanent secretaries must form the most closely knit and powerful association in Great Britain.

Richard Crossman, July 1970.

Next door to the ministers in less spectacular rooms sit the permanent secretaries, the official heads of departments. The relationship between the permanent secretary and his 'master' is poignant and complex. It is the coming together, not just of politics and officialdom, but of two opposite roles. Even the permanent secretaries who are politicians *manqués*—a large contingent—often like to cultivate the style of the servant, the shambling walk, the slight stoop and the quizzical expression which stresses that they are just secretaries: that they are owls and not eagles. Politicians, as we have seen, can derive great emotional satisfaction from their permanent secretaries; Disraeli was rhapsodic about it: 'The relations between a minister and his secretary,' he wrote in *Endymion*, 'are, or at least should be, among the finest that can subsist between two individuals. Except the married state, there is none in which so great a confidence is involved, in which more forbearance ought to be exercised, or more sympathy ought to exist.' But the play of master and servant is nowadays not easy to preserve; 'The fact is,' one Labour minister burst out to his permanent secretary, 'that you're the permanent politician, and I'm just the temporary one.'

Permanent secretaries never write their memoirs; they read the explosions from George Brown or Harold Wilson with amusement or pain, and say to each other 'if only they knew'. In fact much of the history of the last decade is bound up with the views and personalities of civil servants: the influence of Sir Richard Clarke in the late Ministry of Technology; of Sir Douglas Allen in the Treasury, of Sir Denis Barnes in the Department of Employment, have all been central not only to the execution of political measures but (as implied in the words of Sir Henry Taylor, at the head of this chapter) to the measures themselves. Part of their role will eventually come to light in the history books, as the pre-war role of civil servants like Horace Wilson or Warren Fisher later came out. But much will never be known.

Permanent secretaries, like ministers, love talking about the political game—though in a quite different style, dwelling on the ups and downs, the ins and outs, the hopes and disappointments, as if they were spectators at a play. But outside their offices they still revel in their anonymity, which seems to be a passion almost as gripping as fame is for their masters; as they hear a politician proudly produce a phrase that was invented by themselves, they feel a thrill of non-attribution. A few permanent secretaries, following Armstrong's example, enjoy bursting into the limelight, like Sir Michael Cary (the son of Joyce Cary), the head of Public Buildings and Works, who caused a stir in 1970 by attacking the mediocrity of architects. As a group they are nowadays less secretive, and the attacks on the 'mandarins of Whitehall' have left them anxious to show that they are human beings, with nothing to hide. But most of them, I suspect, regard publicity as a distressing disturbance and look forward to the public again becoming bored by them. 'In my view,' said Sir Antony Part of the Department of Trade and Industry, 'we shall cross a fatal Rubicon if we insist on revealing differences of view between departments or exchanges between ministers and civil servants.'

An encounter between a veteran permanent secretary, pessimistic and cautious, and a new young minister, unorthodox and idealistic, provides a classic conjunction. Ministers are full of stories of how they have been told 'it's impossible', 'it's never been done before'. Very rarely the permanent secretary is discreetly removed to another ministry: but 'it's very difficult to get rid of 'em, you know', said one ex-minister, 'things have to get pretty desperate'. Barbara Castle, as Minister of Transport, tried in vain to move Sir Thomas Padmore, the permanent secretary: Richard Crossman as Minister of Housing battled with 'the Dame', Dame Evelyn Sharp, the most formidable of them all, before he came to terms with her. Usually the conflict is resolved in compromise, for the permanent secretary is the repository not only of caution, but of the armoury of facts ('Facts that seem to live in the office,' said Bagehot, 'so teasing and unceasing they are'). Politicians from both parties like to give the impression of battling against bureaucrats: but there are signs that the Heath government are being more successful than the Wilson one—partly perhaps because Labour leaders tend to *like* the bureaucrats.

Permanent secretaries are still very Oxbridge, and communicate easily in that special vernacular. Of the thirty PS's in 1970, two went to LSE, one to Glasgow, and one (Sir Arnold France) did not go to university; twenty-six went to Oxford or Cambridge. But only eleven of them went to public schools; there is only one Etonian (Sir Michael Cary) and one Harrovian (Sir Antony Part) —both unusually formidable and outspoken. Two come from Manchester Grammar School, and two from Christ's Hospital; but the rest come from scattered grammar schools, and one from Wanganui College in New Zealand (Sir Max Brown). Most of the permanent secretaries have worked their way up after Oxbridge through the service; but a few have seen life outside Whitehall. Sir Arnold France worked in the District Bank for eleven years; Sir Samuel Goldman worked for Sebag's the stockbrokers; Sir William Nield, one of the steadfast Europeans once worked in Transport House and for the King-Hall newsletter. But all these were shaken up by the war, and it is now less easy for a man to switch into the service in middle age.

Some secretaries are a good deal more permanent than others, and the position of the stayers is strong. Sir James Dunnett has been at Defence for five years, and has been a permanent secretary in one department or another for the past eleven years; Sir Denis Barnes at Employment has been permanent secretary for five years, and deputy before that. Sir Burke Trend, secretary to the cabinet for eight years, is the personification of 'ongoing reality'. These very permanent secretaries, with their memories of precedents, snags and mistakes, can easily induce in ministers the sense of being very temporary, very rash. In the super-ministries, the permanent secretary is specially indispensible, as the one man who understands the honeycomb. Sir Antony Part, at the Department of Trade and Industry, has been a master-manager ever since he was the second youngest lieutenant-colonel in the war: it is round him, more than the three ministers, that the whole organisation revolves.

The social relations between ministers and permanent secretaries have changed. 'In the old days it used to be thought that the minister was chosen by God and the permanent secretary was just an official,' said Lord Butler, and this servitude was emphasised by the fact that permanent secretaries were much poorer; before the war they earned £3,000 a year against the minister's £5,000 a year, and many ministers had big private incomes. But since 1964 the permanent secretaries have been earning a good deal more than their masters. As from July 1, 1971, they earn

£14,000 a year, and the three top ones get £15,000 a year, compared to the cabinet minister's £8,500, and the difference is made greater by the insecurity of the minister, whose salary can stop dead after a general election, leaving the civil servant still earning away: in this position, a permanent secretary can feel very unservantlike: 'Why should I be at the beck and call of my minister at all times of night?' complained one: 'the politicians are terribly pampered, you know.' Senior civil servants still like to affect that martyred clerical manner as if they were underpaid, overworked and browbeaten; but in fact they are now pretty rich. With cars, chauffeurs, long holidays, large pensions and almost total security, they are among the aristocrats of modern Britain, equipped with power *and* money.

Below are the top grades of the home civil service with their salaries in July 1971 and the numbers of occupants, together with the numbers (in brackets) of specialist and professional civil servants of equivalent rank:

3 super permanent secretaries	£15,000
17 (+8) permanent secretaries	£14,000
8 second permanent secretaries	£13,000
74 (+40) deputy-secretaries	£9,000
302 (+146) under-secretaries	£6,750
1020 (+2434) assistant secretaries	£4,390–£5,640 (under review)

Most civil servants stop at the level of assistant secretary. It is the next jump, to under-secretary, that is the difficult one—like the jump to Flag Officer in the Navy—and it is at this point that the civil service department has its eye on the talent, to find men for top jobs and to move them from one department to another. Promotion, which is supervised by Armstrong and the prime minister, is an intricate chess game, with too many pawns and not enough queens, and all kinds of bureaucratic laws at work to prevent the best people from getting up to the top. There is the time-honoured principle of 'Buggins's turn'. There is the Peter Principle, which holds that everyone rises to the level of his own mediocrity. And there is the law expounded by the late Lord Normanbrook, the former head of the civil service: that, in any promotion, 'either there was nobody else, or there *was* somebody else'. Nobody-else is quite often the case: and Roy Jenkins explained to the Select Committee on the Bank of England that permanent secretaries tend to be self-selecting. Then there is the recurring problem of what to do with the Spent Force, the Burnt-out Case, the man who became senile too soon. In the old days the empire was full of resting-places for deadbeat civil servants, who could be sent off as governors or residents without messing up departments at home. But as the empire dissolved, so the sinecures disappeared: as Lord Bridges said to a colleague: 'All my mattresses are going.' There have to be new ways of discreetly demoting or displacing the dead wood; and the problem of how to widen the narrow top of the pyramid, or to find little pyramids alongside it, is harder in the civil service than in industry, where high sounding sinecures can be created without trouble from shareholders.

To many politicians the network of permanent secretaries is a kind of knightmare—a mysterious negative force which stops things happening, by pulling invisible levers. They work more closely together than ministers, who are more preoccupied with competing with each other: they see each other in interdepartmental committees, and in such places as the cabinet office mess, the informal hub of the Whitehall world, where men from the top departments of Whitehall can meet for macaroni cheese and Dutch lager, and where Sir Burke Trend has his special table reserved in the corner. Every year all the permanent secretaries go to the Civil Service College at Sunningdale, for a weekend conference to discuss their common problems, and to walk round Windsor Great Park (while Sir Douglas Allen plays tennis). It is enough to bring out the worst fears of government by mandarins.

If all the permanent secretaries are against something, they can certainly make it very difficult for the new ministers to carry out their plans; on moves which threaten their own profession, they can be very solid (they were specially worked up about Enoch Powell's allegation about 'enemies of the State'). But they have their own rivalries and extreme differences of opinion: they are left-wing and right-wing, European and anti-European, interventionist and anti-interventionist; and in their sympathies with Labour or Conservative they probably (as far as one can penetrate their elaborate cynicism) divide roughly equally.

THE GREAT AND THE GOOD

In any speculations about 'The Establishment' or 'They' the permanent secretaries will always be a favourite target, with the heads of the civil service department and the Treasury in the bull's eye. They not only settle economic and financial policies and regulate the civil service; they have also a large influence on quasi-government appointments (ranging from a director of the Tate Gallery to a director of British Petroleum) and on the process of talent-spotting and approval of all the hundreds of men from outside the civil service who serve on committees and commissions. A secret tome of The Great and the Good is kept in the civil service department, listing everyone who has the right qualifications of worthiness, soundness, and discretion; and from this tome come many of the stage army of committee-people who are scattered through this book. For anyone who feels neglected, persecuted or underestimated it is not difficult to imagine his name in a Book of the Bad. The tome is in fact a whole row of loose-leaf volumes, looked after by young civil servants, who keep track of likely men through official appointments, press cuttings and news from other departments. The limitations are evident in the difficulties the government has in finding the right men—particularly for nationalised industries (see chapter 35). 'The trouble is,' said one permanent secretary, 'that civil servants don't really meet other people until they get to the top. We can't really find out who are the able men in their thirties or forties before they become famous.' Too often the Book recommends someone whose career on paper looks immaculate, but who turns out, like Lord ——, to have been kicked up one lot of stairs after another.

Permanent secretaries themselves are of course assumed to be the Greatest and Best, and their opportunities are extended by their easy access to jobs outside the civil service. Some go into other parts of the public service—like Sir Richard Way, who went from the Ministry of Aviation to be chairman of the London Transport Executive; or Sir John Winnifrith, who went from Agriculture to run the National Trust; or Sir Alan Marre, who became the Ombudsman. In the last ten years, with the growth of planning and interventionism, the permanent secretaries have become much closer to private industry, and many more have moved into top industrial jobs, like the 'parachuting' of the French *inspecteurs des finances* into private industry. The main cause (as in France) is money. Permanent secretaries can earn more than their £14,000 a year in industry: and they are now allowed to keep their pensions if they leave early. The life of a tycoon is easier—there is less pressure of work, no parliament watching you, no minister in the way. There are fewer committees and less frustration, and some civil servants become visibly impatient with the Whitehall machine. The exodus began in 1951, when Sir Henry Wilson-Smith left to become deputy-chairman of Powell Duffryn, but it gathered pace in the sixties. In 1960 there was a greater shock when Sir Leslie Rowan, one of the Treasury knights, left for Vickers; and the next year Sir Edward Playfair, the head of Defence, became (rather briefly) chairman of International Computers. In 1969 Sir Richard Powell, former head of the Board of Trade, became chairman of Albright and Wilson. In one firm, Tube Investments, one Treasury man—Lord Plowden, a former chief planner—has worked hand-in-hand with another, Sir William Strath. But it cannot be said that permanent secretaries have had a dynamic effect on industry through their closeness to it, and their network has not been notable for bringing in bright young men or ideas: Vickers, Albright and Wilson and International Computers have all been in the doldrums.

In the reverse direction there have been a few more intruders from outside into the civil service; some of them are short-term professional exchanges, from banking, industry or the Bank of England; others are more political invasions. The Labour government brought a little army of economists into Whitehall departments; and the Conservatives in 1970 invited a small band of businessmen into the civil service department—including Richard Meyjes from Shell, Derek Rayner from Marks and Spencer, K. F. Lance from Rio-Tinto-Zinc, and Mark Schreiber via the Conservative Research Department. The prime minister was quick to stress that they would work 'with the grain'. The most spectacular result was in April 1971, when Derek Rayner was promoted to be head of the new 'Procurement Executive' in the Ministry of Defence, in charge of buying equipment worth £1,000 million a year, and indirectly responsible for 52,000 people. Rayner, a bachelor of 45, had begun as a theological student at Cambridge, decided on Marks and Spencer instead of the ministry, and rose to be a director in that legendary family firm after only fifteen years, specialising in food. Like others of the new businessmen in Whitehall, he first met the Tory leaders at their special Sundridge Park conference in September 1969, and was loaned to the government by Marks and Spencer for two years. It remains to be seen how far he can transfer his buying skills from sausages and cheese to rockets and guns: if he succeeds in producing real value for money in the Ministry of Defence, it will be a historic achievement.

But few outsiders have ever been able to work the Whitehall machine effectively: as Samuel Brittan (himself an 'irregular'—as George Brown described the temporary recruits—in the Department of Economic Affairs) says, 'Irregulars inevitably run with leaden boots in any race against professionals.'[1] And with businessmen in Whitehall, there is always a lingering suspicion that if a man were *really* top-class, his firm would not have let him go.

It is in the dark forests between policies and their execution, between ideas and realities, between doctrine and its application, that the trails of the investigator finally become hopelessly lost: the member of parliament, the journalist, and even the historian has to admit that the truth will never fully emerge. Most ministers and all prime ministers like to depict themselves as master organisers, and when they write their memoirs they show few doubts about the effectiveness of their decisions. Denis Healey, Anthony Wedgwood Benn or Peter Walker set themselves up as master technocrats, able to convert whole ministries into new kinds of organisations, to infuse them with new enthusiasms and incentives. But that is never how it looks from inside. From there, nearly all ministers appear bored with the whole question of internal organisation; they will make speeches at the drop of a hat about technological revolutions, participations and mergers, but once inside the engine room they will show a distinct withdrawal of interest. In cabinet and in public speeches, they will speak passionately about the need for economy and cutting down staff; but within their own department they will defend every pound and every person as a part of their personal power. Even those ministers who have come into Whitehall with the reputation from outside it for ruthless business efficiency—like Lord Chandos, Ernest Marples or John Davies—usually turn out to be far more interested in talking about it than doing it. And that is not surprising; for the real problems of efficiency, of getting one man to do the work of two or of enforcing economies, can only be solved by patient long-term reorganisation, balancing the spirit of change with a sense of security. The outcome will only be seen ten years later, long after the politicians have left their jobs; and it will be achieved not by political speech-making but by a slow, unacknowledged adjustment in the attitudes of tens of thousands of unsung individuals.

[1] Samuel Brittan: *Steering the Economy*, Secker and Warburg 1969, p. 30.

13

Honours

Men are led by baubles.

Napoleon.

Even now, the number of those who are not knighted exceeds the
number of those who are. Time doubtless will reverse these figures.

Max Beerbohm, 1899 (later Sir Max Beerbohm)

THE most visible link between the fantasy-world of monarchy and
the practical world of administration is in the system of honours.
The Queen still has to be regarded as the 'fount of all honour';
and however much everyone knows that it is the prime minister,
the Conservative Central Office or the permanent secretary who
fixes honours up, the sense of historical continuity, the touch of
royal magic, still gives them a special kind of fascination. In
official lists at international gatherings most foreign dignitaries
appear simply with their names: but British delegates will be
cluttered with GCBs, GCMGs, KBEs, CHs, and they can always
have fun about how foreigners always get them wrong, talking
about Sir Home or Baron Carrington. However ridiculous they
may seem to foreigners, these titles still have some mystic importance to the British, of a different order to a Chevalier or a
Commendatore. There are still faint emanations from King
Arthur's Round Table.

Twice a year, a few weeks before January 1 and June 6, a few
thousand letters marked Urgent, Personal and Confidential,
arrive at British homes from a private secretary at 10 Downing
Street. A typical letter reads:

Sir,

   I am asked by the prime minister to inform you that he has it in mind on the occasion of the forthcoming list of Birthday Honours to submit your name to the Queen with a recommendation that she may be graciously pleased to approve that you be appointed a Companion of the Order of the British Empire (CBE).

   Before doing so, the prime minister would be glad to be assured that this mark of Her Majesty's favour would be agreeable to you.

   I should be obliged if you could let me know at your earliest convenience.

I am, sir,
Your obedient servant,

   The expression 'has it in mind' (one honorand pointed out to me) is an invaluable piece of civil service phraseology. It infers that the prime minister can quite easily put it *out* of his mind if the offer is rejected: but that in the meantime all those potential baronies or Orders of the British Empire are revolving slowly and quietly in the back of his head, waiting to be crystallised.

   The multiplicity of the 'orders of chivalry' is enough to baffle the most loyalist Englishman: Queen Victoria, King Edward VII, King George V all founded new orders—each with slightly different nuances of glory. To many, the grandest is thought to be the Garter, founded in 1348, as a reward for skilful jousting: it has not more than twenty-six members who at their investitures wear dark blue velvet garters bearing the inscription 'Honi soit qui mal y pense'. Lord Melbourne (who never accepted the Garter) said 'there's no damned merit in it', and that is still roughly true: the Garter includes royal favourites, such as the Duke of Beaufort, and a tiny band of fellow-monarchs, including the Emperor of Ethiopia and the Emperor of Japan (his garter was taken away during the war, but is now restored). The genuinely illustrious war leaders were given the Garter, but most are now dead, and their place has been taken by politicians or obscure Lord Lieutenants like Sir Cennydd Traherne or Sir Edmund Bacon. Some people prefer the Thistle, the Scots order, with a similar mixture, including the King of Norway, two Dukes and Sir Alec. Other very cosy orders are the Royal Victorian Chain, mainly for royalty, but including Lord Fisher of Lambeth; and the dwindling Imperial Order of the Crown of India—only twelve left—for Maharanis and ex-Vicereines of India. There is also the Royal Victorian Order, awarded personally by the Queen, in varying degrees from GCVO to MVO, fifth class (even

269

the honours system is riddled with class divisions). It is given to such people as royal doctors, the Keeper of the Privy Purse, the Extra Groom in Waiting, and the Keeper of the Swans.

In contrast to the Garter are the twenty-four members of the Order of Merit whose name itself suggests a side-swipe at other orders. OMs have no association with empire or jousting, and are meant to be merely distinguished. A lot of people who turned down everything else (like Earl Russell) accepted the OM: it is a permissive order, and divorce, promiscuity and atheism are no bar to it. The OM is an odd little band, including an architect (Spence), a sculptor (Moore), two musicians (Britten and Walton) and lots of scientists: it has one mysterious member, John Caute Beaglehole, who turns out to be a New Zealander who told the Queen a lot about Captain Cook on her tour. Another side-swipe is the Companionage of Honour—founded in 1917— which likewise suggests that other companions are not wholly honourable: but the distinction between honour and merit in the two orders is sometimes rather obscure. The sixty-five Companions comprise numbers of eminent writers, artists and scientists, including Graham Greene, but recently they have been rather swamped by ageing Labour politicians.

Other orders are much more mundane, mainly concerned with rewarding public servants and conferred not (like the preceding ones) by the Queen, but by the prime minister in her name. The most senior of the civil service orders is the Bath (CB, KCB, GCB), mainly for military men and civil servants; but since 1971 it has included a few women, who can provide jokes about mixed bathing. The St. Michael and St. George, whose sad motto is 'token of a better age', was originally established in 1818 for the natives of the Ionian Islands and Malta, but is now distributed (in the way the Victorians appropriated other people's mythology) to British diplomats, colonial servants and overseas officials; members rise from CMG (known sometimes as 'Call Me God') to KCMG ('Kindly Call Me God'), to GCMG ('God Calls Me God'). To these older orders was added in 1917 the Order of the British Empire, invented by King George V with the motto 'For God and the Empire' and with five grades, rising from the MBE to the OBE to the CBE to the KBE to the GBE. As the British Empire has dwindled, so its orders have multiplied (though the inflation is not acute as in France, where Napoleon's 2,000 members of the Légion d'Honneur have grown to hundreds of thousands, all with their ribbons in their coat lapels). The Commanders of the British Empire—the stage before the knighthood—are an extraordinary mix-up of people; they include, among the aldermen and public servants, Angus Wilson, Stephen Spender and V. S. Pritchett. The OBE is thought more appropriate for pop figures like David Frost or Bobby Charlton, or, more oddly, Muriel Spark (it 'must have been actuated by a desire to make me feel deeply embarrassed', said Rebecca West, Dame of the British Empire, 'and indeed I do'). The MBE is for the most pop of all, the Beatles (though Lennon sent his back). It is a pleasant fantasy to think of them all belonging to a single unified order, embracing aldermen, sculptors and dockyard managers, all jostling among each other, discussing imperial questions and occasionally raising a glass and muttering 'for God and the Empire!'

In the past the awards of CBEs, CMGs and CBs have come to be regarded as part of the bureaucratic machine, registering each stage of a civil servant's progress; but in the last few years the fount of honour has been less gushing. In 1957 there were 267 civil servants in the honours list, but in 1968 there were only 153; nowadays only permanent secretaries can expect to get a K, and deputy secretaries must put up with a CB—though the Foreign Service still bristles with initials. The old argument that honours for civil servants were a kind of substitute for higher salaries is less cogent now that senior civil servants are very well paid, and the current idea, I am reliably informed, is that 'promotion in the career is its own reward'.

The most visible recipient of honour—apart from a peer—is a knight: overnight Mr J. M. Smith will be transformed into Sir John and—more important—his wife will become Lady Smith. (Baronets, who inherit their Sir, went out with Sir Alec Douglas-Home). Through all Britain's social revolutions, the charms of knighthood have remained undiminished: echoes of Sir Lancelot and Sir Galahad mingle with more practical advantages: 'Expect clients to pay sir charge' cabled one witty architect after his knighthood had been announced. Nor has the knightage swelled quite as Max Beerbohm forecast: there are about 3,500 knights today—roughly the same number as in 1935—though fewer of them are Empire knights. The bulk of the knighthoods still go to civil servants, local worthies, heads of professions, and dignified businessmen. But the field of knightworthy activites has been enlarged. There are acting knights, cricketing knights, football knights and even now publishing knights (Weidenfeld, Lusty and Collins): advertising men still feel aggrieved at their lack of recognition.

It is in the peerage that the inflation of honours has been most spectacular: Harold Wilson, in his six years of power, created no fewer than 140 Life Peers, increasing the membership of the House of Lords by twelve per cent (see Chapter 1). The justification for this boom in lords was a valid one: that there had to be more peers on the left, drawn from a wider cross-section of society. But the promotions also had the effect of enhancing the prime minister's power of patronage, and revealing more nakedly how much the honours system is the tool of politics.

Theoretically anyone can recommend anyone for an honour, and thousands of people write to the prime minister suggesting their friends or themselves. But the weighty recommendations come from Whitehall departments, from the Conservative Central Office or Transport House, and from the parts of the Commonwealth which still care about honours. They are sifted and weighed by Sir William Armstrong and scrutinised by Stuart Milner-Barry, a former chess champion who is now secretary of the Political Honours Scrutiny Committee—the body set up after Lloyd George's exploitation of honours—to make sure that the system is not being abused (though there is doubt as to how effective they are). Only the more important recommendations are passed on to the prime minister. Harold Wilson was expected by many followers to cut the honours system right down; but once in office, he found it far too useful and too much fun. He did, however, announce in 1966 that he would 'discontinue the practice of making recommendations concerning honours for political services . . . it will be public service which will be recognised, irrespective of party'. The distinction was not as clear as it looked, since the typical Labour Party activist is often also involved in local government; but Wilson did cut down political rewards, and Labour ministers grumbled about the difficulties of getting honours for loyal constituency workers. Only in his resignation honours did Wilson break his own rule, doling out knighthoods to his press secretary, his doctor and his mackintosh-maker, and showering Transport House and his Downing Street staff with CBEs and MBEs. But resignation honours have always been an occasion for a last fling: 'The last and least glorious exercise of power,' as Disraeli described it, 'making peers, creating baronets, and showering places and pensions on a rapacious crew.'[1] Sir Alec Douglas-Home, having himself off-loaded his earldom, celebrated his departure in 1964 by creating the last six hereditary barons and the last hereditary viscount, Lord Dilhorne.

When Edward Heath came to power in 1970 he stated firmly 'I do not believe it's right to exclude from the honours list citizens taking part in political work'; but his first list in the New Year was not generous to political workers—only six out of eighty-nine CBEs, eight out of 187 OBEs, only one political knighthood (Sir Gerald Glover)—and he disappointed many romantic Tories by not bringing back hereditary peerages, which Wilson had stopped (the first prime minister to do so). Heath's list was altogether a remarkably dull one, suggesting that he was extending his technique of 'government by boredom' to the honours system—perhaps not a bad thing.

How many people reply that Her Majesty's favour would *not* be acceptable? There is no reliable information, since publicly to refuse an honour is at least as vain as to accept it, but it seems clear that among intellectuals and artists—who used to be regarded as outside such ladder-systems—honours have become recently much more acceptable. I asked one newly-dubbed professor why he had taken his knighthood, and he explained: 'You're only justified in refusing it if you can keep quiet about it. I knew I couldn't. So I said yes.' Other honorands justify their acceptance more grandiloquently: as Sir Neville Cardus put it, 'It is not for the likes of me to go counter to the pleasure of Her Majesty the Queen.' The motives for refusal are often suspect: 'Fourteen out of fifteen of the people who write back to refuse are obviously annoyed because they weren't offered something better,' said one man at Number Ten: 'It's a relief when you come to the fifteenth who really honestly doesn't want it.' Before the war many intellectuals, including Professor R. H. Tawney, Bernard Shaw, Rudyard Kipling and H. G. Wells, refused honours. A few people still turn them down, such as Frank Cousins, J. B. Priestley, John Freeman and Christopher Soames: Sir Roy Welensky refused a peerage; that would be embarrassing for a Rhodesian. But today most prominent artists and intellectuals have accepted honours of some kind, and nearly all the former Labour leaders have accepted peerages. The one honour that appears to be almost irresistible is a privy councillorship (PC) which gives its

[1] Robert Blake: *Disraeli.* Eyre & Spottiswoode 1966, p. 713.

recipient the right to the prefix 'Right Honourable', but is otherwise wholly meaningless.

Honours still retain their ancient lure. Men and wives approaching retirement, often after a lifetime of apparent indifference, become mysteriously fascinated by the possibility of a C or a K; in a suburb or country village a knighthood can make the difference between an unwanted old bore and a resplendent national figure, always in demand: the strongest argument for retaining knighthoods is that they make people happier, and sometimes nicer. Honours can still act as a brokerage-system between money and status, converting an aggressive self-seeking tycoon into a confident dignitary: it is in honours that the need for *belonging* reasserts itself. The soothing qualities of the honours system make it hard, probably impossible, for any prime minister to abolish them. But the honours have long ago outgrown the purpose for which they were created; and in contemporary Britain, without an empire and with great need to look outwards, this device of synthetic patriotism has absurd side-effects. The value-system of any distribution of honours, however well-meaning, must always be corrupt: how can any small group of people in Whitehall discover who is really honourable? It would be pleasant to imagine a committee of wise, just men, quite outside politics, deciding who was *really* worthy. But in the end the only judges of a man's achievement can be his immediate friends, who will honour him with a K or without.

14

Treasury

———

Surely the lesson of the past twenty years is that all economics are politics. We should really once more be talking about 'political economy'.

Harold Lever (New Statesman, October 30, 1970)

OF all the civil service departments, the Treasury has always been the most abused, mocked and disliked: for it is its job to say No. It is responsible not only for taxing the public, but for cutting down government expenditure, and for questioning every new project. It is abused not only by the taxpayers but by every other Whitehall department. 'The Treasury can never be popular among departments in every way,' Lord Helsby, the former head of the civil service said, 'and indeed it would probably denote a serious failure on the Treasury's part if it ever did become popular.' Treasury men adopt, like judges, an attitude of resigned immunity in the face of the odium and debate. And no question of government has been more debated over the past few years than the proper role of the Treasury. For the organisation of the Treasury involves the duality that has been at the heart of all governments since the impact of Keynes—that it should on the one hand save and control, and on the other hand lead the country towards expansion and growth.

The Treasury does not inspire quite so much awe since the civil service department was split off from it, for it no longer controls both money *and* men. But the money is the ultimate weapon, and the Treasury still has a large proportion of the cleverest men in

Whitehall among its thousand; it can take the pick of recruits, and they can later steal men from other departments, or send its own men to run departments. 'We can match other departments four-to-one in ability, at any level,' one of the heads of it said to me. Treasury men are known to be members of a chosen race, which gives them—quite apart from their actual power—an edge over the un-chosen. They operate in a close collegiate atmosphere, in which everyone knows everyone by Christian names. 'Our strength comes from the fact that we cohere,' I was told: 'I can get everyone who is an under-secretary or above round that table. People are close enough to be able to see the important connections—between taxation and balance of payments, between taxation and inflation; it's the *connections* that matter.' But this awareness of connections can easily turn to arrogance: as one Treasury correspondent put it:

> The collegiate atmosphere is very important indeed. It is a compound of small numbers and close, informal relations on the one hand, and a quite surprising degree of unconscious superiority (as one might find in a real, Oxbridge, college society) not so much intellectual superiority but what I'd call *patriotic* superiority. Many of my colleagues do believe, deep down, that they have a near-monopoly of knowledge on what is good for their country. Advice and argument from other quarters, whatever the source, tends to be regarded as suspect, partial, interested; only the Treasury itself sees the whole national interest plain, unvarnished, compelling, without bias! At the best, this attitude is arrogant; at worst it is positively dangerous in its complacency.

The Treasury is an operational, not a social elite; few of them come from aristocratic families, or are likely to be seen in the drawing-rooms of 'Society'. Most of them live in suburbs, and return in the evening, with bulging briefcases, on late trains ('a breakdown on the Southern Region can bring the civil service to a halt'). At lunch time they will either go to the cabinet office mess, for macaroni or chops, or walk across the park, down the Clive steps and up the Duke of York steps, probably to the Reform Club, when they can be sure of seeing other Treasury men.

The corporate spirit of the Treasury is still expressed in its legendary passion for music, which seems to fit with its withdrawn world, and unmusical men in the Treasury have an uneasy feeling that music is important to promotion, still more so since the coming-to-power of an organist, with his musical secretary (see chapter 5). There is still a flourishing Treasury choir, which sings

Bach and sometimes performs at the Guards Chapel across the park. Perhaps music encourages the quiet detachment of Treasury men, which is their dominant characteristic. As Samuel Brittan has put it: 'It is not done to show enthusiasm for any idea, or to take too seriously the national objectives discussed in the newspapers . . . The words "there is nothing new under the sun" seem to be written on the walls in invisible ink.'[1]

They have few opportunities of meeting people from more ordinary walks of life. They may encounter economists from outside, in the Reform Club, Nuffield College, or the National Institute for Economic and Social Research (NIESR) which the Treasury helps to finance. They may belong to dining clubs like the Tuesday Club, where they can meet with businessmen or economic journalists. But most of them move in a milieu which is at one or two removes from practical problems, and they see life through a pane of frosted glass. The distortion is enhanced by the fact that the Treasury, in finding out about 'the outside world' always has to deal through the other institutions of Whitehall; its knowledge of unions comes from the Department of Employment and the *Financial Times*, of industry through the Department of Trade and Industry or sometimes through Neddy. Like Lord Lugard with Nigerian tribes, they operate through indirect rule, and this adds to the sense of unreality: 'I think it's a necessity imposed on us,' said one Treasury man: 'You can't double-up the direct contact with hospitals, schools, roads, ports.' Every head office in industry is (as Lord Heyworth once said of Unilever's) 'a half-crazy place': but the Treasury, the head office of head offices, has the special oddness of shy men who express themselves more on paper than in talk, and who have lived in the same building for most of their lives. Outside Oxbridge common rooms, they must be one of the most etiolated group of men in the country.

CHANCELLOR VERSUS OFFICIALS

Behind the curving corridors of the 'Inner Circle' of the Treasury building, out of earshot of parliament, or anyone but a few private secretaries, take place the encounters between the politicians and the senior civil servants romantically dubbed the 'Treasury Knights'—the bogies and scapegoats of successive governments. Harold Wilson blames them in his memoirs (p. 464)

[1] Samuel Brittan: *Steering the Economy*. Penguin 1971, p. 43.

for his phrase after devaluation about 'the pound in the pocket'. It is at the meetings with Treasury men that so many political ideals have been defeated, so many bold promises gone sour; 'The power of the Treasury knights,' complains one Treasury man, 'is journalese for facing the promises of opposition with the problems of government.' It is in these meetings that secrecy becomes almost total, and the enquiring eye of parliament or the Press finds the doors slammed in its face.

The arrival of any new chancellor provides new scope for the assessment of the balance of Treasury forces, and however much pessimistic politicians may complain about Treasury rule the personality of a chancellor still has some noticeable affect on the assumptions behind the decisions. The entry of Anthony Barber in July 1970—after the one-month chancellorship of Iain Macleod —was the cause of special speculation; for Barber had a very sudden promotion. He had risen to the top under the aegis of Edward Heath, to whom he had been monotonously loyal. His slight, boyish build, his hearty manner, his eager smile, his love for his Jensen Interceptor, all contributed to a picture of a bantam-weight: at conferences, clapping and grinning at his leader, he appeared almost overcome with hero-worship.

Barber is, of course, rather tougher than he looks; and he began by pushing his own way into politics. The son of a Doncaster sweet-manufacturer and his Danish wife, he was determined to make a mark—like his brothers Noel Barber, the *Daily Mail* journalist, and Kenneth Barber, Secretary of the Midland Bank— and he had plenty of courage. In the war he was captured as a pilot, took a first in law from the prisoner-of-war camp, and later escaped from Poland. He went into parliament in 1951, and became Macmillan's private secretary by 1958—just getting into the cabinet, as Minister of Health, before the Tories fell in 1964. In opposition he soon emerged as one of Heath's new men, and took over the chairmanship of the party in 1967; but he never said or did anything very memorable, and there was never a recognisable Barberism as there was Heathism or perhaps even Walkerism. In the Treasury his political lieutenants, Maurice Macmillan, Patrick Jenkin and Terence Higgins, were all men of greater intellectual and economic equipment, and in parliament he was soon mocked by the opposition for his fumbling performances.

Barber has appeared to hold his own with the Treasury men. He was determined to produce his 'mini-budget' by October 1970, and in his full budget in April he was able to announce—apart from the ruthless redistribution of income—an overhaul of the tax system, of the kind that Roy Jenkins had failed to push through the Treasury objections. Barber emerged as an effective administrator; but it is doubtful whether he could have achieved the changes without the driving force of Ted Heath, who had first planned Conservative tax reforms six years before, when he was shadow chancellor under Sir Alec. Heath had left no doubt that he was ultimately in charge of economic policy, whether it concerned the budget or the common market negotiations.

Advising the Chancellor are the array of finance experts and economists shown in the chart overleaf, some of them with their own departments. A few of them have come from outside. Francis Cuchfield was a former inspector of taxes who moved out to take over Boots the Chemists, and then came back to advise the Tories on tax changes: he was largely responsible for their 1971 reforms. Sir Samuel Goldman took a first in economics, rose up through stockbroking and the Bank of England, and later became chief statistician in the Treasury. Sir Donald MacDougall has moved between academia and Whitehall over the last twenty years, and was director-general of George Brown's Department of Economic Affairs throughout its four-year wonder. But the most impressive economist in the building—an unprecedented situation—is the permanent head of the Treasury, Sir Douglas Allen, who read economics and statistics at the LSE and has kept well abreast of both subjects in his quarter-century at the Treasury. Allen is a striking example of one of the new meritocrats; like Armstrong he worked up from very modest beginnings—his father was killed in the first war, he was brought up in some poverty, and he now lives unpretentiously in Croydon, playing bridge and enjoying do-it-yourself. He has the same grey, burdened look as Armstrong. He is shortish, white-haired, slightly paunchy, but he walks springily and plays a lot of tennis; he has a twitch suggesting concealed energy. He is respected and liked by his colleagues. The fact that the men at the two peaks of the civil service should both come from very humble backgrounds has finally bonked on the head the old image of the civil service as a public school preserve: such men are still often described as being 'not at all typical', but nowadays they are quite typical. In other ways Sir Douglas is the opposite of Sir William; he dislikes any idea of opening-up Whitehall to public

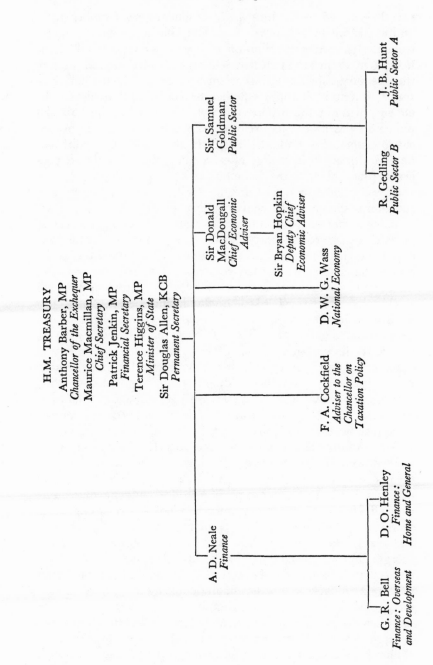

H.M. TREASURY

Anthony Barber, MP
Chancellor of the Exchequer
Maurice Macmillan, MP
Chief Secretary
Patrick Jenkin, MP
Financial Secretary
Terence Higgins, MP
Minister of State
Sir Douglas Allen, KCB
Permanent Secretary

A. D. Neale
Finance

G. R. Bell
*Finance: Overseas
and Development*

D. O. Henley
*Finance:
Home and General*

F. A. Cockfield
*Adviser to the
Chancellor on
Taxation Policy*

D. W. G. Wass
National Economy

Sir Donald
MacDougall
*Chief Economic
Adviser*

Sir Bryan Hopkin
*Deputy Chief
Economic Adviser*

Sir Samuel
Goldman
Public Sector

R. Gedling
Public Sector B

J. B. Hunt
Public Sector A

exposure, not simply for security reasons, but temperamentally and in that respect he *is* typical of both the old and the new Treasury. He emerged painfully into the public eye in January 1971, when he gave evidence to the Wilberforce Enquiry into the power workers' pay dispute, and was questioned about his own salary of £15,000 a year and other top people's increases by Frank Chapple, the power workers' leader: 'how does it come about that people who are not poorly off can get such splendid, such magnificent, increases in wages, without there being any criteria by which to measure their productivity? . . . do you think it is right to give judges £84 increases in some instances, and £50 increases on average? Do you support that claim?' 'You are asking me what advice the Treasury gave', replied Sir Douglas: 'I cannot say that'.

The heart of decision-making remains the most opaque, least penetrable part of the British anatomy; the Treasury men have effectively defied parliament's stethoscopes, cardiograms or X-rays. Recently there have been eloquent pleas for a select committee for economic affairs, to question Treasury officials about economic policy, partly on the lines of the joint economic committee of the American Congress. In a persuasive memorandum pleading for such a committee, the two leading economic journalists, Samuel Brittan of the *Financial Times* and Peter Jay of *The Times*, made a powerful case:

> We believe that the conduct of public policy and the quality of politics improves or deteriorates in direct relation to the quality of public debate about it. The quality of public debate in its turn varies directly with the quality of information and understanding deployed, not by the government, but by its chief interlocutor. For the level of debate, like that of tennis or chess, tends to be set by the weaker participants.[1]

Senior Treasury men insist that such a probe into this central area would make their position impossible; 'What you must never do,' one of them explained to me, 'is to drive a wedge between the minister and the official and to find out what the official advised. How can we say what we think about the Selective Employment Tax when we know it is anathema to the Tories and the darling of the Labour Party?' But it should be quite possible to discuss systems of taxation, and possible changes in monetary policy, without nailing officials to a political view; the members of the select committee themselves are quite aware of the

[1] Select Committee on Procedure: Report for 1969-70 Session.

rules of the game. Without some more effective instrument for parliament, and without some preparedness by the Treasury to open up their arguments, there is little prospect of the public feeling themselves involved in the central issues of our time; the pressing questions about inflation, about the common market or regional development, are automatically assumed to be too delicate or too complicated for public debate, and the answers are pulled out, ready-mixed, and pre-packed, from the secret oven of the Treasury.

PLANNING AND NON-PLANNING

Round the Treasury has swirled over the last decade the flooding and ebbing tides of planning and anti-planning, interventionism and anti-interventionism. Notions of planning have had many rises and falls since before the war. The first high tide was in 1947 under the Labour government, when Sir Edwin Plowden (later Lord Plowden) was Chief Planning Officer. Even before the end of Attlee's government, planning fell into disrepute, discredited by miscalculations and economic crises. Then, after a long lapse, it became fashionable in Conservative as well as Labour circles in the early sixties. 'Planning has become an emotional word,' said Harold Macmillan in December 1961; 'for myself I have always rather liked it'; and in the following year he set up the first major attempt at voluntary planning on a national scale, a pale copy of the French *commissariat au Plan*. The National Economic Development Council, generally known as Neddy, was established with a mixed membership of ministers, industrialists and trade unionists, to map out the industrial future of Britain. Neddy had some success and made everyone feel better, but in 1964 the Labour government came in with far bolder schemes. They kept Neddy and added the ambitious Department of Economic Affairs as the main instrument of national planning, with George Brown as its dynamo, to stimulate the Treasury and to generate 'creative tension', or 'symbiosis' as it was fashionably described: there was certainly no lack of tension. The DEA had its temporary triumph in September 1965, when the National Plan was proclaimed, predicting a growth rate of four per cent a year: but nine months later, with the crisis of July 1966, it had collapsed, and the department never recovered. It was finally disbanded in 1969 and reabsorbed into the Treasury, with only an enlarged economic department as its memorial, though former DEA men in the Treasury still show a nostalgic *esprit de corps:* they wear their own club tie and have a commemorative drink on the DEA's birthday. The mention of 'creative tension' nowadays raises a laugh, and the orthodox Treasury men are confirmed in their suspicions of any disturbance.

In the meantime, under the Labour government, to the notion of national planning had been added interventionism. The new Ministry of Technology was set up in 1964 as the instrument of 'selective intervention' to enable the government to stimulate and modernise industry; and as its protégé the Industrial Reorganisation Corporation was founded in 1966 (see chapter 32) to induce rationalisation of industry, if necessary with the help of government money. But while the IRC was merging and subsidising companies, the Conservatives were coming out more solidly against it; and after their return to power abolished it. The pattern of institutions was back where it had started eight years ago with the Treasury as the sole guardian of the economy, and with only old Neddy as the forum for 'voluntary' planning. Ted Heath, who was involved in its early years, came back to its meetings as prime minister.

Neddy still has some importance as the chief meeting place between the three sides of industry, and its members constitute a minor Establishment, of over-familiar names ('Are there too many occasions,' asks Sir Antony Part, 'on which the same stage army from government meets the same stage army from industry to discuss more or less the same problems?').[1] Apart from the government members, normally headed by the Chancellor, the council in June 1971 consisted of:

Sir Frank Figgures	Director-General
Michael Clapham	Deputy Chairman, ICI
Lord Netherthorpe	Chairman, Fisons
Gordon Richardson	Chairman, Schroders
Sir Arthur Norman	President, CBI
Campbell Adamson	Director-General, CBI
Sir John Partridge	Imperial Tobacco, Chairman CBI
Jack Jones	Transport and General Workers' Union
Alfred Allen	Union of Shop, Distributive and Allied Workers
Lord Cooper	National Union of General and Municipal Workers

[1] Speech to Industrial Educational Foundation; July 3, 1969.

Sir Sidney Greene	National Union of Railwaymen
Victor Feather	Secretary-General, TUC
Lord Melchett	British Steel Corporation
Hugh Scanlon	Amalgamated Union of Engineering and Foundry Workers
Professor McClelland	Manchester Business School

After the consultation and consensus of the two Harolds, there is once again a mood of anti-planning and anti-interventionism, and Heath and Barber regard Neddy more as a sounding-board than as an instrument of national policy-making. The former director-general, Sir Frederick Catherwood, a convinced planner with a rare kind of Calvinist zeal for the reconstruction of British industry, has returned to private industry (to run the building firm, Laing's); and his place has been taken by an ex-Treasury man, Sir Frank Figgures, the former secretary-general of EFTA: a numerate man as his name suggests, but without great planning ambitions. Neddy is not what it was; but behind the political posturing the pressures towards planning and state involvement in industry are bound to continue. And however much businessmen may protest about government interference, they all know (as Catherwood puts it) that the government will have to make its own plans, and that if the government is planning anyway, they had better be in on it.

INTERDEPENDENCE

In economic affairs more than in any other sector, it has become difficult to distinguish the national anatomy from the international one. When Britain is heavily in debt the scope of her spending and the priorities of her budget are limited as surely as that of a customer with an overdraft by his bank manager; and in the late sixties the restrictions became painfully obvious. The controlling factors have been not so much the Treasury officials and the Chancellor, as the web of international agencies in Washington, Paris or Basel. There is the OECD in Paris (the Organisation for Economic Co-operation and Development) which surveys the economies of twenty-two nations, and its offshoot Working Party Three (WP 3), almost identical with the Group of Ten below, which meets once a month to try to co-ordinate the members' economies. The OECD includes several ex-Whitehall men, and has been called 'the Treasury in exile': its criticism of British policy in its report on inflation late in 1970 caused great annoyance among Tories. There is the Bank for International Settlements (BIS) which organises the monthly meetings of Central Bankers in Basel. And most important of all is the International Monetary Fund (IMF), based on Washington under Pierre-Paul Schweitzer, and its sub-committee of the richer industrial nations, the Group of Ten—a kind of inner cabinet of the IMF, which has been responsible for organising the big loans to Britain. As Britain's debts mounted through the sixties, the pressures of the international creditors became greater; and Roy Jenkins had to publish his 'letter of intent' to the IMF to explain his policies; it promised that 'before making a request for a further purchase under the standby arrangement, the government will consult with the fund and reach understanding regarding the circumstances in which such purchases may be made'. The pressure from the world's bankers and their advisers influenced not only Britain's deflationary policy after 1967, but also the attitude to trade unions and strikers.

As and when Britain settles her huge debts, the pressure from foreign bankers will be less evident; but in any case the whole interdependence of all rich countries is becoming closer. Speculation in one currency sets off another, inflation spreads across frontiers and and a boom in Germany or a slump in America can shut down factories and cause unemployment in remote parts of Britain. The common market, if Britain joins it, will increase the interdependence: the Six are starting hesitantly on the road to a joint monetary policy, and the Werner Plan envisages a common currency by 1980—to which Britain would have to subscribe. But it is exaggerating to say (as Peter Shore, the Labour anti-marketeer says) that this is 'the surrender of the substance, if not the form, of national economic self-determination'. For Britain has long ago ceased to be economically autonomous; and with or without a common currency or a common market her future is inextricably bound up with the economic policies of Bonn, Paris or Washington.

15

Diplomats

If foreign ministries did not already exist, they surely would not
have to be invented.

Zbingniew Brzesinski, 1970.

The idea that all the meaningful relations of any people, with others
who live in other countries, can be squeezed through a network of
narrow channels called foreign offices is at least a hundred years out
of date.

Anthony Wedgwood Benn ('The New Politics'), September 1970.

BETWEEN Treasury men and diplomats, the twin elites of Whitehall, there is an old unfriendly rivalry: they live in worlds as
separate as the army and the navy. You can see both kinds
walking across St. James's Park at lunch-time, but the Treasury
men make for the Reform, while the diplomats go into the
Travellers' next door—the 'works canteen' of the F.O. At home
the diplomats are still likely to be richer than their Treasury
counterparts; some of them have married rich foreign wives as a
reward for spending much of their lives in expensive society
abroad. Diplomats are less dependent on the Treasury than other
departments for promotion and policy, and they talk with special
scorn of the *home* civil service: they like to call themselves 'The
Office' or simply 'The Service'. They used to be less separate:
from 1919 to 1956, Sir Warren Fisher, Sir Horace Wilson and Sir
Edward Bridges were heads of the whole civil service including the
diplomats, and they liked to interfere. But when Sir Norman
Brook took over in 1956, he was announced as head of the *home*
civil service, and the Foreign Office were left to themselves, with
their own private pyramid. The Treasury still have their revenge
in 'teasing' the diplomats over their expenses.

Diplomats are aware of being, if not aristocrats themselves, the heirs to an aristocratic tradition: not clerks, but knights. Only since 1919 has it been possible (though not common) to enter the Foreign Office without a private income, and there is still a family-circle feeling—a closer circle than the Treasury's. Diplomats exchange chatty telegrams, cosier than Treasury memos; unlike permanent secretaries, who remain ever anonymous, senior diplomats often write *belles lettres*, or biographies: in the end they may come to roost in their old school or college like Lord Caccia at Eton, or Sir William Hayter at New College, Oxford.

Diplomats abroad are inclined to regard themselves as representing not the United Kingdom but the Foreign Office; in London (one civil servant complained) they regard every other department—including 10 Downing Street—as a foreign power. Treasury men, on their side, like to imply that the diplomats are not altogether patriotic, that they mix too much with foreigners to be aware of the national interest, and that they don't understand the needs of the national economy. Certainly in London the diplomats (as one of them put it) tend to see themselves as ambassadors *from* the country they deal with on the desk—defending one Sheikh against another represented by the desk down the corridor.

Since October 1968 the exclusiveness of the diplomats has been diluted by the merger with the Commonwealth Relations Office to produce the Foreign and Commonwealth Office. The CRO brought with it many senior men who had by Buggins's rules to be placed in senior jobs (many of them in Africa). The merger caused some healthy disruption of the old chess-game of Foreign Office promotion; backwoodsmen from Ghana or Ceylon have found themselves in the European chancelleries, and chandelier people have been pushed off to Zomba or Lagos. But the Foreign Office men have been able to complain with some reason that the Commonwealth men are inferior, and the old-style diplomats are held together by the sense of shared experiences, the suspicion of other groups, that marks boarding-school life. Their intimacy is strengthened by their Oxbridge background, by the 'third rooms' which they share when they begin their career, by the flow of telegrams which provide a kind of school magazine, and by their cut-offness from the world outside the walls. The British diplomatic service has a collegiate spirit only rivalled, perhaps, by that of the barristers and judges. No other country's diplomatic service has the same confident segregation—not even the French diplomats, for they are not traditionally superior to the other *Grand Corps* at home. The closed tradition of British diplomacy has its boons and its snags. The familiarity allows its members to communicate freely and frankly, to exchange mmms and errrs, catching nuances of meaning, and to avoid the kind of cross-purposes and Parkinsonian tendencies that muddy the waters of (for instance) American diplomacy: decisions in the Foreign Office are taken much more quickly than in other departments. But the corporate strength, like that of the Treasury, has dangers in a changing world. The diplomats have a double insulation from the rest of the country, both professional and geographical, and they can become amazingly out of touch with changes at home: talking about the old country, they sometimes seem to have been whirled backward in a time-machine, into a nostalgic land of the forties or fifties. And they can easily become caught up in their short-term diplomatic games and hysterics—like school hysterics—as they showed in their reaction to de Gaulle, culminating in *L'Affaire Soames*.

In the last few years the diplomatic service has become less separate in its class basis. In 1964 the Plowden Committee showed that, between 1952 and 1962, 70 per cent of the successful applicants for the senior branch came from independent public schools, 8 per cent from direct grant schools, and 20 per cent from maintained schools. The range of universities was even narrower; during the same period, 94 per cent came from Oxford or Cambridge, and 59 per cent from Oxford alone. But since then the numbers of redbrick or grammar school diplomats have gone up quite sharply. By 1968 the proportion of Oxbridge entrants was 65 per cent, and the proportion of ex-public schoolboys 54 per cent—not very different from the home civil service (see Chapter 12). But the upper ranks still have a very heavy public-school, Oxbridge bias; of the thirteen Grade 1 ambassadors in May 1971, all but one (Sir Arthur Snelling) went to public school: eight went to Oxford, two to Cambridge. Non-Oxbridge men have tended to find themselves in small or poor countries, like Gambia, Costa Rica or Somalia—so that the countries of the world seem quaintly aligned with the British class system.

The diplomatic service is an expensive apparatus both in money and in top manpower. Overseas representation in 1969 cost about £107 million, or one per cent of British government spending; of which £63 million was spent on the diplomatic service (£37 million of it in much-needed foreign currency). More worrying is the consumption of brains; of 3,700 members of the old administrative class in the whole civil service, more than a quarter are diplomats. The Duncan Report of 1968, the most recent examination of diplomats, which provides these figures, was confident that the 'diplomatic service does not waste manpower';[1] but many clever young men have been leaving it, complaining that it does not use their abilities. The service has a top-heavy structure (in the next class, the executive class, there were only 1,900 people in 1969 compared with 84,000 in the home civil service) and many of the young men are put into 'fagging' duties which do not stretch their abilities, while they wait in the long slow queue to the top. At the top, too, there is a surplus of manpower; and in 1969 thirty senior diplomats were discreetly retired in their early fifties, to try to clear the bottleneck. With such wastage of brains, such slow promotion, and the risk at the end of being put out to grass, it might seem surprising that the diplomatic service can still attract the best men. But there is still the old gap between prestige and power, between the glitter on the surface and the dullness inside.

There is a large element of absurdity in all countries' diplomacy; watching international diplomatic occasions, with their mirthless laughs, their automatic smiles, their relentless handshakes, one is tempted to think that diplomats become more like each other than like anyone else; that they have become caught up in a special kind of idiots' limbo, whirled round in a subtle torment of asparagus-tips and duty-free whisky. Diplomats from all countries, most of all from the young countries, tend to become very cut off from their own people, closer to other diplomats: the inflation of new countries, new embassies and new national day celebrations has multiplied the permutations of diplomatic encounters.

The arrival of a large number of grammar-school men into the British foreign service corresponded, poignantly enough, with the issue in 1965 of a special guide to etiquette for British diplomats, a comic and revealing document, beginning with Talleyrand's motto: 'Only fools make fun of etiquette; it simplifies life.' The rules do not *look* very simplifying; and for the young diplomat's wife they are specially alarming. She is told how she must leave three cards on other married women, with their top left-hand

---

[1] Command 4107, 1969, p. 23.

corners turned down; she must discover what kind of clothes the ambassador's wife likes her to wear, she must keep the right-hand side of the sofa for the top guest, avoid dinner parties of fourteen (in case one guest drops out); if a guest uses a spoon instead of a fork, she should do the same too, to put him at ease; she should beware the 'temptations of wit, and the dangers of humour'. Every diplomatic drawing-room, it turns out, is a minefield: you must 'never trifle with *placement*'; if you place an official guest wrongly, he may leave after the soup. In inviting guests you should keep to your own level, and not ask incompatible people; the terrible story is told of how one hostess asked the chief of protocol to advise her beforehand about seating her guests: 'Madam,' he answered, 'I can only advise you not to give that particular dinner.' The ambassador himself emerges as a minor monarch, whose invitations should never be refused, and who should only be invited after special consultation. 'You may be wondering,' the booklet says at the end, 'whether you are not about to step backwards into the social world of the Congress of Vienna'; it then explains that new countries need the rules more than old ones do. The interest of the book is that it implies that British diplomats *need* to be told the rules, and that diplomacy is no longer a natural extension of upper-class society where any outsider will be made to feel gauche; but a special profession whose rules anyone can learn.

AMBASSADORS

It remains true that the Foreign Office is a club, and nobody who is a member of a club is going to help you identify the misfits.

George Brown, April 1968.

An ambassador is an honest man sent to lie abroad for the good of his country.

Sir Henry Wotton (Ambassador to James I).

The divisions and titles of the diplomatic service might have been designed to confuse the outsider. The Foreign and Commonwealth Office itself is a 'department' of state: but it is divided into many sub-divisions, ingeniously called 'departments'. Most people, from the Foreign Secretary downward, are called secretaries (there is a principal private secretary to Her Majesty's principal secretary of state for foreign affairs). A young man works his way up from being third secretary to second secretary to first secretary (no relationship to a first secretary in the Treasury), to counsellor and then—if he is lucky—to minister, and thence to ambassador.

The hierarchy of the diplomatic service, though parallel to the civil service with equivalent rates of pay, has a special nomenclature, with titles of misleading humility. These are the top grades, with their salaries and home equivalents:

Grade	Example of job	Home civil service equivalent
1	Permanent Under-Secretary	Permanent Secretary
	Senior Ambassador	
2	Deputy Under-Secretary	Deputy Secretary
	Ambassador	
3	Assistant Under-Secretary	Under-Secretary
	Consul-General	
	Junior Ambassador	
4	Counsellor	Assistant Secretary
	Consul-General	Principal Executive Officer
	Head of Department	
5	First Secretary	Principal or
	Consul	Chief Executive Officer

Ambassadors of all nationalities live in nineteenth-century surroundings, as a kind of temporary subsidised aristocracy. They are called 'Your Excellency' and about half of the British ones are knighted, with a KCMG. Abroad, they represent the Queen, taking precedence (in theory) over cabinet ministers; but at home they have to live much like ordinary people, and in this up-and-down situation their wives often find it difficult to remain altogether sane. Ambassadors are not as special as they were: before 1914 there were only nine: in 1939 there were still only 17: now there are 103. Small states feel insulted if they do not have an ambassador, and Iceland has a British ambassador with a staff of four, and a consul and two vice-consuls, for a population of 170,000 —rather less than Croydon's. The grandest ambassadors are not necessarily now the most important: their diminution began with the electric telegraph (the line to Constantinople was built as early as 1870), and has been accelerated by jet planes and telephones. This produces a discrepancy between the dignified and the efficient parts of the Foreign Office. On the one hand are the ancient embassies, with pomp and protocol (as codified by the Congress of Vienna), chandeliers, colossal *frais de représentation*, but dwindling political importance. On the other hand are the small new embassies in remote capitals, sometimes looking after three or four countries, without protocol but with perpetual challenges and crises. Gorgeous but unimportant posts are useful to the Foreign Office, for they provide a dignified upstairs, a kind of House of Lords. On the other hand, dumping deadbeat diplomats in remote capitals is now tricky, for the most unlikely countries in South America, can suddenly explode: and the new practice of kidnapping diplomats adds an extra hazard. If kidnapping continues, it may change the whole character (and pay-scale) of diplomacy.

The deployment of top diplomats is the most delicate part of the Whitehall snakes-and-ladders; for ambassadors, however ineffectual, have a more visible prestige than permanent secretaries or managing directors. The Foreign Office has always been a stronghold of the ancient principle of Buggins's Turn; senior men who have become exhausted and apathetic are promoted to yet more senior ambassadorships, because they cannot go downwards or sideways. One Foreign Secretary, George Brown, rashly laid into what he called this 'self-perpetuating hierarchy', at that time dominated by the 'class of 1909', of men in their late fifties.[1] He displaced the modest professional diplomat in Paris, Sir Patrick Reilly, with an outsize politician, Christopher Soames; he sent an ex-journalist John Freeman, to Washington; and he refused to promote Sir Con O'Neill, a veteran diplomat who wanted to be ambassador to Bonn—and chose instead a more orthodox career man, Sir Roger Jackling. The hierarchy were furious: Sir Con O'Neill resigned from the service, and one ex-ambassador, Sir Cecil Parrott, class of 1909, launched a public attack on Brown's bad manners: 'We must never forget what happened when Khrushchev took his shoe off at the United Nations and hit the table with it.' But the professionals had their revenge: George Brown resigned in a huff the next year; and Sir Con came back to the Foreign Office under contract to lead the common market negotiations.

The twin peaks of the diplomatic profession are Paris and Washington. The Paris embassy is the grandest of all: the ambassador occupies a superb mansion, bought from Napoleon's sister and once inhabited by the Duke of Wellington, whose huge cost is now much resented by the Treasury. It has a courtyard in the Faubourg St. Honoré, a hundred yards from the Elysée Palace,

[1] See *Sunday Times*, April 7, 1968: 'Why I shocked the F. O. Mandarins.'

and a long garden leading down to the Champs Elysées. There is a large ballroom, a row of reception rooms full of flunkeys, and a famous chef. It is a far more lavish establishment than 10 Downing Street, and it is notorious for inducing *folie de grandeur* in its incumbents. It is not easy to find anyone big and confident enough to fill the immense rooms, or to make themselves heard across the dining table. But when Christopher Soames arrived in 1967 he made the place look, if anything, too small: his bulging frame strides through the rooms and he rules the place like a prince with some of the grandeur of his father-in-law Churchill—which seems to suit the French. In the new Tory Party he appears something of a throwback to the *ancien régime*, and his links with the new Heath men are not very close. But he has the Tory quality of robustness, and he brings to the dry technical operation of Britain's entry into Europe a much-needed panache, a refreshing contrast to the sulks and withdrawal symptoms of the embassy before he arrived.

In a class by itself is Washington: for since the war the one central plank of British foreign policy—albeit a wobbly one—has been the maintenance of the Anglo-American alliance. The Washington embassy has a staff of no fewer than seven hundred, including 92 members of the diplomatic service, and not including the web of consulates and information offices spread throughout the States: its staff is twice that of any other Western European embassy. ('What criteria determine the number of footmen at the British Embassy?', asked Tam Dalyell in parliament in March 1971: 'I know Mr. Dalyell will scarcely believe it,' replied the under-secretary, Anthony Kershaw, 'but most normal people do not object to having discussions over a good meal, properly served in agreeable surroundings.') The embassy itself, a huge pillared place designed by Sir Edwin Lutyens with a gloomy office block attached to it, is like a government department itself. For the last decade it has been recognised that the Washington ambassadorship is such a political job, needing such close relationship both with the president and the prime minister, that it calls for a political appointment: Harlech for Macmillan, Freeman for Wilson, and now, for Heath, the very political banker Lord Cromer. Cromer's career has been professionally successful: he has been Economics Minister in Washington, Governor of the Bank of England and head of the family bank, Baring Brothers. But he has not tried to disguise his right-wing Conservativism; and he came out most openly during the 1970 election, attacking the Labour Party for misrepresenting the balance of payments. He trod the primrose path—Eton, Cambridge, the Guards, the family bank: he married the daughter of Lord Rothermere, owner of the *Daily Mail*. He is thick-set and portly, with the look of a boxing promoter, and his style is blunt. Once in Washington he soon set himself up as a propagandist for the new Heath-type government: 'they are men who have succeeded in their chosen careers,' he told the National Press Club in Washington in February 1971, 'and know to the full the frustrations of excessive collectivism and swingeing progressive taxation on successful endeavour. They do not owe their jobs to preferment, heredity, or privilege but to their own ability.' And meanwhile Lady Cromer was explaining the Viet-nam war: 'It's a long and terrible war, but saving face means so much more to the Asians than life. Life means nothing, but nothing to them.'

THE PALAZZO

At the centre of the world web of embassies and high commissions is the astonishing building in Whitehall, now awkwardly called the Foreign and Commonwealth Office (FCO). You come at it through an arch in Downing Street, opposite the prime minister's house, leading into a great square Italianate courtyard surmounted by statues: at the north-west corner is a rather beautiful tall tower, looking over the lake in St. James's Park. Inside, the building has the atmosphere of an eccentric Italian museum. You walk through a hall of purple wallpaper, along long arched corridors and crumbling mosaic floors, past a room filled with ancient pneumatic tubes, till you come face to face with a marble grand staircase, with two tall alabaster statues at the bottom (one of George Villiers, Earl of Clarendon: one of the third Marquess of Salisbury). At the top of the staircase are huge faded frescoes: one of them 'Britannia Sponsa', apparently depicts a rape, though it is called 'The Sea-farers claim Britain as their bride'; another called 'Britannia Nutrix' shows a young mother suckling a disagreeable baby: a third shows a buxom girl pointing with a flourish to the word 'Silence'.

Amidst these amazing surroundings British foreign policy is devised and run. The building is so preposterous that some people have been tempted to blame it for the periodic absurdities of

British diplomacy. Lord Chalfont, who was one of the Labour ministers at the Foreign Office, has blamed the architecture—as well as the officials—for the Labour Party's failures. The architecture is certainly extravagant: the Duncan Committee reckoned that a new building could save five hundred people, and a million pounds a year. But the failures of British diplomacy have much deeper causes than architecture.

While the ambassadors abroad have pomp but doubtful power, the senior diplomats in London are very little heard of, disguised with clerkly titles as deputy-under-secretaries; but their influence on policy is likely to be greater than their excellencies'. In the nineteenth century the London diplomatic staff was tiny and unimportant; Lord Salisbury in the 1890's never consulted his permanent under-secretary on any matter of importance. Only since the first world war have the PUS and his staff emerged 'from clerkly bondage', to become advisers of recognised importance.[1] But since then the bureaucracy in Whitehall has galloped ahead, and no one seems to know what they all do. The Duncan Committee discovered with some dismay that about half the six thousand people in the diplomatic service were based on London, of whom 376 belonged to the administrative class—an amazingly high figure compared to the 126 equivalent men in the Treasury—and they detected signs of extreme Parkinsonian tendencies: 'The political officers in the chancellery at Strelsau and the Ruritanian desk officers in the Foreign and Commonwealth Office may make more work for each other than the intrinsic importance of Anglo-Ruritanian political relations really justifies; and this tendency will only be increased by the likelihood that each group contains able and energetic men who will not be content to produce less than a full day's work'.[2] But after this devastating comment, they stopped short of prescribing a major reduction of numbers.

At the top of the bureaucracy is a bevy of knights, each with the title of deputy under-secretary, falling over each other to give advice to the politicians, or to administer bits of the building. Above them, at the peak of the diplomatic profession, is the permanent under-secretary, the closest official adviser to the Foreign Secretary. The job has usually gone to one of the grander ambassadors, usually an old Etonian, and when Denis Greenhill took over in 1969 he was heralded as a man of the people. He

[1] Lord Strang: *The Foreign Office*, Allen & Unwin, p. 147.
[2] Command 4137, p. 56.

looks, certainly, more like a rugged businessman than a diplomat: stocky, with straggly white hair and a leathery face. His father was a Congregationalist, a general manager of Westminster Bank, and he himself, after a minor public school and Oxford, went into the old LNER as a railway trainee. He became a colonel in the war, and was then recruited to the foreign service for special assignments; he was sent to Bulgaria and was thrown out two years later, accused of trying to extract secret information from a Bulgarian priest; he was sent to Washington, Paris, Singapore and back to Washington again, where he became political minister, and then returned to London to run the intelligence network. He was a hard-liner, outspoken, determined on a tough line with the Russians, and sceptical about aid; he got on well with George Brown, and could keep him under control and Brown promoted him to the top job. He fits in too with the current Tory mood, of not-letting-Britain-be-messed-about-by-foreigners.

The PUS, like his opposite numbers in Whitehall, is proverbially overworked; he is, as Lord Strang (a former incumbent) has put it, at the top of a gently-sloping pyramid: 'The apex of a pyramidal structure of the administrative kind becomes the more uncomfortable to occupy, the more gently the sides of the structure slope.'[1] Greenhill does not give his colleagues the impression of being harassed by work, but in the bombardment of telegrams and crises, no permanent secretary has much opportunity for thinking about the future of the world: much of the time he has to be more like a nanny, trying to keep his difficult children happy, and keeping the office running smoothly. Men with strong, far-seeing ideas are apt to find themselves *not* becoming permanent under-secretary, and in this finely-tuned, well-oiled machine, smoothness is all.

The intrusion of a new Foreign Secretary into this china-shop, this delicate hierarchy of knights and excellencies, is always a dramatic entrance. When a man of spirit comes in, the sound of breaking china reverberates down the street. As George Brown, the most obstreperous arrival since Bevin, put it: 'The fact of the matter is that if, faced with such a smooth machine, you did not occasionally act rough, one of two things would happen. Either you would make a decision which was wrong and start a calamity; or, much more likely, you would make no decision at all.'[2]

[1] *The Foreign Office*, Allen & Unwin, p. 198.
[2] *Sunday Times*, April 7, 1968.

The arrival of Sir Alec Douglas-Home in June 1970 was a much less spectacular event; it seemed more like a flash-back to ten years before, when Sir Alec, under the name of Lord Home, had first turned up as Foreign Secretary. His policies had changed little since then; 'I must warn people that there is a challenge from communism on an unparalleled scale, which will be pursued quite relentlessly,' he said in 1961; and in 1971 his attitudes were still based on the determination to uncover and fight communism everywhere—particularly in the Middle East. The main difference was that he was ten years older, more rigid and less attentive, so that he sometimes seemed to miss the thread of his officials' arguments. In his first weeks he seemed determined to press through strong Tory policies, and he was convinced of the need to maintain close relations with South Africa to safeguard the Indian Ocean against communist ships; an opportune visit by the South African foreign minister, Hilgard Muller, persuaded him to resume quickly the sales of arms to the Republic. Most advisers, not only in the Foreign Office, but also in the Ministry of Defence, were firmly against it, and very sceptical about the relevance to any communist dangers, and Sir Alec began to be persuaded of the unwisdom of selling arms. But Ted Heath was determined to show his followers that Britain could maintain an independent foreign policy, and not be pushed around by black and brown men; and at the Singapore Conference in January 1971 made no apparent concessions. In fact, Heath *did* modify his policy, and confined arms sales to certain categories; but in the meantime he had successfully antagonised most of the rest of the Commonwealth, to very little purpose except to show his independence. What he did demonstrate was that the prime minister was in charge of foreign policy, and that Sir Alec was in a less independent position than he had been ten years before.

REFORMERS

In the nineteenth century foreign policy was described by John Bright, in a famous phrase, as 'neither more nor less than a gigantic system of out-door relief for the British aristocracy'. During the last thirty years successive attempts have been made to modernise the service, and to adapt its structure to modern conditions; but the reforms never catch up with the conditions. The first and most drastic attempt began in 1941, in the worst part of the war, when

Anthony Eden, with support from diplomats, set up a committee to advocate reform. It was the time of the Beveridge Report, the Colonial Development Corporation, the Fleming Report on public schools, and other radical thinking. ('When a man is about to be hanged,' Dr. Johnson said, 'it concentrates his mind marvellously.') The committee produced an outspoken white paper, and as a result the 'Eden-Bevin' reforms emerged after the war. Four separate branches—diplomatic, consular, commercial, information—all became interchangeable. Recruits were to be chosen not simply by written examination and interview, but by thorough psychological tests. A second language was no longer required before entering. And *women* were admitted to the senior grades. The reforms seemed impressive: but the complaints in the 1943 White Paper—about the narrow circle, the lack of specialists, the seclusion—were still heard.

Twenty years later, in 1962, a new committee was set up under the chairmanship of the ubiquitous Lord Plowden, and including two former diplomats (Lord Inchyra and Sir Percivale Liesching), a banker (Lord Harcourt) and a director of Unilever (A. D. Bonham Carter). They were much more cautious and circumlocutory than their predecessors; but they improved conditions in the service—for instance by allowing a special grant of £500 a year per child to educate diplomats' children at boarding schools. They were worried about the amateurism and suggested that diplomats should spend up to three months learning about a country and its language before being sent there; they also recommended that diplomats should even stay in one place for four or five years.

The Plowden Report in its turn was acclaimed as right-minded, but once again the foreign service mysteriously did not seem to change as much as was hoped. Only six years later *another* committee was set up, largely as a result of Treasury insistence on expenditure cuts. It was headed by a mining entrepreneur with a reputation for ruthlessness, Sir Val Duncan (see Chapter 34) accompanied by Sir Frank Roberts (the ex-ambassador in Bonn and Moscow), and Andrew Shonfield (now Director of Chatham House, see Chapter 20). This lively trio were quicker, more daring and more interesting than the Plowden lot; they raced round the embassies, commissioned elaborate calculations, and came out in July 1969 with some bold-sounding reassessments of Britain's role overseas. They decided that:

Britain is nowadays a major power of the second order. We believe
that in this role she has much to offer the world, as well as much to
gain from it; and that her international future will be quantitatively
as distinguished as her past. . . . If Britain may be compared to a man
who decides that his requirements no longer justify the upkeep of a
Rolls-Royce, the choice lies between replacing it by a smaller car of
high quality or a lower quality car of the same size. We are sure that
the former option is to be preferred. But it must be accepted that the
new car's capacity will be less than the old one's was.'

The Duncan trio discovered a good deal of waste and absurdity:
they reported that much accounting at embassies was 'in or near
the quill-pen era', that the information staff could be halved, and
that there was a petroleum attaché in Washington costing
£20,000 a year whose job was unnecessary. They suggested that
some jobs could be done just as well, and much more cheaply, by
men flying out from London. They calculated that a counsellor
could visit Washington for twenty-seven separate weeks in a year
without costing more than an officer of the same rank permanently
stationed there.[1]

They made some devastating criticisms of other departments,
concealed still in the cryptic language of white papers—of which
this report is a connoisseur's piece (the more drastic the criticism,
the more circumlocutory the language). Of the Board of Trade,
they said, 'Again and again we felt the lack of a meaningful
dialogue on export policy' (They don't know what they're doing).
Describing the agricultural attachés, they said, 'We doubt
whether an adequate job analysis has been made of these posts'
(Nobody knows what they are for). Of the 297 members of the
British defence staff in America: 'There are a number of factors
which make it difficult for the committee to accept without demur
that these staff represent full value for money' (Most of them are
completely superfluous). These discreetly devastating comments
have had little apparent effect on the Foreign Office since.

The most controversial part of the Duncan Report was its
drastic division of the world, which followed on the Labour
government's recent withdrawal from East of Suez and its
commitment to Europe. There was to be the 'Area of Concentration', consisting of the industrialised nations of Europe and
America, and the tactlessly named 'Outer Area', of nearly everywhere else. The area of concentration, they explained, had a

[1] Command 4107, p. 39.

common social structure, a way of living and of conducting business, which led (as they put it) to 'increasing regular contacts at all levels between specialists from various countries in the complicated techniques of modern life, and the switch to multi-lateral organisations . . .' To this they gave the name 'the New Diplomacy'.

THE NEW DIPLOMACY[1]

The activity and exchanges between nations have multiplied all through Western Europe; it is like a change from two-dimensional to three-dimensional chess. Nearly every Whitehall department now has some relations with opposite numbers abroad, and a cluster of international organisations have grown up, each with its own polyglot bureaucracy. NATO is overseen both by the Foreign Office and the Ministry of Defence. OECD, as we have seen, is a disconcerting shadow to the Treasury. GATT and EFTA are the business of the Board of Trade, and UNESCO is linked to the Department of Education and Science. The Council of Europe, jealously watched by the Foreign Office, embraces a huge range of subjects from air pollution to vaccination which involve nearly every ministry of Whitehall. As for the common market, even those countries who are not in it need experts on tariffs, agriculture, industries and mergers to watch it: if Britain goes in, the Ministry of Agriculture alone will need four hundred extra men.

Each international organisation requires a separate British delegation, and the embassies themselves have been smothered by men from other departments, so that the biggest become mini-Whitehalls, complete with labour attachés, military attachés, scientific attachés, each acting as the guardian of his own ministry's interests, exporting their inter-departmental muddle. And other big British organisations feel a need or a taste for representation abroad. The TUC, BBC, NFU, CBI, all have their own kinds of diplomats, hobnobbing with their opposite numbers, and with *their* international clubs, like the International Labour Office and the European Broadcasting Union. The industrial giants like ICI or Shell are establishing in Brussels or Geneva their own commercial diplomats to safeguard their interests.

[1] I have discussed this subject at greater length in a chapter on 'Institutions of British Foreign Policy' in *Britain and West Germany: Changing Societies and the Future of Foreign Policy*. Oxford University Press, July 1971.

The interdepartmental rivalries and confusions within Whitehall are intricate enough: but once extended into international bureaucracies, the scope for muddle is multiplied. Education is covered by three or four bodies—OECD, linked to the Treasury; the Council of Europe, linked to the Foreign Office; UNESCO, linked to Education; and the common market, linked to almost everyone.

The most evident new kind of diplomacy is economic. Ever since the end of the war the Treasury has emerged most strongly as the ultimate arbiter of foreign policy. The Suez escapade may have started at the Foreign Office, but it was the Treasury that stopped it. In the sixties the Treasury seemed to be everywhere. The import surcharge of 1964, which reverberated through EFTA; the successive rescues of the pound; the non-intervention in Rhodesia; the bids to join the common market; the devaluation of the pound; the gold crisis—they all involved the Treasury more than the Foreign Office (though the Treasury's ignorance of the international repercussions was frequently dangerous). At the time of devaluation, in November 1967, every major embassy found its relationships transformed overnight by the Chancellor's secret decision.

The interlocking of experts—sometimes rudely called 'bureaucratic interpenetration'—can make the professional diplomats feel very left out; and they may feel more so if Britain comes into the European Community. For by its nature the community, if it progresses, must merge foreign policy with economic policy, and at Brussels it is often the economists rather than the diplomats who end up on top. The *raison d'être* of the diplomat is the defence of the national interest: as an Israeli observer, David Vital, has written, 'the making of foreign policy is founded on ego-centricity'.[1] To quote an American student, Laurence Scheinman: 'It is probable in the long run that as the EEC develops and expands, the foreign ministries will continue to lose influence and authority, for as common policies develop they become internal policies no longer the subject of traditional diplomatic negotiators.'[2]

The Duncan trio realised the importance of this new diplomacy, inside the area of concentration; but their prognosis, it seems to me, did not fit their diagnosis. They seemed confident that the diplomatic

[1] David Vital: *The Making of British Foreign Policy*, p. 19.
[2] Laurence Scheinman: 'Some Preliminary Notes on Bureaucratic Relationships in the EEC': *International Organisation, Vol. XX, no. 4* (Autumn, 1966).

service, by absorbing some outsiders and by modernising its techniques, could cope with the interpenetration; they even recommended a redoubling of diplomatic effort inside this area at the expense of posts elsewhere. But they stopped well short of suggesting that the diplomats should be more closely integrated with the home civil service, or that Whitehall itself should be reorganised to this end. (The Fulton Report of two years before was regrettably not allowed to include the foreign service.) Yet this is surely the only effective way of grappling with the new diplomacy—to make civil servants into diplomats, to cross-fertilise between embassies and ministries. A concentration of diplomats can cause more problems than it solves. The more direct the contact between the source of policies and the foreign capitals, the more efficient the machinery of diplomacy is likely to be; and there is no reason why senior home civil servants should not become more interchangeable with the foreign service—allowing nomadic diplomats to have long spells in London, and giving Treasury men a much-needed experience of abroad. The task of every commission on diplomats since the war has been how to define the role of this separate breed in the changed and more complicated world: but they have jibbed at the most obvious remedy—that the breed should no longer be separate.

16

Defence

Army, Navy,
Medicine, Law,
Church, Nobility,
Nothing at all.

Cherry-stone rhyme.

Few changes have been more marked in the British atmosphere than the fading respect for military values and castes. Britain, it is true, has never been as obsessed by martial glories as France or Germany: she has turned away from her soldiers in peacetime, and (like no other European country except Luxembourg) refuses to have peacetime conscription. Since Cromwell's major-generals, the top soldiers have been suspected by politicians, and the last and only general to become prime minister was the Duke of Wellington. But the second world war left a wake of respect for military men, and up till the late fifties retired heroes occupied key emplacements in civvy street: Sir Brian Robertson commanded British Railways, Sir Ian Jacob led the BBC, Lord Douglas was C-in-C of BEA. Lord Portal took charge of British Aluminium, Major-General Dunphie marched into Vickers, Captain Brownrigg, R.N., paced the quarter-deck of Associated Rediffusion. In the Tory Party, Captain Macmillan took over from Captain Eden, in a regiment that included Brigadier Lloyd, Brigadier Powell, Major Macleod, Captain Soames and Colonel Heath. The Tories made a point of despising the politicians, like Butler, and particularly Labour ones like Gaitskell and Wilson, who had not borne arms. Generals' memoirs were the best-sellers, and the armed forces themselves were still defending one residue of empire after the other—Malaya, Cyprus, Kenya, Suez.

By the late sixties, there was not much left of the glory. A few lingering chairmen, like Lord Harding of Plessey; a clique of backbench colonels and captains in parliament; a flotilla of naval officers in public relations. And in the meantime a new generation had cheekily rejected military values, with satirical war-films, old military uniforms in frivolous contexts, and Union Jacks on shopping bags or aprons, bought in shops like 'I was Lord Kitchener's valet'. Even Colonel Heath has started growing his hair long. For the first time since 1914 a generation saw no likely prospect of being called up, and the whole point of the imperial burden had collapsed with the last parts of the empire. The youth responded by going back to a style of dandyism, mockery and sexual confusion, a throwback to the Regency Style,[1] before the empire was established. In this fierce rejection there was a good deal of love-hate, and a fascination with the confidence and cruelty of a parents' generation (as in the melodramatic film debunking public schools, *If*, directed by Lindsay Anderson, son of General Anderson): a new school of young military historians—Corelli Barnett, Alan Clark, John Terraine—showed some of this ambivalence in writing about the two world wars. In fact the old martial stereotypes—Colonel Blimp, the general from Poona, the crusty old sea-dog—had almost disappeared over the horizon, except in letters in the *Daily Telegraph*. Many of the new iconoclasts, with their contempt for old age and their fascination with violence, could be much more frightening than they.

This change in social attitudes reflected a real and spectacular change in economic priorities—one of the most basic changes of the sixties. Defence expenditure dropped during the last government from 8·3 per cent of the national income in 1963 to an apparent 5.1 per cent in 1969: though part of the drop is due to items being removed from the defence expenditure and charged to the Ministry of Technology or Public Building and Works. For the first time, spending on education exceeds spending on defence, and there are more teachers than armed forces (see chapter 7). This is how the estimated Defence Budget was divided in 1969–70:

[1] It has been argued by Lord Blake that dandyism is 'characteristic of an era of social flux, when aristocracy is tottering or uncertain, but when radicalism has not yet replaced it with a new set of values': Robert Blake: *Disraeli*, p. 78.

	£	*Men*
Central	87,618,000	
Army	661,300,000	190,000
Navy	685,797,000	87,000
RAF	638,235,000	113,000
Royal Ordnance Factories	48,750,000	
Total:	2,121,700,000	
Ministry of Technology	236,417,000	(Defence share)
Ministry of Public Works	193,734,000	(Defence share)
TOTAL:	2,551,851,000	

The blustering old martial style is out of step with the rest of the country, but the military tradition is not quite as irrelevant or washed-up as it looks. For the armed forces have become much more closely inter-connected with industry and technology; and in the process they have influenced them as well as been influenced. Behind the theatricality of the mess or the wardroom, the military tradition and discipline can still make its mark on more confused and doubting occupations. The army officer may be more stupid and less analytical than the university post-graduate; but he will not suffer from 'analysis-paralysis', indecisions or blockages. The more industry is worried by doubters and drop-outs, the more important it is for them to have men who have confidence and a sense of command. The Army have advertised themselves shrewdly as providing a way out of what Sir Paul Chambers calls 'the wilderness of the unpromotable clever boys'.

The services are beginning to see themselves as large employers competing with industry for men of calibre. Recruitment centres are being brought on to the high street, the services are now more subject to market pressures, and as with the civil service or industry, the need for recruits has begun to change the service itself. As one Admiralty officer put it: 'I joined as a vocation—I've an awful feeling that young people today look on it as just another job.' Or as Sir John Hackett—former C-in-C of BAOR, and since 1968 the principal of King's College, London—has described the 'profession of arms':

> As the profession grew more professional, first at sea and then on land, the sailor and the soldier moved farther apart from each other and the functional area in which both operated, the military, grew more sharply distinct from the non-military. The movement away from the civilian has now been reversed. They have come closer together, military skills are less exclusively specialist. The military community lives less apart. Uniforms are less worn in civilian society.

305

The working clothes of a general are very like those of a machine minder, though he still has something rather more grand put by for special occasions. How far will this tendency towards reintegration go? Not, I am sure, as far as a complete merger. The special nature of the military calling will persist, and although the threshold between civil and military has in recent years got lower, and may get lower still, it is unlikely to disappear. The task of those in charge is to determine its optimum height, or, to put it another way, to see how close the military can be brought to the civilian without destroying the value of the soldier to society. One thing is particularly important: to facilitate reintegration when the soldier wishes to cross the threshold and become a civilian.[1]

Attracting the young to the services is the over-riding problem, which has affected their whole character: 'A major change has occurred'; said one military man; 'the army realised that they must go out and meet people—they can no longer afford only to wait for those who will forge their own path in.' The British hatred of conscription and (till recently) the low rate of unemployment have meant that the services depended on the goodwill of the community for their recruits; without recruits there can be no defence policy. A 'hearts and minds' campaign has been waged in Britain, as it has been waged in other countries inhabited by British armies. Public goodwill is the aim of much of the advertising, on which the army spent a total of £1¼ million in 1970, and of new schemes to bring the military into closer touch with civilians. They offer Military Aid to the Civil Community (MACC) at times of disaster, they mend broken bridges and build roads. They plan to move married quarters from military deserts like Bovington Camp, to put them in the midst of towns and villages.

ARMY

Conscription may have been good for the country, but it damn near killed the army.

General Sir Richard Hull, 1962.

The transformation of the army might be measured by the decline of the regiment, which has been (far more than a ship or a squadron) the repository of loyalty. Regiments in their modern form were invented—like the civil service—in the dynamic 1870s. They were the administrative unit devised by Col. Cardwell, the Secretary of State for War, as a way of ruling the

[1] 'The Profession of Arms': Lees Knowles lectures at Trinity College, Cambridge, November 1962.

empire: there were seventy-five regiments each with two battalions —one at home, the other guarding a distant outpost—and in their static isolation they developed powerful and splendid characters of their own, which were not necessarily very relevant to military efficiency. 'I hope you won't disband the regiments too quickly,' Churchill said to Macmillan, as Minister of Defence, in 1954, 'I want plenty of brass bands for my funeral.' Churchill lived too long: 23 pairs of regiments were merged between 1958 and 1961. Amalgamations and disbandments, bringing bitter resentment in their wake, continued to streamline the fighting units. The 77 infantry battalions existing in 1957 had dwindled to 52 by early 1970. Before the 1970 election the tiny Colonel Mitchell, 'Mad Mitch', became the champion of the regiments, particularly the one in which he served, the Argylls. After the election, four battalions and one regiment at the eleventh hour escaped (as Mitchell put it) 'hanging by the Socialists, to suffer drawing and quartering by the Conservatives'. Three more battalions have had their blow softened by being put into 'suspended animation' (like putting a warship in 'mothballs'), which is a polite word for death: only the Regimental Colours are preserved to allow for resurrection. In 1970 the army was made up this way:

58 infantry battalions (including 6 Gurkha)
 3 parachute regiments
19 armoured car and reconnaissance regiments
28 artillery battalions
13 engineer regiments

THE GUARDS

The regiments' strict 'pecking-order' lingers on. The richer ones used to insist on private incomes, and through bequests and private enterprise they acquired large funds. The younger, poorer regiments fell behind. At the top of this pecking-order is the Household Division, the five regiments of the Guards Division and the Cavalry—the newly-merged 'Blues and Royals', made up of the Royal Horse Guards and the Royal Dragoons, and the Life Guards. They are entrusted with guarding the Queen, including marching outside Buckingham Palace in black bearskins, and with the most prominent role on royal and public occasions, such as the state funeral of Sir Winston Churchill, with plenty of brass bands.

The three oldest foot regiments—the Grenadier, Coldstream and Scots Guards all date back to the time of the Civil War, when they helped to restore Charles II to the throne (though the Coldstreamers, the oldest of the three, had originally been raised as part of Cromwell's New Model Army). The Irish Guards were founded in 1900, to commemorate the Irish bravery in the Boer War, and the Welsh Guards (whose Colonel is Prince Philip) in 1915. Since the war, the Guards have modified their requirements; officers need no longer buy their own headgear or horses, and men need be only 5 feet 8 inches tall. They protest that they have no secret or tribal supply of recruits. Like other regiments they drum them up as best they can: they encourage the lads with the help of success stories of cricketers and World Cup football players (Jackie Charlton was a former member of 'The Blues'). Even the Irish Guards now recruits from London, the Midlands and North-West, as well as Ireland (they maintain their recruiting has not been set back by the army's involvement in Northern Ireland).

There are 380 regular Guards officers with 'the privilege of being commanders of guardsmen'. The Guards pride themselves on being the finest fighting force. 'Like all establishments possessed of infinite self-confidence,' writes Anthony Verrier, 'the Household Brigade's members are either totally conformist or completely outspoken.' The ceremonial role is still an integral part of the way of life. Many officers are from Ampleforth, Downside or Worth— Roman Catholic schools where ceremony and hierarchy may be considered more important. The Guards claim nowadays that they are much more democratic, and that their officers come from the widest possible spectrum of schools—by which they mean fewer from Eton and more from other public schools. One or two grammar school boys have been reported recently, and fourteen officers are currently at university—including ten at red-brick ones. But Guards officers still like to cultivate careful snobberies and, like courtiers, a rigid code of what is and is not said, of a Nancy Mitford kind—like not saying 'cheers' before drinking, not using public transport, always having a hat. (These codes have been threatened since the 1970 pay deal—which separates the living allowance, and thus makes it cheaper for officers with family houses in London to live in them.) The mystique of the Household Brigade—as the standard bearer of the whole army—is much reinforced by their huge barracks in some of the most splendid and expensive sites in London, ostensibly to enable them to protect the Queen: this visible link with the monarchy probably helps to maintain their social confidence. The expense of these metropolitan barracks is sometimes excused by their importance for tourists, who rate pageantry as one of Britain's greatest attractions: but the Guards are not keen to step up their ceremonial; the British Travel Association wanted to arrange two Changings of the Guard each day, but the Guards refused, on the grounds that 'the ceremony would no longer be meaningful'.

OFFICERS

There is no such thing as the Sandhurst type.
Major General Philip Towers (Commandant of Sandhurst), 1970

The army college at Sandhurst finds itself rather lost with the waning of the military ethos. The traditional Sandhurst recruits, the public schoolboys, are going elsewhere and the college was not even filled in 1969: in that year the most military school, Wellington, sent only seven boys to Sandhurst. The famine of recruits forced the army as early as 1964 to call in the advertisers, in the shape of Benson's, who put together a famous heretical advertisement headed 'Does it matter what school you went to?' It featured several 'non-U' officers, as well as 'U' ones, lolling over the messroom's red leather chairs by the brass hearth fender, with a floppy-eared mascot dog. It provoked strong reaction in the upper echelons of the army: but it was true that fewer public schoolboys entered Sandhurst in 1969—57 per cent compared with 70 per cent in 1961, and more boys from maintained schools have made the grade, a not very high one (more than 40 per cent in 1969 had only five 'O' levels).

The army makes no secret of trying to get back into the public school anterooms. 'What is the use of receiving a thousand applications as the result of *Daily Mirror* advertising, if we don't select any of them?' The proportion of public schoolboys selected by Sandhurst is sixteen per cent higher than the overall number applying. Seventy-three per cent of the school entrants to Mons (the short-service training college) are public school; the training period there is only five months and so 'leadership potential' must be more highly developed on entry. Over sixty per cent have fathers who were officers and over fifty-five per cent come from the south of England. The army still regards the public school 'as the natural breeding ground for any type of leader'.

'Is the service of the Crown in this country's land forces to be left in the hands of those whom industry would reject, young men too dull to get into Shell or ICI, or Glaxo?' asked Sir John Hackett in 1960: he foresaw a future army in which all officers will have taken degrees or their equivalents. Whether this will be so it is too early to say, but the army, like everyone else, has become degree-conscious: in 1970 they had twenty-eight university cadets whom they pay very well to study what they like (except useless subjects 'like music') if they commit themselves to the army. A pre-university army scheme has been started, to encourage some young people to try out the army for a few months. Advertising is trying to combat the image of a 'tough but thick' army; one advertisement in 1970 even showed 'part of the army's new training area' as the Bridge of Sighs at Cambridge. But the army has not dared to follow the air force's example in going only for graduates.

The army competes with industry for the same kind of manpower, and when many officers were sacked between 1958–61 industry found some of them excellent managers. 'We feel,' a Shell man said, 'that for the right people a military training gives a certain maturity it would be impossible for them to attain in industry—an edge if you like.' Shell have even sent three junior managers already on their payroll to short-service commissions. Many short-service people are part of a joint scheme assisted by the CBI, with 120 firms guaranteeing jobs at the end of three years. While the army has great difficulty in catching long-term recruits, many people enjoy a much shorter commitment of three years, and Mons was filled in 1970 for the first time for several years. Only one-tenth of these officers transfer to a regular commission, but the army console themselves with the military goodwill that the other nine-tenths take into the outside world.

For other ranks, recruitment has been very difficult since the ending of conscription in 1962. In 1970 Britain needed 23,000 more soldiers then she recruited: there has been a dearth of 17 to 20-year-olds (who make up eighty-eight per cent of recruits) after the previous post-war 'bulge' of births. 'We're competing with industry now,' said one man at the Ministry of Defence, 'and we have to take a different attitude; it's no longer a question of go and get yer 'air cut.' Advertising is the obvious means of changing the image of the army, and has met with some success; but the most effective boost is a skirmish, which pushes up recruitment figures.

Nothing is more frustrating to an organisation dedicated to fighting than not being able to, and nothing more morale-boosting than action. The ranks do not want to commit themselves, any more than officers do, to long periods of service, so a three-year period was introduced; 'only three years' and 'professionalism' are the two current advertising themes. In the last few months the new pay scales—together with higher unemployment, that old godsend of the army—have helped to boost recruitment. These are the pay-scales in 1971:

Officers	£ p.a.	Other Ranks	£ per week
2nd Lt.	1,606	Private	17·50
Captain	2,245–2,555	Lance-Corporal	25–30
Major	2,920–3,322	Sergeant	31–36
Lt.-Colonel	3,833–4,234	Warrant Officer	35–42 +
Colonel	4,654–5,265		
Brigadier	5,750		
Major-General	7,250		
Lt.-General	9,250		
General	12,500		
Field Marshall	14,000		

At the top levels the army has always been very tribal. Seven out of the ten full generals still come from army families; the last Chief of the General Staff, Sir Geoffrey Baker, was the son of a colonel, married to the daughter of a major. But the present Chief of the General Staff, Sir Michael Carver, represents more than any other general the new army intelligentsia: he is another product of that cerebral school, Winchester. His heresies began early when he joined the Royal Tank Corps, not from choice, but because, as he has said, 'I saw the army as the quickest way of gaining economic independence. I meant to study and get out, but the war finished that.' He joined the tanks because he could earn more, and because they were the vanguard of the professional revolutionary. He spent his war service in North Africa and in 1944 at the age of twenty-nine he became (it is said) the youngest brigadier in the army. In 1967 the Minister of Defence, Denis Healey, sent him as C. -in C. to the Far East. Healey was very impressed by his brilliant logical mind—not unlike his own—and pushed him up to be CGS; but his ruthlessness and lack of common touch made him unpopular with his more conventional colleagues and with the Tories. He is associated with the demise of the Territorials; he is anti-conscription. He has written books on El Alamein and Tobruk and a modern history of the Royal

Scots Greys, whose purpose was to remind future soldiers of 'a tradition of high efficiency'. He sees a modern army in which merit takes precedence over seniority: his career bears this out.

NAVY

Stick close to your desks and never go to sea,
And you all may be Rulers of the Queen's Navee!
Sir Joseph Porter, in HMS Pinafore.

Traditions of the Navy? What are they?
Sodomy, rum and the lash.
Sir Winston Churchill.

In 1914, when the navy was at its peak, it had 389 ships, including 71 battleships and battle-cruisers and 148,000 men. In 1939 it was still the largest navy in the world, with 300 ships and 161,000 men. By 1970 there were 200 ships and 87,000 men.

The old symbol of naval glory was the battleship, the grey floating fortress which was Britain's ultimate weapon. It had the protocol of a floating court, and its own mythology of rum, beards and quarterdecks. Battleships lingered like dinosaurs until 1960, when *HMS Vanguard*, the pride of the post-war fleet, was towed to the scrap-yard. With it went a way of life. The new kind of navy is as different as porpoises from whales. The new symbol of naval might is a much more secretive and unattractive machine— the nuclear submarine, which spends three to four months under water; the crew are cooped up in their floating cigar, living on top of each other, without seeing anything except film-shows and the sea and each other, which gives a new poignancy to the old song:

We joined the navy
To see the world
But what did we see?
We saw the sea.

The great majority of naval men—three out of four—are on dry land, in that fantasy-nautical world where barracks are ships, office blocks are called HMS, cars come alongside, files go adrift, stairs go aloft, and ratings go ashore by walking out through the gates. But there are still enough ships left to make recruiting even more difficult than for the other services, mainly because of the problems of wives; the navy has become much more accommodating, but it stops short at allowing wives afloat. 'The only recruiting slogan I could think of,' said one top naval man, 'was: join the navy to get away from your wife.'

The navy has traditionally been the least democratic of the services, with officers from the younger sons of the gentry, and the lower deck recruited by press-gangs. The tradition of coercion still survives in the recruitment of boys who want to 'run away to sea' at the age of fifteen, and who cannot then buy themselves out until they are twenty-three: nearly half the lower-deck recruits in 1969 came from this 'junior entry'—a system which Gerry Reynolds, the former Minister for the Navy described as 'morally indefensible': but the abuses *should* soon be rectified, after the publication of the Donaldson Report. The recruitment is still very regional, mainly from the areas round the south coast, behind the ancient naval bases of Devonport (Guzz), Portsmouth (Pompey) and Chatham (Chats); the ancient dockyards still dominate those towns, and one of every four of the men in Devonport works in the dockyard. The entry of naval officers has shown a great change in the last few years; the traditional gangway has been through Dartmouth, which took most of its recruits from independent schools; but that source of supply (as for Sandhurst) has been drying up quickly, as the naval future has looked less certain. On the other hand, the navy has had far more applicants from the universities, as graduates have been faced with unemployment; so that in 1971 the navy aimed to recruit *five* times as many graduates—up to 100 a year—and the navy is steaming ahead of the army in its 'graduatisation'.

At the top of the navy there has always been a mixture of radicalism and orthodoxy, and the First Sea Lords are apt to alternate between the two; the previous one, Sir Peter Hill-Norton (now Chief of Defence Staff) was quite radical; the present one, Sir Michael Pollock, is much more conventional, with the standard naval background—educated at Dartmouth, lives in Hampshire, and has risen up through naval establishments rather in the wake of Hill-Norton, without much experience of the larger issues (apart from commanding HMS *Tiger* during the Smith-Wilson talks). But his successor is likely to be Edward Ashmore, a more unusual phenomenon; his father and his brother are admirals; he married (like his brother) an admiral's daughter; and he has been equerry to King George VI and the Queen. But Ashmore is also half-Russian, with an outlook much wider than most sea-dogs; at forty-nine he belongs to a younger generation of men who came into the Navy in the late thirties, noticeably abler than their predecessors.

This was the navy's strength in 1970:

4 nuclear-powered Polaris submarines
5 nuclear-powered fleet submarines
27 diesel-powered submarines
2 aircraft carriers
2 commando ships
2 assault ships
3 cruisers
8 guided-missile destroyers
2 other destroyers
66 frigates
76 minesweepers and hunters

AIR FORCE

Ten years ago it seemed that one generation of airmen might see the birth, triumph and death of the Royal Air Force. With the advent of missiles, H-bombs and nuclear submarines, the days of manned fighters and bombers—the very soul of the air force—appeared to be numbered; the main business of a future airman looked like being the transporting of the army. But since then the airman has reasserted his role, and the air force prefers to keep the human being with his skill and his brain—more discriminating than a computer—to finally decide when to press the button. The fighter still has a role; and the spectacular Israeli air victory in 1967 revived faith in the hearts of air-minded boys.

The changes in the organisation of the air force have roused less noisy protest than those in the army: in 1968 Bomber Command, of Battle of Britain fame, was amalgamated with Fighter Command to make one Strike Command. The 113,000 men are now in four Home Commands (Strike, Air Support, Training and Maintenance) and four Overseas Commands (Near East, Far East, RAF Germany (6,500 men) and RAF Gulf).

The 720 combat aircraft break down thus:

70 Vulcan bombers (with bombs or Blue Steel air-to-surface nuclear missiles)
160 F-4 Phantoms in interceptor and strike roles
130+1 squadron of Lightning interceptors
35+ Buccaneer strike aircraft
V/STOL Harriers
160 Phantom strike/interceptors

314

64 Canberra strike aircraft
30+2 squadrons of Canberra PR-7s for photo-reconnaissance aircraft
45+1 squadron of Shackletons
6 Nimrod maritime patrols
12 Victor 2 reconnaissance aircraft
24 Victor 1 tankers

Air support includes 22 Britannias, 12 Belfasts, 5 Comets, 14 VC-10s, Hercules, 15 Argosys, Andovers, Whirwind and Wessex Mark 2 helicopters
Bloodhound and Tigercat surface-to-air missiles[1]

The air force, unlike the other two services, has never had a settled existence. Born in the first world war, it was bitterly resented by the army, and still more by the navy: the fierce battles over who should control the Fleet Air Arm have deepened the feuds. Today, in the era of tri-service diplomacy, the navy are annoyed by the airmen's abilities: 'Naval officers are just not crooked enough,' protested one. 'These air marshals are very persuasive. A lot of them have had the benefit of university education. Even in Whitehall that sort of thing pays in the end.' The old separation between the teeth and the tail—the fighting men at the front and the technicians at the back—was never viable in this very technical service, and airmen are still often looked down on as technicians—'No one *leads* anyone in the RAF,' said a Guards officer. Airmen were regarded by the others as upstarts, non-gentlemen, raffish and undisciplined. They reacted by being aggressively air-minded. 'We don't believe in bull—planes have their own discipline.' The string and glue period, the triumph of the daring individualists who were called to their fighters at a moment's notice, is over. Now jet planes are much faster, more expensive and complex, and discipline and technical certainty have become much more crucial: a Nimrod has a crew of eleven.

The new kind of pilot is a different animal from the old Flying-Officer Prune. A pilot is likely to find himself, not alone in the clouds, but flying in a bomber like a power station, watching a row of black boxes, always in touch with his base. The pioneering is over. A pilot is a technologist—the training of one Phantom pilot is said to cost £350,000—and he is the kind of person so insistently wooed by industry and commercial airlines; a Boeing 707 pilot gets £11,400—which is more than an Air Vice-Marshal. The tremendous costs involved in training RAF

[1] Institute for Strategic Studies: *The Military Balance, 1970.*

personnel require a long commitment—sixteen years minimum, but in spite of this they have been able to recruit up to par.

The RAF is much more meritocratic than the other two services: 'Snobbishness of any kind won't work,' said one recruiting officer. 'If a chap comes up to Biggin Hill with a yellow shirt and long hair,' another recruiting officer said, 'we take it at face value.' They regard recruiting in comprehensive schools as a challenge, which to the army is a 'bloody nuisance'. They are looking for men, U or non-U, to do highly technical work: they even recruit *women* as engineer officers. In 1966 413 officers were commissioned from the ranks, compared with only 75 in the army in 1970. Of the total RAF commissions, far fewer are from public schools than in the army; in 1969 only 13 per cent were from Headmasters' Conference schools (compared with 43 per cent to the army).

The RAF goes much further than the others in recruiting from the universities, and it has just wound up its own 'university of the air' at Cranwell. The army and navy are sitting on the fence watching anxiously for the success or failure of the new graduate entry scheme, which for the air force could be the fulfilment of Hackett's dream for the army. It seems to be succeeding: in 1970, 58 officer recruits came from Cranwell, and 248 came from universities. At the end of 1970, 360 acting pilots, who had managed to get their own places, were reading for degrees. A lot of noises are made about 'wastage of the defence budget'—since many sponsored graduates leave after sixteen years—but the recruiting officers maintain that the £1,000 a year to educate a cadet should be charged up to general education, not to defence.

The RAF still has to work hard to sell itself to the young, and it is against any suggestions of joint service recruiting. Its very professional sales organisation is greatly admired by other public organisations, like the fire brigade and the metropolitan police. The recruiters jealously guard their professionalism against their own top brass: 'The attitudes of our own brilliant leaders must change. It's no good Guinness liking the beer if no one else does.'

Fewer of the top officers in the air force (not surprisingly in view of its newness) come from military backgrounds, and there have been many unorthodox men, particularly from the Commonwealth. The previous Chief of Defence Staff, Sir Charles

Elworthy, was a New Zealander who took a law degree, one of the ablest men in Whitehall. The previous Vice-Chief of Air Staff, Sir Peter Fletcher, was the son of a Rhodesian tobacco-farmer, married to a South African, and also a lawyer. But the Commonwealth links of the RAF are fewer than they were (partly because of the loyalty problem, partly because the Australians are building up their own air force); and the current Chief of Air Staff, Sir Denis Spotswood, is impeccably British to the tips of his handlebar moustaches; he has even been ADC to the Queen.

MINISTRY OF DEFENCE

Since the last war the services have found themselves constantly engaged in combined operations. In the amphibious state of modern warfare the air force can carry the army, the navy protects the air force, and all three often operate together. Successive governments have tried to bring them closer together, and to compound their individual loyalties in the 'tri-service outlook'. But the problem of merging them is probably the most complex of all organisational problems, psychologically as much as logistically. For the ideal of a streamlined single service, integrating all the elements into a single pyramid, is in the end a meaningless one; the service loyalties, and the loyalties to battalions, squadrons or ships, are an essential part of the fighting spirit, an example (as one defence politician put it) of the 'territorial imperative'. Without some conflict within the organisation, even a bit of 'creative tension', the morale of the forces would collapse in confusion, and the new bureaucratic muddles could be more crippling than the old ones. British officers, when threatened by a new phase of coming-together, like to point to the example of the Canadian Armed Services, which were brought together in 1968, all with the same bright green uniforms with naval stripes, inside which the morale is reported to be at rock-bottom.

There have been many attempts to bring the services closer together: as long ago as 1856 Disraeli had a scheme to bring the army and the navy together under a single War Minister. In 1946 the Ministry of Defence was first created, to co-ordinate and control the three services; but the three service ministries remained very separate and at constant cross-purposes. It was not until 1962 that a real reorganisation took place, one of the most important achievements of Harold Macmillan. All three services were brought together into one 'main building', the big stone office block between Whitehall and the river, one of the ugliest piles in London. The political heads of the three services lost their autonomy, and the post of 'First Lord of the Admiralty', first held in 1673, was abolished: in its place was the 'Minister of Defence for the Royal Navy', alongside his counterparts for the army and air force. And at the head of them was the minister himself, renamed the Secretary of State, with much greater powers over the combined services. Lord Attlee protested that 'by destroying these old landmarks they may destroy the spirit of the services'; Lord Teynham complained that they were creating 'a post for a superman'.

The power of the Secretary of State is certainly unparalleled in a peace-time ministry. He regulates not only £2,500 million a year, but a force of 390,000 service men and women, and another 348,000 civilians—more than the total employees of the National Coal Board. The job requires not only mastery of the problems of strategy and nuclear chess, but a deep insight into the workings of large bureacracies—complicated by the inter-service rivalries. At the same time the defence complex is still more cut off from the public, parliament and the Press. The secrecy about defence plans is increasingly effective, and fiascos usually only become apparent after it is too late. In the past angry admirals or generals used to leak information, in their wars against each other; now, together in the same big building, there is more watchfulness, if not more solidarity. The Ministry of Defence is the first and biggest of the 'monster ministries' which have grown up beyond the ken of MPs.

At the head of the ministry are three men—a warrior, a civil servant and a politician—together with a chief scientific adviser, Hermann Bondi (see next chapter). The top job in the services is appointed by an absurd system of rotation between the three services, the most formalised and inefficient example of Buggins's Turn, which often causes this crucial post to be occupied by a man who is too old and too tired. The present occupier is vigorous enough, but not a man with a natural 'tri-service outlook': Sir Peter Hill-Norton is thoroughly naval, the son of a naval captain, and the father of a naval lieutenant; like nearly all of his fellow-admirals, he came up through Dartmouth, and rose quickly in the war, where he served in Arctic convoys. In the ministry he is known as a 'fire-eater' (a favourite services phrase) who speaks out shrewdly and with rare articulation; but he looks down on the air force, and the air force returns his scorn; so that the wasteful rivalry between airmen and sailors has not been made easier. The top civil servant, Sir James Dunnett, is a rugged Scot, the son and brother of a civil servant, who has been a permanent secretary for the last eleven years—first in Transport, in Labour and in Defence. He has spoken out boldly about civil service reform, does not mind making enemies, and can intimidate politicians: but in the last years he has lost some of his fire.

In the ten years up to 1964, the Conservatives had seven Ministers of Defence; the job was always a stepping stone. In the five-and-a-half years of the Labour government, there was only one minister, the black-browed Denis Healey, whose lone role in the contemporary Labour Party has already been inspected (Chapter 3). Healey's actual defence policies could not be accused of consistency; he began, like the Grand Old Duke of York, by insisting firmly that Britain should maintain her forces East of Suez, and after devaluation (to which that costly policy contributed), he switched with equal firmness to retreating from the East. But he did succeed in pushing through the unification of the services, with a steady ruthlessness throughout his term. He was often compared to McNamara in Washington, the arch-rationaliser of the Pentagon. Certainly he established his personal command over the ministry in a way few ministers have done. He created central committees made up of all three services, which over-rode the individual service boards, and which he could dominate; the junior ministers were reduced to his lackeys, and if they resigned (like Christopher Mayhew) they sank almost without trace; while the admirals, generals and air marshals were outfoxed by his arguments and exhausted by his combative energy.

The services have always, not surprisingly, looked to the Conservatives as their natural allies and defenders of their traditions; and in 1970 their return to power was awaited with special relish, for they were committed to restoring the presence East of Suez and even (perhaps) to saving some regiments. The five new political incumbents at the ministry were from the very best stock. Lord Carrington was descended from George IV's banker; Lord Balniel was heir to the 28th Earl of Crawford; the junior ministers were Antony Lambton, alias the 6th Earl of Durham; Ian Gilmour, the rich son of a brewer and brother-in-law of the Duke of Northumberland; and Peter Kirk, the son of a bishop. To these were added in April 1971 another publicist, the

TV salesman of the Tory Party, Geoffrey Johnson Smith; and the man from Marks and Spencer, Derek Rayner. The politicians are a bit more up-to-date and questioning than they might seem; Kirk was one of the first Tory Europeans, and a man of political courage; Gilmour owned *The Spectator* in its heyday, and wrote a learned book on British government; Lambton, a supercilious journalist, was one of the deadliest critics of Harold Macmillan. The minister himself, Lord Carrington, is one of those mysterious Tories who float without apparent effort to the top. He is a charming, equable man behind big glasses, whose manner has a touch of Bertie Wooster. He went from Eton to Sandhurst to the Grenadier Guards; he was given small jobs in the Tory government, and then became High Commissioner to Australia, where Macmillan discovered him and soon made him First Lord of the Admiralty—the last-but-one, as it happened. In opposition he came in handy. He was conscientious and trusted by Heath, and raised funds for the party; he was rewarded with one of the top jobs in the cabinet. He is outspoken and fearless: he has become the chief trouble-shooter in the cabinet, dealing with Northern Ireland and Rolls-Royce as well as defence. He has argued against his leader's most glaring mistake—of selling arms to South Africa. He has the gift Heath lacks, of reassuring others. It remains to be seen how far he has the intellectual mastery to cope with the internecine battles of the ministry.

For the services remain very far from unified, and inside the ministry the skirmishes continue between soldiers, sailors and airmen, as deadly as anything designed for the enemy—fought with memos, committees and, above all, with the secret weapon of all the services: Muddle. A few months before the 1970 election, a headquarters committee, under Sir James Dunnett, had recommended that there should no longer be ministers for each of the three services, but one or two junior ministers looking after all three services; Healey agreed, and wanted to weaken the influence of the 'Service Boards'—the top committees in each service, which could still obstruct the tri-service arrangements, and pressurise the politicians in their favour. But the Conservatives, once in power, retained the three ministers, to the relief of the military men. 'It takes a strong junior minister,' said the ex-minister for the navy, David Owen, who had been involved in pushing through the reforms, 'to resist the temptation to connive with this pressure for the accretion of single service power. The central machinery grafted initially on top of the single service machinery still exists too frequently merely as an addition, and the co-ordinators often seem to outnumber the decision makers.'[1]

The Ministry of Defence is a caricature of all those organisations where a central command tries to merge rival components—BMC and Leyland, GEC and English Electric, English Unilever and Dutch Unilever. At the top the merger looks plausible, but underneath the traditions and rivalries can continue for decades. Bureaucrats thrive on such rivalries; for they require co-ordinators, liaison officers, committees, committees and more committees. It should not be forgotten that the great Professor Parkinson's original law, that 'work expands so as to fill the time available for its completion' began with the professor's examination of the navy estimates, which revealed that the fewer the ships, the more people were required to administer them. The formation of a single Ministry of Defence was expected by naïve observers to economise in staff, even perhaps to allow one man to do the job of three: 'I have taken certain actions,' said Peter Thorneycroft, the Minister of Defence in 1964, 'which ensure that Professor Parkinson is removed from the building.' But the ministry provided a haven for bureaucratic proliferation of which the Professor could be proud. In August 1970 there was a gallant outburst from Colonel Acland of the Scots Guards to *The Times*, protesting that the recent economies had heavily cut down the most crucial fighting arm, the infantry, but had not reduced at all the civil servants and staff officers who 'push the paper around the headquarters'. Retired colonels and admirals joined the attack, in full cry against what the Duke of Wellington called 'the futile drivelling of mere quill-driving'. But the military men overlooked the fact that the real trouble was their own rivalries. As Michael Howard, the military historian, summed it up: 'The cause of the grossly inflated headquarters of our defence services is fairly simple: the determination of each of the armed forces to retain an independent bureaucratic infrastructure in addition to that provided by the central authorities of the Ministry of Defence. Whereas the civilian element in the ministry has now been effectively streamlined, the military has not, and as a result now has the worst of both worlds.'[2]

The most immediate worries of the ministry are how to inte-

[1] *The Times*, July 27, 1970.
[2] *The Times*, August 21, 1970.

grate the three British services; but the long-term problem is a still harder one—how to integrate the British defence forces and their equipment with the rest of Nato. For as the cost of military equipment sails up on an exponential curve, Britain can no longer afford to build aircraft or guided missiles for herself alone; and the likelihood of Britain 'going it alone' in a major war becomes more remote. The attempts to standardise Nato equipment and to integrate Nato armies have made up a melancholy story; there are still twelve armies, eleven navies and eleven air forces, many of them as unequipped to fight any likely enemy as pre-war Balkan armies. As America becomes less certain as the defender of Europe, the Europeans are coming to collaborate on joint projects, like the current Anglo-French Jaguar strike trainer, the Martel guided weapon, and the European Multi-Role Combat Aircraft (MRCA). The British and Dutch navies already co-ordinate closely in joint manoeuvres, and the British navy trains all the Dutch fleet. Whether or not Britain enters the common market, her fighting forces will have to come closer to the continent's. Already the decisive figures in Britain's defence policy are not so much the Chief of Staff or the Secretary of State, but the Americans, Germans or Italians who control the Nato commands, with outlandish names like Saceur, Comanaucent, Chinchan. The most important of all is Cincent; he is the German General Bennecke, Commander-in-Chief of the Central Region, who commands the five-hundred mile frontier from the Elbe to the Swiss frontier. On these frontiers of defence the concept of British sovereignty has long ago become meaningless.

17

Scientists

For the scientists the party is over.
Shirley Williams, February 1971.

In the whole territory of government, and most notably in defence and diplomacy, the traditional non-specialist administrators have had, whether they liked it or not, to deal with weird, inarticulate men who were undermining many of their assumptions. For the last twenty years the relationship between scientists and the other British estates has become increasingly uneasy; they have not known whether to regard scientists as priests or pariahs. From Victorian times, almost up till the last war, there seemed no great complication. Science was Progress, and the identification was commemorated in the allegorical figures, the heroic friezes and the muscular statues which adorned ambitious new buildings. Scientists were a separate incomprehensible breed, often regarded as boring or boorish by arts graduates or politicians; but they were an inevitable part of the progress of mankind, and since they were mostly politically naive, they could be kept in their place, divided and ruled by skilful managers, and there was not much cause for alarm.

But the last war—far more than the first—transformed their position; they turned out to be far more important than either politicians or businessmen had expected, not simply for making bombs, jets or radar, but for the whole economic progress of the nation. In the following two decades scientists were anxiously lured into the ante-rooms of power, whether into Whitehall, into boardrooms or into university administration; and the top scientists found their status up-graded. From being an under-paid eccentric fringe to the world of power, they now found themselves in constant and lucrative demand, whether as government advisers or consultants to companies, showered with honours and paraded as symbols of Britain's greatness.

In this triumph of scientists there was some unease under the surface; they were a priesthood perhaps, but they might also be a coven of necromancers. The invention of the atomic bomb had left its searing marks on the consciences of many top scientists; that explosion had finally destroyed the assumption that science was necessarily associated with progress and improvement, and the 'guilt of Hiroshima' worked away in the minds of that generation. But governments could not afford to be troubled by these thoughts, and nor could most scientists; and there were new dreams of peaceful atomic energy bringing prosperity to the starving millions of the world, to repay the debt of guilt.

The fact that non-scientists could not understand a word of the new language increased the prestige of its practitioners, and in the sixties it became much less respectable for politicians or company directors to speak slightingly of 'boffins' and their equations. Lord Crowther attacked the 'innumeracy' of the arts graduates, and the ponderous shape of Lord Snow briefly but effectively made itself felt as the scientists' champion, attacking the laymen for not understanding the second law of thermodynamics. Public schools, which had been a bastion of Latin against Science, began to embrace scientists eagerly, helped by generous grants for laboratories from industrialists.

But while the arts men were feeling guilty about not understanding science, there was a greater but less noticed failing; the scientists not only did not understand arts subjects, but were very out of contact with the condition of society as a whole. Both their education and their inclination cut them off from social and political problems; at university they had to spend afternoons and evenings with their retorts and test-tubes, while their arts contemporaries were politicking or drinking. Many by temperament preferred things (reliable, predictable, mathematical) to people (irrational, variable, temperamental). To them society and politics looked like lamentable aberrations from rational laws, only to be remedied by rigorous scientific methods.

The politicians continued to embrace the scientists uneasily. Shirley Williams has compared the relationship to the treatment of financial problems before the second world war—'a kind of awestruck but indignant acceptance of the city as a closed world. Science today is too much a closed world, and I believe the scientific establishment has an obligation to society to let more light in'. (*The Times* Feb 27, 1971). In the meantime scientists were developing much greater doubts about their own role in the power-structure. The Vietnam war, the American civil strife, and the wave of concern about the problems of pollution and the environment engendered great new worries in America, which soon crossed over to Britain. Even older scientists became much more concerned about their social responsibilities. Some changed over from the more discredited areas of science, like physics, into the more hopeful ones, like molecular biology; others moved away from science altogether. Many younger scientists complained about the narrowness of their own curricula, and their separation from social sciences which had grown right apart since the beginning of the century (when they had first been excluded from the Royal Society). Young people became aware that science created as many problems as it solved, and that scientists had no solution to the real problems of humanity; and this, together with the exclusiveness of the scientific education, contributed to the 'swing away from science' in schools in the late sixties, after the earlier swing towards science in the late fifties. As Professor Dainton has described it:

> In the course of many discussions with students I have become sharply aware of a prevalent image of science and scientists. The general picture of the man is of someone voluntarily withdrawn from human contact; dissociating himself from personal and societal problems, only really at ease with soulless machines and computers; busy amassing, storing and correlating facts, mainly about inanimate matter, and if he is forced to deal with living creatures, doing his best to analyse and codify them without regard for their feelings and individuality and also one who is insensitive to aesthetics (though acknowledged occasionally to have an interest in music where it has a clear structure as in the works of Bach). In short, he is a 'cold fish' whom any warm-blooded emotional human being would avoid as a companion, and never befriend; a man who is 'objective' to an objectionable degree. His scientific method is thought of as a calm logical

progression from observation and measurement, through collation and rational analysis to an inexorable conclusion.

Of course this image is a travesty of the truth. But whom have we to thank for creating this false picture? Principally the scientist himself, who for some extraordinary reason wants to be seen in this light. By creating an intellectual framework for his subject (in itself an entirely laudable goal), more often than not he offers his undergraduate pupils a neat logical, or near-logical package, and perhaps unintentionally gives the impression that this is how the subject really grew. Most scientists compound their felonies by communicating their own research findings to their colleagues in highly ritualistic form into which no personal enthusiasm is allowed to intrude, and the charade of logical progression is dutifully maintained.[1]

Scientists have become much less secure as a result of erratic swings in the demand for them, both from industry and government—which do not correspond with the swings in supply. From the early fifties, there was thought to be an acute shortage of scientists; the big industrial companies, the Atomic Energy Authority, and all kinds of new government research stations were crying out for more scientists, and the universities needed more teachers as they began to expand more and more rapidly in the early sixties. Research was regarded as the solution to many of Britain's problems, and great efforts were made to persuade schoolboys to swing to science—with increasing success. By the mid-sixties the shortage seemed at its most serious, made worse by the 'brain drain' of scientists to America; a drain which seemed irreversible and international, drying up the supply from countries like India as well as from all over Europe. Then, after 1968, the balance quickly began to change. In America the recession affected the big scientific projects, and left foreigners out of work; while the uglier political climate in the States, the student riots and the Vietnam war made many British scientists decide that poverty and peace in Britain were preferable to riches and riots in America. The drain became a two-way flow, and even some American scientists applied for jobs in Britain. But in Britain, too, there was beginning to be a surplus of scientists. By 1970 the Labour government was disillusioned by the lack of effect of the huge increase in research spending on the gross national product. The government was cutting down, and the universities were expanding less fast; industrialists found post-

[1] Sir Frederick Dainton: 1870 Centenary Commemorative Lecturer: Central Hall, Westminster. May 1, 1970.

graduates often too unadaptable for their commercial needs. The numbers of Chemist Ph.D.s had almost doubled in the five years to 1969, from seven hundred to twelve hundred; but many of the new post-graduates found that the demand for them had evaporated. Among new graduates in 1971, it was reckoned that 3,000 could not find jobs in the field for which they were trained. It has been a bitter discovery. But it may have some benefits for the country; for more scientists are likely now to go into unscientific jobs, in government, industry or even banking, and may thus help to bridge the gap between the administrators and the specialists, and to forge links between scientists and the rest of society.

BRITISH ASSOCIATION

The scientists' recriminations have even begun to explode into the stately 'scientists parliament', the British Association for the Advancement of Science. The 'British Ass' was founded in 1831 by David Brewster, modelled on a German scientists' society, to rescue science from its low status at that time: 'Can we behold unmoved the science of England,' asked Brewster, 'the vital principle of her arts, struggling for existence, the meek and unarmed victim of political strife?'[1] It was mocked by *The Times* and by Dickens, who called it the 'Mudfog Association for the Advancement of Everything'; but in mid-Victorian times the B.A. became the great battleground for scientific debates, and in 1860 it was the setting of the great argument between Huxley and Bishop Wilberforce on the subject of Darwin's *Origin of Species*. In the last decades the British Association has become a much more cautious and uncontroversial body, and its annual summer meetings, rotating through British cities, have developed into a kind of genial festival of scientific progress, full of readable papers by popular professors, which catch the headlines in the silly season.

But in 1970 the BA meeting at Durham was loud with the political ground-bass, and social issues broke suddenly into the open. The year's president was one of the most controversial of the old guard of science. Lord Todd of Trumpington—Nobel laureate, Master of Christ's College, Chancellor of Strathclyde University—is a tall, proud Scots chemist, now sixty-three, who rose up through the universities of Glasgow, Frankfurt and Oxford to become one of the powers in the scientific establishment,

[1] O. J. R. Howarth: *The British Association*, 1931, p. 6.

and for twelve years, until it was reorganised in 1964, he was chairman of the Advisory Council for Scientific Policy. Todd sees scientists as a special elite of highly-trained, privileged men: appropriately, he married the daughter of another Nobel prize-winner, Sir Henry Dale. In his earlier days he was compared with his more modest rival, Sir Neville Mott (now Professor of Physics at Cambridge) in the rhyme:

> Todd
> Thinks he's God.
> Mott
> Knows he's not.

As president of the BA, Todd made an opening speech which confidently reasserted the separateness and seclusion of science:

> Although science has expanded enormously and with increasing speed during the past couple of centuries, it has had of itself little or no direct effect on society. Nor could it have, since it is a cultural pursuit akin, indeed, to music and the arts; it seeks only to enlarge our understanding of the world in which we live and the universe of which our world forms a tiny part.

He went on to advocate that schools should teach science, like English or history, as part of the compulsory curriculum, to produce a 'scientifically conscious democracy'; but also that higher education must become more clearly divided in future between the needs of the majority, whose 'education must have a vocational content that will lead to suitably lucrative employment'; and the special requirements of the all-important intellectual elite: 'That such a group or elite exists must be clear to anyone who has been concerned with higher education, and it should, indeed must, be given every opportunity to develop its power to the full.'

Lord Todd's proclamation in the splendour of Durham Cathedral was a perfect cue for scientific radicals; they were already organised in the British Society for Social Responsibility in Science (SRS) which had been founded in 1969, proclaiming its belief that 'the development of science is not predetermined but should depend upon the social choices of the community and the individual choices of the scientist': their president is Professor Maurice Wilkins, a Nobel prizewinner and molecular biologist who worked on the atomic bomb during the war. They have organised studies of toxic gases, defoliants, pollution, the role of universities, and by 1970 they had a thousand members, with quite high voltage. Todd gave them their opening. They distributed copies of his speech with their own annotations, and tried with limited success to stage a nerve-gas happening in the cathedral precinct; later in the conference they organised an eight-hour teach-in on the theme 'Science is not Neutral', and distributed pamphlets raising awkward questions:

> Some of the uses of deuterium and tritium are on the programme for the Thursday meeting of Section B—Chemistry. But there is one use of them which seems to have been overlooked: the manufacture of H-bombs.
>
> When will the BA invite a poor tenant farmer to talk on the conservation of the landlord's rights (look at the list of the BA's VIPs for the local gentry) or trawlermen to talk about productivity?
>
> Do you feel that science is morally and politically neutral and that scientific work is an end in itself, enquiring no further justification to society? If the answer is 'Yes' to such questions, we think that your view of science and of the scientist's social role are unrealistic.
>
> Aerospace is a limited perspective. We must see beyond it. As the Nobel prizewinner Max Delbruck said recently, 'the frontier of science is not on the Moon or Mars, but here'.

The radicals did not seriously disturb the stately progress of the 132nd annual meeting; but they did reflect the worry of a growing number of scientists who are determined to break out of their social insulation, and to bring science into the political field. The movement still only represents a small proportion of scientists— most of whom remain political innocents. But in the next decade, the relationship of science with society is likely to become more anxious, not only in the universities, but in all the research establishments through the country which interlock with defence. Among the many demands for workers' control and participation, the scientists' demand to be involved in the political results of their research may prove the most far reaching of all.

ROYAL SOCIETY

The new mood of doubt has not had too much effect on that ancient citadel of mutual admiration, the Royal Society, the club of seven hundred top scientists. Its tercentenary was celebrated in 1960 culminating in a rally at the Albert Hall, and in 1967 they proudly moved into four splendid houses in Carlton House Terrace —at a rent of £43,000 a year—overlooking St. James's Park in the midst of palace-land (they even published a paper on the building).

In the seventeenth century 'the Royal' was the hub of scientific discovery; Newton, Halley, Dryden, and Pepys gathered to chat about inventions, and even though Pepys (who was president) couldn't understand Newton's *Principia*, they could all enjoy telescopes and comets. Since then specialists have learnt more and more about less and less, and the renaissance ideal of the 'universal man' has faded. It was in 1901 that the fellows decided to exclude altogether the 'human' sciences—economics, for instance, or philosophy—and their proceedings have become steadily less intelligible to the layman. The society was split into two sides— the 'A' side (mathematics, physics, chemistry, etc.) and the 'B' side (geology, botany, physiology, etc.). But in the last decades the demands of the subjects themselves have been breaking down the rigidity of 'A' and 'B', and now demographers, archaeologists and even human psychologists are eligible for membership. A new medal, 'the Royal C', has been awarded to applied scientists— including Sir Christopher Cockerell, the inventor of the hover-craft, and the bridge builder, Gilbert Robins: and there is now even a medal for contributions 'leading directly to national prosperity' which has been given to Dr Alastair Pilkington, the glass man. The annual quota of fellows has been increased from twenty-five to thirty-two, to include applied scientists: among the astronomers and higher physicists there are now technical direc-tors and such worldly men as the chairmen of Hawker-Siddeley (Sir Arnold Hall), Glaxo (Sir Alan Wilson) and Courtaulds (Lord Kearton).

From 1965 to 1970 the president was the most awesome and revered of all living British scientists, the physicist and Nobel prizewinner Lord Blackett of Chelsea, now seventy-three: he was a key figure in the Labour government's reorganisation of science in 1964, and served on the Advisory Council of the Ministry of Technology. In 1970 he was succeeded by Alan Hodgkin, Professor of Biophysics at Cambridge, where he has spent most of his career. He worked on radar during the war, and later did research into the conduction of nerve impulses, for which he won (jointly) the Nobel prize for medicine: he married the daughter of an American cancer research pioneer, Peyton Rous—who won the Nobel prize for medicine three years after his son-in-law (another spectacular example of scientific in-breeding). Once a month as the Royal Society, Hodgkin chairs the council meetings at the long oval table in the council chamber, below a modern Zulu tapestry depicting 'The Beginning': beside him are the treasurer, Sir Frederick Bawden, two secretaries—Sir Benjamin Katz and Sir Harry Massie—the foreign secretary, Sir Harold Thompson (also vice-president of the Football Association) and sixteen councillors. In the lecture hall are portraits of Hodgkin's predecessors as president, including Wren, Newton, Davy, Huxley, Kelvin, Thomson, Rutherford, Bragg, Dale and Adrian.

The Royal Society has grown up alongside monarchy, government and church over the last three hundred years, and it is in constant danger of being lured into the sleepiest regions of the establishment. It can easily get absorbed in its own mumbo-jumbo, and it has been accused of having lost every faculty (like the Pacific Palolo Worm) except that of reproduction. But over the five years of Blackett's presidency it became more relevant and adventurous. It has made links with the developing countries: Ghana could ask it, as a non-governmental body, for help in its research institutes. It made its voice heard quite loudly over Aldabra, the island that was threatened with a defence base, and now runs a research station there. And among its seventy-three committees there is now an education committee which has been trying to improve science education at all levels.

The Royal Society typifies the older scientists' self-portraiture as a priesthood with their own rituals and missions. The scientific establishment is one of the most separate and enclosed of all the sub-divisions of the British power-structure: while lawyers and economists—the earlier prophets—have been tamed and brought into the heart of government, scientists remain stubbornly resistant to bureaucratisation and integration. The separateness can make them intimidating, but also often engaging. I have usually found conversations with scientists a relief after the more guarded responses of managers and bureaucrats: many of them talk freely and wittily, and maintain a cheeky attitude towards Whitehall or Head Office. Most of them remain unpompous, do-it-yourself people with boyish enthusiasms and little snobbery, enjoying living down to their image, in reach-me-down suits with baggy trousers.

NOBEL LAUREATES

The British scientists have some reason to be proud of their international achievements. One index is the number of Nobel Prizes for Science, first set up in 1901 by the Swedish dynamite king: the arrival of a telegram from Stockholm is the dream of most ambitious researchers. These are the prizes won by the leading scientific countries in the subsequent seventy years:

	Physics	*Chemistry*	*Physiology or Medicine*	*Total*
USA	27	16	35	78
Germany	14	22	10	46
Britain	15	17	15	47
France	8	6	6	20
Holland	5	2	2	9
Sweden	2	4	3	9
Austria	3	1	3	7
Switzerland	—	3	4	7
USSR	6	1	2	9

In spite of the emergence of America and Russia as super-powers with enormous resources and four times Britain's population, Britain has maintained its proportion of Nobel laureates in the second half of the twentieth century at the same level as in the first half. Since 1901 Britain has won more than a sixth of the scientific Nobel prizes; in the last twelve years she has kept up the proportion with seven winners of the chemistry prize, five physiology and medicine—though none in physics. The factors that generate this inventiveness are complex and fascinating; some idea of the odd mixture of creativity, concentration, team work and luck can be gained from that extraordinary book *The Double Helix* by James Watson, who won the prize with Francis Crick in 1962. A tradition of scientific discipline and great teaching is a very large element in producing prizewinners: the Cavendish Laboratory at Cambridge—where Lord Rutherford worked—has produced no fewer than fourteen Nobel laureates. The scientific concentration in the London-Oxbridge triangle out-strips all other parts of the country: in 1960, out of 616 Fellows of the Royal Society, 126 were at London, 107 at Cambridge, fifty at Oxford, while all the other universities together produced only 113. Cambridge remains the most phenomenal seed-bed of British science. But Britain also owes five of her Nobel prizewinners—Max Born (now returned to Germany), Ernst Chain, Sir Bernard Katz, Max Preutz, and Hans Krebs—to the pre-war escape from Hitler; and no fewer than forty-nine out of the seven hundred members of the Royal Society are Jewish immigrants. In science, as in other fields (banking, property, growth industries, medicine), Britain without immigrants would have been a much sleepier country.

GOVERNMENT AND RESEARCH

About £1,000 million a year is spent in Britain on 'Research and Development'—about 2½ per cent of the Gross National Product. It is a higher proportion than is spent by any other European country, though a lower percentage than is is spent by the United States. The fact that Britain spends so much on research, with so little apparent benefit in terms of economic growth, is one of the facts that annoy politicians and administrators who try to control the purse-strings.

The biggest single slice of this money—a third of it—is spent by the Ministry of Defence, the giant patron of science. This is the murkiest region of all, for what really happens to that money is known to only a handful of people. Most of the scientists work in isolated stations, scattered over the country, knowing little about each other. Secrecy is anathema to scientists. Discovery depends on communication. Scientists have, since the end of the seventeenth century, been internationally-minded. Science knows no real frontiers; and a Russian scientist can soon find himself at home in the Royal Society. The creeping expansion of secret research, largely devoted to means of destruction, has depressed scientists all over the world.

Defence is an area of preposterous waste. Extravagant projects can take nine or ten years to complete, rolling on with their own massive inertia, only to find themselves hopelessly unwanted, for either political or technical reasons. 'Research' still conjures up test-tubes or microscopes, but more often it means gigantic engineering contraptions, lumps of radio-active hardware, and intricate electronic devices—enough to build a whole town, and all liable to be scrapped. Only momentarily does parliament and the public glimpse the waste—as when Denis Healey abandoned the TSR2 aircraft in 1965, writing off £120 million.

The decisions for these vast outlays are taken by the chiefs of staff, the Minister of Defence, and ultimately by the cabinet. But a key position is held by the man with the unpromising title of Chief Adviser (Projects and Research), who is the main link between science and war. The new occupant, Hermann Bondi, who took over from Sir William Cook in January 1971, is a mathematician and astronomer with a very academic background for such a practical and political job. He was brought up in Vienna, and moved before the war from the Realgymnasium to Trinity College, Cambridge—another scientist whom Britain owes to the escape from Hitler. He married a civil servant's daughter, and has been lecturing in mathematics or astronomy for most of his career, in Britain and America; he only became involved in government in 1964, first on the space committee of the Ministry of Defence, and then as director of the ill-fated European Space Research Organisation (ESRO) in Paris. He has the reputation of a compassionate man, fascinated by war-games as an intellectual exercise: his coming into the defence ministry after working so long in the stratosphere raised the eyebrows of the hard-headed experts on weaponry and costings.

The most expensive part of defence research is concerned with atomic energy: and here the ministry delegates its task to the mammoth nationalised concern, dealing both with peaceful and warlike applications—the Atomic Energy Authority. It is the most impenetrable industry. The annual report of the 'Atomic Iceberg' has revealed little about how its fifty millions from the Treasury has been spent. It is divided between two main clients— the Ministry of Defence, for whom it makes weapons, and the Electricity Generating Board, for whom it designs power stations. Between them the AEA manages to be accountable to no one. The basic research centre is at Harwell in Berkshire, which, like so many modern research centres, is remote and isolated. It looks like, and was, a war-time air force base, sitting by itself in the Berkshire countryside, with rows of married quarters, a high fence all round, and inside a mass of fantastic ironmongery, like a deserted fairground. It is dominated by the reactors, built inside concrete cubes and echoing with strange noises—beeps, tapo-catas, boinks and pssts. Thick double doors lead into a jungle of engineering round the central reactor. It is a world on its own: there are TV screens, dashboards of dials, and a travelling crane. Bits of radioactive metal are taken out of the reactor and carried in lead caskets to laboratories where scientists in rubber gloves study them behind glass screens. It is a long way from the conversaziones at the Royal Society and the idea of the universal man. It is typical of the fragmented state of science, where one man can spend a lifetime experimenting with one vast, possibly fruitless, contraption.

Until 1967 the chairman of the AEA was one of the most original British scientists, Sir William Penney (now Lord Penney), who had been leader of the British team which developed the British H-bomb; with his unkempt fair hair, his shambling walk and his cracked voice, he looked like the traditional absent-minded English scientist, strayed by accident into the centre of power. In 1967 he left to become head of Imperial College, the biggest scientific educational complex in the country; and his place was taken, to many people's surprise, by a much more commercially minded man, Sir John Hill, who had been in charge of production at the AEA and had applied quite drastic economies to its white-elephantine operations. Hill has supervised the 'hiving off' of the production group into two new state corporations in 1971: one, called British Nuclear Fuels, based near Warrington, will sell 'enriched fuel' to the world market (which is expected to reach £1,000 million a year by 1980). The other, the Radiochemical Centre at Amersham, will trade in radio-isotopes —which at present brings in about £4 million a year. The AEA has left behind its pioneering days of wild hopes, and has become a much more workaday and less extravagant part of the industrial system.

The AEA's trading corporations are one example of the rapid internationalisation of science, which compels national organisations to look further abroad. Scientists, with their symbol-language as a kind of lingua franca, make foreign contacts more easily than politicians, and develop their own international networks. Whenever defence or politics is involved—as in the ill-fated European space projects, Esro and Eldo—international projects are likely to come into recurring cross-purposes; but in more harmless projects, or in pure research which politicians don't care about, scientists can co-operate freely and relatively happily. The most striking example is the European Centre for Nuclear Research at Geneva (CERN), in which thirteen countries collaborate in investigating the obscure behaviour of neutrons and protons, propelling them at high speed through a huge circular tunnel. A vaster 'accelerator' was planned, to cost £150 million, to which Britain refused to contribute; in 1969 an English scientist, John Adams, took over the project—a remarkably independent-minded man, who rose to be FRS without ever taking a degree. He showed his inventiveness in research stations, including Harwell, and ran CERN in its earlier days. Adams had found a way of

335

building an accelerator more cheaply, and more effectively, and Britain can now pay its share towards CERN.

Outside the huge lump of defence spending, the government spends about another £300 million a year on civil research, covering a vast range from bricks to sugar-beet. This is how the total central government expenditure of £309 million on civil projects was divided in 1968–9 and 1966–7: the comparison gives an indication of the increase in every field except Atomic Energy during that time—the heyday of scientists and technologists:[1]

	1968–9	1966–7
Technology:		
Aerospace	88·6	57·1
Atomic Energy	47·8	50·5
Industrial Services	15·9	9·8
Research Councils:		
Agricultural R.C.	13·4	9·9
Medical R.C.	14·8	11·6
Science R.C.	37·4	30·0
Universities	52·4	41·8
Roads and Transport	2·9	2·3
Agriculture, Fisheries, Forestry	8·5	6·2
Housing and Environment	·5	·2
Law and Order	·6	·4
Health and Welfare	2·8	1·5
Financial admin. and common services	6·7	5·1
Northern Ireland Government	1·2	·9
External Relations	2·9	2·3
	309·1	237·7

Whitehall, partly because of its lack of scientific expertise, partly out of respect for autonomies, has hesitantly approached the control and coordination of research. As far as possible the government has left the scientific dons to themselves, while giving them large grants: 'In our view,' wrote the Zuckerman Report of 1961, 'pure basic research is best carried out in the environment of a university rather than in that of a government research establishment. It is characteristic of universities that they provide their members with the necessary freedom to pursue any line of enquiry they wish to follow and, broadly speaking, at whatever pace their inclinations dictate.'

Applied government research is controlled by a whole cluster of councils: this is committee-country with a vengeance, and a single

[1] Economic Trends, No. 205: Nov. 1970. Table II.

scientist may sit on a score. The main councils are run on the same principle as the University Grants Committee, of allowing 'indirect rule' to the academics. But at a lower level there are webs of committees who can only advise civil servants and ministers, and it is in this tangled region that scientists have felt most cheated and wasted. Lord Blackett, who tried to reform the committee system for the Labour government, described in 1964 how the Whitehall system 'seems almost designed to ensure the giving of advice without the responsibility of action and the taking of action without real knowledge' and he compared the advisory councils to the story of the FAO bull:

> Once upon a time, not long ago, the Food and Agriculture Organisation of the United Nations sent a prize bull to some developing country to improve the local breed of cattle. When the bull arrived it showed amiable interest but no more in the cows presented to it. When asked why he did not get on with his job, the bull replied: 'You forget that I am an FAO bull—so my role is solely advisory.'

In the centre of the web of councils is the central Council for Scientific Policy (CSP) set up by the Labour Government in October 1964, as the successor to the old Advisory Council (ACSP). Its job was to allocate the spending of the other councils —to act as the main funnel between the government's money and the research stations. It is the closest thing to a scientists' cabinet, and it is meant to be (as Blackett described it) 'the main decision-making body for matters scientific'. These were the members of the CSP with their principal jobs in July 1971:

Chairman:	Sir Frederick Dainton, FRS
	Physical Chemistry, Oxford
Deputy-Chairman:	Dr J. C. Kendrew, FRS
	Molecular Biology, Cambridge
Professor A. H. Bunting	Agricultural Botany, Reading
Dr T. L. Cottrell	Vice-Chancellor, Stirling
G. B. R. Fielden, FRS	British Standards Institution
Dr P. E. Kent, FRS	Chief Geologist, BP
Dr A. W. Merrison, FRS	Vice-Chancellor, Bristol
Professor F. H. Stewart, FRS	Geology, Edinburgh
Dr M. G. P. Stoker, FRS	Imperial Cancer Research Fund
Dr R. G. West, FRS	Quaternary Research, Cambridge
Professor P. B. Hirsch, FRS	Metallurgy, Oxford
Professor A. L. Hodgkin, FRS	Biophysics, Oxford
Dr M. Jahoda	Social Psychologist, Sussex

The chairman, Sir Frederick Dainton, is a scientist-administrator who insists on keeping one foot in each camp. He is a sensitive, unobtrusive man with a rare capacity to see science in a wider context; he talks quietly but very openly, and is not afraid of emerging in public. He remains a dedicated scientist (his wife and three children are scientists) and he has always managed to keep going his physio-chemical research. He believes that scientific administrators are more effective if they remain scientists; in his five years as vice-chancellor at Nottingham—a stormy spell—he still kept his research unit at Leeds; and now he combines his chairmanship of the scientists' cabinet with a professorship of chemistry at Oxford. For the last eight years he has been mixed up in government committees, and he is now at the peak of scientific civil policy-making.

When he took over the CSP in February 1970 he talked about 'the growing mistrust of scientists by the public' and pledged that during his term of office his first priority would be to try to reverse the trend. He insists that science is 'one of the great humanities', and he is trying to bring scientists closer to the social scientists (who are not within the scope of the committee, though they are represented by Harry Johnson and Andrew Shonfield). He is quite hopeful that scientists will face up to their social problems: 'The swing away from science has done us a power of good,' he said to me in 1970; 'There's much more concern about broadening the curriculum, and every university now has consultations with the students about it. In the past scientists have been rather austere, rather like the Church in their relations with the outside world; now they are beginning to realise their responsibilities.'

ENGINEERS

There are three ways of losing your money—women, gambling and engineers. The first two are pleasanter, but the last is much the most certain.

James de Rothschild[1]

The separation of scientists from the rest of society is most evident in the most practical frontier, engineering. In general the less practical scientists are, the higher is their prestige, which may

[1] Quoted in Eric Hobsbawm: *Industry and Empire*. Weidenfeld and Nicolson 1967, p. 26.

help to explain the unsatisfactory status of engineers. In Victorian times names of great engineers like Brunel, Nasmith or Telford were national heroes, and many were entrepreneurs as well as technologists: in the railway boom, ambitious engineers set up their offices in Victoria Street, close to parliament where they pushed through their Bills. The consultants are still there, several of them earning as much as £20,000 or £30,000 a year: but far less noticed by parliament or the public. The Institute of Civil Engineers, a stately palazzo off Parliament Square, still evokes the grandeur of Victorian technocrats, with rooms full of portraits of past presidents. But contemporary engineering has become much less associated with individual names. The men behind new projects in Britain, like the Milford Haven bridge, high-rise flats or the Concorde, tend only to become famous when their projects collapse. Since Victorian times engineers have no longer dealt with single patrons like the Duke of Bridgewater, but have become involved with teams and committees, and this has helped to weaken their influence. Engineering has lost a good deal of its panache and immediacy in the last century: the Crystal Palace took a few months from drawing board to completion, and the first fly-over, the Holborn Viaduct, was built over a century ago— without the delays, committees and qualifications of modern engineering. The Victoria underground extension was at the discussion stage for over ten years and the Channel tunnel, having been actually *started* in 1880, is still being discussed. Much of the slowness is due to the delays of democracy, and the penury of modern Britain: but it is partly, too, due to the lack of broad-minded engineers at the top. Compared with the continent, the *average* British engineer is as well trained; but there is no British equivalent for the rigorous two-year course of the French *polytechniciens* who have had such a large influence on their industry and civil service, and the British schools lack their high standing. Continental engineers have a strong schooling in theory, which helps to give them a daring and enterprise, shown in the French aerotrain, Orly airport, or the Citroen cars. Initiative for the Channel tunnel has come from the French engineers, with less interest from London. The very word 'engineer' in Britain, embracing everyone from a mechanic to a professor, has a more modest meaning than the strictly professional French *ingenieur* or Italian *ingegnere*, and a confusion that goes back to the rough roots of the industrial revolution.

339

The scope of engineers has been further limited by the fragmentations of the profession which, like the Inns of Court, has produced complicated internal rivalries. These are the principal technological institutes with their memberships (excluding overseas members) in July 1970:

Institution of Mechanical Engineers	45,395
Electrical	30,157
Civil	26,503
Marine	13,290
Production	11,991
Structural	8,513
Royal Aeronautical Society	7,923
Institution of Municipal Engineers	7,144
Electronic and Radio	5,339
Institute of Fuel	5,410
Royal Institute of Naval Architects	4,297
Institution of Chemical Engineering	4,168
Mining	3,674
Gas	3,393
Mining and Metallurgy	2,708

The oldest of the institutes, the 'Civils' (bridges, roads, dams), took a high-handed line with newcomers, and actually refused to elect George Stephenson a member, which led to the foundation of the 'Mechanicals' (trains, cars, aeroplanes). Others, the Electricals, Chemicals, etc., followed, so that by 1929 there were already more than a hundred societies for engineers. And since 1900 the architects have stolen some of the engineers' thunder: the two professions have been at daggers drawn, and much more separate than on the continent. But the different branches of engineering are now, more than ever, interdependent; a dam can involve Civil, Mechanical and Electrical—and engineers are aware that this fragmentation has weakened their scope.

A bid for unity was made by Sir George McNaughton in his presidential address to the Civils in 1961. 'If engineers are to gain their old position of policy-makers and financial controllers in the work they undertake,' he said, 'they must be able to express views on wider fields than the purely technical.' He suggested that there should be a high-level co-ordinating body between the Civils, Mechanicals and Electricals. Talking about the decline in engineers' influence, he said: 'One can only speculate as to the cause of the present position. Can it be the absence of a higher standard of education in the humanities and the social sciences amongst the entrants to the profession?' A further attack came in July 1963 with the publication of a report on engineering design, under the chairmanship of G. B. R. Feilden, then group technical director of Davy-Ashmore. The report made strong criticisms of the professional institutions—particularly the Mechanicals—with their narrow attitudes and lack of interest in design, and recommended that 'A much greater number of first-class people must be recruited, trained and kept in the field of mechanical design.' Partly as a result of McNaughton's criticisms, the leading institutions agreed to combine to form a Council of Engineering Institutions, set up in 1962 to represent the joint interests of engineers. With a board made up of officials from the fifteen affiliated institutions, their current chairman is Sir Eric Mansforth, whose own career has spanned mechanicals, aeronautics, production and electronics. The Council has managed to establish a common educational standard, and to cut out some of the overlapping between institutions; but it is not a very high-powered body and the feuds between the sub-professions continue. In spite of much talk about widening their education, the engineers continue to be very cut off from problems of management and design—a fact which is all too evident, for instance, in the British car industry.

In the sixties the engineers, like the scientists, became the special favourites of governments who were determined to narrow the 'development gap' which was blamed for Britain's poor industrial performance: it was one sign of the new respect that the old technical colleges were promoted (see chapter 8) first to Colleges of Advanced Technology, then to full universities; and in their wake, the polytechnics and institutes were up-graded and merged into 'New Polys'. Under the Labour Government, pursuing the 'white hot technological revolution', a succession of reports analysed the relationships of engineers and scientists, including the Dainton Report in 1968, on their flow into universities, the Swann Report of 1968, on manpower for scientific growth, and the CBI's report of 1970 on industry, science and universities. In many great export companies, like BMC or AEI, engineers were all-powerful: new government projects like TSR2 and controlled nuclear fission reactors put great hopes on engineers; and the greatest pride of British exports was Rolls Royce with its team of engineering perfectionists, headed by the hero of the profession, Sir Denning Pearson. In their awe of the engineers, politicians and accountants hesitated to interfere or question their prophecies. The honeymoon was short-lived. One blow for the engineers' pride came with the takeover of AEI by Arnold Weinstock (see chapter 32): another with the cancellation of TSR2. But the real humiliation came with the bankruptcy of Rolls Royce (see chapter 32). The collapse of the company seemed to bear out all the criticisms made against the impracticality of engineers—and it was a disaster not only for the Rolls Royce perfectionists, but for the whole engineering profession.

COURT SCIENTISTS

In spite of, or perhaps because of, the proliferation of committees and the elaborate new pyramids, the kind of scientific advice that reaches the top still depends very much on who has the prime minister's ear. There is only one scientist (or ex-scientist) in the present cabinet: Margaret Thatcher. So long as cabinets are scientifically ignorant, and frightened or bewildered by equations and symbols, so they tend to rely heavily on whichever boffin is closest at hand, who can explain problems simply and forcibly. Most prime ministers have encouraged a 'court scientist'. The most celebrated was Lord Cherwell, Churchill's very personal adviser. His modern equivalent, less dominating but very persuasive, has been Sir Solly (now Lord) Zuckerman, who was the personal adviser to four prime ministers. For six years until 1966 he was adviser to the Minister of Defence, and extended his influence from there; then he became chief scientific adviser to the government. This tireless and talkative zoologist was one of the strangest phenomena of Whitehall. Throughout his government jobs he remained Secretary of the Zoo and loved to escape from committees to go off to discuss animals: for years he kept his job as Professor of Anatomy at Birmingham, and he is now attached to the University of East Anglia, with the apt title of Professor At Large. In Whitehall he provided the successive prime ministers and their cabinets with advice they could understand, with a shrewd assessment of the political implications of projects; but his scientific colleagues resented his political agility, and his preoccupation with his own public and social prestige, and he became more out of touch with the complexities of science itself.

Zuckerman's successor as Chief Scientific Adviser in 1971 was his former deputy, Sir Alan Cottrell, a man much less interested in the socio-political aspects of the job. He is unassuming and straightforward, with big eyes under bushy eyebrows. He began as a lecturer and professor of metallurgy at Birmingham, and then moved through different areas of government science—first in the atomic energy authority, then in the Ministry of Defence, where he worked with Zuckerman; their relations were not easy. In advising the cabinet, Cottrell may find a rival in the form of Lord Rothschild, the director of the Central Capability Unit—a man with disruptive, brusque views of his own (see chapter 4); though Rothschild insists he has no desire to play a Zuckerman role. If there is no single court scientist in the future, that will be no bad thing; for there must always be conflicts of views between scientists, which need to be reflected by politicians; as Shirley Williams puts it: 'Science is not a monolith. There are strongly felt disagreements within it, especially about priorities for financial support. It would be better in my view if ministers knew about these disagreements, and were in a position to weigh one argument against another.'

18

Law

You'll find me a very conservative man in matters of the structure of the legal profession.

Lord Hailsham, 1970.

I think all lawyers are conservative.

Lord Gardiner, 1964.

THE legal profession occupies a place in the power-structure which is both in the midst of it yet is—or at least should be—detached from it. When judges are appointed to tribunals or commissions in political crises, as when Sir Patrick Devlin investigated Nyasaland in 1959, or Lord Denning reported on the Profumo affair in 1963, their reports are sent from the Royal Courts of Justice, in W.C.2, to the prime minister, down the road in S.W.1, as if they came from a foreign country. The independence can be desperately embarrassing: when Bernadette Devlin was sentenced to six months' imprisonment in July 1970, it could be predicted, and was, that such a sentence would lead to riots and deaths (there were five); but no politician could prevent or reverse the sentence (unless by a free pardon granted by the Queen).

Britain can claim that its judiciary is more independent— even if they are more narrow-minded—than most other benches of judges in the world. It would be taking a low view of their honesty to suggest that only by cocooning can they remain uncorrupt. Yet the difficulty in discussing the law is to analyse how far its self-centred rituals and restrictive practices are necessary for its sense of security and disinterestedness; and how far they could

344

be demolished while still maintaining the splendours of legal independence, and the search for justice.

The profession of the law is the most extreme example of a closed and ancient community, with its uses and abuses. It is hard for a democrat not to feel some dismay at the construction of the British legal profession. It has built into it more restrictive practices, more privileges and defences than any other trades union, disguised by its elaborate rigmarole: barristers cover their ordinariness with horsehair wigs and flowing gowns, and judges clothe themselves with the paraphernalia of intimidation that goes under the name of 'the majesty of the law'. Judges are uniquely protected from the troubles of most other people's lives: their limitations emerge clearly enough in their language, enunciating moral judgments redolent of an earlier age.

The whole conduct of a British court case is like an elaborate confidence trick: anyone who enters the high hushed room is conditioned through the pageantry and protocol to accept that judges have an authority above their reasonings and their laws. Yet it could be argued that only by this conspiracy of pomp can the notion of legal authority be maintained: and that once the confidence-trick collapses, it turns into an open show of violence (as in the Bobby Seale case in America, when the accused was manacled and gagged). The law's relationship with society is at best delicate; a judge's position cannot rest alone on the naked threat of force behind him. If he requires the element of play-acting to persuade a murderer to go quietly to his twenty-year sentence, should he not be allowed his harmless disguise?

LAWYERS

The conservatism and theatricality of the British law is aptly exemplified by the architure of the Royal Courts of Justice in the Strand, which suggests that the legal machinery has got stuck in the nineteenth century. The medieval palace was built in 1880 by the architect G. E. Street, when the legal profession was at its height. A broad doorway leads into a fake-medieval hall, like a stripped-down cathedral, adorned with big black-letter notices announcing 'Lord Chief Justice's Court', or 'Wash and Brush Up'. Dark-suited men carrying blue or red bags walk into a room by the entrace, and emerge a few minutes later solemnly wearing gowns, tabs and horse-hair or nylon wigs.

345

The 1880s were the heyday of private property: lawyers were the advisers and protectors of the rich men's estates and the law courts were their battleground. With the rush of reforming legislation between 1830 and 1880, the great Victorian lawyers had been interlocked with politics: they could argue in court in the morning and in parliament in the afternoon. But in the past ninety years rich individuals have been replaced by the big business corporations, trade unions, insurance companies and civil service departments, and the immense new area of state administration has crept up on the old powers of the law. Eighty per cent of the common law cases fought in the courts are now about compensation for accidents—in factories or in motor-cars— often fought by one institution against another; for instance, a trade union against an insurance company. The whole territory of taxation, which has enveloped both corporations and individuals, has been largely neglected by lawyers (who proverbially have never been good at sums) and annexed by the new profession of accountants.[1] While accountants have multiplied, the proportion of lawyers has fallen in sixty years from about one in 1,400 to one in 2,000. There are now three times as many accountants as lawyers. Recently the law has become increasingly worried by its image and has tried to make itself more attractive to the public, on whom ultimately it depends: there have been a few cases of neighbourhood law centres in poor districts, to bring lawyers closer to ordinary people. But the gap remains very wide. As Brian Abel-Smith and Robert Stevens described the profession in the mid-sixties: 'The lawyers were still reluctant to regard themselves as providing a service to consumers, let alone a *social* service *for* consumers. The law had remained the last citadel in a capitalist economy where the concept of consumer sovereignty has failed to penetrate. Moreover, the idea that the courts were public services like hospitals, assistance board offices or fire stations was not one that lawyers felt readily able to accept.'[2]

British lawyers (with exceptions such as Lords Goodman, Shawcross or Tangley) do not have the same influence as their American counterparts in big business decisions. Nor do the British courts have the same obvious impact as in countries with a written constitution and a court to interpret it (though ironically it is Britain which has *exported* more written constitutions than any

[1] See Chapter 27.
[2] Brian Abel-Smith and Robert Stevens: *Lawyers and the Courts*, 1967, p. 463.

country). The United States Supreme Court can visibly affect the lives of ordinary men and can openly contradict the government, but in Britain few ordinary people know the names of the ten law lords. Compared to America or the continent, the law in Britain is less closely related to society and its problems. At the time of *Blackstone's Commentaries*, in 1787, the law was regarded as revealing the pattern of society, and lawyers were the great interpreters and prophets. Today, it is the economists, the historians and the sociologists who interpret society, while the lawyers seem to be relegated to the position of long-stop.

The conservatism of English lawyers is reinforced by their strict division into solicitors and barristers—found only in Ceylon, South Africa, parts of Australia, Rhodesia and Great Britain. Only solicitors are allowed to deal directly with the public. There are about 25,000 practising ones and they perform all the routine business: but when they have to take a case to the high court, they must ask a barrister to plead—much as a GP asks a surgeon to operate. It has its advantages. Solicitors find it useful as a form of sub-contracting which often makes for lower total costs. Barristers provide a corps of specialists, none tied to a particular firm, all individualists and carrying only minimal overheads, skilled in court procedure and trusted by judges. But the division, and the traditions that have grown round it, have produced a web of archaic restrictive practices designed unashamedly to maintain the employment of lawyers. A client, having engaged a barrister, cannot even talk to him except in the presence of his solicitor: in court he has to employ both solicitor and barrister together. The bar often seems designed more to maintain full employment for lawyers than to meet the needs of clients.

SOLICITORS

The old 'family solicitor' was designed as the adviser to prosperous middle-class clients. He worked in an office which closely resembled a Victorian gentleman's study, and he regarded himself strictly as a legal adviser as a doctor was a medical adviser. He shrank, like a good professional man, from giving general opinions. But nowadays both companies and individuals need not merely an occasional adviser, but an agent, to take charge of their affairs, and to advise on policy as well as procedure.

Large partnerships have grown up to deal with a specialist age.

Four huge ones, each with more than twenty partners, dominate the City of London, with stately Dickensian titles which—like the big auditors or bankers—have become stamps of respectability. They are, with their numbers of partners:

Slaughter and May	28
Linklaters and Paines	25
Allen and Overy	25
Freshfields	21

The new kind of lawyer is a more adaptable and positive person: he is staking his claim in the new corporate world, and prepared to deal with any business, including tax, pensions and hire purchase, that his client might need. The new role is encouraged by the Law Society—the great stone building in Chancery Lane, which serves as the solicitors' lunch-club and professional head-quarters. The Law Society is primarily a trade union, bent on defending such restrictive practices as the solicitors' monopoly in conveyancing. But it also does something to coax its members into more up-to-date habits.

Solicitors' education is still very backward: 'As far as I know,' said Lord Gardiner in 1964, 'we are the only Western country in which a law degree isn't an essential qualification for a lawyer to have.' Less than half the *new* solicitors are graduates. In 1967 Lord Gardiner appointed a committee under Lord Ormrod to investigate legal education, which reported in 1971 (Command 4595) deploring the narrow qualifications of the profession, and recommending that university law schools should be expanded—which would result in nearly all new entrants being graduates.

BARRISTERS

Solicitors remain the 'junior branch of the profession': most of the mystique of the law settles on barristers, and only a barrister can reach the top of the pyramid—a high court judgeship. In 1970 there were 2,548 practising barristers in England and Wales—a record number, and a third more than ten years before. More than half of them work in an area of London half-a-mile across, in one of the four Inns of Court. There they enjoy a recondite life of their own. At lunch they sit at long wooden benches in big hammer beam halls, like the halls of a public school or an Oxbridge college. They have offices in 'chambers' approached by stone steps with their names proclaimed in elegant eighteenth-century lettering. The Inns have their own elaborate snobberies and pecking-order. The oldest and richest is the Inner Temple, alongside a round Saxon church, which has produced the largest number of judges. Next to it, the Middle Temple is less exclusive. Across the road, Lincoln's Inn is almost entirely frequented by Chancery lawyers: while Gray's Inn, the newest of them, is known for its numbers of provincial barristers.

The Inns, like Oxbridge colleges, have strong autonomy and privileges: they are responsible for admissions and discipline, and have refused to delegate real power to the Bar Council. They are a 'survival of medieval republican oligarchy, the last to be found in Europe'.[1] They have large endowments in land, but no one knows the extent of their wealth since, unlike other institutions, they are exempted from publishing their accounts. They are ruled by benchers—a self-perpetuating group of senior lawyers, who sit at a high table at one end of the hall, and run the Inn. To be elected a bencher brings a barrister into the heart of the small society of the bar. The closed and self-confident world of the Inns of Court helps maintain the discrepancy between lawyers' priorities and those of other citizens. There was a demonstration of this when the former Lord Chief Justice, Lord Goddard, was attacked in *The Times* by Bernard Levin just after his death in June 1971. Eminent judges and barristers rushed to his defence, praising his excellent legal mind, his loyal friendships and club-bable habits, while ignoring the terrible consequences of his reactionary views and death sentences.

The most striking characteristic of barristers is not so much their corporate life as their loneliness. In an age of organisation men they remain individuals—which gives to the profession both its charm and its hazards. By their own decree, barristers cannot, as doctors or solicitors do, share their risks with anyone else. If they make money, they make it only for themselves, and if they fall ill they have no one to take their place. They are the only professional group (apart from physicians) who cannot sue clients for their fees—a relic from the days when they preferred not to be paid fees, but only given an *honorarium* which was slipped discreetly by the client into the pocket-flap (which still survives) in their gown. They are also the only profession who cannot be sued for negligence in court—a monstrous exception that was

[1] Sir Frederick Pollock: *Essays in the Law*, 1922.

upheld by the law lords in 1967. Barristers have the self-indulgent and idiosyncratic appearance of men who work by themselves, with none of the sameness of bureaucrats. They love discussing their profession and its faults, provided they don't have to change it. Living, as some of them do, a quarter of their life in the court-room, they have an odd mixture of scholarship and showmanship. There is an old fellow-feeling between the bar and the stage, and at the Garrick Club, which they share, it is hard to tell them apart. The last Lord Chancellor, Lord Gardiner, once explained that: 'I really went to the bar because I thought it would be easier to go on to the stage after failing at the bar than to the bar after failing on the stage.' The present Lord Chancellor, too, often gives the impression of being an actor *manqué*, and not all that *manqué*; he was recently photographed talking to his stage counterpart in Gilbert and Sullivan's *Iolanthe*.

In the past thirty years the barristers have had to come to terms with a more humdrum age, and histrionics have been at a dis-count. They are more likely to be recounting the details of a factory accident to a sceptical judge, than passionately urging the innocence of a client to a weeping jury; even to juries their style is now likely to be cosy and confidential. The decline in numbers of juries, and their better education, has discouraged acting, and full-throated advocates have found themselves without much of an audience. In 1933 thirty-six per cent of common law cases were tried by jury: today less than three per cent have juries.

Barristers, like senior civil servants, still like to give the impres-sion of being overworked and underpaid, snowed up under a pile of unprofitable and public-spirited briefs. The posture might have been faintly plausible ten years ago, when business was bad; but now, with the great new bonanza from legal aid, barristers' earn-ings have shot up, bringing a wave of new recruits to the bar. Legal aid can assure even the most incompetent barrister—and some are very incompetent—of a minimum wage, while a top advocate can earn between £25,000 and £60,000 a year. But the biggest oppor-tunities for barristers are in the city or in industry, as tax or legal advisers; a survey in November 1970 (conducted for the Bar Association for Commerce, Finance and Industry) showed that the earnings of barristers in business had gone up by forty-four per cent in the previous three years—an increase which 'no doubt reflects the growing awareness in industry and commerce of the ways in which legal issues impinge on every aspect of business'.

Some of the cleverest barristers have left the bar for big business, like Lord Shawcross (now a director of Shell), Mark Littman (now one of the triumvirate who run British Steel), Philip Shelborne (a tax expert who now runs investment trusts), or Gordon Richardson (chairman of the merchant bank Schroder Wagg). And in 1970 there was an almost unthinkable translation of a *judge* into a businessman: Sir Henry Fisher, son of the former Archbishop of Canterbury and a high court judge, announced his appointment to Schroder Wagg; a move which Lord Dilhorne, the former Lord Chancellor, described as 'unprecedented and unacceptable'.

JUDGES

The judiciary has probably been more resistant to change than any British institutions except the monarchy and the church. For centuries judges have been travelling round the country in Chaucerian fashion, accompanied by their clerk and their cook, staying in medieval towns, not in hotels but in castles and mansions, and received with pomp by the Lords Lieutenant of the County: 'It is not too much to say,' said the Lord Chancellor, Lord Hailsham, in November 1970, 'that the basic framework of sessions and assizes was laid down when barristers and judges rode around the circuit on horseback with their briefs in their red and blue bags and their circuit files in hampers—before the days of trains let alone motor-cars or aeroplanes.' But at last, in the mid-sixties, the system had become so congested and seized-up that it was hard to avoid some reform. Lord Beeching, the notorious re-organiser of the railways, was asked to head a Commission on the Assizes, and recommended in 1969 that the whole structure of the courts should be changed, that the civil and criminal parts of the high court should be separated, that there should be proper centres for the courts instead of the old medieval towns, that there should be 'circuit judges' in place of the Recorders, Chairmen of Quarter Sessions and County Court Judges, and new Crown Court Judges. Beeching's proposals were for the most part incorporated in the Courts Bill of 1970, with the support of the new Lord Chancellor and the old one, Lord Gardiner, who described it as 'the greatest reform in the administration of justice this century, and possibly in legal history'.

But the new Bill, as Lord Hailsham made clear, was 'about the structure of the courts and not about the structure of the legal profession'; and it left almost untouched the controversial question of how the judges themselves should be selected. There are not many British judges compared to other countries—eight judges per million of population, compared with seventy-six in Canada and thirty-four in the United States (though the figures are not strictly comparable, and the 16,000 magistrates in Britain fill part of the role of judges abroad). The former Attorney-General Sir Elwyn Jones could boast that 'the population in these islands are the least judged, or rather the least professionally judged, in the world'. The British judges are all chosen from the tiny profession of barristers, and it is not difficult for any barrister who wants to, to become a judge by the age of fifty-five. Every profession likes to appear more competitive than it is; but judges, who are thicker on the ground than admirals or bishops, have been unusually successful in projecting their splendour. The appointment of judges has never undergone the kind of radical reorganisation that senior civil servants experienced in 1870 or 1970. Many of the senior judges are certainly exceptionally able; but the rapid inflation in total numbers of judges has led to some very second-rate appointments. Lord Hailsham at first refused to accept Lord Beeching's proposal that some judges should be appointed from the ranks of solicitors, but after an angry debate in the House of Lords, Lord Goodman and Lord Tangley, the solicitor-peers, succeeded in extracting an amendment to the new Courts Bill, allowing solicitors to become recorders, and thus eventually to become circuit judges. The barristers will retain a virtual monopoly of the bench, perpetuating the suspicions that judges are part of a cosy circle of Buggins's Turn. As Lord Goodman said in the debate (November 18, 1970):

> So far as I can see, this is an issue between the bar and the civilised world. There is a nominal roll of two thousand barristers. If one takes from that number those who, for a variety of reasons, must be ineligible for judicial appointment because they were too young, too foolish, too clever, too rich or did not want to take an appointment in Warrington or Cullompton, and deducts the number who did not want the job, the high number of specialists who could not be chosen because they did not practise—a tiny handful was left to fill the nine hundred judicial appointments at the moment exclusively reserved for the barristers. The arithmetic is overwhelming and the public interest cannot be served by continuing a restrictive practice of this character.

Judges do not have any special experience to furnish their

wisdom. They rarely visit prisons to which they sentence criminals. Their own lives revolve round medieval institutions. Most of them have followed the precept of Francis Bacon who said: 'Judges ought to remember that their office is to interpret law, and not to make law, or give law.' Or as Lord Devlin has said: 'The judges of England have rarely been original thinkers or great jurists. Many have been craftsmen rather than creators. They have needed the stuff of morals to be supplied to them so that out of it they could fashion the law.' For two hundred and twenty-five days in the year they sit in their wigs from 10.30 to 4.15, listening to barristers arguing abstruse points of law. Their long vacation lasts for two months of the summer. Their presence is deliberately surrounded with pomp, to emphasise the majesty of the law, and even in their private lives they are expected to remain fairly remote. Judges are not seen in pubs or cafés (though Lord Wilberforce has been spotted reading *Sporting Life* in the ABC Café in Chancery Lane). Their habitat is a cavernous office in the Law Courts, the high table of an Inn of Court, the Reform Club, the Garrick or the Oxford and Cambridge, a house in the country and a London flat. Much more than American or continental judges the British bench has grown up detached from society and social developments.

Judges, more than any other sub-profession, come from a tiny section of the community, and unlike the higher civil service or the Foreign Office they have shown little change in their educational background in the last decade. When one sociologist, Kevin Goldstein-Jackson, made a survey of the judges named in the Law List for 1968, ranging from Lords of Appeal to metropolitan stipendiary magistrates, he found that out of the 359:

> 292 went to public schools
> 152 went to Oxford
> 121 went to Cambridge
> 20 went to London
> 28 went to other universities

The pattern had varied very little over two decades. In 1947 and in 1967 seven new county court judges had been appointed; in both years six had been public school, and four from Oxbridge. The more senior the judge, the more likely he is to have been to Oxbridge: of the nine members of the Chancery Division of the high court all but one has been either to Oxford or Cambridge, all but one had attended a public school.[1] The law, with its rarefied

[1] See *New Society*, May 14, 1970: also Dr Philip Abrams' survey of 1963.

rules, and its intimidating entry system, is likely to be the last bastion to fall to the grammar schools. It has even been suggested that judges must come from the old elite in order to command authority. Thus William Plowden, investigating legal education, curiously explains:

> As long as British social structure is such that the traditional ruling class can still command some deference, the law, to be sure of respect, must partake of the style of that class. Until the thought of a high court judge pronouncing a life sentence in a Birmingham accent no longer seems incongruous, high court judges must speak with the tones of Oxbridge, and so must ambitious barristers, and so must solicitors who do not wish to be thought inferior to barristers. This situation cannot be changed unilaterally by reforms in the legal profession, including changes in its members' education.[1]

Most judges come from professional backgrounds, and many are sons of judges or barristers; Sir Charles Russell is the son of a law lord and grandson of a Lord Chief Justice. It would be rash to make any firm equation between judges' backgrounds and their moral or political attitudes; but the two judges who now set themselves up as the bulwarks against the permissive society are both interesting psychological studies. Sir Melford Stevenson, who pronounced the savage sentence on Cambridge undergraduates in 1970, is the son of a vicar; he was once a conservative candidate, and now lives in a house called Truncheons. He specialises in fierce sentences and offensive remarks, and once had to be reproved by an appeal judge for failing to put a crucial piece of pathologist's evidence to a jury; like most authoritarian judges, he is said to be personally very kind. Sir Frederick Lawton has a much more disciplinarian background: his father was a prison governor; at Battersea Grammar School he became a keen militarist; at Cambridge he moved to the far right and became a Catholic; and as late as 1936 he stood as a Fascist candidate for Hammersmith. His judgments have been consistently stern, and when fourteen Welsh students invaded his court, singing 'We shall overcome', he immediately sentenced them to jail: three weeks later however Lord Denning, while agreeing with Lawton's instant judgment, reduced all their sentences. Denning himself represents the opposite kind of self-made judge; he won a scholarship from Andover Grammar School to Oxford, and moved from mathematics to the law; his brothers, General

[1] 'What's Wrong with the Law?' BBC, 1970, p. 124.

Denning and Admiral Denning, were almost equally successful. He made his public name with his report on the Profumo affair in 1963—which he wrote with an almost embarrassing sense of drama—and his judgments are notable for their compassion and wit. He once upheld a complaint against a fellow-judge, who had interrupted a case so often that the witnesses could not be properly examined, quoting Lord Bacon: 'Patience and gravity of hearing is an essential part of justice; and an over-speaking judge is no well-tuned cymbal.'[1]

The Lord Chief Justice of England is, next to the Lord Chancellor, the senior judge. He can sit in any court, from the Queen's Bench to the House of Lords: he can decide which judge hears which case, he can make bold public statements, and he has the ear of the government: since July 1971 he earns £16,750—more than any civil servant or minister—and he need not retire till he is 75. Most days he can be seen in his own large green court, with chandeliers and velvet curtains, sitting with two of his colleagues in red robes and flapping white tabs, in front of a carved lion and unicorn. The previous 'Chief', Lord Parker of Waddington, had twelve years in the job, during which he was generally regarded as fair-minded and comparatively progressive, in the face of the massive increase in crime (though he passed a record sentence of 42 years on George Blake, who thereafter escaped to Moscow). In April 1971 he retired at the age of 71, to be replaced by Lord Widgery, a well-respected judge who has the distinction—significant in view of the current row between the two branches of the profession—of being the first Lord Chief Justice ever to have been a solicitor. He switched to the Bar after the war, and became an expert in the much-expanding field of town-and-country-planning: he became a silk twelve years after being called, and three years later was a judge in the Queen's Bench division. He has been concerned with trying to improve legal education, as first president of the Inns of Court Senate, and in trying to standardise sentencing in the Courts. In legal circles he is regarded as very clever, very efficient, but very orthodox, impenetrable and cold: 'like an iceberg', as one barrister put it: 'the ice above the surface conceals a lot more ice below.'

The progress of a judge is elaborate, and marked by an archaic confusion of titles. A barrister after ten years or more may become a Queen's Counsel or 'take silk', becoming known as John Smith,

[1] Quoted in *The Language of the Law*, edited by Louis Blom-Cooper, 1965, p. 317.

QC, with higher fees and the assistance of a junior. He may be appointed one of the hundred new 'circuit judges', when he will become known as His Honour Judge Smith, with a salary of £5,700 a year. Alternatively, a QC may be chosen for the High Court, where he becomes known as 'The Hon. Mr Justice Smith', or 'Smith, J.', or 'Sir John Smith' (acquiring a knighthood automatically) earning £11,500 a year. From there he may become one of thirteen judges in the Appeal Court, where he will wear black robes, become a privy councillor, and be known (although he is not a Lord) as 'Lord Justice Smith', 'Smith, L. J.', or the 'Right Honourable Sir John Smith'. Finally, he may become one of the ten law lords or 'Lords of Appeal in Ordinary' who are life peers, sitting in the House of Lords, earning £15,000 a year, and known as 'the Right Honourable Lord Smith'.

The law lords are the supreme judiciary of Great Britain: the Scottish courts have a separate hierarchy of judges, but two Scots lawyers, Lord Reid and Lord Guest, sit as judges in the House of Lords. They are a very homogeneous group, and they can often be seen lunching together at a special table in the House of Lords. Several have political pasts: Morris was a Liberal candidate, Guest and Wilberforce were Conservative candidates, Reid was a Unionist MP, Donovan a Labour MP, Dilhorne a Tory MP and Lord Chancellor: but they are much less political than law lords used to be.[1] Their sittings are undramatic and impressive; a group of five men, not in wigs and robes but in plain grey suits, sit in a committee room in the House of Lords, listening to the intricate arguments of counsel, which have by now reached a rarefied plane. They hear about forty appeals a year, sitting a hundred days. These are the present law lords with their places of education and their ages in 1971:

Lord Reid	Edinburgh Academy; Cambridge	81
Lord Morris of Borth-y-Gest	Liverpool Institute; Cambridge and Harvard	75
Lord Guest	Merchiston Castle; Cambridge	70
Lord Donovan	Brockley Grammar; private coaching	73
Lord Wilberforce	Winchester; Oxford	64
Lord Pearson	St. Paul's; Oxford	72
Lord Diplock	Whitgift; Oxford	64

[1] For a full study of the Law Lords see Louis Blom-Cooper and Gavin Drewry: *House of Lords: A Study of the Final Court of Appeal.* Clarendon Press, to be published in 1972.

Lord Dilhorne	Eton; Oxford	65
Lord Cross of Chelsea	Westminster; Cambridge	66
Lord Simon of Glaisdale	Gresham's, Holt; Cambridge	60

The law lords are the head of the legal profession, but increasingly some of the cleverest judges spend the last years of their careers not in the courts, but serving as the 'wise men' of governments; and many of them seem relieved to get away from the claustrophobia of the courts. Lord Pearson has reported on the docks dispute, Lord Devlin has been chairman of the Press Council, succeeded by Lord Pearce; Lord Wilberforce presided over the court of enquiry into electricity workers' pay. Outside the law lords, Sir Leslie Scarman has reported on riots in Northern Ireland, and Sir Eustace Roskill has reported on London's third airport.

What marks a judge from a barrister, a civil servant or a leader-writer is that he has to *decide*. The judge's bench is one of the few places where it can be said 'the buck stops here'; what matters is the quality of the decision. 'Ability isn't the most important thing,' Lord Devlin once told me: 'In most cases the facts aren't really very difficult to get at: no, the most important thing for a judge is—curiously enough—judgment. It's not so very different from the qualities of a successful businessman or civil servant. I'm always struck by how alike men in high positions seem to be. It's rather like seeing a lot on different parts of the stage, and finding that they're all Gerald du Maurier in the end.'

LORD CHANCELLOR

The Law is the true embodiment
Of everything that's excellent
It has no kind of fault or flaw,
And I, my Lords, embody the Law.
Lord Chancellor in 'Iolanthe'.

Lawyers have excelled in politics, but not often reached the peak. The last career barrister to become prime minister was Asquith: the last (and only) solicitor was Lloyd George. The only law officer who ever became prime minister was Spencer Perceval in 1809, and he was shot dead two years later. But nevertheless lawyers—more than any other profession—have gravitated to politics, and barristers now make up almost a sixth of the House of Commons: 93 of them, compared to only 78 in 1966. For successful barristers politics has been a natural climax, and they have been able to combine a lucrative practice with a prominent political career. It is most doubtful nowadays whether this close connection can continue. Both careers are more specialised and professional: to maintain a successful bar practice while sitting on the back benches is much more difficult, and first-class barristers are more inclined to keep out of parliament. It will be more difficult to find future Lord Chancellors who can be both politicians and judges, and this oddly intertwined job may have to be disentangled.

At the top of the intricate legal pyramid is the ancient and confusing position of Lord High Chancellor. For the Lord Chancellor (as usually abbreviated) combines three quite separate functions: he is the head of the legal profession and senior judge—selecting judges, Queen's Counsel, 16,000 magistrates or justices of the peace, 35,000 members of tribunals, and presiding (if he wishes) over the hearings of the law lords. He is Speaker of the House of Lords, sitting on the Woolsack. He is also a member of the cabinet, and the government's chief legal adviser. He is the only man who combines the powers of the cabinet, the judiciary and the executive: he helps to make the laws, to carry them out, and to interpret them (the combination is the negation of Montesquieu's theory of the separation of powers). While it has obvious advantages, it also has obvious perils; the legal side of the Lord Chancellor is always in danger of being over-influenced by the political side.

The Lord Chancellor's post is the most ancient one in the government, five centuries older than the prime minister's, dating back to the medieval court where the Chancellor was the 'Keeper of the King's Conscience': and this seniority is still reflected by his salary of £14,500 a year, the highest in the government and £500 more than the prime minister's (though oddly less than the Lord Chief Justice's). At formal dinners or royal processions he walks in front of the prime minister. He lives in a Victorian house inside the Palace of Westminster, above a special 'Lord Chancellor's Courtyard' adjoining the House of Lords, and he works in a long high room overlooking the Thames, with heavy Gothic lamps hanging from the ceiling, and a tapestry at one end.

Lord Chancellors, arriving in their illustrious position in their sixties, are unlikely to be bold reformers. When Lord Gardiner took over in October 1964 at the age of sixty-four, there were many—including myself—who expected him to make far-reaching reforms, both in law-making and in modernising the profession. In the first, he achieved his main aim, of setting up a law commission to design the future structure of the law, and to deal with the defects in the law exposed by the courts. The commission, sitting under Mr Justice Scarman, has five commissioners and twenty-one lawyers, and after five years it has submitted eighteen reports of which eleven have been implemented by parliament, including the major Bill on Divorce Law Reform. Scarman himself hopes that the commission will eventually develop into a kind of Ministry of Justice[1]—a whole department concerned with law-making machinery, such as exists in most continental countries. The law commission is a monument to Gardiner's Lord Chancellorship: but in dealing with the legal profession, Gardiner showed himself loth to make changes. He spent a great deal of his time rather unnecessarily sitting on the Woolsack, and he decribed lovingly his daily routine:

> At two o'clock I start to change into knee breeches, a pair of black cotton stockings and a pair of black silk stockings. At 2.15 the Clerk of the Parliaments arrives to go through the afternoon's Order Paper. At 2.27½ I leave my room for the Woolsack preceded by the Mace and by the Pursebearer and with the Trainbearer behind me. And there I am more or less stuck until the House rises.

The new Conservative Lord Chancellor, Lord Hailsham, seemed in many ways much less likely than Gardiner even to try to transform the structure of the law. His father had been Lord Chancellor before him—the only father-son team since the Bacons in the sixteenth century—and he insisted from the beginning that he was very conservatively-minded. Ever since he was a scholar at Eton, he had moved without difficulty up the old road—Christ Church, the bar, a seat in the house. He came into parliament at the age of thirty-one in the famous Oxford by-election in 1938, committed to appeasement, against the independent candidate, A. D. Lindsay, who enjoyed the support of Tory radicals like Harold Macmillan and Ted Heath. But against this conventional background there is always an element of individuality and unpredictability in this curious man. He has a superiority complex which makes him blithely indifferent to what other people think, and he is still, at the age of sixty-four, amazingly excitable. He has had a hot temper since his Oxford days, when as a rather priggish

[1] 'What's Wrong with the Law?' BBC 1970, p. 80.

undergraduate he was a target for bullying and teasing: since then he has learnt to control and sometimes to exploit his temper, letting go on television with side-glances to make sure of his effect. But he can still suddenly burst out in a way that can be refreshing or disastrous: when he had a chance to become prime minister after Macmillan suddenly resigned in October 1963, he dished his chances by leaping forward in television postures of blatant demagogy. In the new Heath-type Conservative Party he seems an antique, fustian figure, one of the relics of the Macmillan age tradition; but he still has fight in him, and can embarrass his cabinet colleagues by (for instance) his sudden outburst about inflation.

As Lord Chancellor, Hailsham has shown himself less obsessed than Lord Gardiner with sitting on the Woolsack: 'It is not a particularly efficient use of manpower,' he explained (to Michael Zander), and he quickly asked the Queen to appoint five more deputy-speakers (on top of the existing twenty-one) to allow him to get on with other things, including sitting as a judge among the law lords, which he enjoys. He has tried to stop solicitors becoming judges, and he does not apparently have many criticisms of his own profession: but he accepted the importance of the law commission, and the need to codify large areas of the English law, and he has shown special enthusiasm for a Bill of Rights to safeguard the liberties of the individual against the inroads of legislation—a national form of the European Convention. It is still possible that Hailsham, with his independent logic, will prove a more effective reformer than Gardiner. As he put it: 'My fundamental philosophy is very akin to Lord Melbourne's—if it works, leave it alone. But sometimes a stage comes when things cannot be left alone any longer. Very often when that stage is reached the most conservatively-minded person turns out to be the most radical in practice.'[1]

[1] *Sunday Times,* July 19, 1970.

19

Police

We are accused by the French of having no word in our language
which answers to their word 'police', which therefore we have been
advised to adopt, not having, as they say, 'the thing'.

Lord Chesterfield, 1756.

To a large part of the British population 'The Law' means not the
courts, or the judges, but the police. The cry of the Law, or the
Fuzz or the Cops or the Pigs is the cat-call for any appearance
of uniforms and helmets, representing the world of authority,
discipline and the punitive machinery of the state. The fact that
the police are separate from the state or the judiciary, that their
prosecutions are frequently rejected by the higher courts, is not
one that is evident to most citizens (not least because magistrates
too readily accept police evidence). But that separation is the
most critical element in any democracy.

The police have acquired new connotations in advanced countries where wars have receded into the past, and where a new
generation feel a need for a visible enemy, to be a symbol of their
parents' generation, or of the society that they are rebelling against.
All over Western Europe and America, the police have found
themselves in the last five years becoming bogies to the students,
required to play out a part which they cannot fully understand. Demonstrations take on the form of a national ritual
in which the police are expected to behave in formalised pre-
ordained ways: in France, to charge with batons across barri-
cades; in Germany, to line up in battle formation; in Britain, to

march at the head of processions, or to link arms with helmets ready to be stolen. The students even more than the rest of society require the police to be something quite separate from themselves, to attack and bring down.

However strained the relations between British police and the public, they are more relaxed than the confrontations of most continental police, as suggested by the style of demonstrations in London, Paris and Berlin. There are probably many reasons: the comparative sophistication of the British police, their lack of firearms, the more tolerant political tradition. The wave of student demonstrations has not led to any apparent backlash of anger by the police, as many had warned: it may have caused the opposite. 'I think two things have helped to improve police morale in the last few years,' said one senior officer: 'the first was the Shepherd's Bush murders of policemen, which showed the depth of public sympathy, the second was the students' demonstrations, which made people see how better our police were than those of other countries.'

There is also, however, an important constitutional difference. Britain is one of the few countries where all the police are in theory the servants of the public, subject to common law and with no special arm, like the CRS in France or the Carabinieri in Italy, who come under the direct control of the government. The absence of any 'third force' of that kind in Britain to be invoked in times of civil disturbances must have some relevance to the national psychology; both police and government know that they have no extra force to fall back on, except the army. The police are the most vulnerable part of that elaborate confidence trick which is government. Ministers, judges or civil servants require the passive obedience of the population; but the police are required to go out and do things—to be the sharp end of the instrument. The fact that the police are a flimsy force of only ninety thousand people, one in six hundred of the population, is something that must be concealed by a process of bluff.

The oddity of the relationship between police and public shows through in thrillers and whodunits: the police have always had a fascination in fiction whether as villains, butts or intrepid detectives, and the real police have had to get used to these phantom colleagues, flat feet or sleuths, as civil servants became accustomed to *their* ghosts with bowler hats and umbrellas. Television has brought a new intimacy to the fantasies. 'Z Cars' was first based on

Lancashire, with the cooperation of the then chief constable, Eric St. Johnston (later Chief Inspector of Constabulary for England and Wales). When the series began he, like others in the force, was appalled: and he rushed down to London to complain. 'Z Cars' (and its sequel 'Softly Softly') broke with the old clichés of 'Dixon of Dock Green', and showed police with human failings like any other group of men. Some police still complain about the characterisation: 'I suppose if you search the whole country, you could *just* find four people like that,' said one. 'Anyone who treated his men as Inspector Barlow does, wouldn't last another day in the force,' said another. A more serious objection has been that 'Softly Softly' perpetuates the legend that the police always get their man; while the real problem of the force is that they usually don't, and that if they do, he often gets off in the higher courts. But the police are thankful that television serials have at least helped to drive home the fact that they are ordinary people, with ordinary homes, wives and problems.

Many problems of bureaucracy—of centralisation, of 'we' and 'they', of maintaining authority while belonging in society—reach a kind of apex or caricature with the police, who are in the midst of society yet regarded as being right outside it. The ambivalence was clear in their very beginnings. Like bureaucracy, the idea of the police was regarded as foreign, specially French and therefore specially undesirable. It was not until Peel's 'new police', founded in 1829, that the word policeman, as opposed to the old English word constable, came into existence; the first reference in the New English Dictionary is to the quotation: 'I find a general opinion prevailing, that your policemen are not paid sufficiently.' The notion of abstracting people from civilian life into a separate force, instead of using part-time constables (like Dogberry and Verges in *Much Ado About Nothing*) was not popular, and ever since there has been a public confusion of attitude about the police, expected at the same time to impose authority from above, and yet to be responsible to the community.[1]

LOCAL OR NATIONAL

The organisation of the police raises the most fundamental argument between national and local control. There are now, after a succession of mergers, forty-seven chief constables in England

[1] See Ben Whitaker: *The Police* (Penguin), 1964, p. 18.

and Wales; most of them have charge of a county, though a few embrace several—like Thames Valley Constabulary, Mid-Anglia or West Mercia. The 'Chief' still has a large measure of autonomy; he is responsible to the local 'police authority', made up of a committee of councillors and magistrates, but his own personality has great scope. He is a grand figure in the county, with a big subsidised house, a fast car and driver, and a salary of £7,000 or £8,000 a year: the councillors may well be in awe of him, and his own views, about students, drunken driving, traffic or pot, may affect the deployment of police through the whole country. The chief constables are Conservative voters almost to a man, but they vary a great deal in their background; some like Sir Dawnay Lemon of Kent, or Peter Garland of Norfolk, come from public schools; others have worked their way up through the force, from modest beginnings. The police is one field where an intelligent and ambitious man can move up through the social scale quite easily, ending up in the very centre of 'county' society, alongside the lord lieutenant and the high sheriff.

The arguments against a national police force were eloquently stated in the select committee of 1822 with Robert Peel as its chairman; it reported in a classic sentence that 'it is difficult to reconcile an effective system of police with that perfect freedom of action and exemption from interference which are the great privileges and blessings of society in this country.' Six years later Peel stated the other side of the case, saying: 'It has always appeared to me that the country has entirely outgrown its police institutions,' and set up another committee which took the bold step of creating the Metropolitan Police, embracing a very large area of London. But the provinces were left to look after themselves. Gradually the central government found the need for more co-ordination and in 1856, in return for contributing half the cost of their expenditure, the government was allowed to inspect each constabulary, with three inspectors responsible direct to the Queen. But the inspection was often very perfunctory (one inspector used to investigate the Carlisle police by having them lined up on the railway station as his train passed through to Scotland): not till 1919 did the Home Secretary have power to regulate pay, clothing and conditions. There are now, under the Police Act of 1964, seven inspectors who between them visit each police force in the course of a year; the chief inspector, John McKay, is a Glaswegian graduate, a Catholic respected for his integrity: he began in the Metropolitan Police, and rose to be chief constable of Manchester before becoming inspector. He insisted to me that his influence over local forces is essentially through persuasion and argument; but behind his persuasion is the fact that all new grants have to be approved by his office, and all short lists of chief constables must be approved by him. He inspects all the forces except—a huge exception—the Metropolitan Police.

The Metropolitan Police, 'the Met', who have a quarter of the total policemen—20,000 out of 90,000—are very much a law to themselves, with their own large bureaucracy at New Scotland Yard, an extravagant new office block in Victoria. Ever since Peel set them up, they have been directly under the home secretary, who appoints the commissioner, deputy commissioner and four assistant commissioners; when they are appointed, the commissioners give up their police status and become technically magistrates, known as plain 'Mr'. The commissioner himself is in a position of almost unique personal power. He is very difficult to control, almost impossible to sack, and subject to inspection by no one: he and the chief inspector (half-a-mile down Horseferry Road) are the twin heads of the police, with no control over each other. The present commissioner, Sir John Waldron, came into the force from Charterhouse and Cambridge, and rose to be chief constable of Berkshire before moving back into the Met; he is an orthodox, independent-minded authoritarian, more popular with the police than the politicians, very wary of reforms. His deputy, Robert Mark, is quite heterodox, and he may play a large role in reforming the police. Mark went straight from grammar school into the Manchester police, became a radical chief constable of Leicester, and was brought into the Met by Roy Jenkins in 1967. He has a questioning and analytical approach to his job which sounds almost too like *The Guardian* to be true: he has written and lectured about police reforms, and combines firm views about an effective complaints system with an insistence that the law must be revised to enable the police to prosecute more effectively.

As the crime rate has increased, criminals have become more organised, and communications faster, so the case for establishing a national force has seemed stronger. The argument came to a head in the Royal Commission of 1962, under Sir Henry Willink; the majority of members eventually decided that the chief constable's position should not be changed. 'In our opinion the present police system is sound because it is based upon, and reflects, a political ideal of immense practical value which has gained wide acceptance in this country, namely the idea or partnership between central and local government in the administration of public services. This idea, working itself out in a variety of ways in our education, health, housing and other services, admirably suits the British temperament.'[1]

But a withering rebuttal came from a dissenting member, Dr. Arthur Goodhart, Professor of Law, in a separate memorandum; he insisted that the case for local constabularies was based on sentimental misconceptions, and that efficiency demanded a national force which would strengthen, rather than damage, the public's confidence: 'It has been suggested that the recent dictatorship on the continent ought to be a warning against the establishment of a strong, centrally-controlled police force here. I believe that the lesson is the exact opposite. The danger in a democracy does not lie in a central police that is too strong, but in local police forces that are too weak. It was the private gangs of the Fascists and of the Nazis that enabled Mussolini and Hitler to establish their dictatorships.'

The argument still rumbles on, both inside and outside the police. Whatever the political opposition, it is probable that the police will gradually become more nationally organised. The Metropolitan Police, who are already responsible for such national organisations as the special branch, the fraud squad, and the connections with Interpol, are likely to extend their influence still further; yet the Met, with its conservative, inward-looking attitudes, and its adamant refusals to be inspected by other police forces, is not itself a reassuring advertisement for a national force. The case for a national police is not as over-riding as it looks; partly because there is a great deal of co-ordination already and partly because the prevention of crime depends on changes in the law as much, or more, than changes in police organisation. Robert Mark maintains that 'Whilst nationalisation or regionalisation may confer administrative benefits, neither would have any effect at all on the incidence of crime or the proportion of crime cleared up.'[2] Any concern about crime waves and crime prevention is usually discussed as if it were purely a police matter: in fact

[1] Command 1728, para 142.
[2] Robert Mark: 'The Police, the Public and the Law', talk at the Inns of Court School of Law, October 9, 1968.

the police are only effective insofar as they can obtain convictions in the courts, and they cannot enforce laws which (as may become the case in the prohibition of cannabis) do not have the great majority of the population behind them.

A centralised police force may not in itself be a move away from democratic control: but the general question of centralisation is bound to loom larger, in terms not of retaining the autonomy of chief constables, but of defending individual rights against the use of centralised information, strengthened by the use of computers. Here again the British have a strong instinctive resistance, symbolised by the absence of the identity card; Britain is one of the few European countries whose citizens have no number, and are not required to carry any indication of who they are; many police, not surprisingly, deplore this lack of basic codification. But the development of computers will make it much easier for the police to assemble files of information about individuals without anyone outside their headquarters being aware of it; and it is this kind of centralised power which calls for constant oversight and scrutiny by parliament or its representatives.

POLICING THE POLICE

The investigation of complaints against the police has become a far more urgent question in the last few years, precipitated by the increase in crime, the under-manning of the force, the rebelliousness of youth, the prevalence of drugs and the general decline in respect for authority. The distrust of the police, and the allegations of persecution, may sometimes be ascribed to a psychological need for enemies or hate-figures, and the police, as Ben Whitaker puts it, 'are the most accessible personifications of Fate'.[1] Militant demonstrations require policemen as an essential part of their ritual, to be sworn at, mocked and hated as convenient substitutes for the government, vice-chancellors or foreign dictatorships. But behind the subjective distortions, there have been very real causes for worry about the police; a succession of very ugly cases, like the Sheffield whippings in 1963, or the Challenor case in 1964, have shown the willingness of police to cover up for each other, against any outside accusation. Complaints against the police have risen steadily; in 1969 there were 10,600 complaints, of which 1,240 were found to have some substance. One hundred

[1] Ben Whitaker: *The Police*, p. 135.

and ten policemen, about 0.1 per cent of the total force, were either sacked or forced to resign.

Much of the public's distrust of the police stems from their refusal to allow investigations by outside bodies—so that even when a complaint is unfounded, it is not proven to be so. All serious complaints are supposed to be dealt with by police from a different area; but the Metropolitan Police refuse (as in the enquiry into allegations by *The Times* against detectives) to allow other forces to investigate them. The ombudsman—who could play a useful role as an independent enquirer—is not allowed to look into police complaints. In 1969 James Callaghan set up a working party to review the system of complaints, which includes Robert Mark, the deputy commissioner who is known to be pressing for a system of independent review; and many other senior police officers favour it. But the working party is still sitting, and the Home Office moves reluctantly towards reform. The Home Office itself is empowered to ask for an enquiry, either in public or private, into 'any matter connected with the policing of any area' under the Police Act of 1964 (Section 32); but this power has not been publicly used since the investigation into the Challenor case, and the Home Office is easily frightened of alienating the policemen, and making recruitment still harder.

It is inside the Home Office—that slow-moving and hierarchical department—that the question 'who runs the police?' becomes lost. Of all the responsibilities of parliament, the responsibility to discuss, investigate and, if necessary, control the police is one of the most obvious; but MPs soon become entangled in the elaborate confusion about where the power actually lies. The 1962 commission rejected any arrangement under which the police should be placed under the control of the government, but it did recommend that the Home Secretary be made statutorily responsible for the efficiency of the police. The Police Act of 1964, however, did not follow that recommendation, and the Home Secretary is still able to answer criticisms of the police by saying that since he does not have full power over them he cannot be held fully responsible. Certainly there is a strong case for the police not being directly controlled by the government. But the present solution is a classic piece of British humbug, in which the Home Secretary's officials can and do interfere with a large range of police questions, but can still shelter behind the appearance of local autonomy.

20

Antibodies

Antibody. Kinds of substance in the blood tending to neutralise others that are harmful.

          Oxford Dictionary.

FACED with the embattled bureaucracies that we have seen in the last chapters, the task of parliament in supervising and checking them becomes increasingly difficult. The ordinary MP, representing the ordinary voter, finds himself faced by these citadels whose conflicts are obscurely resolved inside their walls. The parliamentary question is an inadequate weapon, for an effective question itself requires considerable knowledge. The political journalist is easily distracted by the parliamentary intrigue, the mock-battles and shadow-boxing, which conceal the real battles inside the committee-rooms. The secrecy which is characteristic of all bureaucracies becomes easier to enforce, more part of the seemingly natural order of things, as the huge ministries become wrapped in on themselves, and can define 'security' as anything that might cause embarrassment of the government. 'It is no business of any official,' said a Foreign Office witness, John Welser in 1970 in the Official Secrets trial of Jonathan Aitken and others, 'to allow the government to be embarrassed. That is who we are working for. Embarrassment and security are not really two different things.'

SELECT COMMITTEES

Parliament has repeatedly searched for ways of scrutinising and checking its 'servants'. Its traditional weapons are 'select committees', made up of members from both sides of the house who are empowered to co-opt and question anyone they wish. The committees' verbatim reports, little noticed by the public, give fascinating glimpses into the workings of government. It is here that we see most vividly the ordinary MP pursuing, through thousands of questions and answers, the 'will o' the wisp of power'.

The most ancient and prestigious is the Public Accounts Committee (PAC), instituted by Gladstone in 1861, with powers to scrutinise all government accounts and to criticise them on behalf of parliament: the chairman is always a prominent opposition member: for years Harold Wilson had the job; now it is Harold Lever. For their scouting, the PAC make use of the chief watchdog of Whitehall, the Auditor-General, or (to give his full title) the Comptroller-General of the Receipts and Loans of Her Majesty's Exchequer, and Auditor-General of the Public Accounts. The Auditor-General is a unique civil servant; he is appointed for life, in theory by the Crown, and like a judge he can only be sacked by an address from both houses of parliament. He comes from the safe stable of top civil servants: the current Auditor-General, Sir Bruce Fraser, worked his way up through the Scottish Office and the Treasury, and became a permanent secretary before he moved over in 1966. But as Auditor he is deliberately separate; he works in 'Audit House', a building looking over the river, appropriately placed half-way between the Bank of England and the Treasury. It is part of his job to underwrite the cheques drawn by the Bank of England on the Treasury Account, to make sure that the money is properly spent; but the more important part of his business is the auditing of the accounts, for which he has a specially-trained staff of five hundred. Much of the Auditor-General's job is dull and routine, like that of any company auditor, but from time to time a wonderful scandal is unearthed in Audit House. In 1964 the Auditor-General (then Sir Edmund Compton) exhumed from the books of the Ministry of Aviation the extraordinary discrepancy in the contract with Ferranti Ltd. for producing Bloodhound missiles, which enabled Ferranti's to make a profit of over five million pounds. It was taken up by the Public Accounts Committee, and eventually Ferranti's had to repay a large part of the profits. But the only effective check that the Auditor-General has on government departments is through the accounts; he cannot investigate what a department *does*, how efficient it is, or whether its staff is justified; and advisory and exhortatory departments who have no measurable output, such as the Board of Trade, cannot be effectively checked.

Other committees of MPs have made some marks on the bureaucracies. The select committee on nationalised industries has produced quite penetrating reports and in 1969, under the left-wing MP Ian Mikardo, they even dared to investigate the most secretive institution of all, the Bank of England.[1] But the select committees are limited by their lack of knowledge: they move on from one specialised field to another, spending little time on doing homework between meetings, and they can easily be baffled by boffins. A new kind of weapon was fashioned in 1966, under the Labour government, in the form of 'specialist committees' made up of members with more intimate knowledge who could watch particular ministries. Two committees were set up, on agriculture and science, which soon ran into difficulties; when the agriculture committee tried to visit Brussels to investigate common market farming policy, the Foreign Office did their best to prevent and delay them. The committees themselves lost their zeal, and only three now operate—on science and technology, on race relations and on Scottish affairs.

Another inquisitor has been the select committee on estimates, which cross-examines departments about their annual budgets; but it has been too preoccupied with watching short-term spending to keep an eye on the long-term plans which consume the big money. In 1970 the Conservative Leader of the House, William Whitelaw, announced that it would be expanded into a select committee on expenditure (a recommendation made two years before, by the select committee on procedure); it would have forty-five members, could investigate five-year plans ahead, and could appoint specialist sub-committees, and have its own research staff. This new body should throw some new light on two of the darkest places, the Foreign Office and the Ministry of Defence, which will be in their scope, as well as on the Treasury; and they have co-opted one of the ablest ex-Treasury men, Wynne Godley, to advise them on public expenditure.

[1] See Chapter 30.

OMBUDSMAN

The select committees cannot be concerned with an individual's wrongs at the hands of the civil service; they cannot assuage the ordinary citizen's sense of helplessness in the face of the state. In the late 'fifties a lobby of enlightened British lawyers became interested in the remarkable institution of the Ombudsman, which had been devised in Scandinavia as early as 1713. The Ombudsman tours round Sweden, investigating complaints from the public, sometimes pouncing on government institutions at a day's notice. The British proposal met with heavy opposition from MPs, who resented this intrusion on their guardianship of their constituents, but eventually a Bill was passed appointing a 'parliamentary commissioner', a kind of half-baked ombudsman. He could not report on fields outside the civil service, not on the police, nor on local government, nor on nationalised industries: he could not deal with citizens' complaints direct, but only through members of parliament.

The first ombudsman was Sir Edmund Compton, a musical ex-Treasury man who moved over from that other watchtower, the Auditor-Generalship. He set up a staff of sixty in Church House in Westminster, but looked at every case himself. He was very conscious, perhaps too conscious, of the limitations of his job. 'I can't give any orders,' he explained to me in 1969; 'reform can only be achieved through the political machine: the ministers' responsibility has to be maintained.' His first reports took the key word 'maladministration' in its narrowest civil service sense—failing to go through the proper channels. In 1968 he received 1,340 cases from MPs, rejected over a half of them, and found 'maladministration' in thirty-eight of them; the Inland Revenue were the worst (13), the Department of Health and Social Security the next (7). Most of the complaints had to do with property and tax—the worries of the bourgeoisie. In 1971 a new ombudsman took over, Sir Alan Marre, another senior civil servant, with a less conventional background: he was the son of a Russian immigrant (an East End barber) and he worked his way up through Cambridge to be permanent secretary. Marre is known as a meticulous man, with a sense of social injustices; but there is doubt whether he has enough controlled aggression to make the ideal ombudsman.

In a proud parliamentary democracy, the position of an

ombudsman must be delicate, for he is doing just what MP's like to think *they* can do. But in reality MPs (as John Mackintosh said on page 21) have little desire to battle with the bureaucracies; an ombudsman, with greater scope and powers, could give ordinary citizens more confidence that they were not the passive dependants of the state machine. It is one of the most maddening weaknesses of Westminster, that it pretends to have powers that it has long ago lost, or never had; and that it likes to pretend that bureaucracy does not exist as an entity outside its control. On the continent, where bureaucrats were entrenched before parliaments, it has often been easier to set up countervailing powers, like the ombudsman or the French *Conseil d'Etat*, and to learn the lesson that to catch a bureaucrat you need a counter-bureaucrat.

INSTITUTES

Many politicians and even some civil servants have worried about how to build up counter-weights to the great centres of bureaucratic power, how to provide interlocutors (in Peter Jay's phrase) to raise the level of debate; above all how to construct a challenger to the Treasury, with its collegiate confidence, patronage and capacity for 'connecting'. As soon as a party goes into opposition its leaders become aware of how heavily they depended on the government machinery of research and information.

An academic alternative, or extension, to the world of Whitehall is attempted by a cluster of institutes, most of which have been set up in the last twenty years, as a kind of shadow civil service, a doppelgänger to the government departments. Many have been set up with the help of American money—institutes are a favourite American idea—and supplemented by funds from British big business. The grandfather of them all was the Royal Institute of International Affairs, usually known as Chatham House after Lord Chatham's mansion which it inhabits in St. James's Square: it was founded in 1920 by a group of rich benefactors including Lord Astor and Sir Abe Bailey, but is now heavily dependent on American foundations. After the war Chatham House was in the doldrums, and distressed by the future; it was even slower than the Foreign Office in realising the importance of the common market, and when a Race Relations Department was set up with its own large sources of funds, the then director Monty Woodhouse insisted that it should be hived off into a separate institute—which now exists round the corner in Jermyn Street. In the last few years, under Kenneth Younger, an ex-Labour minister, Chatham House has become more lively and adventurous, and has cleared away some of its dead wood; and it is soon to be run by a very articulate economist, Andrew Shonfield, who has a rare gift for presenting complicated arguments with dramatic clarity. The son of a Rabbi, Shonfield has been journalist, TV commentator, and chairman of the Social Science Research Council. He has written a study of world poverty, contributed much of the Duncan Report (see chapter 15) and wrote a hard-headed book on Modern Capitalism.

Chatham House is inclined to see itself too easily as a temple for the consensus, an annexe to the Foreign Office, rather than as a seriously challenging antibody. Its sedate lunches, its sherry parties and its stately interiors encourage the style of an austere country house party; there is a large supply of diplomats, visitors from the city or industry trying to sound like diplomats, men with wavy hair and fastidious voices reminiscing about abroad, occasionally interrupted by emigré accents and querulous blue-stockings. The lectures and discussions have their own ritual, like operas, with an overture, arias and occasional duets in well-modulated voices; every performance must have its happy ending, with a kind of recognition scene in which everyone turns out to have a great deal in common. Marxist views are rarely uttered by speakers at Chatham House, and its policies are committed to Transatlantica, which gives a certain monotony to its standpoint. An attack on the Foreign Office or a statement of defiant dissent is regarded as embarrassing; so that its role as an interlocutor remains limited.

Some of the muffled thunder of Chatham House has been stolen by a much newer body, the Institute for Strategic Studies (ISS), also dependent on American money; it was founded in 1958 and built up by Alastair Buchan, a journalist-diplomat and son of John Buchan, who has now gone over to the Imperial Defence College. The ISS is now run by François Duchêne, an Anglo-Swiss journalist with a remarkable background: his father was manager of the London Ritz, he worked for Jean Monnet and remains a keen European. The ISS is less nationally-based than Chatham House (which excludes aliens from its membership) and is a kind of shadow, not just to the Ministry of Defence, but to Nato and the

State Department. It specialises in the abstruse regions of nuclear chess and strategic scenarios, and in that field it has become very influential. As one Israeli student of diplomacy has put it: 'What in previous times would have been restricted to limited official circles, and discussed primarily in departmental terms, became topics of general interest, inquiry and debate, both public and private, in a manner that could not fail to be registered by—and therefore affect—the departments.'[1] But its patronage by the ministries, and its preoccupation with strategy, puts it outside the ken of the public, and of most parliamentarians.

These are some of the most important institutes, with their directors, and their governmental counterparts:

Royal Institute of International Affairs (Kenneth Younger)—Foreign Office
Overseas Development Institute (Anthony Tasker)—Foreign Office
National Institute for Economic and Social Research (G.D.N. Worswick)—Treasury
Institute for Fiscal Studies (Dick Taverne, MP)—Treasury
Institute for Strategic Studies (François Duchêne)—Ministry of Defence
Institute of Race Relations (Hugh Tinker)—Community Relations Commission

Another foundation which sets itself up as a kind of shadow-government is Nuffield College, Oxford. Its warden is Norman Chester, who served in the wartime cabinet secretariat and for twenty years edited the worthy journal *Public Administration*; his deputy and likely successor is David Butler, the most exhaustive of the psephologists, who emerges in the public eye each election night to explain the swings, and later to chronicle the campaign. Nuffield likes to regard itself as being worldly and well-connected, and its visiting fellows constitute a miniature establishment, including Sir William Armstrong, Robert Mark, Jim Slater, Jack Jones, William Rees-Mogg, Shirley Williams, and William Whitelaw. But the college is too concerned with its respectability and its Whitehall connections to make bold use of its academic freedom; and to the disappointment of many, it has become more an anteroom of government than an alternative source of policies and ideas.

Some of the institutes are committed to a particular viewpoint: the Institute for Economic Affairs (IEA), for instance, founded in

[1] David Vital: *The Making of British Foreign Policy, 1968*, p. 87.

1957 and run by Ralph Harris and Arthur Seldon, unfolds the wonders of the free enterprise system or in its own words 'specialises in the study of markets and pricing systems as technical devices for registering preferences and apportioning resources': but its commitment has not prevented it (see chapter 6) influencing both Labour and Tory policies. On the other side, after the 1970 election a group of economists gathered round Nicholas Kaldor, the former adviser on taxation to the Labour government, to provide a kind of brains trust for the Shadow Chancellor of the Exchequer, Roy Jenkins. In theory the group's expertise is available to whichever party happens to be in opposition; but in fact it has an unmistakable left-wing character.

IN AND OUT

The tightening of Whitehall security and the proliferation of government activity have made the opposition's task much harder than it was, for instance, when Churchill before the war was able to draw on his private information network to puncture the government's complacency. Nor is it simply their lack of information; the whole spell, the aura of government—networks, receptions, cars, contacts, the cosy sense of being 'in-the-know'—reinforces the contrast between the Ins and the Outs. The health of a two-party system must depend not only on the swing of the pendulum but on a balance of resources which can enable oppositions to mount effective attacks without being humiliated by their ignorance. The power-world of Whitehall is exclusive and secretive not only because of the natural defence system of the ruling political party; it is made more so by the old collegiate tradition of the civil servants, and their inherited suspicion, not only of the opposition, but of the public at large. The implied contempt for the outsider and the refusal to communicate might be justified in the age of Bagehot, when the 'men in the second-class railway carriages' found the pretence of monarchy such a useful disguise. It is desperately inappropriate to an age when a pressing problem is how to involve the rest of the population with the debates of government, and how to prevent the disillusion with politics and government spreading to the point when the whole confidence trick, the whole stately façade is seen through and discredited.

PART

FOUR

————

Communications

21

Press

We cannot admit that a newspaper's purpose is to share the
burdens of statesmanship or that it is bound to the same limitations,
the same duties, the same liabilities as those of Ministers of the Crown.
The purpose and duties of the two powers are constantly separate,
generally independent, and sometimes diametrically opposed.

John Thaddeus Delane
(editor of *The Times*) to Lord Derby, 1852[1]

THE oldest and most organised intruders on government secrecy,
and potentially the most effective antibodies, are the people whom
bureaucrats like to describe, with heavy irony as the 'gentlemen of
the Press'. The importance of the 'Fourth Estate', as Carlyle first
described the Press, referring to the reporters' gallery, has become something that politicians, civil servants and even judges
have to acknowledge: their enthusiasm tends to evaporate when
confronted with the actual likelihood of disclosure and (that
essential bureaucratic word) *embarrassment*. 'Newspapers,' said the
great Delane, 'live by disclosure.' But they find themselves severely
restricted as to how much important news they can uncover, or
print; partly because of their commercial limitations which we will
note, but—more importantly—because of the growing difficulty of
extracting the most crucial information from the secret recesses of
the government bureaucracies. Governments are becoming more
skilled in controlling the sluice-gates of news, and thus managing
the news to suit their own political ends. The newspapers, having
won their great victory in the eighteenth century by penetrating
the secret meetings of parliament, now find themselves like

---

[1] Quoted by Anthony Howard in 'The Role of the Lobby Correspondent': *The
Listener*, January 21, 1965.

parliament itself still excluded from the real centres of decision-making, which lie inside the Cabinet, in Ten Downing Street or in the Civil Service. The centres of decisions are well defended by the Official Secrets Act: and the mass media like the parliamentarians can easily be distracted from the real issues, into reporting the day-to-day ups-and-downs and ins-and-outs of the parliamentary game, while serious long-term decisions and issues are well hidden. The outward show of politics is presented as a steeple-chase, with constant speculation on the next day's events in a 'will-he-won't-he' style; and the general election is the Grand National.

The control of the bureaucracies over the mass media works subtly. News and comment is 'inspired' by press conferences, off-the-record talks and briefings, which provide the context of the news; the Foreign Office provides its daily talk for diplomatic correspondents; the Ministry of Defence cultivates defence correspondents; and journalists are welcome to the whole apparatus of government entertaining and 'facilities'—which stops them from finding out about other things. Most effective of all is the system of the parliamentary 'lobby'—a group of favoured journalists, one or two from each newspaper, who are allowed free access to the members' lobby in parliament, and are given off-the-record briefings by cabinet ministers and the prime minister, on the understanding that they do not disclose their source.[1] These briefings find their way into the newspapers with phrases like 'it is understood that', or 'it is believed that'—whereas a truthful report would say 'the prime minister's press secretary told me that'. The distortion conceals the fact that the news is being managed, and also implies that the newspapers' perspective is the same as the prime minister's: Harold Wilson, at the beginning of his premiership, inspired most of the Press with his picture of dynamic leadership and reform, while making it appear that each paper had its own independent source of news. Wilson's extreme exploitation of the lobby system produced protests and some reaction against it; but newspapers still do not dispense with the lobby, because it provides a ready-made source of news, tailored to make headlines. Ted Heath has protested in the past that 'it is only when the opaque windows on to Whitehall and around our working lives are opened . . . that we shall find ourselves braced to

[1] For the Rules of the Lobby see Jeremy Tunstall: *The Westminster Lobby Correspondent*, 1970.

make the immense efforts which are required in Britain today'
(1966), and he has talked a good deal about 'open government'.
But Heath's interpretation of that phrase is now very limited (see
p. 96), and since 1970 the windows on to Whitehall (in my
experience) have become more opaque.

No part of the British power structure has been more closely
scrutinised over the last decade than the instruments of communication. Part of this can be ascribed to the introspection of
the communicators themselves, and the parochial concern of
people in one medium for the workings of another. Politicians,
too, when lacking issues or events to divide them or absorb
their ambitions, become still more bemused by their image as
reflected in the bright mirrors of the newspapers and television.
The cosy circle of politicians, journalists and telly-men, like the
showbiz world, often turns into a mutual admiration society which
reduces great issues to small gossip and show-off: and the cut-
offness appeared very clearly in the mass-miscalculations about
the 1970 general election.

But even discounting this distortion the communicators, as part
of both industry and politics, have taken over some of the 'commanding heights' of British life from the steel masters and captains
of industry who preoccupied politicians twenty years ago. In
purely financial terms, Associated Television and the International
Publishing Corporation are among the biggest companies in the
country, and with the expansion of 'the knowledge industry', their
scope may grow further. But the deeper interest in communications lies in their social and political power, and in the connections
they make between the wheels of government, institutions and the
public: the whole process of government and control is exercised
through language and pictures. The intrusion of advertising has
increasingly involved the mass media in conniving to draw a
specious picture of society.

In this connivance, the actual power of the Press or television
has become less blatant, but more important. The old public
hatred of the Press lords, of Beaverbrook or the first Rothermere,
was associated with their political ambitions and with the ruthless
exploitation of their ownership to swing their readers in their
direction. That power began to be undermined with the coming of
radio, and was still further diminished by television. The new Press
Lords, even if they have views, now have less scope to misinform

their readers. The influence of their newspapers lies much more in creating a climate and in conditioning readers to a set of assumptions, an influence harder to pin down than the old one of slanting editorials and suppressing the news. A comparison of the quality papers of 1970 with those of 1960 shows the extent of the process of coming-to-terms with advertising, and with what is loosely called 'the consumer society'. To a new generation of left-wing students the newspapers are not to be trusted as vehicles of news: they are seen as the 'manipulators', the means by which a population is kept in a narrowly competitive state, harnessed to a set of material values.

THE BIG FIVE

The fortunes of newspapers have always been fickle, but in the last decade the ups and downs have been still faster and fiercer. Newspapers like to regard themselves as institutions, with solid buildings and hierarchies, pension rights and long-term responsibilities. Yet as soon as they harden into institutions, and outgrow their flexibility and mobility, they lose contact with their readers and become vulnerable to more daring rivals. Journalists, as they grow older, tend to lose the curiosity, ferocity or resentments that used to fire their writing, and begin to address themselves less to the readers than to each other, to politicians, diplomats or TV men, writing in a private code which can only be cracked by their colleagues. Respectability has been the undoing of many Press empires: like battleships, they become so stately and so unmanœuvrable that they are sitting targets for submarines and torpedo-boats.

These were the main national newspapers, their groups and effective bosses, with their average sales for July-December 1970:

International Publishing Corporation (Don Ryder):

| *Daily Mirror* | 4,443,584 | *Sunday Mirror* | 4,797,436 |
| | | *People* | 5,037,589 |

Associated Newspapers (Vere Harmsworth):

| *Daily Mail* | 1,814,331 | | |

Beaverbrook Newspapers (Sir Max Aitken):

| *Daily Express* | 3,518,664 | *Sunday Express* | 4,244,821 |

Telegraph Newspapers (Lord Hartwell):

| *Daily Telegraph* | 1,415,656 | *Sunday Telegraph* | 770,736 |

Thomson Newspapers (Lord Thomson):

| *The Times* | 375,055 | *Sunday Times* | 1,414,777 |

News of the World (Rupert Murdoch):
The Sun	1,721,533	*News of the World*	6,242,270

The Observer (David Astor):
The Observer   796,421

The Guardian Newspapers (Laurence Scott):
The Guardian   304,102

The Financial Times (Lord Drogheda)
The Financial Times   165,047

The list shows some spectacular changes. Ten years ago two big groups, built round the *Daily Mail* and the *Daily Express*, were especially confident of their future. The *Daily Mail* founded by Lord Northcliffe in 1896, and passed on to his nephew Lord Rothermere, seemed still to hold its own in the middle mass market, straddling the classes. Across the street, Lord Beaverbrook, the owner of the *Express*, seemed to have captured forever the magic formula: the *Express* was the great classless, fun-loving paper, whose outrageous right-wing views fascinated left-wing readers. Yet ten years later, both Rothermere's empire (now inherited by his son, Vere Harmsworth) and Beaverbrook's (inherited by *his* son, Sir Max Aitken) were facing crises. The middle ground of middle-class readers which they occupied seemed to be slipping away, towards mass popular papers on the one side, and 'posh' papers on the other. They were committed to big circulations for their advertisers, but maintaining those figures was increasingly expensive and precarious. The polemical, patriotic style had lost its resonance in a world where the Empire had disappeared, and where Britain was becoming just another not very successful commercial country.

In the meantime new Press Barons had come up from nowhere, offering more saleable and down-to-earth wares. Lord Thomson had emerged from Canada in a decade to buy the most prestigious prize of all, *The Times*. And a pugnacious young Australian, Rupert Murdoch, had in the course of eighteen months acquired the biggest Sunday newspaper and revived an unprofitable daily so rapidly that he challenged the whole popular Press. The stories that follow, of the newspapers at the bottom and the top of the market, may illustrate the extreme difficulties of combining large-scale commercial organisation with that close contact with readers on which the health of newspapers depends.

INTERNATIONAL PUBLISHING CORPORATION

You know what Fleet Street is. It's a bit of a jungle.
Cecil King 1968.

The fragility of newspaper empires is exemplified by the vicissitudes of the biggest of them, the International Publishing Corporation, which behind its ponderous name has been kept going by a single tabloid, the *Daily Mirror*. In the thirties the *Mirror* was the first proletarian mass paper, and with its thick black headlines, sensational photographs and very short sentences it romped up to the biggest circulation (outside Russia and Japan) in the world. In 1951 its new chairman was Cecil King, nephew of the mad Lord Northcliffe: in the next twelve years, with the help of the *Mirror*'s vast profits, King branched out everywhere. He bought a share of Associated Television, and two jumbled groups of magazines—Amalgamated Press and Odhams, which included the *Daily Herald* and the *People*. He found himself in control of the biggest newspaper empire in British history.

It looked secure enough. The group moved into a new red glass building looking over St. Paul's, and behaved with patronising aloofness towards the rest of Fleet Street: while some other papers tried to battle with the printing unions, the *Mirror* could always afford to give way to their demands. When the Labour Party came to power, in October 1964, the *Mirror* was in its element. King, convinced that he had contributed to the victory, expected to be offered high office; when nothing materialised, the paper's editorials took a sourer note. The group rested on a strange duumvirate; alongside King was Hugh Cudlipp, an explosive and volatile Welshman, the son of a grocery-traveller who had begun work at fourteen on the *Penarth News*. King patronised Cudlipp, was embarrassed by his noisy outbursts, and tried to educate him as they drove together in King's Rolls-Royce. Cudlipp resented King's icy arrogance, and the growing autocracy of his style; but they were dependent on each other. Cudlipp's style of bloody-minded candour had been part of the *Mirror*'s tradition. But alas, he was becoming mellow and cautious with his new responsibility; in 1964 he supervised the launching of a new paper, the *Sun*, out of the ashes of Odhams' old *Herald*. There were enormous fanfares and promotion costing half-a-million pounds, but the *Sun* slowly sank.

The *Mirror* itself rode high, topping the five million mark, while its more bourgeois rivals, the *Express* and the *Mail*, declined. Confident of its supremacy, and very self-conscious of its political importance, it became more respectable, 'trading-up' with special educational features and long editorials addressed to the government. But the rest of the group had troubles. The magazine groups never properly merged, and many of their circulations slipped; the most successful of them, *Woman*, fell from four million to two million sales. The book section of the group, bought from a young millionaire, Paul Hamlyn, got tangled up in computers. And the *Sun* was still sinking. King remained loftily preoccupied with politics. In 1968 he wrote a leader attacking Harold Wilson, called 'Enough is Enough', which maddened many of his colleagues, and secretly the other board members began plotting. In May 1968 they sent him a letter telling him he had been sacked: and Hugh Cudlipp got his job.

After Cudlipp took over, the group's worries became worse. The board still could not put the messy empire into order; they launched a weekly colour magazine with the *Mirror* and then folded it up. And they made a historic blunder; they sold the *Sun* to Rupert Murdoch. The turnover of IPC was shooting up, but not the profits. The big investors were critical of the management, the pressures mounted, and finally in January 1970 a shot-gun marriage was announced, which was far from a love-match: the boards of the IPC and the Reed Paper Group—of which IPC owned 27 per cent—announced the terms of a what was described as a merger, but which was virtually a take-over. Reed's chairman Don Ryder—a hard-edged old protégé of King's—became chairman of the new giant, committed to drastically reorganising the *Mirror* group; and Cudlipp had the title of Deputy Chairman (Editorial). 'The takeover is to be seen,' commented Cecil King with unconcealed gloat, 'as a palace revolution to forestall attack from outside.' The proud newspaper palace was now part of a conglomerate of newsprint, paints, wallpapers and do-it-yourself gadgets; and its centrepiece, the *Mirror* itself, was increasingly challenged by the *Sun* which it had sold off as unprofitable.

MURDOCH

The development of the *Mirror* group was in keeping with a familiar pattern of newspaper ownership in Britain: in one generation a brash newcomer exploits a new mass market, with supposedly disreputable techniques, daring to go further than his rivals. In the next generation the newcomer becomes integrated and respectable, and wants to be taken seriously by politicians and his peers; leaving the way open for a new outsider to outbid the old one. Thus were Northcliffe and Rothermere outbid by Beaverbrook; Beaverbrook outbid by King and Cudlipp; and now Cudlipp by Murdoch.

At the end of 1968 Rupert Murdoch was unknown in Britain, and he came into Fleet Street as an odd by-product of a quite different struggle. It began with an unsuspected crisis in the Carr family, an easy-going dynasty of golfers, who for nearly eighty years had controlled the old-fashioned sport-and-scandal Sunday paper, the *News of the World*. Professor Derek Jackson, a cousin of the Carrs who owned a quarter of the stock, decided to sell his shares, through his bankers Rothschilds, to one of the most dreaded of all intruders, the Czech-born tycoon Robert Maxwell—then head of the scientific publishers, the Pergamon Press. The rest of the Carr family were so appalled by the impending take-over of their very British paper—'as British as roast beef', as their chauvinist editor described it—by a 'foreigner', that they desperately searched for almost anyone else, as a match for Maxwell. Meanwhile, in Sydney, the young Rupert Murdoch saw the chance he had been waiting for, to step into Fleet Street. His father, Sir Keith, had been a successful Australian newspaper executive but had only been able to bequeath his son an evening paper in Adelaide. From this base Murdoch quickly built up a group of papers of unusual awfulness, including *Truth*, a notorious twice-weekly sex-and-racing paper. By 1968 he had the third biggest group in the sub-continent, including a highbrow but boring national newspaper, *The Australian*.

Seeing a slim chance to capture the *News of the World*, Murdoch flew to London and began secretly buying some shares. The Carr family welcomed him, and even though he had only bought 3½ per cent of the shares—dealings were soon suspended by the Takeover Panel—Murdoch found himself in a position to drive a tough bargain, for if he moved out, the hated Maxwell would move in. Even so, the eventual agreement astonished most people; in return for his small stake, and a complicated deal with his Australian group, Murdoch was to become sole managing director of the *News of the World*; in their hatred of Maxwell, the Carrs had virtually given away control to Murdoch. (I watched the stormy extraordinary meeting, where the shareholders in a mood of high xenophobia defeated Maxwell's bid, while the share prices toppled.) Murdoch swiftly made himself felt. Sir William Carr soon resigned as chairman; a year later the moralising editor Stafford Somerfield was sacked with a £100,000 handshake. Murdoch preferred his men to be (as he said) 'young, lean and hungry', and a new gang were moved in, to tart up the ancient property. The *News of the World* rapidly lost its old-fashioned mixture of morality and salaciousness, and became a straightforwardly muck-raking paper, including re-hashed memoirs of Christine Keeler and an exposure of three-in-a-bed practices in the suburbs. The circulation went up by 800,000 in Murdoch's first year.

In the meantime Murdoch was already looking for new properties, and he soon found one in the form of the *Sun*. Murdoch put in a bid and, after long negotiations with the unions, the *Mirror* people gladly parted with it in December 1969, convinced like most of Fleet Street that it was a dead duck, with its circulation down to around 900,000. Murdoch turned it into a tabloid, put a pin-up on nearly every spread, devoted a third of the paper to sport, and introduced a comic-strip about a girl called Scarth, a sexed-up version of the *Mirror*'s Garth. He spent £600,000 on promoting it. There was nothing very new about the new *Sun*; it was based on the same kind of contempt for the readers as prevailed in Murdoch's Australian tabloids, and in the pre-war *Mirror*, without any of the *Mirror*'s political idealism. Its attitude to politics was appropriately mindless: at the beginning of the election campaign in May 1970 it said: 'The *Sun*'s growing army of readers are entitled to know which side their newspaper is on. The answer is simple. The *Sun* is on *your* side.' Murdoch believed that the *Mirror* was over-estimating the intelligence of its market, and that the readers would not necessarily raise their tastes as they raised their incomes: he did not agree with Hugh Cudlipp's theory that the permissive society had diminished the public's taste for vicarious stories of sexual scandals. He was right. Eighteen months after he had bought the *Sun* its circulation had more than doubled, to two million. It had taken some of its extra readers from the *Mirror* itself, which after busying itself with party politicking and self-improvement, now came back into the fray re-armed with pin-ups, scandals and sport. The *Sun* took more readers from the *Sketch* which finally in May 1971 packed up under the strain, to be

merged into a new tabloid version of the *Daily Mail*—which however had a distressing resemblance to the old *Sketch*. Murdoch had
knocked on the head the idea that the level of popular journalism
might be gradually rising.

LORD THOMSON AND HIS TIMES

No one can understand *The Times* who does not understand that it
is an institution.

The Times, January 18, 1967.

While the mass newspapers have been fighting each other with
pin-ups and comic strips, there has been a subtler struggle at the
top end of the market, where the 'heavies' have found themselves
enmeshed in the world of big business. The change has been most
acute in the case of the most influential British newspaper, *The
Times*. The self-mystifying style of *The Times* has always encouraged readers to believe that it is, like Eton or Buckingham Palace,
a permanent part of the landscape which has no real connection
with commerce or change; and part of its influence rests on this
assumption. Certainly none of its three owners during this century
has made money out of it, and it might be said that it is the historical role of *The Times*, like that of a great courtesan, to lure the
richest newspaper owners into sacrificing their fortunes for the sake
of deeper pleasures. But the demands of this mistress have become
outrageous, and *The Times*'s losses are now too big to be borne
indefinitely by any multi-millionaire. Its predicament has become
a national problem.

The Times has for the whole of this century been an intractable
property. Northcliffe, who owned it for fourteen years, could not
bend it to his will; he was baffled by the 'black friars', as he called
its stately leader-writers, and talked of writing over its door,
'Abandon scope all ye who enter here'. It was then bought by
J. J. Astor, later Lord Astor of Hever, for £1½ million, who later
handed on the chairmanship to his son Gavin Astor. The Astors
ran it in a dignified and secretive fashion, with a heavy sense of
their own burden, as if it was a private estate or foundation; and
the editor for fourteen years from 1952, Sir William Haley, had the
same stiff sense of duty. It was known that the great paper was
losing money and not gaining readers, but the Astor court kept
their worries to themselves. They made a few changes, which at the
time seemed revolutionary. The gloomy old pile of 'Printing House

Square' was knocked down, to make way for a gloomy new pile; and in May 1966 after years of heart-searching they put news instead of advertisements on the front page, and heralded it with a massive promotion campaign. The circulation crept up to 290,000, but the company was still losing a quarter of a million pounds annually. The Astors made secret approaches to possible buyers; there were talks with Lord Cowdray, the multi-millionaire behind the *Financial Times*; and once or twice the unmistakeable shape of Lord Thomson was spotted in the lift. Later in 1966 it was announced that a new company had been formed, called Times Newspapers Ltd., to publish both *The Times* and *The Sunday Times*. Behind the contorted announcement of the 'partnership' it soon emerged that, not to put too fine a point on it, Lord Thomson had bought *The Times*.

Lord Thomson, or 'Uncle Roy', had already in the previous ten years made a great dent in Fleet Street, and his impassive presence, behind pebble glasses, had become a symbol for the faceless commercialisation of the quality Press. He had only arrived in Britain in 1953, when having made a modest fortune in Canadian radio stations and small newspapers, he decided to buy *The Scotsman*, and to settle in the land of his great-grandfather. He was a lonely widower of fifty-nine and was assumed to be quietly retiring. He soon discovered that it was difficult, in the non-competitive atmosphere of Britain, to stop making money: 'There must be something wrong with this country if it's so easy to make money in,' he said. He bought eighty per cent of the shares of Scottish Television, which made him two million a year, so he looked around for another newspaper; and in 1959 he got his chance when the ageing Lord Kemsley decided to get rid of *The Sunday Times*. Thomson bought it, together with a lucrative provincial chain, for what looked like a very high price, and moved down to London where, as the owner of a big national paper, he found himself late in his life in the Big Time. *The Sunday Times* soon got fatter and fatter, with more and more readers, and Thomson went on buying up newspapers, magazines, travel agencies, aeroplanes, publishers.

Thomson and his managers showed no creative instinct for journalism, as Northcliffe or Beaverbrook had. His team of market researchers and advertising salesmen had the capacity to demoralise the most enterprising editors: when the managers had the chance to launch or transform a magazine, like the *Illustrated*

London News or *London Life*, the results were disastrous. Thomson enjoyed shocking people about his money-mindedness—he lists his hobby as 'balance sheets'—in the way that some people enjoy exhibitionism about sex. 'Newspapers and television,' he once said 'appeal to me as the most fascinating forms of business enterprise. I do not regard them as instruments for securing or wielding personal power.' His politics were naïve; he regarded himself as an independent Tory because (he once told me) 'I've got money so I'm a Conservative.' He did not commit his papers to a strong party line, but nevertheless he got a barony: thereafter his speeches became less provocative, his style more sedate. He became more ambitious to buy a London daily paper, to crown his career. But not many people suspected it would be *The Times*.

The announcement of Thomson's coup led immediately to the setting up of a special committee by the Monopolies Commission, including Donald Tyerman and Lord Annan; and in the meantime all kinds of rival schemes were put forward, including a consortium of *The Observer* and *The Guardian*, and a plan for a BBC-type of *Times*, owned by the state but run as an independent corporation. The committee revealed that *The Times* might well, if it had acted earlier, have rescued itself; but that 'the company no longer has confidence in its own ability to carry on successfully'. They decided that Thomson was the only real alternative.

So in he moved, and a board of dignitaries was set up to supervise the joint company, with *The Sunday Times*, tactfully excluding Lord Thomson himself, but including his son, Kenneth, his editor-in-chief, Denis Hamilton, and (very temporarily) Sir William Haley. The others were rather like a potted Court of the Bank of England:

> Sir Kenneth Keith—Deputy Chairman, Hill Samuel
> Sir Eric Roll—Director of Warburg's
> Lord Robens—Chairman, National Coal Board
> Sir Donald Anderson—Shipowner
> Lord Shawcross—Director of Shell, etc.

Thomson had a quick choice to make, between cutting costs and leaving the paper at its existing small circulation (which the Monopolies Commission had favoured), or of making a bid for a much bigger sale; and he rashly opted for the second. He reckoned it would cost five million to make it break even, and he set about spending money, as he put it, 'like drunken sailors'. *The Times* was jazzed up, with bigger headlines and more photographs. In a classic editorial, in January 1967, it compared itself to other institutions like the Russian Monarchy and the Catholic Church, and explained that 'an out-of-date newspaper is far more of a contradiction in terms than an out-of-date regime'. A separate business supplement was introduced, full of flattering accounts of British tycoons. Advertisements of embarrassing crudity showed how far the admen had penetrated into Printing House Square. One of them said:

> On a darkening evening last January anyone looking across from Blackfriars station to the lighted windows in Printing House Square might have been pardoned for imagining he saw the whole edifice crouching down on its haunches ready to spring. The first change was a radical one. *Times* correspondents were told to take off their masks and come out into the open, by-lined and vulnerable to praise and blame instead of sitting in oracular anonymity. The effect in the Square was immediate and stimulating; journalists share the frailty of all humanity; they like to be known by their deeds.

The promotion pushed up the circulation, but it was a pyrrhic victory. The total cost of rescuing *The Times* seemed likely to be at least £10 million; by raising the stakes to a higher circulation, its position had become more, not less, perilous, and advertising now accounted for three-quarters of the revenue. Faced with still greater risks and losses, Thomson decided in the summer of 1970 virtually to reverse his policy, and to change back the paper to its old serious style, with small headings and unbroken type, designed to maintain its intellectual readers rather than to entice lowbrow ones. The new style was proclaimed as confidently and eloquently as the previous new one; but it was basically a return to the old *Times*, with some of the old confidence and arrogance gone: Lord Thomson, at 77, had explored the limits of his Midas touch, and *The Times* had finally baffled him, as it had baffled Northcliffe fifty years before.

The chief continuity-man between the old *Times*, the new *Times* and the new-old *Times* has been its editor William Rees-Mogg, whose own style can be regarded as either old or new. He is only forty-three, but he is a man who has always seemed old; indeed he now seems rather younger in manner than when he was President of the Union at Oxford. He has always had a *gravitas* which required a position worthy of it. His background is ample. He comes from an old Somerset family, which had turned Catholic; he lives in Lord Butler's old house in the division bell district of Westminster, and in a Palladian country house with several hundred acres; he spends his spare time collecting books and talking politics with old friends, including other ex-Presidents of Unions, Humphry Berkeley and Norman St. John Stevas. His career rolled on, from Charterhouse to Balliol to the *Financial Times* to the *Sunday Times*, and thus to *The Times*. Mogg had always been fundamentally a Tory, of the nicest kind; he had stood as a candidate in Durham and hoped for a safe seat. He still gives the impression that he would prefer to be in parliament (successful journalists are prone to wishing they were someone else—politician, novelist, diplomat or tycoon).

Arriving in *The Times* the new editor comfortably delegated whole areas of the paper, and he spent much time in editorial conferences, rocking up and down in his chair as he talked at length about politics. He loved writing the editorials: the leaders of 'the Thunderer' have always had a special mystique, and have often been credited with the power to make or break governments (indeed it is thought that *The Times*'s final attack on Macmillan on his sickbed in October 1963 gave him the final push). Mogg was adept in the special linguistics of leader-writing, which imply that the writer's views are held by the whole staff of the newspaper, and most of the readers. The editor of *The Times* feels obliged to regard himself, through his leaders, as one of the prime minister's most important advisers, but the relationship is a fickle one, and when the government fails to take the advice, the editor is apt to turn nasty; thus was Haley locked in combat with Macmillan, and Mogg with Wilson. On December 9, 1968, there was a historic attack on Harold Wilson, beginning 'if one is British one can only feel heart-sick about the state of the country', going on to advocate a coalition, and laying into the prime minister: 'No need to condemn him; scarcely now any need to discuss him; his astonishing complacency at every stage of his disastrous adminis-tration condemns itself.' But only ten months later (October 18), *The Times* decided that 'Mr. Wilson himself now looks stronger as the leader of his team ... It looks now like an administration which has passed the follies of youth and entered a putatively healthy and certainly more mature middle age.' And on May 18, 1970 the day after the general election was announced, *The Times* said sadly: 'It is hard for a Conservative Party to challenge a government that appears to answer so well to the conservative instincts of the voters.' When the Conservatives had won, *The Times* emerged more openly as a straightforwardly pro-Tory, pro-Heath newspaper, as the prophet of the new era. But soon Heath, in his turn, was refusing to take *The Times*'s advice, either in combating inflation or in renouncing arms to South Africa; and the process of disillusion and remonstrance began once again.

THE HEAVIES

The Times's predicament is only part of the greater competitiveness between the 'quality newspapers' or 'heavies'. *The Times*'s most obvious rival in political weight is *The Guardian*, formerly of Manchester, which, even though it moved its headquarters to London ten years ago, still has a seriousness quite separate from the rest of Fleet Street. It still retains much of the solemnity of its great editor, C. P. Scott. Its leaders still bristle with confidence in their ability to change the world, particularly the ex-colonial world; and the feature pages have resisted the glamorisation and trivialisation that overcame *The Times*. In the first years after Thomson's takeover, *The Guardian*'s position looked perilous; it had far less capital, and fewer journalists earning much lower salaries, and *The Times* was partly aiming for their readership. But *The Guardian* had loyal staff and loyal readers, and a determined editor, Alastair Hetherington, an austere Scots intellectual who took it over fifteen years ago, at the age of 36. It retained its sense of identity and its intellectual integrity, while *The Times* was uncertain of itself. It was also able to lose a million pounds a year, from the profits of its sister-paper, the *Manchester Evening News*. When *The Times*'s circulation began slipping in 1969, *The Guardian*'s turned up; and it now has some prospect of actually overtaking its ancient rival.

The soundest quality paper commercially is the *Financial Times*, 'the pink paper', which has a far lower circulation, but a higher price and very high advertising rates, which contribute eighty-five per cent of its revenue. Its position is almost impregnable, since it is part of a monopoly of financial papers, including *The Economist* and the *Investors' Chronicle*, and is linked with the financial empire of one of the richest men in Britain, Lord Cowdray.[1] The pink paper, in the last twenty years, has emerged from the city ghetto to become a more general newspaper under the control of one of the most remarkable editors, Sir Gordon Newton: it now includes

[1] See Chapter 26.

wide reporting of politics, foreign news and arts, and it enjoys intellectual prestige among 'tough-minded' men of the Left. But its political limitations remain essentially those of the bankers' parlours from which it graduated. Its view of the world is finely geared to gross national products and profit margins. The word *good* usually means simply profitable; its reporting of takeovers, mergers and maximisation shows little interest in the effects of financial jugglings on ordinary people; and its immense dependence on advertising makes it hard for it to discuss objectively—even if it wanted to—the problems of advertising and the consumer society.

By far the biggest circulation among the daily 'heavies' is that of the *Daily Telegraph* which has grown rich on the formula of looking like *The Times* while being cheaper, less demanding—and unswervingly Conservative. It is owned by the private company of the Berry brothers, whose father, the first Lord Camrose, built up its success, and is edited by a man from *The Times*, Maurice Green. Its popularity is an index of the massive conservatism of a great body of white-collar workers. In its coverage of news, particularly foreign news, it is more thorough and often less biased than any other daily. But it is curiously uninterested in provoking serious discussions: its letters column still splutters with complaints from Surrey suburbs; and its editorials echo with petulant, almost paranoid conservatism.

The newspaper battle is still more hectic among Sunday newspapers, which in Britain (as in no other country) combine the elements of news magazines, *feuilletons* and weekly newspapers in one big package. Their development has been sudden; before the war the posh Sunday papers had tiny, gentlemanly staffs and a few literary contributors who sent in long articles from the country. The war, the rise in the school-leaving age and the expansion of universities have changed all that, and the more literate Sunday readers have become a valuable prize to be fought over by newspaper owners, advertisers and purveyors of luxuries.

The oldest of them, *The Observer*, founded in 1791, is the only paper in Fleet Street which still has an owner-editor (technically it is owned by trustees, whose chairman is the ubiquitous Lord Goodman). It was bought by the second Lord Astor in 1911, and for the past 22 years has been edited by his son David Astor, who re-moulded its character, as a high-minded paper defending a large range of underdogs, from Africans and Nagas to prisoners or homosexuals. Astor ran it like a kind of intellectual Medici, with a court of exotic contributors reflecting different facets of his own complex character. In the late forties and early fifties *The Observer* was a uniquely independent newspaper, revolving round its editor, and it had an outspokenness and a Whiggish confidence which made it unusually able to excite or infuriate readers. But since 1956—when it bravely attacked the Suez escapade, and lost readers from it—*The Observer* has been in a less confident mood, and it faced growing competition from the more commercially-organised *Sunday Times*.

The Sunday Times, the most phenomenal success in Lord Thomson's newspaper empire, has a more extrovert character; it is driven on a loose rein by a 43-year-old editor, Harold Evans, pulled in several directions by a team of ambitious and professionalised journalists, competing fiercely with each other for exposures and scoops. There is an uneasy tension between the 'gentlemen', who hold forth in classical style, and the 'players', including a large Australian 'Mafia', who enjoy offending all sectors of the British establishment. *The Sunday Times* likes to give something for everyone: it has left-wing politics and right-wing politics, exposures and court circulars, and it has romped ahead on this formula. But its corporate character, partly as a result, is uncertain. Its writers and crusades—particularly in the field of race relations—are predominantly left-wing; but in June 1970 it firmly advised its readers to vote Tory.

Since 1961 these two old Sunday rivals have been disturbed by the arrival of a third, *The Sunday Telegraph*. It was the special brainchild of Michael Berry, now Lord Hartwell, who inherited the immensely profitable *Daily Telegraph* from his father, and was determined to create his very own paper. *The Sunday Telegraph* broke into the Sunday market to 'fill the gap' (as it proclaimed) between the popular and posh papers. It is cheaper and more straightforward than its quality rivals, and it projects an unashamed Conservatism, with the nostalgic Tory intellectual Peregrine Worsthorne as its regular commentator. The *Sunday Telegraph* proved to be an expensive adventure for Hartwell and the Berry family, losing over half a million pounds a year; and it was often said that three newspapers were competing for a market which could only be profitable for two. If the competition were only for readers, it might be to their benefit; but the papers were competing more fiercely for advertising, which was changing their whole character.

MAGAZINES AND ADVERTISING

Avaunt this vile abuse of pictured page!
Must eyes be all in all, the tongue and ear
Nothing? Heaven keep us from a lower stage!
William Wordsworth.

The battle of the Sunday papers has become more expensive and more perilous—like wrestling on a cliff-edge—through the addition of colour supplements, which represent a brittle new stage in the development of picture journalism. It has a long history. Wordsworth's appalling lines above, written in 1846, were in protest against 'Illustrated Books and Newspapers', including the *Illustrated London News*, the weekly news-magazine founded in 1842. The picture magazines got a great new fillip from the development of photography, and from the heroic subject-matter of the first world war; they reached their peak during the second world war, when such general magazines as *Picture Post, Illustrated, John Bull* and *Everybody's* all had circulations over a million. Since then the coming of television and the expansion of the women's magazines and Sunday newspapers have killed off all those four. In place of the old British magazines there has arrived the new phenomenon of colour magazines, wrapped up in existing newspapers, and intended to be paid for exclusively by the advertisers. They thus represent a new and ominous departure from the traditional financial structure of the British newspaper industry. They owe their existence to the search for advertisers more than readers. With their high costs of production, and their need for quick new revenue, they raise the financial stakes still higher. Intended partly to compete with television, they brought newspapers closer to the hectic competition of TV.

The first of these new-style magazines was launched in February 1962 by Lord Thomson and *The Sunday Times*, true to his principle that whatever can be done in America can be done in Britain. It lost nearly a million pounds in its first eighteen months, but thereafter made a profit. *The Observer* was forced to start up its own, and the *Daily Telegraph* joined in with a Friday one; in 1969 even the *Daily Mirror* started *its* magazine, which folded up the next year. The attraction of the magazines to the readers was that they were 'free'—that is, like commercial television, their cost was entirely borne by the advertisers, who insisted that they would not interfere with the editorial. But advertisers could, with their mastery of colour techniques, present the whole context and background against which the editorial was read—a context of romances beside mountain streams, of imminent seduction in candle-lit dining-rooms, of car-worship and obsession with all consumer durables. The editorial pages, if they wanted to be serious, found themselves like preachers at a champagne party; photographs or articles about the poor or the starving looked merely absurd opposite trendy young marrieds eating succulent meals. The dominating effect of the advertising—which often accounts for fifty per cent of the pages, much of it in colour at £3,000 a page—makes the colour magazines (whatever their editorial says) look like handbooks of contemporary materialism and social ambition.

In their eagerness to attract more advertising, the editorial pages began increasingly to play along with their ultimate sponsors, with special features on Harrods, Selfridges, or holidays in South Africa; so that the boundary between advertisement and editorial is often difficult to detect. As one critic of the colour magazines, Karl Miller (editor of *The Listener*), has put it: 'Advertising is now in a position to compete with journalism, and to secure alliances with it, in describing the society to which they belong. Advertisements are not only consulted, they are read and enjoyed. Advertising is not only an instrument of the economy; it also gives a compelling account of the lives people lead.'

The colour magazines, moreover, had an indirect effect on their parent newspapers; for they caused the proportion of revenue that came from advertising to increase to about three-quarters, thus making the newspapers much more vulnerable to the ups and downs of business booms and recessions. It was Lord Thomson who, by launching the first magazine, had encouraged this greater dependence on advertisers; but eight years later it was he who was insisting that newspapers, to be secure, should redress the balance away from the advertisers. The colour magazines are only the most extreme form of dependence on advertising which now influences all quality newspapers, and the view they present of the world. The reporting of company news in the more radical papers shows a quite different value-system from the rest of the reporting; news of South African gold-mines or of profits in Brazil will be presented on the straight-forward assumption that all profits are

397

good, all losses are bad. Travel articles will report the beauties of Portugal or Greece without reference to the political system or the lives of the ordinary inhabitants. In the context of this commercial acceptance, the strictures of the editorials or news reports lose a good deal of their force. The advertisers' needs, much more than the readers', dictate the allocation of subject matter, so that business, fashion or travel pages proliferate, while foreign news or cultural reporting remain restricted. The size of newspapers goes up and down according to the advertisers' calendar, and just when readers have most time to read (as in August or at Christmas) they dwindle to a few pages.

Newspaper owners have always been two-faced and self-deceiving about advertising, hoping that they could collect the money and remain quite uninfluenced by it. The pattern was set by Lord Northcliffe, whose *Daily Mail* got rich on advertising: 'It shaped the advertising future,' said Northcliffe's biographers, 'by encouraging the art of salesmanship through print.' But Northcliffe knew that they 'spoilt the paper', and he kept on trying to keep advertisers in their place: he once complained that an advertisement made him feel 'like a bird wounded with an arrow'. Just before he died he was so appalled at the 'coarse, abominable and offensive' advertisements in the *Daily Mail* that he appointed the 18-stone hall porter, Mr. Glover, to be chief critic of advertisements: 'I can make the only appeal left, and that is to force.' Mr. Glover's regime, of course, did not last, for Northcliffe was all too aware that he depended on advertising revenue: as he wrote to *The Times*, 'It is not pleasant to think that, owing to the gigantic wages paid in newspaper offices and the high price of paper, newspapers are now, for the first time in their history, entirely subordinate to advertisers.'[1]

It has been argued that advertising, far from encroaching on the freedom of the Press, protects it by subsidising it; thus *The Times*, in an amazing editorial in May 1964 (before Thomson bought it), wrote that 'the British Press is sustained by the independence that is guaranteed by diverse advertising revenue. They release newspapers from that moral Danegeld of the politically subsidised. Advertising (which is itself news) is the foremost bulwark of the freedom of the Press. Newspapers, great and small, in democratic societies owe to advertising the liberty that safeguards liberties.' This view was properly denounced by George Wigg,

[1] Reginald Pound and Geoffrey Harmsworth: *Northcliffe*, pp. 214, 259, 776, 847.

then Paymaster-General, in a speech to newspaper editors in September 1967: 'I can imagine the hoots of delighted derision with which *The Times*'s implied tribute to their noble motives was greeted by the pedlars of pills, unit trusts, cosmetics for men, and those spots of sweet oil behind the ears of women which are foxed-up with scent and sold in expensive packets as perfume . . . It is, I suggest, possible to argue that the Press has exchanged the tyranny of the political establishment for that of the commercial establishment, and that the "moral Danegeld of the politically subsidised" has given way to the contemptuous pay-off of the commercial advertiser.'

WEEKLIES AND THE FRINGE

The big 'quality' newspapers are all now competing for a broader readership, outside the coteries of administrators and intellectuals for which they were first designed; and they are all competing anxiously for advertising. The two pressures push them towards the acceptance of the values and rules of the consensus and the consumer society, in which spending, high profits and high salaries are assumed to be important for their own sake. They have all, in their characters, become more like department stores, dedicated to the proposition that 'the customer is always right', and providing something for everyone, but nothing very special for anyone. Faced with these rich but cumbersome giants, there are still some opportunities for smaller political papers to hold their own, like boutiques next to Harrods.

The traditional intellectual strongholds are the weeklies, which can trace their origin back, rather fitfully, to *The Tatler* and *The Spectator* in the early eighteenth century. *The Tatler* is now, after a long hiatus, a picture-chronicle of fashionable weddings, balls and county occasions; *The Spectator*, which was founded in 1828, has after several reincarnations emerged as the organ of the intellectual right—a force which seemed dormant until the late sixties. It is edited by one of the 'characters' of Fleet Street, George Gale, a huge, haggard figure with a wild shock of red hair and a husky voice, who wrote a column in the *Daily Mirror* and now proclaims the follies of liberalism in robust and intolerant style.

There are at least three other influential general weeklies— apart from a host of specialist ones, like the Catholic *Tablet*, the pacifist *Peace News*, or the left-wing *Tribune*. The most successful commercially is *The Economist*, the businessmen's fat weekly, which was founded in 1843, and was enormously expanded in the forties and fifties by Sir Geoffrey Crowther, now Lord Crowther and chairman of the Royal Commission on the British Constitution. His legacy has left *The Economist* with great self-confidence, and a pontifical anonymous style which suggests (as Alastair Buchan has put it) that it may at any time be called in as an alternative government. But it has lost its intellectual edge. It is edited rather loosely by a right-wing economist and television commentator, Alastair Burnet; and it attacks British trades unions with a crude insensitivity reminiscent of old class-warfare. It leaves the broader interpretation of society and sociological questions to its left-wing rival *New Society*, set up in 1962.

Probably the most influential of the weeklies has been the *New Statesman*, founded by Sidney and Beatrice Webb in 1913 as the organ of Fabian socialism, and later absorbing *The Nation* and the *Weekend Review*. For thirty years the 'Naggers and Staggers' was edited by Kingsley Martin, a passionate dissenter, who distilled the austere spirit of intellectual Socialists through long years of opposition. The paper, as its nickname suggested, was like a club; and in the years of the retreat from Empire its name had a special magic for Afro-Asians and radical exiles. But after the departure of Martin in 1960, and the victory of many of its causes, its identity was less sure; it was edited first by John Freeman, later Ambassador to Washington, then by Paul Johnson, a brilliant but contrary polemicist, who stolidly defended Wilson through his troubles. Then, after the 1970 election, it was taken over by Richard Crossman, for whom the job had been his life's ambition throughout his time in politics. Crossman quickly impressed his outsize personality on the paper, and turned it into a kind of shadow cabinet, with his old colleagues Barbara Castle, Harold Lever and Lord Chalfont as contributors. Crossman's rumbustious and bullying tactics caused some anguish in the *New Statesman* offices; but his intellectual power and his revelations brought a new distinction to weekly journalism.

The third rival is *The Listener*, which was set up in 1929 to print broadcast talks, and is still subsidised by the BBC. Before the war it was regarded as a great instrument of popular education. Now, under a new editor, Karl Miller, it has become consciously highbrow, and a house magazine of communicators and critics; Miller is a distinctive intellectual—an austere Scots critic of English literature who has impressed *The Listener* firmly with his own characteristics—long articles about football, astringent reviews of poetry, and articles by a close coterie of Cambridge contemporaries (Jonathan Miller, Nicholas Tomalin, Mark Boxer, Alan Bennett, George Melly, etc.) generically known by their postal address as 'N.W.1'.

These traditional weeklies have held their own against mass papers and television by offering a more intimate and defined relationship with readers. But a more drastic antidote comes from the new 'fringe' or 'underground' papers which appeal to a radical generation fed up with the measured tread of the heavies, who like papers to be closer to their own language. They identify themselves with the crude radical newspapers of the eighteenth or early nineteenth century, before the commercialisation of the Press replaced them with the 'safe' mass newspapers (as cartoonists like Scarfe or Steadman have looked back to Hogarth and Rowlandson); and like those earlier papers, they come and go. The neo-Marxist *Black Dwarf* was founded in 1968, in the euphoria following the 'May Revolution' in Paris, taking its name from the radical paper set up in 1817 by T. J. Wooler (it cheekily said 'Established 1817' on its front page.) But it was much more introverted than its predecessor, with gilded contributors pretending to be proletarian, talking to each other more than to potential new readers, and it ran into ideological troubles between one faction, the International Marxist Group, and the rest. In 1970 *Black Dwarf* collapsed, and the IMG set up a new paper *Red Mole* (named from Marx: 'We recognise our old friend, our old mole, who knows so well how to work underground, suddenly to appear: the Revolution').

The underground Press is in a state of perpetual flux, and is now less confident than two years ago. As one of them, *Friends*, put it in November 1970: '*Cyclops* has died. *Strange Days* has died. *Grass Eye* and *Zig Zag* ail. The alternative Press is in trouble all round.' The two veterans in the field are *It* and *Oz*: *Oz* is edited by yet another Australian, Richard Neville, and was prosecuted for obscenity in June 1971; he was also involved in setting up in May 1971 a more ambitious weekly called *Ink*, aiming to fill the gap between the 'guerilla' press and the 'uneasy Fleet Street giants'. Another semi-underground paper, *Time Out*, dealing honestly with entertainment, has emerged overground as a big magazine with conventional advertising. But once an underground paper comes above ground, its success may be self-defeating, as it conforms to the requirements of advertising and mass readers.

The best known of the fringe papers, with most influence on other journalism, is the fortnightly *Private Eye*, first launched in 1962 as a 'lampoon', with satirical gossip, lavatorial jokes and naughty cartoons, owned by Peter Cook. It produces serious as well as frivolous scoops, which it obtains (like *Le Canard Enchainé*) by publishing what other papers dare not or will not print. Every Wednesday 'the Eye' holds a lunch at the Coach and Horses in Soho, presided over by two very opposite personalities. At one end is Richard Ingrams, the hearty editor, full of jokes against foreigners, liberals and homosexuals; at the other end is Paul Foot, the Trotskyist son of Lord Caradon, who has published well-documented exposures of Harold Wilson and Enoch Powell, and writes the most important scoops, the 'Footnotes' at the back of the paper. Between them are an uneasy mixture of discontented journalists and politicians, from right and left, leaking damaging stories over steak and Beaujolais (even Mrs. Thatcher has been seen there). *The Eye* can be very inaccurate and vengeful; its humour is often based on public-school snobbery, like the jokes about 'Grocer' Heath and the mocking of Mrs. Wilson for her lower-middle-class habits. Its importance lies in the fact that—partly because it is too poor to be worth most people suing—it can expose humbug and corruption with a freedom given to no other paper. It goes back to the rough roots of journalism, and politicians cannot resist reading it.

WHO CONTROLS THE PRESS?

Those who run the Press are at the moment running it steadily into the ground. It is for the journalists and printers themselves to save it. The long-term perspective is that those who make newspapers should own and run them.

Free Communications Group, 1970.

Your connection with any newspaper would be a disgrace and a degradation. I would rather sell gin to poor people and poison them that way.

Sir Walter Scott to Lockhart, 1829.

The question of who runs newspapers is much more complex and interesting than it was twenty years ago, when most of them were firmly run by either the proprietors or the editors. Today much of that personal power has been eroded: the intensity of competition and the divided ownership have made the Press lords more dependent on accountants and market researchers, and the editors have become more limited by managements, and less able to control and influence journalists. Bagehot in the nineteenth century foresaw that signed articles would be the end of strong editors; and the proliferation of signed columns in the quality Press has made the confidence of the anonymous editorials, supposedly speaking on behalf of the whole paper, sound less convincing.

But journalists have remained in a weak position, and their weakness is shown by the fact that, while most of them are on the left, the majority of newspapers, like their proprietors, are predominantly on the right. Licensed rebels can hold forth in Conservative newspapers like the *Daily Mail* or the *Evening Standard*, but they are like eccentric radicals invited to amuse or provoke a Tory dinner-party. The 25,000 journalists are caught unhappily in the commercial cogs of Fleet Street. British journalists are aware of being less respected than Americans; there is no British equivalent to the American journalist-pundit— Reston, Lippmann, or the Alsops. American newspapers helped to create their democracy, spreading news from coast to coast —in a country without traditional social networks, journalism was crucial. But in Britain, the secretive ruling classes in the eighteenth century had no love of journalism, and it began as an eavesdropping profession, where even parliamentary reports had to be smuggled out. In spite of such eminent journalists as Churchill, Milner or Dickens, journalism has never quite recovered from this backdoor complex.

The pressure of profits and the shortage of space make newspapers unwilling to employ good reporters for the sake of prestige, and the business of reporting has become more mixed with entertainment and comment. Television has infected much of journalism with its hectic aggressiveness: jet planes and TV cameras between them have made news seem more like a series of sudden and disconnected crises and spectaculars. Journalists in Britain have never had the cosy sense of profession, nor the sense of duty, which Americans enjoy. In America journalism is apt to be regarded as an extension of history, in Britain as an extension of conversation. As the Alsop brothers (perhaps oversimply) described the difference, in Britain 'the national debate can be and actually is quite largely carried on in the House of Commons itself. The British Press therefore has far less national responsibility than the American Press.'[1]

British journalists, conscious of their insecurity, have in the last two years taken up the demand of workers' control. They have looked abroad for models of self-governing newspapers: for instance, to *Le Monde*, where the majority shares are held by the senior journalists, or (more misleadingly) to *Le Figaro*, where fuddy-duddy journalists have battled for control with a rather less fuddy-duddy proprietor. The more militant members of the journalists' union, centering round the Free Communications Group[2] have resolved to set up elected editorial councils, to share all the crucial information with managements, and if necessary to take over newspapers by direct action. A proper participation by journalists in their newspapers could bring much greater honesty to the Press, and counter its commercial motives; but the claims for journalists' control are mixed up with the question of whether journalism is, or should be, a closed profession. A closed shop of journalists could exclude some of the most interesting talents (as the *Mirror* journalists tried to exclude Clive Jenkins from writing a weekly column); and it could turn newspapers further in on themselves, losing touch still further with the curiosities of their readers.

Two other groups of people are involved in newspapers, and both are now more vocal. The first are the printers, whose unions are among the oldest in the world, with a special dignity and pride. A new generation of more politically-conscious printers are much more aware that what they are producing has political implications: so that printers have sometimes refused to print editorials or cartoons which are directed against them or other workers. The argument is not new; many idealists in the nineteenth century, like William Morris or Michelet, lamented the dissociation between printing and writing. There was a political showdown in 1926, when the printers of the *Daily Mail* went on strike when the editor wanted to appeal for strike-breaking volunteers; and the *Daily Mail* strike set off the whole General Strike. The printers' objections have been regarded by most journalists and editors as a basic threat to freedom of expression; but how far should an intelligent printer be expected to set up copy which he believes to be wrong? Here, as in other fields, there

[1] Joseph and Stewart Alsop: *The Reporter's Trade*, Reynold, New York, 1958, p. 11.
[2] See Chapter 24.

are signs of a harking back to the pre-industrial age, when the writers were much closer to the printers or scribes; as they are today in the 'fringe' papers.

There are also the readers themselves: who are not only the final arbiters of a paper's success, but who often—in their own letters—write the most interesting part of the paper (a worrying challenge to the profession of journalists). *The Times*'s correspondence columns are the core of the paper, containing all the ingredients of a successful journal—scoops, comments, information and outspoken argument: the letters page is like an extra lobby to the House of Commons, where questions are aired and debated before they are taken up by the politicians; and other papers, too, find their letters columns are among the best-read parts of the paper. The fondness for writing to the papers is specifically English; and the readers' letters, even though they come from a restricted stratum of professional men, help to make the notion of 'public opinion' more credible in Britain than on the Continent. The readers' preference for reading each other's letters, instead of the more formalised parts of the papers, is one sign of the danger of an over-organised Press. Here again journalism may be looking back to its origins, when newspapers were first made up of correspondents in the literal sense of the word, writing letters to people with common interests.

All these claimants for influence are disputing the traditional authority of the editor and the owner. But any dreams of a shared endeavour, or of real participation between all the elements that produce a newspaper, are limited by the harsh commercial facts which govern all mass newspapers in their present predicament: that whoever controls them, they have to play in with the forces of advertising as well as of readership, and that they cannot afford to offend the majority of either.

22

Advertising and Consumers

The trade of advertising is now so near perfection that it is not easy to propose any improvement.

Dr. Johnson, 1759.

I don't drink Guinness because the advertisements tell me to; I drink it because it's good for me.

Old joke.

HOWEVER convenient advertising men may be (as in the previous chapter) as scapegoats for journalists and other communicators, it is useless to regard advertising as separable from the rest of industrial society. As industry moves closer towards the consumer —gearing its factories, structures, and managers to understanding and mastering the housewife—so its production lines and pay-packets depend on creating demand for new products. With the development of the 'consumer society', the advertising man enters his restless kingdom, as the man who understands how to create desires, how to communicate between the producer and the consumer. Arguments against advertising have been a favourite intellectual pastime, but most of them turn out to be arguments against the whole nature of the capitalist economy and of modern society. The techniques and images of contemporary advertising have spread out to other art-forms. The disconnected surrealism of television commercials influences serials like *The Avengers* and films like *Women In Love*: many film directors, like Dick Lester, Clive Donner or Lindsay Anderson, learnt their business by making commercials; the glossy sex-symbols of posters fascinate serious pop artists. The pervasiveness of advertising is strengthened by its internationalism; and as industry crosses frontiers, so advertising, its standard-bearer, has begun to create images which can repeat themselves all over Western Europe and America. The heralds of European integration have been Esso's Tiger in the Tank, Colgate's White Tornado, Peter Stuyvesant's cosmopolitan smokers. Western Europe's involvement with advertising becomes evident as soon as one gets out of it, into Eastern Europe or Russia, where (though advertising is now slowly developing) the newspapers have no displays, the undergrounds have no brassières or bikinis, and the cities without hoardings or neon lights hardly seem cities. Coming back from this world of silence and darkness, a Western European is reminded how far advertisements have become not only the daily goads, but also the familiars.

The serious debate about advertising is a very political one. On the one side, Raymond Williams, the Marxist professor of communications, describes how 'We get an idea of a society in which we need ask no other questions than the name of the brand, and in which the relative importance of this man's marginal product to another man's desperate need is never questioned, while the game and the music last.'[1] On the other side, Enoch Powell sees advertising as the protection from dictatorship: 'Remove advertising, disable a person or firm from preconising its wares and their merits, and the whole of society and of the economy is transformed. The enemies of advertising are the enemies of freedom. . . .'[2] These are the two extreme views. In the spectrum between are different shades of the characteristic British belief, that it is possible to maintain a balance between state enterprise and free enterprise, as between the BBC and commercial television: both to have the benefits of advertising, and yet to keep it in its place. This balance, I believe, is essential to honest communications, and it could be achieved. But it requires a continuous questioning and resistance to advertising pressures, and in the last decade the balance has been seriously tilted. The pressure of commercial interests on television and the Press has increased the leverage of advertising, and many defences have crumbled.

ADMEN

Advertising has no direction, no centre, no obvious tycoon. It

[1] *May Day Manifesto* (edited by Raymond Williams), Penguin Books, 1968. P. 41–3.
[2] *The Listener*, July 31, 1969.

exists as a hectic go-between, connecting the two great wheels of producers and consumers, taking a succession of quick and temporary decisions, existing from hand to mouth, and still surprised by its own existence and wealth. This dependence of advertising men, who are frequently on the defensive as the scape-goats of capitalism, is part of their self-justification. As one of their pundits, John Hobson, has put it: 'Advertising is not (as some people seem to imagine) something in its own right, some separate estate of the realm, like civil administration, or the services, or law. Advertising is an integral part of industry.'[1] They like to see themselves as 'consumption engineers' who (says one of their apologists, Jeremy Tunstall) 'are likely to take over from the manufacturers as the predominant group of business managers within the next generation'. The word 'engineer' is their let-out, for it implies an accepted machine; and the introduc-tion of computers has strengthened the alibi, by suggesting that men are powerless in the face of unchangeable facts. ('What can we do? If you feed the facts into a computer . . .') Only occasion-ally do they get together to defend their trade or extend their influence. In the one great recent advertising revolution—the creation of commercial television—a few agencies took an important role, but most were more alarmed than exhilarated by the prospects (see Chapter 24).

Modern advertising was an American invention. There were British pioneers, like Lever and Lipton, but the pace was set by New York. High-pressure advertising began with a young Texan-Jewish salesman called Albert Lasker, who in 1904 first developed the principle of 'salesmanship in print'. He trans-formed advertising from a series of sedate announcements into a cunning art of appealing to secret desires, and in the next forty years he made forty-five million dollars out of it.[3] But as the business became more complicated, so advertising became less of an art, more of a science. On to the original wagon of salesmanship was loaded an extraordinary baggage of statistics, pollsters, committees and analysts: the technique of probing and goading the human mind became itself a major industry. 'Advertising,' complained Lasker, 'has been lost in the advertising business'.

In spite of its impedimenta, advertising still has its own

[1] John Hobson in the *Journal of the Royal Society of Arts*, July 1964, p. 566.
[2] *The Listener*, March 12, 1964.
[3] See John Gunther: *Taken at the Flood*, 1960.

histrionic atmosphere, like a second-hand Hollywood. Advertising agencies are a compound of ballyhoo, calculations and creative energy: in their curious caravan are included accountants, film producers, salesmen, poets, artists, showmen and straightforward businessmen. Nothing is actually *made* in an agency building except words and pictures, and when all the committees are finished, the advertisement still depends on someone to write it. The copy-writers who compose the advertisements and the artists who design them make up the neurotic centre of the advertising business. Advertising and television between them have created a sudden and insatiable market for the more malleable kinds of creative talent: and a talented copy-writer in his early thirties *can* earn £10,000 a year. Any creative talent is in furious demand, and anyone prepared to bend his talent to commerce is more likely to collapse from overeating at the Terrazza than from starving in an attic.

In the first few years of a career, advertising can be a glorious romp, a kind of glorified Scrabble or heads-bodies-and-legs, fitting words or pictures into a competitive game, and being very highly-paid for it; but in middle age the game palls. Advertising is no longer a kind of bohemia—disreputable but excitingly wild. As one copywriter put it to me: 'Ten years ago, if you said you were a copy-writer they thought you meant a copy-typist or an under-writer. Now they know. Copy-writers used to be rather shabby men with leather elbows and cars with names like Margery which wouldn't start. Now they're trendy and carefully dressed, and they drive Volvos and Saabs.' Or to quote one ex-adman turned playwright, John Bowen:

> Advertising has not been a profession very long, but already, among the older, toping generation, among the directors of some of the smaller agencies growing senile together in golfing suburbia, there is talk of the good old days. All the successes of advertising in the good old days, they would tell you, were sudden flashes—advertisements printed upside down, pages left almost entirely white, slogans which swept people into the shops where they bought and bought and bought again, puns which passed into the public language.[1]

Advertising is now a disciplined and demanding sub-profession, cut off from the literary or journalistic world, with its own territory, its own values, its own intermarriages. The cockiness of its world can be sampled in its gossipy magazine *Campaign*,

[1] John Bowen: *Storyboard*. Faber and Faber, 1960.

bursting with news of accounts changing hands, bright young men climbing up, and men in their forties being discreetly shoved out ('taking an extended holiday ... looking for other challenges'). Here the adman's language appears in all its splendour, with the messages lost in the media: 'Ronnie Corbett in voice-over handled a nicely-judged crescendo of what sounded at first like anti-sell.' The rest of communications are confidently judged in terms simply of circulation and impact ('*The Times*, with its new personality, has really kicked life into a whole dead area of journalism').

Advertising has become trapped in a tradition of extravagance and showmanship which seemed gaily appropriate in the boom years of expansion, but looks slightly absurd—even mocking—at a time when business is bad; behind the gloss and the glamour, the pretty secretaries and wallpapered corridors, worried men bite their nails over last year's billings. In the last few years, cold winds have blown through the plush; in 1966 (a peak year) there were 20,000 people employed in the agencies, in 1970 there were only 17,000; and there were twice as many applicants for each job. The sluggish state of the economy, and the depression on Madison Avenue, had helped to slow down the business; but there were also more serious threats to the admen. The big chain-stores and supermarkets took to spending more money on discounts, competitions and promotions, and less on national advertising; the 'private labels' of Tesco, Sainsbury's or Fine Fare were threatening the old brand names, and there were signs of a retreat from massselling, back to the ancient ballyhoo and bargaining of the bazaar. And the growth of the resistance movement called 'consumerism'— as we will see—disputed the credibility and conviction of advertising. In this harsher climate, the lunches at the Connaught and the clients' treats have macabre overtones. The admen's predicament is made more difficult because many clients—and other observers of their scene—would rather *like* them to be gay, wicked and corrupt, and to provide psychiatric good cheer. Like sad clowns, they are expected to keep on living it up in the face of gloomy statistics.

There are about three hundred advertising agencies in Britain, but about half of them do 90 per cent of the business. These were the ten biggest agencies, together with their 'billings' (the total cost of the advertising they placed and the proportion spent on television), in 1969:

	Agency	Billings (£m)	TV (£m)
A	J. Walter Thompson	24·3	17·4
	Masius, Wynne-Williams	18·5	12·6
A	Ogilvy and Mather	13·6	8·2
A	Young and Rubicam	10·8	8·5
A	Hobson Bates	9·7	7·7
	S. H. Benson	8·3	4·6
	Lintas	8·3	6·6
	Leo Burnett LPE	8·0	5·6
A	Wasey Pritchard Wood	7·1	3·0
A	McCann-Erickson	7·0	3·8

Six of them (marked A) are American-owned and over a third of the British agency business is now American-owned, compared to a fifth ten years ago. Admen periodically complain that the American invasion is destroying the authentic British way of life: but others are doubtful whether there is any longer such a thing as a British approach in such a very international business. Consumers, whether in Britain, America or Germany, show signs of becoming increasingly alike, increasingly vulnerable to tigers, white tornadoes or Lux film stars.

The dominating agency in Britain—as in many other parts of the world—is the giant American firm of J. Walter Thompson, which celebrated its centenary in 1964. 'The great days of advertising are over,' said Commodore James Walter Thompson, the bearded pioneer, when he sold his agency in New York in 1916: since then the turnover has multiplied by nearly 200. J. Walter Thompson is not a typical agency (there is no such thing) but, both in America and Britain, it has set the pace for others. It was the first agency to develop exhaustive research about markets— ever since 1912 when it produced a small dry book called *Population and its Distribution*. JWT men in New York like to think of themselves as part of a serious profession: they are opposed to nepotism, and there is hardly a son-in-law in the business. They have imposed bureaucracy and science on the young wild trade of advertising: the poets and artists, like scientists, bishops or trade unionists, have found themselves sucked into committees. Thompson's pioneered 'Reason why' advertising, which tries to make claims credible on a rational basis. They go in for scientific evidence, and they have a whole team of highly-paid consultants from universities to help them with special ingredients and secret formulae, with that zeal for technical perfectionism which characterises the advertising profession, as a kind of substitute for any more serious aim.

The London office of Thompson's, though ultimately controlled from New York, is determined to be very British. The chairman is Dr. John Treasure, a beady-eyed and articulate market research expert, who was once an economics don, and spends much of his time explaining the role of advertising in the capitalist system. (The doctor bit fits well with the adman's contemporary image, as the bed-side physician to industry, diagnosing unpronounceable diseases.) The managing director, Denis Lanigan, worked in the Bank of England after reading economics. They are both in keeping with the Thompson idea of being a 'university of advertising'.

In spite of its cult of high seriousness, Thompson's two buildings in Berkeley Square, like other agencies' offices, project a heightened atmosphere of theatricality and tension. Creativity is the catchword, and hard-headed executives pride themselves on being able to cope with the most difficult employees; notice boards are full of quips and slogans, and walls are hung with contemporary lithographs or old Guinness posters. Some offices, with thick pile carpets, soft lighting and luxuriant wallpapers, have the look of an expensive bordello; in the ante-rooms fashionably lace-booted girls are ready to indulge their bosses with Scotch and sympathy. Other offices, with comic pictures on the wall and photographs on the floor, look like some grown-up's playroom. At the Thompson's pub round the corner, the Coach and Horses, young admen talk success stories to each other, ending with their arm held up at a gradient: 'And the sales went up like this'. In their own parties the admen seem determined to live up, not only to the clichés of advertising life, but to the world they depict in their advertisements, of trendy couples always on the point of seducing each other, of fun people endlessly drinking, eating and changing their clothes, of moments of ecstasy at candle-lit dinners; so that one expects any moment a White Horse to come into the room.

ADVERTISING AND INDUSTRY

There have been many painful collisions between the boastful world of advertising and the inarticulate world of business. In Britain, in contrast to America, businessmen have inherited a distrust of advertising and a feeling that if what they make is good enough, there will be no need to boast about it. Many have regarded advertising as a useful luxury, not an essential tool. An elderly director of a family firm and a young advertising executive from Mayfair talk different languages. But in the last decade the admen and salesmen have come much closer to industry: 'Thirty years ago people were shocked at the idea of a marketing man on the board,' said Dr. Mark Abrams: 'Accountants and engineers were all right, but not people who *sold* things. In those days an advertising man was likely to have a chat with a manager at Lyons Corner House: now he'll be talking to a member of the board in the directors' dining-room.'

Like professionalised industrial managers, advertising men are dedicated to the kind of drastic change which can only be effected by operating outside the traditional national structures. The moment when an entrenched British institution, like the Army, the Police, or *The Times*, decides it has to advertise, to improve its image or to whip up recruits, is a moment as laden with significance as the first assignment with a call-girl. From then on the institution enters into a dialogue with the outside world: it has to think what it is *for*, how it can be liked, how it began and where it is going. The process of self-questioning and self-doubt, which the admen induce, can change the whole outlook of an old institution; it can sometimes also—as with *The Times*—lead to a loss of identity from which it is not easy to recover.

But many industries in Britain have been built on advertising and can never forget it. Margarine, patent medicines, cigarettes or cosmetics were born into an age of posters, and the firms which make them, like Unilever or Beechams, are dominated by marketing men. The sales ebb and flow with the effectiveness of the advertising, and the agency men can move into the company like mercenaries upholding feeble regimes. In advertising circles a special magic surrounds products which spend more than a million pounds a year. These were the ten products which spent most on advertising in 1970, and the firms that made them:

C & A Modes	£1,587,000
Radiant (Unilever)	£1,454,000
Weetabix	£1,346,000
Persil (Unilever)	£1,221,000
Kelloggs Corn Flakes	£1,100,000
CWS	£1,070,000
Ariel (Procter and Gamble)	£1,052,000

413

Milk Marketing Board	£1,018,000
Maxwell House Coffee	£1,006,000
Daz (Procter and Gamble)	£992,000

Advertising men can also reassure industrialists by improving their image, both to the outside world and to their own workers; and many big companies like to project themselves to the public with 'corporate advertising' or 'prestige advertising' or 'good-will advertising' (the multiplicity of names, as for lavatories, suggests some embarrassment). 'Company advertisements,' said a pamphlet issued by the Institute of Practitioners in Advertising, 'can influence the public to regard the company in a certain way: as forward-looking people with a vigorous policy of scientific research; as friendly, helpful people with enough humanity to laugh at themselves; or as craftsmen in the English tradition to whom "automation" and "assembly line" are naughty words.' Corporate advertisements can be seen basking on the pages of *The Economist* and the *New Statesman*, explaining in honeyed words the pioneering spirit of banks, the compassion of airlines, or the deep concern of chemical companies with ecology and the environment. As industry becomes more international, so advertising a company becomes mixed up with advertising a country; and commerce merges with nationalism. Lufthansa is part of the German way of life, Swiss watches are a part of the splendour of Switzerland. The statements of faith seem to be designed to reassure the company's employees, the board and the chairman, as much as the public. How much this corporate advertising achieves, no-one ever knows; it may make companies still less loved, by drawing attention to their size; and some giants (like Unilever) prefer not to display themselves.

PUBLIC RELATIONS

Organised lying.

Malcolm Muggeridge.

The deliberate, planned and sustained effort to establish and maintain mutual understanding between an organisation and its public.
Definition by the Institute of Public Relations.

The first public relations officer was Ivy Lee, an American who was employed by the first Rockefeller in 1914 to explain away the massacre of strikers in Colorado: in 1934, when he was had up in court, he turned out to be acting as PR man to the Nazi government. The first public relations officer in Britain was Sir John Elliot, who began on the *Daily Express*, became the first PRO for Southern Railways, and later chairman of the London Transport Executive. It was the second world war that made public relations, like advertising, respectable; Whitehall found PROs very convenient for explaining unpopular actions. Since the war the trade has raced ahead and today there are about 8,000 public relations men: the Church of England, the MCC, the Archbishop of Canterbury, the Queen, Paul Getty, the Aga Khan, all have their PROs.

In America PR is a trade very separate from advertising, with its own large firms: in Britain most advertising agencies have their own PR departments, which they use to supplement their advertising, but which they look down on. As one adman described them: 'Most PR people are either queers or women—over-trendy women with caked make-up, red lips, and poofy hairdo's, with all the glitter of advertising but none of the professionalism.' Public relations men are always expecting to come into an era of total respectability, but it has not yet come. Businessmen like to talk about the importance of good public relations, but baulk at actually opening up their worries to an outsider; so that though the numbers of people in the trade are still increasing, they are still conscious of being a pariah profession.

Public relations men, it is sometimes said, can improve anyone's image except their own. The general tattiness of the British trade was reflected in the survey which the Institute of Public Relations rather rashly published in 1964. A thousand of their members answered a questionnaire, and the replies revealed that

> 32 per cent went to public or private schools.
> 32 per cent of members went to university,
> 19 per cent graduated,

The Institute, founded twenty years ago, does what it can to improve the standing of the trade; but only about half the public relations men are members (the membership is about 1,400), and the Institute's discipline is not strong. In 1965 they tried to insist that all their members should pass an examination, but the experiment was disastrous; not many members sat for it, still fewer passed, and the older members were indignant; so that in 1968 the exams were dropped. The Institute's rules include a controversial

Clause Four, which says that members are forbidden to engage in 'any practice which tends to corrupt the integrity of channels of public communication', but that offence is not an easy one to prove. The Institute was obviously embarrassed in 1969 when one of its members, Maurice Fraser, was found to have been promising the Greek government under-cover political support from a British MP.

Hundreds of public relations men are pensionably employed by large corporations and government departments, keeping newspapers and television informed of their employers' achievements, suffused through a rosy light. The chief PR man in a big company is sometimes both an image-maker for his chairman and a universal fixer, ready to flatter a recalcitrant sheikh, to find a hotel suite, or to arrange meetings with amenable girls. But there are also more independent practitioners, who like to call themselves 'consultants'. They now have their own Public Relations Consultants Association, representing about 600 firms: they conducted a survey in 1970 which showed that up to twenty of them had fee incomes of over £100,000 a year: the biggest companies by turnover in 1968 were Lexington (£227,000), Planned PR (£200,000), Bensons PR (£153,000) and Michael Rice (£153,000). Many of the consultants favour names which stress their friendly brokerage, like *Interflow*, *Interlink* or *Link*. They work among thick carpets and marble mantelpieces, telephoning, entertaining, introducing, arranging, conciliating, explaining—lubricating the relationships between big business and the public. Sometimes they make use of institutional advertising, but their real art consists of *unseen* promotion—inspiring headlines, television programmes, questions in parliament, letters to *The Times*. The aristocrats of the profession are the public relations advisers to the big corporations and government departments: men like Sir Harold Evans, who as PR man in Downing Street put across the image of unflappable Macmillan, and now tries to improve Vickers' faded image; or Donald Maitland, the former ambassador to Libya who looks after Heath's press relations; or Will Camp, the novelist-publicist, one of the most sophisticated operators, who looked after the promotion of High Speed Gas, and now defends the interests of British Steel and Lord Melchett against the attacks of Tory politicians.

Several of the PR consultants are employed by foreign governments (a practice regulated in America), and are taking over part of the role of ambassadors. Public relations can offer foreign governments much more comprehensive and visible benefits than any diplomats; they can nobble MPs, journalists and television, and they can use advertising as a means of pressure on editorial comment ('of course if you insist on unfair attacks on Franco, you can't expect us to go on advertising Spanish tourism'). Tourism advertising looms large with such dictatorships as South Africa, Greece or Spain, and advertisements or sponsored articles about travel can be deployed to convey the stability and general happiness of those countries.

The para-diplomats of public relations are a theatrical crowd; one of the doyens of the trade is the soft-voiced Toby O'Brien, who cultivates an old-fashioned languor, with monocle and striped trousers, and claims to be descended from the Monarch of All Ireland. He was PRO for the Conservative Party after the war, and has since championed many of the most right-wing governments, including the Yemen, Saudi-Arabia, and the Portuguese African colonies. Prince Yurka Galitzine looked after Nigeria and Greek tourism, and has run the British campaign for Nixon as President. Lex Hornsby, a veteran from Glasgow, handles East Germany's trade and culture; Michael Rice, a smooth Tory, promotes the Arab League and Bahrain, and has an MP, Patrick McNair Wilson, on his board.

The contacts between journalists and public relations have the barbed complexity of any two occupations, like police and criminals, which are hostile yet interdependent. Journalists shout abuse against PR men, while becoming increasingly dependent on them; there was a short-lived Society for the Discouragement of Public Relations which in 1961 held some indignant dinners to protest their independence; but a lot of the members turned out to be knee-deep in all kinds of obligations, and at the last dinner the founder of the society was ignominiously absent on a public-relations trip. Journalists are dependent on PR's not only for their news, doled out in an easily-usable style, with handouts, press conferences, pseudo-events and ready-made stories: but also for providing context of the discussion, which brings the argument on to the PR's home ground. The ultimate victories of public relations are to be found in the women's pages of newspapers, where the whole calendar of fashion events is set by the promoters; where shopping hints are virtually an extension of the marketing industry; and where advice about food, drinks and restaurants is heavily influenced by hospitality. The battle between the two armies, of journalists and public relations, is unequal; for the effective PR has both money and information on his side.

OMO V. DAZ

Far too many people are allowing their dislike of plastic daffodils to blind them to what advertising really does.

The Economist, August 1966.

One sector of industry's dependence on advertising was revealed in the tragi-comedy of the detergents, Omo and Daz. In advertising battles the products are apt to emerge with stronger personalities than the people selling them: in this story the real heroes are powders. Two giant companies, the American Procter and Gamble and the Anglo-Dutch Unilever, have for two decades dominated the soap-and-detergent market, and in Britain they have captured ninety per cent of the business: in the sixties their biggest detergents, Omo (Unilever) and Daz (Procter) were locked in fatuous combat; each of them, year after year, spent over a million pounds on advertising. By the early fifties there were already rumblings of political disapproval at this colossal wastage: between them they spent more on advertising than the annual cost of the Queen, with all her castles. For the next decade, Omo fought Daz through the sinks of England: Omo's advertising agency was the all-British S. H. Benson, one of whose copywriters, Gilbert Hughes, conceived the slogan 'Omo adds Brightness to Cleanness and Whiteness'; before long he found himself managing-director. Daz's agency was the American giant, Young and Rubicam, who thought up the sinister 'Brand X', which was always so much less white than Daz. With the help of commercial television advertising for Omo and Daz romped still further ahead: they competed with jingles, innuendoes, give-away coupons, washing-up cloths and plastic daffodils. By 1966 Daz's sales were £8.4 million a year, and Omo was £6.2 million; each of them was spending about 20 per cent of its sales on advertising. Altogether, including their give-aways and 'door-step jamborees', detergents were spending £18 million a year on advertising and promotion.

Even Tory politicians were distressed, and Unilever men, who are not very convinced capitalists, showed symptoms of a guilt-complex about their advertising. In 1963 as a partial concession they introduced 'Square Deal Surf', which had no free gifts and more powder, heavily advertised with half a million pounds a year; but after three years it only got six per cent of the market: housewives evidently preferred a crooked deal to a square one. By 1966, with the Labour government in power committed to cutting down advertising, detergents were becoming a hot political question. But the challenge came from a non-political quarter. The usually cautious Monopolies Commission had been quietly studying the contenders, and came out with a sensational report in August 1966: they recommended that the two big companies should immediately cut their selling expenses by forty per cent, and that the government should try to tax their promotional spending. The economists were indignant or contemptuous: the right-wing 'Economists' Advisory Group' pointed out that it was advertising that had first enabled Procter to break the Unilever monopoly.[1] But the Board of Trade, then under the austere rule of Douglas Jay, felt it had to do something. After painful negotiations, Jay was persuaded that the Commission's idea was unworkable, and the companies refused to cut advertising on Omo and Daz. But they agreed to freeze all their prices for two years, and to sell two 'extra value' detergents, which would cost a fifth less than the existing brands—equivalent to deducting the cost of the advertising. Unilever produced Surf, as a new version of Square Deal, with the same powder as Omo but a fifth cheaper. Procter produced Blue-and-White Tide, a fifth cheaper than Daz.

But the main warfare between Omo and Daz was unabated, and even intensified. By July 1967 the total advertising expenditure of the two big companies had gone up by forty per cent. It is doubtful how genuine the companies' intentions were to promote the cheap packets; most of the extra advertising was spent on the familiar packets, and only a quarter of the housewives were using the new cheap powders. The following May Lord Cole of Unilever pronounced the cheap powders a failure, because they made up only a fifth of Unilever's sales. The magazine *Which?* explained that there was now such confusion in the supermarkets that people didn't know which brands were cheaper: they called unsuccessfully for a counter-advertising campaign. The next month the Board of Trade (by then under Anthony Crosland) capitulated, and allowed the big companies to raise their prices, partly because of devaluation. A few months later many of the

[1] *The Economics of Advertising.* Published by the Advertising Association, 1967, p. 61.

cheap brands were no longer in the supermarkets at all, and Omo and Daz still led the field. Soon a new competitor from Procter, called Ariel, the 'biological washing miracle', armed with enzymes, entered the field: Unilever, after a dangerous time-lag, counter-attacked with their Radiant. The war of the sinks started all over again, on an even more extravagant scale. (Though in the meantime enzymes were under heavy attack, and detergents were being increasingly blamed for water pollution.)

Advertising men and economists were not slow to point their moral of Omo and Daz. 'The plain fact,' said *The Times*, 'is that consumers, exercising their free choice, chose in overwhelming numbers to buy the heavily promoted brands.' A scholarly pamphlet by the Institute of Economic Affairs, the academic champions of free enterprise, persuasively argued that advertising had been the spearhead in innovation among detergents, and had brought down the costs; and decided that the only way to break up the monopoly was 'by some form of special intervention by the state to create additional countervailing power and to challenge the two market leaders'.[1] Certainly it had become evident that it was no use tinkering with the advertising business without going to the heart of the capitalism system; and that if the state wanted to break up the clinch of Omo and Daz, Ariel and Radiant, they would have to intervene much more seriously.

CONSUMERS

A great constituency is still awaiting its representatives; a new interest—the consumer interest—is still awaiting its champion.
Michael Young, 1970.

In the last decade the massed armies of advertisers and manu-facturers have encountered some heavy sniping on an effective but narrow front. In the early sixties ordinary people began to be talked of as 'consumers'. It was after the 1959 'washing machine election', in the middle of the first great boom in 'consumer durables' (how can a durable be consumed?). The cult of the consumer was two-edged: on the one hand the 'consumer society' implied that the voter was locked into the industrial system, and enmeshed in the machinery of production and growth; not very encouraging for individual dignity. But 'consumer' also became

[1] George Polanyi: *Detergents: A Question of Monopoly?* IEA, 1970.

the battle-cry of people determined to resist and expose the deceptions of advertising and manufacturers.

The most spectacular sign of this awareness was the foundation in 1957 of the magazine *Which?*, by a group called the Consumers' Association, led by a remarkable back-room socialist, Michael Young—a man with a rare combination of idealism and tycoonery who has been called 'the Charles Clore of the do-gooder business'. Young was a confirmed outsider: he came from an Irish-Australian background, and was a prize pupil of the avant-garde school of the thirties, Dartington Hall. He detested British inefficiency and complacency, which he attacked in a pamphlet called The Chipped White Cups of Dover, and wanted for a time to set up a Consumers' Party. Seeing the success of the American 'Consumers Union', which had been already going for two decades, he introduced *Which?* in Britain, with its own flourish of public relations. Its success was spectacular; in twelve years its circulation has zoomed up to 620,000—far more than *The Times*. The turnover of the association is now nearly two million pounds a year: on testing a major piece of equipment, like central heating, they could spend £30,000. They employ a staff of 300, mostly in a big Georgian house off the Strand. *Which?* produced offshoots, *Motoring Which?* and *Money Which?*, and (in a separate organisation) a guide to schools called *Where?* Michael Young himself became president, and was preoccupied with other new causes, leaving the running of the Association to an ex-head of the Conservative Political Centre, Peter Goldman. *Which?* is edited by a militant housewife, Eirlys Roberts, who rallies the faithful once a month with stirring editorials about soapsuds, weedkillers or fridges.

The achievement of *Which?* was notable; it made manufacturers more watchful, advertisers less mendacious, and products safer and more reliable. It helped to give a new militancy to housewives, and a new menace to the word consumer. The Consumers' Association succeeded emphatically in its main object: 'To promote and advance public knowledge in all matters concerning users and consumers of materials, goods and services of all kinds.' But in terms of any broader idealism of improving the quality of life or of educating the masses, *Which?* has been disappointing, for it has settled into limited ambitions which are, in their way, almost as depressing as the values of advertising which they set out against. Over the years they have turned increasingly to the accoutrements of upper-middle-class homes—deep-freezes, stereo record players, colour television, au pair girls; even burglar alarms and advice on how to make a will. The bourgeois impression has been reinforced by the merger of *Which?* with the *Good Food Guide*—an annual which had conjured up a gloomy picture of ageing radicals from Hampstead or Chelsea rolling through England in search of *haute cuisine*, their appetites and waistlines enlarging as their ideals recede, demanding French cooking and wine in rural outposts. (Can you eat lobster thermidor in Abersoch? asked one of the *Guide*'s advertisements.)

Which? claims to have three million readers, but only about a third come from the lower middle and skilled working classes; and they admit that they have not reached the market that most needs them: 'It is precisely the educationally underprivileged who are most vulnerable to misinformation,' Peter Goldman has written.[1] He has recently done something to try to widen the counter-attack; he has opened a centre in Kentish Town, modelled on the Viennese Consumers' Association, where working-class shoppers can call for advice; and the Association is encouraging research into new kinds of products, by establishing an 'Institute of Consumer Ergonomics' at Loughborough University. But the assumptions of *Which?*, with its rather smug campaigning for material comforts for the middle-classes, seem to be symptomatic of the psychological retreat from the broad ideals of the forties into the consumer cosiness of the sixties and seventies. It is not able to question the basis of the consumer society, or to try to deflect the public away from gadgetry and new luxuries, for its approach is based on taking the goods and shops as they are.

A short-lived alternative shoppers' champion was the Consumer Council, set up in 1963 by the Conservative Government, on the recommendation of the Molony Report on Consumer Protection. 'The producer is dominant, and his voice all-powerful,' said that report: 'his interests easily prevail over the welfare of the consumer and will continue to do so until the consumer is provided with an organisation of equal weight to protect and represent him.' But the new Council grew up too close to the aura of Whitehall; its members were appointed by the Board of Trade (which was like asking the Great Train Robbers to appoint a committee on British Railways Security) and it was prevented, by its statute, from testing products or receiving individual complaints. It was

[1] *The Spectator*, September 30, 1966.

showing signs of stirring itself: but just as it had appointed a new director, Des Wilson, who is one of the most adept publicists in the country, it was shut down by the new Tory government.

The consumer organisations and the militancy which they have unleashed have made their impact on big business, and the idea of 'consumer opinion', which ten years ago was hardly imaginable, has become quite a maddening reality for industrialists. As Goldman puts it: 'I think we've got the capitalist system a good deal tamer in this country. Not as tame as in Sweden, where it's pretty well crushed, but much tamer than in America.' One sign of industry's sensitivity appeared in 1969 when American research (since much questioned) suggested that cyclamate sweeteners in food and soft drinks might be dangerous; the Labour government quickly banned cyclamates, which caused a loss to Unilever (the main user) of around a million pounds. Food manufacturers now live in some dread of the consumer militants, and the chairman of Birdseye James Parratt squawked in 1970: 'Ours is an honest and straight-dealing industry. We are quite justified in resenting any suggestions that are calculated to give the impression that we neither know nor care what our customers eat.'

The consumer organisations have harassed their enemy, but they have not yet mounted an effective counter-attack on a broad front: they have not found a propagandist comparable to Ralph Nader in America, and they have not begun to capture the mass media. Television, which is the scene of most of the victories of advertising, and where most of the battles of Omo and Daz were fought out, sees very little gunfire from 'consumerism'. The BBC, as the only sector of the mass media which is independent of advertising, should be well-placed to give honest information about travel, detergents or cars; but a short-lived programme, run jointly with the Consumers' Association, called *Choice*, collapsed from timidity; and the BBC motoring programmes are full of long-winded bores extolling the cars they have been lent by the manufacturers. When Panorama *did* expose the motor industry at the 1970 Motor Show it showed how much the BBC could do if it regarded itself as the medium of truthful consumer information, as a mass critic of mass advertising.

Perhaps the greatest challenge for consumer organisations— which has not yet been met—is to grapple with the nationalised industries which provide most of the country's services, and which affect the whole population. The miseries of the underground, the inhumanity of council estates, the inefficiencies of the Gas Board, should all be potentially vulnerable to the pressures of consumer opinion. As Des Wilson put it, before not taking over the Consumer Council:

> In his discomfort and frustration the commuter complains bitterly, but it is surprising how few know whom to blame, and direct their anger to where it can be felt. It is almost as though people believe that British Railways are a huge, monolithic, inhuman machine, without social or public responsibility, and there to be obeyed. But British Railways is run by people—people sitting in parliament, on committees, in offices, and people on the station platforms. They are employed to serve the public and should be accountable. They are get-at-able. They are vulnerable. They can be forced to face up to the realities of their inadequacy. The exploitation can be stopped . . .

Each of the nationalised industries has its Consultative Committee, supposed to serve as spokesmen for the consumers; but the members (absurdly) are appointed by the appropriate minister, as part of his overblown patronage, and they are not usually men who enjoy making a row. The committees are apt to be consulted at so late a stage that nothing, anyway, can be done. 'It's only by changing the management structure that you can change the nationalised industries,' says Goldman: 'You have to get consumers on the board, along with the managers and trade unions, so that they can influence decisions before it's too late.' *Which?* does not often venture into the nationalised industries, and when it *did* investigate Heathrow Airport, at the invitation of the Airports Authority, their findings were much too polite. The consumer organisations have followed the patterns of society as they exist, and they have concentrated on the minor shortcomings of private affluence, not the basic miseries of public squalor. It is only when the idea of the consumer is really widened, to include not just the middle-class comforts but the community at large, to embrace housing, hospitals, public transport or social services, that the consumer movements will have major political significance, and can challenge the world of advertising on its most vulnerable front: not for what it says, but for what it leaves out.

23

Arts and Leisure

The day is not far off when the economic problem will take the back seat where it belongs, and the arena of the heart and the head will be occupied or reoccupied, by our real problems—the problems of life and of human relations, of creation and behaviour and religion.

Lord Keynes, First Annual Report of the Arts Council, 1945–46.

As leisure becomes a more marketable commodity, so the mass media, which themselves take up many hours of people's spare time, are becoming increasingly involved in boosting other forms of leisure—whether urging their readers to rush off to Greece, to buy a fast car or to give a trendy cocktail party. Both advertising and editorial pages persuade their customers to connect leisure with spending; so that a leisure supplement or magazine, whose main object is advertising, will tend to avoid anything which suggests that 'the best things in life are free', and even sex—their obsessive theme—is associated with extravagance and spending. The world of free leisure, of parks, countryside, or, till recently, art galleries and museums, takes second place to the world of expensive leisure, obsessed with the acquisition of *things*.

The commercial interest is two-fold; to encourage people both to spend their time expensively, and to spend it in the same ways— to migrate *en masse* to the same holiday resorts, to buy the same records and books, to drink the same drinks, so that leisure can become a mass industry like any other. 'Leisure industries' have been booming, led by television and tourism, and including do-it-yourself shops, gardening centres, boat-builders or caravan companies. Many modern success stories, like Forte's snack-bars, Polycell do-it-yourself, or Pontin's holiday camps, come from the exploitation of the new leisure, and the money that goes with it. Big businesses conspire with each other to provide uniformity of habits, so that (for instance) BEA goes into partnership with Forte's hotels to provide packaged tours: 'Enjoy your flight with us, then spend the night with us.' One recent merger, between two big 'leisure companies', Grand Metropolitan Hotels and Mecca, means that a man can gamble with Ace fruit machines or City Tote betting shops, dance at a Mecca dance hall, eat at a Berni Inn and stay at the May Fair Hotel, all under the aegis of the same company. Advertising (as we have seen) is now concerned with portraying a whole way of life and leisure as much as a saleable object: the leisure-land they promise has an insistent sameness, as if all the make-believe people could be consolidated into a single clique of lecherous socialites; of Gordon's Gin people, Badedas people, Yo-ho-ho people. Eccentricity is tolerated and even encouraged, provided that it is exhibitionist and expensive—like drinking champagne in the bath.

There is total cross-purposes between this commercialised vision and the vision of leisure as a means of private relaxation and self-discovery. The British have always prided themselves on the eccentricity and individuality of their leisure pursuits; what George Orwell called the privateness of English life: 'we are a nation of flower-growers . . . of stamp-collectors, pigeon-fanciers, amateur carpenters, coupon-snippers, darts players, crossword puzzle fans'.[1] This private variety is still jealously guarded; anyone who doubts it need only look at the mass of hobby magazines, or watch customers at a do-it-yourself shop lovingly choosing their strip of two-by-four, or survey the tiny gardens, each one quite different, in back-to-back terraces. The fronts of houses proclaim the public face of their occupants, which can be subjected to all kinds of generalisation about class, status and background. The backs of houses proclaim the insistent escape from that pattern, with outhouses, bird-cages, chicken-runs or prize chrysanthemums.

Statistics confirm that the British lead a more domestic, eccentric life than other Europeans, revolving round the house and garden, rather than the apartment and the café. A European survey in 1969 revealed that 73 per cent of the British lived in two-storey buildings, and only 13 per cent lived in flats; while 56 per

[1] George Orwell, *The Lion and the Unicorn*, 1941.

cent of Italian families lived in flats, and 68 per cent of the Germans.[1] The British house provides a setting for British hobbies: 78 per cent of British households have gardens (more than any other European country except Luxembourg); and with gardens come lawn-mowers, pets, caravans and, inevitably, do-it-yourself. Britain is the greatest nation in Europe for handymen and potterers-about; it has the highest proportion of people who do their own wallpapering, painting, drilling and plumbing, and the highest proportion who buy second-hand cars. A broad picture unfolds of the British living a withdrawn and inarticulate life, rather like Harold Pinter's people, mowing lawns and painting walls, pampering pets, listening to music, knitting and watching television. If one wanted a symbol of what distinguishes contemporary British life from that of other countries it might well be a potting shed.

Three occupations prevail over all others—gardening, sport and (above all) watching television. A survey in 1965-6 commissioned by the Department of Education showed the young people spending much time in sports, dancing and cinema-going; as they grow older they turn to gardening and do-it-yourself; and retired people do still more gardening and walking. In new towns there is a special passion for gardening and (among women) for knitting. But television predominates everywhere. This table, from the survey,[2] shows 'the average proportion of leisure periods when each activity was cited as the chief leisure pursuit':

Activity	Men %	Women %
Television	23	23
Reading	5	9
Crafts and hobbies	4	17[3]
Decorating and house/vehicle maintenance	8	1
Gardening	12	7
Social activities	3	9
Drinking	3	1
Cinema and theatre	1	1
Non-physical games and misc. club activities	5	4

[1] 'A Survey of Europe Today': *Reader's Digest*, 1970. The findings are broadly in line with official statistics as published for instance by the Common Market's *Basic Statistics of the Community*.

[2] K. K. Sillitoe: *Planning for Leisure:* Table 8, page 41. HMSO 1969. The survey was based on a sample of 2,682.

[3] Knitting makes up the greater part of this category for women.

Activity	Men %	Women %
Physical recreation—		
(a) as participant	11	4
(b) as spectator	3	1
Excursions	7	7
Park visits and walks	5	5
Anything else	7	7
No answer or don't know	3	4

The private life of Britain is beyond the scope of this book, which is about power and institutions. But increasingly the 'problem of leisure'—as it is depressingly called—has had to become a responsibility of governments, local councils or companies. Because many pursuits depend on facilities which people cannot provide for themselves; because if everyone were allowed to follow their own bent, the countryside would be ruined; and because the use of leisure, particularly among young people, will affect the whole character of society. In the last few years the words quality of life, pollution, environment, or amenities, have become political catch-phrases, part of the stock-in-trade of manifestoes and election addresses.

The British always like to imagine themselves as specially insistent on leisure: they invented the word and the idea of the weekend and the long weekend. But the British are behind most of Europe in their annual holidays. The British trade unions have been notably uninterested in extra weeks' holidays; while the French workers, as long ago as 1936, demanded and got a three-weeks' holiday a year, which has now, in most French companies, been increased to four weeks. In Italy, the most holiday-conscious country in Europe, workers have a minimum of 29 to 47 days paid holiday a year, and even in Germany the minimum is between 25 and 37 compared to the 16–21 for Britain. Le weekend, il weekend, have become part of the language and thinking of the continent; and most continental countries have many more Bank Holidays and saint's days scattered through their year, so that they can take frequent long weekends, or 'make a bridge' to provide four-day holidays.

ARTS AND GOVERNMENT

Quite suddenly, all round the world, governments are at work on
policies to reshape the environment and to put new life into the arts.
Lord Eccles, October 1970.

Over the last two hundred years the people have gradually
gained access to the territory of the rich: parks, palaces, galleries
and estates have opened up. A great expansion in public amenities
—more spectacular than anything in our own time—came with the
Victorian zeal for improvement, helped by the Prince Consort and
the vast profits from the Great Exhibition, which financed the
cavernous South Kensington museums. The Victorian expansion
was made easier by the loot and wealth of the Empire and the ease
with which great treasures like the Elgin Marbles could be pinched.
Most of the great museums, in their present form, date back to the
Victorian age, or earlier: these are the biggest, with their estimated
annual cost in 1970–1, and their directors (most of whom are
appointed by the Trustees, though sometimes heavily influenced
by Whitehall):

British Museum	Sir John Wolfenden	£3.4 million
Natural History Museum	G. F. Clarionbull	£1.2 million
Science Museum	Sir David Follett	£0.7 million
Victoria and Albert Museum	Sir John Pope-Hennessy	£1.0 million
National Gallery	Martin Davies	£0.7 million
Tate Gallery	Sir Norman Reid	£0.4 million

Their possessions are still almost unequalled in their range and
value; but during this century the first enthusiasm for public
education has evaporated, and the museums have become
increasingly out of touch with the public. The funds for upkeep
and modernisation have been far too small to make the vast
Victorian premises attractive to a contemporary public. Superb
collections of Constables, Turners or Blakes are hidden away in
cellars or remote rooms, while avenues of ironwork and bits of
transplanted churches occupy acres of museum-land. The British
Museum complained bitterly when they were refused an extension
to their complex of buildings, which dominates Bloomsbury; while
their staff was already unable to cope with the existing acreage,
and wild cats had been reported roaming in the basements. Since
Victorian times a bureaucracy of curators has grown up on civil

429

service lines, divided like the army into officers and other ranks, with the 'keepers'—quite unlike the keepers at zoos—as the officer-class, jealously guarding their own territory.

The demarcation disputes between museums are often as bitter as those between trade unions, and can be equally against the public interest; in museums, as in other old corporations, the trustees and officials will protect their interests more narrow-mindedly and selfishly than they would dare to protect their own, and will refuse to co-operate in pooling or rationalising their resources. One Egyptian treasure, the Battlefield Palette, has its top part in the Ashmolean at Oxford, and the bottom half at the British Museum; neither side will collaborate to bring them together. The possessiveness of galleries has been increased by the huge inflation of prices of old masters in the auction rooms, which means that if pictures are loaned from the cellars, the cost of insurance can be prohibitive.

Some museums have tried to become more attractive and accessible to the general public. At the Victoria and Albert, Sir John Pope-Hennessy combines his fastidious scholarship with crowd-pleasing topical exhibitions, to rival those of the National Portrait Gallery and its young showman director Roy Strong, who advertises pop exhibitions for passers-by in Trafalgar Square. But most museums have an instinctive dread of showmanship and self-advertisement, so that a visitor can pass by the National Gallery every day on a bus without knowing what it is, or contains. And the very size of the buildings, like the size of Selfridges, is now a doubtful advantage. Many were built for the age of the railways, when British life was centralising on London, as the heart of the empire. Now in the age of the motor-car the concentration may be not a convenience, but a parking problem; and many of their treasures would be more fittingly displayed in the countryside where they came from—the Mildenhall treasures in Mildenhall, the Constables in the Stour Valley, or the Gainsboroughs in Bath. 'Satellite galleries' could be established in provincial centres, as Jack Lambert of the Arts Council has suggested, to house pictures borrowed in rotation from London collections; 'the thought of a few centralised institutions', he wrote in the *Sunday Times*, 'getting larger and larger, corridor stretching beyond corridor, rooms suffused with imitation daylight succeeding each other in desolating succession, is not to be borne.' But the demands to decentralise the London loot come up against all the entrenched interests of the keepers and curators, who are still pressing to extend their gloomy empires in South Kensington and Bloomsbury. Only a few museum men have shown much interest in creating new kinds of gallery: 'the whole future of museums,' Roy Strong has written, 'lies in their development as social centres relating them to the nascent cultural centres emerging in the regions . . . the Seventies are concerned with the grass roots of our existence and we should listen more seriously to what the public says, rather than turn inward and indulge in the cramping folly of museology.'

Governments have traditionally been wary of involving the taxpayer with paying for the arts. Outside Central London the provision of parks, galleries, museums or entertainment has been mainly the responsibility of local councils, which since 1948 have been allowed to levy up to 6d in the pound for entertainment (though they hardly ever do). But in the last six years, since the Labour Government came to power, there has been a sudden increase. In 1969–70 the government spent altogether £17 million under the general category of the arts, including three million on preserving historic monuments, and seven million on running the national museums and galleries. The biggest slice of spending now goes to a body which is only twenty-four years old, the Arts Council; and the development of this curious body since the last war marks a significant extension of the notion of government patronage. Its precursor, the Council for the Encouragement of Music and the Arts (CEMA), was set up, like so many new government bodies, during the war, and was enlarged into the Arts Council in 1946; but its grant was only very slowly increased, reaching £3 million in 1964–5. The Labour Party was committed to expand it, and Harold Wilson appointed as minister in charge of the arts Jennie Lee, the widow of Aneurin Bevan and the *grande dame* of Socialism, who had a special hold on the conscience of the new cabinet. Her own tastes were not exactly adventurous; she enjoyed brassbands and mass rallies, and sometimes seemed to see culture more as an extension of the Health Service, a kind of therapeutic activity to keep people out of trouble, than as a profound creative experience. But she admired artists and enjoyed their company, and her inexperience in the arts was welcome to many of them, who would have been alarmed by any governmental direction. She was adept, above all, at pressing for money; throughout the economic crises which followed, the grant to the Arts Council increased, so that by the year 1970 it had reached £8.2 million.

The Conservatives, in the meantime, were brewing up a very different philosophy about the arts, which burst suddenly on the public in 1970, personified by the new Minister for the Arts, Lord Eccles. This proud, controversial man has always attracted special abuse; his immaculate appearance, his brusqueness and his tactless remarks have antagonised Tories as much as Socialists. His unassailable confidence may come partly from his fashionable-medical background, partly from his Christian beliefs (he has written a book on *Half-way to Faith*): his father was a Presbyterian Harley Street surgeon, and he married the daughter of the Queen's physician. After Winchester and Oxford, he made a fortune in the city, went into parliament and became probably the most effective post-war Minister of Education. He enjoys administration, with a steely concentration of purpose; and he has in an extreme form the characteristic of many of the New Tories, of not needing to be *liked*. He moved into his new job deliberately keeping his distance; he established his headquarters in a huge house in Belgrave Square, and began delivering occasional broadsides. The main gist of his message was at first sight surprising from someone who was himself a fastidious connoisseur; it was that the arts must be opened up to the people, that government subsidies should be extended to crafts, like marquetry or weaving, that the distinction between professionals and amateurs should be broken down. 'Beware of the bearded men,' he said in August 1970, 'who say that only two or three out of a hundred of us can understand fine art.' But at the same time Eccles was a very convinced Tory; he believed in money as a criterion of success, and thought pleasures were more appreciated for being paid for (what his critics call 'the prostitute principle').

Eccles' first bombshell on coming into office was to announce that the eighteen nationally-subsidised galleries would for the first time impose entrance charges. The curators and trustees were rather slow to fight back, and they were not united in their attitude; but they gradually woke up to the threat. The Tate Gallery, the most democratically-minded of them, wrote to the prime minister, 'that this decision is entirely contrary to the spirit which has guided these great institutions for generations'. Mass petitions were signed, and a new pressure-group called National Heritage, founded by a publisher, John Letts, was pledged to defend the consumers' interest in museums; it was supported by the most enterprising curators, including Roy Strong, Francis Cheetham of Norwich Castle, and John Hayes of the London Museum. After loud protests, the gallery charges went through; the government in return for admission charges of 10p would pay an extra £2 million a year for modernising museums. It was (I believe) a tragedy that the principle of free public amenities should be breached; but the charges may have helped to wake up the museums. There was some sad truth in Eccles' statement in the Lords, that 'the mere proposal to introduce charges had uncorked a concern for the national museums far greater than all the propaganda their trustees and directors had ever made in the past'.

LORD GOODMAN

Lord Eccles' main concern was with the chief government patron, the Arts Council; and here his policies soon proved in conflict with the chairman of the Council who had transformed it during his occupancy over the previous six years—the astonishing Lord Goodman. Lord Goodman calls for a special digression from anyone concerned with analysing the British establishment. He is a phenomenon not only interesting in himself, but throwing light on the whole power-structure; and he crops up in many chapters (more than anyone else) of this book—in the Law, in Corporations, in the Press, in the City. For he is a kind of universal joint, always able to join one bit of scaffolding to another; a broker who understands better than anyone how to conciliate between two sides. He is primarily a very shrewd lawyer, in the American rather than the British pattern, who has become indispensable as an adviser and settler of disputes, cajoling, defining and settling. But he has come to be a conciliator not only between people but between institutions, and hence as a kind of benign prophet of the neo-capitalist consensus.

His presence in any gathering is unmistakable. He is large and hirsute, shaped like something between a bear and a gorilla, with an expressive face that seems lost in the middle of an indefinite head and thick black eyebrows coming half-way round his dark eyes. When he sits down in a chair, it is hard not to catch one's breath. Encountering him is like encountering a physical object, a great rock or tree; and from the middle of it there emerges a voice which is equally unique, a kind of soft growl, firm but subtle, and infinitely articulate, full of elaborate ironies, parentheses, double negatives and understatements, as if it came from the Delphic oracle itself. He talks of the world of power with tolerant amusement, so that he seems to be right outside the arena, simply enjoying a spectator sport. But he is himself in the middle of it; and the ability to keep his detachment in the midst of the fray is a large ingredient of his success and his strength.

For years Goodman was a back-room lawyer whose talents were only known to professionals and friends. He came from a prosperous Jewish family, took a double first in law at Cambridge, and joined the solicitors' firm of Rubinstein, Nash, which specialises in literary libels. In the war he became quartermaster-sergeant in an anti-aircraft battery, where he first showed his genius for arranging the impossible. He went back to law, and in 1954 set up his own solicitors' firm, with some millionaire clients. He became increasingly useful as a lawyer, specialising in libels, to politicians; in 1957 he won spectacular damages for three Labour leaders—Bevan, Crossman and Morgan Phillips—against *The Spectator*, who accused them of drunkenness in Venice. With the coming of commercial television, he proved adept at setting up syndicates for TV stations ('there's been nothing like it since Charles II sold patents for soap').

He was still not a public figure and he refused to be photographed. It was not till Harold Wilson came to power in 1964 that he hit the headlines. At first he was 'Mr. X' who settled the commercial television strike, but by the next year he was transformed with a few waves of Wilson's wand into Baron Goodman, Chairman of the Arts Council, and Lord High Everything-Else for the new government. From then on he appeared much more openly as the chief trouble-shooter; and he even emerged from his shyness to be a gruff kind of social lion. 'Send for Lord Goodman' became the first thought of any top person in difficulties; and often it seemed that the mere mention of his name would make the other side collapse. It was part of Goodman's approach that there was nothing that could not be settled between intelligent men; and he took this to its extreme when in 1968 he flew out to Rhodesia (with Sir Max Aitken) to try to reach a settlement between Ian Smith and Harold Wilson.

He began with the ear of the prime minister; and the more important he became in one province, the more useful he was in others as a crossing; he hurried from one to the other, always late: 'the late Lord Goodman'. He was asked to rescue British Lion, the film distributors, and took it over as chairman, with his own large block of shares; he became chairman of *The Observer*, and then chairman of the Newspaper Publishers' Association, leading the negotiations which ended the strike in June 1970; he became a director of the Industrial Reorganisation Corporation, the Labour government's rescue-operation for industry; and he also went into partnership with the ex-director of it, Ronald Grierson, in a consultancy advising industrial companies. Because he was the friend and legal adviser of Harold Wilson, it was widely assumed that he was a convinced Labour supporter; but he sat on the cross-benches of the House of Lords, and he was sometimes bitterly critical of Wilson's policy, particularly on Biafra. And when the Conservatives came to power in 1970, it soon turned out that he had first met the new prime minister when Heath was seventeen. 'I'm not particularly concerned,' he said on television soon afterwards, 'with the colour of the government.'

He moves in a world of big money, and to his fixing activities he adds a great role as a fund-raiser: he can astonish visitors who need money for good causes by picking up a telephone, exchanging a few words with a very rich man, and extracting a few thousand pounds on the spot; so that 'Goody' can be a kind of fairy-god-mother to the poor as well as the rich. He understands very thoroughly the nature of the fund-raising equation—the bringing-together of millionaires who want public recognition with worthy men who need money—and his own rock-like presence serves as a neutral meeting-place, making both sides feel better. Money is both his skill and his limitation; for, like many businessmen, he sometimes seems to assume that money can do anything.

ARTS COUNCIL

Goodman brought his Midas touch very quickly to the Arts Council, working closely with Jennie Lee. He moved the head-quarters from a small palazzo in St. James's Square to the former *Hotel Splendide* in Piccadilly. He hugely stepped up the spending on music. He appointed a succession of committees to allocate funds, to investigate theatre, literature, obscenity or 'new activities'. He arranged for the Sadler's Wells Opera to move into the Coliseum Theatre in the West End. He raised money to move the Institute of Contemporary Arts, a small avant-garde centre, into big new premises in The Mall (an example, it turned out, of the occasional deadness of the Midas touch; for the ICA in its translation to grandeur lost much of its intimacy). He presided over the Council with benign calm, and generated euphoria. 'If the limitless faith of a Chairman of the Arts Council should ever flag,' he said in his report on the year 1969, 'recommend to him a simple remedy—travel to other places which do not have an Arts Council and observe how much better we order things here . . . I believe that the last thirty years in this country have demonstrated a profound social change. Within our society there is now a widespread feeling that the provision of drama and music and painting and all culture in its broadest sense is no longer to be regarded as a privilege for the few, but is the democratic right of the whole community . . .'

The Arts Council had certainly contributed something towards that social change; but there was a tendency towards self-congratulation between their members; and they sometimes spoke as if they were not only the financiers and impresarios of the Arts, but the Muses themselves. They seemed to prefer communicating with each other to communicating with the public, and they were inclined to regard publicity as vulgar or corrupting; so that they have done little to break down the traditional secrecy of museums, or to proclaim their exhibitions to a wider public. London has no great posters hanging from flagpoles to proclaim its exhibitions and attractions, as Paris has: and the Hayward Gallery, the secret concrete pile on the South Bank which houses Arts Council exhibitions, is unknown to most Londoners. The Council itself, though high-minded and cultivated, lacked the aggressive spirit towards popularising and promotion. These were they in June 1971:

Lord Goodman (Chairman)—*passim*
Sir John Witt (Vice-Chairman)—artistic solicitor
Michael Astor—millionaire art-collector
Richard Attenborough—actor, film producer
Frederic R. Cox—ex Principal, Royal Manchester School of Music
Colonel William Crawshay—Welsh gentleman, art collector
Constance Cummings—actress
Cedric Thorpe Davie—Reader of Music, St. Andrew's University
Lady Antonia Fraser—writer and hostess
Lawrence Gowing—Professor of Fine Art, Leeds
Peter Hall—director and impresario

Intimate Opera at Eltham

Earl of Harewood—musicologist, Queen's cousin
Hugh Jenkins—Labour MP and trade unionist
Frank Kermode—Professor of English Literature
J. W. Lambert—Literary Editor, *Sunday Times*
Sir Joseph Lockwood—Chairman, Electrical and Musical Industries
Dr. Alun Oldfield-Davies—Welsh broadcaster
Sir John Pope-Hennessy—Director of Victoria and Albert Museum
Lewis Robertson—Dundee industrialist
George Singleton—Glasgow cinema-owner

The Council distributes largesse in all directions, ranging from nine orchestras, to scores of small societies, magazines, repertories and galleries; the 1969 benefactions included £60 to the Association of Polish Artists in Great Britain, £60 to the Truro and District Arts Society, £17 to the Little Festival of Poetry at Cley-next-the-Sea, £30 to the Intimate Opera Club at Eltham, £40 to the Ilkley Art Club, and £15 to the Welland Valley Art Society. The Council has steadily increased the proportion of its funds spent on regional centres, subsidising art, drama and music. But the balance is still unequal, between a few extravagant show-pieces, subsidised at colossal expense, and the mass of small ventures, kept going at a minimum level. In drama nearly two million pounds a year is spent in England on subsidising sixty-seven different theatre companies; but a quarter of that is spent on two companies, the National Theatre and the Royal Shakespeare Company, both with reputations for reckless spending. In spite of the increases in the provinces, nearly a third of the Arts Council money is still given to two pursuits associated with a small minority of high bourgeois audiences: Opera and Ballet. The opera-houses raise, in an extreme form, the problem of how far the tax-payers can be called on to subsidise minority tastes.

To go to the Covent Garden Opera, in the midst of the jumble of fruit markets and vegetable stalls, is like a sudden flash-back into the Victorian world of Soames Forsyte, as if the audience had been deep-frozen under the medallion of the young Queen Victoria, when the Opera House was first built. In these surroundings, it is odd to remember that the state pays on average half the cost of a seat. Boxes and seats in the stalls are reserved for great companies and bankers at only twenty per cent more than the normal price: there is still a special 'Bedford Box' reserved for the ground landlords, who get it as part of the rent; and the Royal Box (since the Royal Family cannot stand opera) is usually occupied by one of the governors with a group of friends who are supplied with sumptuous supper in the dining-room behind it. The thirteen governors, with perhaps three exceptions, might all have come from the same Kensington drawing-room; at least one is thought to be tone deaf. They include two earls, at least three millionaires, Lord Robbins and Lord Annan. This curious oligarchy reflects the confusion which has always surrounded opera: it is so expensive, so grand, so associated with spectacle on both sides of the curtain, that there has always been a mixture of motives among opera-goers.

The Arts Council subsidy to Covent Garden, of one and a quarter millions a year, is big enough to infuriate other claimants, but not big enough to reduce the price of seats to a level which ordinary people can afford; and the Opera House still exudes an atmosphere of inaccessibility and elitism. The haughty style of the place can easily demoralise any newcomer, and the opera synopses are written in the incomprehensible language of opera buffs. A move towards popularising was taken when the Sadler's Wells Company shifted from the Angel to the Edwardian light-opera palace, the Coliseum, which is cheaper and less intimidating than the Garden. But the Coliseum feels compelled to compete with its superior predecessor half a mile away, with more expensive voices and more lavish productions.

Much of the high cost of opera stems from the fact that it has become a great international status symbol, requiring, above all, immense fees for top voices—the fragile commodity on which the whole business is based. Covent Garden has to compete with the Metropolitan in New York or La Scala in Milan, who have more wealthy patrons and still greater backing: in opera, as with BOAC pilots or corporation managers, internationalism breeds its own elite. Covent Garden can fairly claim (as it repeatedly does) to be one of the finest opera houses and companies in the world: it can point to the Paris Opera—that magnificent forlorn palace— as an example of Britain's superiority in managing this delicate art. But the fact that three million pounds a year is pumped into this already-rich metropolitan milieu, while so comparatively little is being spent in the provinces or on more popular arts, remains an embarrassment in the face of the taxpayer.

A world away from this chandeliered region, the Arts Council periodically tries to come to terms with the avant-garde, and with the obscure subterranean networks of experiments, happenings, arts laboratories, way-out festivals and freak-outs, loosely known as the Underground. The complexities of this world and its searchings for self-expression are too extensive to be recorded here; some clues to the ramifications can be picked up from the BIT Information Service in London, or the Arts Labs news letter, which conveys the casual flavour of international coming and going, and announces such events as (for instance) the South-West Festival Gathering at St. Ives, with

FESTIVALCARNIVALFAIRSJUBILEEGATHERINGSMASQUE
HAPPENINGLIGHTSHOWTHEATRESCULPTUREEXPERI-
MENTSEVENTS&AUDIENCEPARTICIPATIONDANCING
PUNCH&JUDYENVIRONMENTSNEWSOUNDSCOMEDY
KINETICARTPROCESSIONS&CYBERNETICSFANTASYSUR-
PRISESEXTRAVAGANZAMYSTERIESFARCENEWEXPERI-
ENCECONTRASTGOGOINNOVATIONFUNBALLETBALLOONS
BRASSBANDSJAZZJIVESWINGINGFOLKMUSICSTREET
THEATREFILMARTEXHIBITIONSSUBLIMESOUNDSPOETRY
MIMECONCERTCABARETSPOPMUSICSURPRISECINE
MAKITES

It has been part of Lord Goodman's philosophy that the Council should not try to impose its own pattern on the young: 'It is of the greatest importance that we should not expect them to adopt standards which are our own standards.' But to connect up with the underground was not an easy task, and some idea of the difficulties emerged after the setting-up of a 'New Activities Committee'. The first committee had an improbable chairman, Sir Edward Boyle, and included the tycoon Sir Joseph Lockwood, the head of the giant record company EMI, and the art-collector, Michael Astor. Rather rashly, the committee in December 1968 invited some 'assorted freaks', including the staff of *Circuit* magazine (which gets £225 a year from the Arts Council), to give evidence to them at the House of Commons, and asked them vague questions about mixed media and happenings. The freaks were appalled at the committee's ignorance (one of them, the poet Jeff Nuttall, told them that they all came from 'the paunch belt'), and the next day they formed their own angry organisation called Friends of the Arts Council Co-operative, or FACOP, which held weekly meetings to build up a case against the Arts Council. A few months later six members of FACOP invaded a meeting of the committee to present the case (Lockwood lost his temper, but Boyle seemed to enjoy it) and went on to hold a national conference of artists at St. Katherine's Docks—the then newly-taken-over centre for avant-garde painters—to 'create the beginnings of a political consciousness among artists'. In the meantime another New Activities Committee had been formed, with Michael Astor as its chairman; and Astor soon succeeded in recruiting six members of FACOP to it—to the fury of *Circuit*, who accused him of repressive tolerance. 'The Arts Council of Great Britain,' said *Circuit*, 'disguises itself as the giver (if not the author) of all good things, but it is in fact an essential member of Mammon. It is one of the great organs of cultural digestion; amoeba-like, it extends a pseudopod on either side of "new activities", not to embrace, but to incorporate them.' FACOP insisted that there should be a panel elected by the artists themselves; and later five of them marched into Astor's committee to present applications for grants, wearing dunces' hats and standing in the corners of the room. The committee later accepted most of their applications, which still further annoyed the rebels. 'On the whole,' concluded the revolutionary paper *Black Dwarf*, 'the first round of the battle with the Arts Council has been won by the bureaucrats.'

The attitude of Lord Eccles to this wide-ranging patronage of the Arts Council was awaited with some anxiety in the *Hotel Splendide*. It was soon clear that he and Lord Goodman had very different approaches. But it was not a simple conflict between left and right; Eccles in his own way insisted on art for the people, and wanted to break out of the circle of professionals. 'I don't think art is satisfactory if it is a mutual aid society,' he said, and again: 'The better the professional artists are supported from the centre, the more likely a gulf is to open between them and the general public, so that 2 per cent of the population enjoy subtle, disturbing and often fine works which are incomprehensible to the remaining 98 per cent.' There was a large element of *de haut en bas* in Eccles' attitudes to popularising arts, and a suggestion of moral paternalism; the first major clash came when Eccles complained that it was an abuse of public money to make it available 'to finance works which affront the religious beliefs or outrage the sense of decency of a large body of the rate-payers'; Lord Goodman, in the House of Lords, replied that the problem was trifling and 'almost insignificant'. But the Arts Council, with its distaste for publicity and its tendency towards metropolitan self-congratulation, was vulnerable to Eccles' attacks: and at the same time he was able to show his earnest by raising the grant in 1971 by £2.6 million—more than it had gone up under four years of the Labour government.

LEISURE AND THE WORKERS

With help from the Arts Council, Britain has become a less philistine country; classical music has boomed, art galleries have doubled their attendance in ten years, repertories have grown up in the provinces and nearly every county has its annual festival. But this extension of interest in the arts and in 'creative leisure' still only affects a small fraction of the British people; even the denizens of the Underground, though they look proletarian and impoverished, usually turn out to be very middle-class in origins. The mass of the population has been very little affected by the cultural boom. There are more cars, which give more opportunity to reach the countryside; more gardens; more sports grounds; more holidays abroad. But the weekly pattern of life remains, in most parts of Britain, monotonous in its conformity; cinemas have closed (there are now only 1,600 cinemas, compared to 4,700 in 1946) to give way to television; greyhound racing has declined in favour of bingo; gambling in one form or another remains almost as dominant as ever in the British way of life: in 1968 the Jockey Club published the Benson Report which reckoned that the annual turnover for horserace betting was £850 million.

There have been some brave attempts to project the arts on a grand scale into working-class life. In 1960 the Trades Union Congress passed a resolution, number 42, calling for greater participation by unions in cultural activities, to improve the quality of life; and the playwright Arnold Wesker took up the resolution and proclaimed a 'Centre 42', to be a prototype place to provide art for the people. A small outfit was formed, which put on a few trade union festivals and cabarets; but the trade unions' subsidy never materialised, and the Centre never actually happened. In 1962 Wesker, with the help of a friendly millionaire, got the lease of a magnificent engine-shed in Chalk Farm called the Round House which was to house Centre 42: but neither the TUC nor the Arts Council was interested in it, and Wesker—a difficult idealist—insisted that the Centre should provide only the best, with no concessions to 'the penalty of ignorance'. Eventually some money was raised with the help of Jennie Lee to keep the Round House going, and the amazing building attracted pop groups and exotic theatrical productions, like Nicol Williamson's *Hamlet* and Kenneth Tynan's *Oh! Calcutta!*; which helped to pay for it. But the Round House had lost any special connotations with

Art for the People; and a final blow to Wesker's idealism was delivered in 1970 when it was announced (without Wesker having been consulted) that a luxury hotel was to be built next to the Round House, on part of the trust's land.

Another bold venture was the special protégé of Jennie Lee after her appointment; it was a plan to reorganise six thousand acres of London land—almost as much as the existing open space in London—along the Lea River, a kind of arse-hole of London which flows down the East End of London into the Thames, among factories, sewage farms and gasworks. A bold plan for parks, gardens, and lakes along twenty miles of the river had been prepared in 1963 by the Civic Trust, with a great Fun Palace as its centre-piece where people would be allowed to do almost anything; and the Fun Palace was taken up with special enthusiasm by the new Labour government. But the Arts Council were wary of the showmanship of Joan Littlewood and her friends: and the whole scheme depended on the approval and co-ordination of twenty-nine local authorities, who very soon caused so much difficulty that it had to be dropped. It is a recurring difficulty in improving the British 'quality of life' that so much of the opportunity is in the hands of the local authorities who, though closer to the people, are nearly always less imaginative and far-sighted than the central government. The River Lea, as desolate as ever, is a monument to their intransigence.

The improvement in the 'quality of life' for most of the population over the past two decades has been slender; and the commercialisation of leisure has encouraged mass spectator sports, mass holiday camps, mass camping and the concentration of holidays at the peak seasons. Against the small efforts to bring art or music to the masses must be set the vast and pervasive influence of the dominant leisure activity, watching television: for in the last twenty years the small screen has become the central factor in nearly all people's spare time. Television takes up an average of twenty-three per cent of people's leisure hours throughout the year; ninety-four per cent of British homes have television sets, and British families on average watch television for eighteen hours a week—far more than any other European country, and twice as much as Belgium, Italy or Sweden.[1] Television not only occupies this huge chunk of people's lives, it also affects other

[1] See *Planning for Leisure*, HMSO, 1969 and 'A Survey of Europe Today', *Reader's Digest*, 1970.

leisure activities, generating sudden tastes for fashions, sports or books. If the BBC serialises a book its sales will leap ahead: when they put on *The Forsyte Saga* (which had been out of print) Penguins sold half a million copies of the books. If it puts on an opera, it can be watched (as *Aida* was) by a million people, enough to fill Covent Garden for a year and a half: as Lord Eccles has said, 'the millions watching television could not be squeezed into all the theatres of the world'. The influence of the Arts Council, the Underground, concerts and theatres on the bulk of people is tiny compared to the overwhelming influence of the three television channels; and the nine million pounds a year disposed of by Lord Goodman is small compared to the 80 million disposed of each year by Lord Hill of the BBC. While Lord Goodman and Lord Eccles, in their very different ways, try to improve and uphold the quality of leisure, Lord Hill and his men are preoccupied by appealing to the lowest common denominator of their mass audiences.

24

Television

Through talk we tamed kings, restrained tyrants, averted revolution and ultimately reflected public needs in such a way as to help shape public policy. In this sense, the BBC has assumed some of the role of parliament. It is the current talking shop, the national town meeting of the air, the village council. But access to it is strictly limited. Admission is by ticket only. It is just not enough . . .

Anthony Wedgwood Benn: October 1968.

Since TV transmissions first began in the thirties, the full effects of the small screen have only slowly shown themselves. At first the new invention was seen as a hybrid of other technologies—newspapers, films and radio. Its early rulers were confident that they could control it, without being controlled by it. The arrival of television was so abrupt, like a transplant, that its relationships with society, and with other institutions, were unpredictable. It is only in the last decade that the full consequences of the graft have become clear; it is not an extra limb so much as an addition to the nervous system, which makes everything else not only look different, but behave differently. Many parts of this book have been affected by this new organ: politics, parliament, the prime minister, the Press or the palace—they have all found themselves, confronting not a straightforward intruder, but a subterranean force. Television can no longer be seen as an extension to parliament, an additional platform for politicians; it has become a kind of parliament itself, in many ways more wide-ranging and relevant than the real one. It no longer takes over the newspapers' techniques; it can make its own news, and provide its own values. It is not just a purveyor of ideas and incentives about leisure and life; it makes up, by itself, a large slice of nearly everyone's leisure. Its pervasiveness makes the effects of TV hard to analyse and pin down, and a very awkward study for academics; 'There is a vast gulf,' wrote two recent investigators, 'between what we know about the political impact of television and what television is often supposed to have done to Britain's political life.'[1]

That television surrounds us, as if it were society itself (as for some old people it is) makes it often hard to remember that it is a deliberate pageant, a succession of images which are worked out and controlled by a given number of people; and that it can be improved or worsened by the efforts of individuals, or if necessary by act of parliament. The similarity of the three TV channels, their apparent common notions of 'good television', radiate the impression that television-land is a real territory, where everyone has the same voices, glib questions and answers, and where professors, comedians and bishops meet quite naturally together. The huge omissions of television, in the fields of culture, education or serious discussion, are apt to be forgotten by the viewer who watches television as if it were there like the weather, or (to use the current phrase) like electronic wallpaper. The gap between what television is, and what it could be, is only beginning to become a major grievance. The awareness of the power of the medium is now generating a real crisis of conscience among the practitioners; so that television—more perhaps than any other institution—is faced with the problem of participation, and has become a battleground of ideas about democratic control.

BBC

I believe that the success of a business depends on one man.
Lord Reith.

The revolution in broadcasting can be traced through the transformation of the BBC from an authoritarian institution to a mass-minded competitor. Its thirty-year monopoly, from the royal charter of 1927, seemed for most of that time as inevitable as that of the air force, and it acquired its own massive character. It has some claim to be the first public corporation, for largely through the personality of J. C. W. Reith it succeeded in wresting itself away from the control of the Post Office, its nominal master, to

[1] J. G. Blumler and D. McQuail: *Television in Politics, Its Uses and Influences,* chapter 13.

become a separate organism, responsible to parliament only, who renewed its charter every five years. The BBC had none of the anonymity and apparent headlessness of later nationalised industries, for its whole personality revolved round Reith. He understood well enough that the new corporation's posture of independence depended (like that of the universities) on not exercising that independence too far; and under him the BBC acquired that reverent attitude to British institutions—particularly the monarchy—which made it the most visible and disliked symbol of the Establishment. The Reithian picture of the role of the BBC might be summed up by the grandiloquent inscription that still adorns the entrance-hall at Broadcasting House:

THIS TEMPLE OF THE ARTS AND MUSES IS DEDICATED
TO ALMIGHTY GOD
BY THE FIRST GOVERNORS
IN THE YEAR OF OUR LORD 1931
JOHN REITH BEING DIRECTOR-GENERAL
AND THEY PRAY THAT THE GOOD SEED SOWN
MAY BRING FORTH GOOD HARVESTS
THAT ALL THINGS FOUL OR HOSTILE TO PEACE
MAY BE BANISHED HENCE
AND THAT THE PEOPLE INCLINING THEIR EAR
TO WHATSOEVER THINGS ARE LOVELY AND HONEST
WHATSOEVER THINGS ARE OF GOOD REPORT
MAY TREAD THE PATH OF VIRTUE
AND OF WISDOM

Television, by its sheer complexity and wildness, made it impossible for any single Reith to control it, even if there had been such a man. The old hierarchy of stately 'sound men' continued to appear to run the Corporation from Broadcasting House, the Temple of the Arts and Muses; but a huge new centre was growing up round Shepherd's Bush, which many of the old administrators were terrified of. Hard-swearing young producers, Welsh, Irish or Australian, yelled across the sets with violent jargon, supported by pretty and wide-eyed girls; impresarios, full of the exuberant insincerity of show-business, moved in from films, music-hall or theatre. An atmosphere of youthful extravagance spread through Shepherd's Bush: it was a blend of Fleet Street and Showbiz, quite opposite to the old puritanism of Broadcasting House. TV teams were flown round the world; fleets of cars raced round London every night, picking up celebrities; the news teams cultivated abrasive techniques and shock tactics, descending on

stately institutions with menacing questions. The separate programmes—Tonight, Panorama, Twenty-four Hours, Nationwide
—became distinct empires, competing ferociously with each other,
and only united in opposition to their would-be controllers. The
Shepherd's Bush ghetto became increasingly self-sufficient and
cut off from London, and ordinary people visiting could soon
be intimidated or absorbed by the green-room talk. BBC canteens, BBC restaurants, BBC bars, all buzzed with talk about
last night's shows; and the whole apparatus of cameras, arc-
lights, earphones and monitor screens conspired to turn the
studios in on themselves, like halls of mirrors. The more sensitive
producers were alarmed by their own power: politicians would
travel hundreds of miles to appear on their programmes, and suck
up with Christian names to get on the right side of them. Any
complaints from the outside world could usually be bought off
with an offer to appear on the screen. Faced with the young turks,
the old mandarins of the corporation had to control them as best
they could with budgets, auditors and periodic edicts.

In those first rip-roaring years, money was no great problem;
the BBC lived off the television licence, of £4 a year, and as
the numbers of sets multiplied, so their income increased without
effort. The coming of commercial TV, by doubling the sets,
doubled the money. Staff, salaries and buildings expanded to use
up the income. But as the number of television sets reached
saturation point in the mid-sixties, so the income stopped expanding, while costs continued to go up. By 1967 the BBC found itself,
for the first time in its life, in the red. That simple fact had huge
political repercussions; for the increase in licence fees could only
be sanctioned by the government, and the government, as it
happened, was longing to step in.

CHAIRMEN AND DIRECTORS

The formal rulers of BBC television and radio are a board of
governors with a chairman at their head, who meet once a month
to supervise the executive head, the Director-General. The
governors are chosen for five-year terms by the Postmaster-
General (often influenced by the prime minister, if he so wishes),
on the amateur principle, as representatives of the public, from
familiar areas of the Establishment. These were they in 1970:

447

Lord Hill (Chairman)—ex-cabinet minister
Lord Fulton (Vice-Chairman)—ex vice-chancellor
Glanmor Williams—(Welsh) professor of history
Lady Baird—(Scots) social worker
Lord Dunleath—(Irish) landowner
Sir Ralph Murray—ex-ambassador
Sir Robert Bellinger—ex-Lord Mayor of London
Tom Jackson—trade union leader
Paul N. Wilson—engineer
Dame Mary Green—headmistress
Sir Hugh Greene—ex-Director-General of BBC

The ignorance of the medium of most governors limits their effectiveness, and the real balance of power is usually between the chairman and the D-G. The chairman's powers are very undefined. For the first forty years of the corporation's existence, the director-general was the almost undisputed boss, on the pattern established by Lord Reith; he was succeeded by weaker men, but the chairman was never dominant, and when Sir Hugh Greene was appointed director-general in 1960 at the age of only fifty-one it was thought to be a special victory for the autonomy of the BBC. Greene was the first head to come from inside the corporation; and he enjoyed his apparent independence, deliberately breaking down the BBC's associations with the Establishment with more adventurous programmes, including the short-lived satire shows. 'It's always been my belief,' he told me in 1964, 'that the BBC should not be part of the Establishment—or Establishments—but that it should be looking at the various powers-that-be with an enquiring, a critical, and sometimes a satirical eye.' The chairman, Lord Normanbrook, a former head of the Civil Service, was more conscientious than many of his predecessors, and sometimes put his foot down (as when he stopped Panorama from showing an interview with Ian Smith of Rhodesia). But Normanbrook was impervious to the pressures of politicians, and he was not popular with the Labour government.

Then, in June 1967, Lord Normanbrook died, and after an expectant interval his successor was announced as Lord Hill, who for the previous four years had been the chairman of the Independent Television Authority. Few appointments in the past decade have caused such a furore. 'It was,' remarked David Attenborough, the head of BBC 2, 'as if Rommel had been put in charge of the Eighth Army.' Not only was Harold Wilson, by shifting the same man from the commercial service to the BBC, implying that there was no real difference in their characters; he was also, as it soon transpired, determined to bring the BBC to heel. Hill himself was the kind of elemental politician that the BBC had never experienced. His tough, stocky shape, like a boxer's; his rubbery face, encased in huge glasses; his earthy and plausible voice; they all proclaimed that here was a politician's politician, a man who understood the crude roots of power. He came from a humble home in Islington, and began as a bumptious medical student at Cambridge; but from medicine he turned to medical politics, becoming secretary of the British Medical Association and broadcasting as the Radio Doctor, growling about bowels and constipation. He was persuaded by Beaverbrook to go into Tory politics, and after he got into parliament in 1950 he became a useful public relations expert, representing the democratic, proletarian face of the Tories. By 1957 he had mysteriously arrived in Macmillan's cabinet, in charge of public relations, but he never revealed any clear political ideas, even in his autobiography, *Both Sides of the Hill*. When he arrived at the BBC he knew that he carried a very powerful lever. The BBC was broke, and desperately needed to increase its licence fee; only he, Hill, could achieve that for it.

Hill's appointment was greeted with horror by the heads of the BBC; Greene thought of resigning immediately, but he was dissuaded by his colleagues. Hill presented himself as just another part-time chairman, in the old tradition; and in fact he had another lucrative job as chairman of Laporte Chemicals. But he soon began to throw his weight about; as one of the angry directors later put it: 'The bland progress towards executive chairmanship and gubernatorial power continued.'[1] Hill encouraged his fellow-governors to take firmer stands, and while several of the directors were junketing in New Zealand he prepared a declaration of intent called 'Broadcasting and the Public Mood'. He strengthened his own secretariat, paid impromptu visits to the studios, held his own dinner parties at Television Centre. He may not, in fact, have been stronger as a chairman than his predecessors; but he liked to show his strength publicly, and in doing so changed the whole style of the corporation. Greene was clearly unhappy at this usurpation, but not in the mood to fight. In July 1968 he finally announced that he was resigning as

[1] Kenneth Adam: 'Takeover at the BBC', *Sunday Times*, March 9, 1969; a vivid, vitriolic account of Hill's arrival and the author's premature retirement.

director-general and—an unprecedented sidestep—becoming a governor.

As Greene's successor, Hill and his colleagues chose Charles Curran, another man from inside the corporation, but of a more bureaucratic kind. Curran has insisted repeatedly that the director-general's status has not changed, and he often appears quite a formidable defender. He is a tall Catholic Irishman, the son of an Indian Army officer, a weekend rugger referee. Like Greene, he has spent most of his career—except for a spell with *Fishing News*—in the BBC. But he has climbed up as an administrator, not as a producer; he became the secretary at the age of only forty-two, then director of external broadcasting, then director-general at forty-six—the youngest since Reith. But in his quick rise to the top he has had little to do with television. He seems happiest when talking about management, licences or the experiences of being McKinseyised (those arch-managers, McKinseys, were called in to reorganise the BBC). Certainly anyone who took over the director-generalship would have had to face huge problems of managing 25,000 people with mounting costs and limited revenue, against a background of political discontent both from the right and the left. 'The BBC happened because of a kind of institutional accident,' Curran said to me in October 1970: 'It will stand just so much politics, and no more; there's a danger that the politicians, if they don't think about its value, could almost accidentally destroy it.' Curran appears sensitive to the pressures, very conscious that he is riding a tiger; but in public he purveys too easily the BBC's vices of smugness and smoothness— the bland manner which is much magnified by the vast publicity apparatus, and by the managing director and director of programmes, Huw Wheldon and David Attenborough. In their general talk-in, the heads of the BBC have failed to give any real sense of purpose or dignity to the producers, who feel themselves to be addressing no one in particular, for no particular reason.

The change in the corporate character of the BBC since their monopoly was broken has transformed the background to British culture. The change is most evident, not in television, but in radio; for when the BBC was threatened by pirate radio stations, they resolved in 1967 to form their own pop station called Radio 1, complete with slick-talking disc-jockeys, jingles advertising their own programmes, and some sleazy dealings, which in 1971 were gleefully exposed by Murdoch's *News of the World*. In their determination to hold their own with commercial interests, both on radio and TV, the BBC have often seemed more obsessed with the 'ratings' than their rivals. They often complain that they are singled out for attack by liberals who expect too much from them; and certainly they generate a special love-hate. The BBC remains a more thoughtful and sensitive organisation than its rivals and it can still (as in Panorama and many of its serials) show a confidence in the importance of quality. But the long-term justification for its licence must depend on the aggressive demonstration that it has a more serious purpose than its rivals; and that, being independent of advertising and commercial controllers, it can provide alternative values and a more honest critique of contemporary society.

COMMERCIAL TELEVISION

'Television, this titan of communication between man and man, this surging, sweeping power, rationed and controlled for us before, is in our hands.'

Sir Robert Fraser, September 24, 1955.

It is only sixteen years ago since the first television advertisement, for toothpaste, appeared on the British screen; but already commercial television, like a mobile column through the middle of Britain, has wrought change all around it. It is important not to exaggerate the social effects of commercial TV: in France, after all, there have been more drastic upheavals, and much greater industrial growth, without television advertising. But the impact of the flickering advertisements and the new profit motives behind television programmes played their part in transforming the social atmosphere of Britain in the sixties. They unleashed new ambitions amongst the consumers, quickened the pace of fashion and taste, encouraged mass marketing and supermarkets, and produced a spectacular alliance between the old forces of conservatism and the new ambitions of the consumer—so that Disraeli's 'one nation' seemed to be coming about in a new, greedy kind of way.

Yet this social revolution, which gave such succour to the Tories, was not planned by the political leaders. It was due only to a handful of resolute plotters, much helped by the smugness of the BBC at the time. It may be that the commercial pressures for television advertising would eventually anyway have made themselves felt; but the speed with which commercial television arrived in the fifties, with so much of the Establishment against it, was a rare example of a small conspiracy having a decisive effect on the course of history. The forces against commercial television seemed effective enough. They included not only most of the Labour Party, but a formidable body of Tories, like Lord Hailsham, and Whig paternalists, like Lady Violet Bonham Carter, who saw the BBC monopoly as part of the high-minded tradition of British public life. But the commercial lobbyists were tireless and rich, and they employed the most effective public relations techniques. When the television Bill came up for its second reading in March 1954 it was passed by 296 to 269 votes. 'This study would seem to establish the fact,' concluded Professor Wilson, the historian of the commercial television lobby,[1] 'that a small number of MPs, well organised with good connections, among both party officials and outside interests, and pushing a definite, limited programme, may exert considerable influence and even overwhelm an organised majority in their own party.' His judgment seemed to be corroborated when fifteen years later the Commercial Radio lobby had a similar success—backed by some of the same interests—and in April 1971 the Conservative government announced plans to set up sixty local radio stations financed by advertising.

The supervision of the huge commercial interests of television was the responsibility of a strange public body, the Independent Television Authority,[2] which was set up in 1954 to erect transmitters and to award licences to the companies—a system partly copied from Chicago. The ITA was empowered by the act to 'provide television broadcasting services, additional to those of the BBC and of high quality both as to transmission and as to the matter transmitted', and to ensure that 'nothing is included in the programmes which offends against good taste or decency or is likely to encourage or incite to crime . . .' A chairman and 'members of the Authority' were appointed by the government, not unlike BBC governors in their backgrounds, and like them without much experience of TV: but with a far more difficult responsibility, for they had to hold in check, not a dedicated organisation of public broadcasters, but some of the most powerful commercial organisations in the country. The chairmanship, like that of the BBC, was a job whose scope could stretch or contract;

---

[1] H. H. Wilson: *Pressure Group*, Secker & Warburg, 1961, p. 208.

[2] The use of 'Authority' to describe a public body—a quaint coinage—is believed to date back to Winston Churchill, who invented the Port of London Authority.

the first occupant was Sir Kenneth Clark (now Lord Clark, 'the Lord of Civilisation'), and the second was Sir Ivone Kirkpatrick, the ex-head of the foreign service—neither of whom was at all anxious to intervene.

In the following decade and a half the fortunes of commercial television have shown astonishing swings: compared to the history of the Press, it is as if a hundred years have been compressed into ten. For the first year the losses were colossal, and only the biggest investors could survive. Then in 1957 the tide turned and the advertisers began to realise the immense power of the medium for selling their wares. A whole new breed of millionaires emerged in the course of a few months. The new lords of the air were not only very rich, they also enjoyed, if they wished to exercise it, an almost unprecedented patronage. They were debarred by the Television Act from exerting direct political influence: but they were able to project a whole way of life, a whole background of education and values, on to millions of screens. This patronage had fallen into the hands of a wild bunch, including theatrical agents, financiers, radio peddlers and cinema owners. In cultural terms the first golden years of commercial television left very little behind —only a great heap of money.

NEW FRANCHISES

The period of uncontrolled profits, the 'Hollywood Years', of television, was brief. The Pilkington Report in 1962 (much influenced by its most articulate member, Professor Richard Hoggart) was ferociously critical of the triviality and the debasements of commercial television; it concluded, among other spectacular recommendations, that the planning of programmes should henceforth be taken over by the ITA. This was not implemented, but Pilkington did ensure that the commercial companies should not have a second channel. The new Television Act of 1964 imposed a levy on television advertising, and Macmillan appointed Lord Hill as the new Chairman of the ITA, who was more interventionist than his predecessors. When the companies' contracts expired in 1964 they were all renewed for three years; and they were fairly confident of their further renewal in 1967. But Lord Hill was enjoying the opportunity to shake up the industry, and behind the scenes he was preparing a time-bomb.

With their eyes on the still-huge profits, a number of people were busily preparing syndicates, with the necessary mixture of local bigwigs, professional experts and big businessmen, to bid for new contracts after 1967. Realising that the existing contractors were vulnerable to the charge of not being wildly artistic, the new bidders were specially careful to stress their enthusiasm for the new medium, and to include well-known performers themselves. They prepared glittering names and dazzling manifestos which seemingly had a single object—to impress one man, Lord Hill. Fame on the screen suddenly became a doubly valuable commodity. Two Welsh broadcasters, Wynford Vaughan-Thomas and John Morgan, had the idea of putting together an all-Welsh syndicate to challenge the existing contractors, Television Wales and the West—who were led by the racehorse-owner Lord Derby, operating from London, and who had been insensitive to Welshness. The new syndicate accumulated a plausible and glamorous group of backers, including Richard Burton, Geraint Evans and Lord Harlech, the ex-ambassador to Washington, who became chairman. They prepared their confidential application (not revealed till two years later) which set out, in sickly rhetoric, the glowing future for Wales. 'For a long time,' it said, 'people of the eminence and strength of Richard Burton, Stanley Baker, Geraint Evans, to give only three examples, have been seeking a means of working and expressing their deeply-held patriotic feelings in their own country.'[1] In Yorkshire a more honestly commercial syndicate was put together by Cyril Wilkinson, head of a TV-rental firm, Telefusion: their campaign was organised by the public relations firm of Voice and Vision (a subsidiary of Colman, Prentis and Varley), who assembled the necessary celebrities, including Sir Geoffrey Cox, the then editor of Independent Television News, and Alan Whicker, the itinerant commentator of 'Whicker's World'.

The most flamboyant bid was in London, where David Frost, the most successful of all television personalities, put together *his* consortium. Frost (now 32) is the one most striking case of the television actor-manager. The son of a Methodist preacher in Suffolk, he had unlimited self-confidence and a plain man's style, and at Cambridge he developed a flair for showbiz. He became famous as the compère on BBC satire programmes, speaking other people's lines, and was then given his own show on commercial television, confronting celebrities with rough questions in front of an admir-

[1] See *The Open Secret* No. 1, 1969.

ing audience, with so much publicity-value that cabinet ministers felt the need to submit. His self-confidence and mystique were such that, when he invited a list of famous men to a breakfast in 1966, fifteen of them felt impelled to come, including the prime minister, Lord Longford, David Astor, Cecil King and Len Deighton. 'Frost's Breakfast' was a kind of symbolic homage paid by the old powers to the new. As one of his contemporaries, Phillip White-head (an ex-TV producer) has described him, 'he is an authentic man of our times. As appropriate as Frost's classless suburban accent and appearance is his total ease in the world of the Admass society'. Behind this magic, Frost seems an isolated man, kept going like a top by perpetual motion: nowadays he commutes once a week to New York for his own programme, and gives the impression of hardly touching ground, as if he were floating on his own sound-waves. He avoids answering letters; complaints are replied to by a personal assistant on a typewriter with type even bigger than the prime minister's.

With his nerve and reputation, Frost was well-placed to put to-gether a TV syndicate, and he assembled a fashionable collection, including Michael Peacock, the young controller of BBC 1, Aidan Crawley, the Tory MP and ex-head of ITN; and Clive Irving, a journalist-businessman; their backing was fixed up by David Montagu, of the merchant bank Samuel Montagu. Frost was a master of the art of presenting a case: 'A television bid is a bit like a political campaign,' he explained later; 'i takes organisation, stamina, secret diplomacy and funds.' In one coup he flew to Delhi to recruit the support of the High Commissioner, John Freeman. A stirring application, written by Clive Irving, promised to transform London weekends, with the help of a special public affairs unit, to be run by Irving, a series on the History Makers, and a weekly news analysis, to be edited by Freeman.

These three syndicates, with others, appeared before the assembled council of the ITA to state their case. Hill very quickly made up his mind. Frost's consortium were given London week-ends, Telefusion were given Yorkshire (which took a slice out of Granada's territory); and in the most sensational switchover, Lord Derby's syndicate was dismissed from Wales, to be replaced by Lord Harlech and his band of famous Welshmen. 'The whole thing is absolutely disgraceful,' said Lord Derby. The ITA's powers of patronage were once again breathtaking; again they had apparently created a new race of millionaires. It looked like a repeat performance of the first share-out ten years before, and this time there seemed less risk. By the end of the year the shareholders of the new Yorkshire Television had made a capital profit of 115 per cent on their holdings; Alan Whicker had made £200,000. But the justification of the new bonanza was that this time it included the creative people who actually made the programmes, and there were genuine high hopes of a new era of television.

The hopes did not last long. Harlech began in 1968 with a fiasco of an opening night and a succession of blunders which caused a campaign 'Come back TWW: all is forgiven'. They didn't get round to doing programmes with Richard Burton, or even with Mrs Burton. In Yorkshire the television mast was blown down, and they soon had to resort to lower-grade programmes to recover their ratings (though their standards have remained higher than others'). A strike of all television technicians in the autumn of 1968 was followed the next year by the Labour government's increasing the advertising levy. The expectation of high profits collapsed and the new companies, committed to new buildings and large staffs, became rather meaner than the old ones.

LONDON WEEKEND

> I am a newspaper publisher, not a
> bloody television producer.
> *Rupert Murdoch, February 1971*

The most ignominious turnabout came in London Weekend Television, who had proclaimed most loudly their ability to combine quality with commercial success, and which in the following three years became the *grand guignol* of TV epics. Its board was specially sensitive to criticism; it included David Astor, editor of *The Observer*, Lord Hartwell, owner of the *Telegraph*, Lord Campbell, chairman of the *New Statesman*, and Sir Arnold Weinstock, the austere boss of GEC/AEI. There were real hopes that LWT would become a model commercial station, a kind of BBC 3; for Michael Peacock, the managing director, had brought over several cronies from the Corporation. There was friction from the start, particularly between Peacock and the businessmen, who were amazed by the extravagance. After a fanfare of prestige programmes, London Weekend fell back on low comedy and old films—the usual standby of TV channels in trouble. The 'public affairs unit' never really got off the ground, and by 1969 it was

456

summarily disbanded. The directors, particularly Weinstock and the bankers from Rothschild's and Montagu's, were increasingly impatient with Peacock, who (they complained) was providing neither prestige nor profits, and who told them nothing at board meetings. Peacock seemed bewildered by the conflict of interests, which he had not found at the BBC, and insisted on running the company in a very personal way; he was also in conflict with Frost, who (although not himself a director) had a private empire inside the company and was able to dazzle the chairman, 'Creepy' Crawley. Frost's own shows were the only sure-fire successes, and he also had a network of agencies (called after his middle name, Paradine) which bought up many of the best performers, and sold them back as an expensive package to LWT, to the vexation of Peacock. The board became increasingly embarrassed by the public criticisms and diminishing advertising revenue, and there were even secret discussions about merging with their weekday rival, Thames Television. Then in September 1969, without very careful thought, they prepared a sudden coup, to sack Peacock and promote a more amenable fellow, the business-like Dr Tom Margerison. Peacock's allies rallied, a mass-meeting assembled at the studios, and nearly all the heads of departments (including Frank Muir, Humphrey Burton and Doreen Stephens, who had all come from the BBC) threatened to resign if Peacock were sacked. The board wavered, appointed a committee, but eventually decided once again to sack him: six others resigned in protest (though one came back). The bankers and Margerison the technocrat were in control.

But the company was still financially perilous, and it lacked any kind of strong showman who could reassure the board; Weinstock was fed up with it and wanted to sell his shares. A few months after his elevation, Margerison with astonishing rashness approached a new backer—the Australian Rupert Murdoch who was by now already making large profits with his *News of the World* and the *Sun*, and was looking for an opening in television. Murdoch quickly approached Weinstock, and bought his shares: they gave him only 7.5 per cent of the holding, and he would only be a non-executive director; but he knew (as he had shown with the *News of the World*) how easily he could dominate a company where he had no real rival; and most of the other directors welcomed anyone who could make the company pay. Murdoch offered to pump half a million pounds into the company, which gave him a further hold, and he insisted on joining the executive committee. Only three months after he took over, he had a massive row with Margerison about programme schedules, and Margerison resigned: 'there is only room for one person at the top of any company', he said the same day: 'it was either me or Rupert Murdoch'. Other executives left with him, so that there was virtually no-one remaining, except David Frost, who had been part of the original parade of talents that had been given the franchise. At last the Independent Television Authority felt impelled to act, and required Murdoch to show evidence that LWT would be in keeping with their requirements: David Frost, who still owned 5 per cent of the shares, applauded the ITA's intervention. 'We will completely confound all the bloody critics,' said Murdoch from Sydney, 'but we will never get their acclaim.' The ITA required reassurance that Murdoch would not be in sole control, and eventually the man was found—John Freeman, newly returned from the embassy in Washington, who had been invited to join LWT at the start. Freeman moved in with a salary of around £20,000, protesting his admiration for Murdoch and his friendship with Frost, Aidan Crawley was pushed up to be President, and the battle for the soul of London Weekend began once again. The changes of scene in three years were breathtaking; and Murdoch's invasion, first of newspapers then of television, was more sudden than that of Roy Thomson ten years before ('There must be something wrong with this country if it's so easy to make money in it').

THE NETWORK

The chart opposite shows the fourteen programme contractors as they stood in January 1971, with their main shareholders and chairmen. They each present themselves as autonomous entities, and commercial television is proud of its regional representation. Only one service is common to all the companies, and that is the most remarkable product of Commercial TV, the Independent Television News (ITN): it is jointly owned by all the companies, and is more directly protected from commercialisation by the ITA, with the director-general on its board. ITN, edited by a cosmopolitan journalist, Nigel Ryan, has managed to combine very high ratings (often among the Top Ten) with a sense of

	Region	*Chairmen*	*Main Shareholders*
Anglia	East of England	Marquess Townshend	The Guardian (29%); IPC/Reed (29%)
Associated Television	Midlands	Lord Renwick	Prince Littler (14%); Sir Lew Grade (12%); Beaverbrook Newspapers (8%); Birmingham Post (5%); Lord Renwick (4%)
Border	The Borders and Isle of Man	John L. Burgess	Cumberland Newspapers (23%)
Channel	Channel Islands	Senator Krichefski	Channel Entertainments (51%)
Grampian	North-East Scotland	Captain Iain M. Tennant	Shares widely held
Granada	Lancashire	Lord Bernstein	Granada Group Ltd. (100%)
Harlech	Wales and West England	Lord Harlech	Shares widely held
London Weekend	London (weekends)	John Freeman	Bowaters, ITC Pension Trust, Lombard Banking, News of the World, Pearl Assurance (all 8¼%); Daily Telegraph, The Observer (both 7%)
Scottish	Central Scotland	James M. Coltart	Thomson Organisation (25%)
Southern Independent	South of England	John Davis	Associated Newspapers and Rank Organisation (both 37%)
Thames	London (weekdays)	Lord Shawcross	EMI (50% controlling); Rediffusion Television Ltd. (50%)
Tyne Tees*	North-East England	Professor G. H. J. Daysh	Abec Investments (12%); Renaissance Films (10%)
Ulster	Northern Ireland	Earl of Antrim	Century Newspapers (6½%)
Westward	South-West England	Peter Cadbury	Peter Cadbury (15%); Frederick Corbin (12%)
Yorkshire*	Yorkshire	Sir Richard B. Graham	Telefusion (18¼%); Yorkshire Post Newspapers (11¾%)

* Note: These two companies are now merged and are known as Trident Television.

seriousness, and has challenged and beaten the BBC on its most sacred ground—the coverage of news.

Most companies cannot afford to produce all their own material, and the ITA only requires a small part of their time to be locally generated; so that the bulk of the programmes is bought from other companies, and many serials and shows are shown all over Britain. The pattern of broadcasting is decided by a meeting once a month of all the companies, known as The Network; but the meetings are dominated by the five richest companies. Two of the big five companies—London Weekend and Yorkshire—were newcomers in 1967, under the new franchise. (Yorkshire has now been allowed to merge with the Tyne-Tees company, under the name 'Trident'.) Another big company, Thames, was re-formed as a merger of earlier companies, Rediffusion and ABC. The other two, Granada and Associated Television, were part of the original shareout in 1955; and they are specially powerful in The Network.

Granada, based—at least in theory—on Manchester, has always projected a special personality. Partly because it was the station of the North, of 'Granadaland'—until most of Yorkshire was given to the new syndicate in 1967. But also because it has been under the control of a single showman, Sidney Bernstein —now Lord Bernstein—whose family originally owned 85 per cent of the shares. Bernstein loved to present himself as a left-wing intellectual showman, and as a 'Reithian' with a personal mission to present uplifting programmes. He was relatively speaking an aristocrat of showbusiness (though he looks like a pugilist); he inherited the chain of Granada cinemas from his father, and this ample foothold enabled him to climb into television with one quick heave. Much more than the other original TV tycoons, he had real ideas as to what he wanted to do on the screen: with his profits he has diversified not only into property, TV rentals, and motorway cafés, but also into a group of book publishers, now including McGibbon and Kee, Panther, Rupert Hart-Davis and thirty per cent of Jonathan Cape. Yet his consuming interest, as for the others, has been money, and his real talent has been in discovering the surest formula for the mass-market; Granada's greatest triumph has been 'Coronation Street', which has run through over a thousand instalments. The real heart of Granadaland is not in Manchester but in Golden Square behind Piccadilly, where the Granada accountants and computers supervise the diversified empire.

Duopoly of Entertainment

The most commercially successful of all the companies has been
Associated Television (ATV), which deserves special study as
being one of the twin pillars—with Electrical and Musical
Industries—of the duopoly of the entertainments business. They
have spun a web of interlocking interests which dominates not
only television, but the theatre, records, cinemas, music publishing
and music-hall, and whose affiliated companies include Muzak,
Transworld Bowling Alleys, Century 21 Toys, Joe 90 comics and
Eagle Star Insurance. The ATV-EMI complex, which has spread
out from television in the last fifteen years, presents the most
depressing example of 'leisure industries' becoming dominated by
a near-monopoly of interests; and at the centre of it are two showbiz families who have a natural instinct for the lowest common
denominator; the Grades and the Littlers.[1]

Associated Television was the original brainchild of the
triumvirate who pushed through commercial television; Robert
Renwick (now Lord Renwick), Norman Collins (still Norman
Collins) and C. O. Stanley. The first two are still directors, and
Renwick, a rugged old-war-horse of unreconstructed free enterprise, is now chairman. But the trio very early lost full control;
they did not have enough money in 1954 to satisfy the ITA, and
they had to go into partnership with two prominent showmen, Val
Parnell and Lew Grade (who had been refused their own station,
partly because Parnell's theatre group, Moss Empires, was
considered already quite powerful enough). ATV soon became a
showman's paradise, a kind of Palladium of the Air. Val 'n' Lew,
working in the same office, dominated the company with their
characteristic mixture of expansiveness and meanness; and when
Parnell retired Lew Grade—now Sir Lew—was the undisputed
boss.

Lew became, and still is, the legendary low-brow of television,
the Sam Goldwyn of the new medium, credited with defiantly
illiterate remarks, and eliciting a strange kind of attraction.
'Of course you boys all know I went to Oxford *and* Cambridge,' he
tells his colleagues on The Network. A fat cigar hangs from his
mouth; he slumps in his chair like a bolster; he proclaims unashamedly his pursuit of profits ('The trouble with this business,'

[1] For a more detailed account of the 'Grade Dossier' see *The Open Secret*, issues 2 and
3, 1970, to which I am indebted.

Lew is reported as saying, 'is that the stars keep ninety per cent of my money'). He began his career in showbusiness as a child-refugee, with his two brothers and his father, called Winogradsky, who came to England from Odessa: Lew became the World Charleston Champion, dancing across Europe. Before long Lew and Leslie had built up the biggest variety agency in Britain, while Bernard, who changed his name to Delfont, had his own agency, theatres and managements. When Lew went into television, ATV soon became the most profitable of all the companies. They not only produced programmes like *Emergency Ward Ten* and *Mrs. Thursday*, which reached the biggest audiences in Britain; they also exported series like *The Saint* or *Meet Tom Jones* to American TV, where they could make even bigger profits. They were soon carefully devising their plots, dialogues and settings to be equally comprehensible and acceptable in Buffalo or Bolton. ATV earned as much as £5 million a year from America, and Lew Grade was knighted for his services to exports. The result in terms of TV was a bland mid-Atlantic style with the subtleties and hard edges carefully ironed out. The practice of 'co-production' has now spread on a large scale to the BBC, and expensive serials like *Elizabeth R* or the *British Empire* are jointly financed by American or Continental companies—which tend to encourage nostalgic pictures of Britain.

The profits of ATV enabled them to diversify into records, toys, comics, bowling and property; so that only half their money now comes from television. They also hugely expanded their show-business interests. In 1964 they bought out the Stoll/Moss Empires group of theatres from Prince Littler, and thus owned a chain of London and provincial theatres, including the Victoria Palace, the Palladium, the Hippodrome and Her Majesty's. Lew Grade still kept his share of the Grade agency, now run by his brother, Leslie, and many actors discovered that they were not only dependent on the Grade family for their TV contracts, but also for the agency negotiating them. By 1966 the actors' union, Equity, was so infuriated by the Grade family's 'octopus' that they wrote to the prime minister—without results—asking for legislation. The Grades sounded very hurt: 'I like to think,' Bernard Delfont was quoted as saying to *The Sunday Times*, 'that the only monopoly we have is a monopoly of goodwill.'

The next year another ramified company entered the field: Electrical and Musical Industries, whose main interests were records (HMV, etc.) and electronics, took over the Grade Organisation. The situation was swiftly complicated when, in the next two years, EMI also bought up the whole of the Associated British Picture Corporation, which gave them not only a chain of cinemas but the controlling interest in the new Thames Television. The ITA would only allow EMI to keep their control of Thames if they sold off their agency business, which they did; but the biggest part of the agency, the London Management group, which represents nearly all the top actors, was sold to a company whose directors included Mike Grade, Lew's nephew; and the actors were not reassured to find that all the agencies were in the hands of old friends of the Grades. The octopus was still at large, but it now had *two* heads—ATV on one side and EMI on the other, linked by the Grades and the Littlers.

THE AUTHORITY

ITA—watchdog or lapdog?
*TV producers picketing
the ITA headquarters in 1969.*

The programme contractors have appeared over the past fifteen years to be almost unfettered in their commercial exploitation of the medium. But they are, in theory, controlled by one of the most powerful of all supervisory bodies: the chairman and director-general of the ITA can dictate to the companies, and if necessary dismiss them. The chairmanship has had a chequered history: when Lord Hill was shunted to the BBC, Lord Aylestone, formerly Herbert Bowden, the Labour Cabinet Minister, replaced him. There was some outcry at this political invasion, both from producers and from the commercial bosses; but Aylestone turned out to be much less active than Hill, and not much interested in the standard of programmes; he thus pleased the contractors better. Under the chairman are the nine other members of the Authority: these were they in June 1971:

Lord Aylestone (Chairman)—ex-cabinet minister
Sir Ronald Gould (Deputy Chairman)—ex-secretary National Union of Teachers
T. Glyn Davies—chairman of Welsh Committee of British Council
Sir Frederick Hayday—trade unionist
S. Keynes—director of merchant bank and insurance company
Lady Macleod of Borve—cabinet minister's widow
John Meek—professor of electrical engineering

A. W. Page—chairman of Metal Box Company
Lady Sharp—ex-civil servant
Dr T. F. Carbery—lecturer, Strathclyde University

Their most important job—as for the governors of the BBC—is
to choose the man who is there all the time, the director-general.
For sixteen years this key position was occupied by the same man,
Sir Robert Fraser, a suave Australian who became the great
apologist for 'people's television', a kind of anti-Reith, setting
himself up as a Benthamite in contrast to the Platonic ideals of the
BBC. He was thus well attuned to the ideas of the commercial
magnates. He established the ITA in lush premises next to
Harrods, with penthouse flats and tinkling lifts, and the ITA, far
from maintaining a separate ethos from the contracting companies,
seemed to magnify their Panglossian attitudes; theirs was the best
of all possible worlds. The complacency was ruffled by the TV levy
and by the arrival of Lord Hill; but with his departure, Fraserism
again prevailed, and Sir Robert watched, without apparent
worry, the steady deterioration of standards and the broken
promises of the new companies: 'Catching companies out by
discovering that they had not fulfilled this or that intention'—he
said after the companies' manifestoes had been revealed—'is at
best childish, at worst a bore.'[1]

Sir Robert's impending departure in 1970 produced a flurry of
speculations and applications from TV people, including the
irrepressible Robin Day, the chief inquisitor of the BBC. But the
authority invited an ex-headmaster of Charterhouse, Brian Young,
to apply, and he got the job. Young, who is still only forty-eight,
has the kind of confidence that only a few unchallenged professions (headmasters, judges, surgeons) can nowadays nurture. He
was a wartime naval officer, a classical first at Oxford, a master at
Eton, and headmaster at only twenty-nine. He quickly rebuffs the
suggestion that he comes from a sheltered occupation: 'Are you
repeating the old jibe that a schoolmaster is a man among boys
and a boy among men?'

It remains to be seen how far Young can stand up to the head-
winds that buffet round the ITA headquarters. Most of the commercial companies faced with reduced advertising revenue and the
costs of colour transmission, are in greater financial difficulties, which makes it harder for the authority to press them to
improve their quality. But the director-general, supported by the

[1] *The Sunday Times*, August 3, 1969.

chairman, is in a position of immense power; he can temporarily suspend a company or withdraw a contract. These huge punishments may seem to be too clumsy to be of everyday use, except near the end of a seven-year franchise. But a strong headmaster-director could constantly invoke this implied threat rather as the Governor of the Bank of England, with *his* draconian powers, can generate through the City the sense of 'what isn't done'.

The ITA and its director-general stand on the most exposed position in the current crisis in communications. They could obstruct such interlocking monopolies as the ATV-EMI nexus; they could brake the headlong pursuit of ratings, and thus reduce the pressure on the BBC to outbid their rivals in triviality. It is deep in British thinking that it is possible to have a compromise between state control and free enterprise, by allowing both to compete side-by-side. But the past surrenders of the ITA to commercial pressures have given credibility to Marxist critics who insist that only total state control can resist the pressures of monopoly capitalism, and that any authority, any anti-trust law, will be turned to the advantage of the capitalists. That the ITA *could* be effective is shown by the temporary effect of the Pilkington Committee which, while it was sitting, succeeded in frightening the TV tycoons into producing prestigious 'Pilkington programmes'. There is no reason why the Authority should not present itself as a permanent sitting committee, with much more formidable overseers than the current retired dignitaries. Unless the ITA overhauls itself, and detaches itself from the pressures of commercialism, the greed of the commercial companies will be able to set the whole context for all television on all channels.

WHO RUNS TELEVISION?

Newspapers were born free but television was born in chains, a monopoly created by the state, dependent on the state and in every country regulated by the state.

William Rees-Mogg.

TV has emerged as a medium which colours nearly everyone's life, a 'window on the world', but a half-shuttered window of distorting glass. The more evident its influence, the more the worry from all sides as to who should control it. How do you strike a balance between the only two powers rich enough to finance it—the state and big business? How, given this balance, can you prevent individual ideas and minority tastes being over-whelmed by the bland forces of mass programmes?

The politicians have begun to be vocal, seeing television by-passing their own medium, parliament. A provocative but half-baked attack came from Richard Crossman in October 1968, when he was Leader of the House of Commons; he blamed television for contributing to the prevailing alienation, for weaken-ing the participatory tendencies, and for playing up to the 'gladia-torial aspects of politics'.[1] But his argument was negated by the obvious failure of the politicians themselves, who had refused to allow television inside parliament, and who had carefully avoided presenting the real issues on the screen; the 1970 election showed how the most critical questions—the common market, South Africa, Rhodesia or Anglo-American relations—could be evaded by both sides. Another attack, oddly singling out the BBC, was delivered by Anthony Wedgwood Benn, then Minister of Tech-nology, on *his* participation jag: he complained that 'broadcasting is really too important to be left to the broadcasters', ('The thin end of the Wedge', said the BBC.) Like Crossman, Benn blamed television for omissions, like the failure to discuss seriously the coal industry or the telephone service, which were really the omissions of government and parliament. His most effective complaints were against the uniformity of the BBC: that they funnel all pro-grammes through the same meat-grinder, supervised by a small band of producers who get in the way of genuine participation by outside groups: 'It is as if the only printed material available for us were newspapers—no books, no pamphlets, only newspapers published under editorial control.'

It is the lack of any sense or means of participation in television which makes the new medium such a brassy intruder into the democratic framework. The producers may rope in outsiders, with studio discussions or 'vox pop', but the interviewer and the camera hold the power and have the last word. The camera can be even more misleading than the Press; for it more convincingly presents its view as the real view, and it can so easily ignore the opinions of ordinary people—whether about strikes, race relations or how they will vote. The controllers of television, like politicians and editors, however much they may protest in favour of participation have a natural tendency against it, for their profession depends on being spokesmen for others.

[1] 'The Politics of Viewing': reprinted in the *New Statesman*, October 25, 1968.

While the politicians accuse the producers, the producers themselves have been in smouldering revolt against their masters, and
like the Press, television has begun to surge with theories for
controlling the media. In the BBC, the rebellion burst out most
openly in the Great Radio Revolt of 1969; in commercial television, the anger was stirred up by the broken promises of the new
contractors, and the fiasco of London Weekend. The excitement
of the first commercial years, when producers were learning and
experimenting, gave way to a sense of powerlessness and frustration. One sign of the producers' revolt was the emergence in 1969
of the Free Communications Group, a ginger-group of dissatisfied
journalists and television men who pressed for a measure of
workers' control and social ownership of the means of communication, both in television and in newspapers: their original
steering committee consisted of Neal Ascherson of *The Observer*,
Alexander Cockburn of the *New Left Review*, Gus Macdonald of
Granada, and Bruce Page of *The Sunday Times*. The FCG has been
a fitful organisation, itself an uneasy alliance between revolutionaries and revisionists; but it has already done something to stir
up debate. Its magazine, *The Open Secret*, published the confidential applications of the two TV consortia, London Weekend
and Harlech, and proclaimed the aims: 'The FCG intends to
launch a campaign to inaugurate ideas about democratic media
which have never got above ground in previous debate. The
energy of the communications industry is in those who run it—
who produce the news and entertainment. The FCG intends to
turn that energy into power.'

Another group of broadcasters, the '76 Group', assembled in
1970, founded mostly by people who had resigned from London
Weekend, including Doreen Stephens, Humphrey Burton and
Kenith Trodd. They pressed for a Royal Commission on broadcasting, before the next renewal of the franchises in 1976, from
which fateful year the group was named (the Labour Party did
plan a commission, to be headed by Lord Annan, but it was
scrapped by the Conservatives). 'It is becoming more and more
difficult for the people who actually make programmes to influence what happens,' said Trodd: 'We need a philosophy of
broadcasting, of communication, which we no longer have.' The
sense of a vacuum—filled by commercial interest for want of
others—pervades the medium, and the story of London Weekend
shows how easily the vacuum can be exploited by an aggressive

newcomer. Some producers look back with some nostalgia to the days of Reith, as the only force that had stood against debasement.

In spite of the bitter attacks on British television, both from inside and outside, the characteristic British dual system has worked better than most other countries'. It has avoided both the extreme paternalism and authoritarianism of French television, and the total commercialisation of American stations. Few people, I suspect, would now advocate a return to the days of the BBC TV monopoly. But the British system, to be genuinely balanced, depends on a barrage of criticism and a constant vigilance to prevent the public service being sucked into the values of the commercial rivals; the complacency of the controllers of both the BBC and ITA is in danger of obscuring the fragility of the balance.

PART

FIVE

———

Finance

25

City

In the city
They sell and buy
And nobody ever
Asks them why.

But since it contents them
To buy and sell
God forgive them!
They might as well.

Humbert Wolfe.

WHEN you travel eastwards from the West End of London, as you pass St. Paul's you can sense in the air a certain narrowing and intensifying of ambitions, like the narrowing of the street-canyons themselves. There is little interruption to the rows of bleak grey office blocks, frosted windows and ponderous bankers' façades: only an occasional Wren church with a tiny churchyard or a last-remaining alley with a Dickensian wine-house. The shops are forbidding and utilitarian, selling office equipment, ledgers, commuters' paperbacks, or businessmen's art. The men walk faster, most of them still in dark suits and dark ties, and with umbrellas—though not many nowadays with bowlers. In the mornings and evenings they rush to and from Waterloo or Victoria; at lunch-time, unless they are grand enough to have their own dining-room, they dive down into crowded bars and lunch-rooms, for beery meals, with hardly a girl or any other kind of outsider in sight; the bars still have a college-type intensity about them, and the talk alternates between money, joshing and sport. The girls are emphatically segregated in sandwich-bars or canteens; the austere masculinity of the city frightens away the more sophisticated secretaries, who prefer the brightness and shops of the West End. The city remains the stronghold of male domination, whether social or financial, and women are kept out of nearly all the centres of its power.

Even the bold new buildings of the city have not much lightened the traditional bleakness: the glass boxes of London Wall are monuments to the plot-ratio calculations of property men, with little space wasted on entrances or corridors or even spare lifts: the office workers queue for their lifts in the morning, as they queue for their trains and queue for their lunches. The walkways above the street—intended to be bustling with pedestrians—are almost empty, and many of the shells of the stores are still bare, unable to lure anyone to set up shop. People, it seems, come to the city for one reason only, to make money; and any attempt at a serious diversion is likely to fail.

There are *some* signs of a change in this puritanical or misogynist tradition—a few offices with modern paintings, a few bright ties, an occasional trendy jobber having a drink with a dolly-girl. There is one current city story which may indicate a relaxation of the old segregation. In one of our leading insurance companies (the story goes) a director one day went into the boardroom to discover to his horror one of the clerks and a copy-typist on the boardroom table, in the very act of making love. A board meeting, of course, was immediately called. 'There's only one thing for it,' said the chairman, 'we must get rid of the clerk immediately.' 'Impossible,' said the chief general manager, 'he's the only man who understands the computer.' A long silence. 'Well, there's only one thing for it,' said the chairman, 'we must get rid of the girl.' 'Out of the question,' said the personnel manager, 'she's the only girl in the typing pool who can spell.' An almost unbearable silence. 'Well,' said the chairman (an unusually decisive one), 'there's no alternative. We must get rid of the boardroom table.'

The City of London is still bounded by the 'square mile', which can be crossed in twenty minutes, and which contains most of the important financial institutions in Britain. In the middle of this square is a still smaller area, a quarter-mile across, centring on the Bank of England and the Lord Mayor's Mansion House, which forms the heart of the city: it includes the stock exchange, insurance companies, the commodity markets and nearly all the banks. Concentration, like the concentration of Whitehall, is the most important characteristic of the city: only about ten thousand live there by night—a few more now live in the Barbican flats—

but half-a-million work there by day. Apart from the newspaper workers on the western edge, no city people make anything except money. The propinquity of the financial offices, their steady rubbing, shaping and polishing, has provided the 'sensitive mechanism' (to use the favourite city phrase) on which their reputation rests. 'The city is a village' is a favourite saying: the streets and bars are full of people meeting, recognising, discussing each other. They are pressed closely together by their work, and isolated from the rest of London or the country. Even the different sectors of the city are very introverted: few stockbrokers have even been inside Lloyd's. The city is really a group of villages, with a moat round them all.

The moat cuts them off from the way of life of the rest of the population; and their commuting existence in Surrey and Kent, sitting in the same railway carriage as other city men, makes it rare for them to have contact with any factory worker or manager; so that when there are strikes or redundancies, city men, or even the *Financial Times*, do not often discuss them except in terms of economic repercussions or political dogma. The city remains overwhelmingly Tory, but in an instinctive, inherited way, as part of the tradition of the 'square mile'. There was a brief love affair between some city houses and the new Labour government in 1964 and 1965, but it soon went sour, and the city men who collaborated with Labour, like Lord Melchett or Charles Villiers, are now very suspect with the Tory government. There have been shocks, and may be more, now that the Heath government has pulled away props from firms like Upper Clyde Shipbuilders or Rolls-Royce; but there are only a handful of people in top city places who confess, in tones of some martyrdom, to having voted Labour in 1970.

The city, far more than the regions of government and bureaucracy, has been opened up in the last few years to the influences of the mass media from outside its walls, and linked up to the machinery of journalism and advertising. Business supplements, books on the city, the television money programme, and the huge publicity that surrounds take-over battles, have all thrown light on to the square mile. To some old firms the shock has been sudden, as if they discovered a two-way mirror in their bedroom; and they complain sadly that they are not much good at exhibitionism. But many new financiers have learnt to exploit the mass media, to use newspapers and publicity to 'talk up' their shares, and to project themselves, not just to the rest of the square mile, but to the People—posturing carefully in front of that convenient mirror. There is nothing new, of course, in the process of share-pushing and self-publicising in the city; it is as old as the South Sea Bubble, and all bankers and brokers, behind their rituals, are concerned to promote their wares. The new striving for publicity corresponds to the scope for the city to make money out of new kinds of people, out of small investors who can be persuaded to make use of hire purchase, or to invest in unit trusts—both of them highly profitable to the city and happening roughly thirty years after the Americans. The division in the city between old bankers, preoccupied by dealing with rich people, and new financiers, exploiting new money from small savers, is one contrast that runs through the city villages.

'It doesn't matter what you know, but who you know' has been a favourite city saying. Personal contacts are important in any business; but who-you-know has been used to justify the city's elaborate and unique old boy net—the rituals of Lord Mayor's dinners and livery companies, the social round of Henley, Lord's and Wimbledon, and above all the obsession with good families and public schools, as breeding grounds for men with good connections. The justification is that the city is based on *trust*. 'My word is my bond' is the motto of the Stock Exchange. The speed of operations depends on acceptance of verbal promises, multiplied by the telephone—which carries hundreds of thousands of promises every day. This quick trust, it is argued, depends on knowing to whom you are talking—knowing that he is 'one of us'. New York or Frankfurt are bureaucratic or unreliable, but the city of London has a semi-tribal past, and this can eliminate fuss and lawyers. But the old boy net, left to itself, is essentially a protective arrangement: and over the last two centuries has become a safety net of 'gentlemen's agreements' arranging for banks, insurance companies or lawyers not to steal each others' businesses; the phrase 'it's not done' is still lurking to console the mediocre and frighten the newcomer. In the meantime, the big new developments of the last fifty years—hire-purchase, building societies, industrial life assurance, property development—all of them keyed to the future—have been exploited by men outside the square mile, and outside the old boy net.

In the past few years, a 'new boy net' has begun to assert itself more forcefully, of men who are not related and did not go to school together, but who share the same kind of quick-fire down-to-earth talk, and have contacts, not with the old families, but with people in the Pru, with pension-fund managers, with journalists on the business supplements, or with the property tycoons. The tension between the two groups, the protective and the aggressive, has always been part of the city tradition. The old boys, still with their control of hoards of old money and with their own subtle systems of contacts, can still play very strong cards; sometimes they can break an over-ambitious financier simply by not lending him money at the critical moment; sometimes they bring the clever young men in on their side. The old rich have become much more skilled in the last ten years at making use of the new drive and talent, while still keeping the power to themselves. The city has always depended on some balance between the old rich and the new would-be rich: 'The rough and vulgar structure of English commerce is the secret of its life,' said Bagehot; and with remarkable speed the outsiders of one decade became the insiders of the next.

The city is very conscious of its glorious past, and the banks and insurance companies are full of old prints and mementoes to remind visitors that they have seen better days. From 1815 to 1914—the 'English Era'—London was the undisputed financial capital of the world. Since 1914 the city has suffered a series of shocks—the loss of empire, the disappearance of China, the rise of Frankfurt and Zurich, the crises of the pound. The city has survived these buffets with a resilience which has surprised many critics; the Dickensian-looking men in their mahogany parlours have turned from financing foreign governments to raising Euro-dollar loans; Lloyd's underwriters continue sitting in front of dog-eared ledgers, but now insure giant tankers and jumbo jets. The city can congratulate itself on remaining the leading international market for commodities, chartered shipping, foreign exchange or insurance, and above all on providing the 'invisible earnings' which help to redress Britain's balance of payments. While Britain's industrial performance in the last two decades has fallen further and further back, compared to the rest of Europe, her financial expertise has remained dominant, even while the pound itself has been tottering; the huge and profitable Euro-dollar business has its centre in London, swelling the business of British banks and attracting American newcomers. The British—rather at odds with their image—can claim to be the financial

experts of Europe: and while industrial companies languish or go
bankrupt, the city, which established itself not on industry but on
trade, can still make money out of other countries' wealth. The
Barings and Rothschilds have watched Britain's industrial
supremacy come and go.

STOCK EXCHANGE

The city of London is full of exchanges, buying and selling
things—wool, meat, gold, metals, rubber or spices, each with its
own special smell. But since the joint-stock system was invented
in the seventeenth century, allowing the public to buy shares of
companies, the most important market has become the market for
shares. The stock exchange is rowdier than the insurance 'Room'
of Lloyd's (see Chapter 28)—which may reflect its seedier origins:
the 'rascally' stock-jobbers of the eighteenth century who clustered
round 'Change Alley' were much less solid citizens than the
insurers at Lloyd's coffee-house. The stock exchange has the
atmosphere of a superannuated schoolroom, full of people running,
laughing, waving arms and joking (the stock exchange is assumed
to be the originator of most city rumours and jokes). Looking down
on the 'House', you can see the different parts of the market at
work. Government stock ('gilt-edged') is the most sedate, with a
few men in silk hats—the gilt-edged uniform. In each section are
the 'jobbers', the middle-men (who provide the market and quote
the prices)—a unique English profession, whose necessity is often
questioned. Weaving round the jobbers are the stockbrokers,
trying to buy or sell their shares. From time to time a bell rings
in the House, a notice is put up on a board, and yellow words
begin to move across a big screen on the wall. They may announce
an important dividend or company profits, and now the activity
on the floor becomes more comprehensible: brokers rush to the
jobbers, trying to buy or sell stock after the news, while the
jobbers try to decide how the news will affect their prices.

In the past decade the stock exchange has tried to endear itself
to the public. Visitors can now watch it from behind a glass screen,
and county girls in trendy uniforms answer questions in Knightsbridge voices. A film called *The Launching* is shown regularly,
designed to persuade the timid company-owner that to become a
public company is not frightening or crooked; it shows a small
boat-builder considering whether to go public, talking to his

solicitor, his accountant, and then to a stockbroker, working out his presentation to the stock exchange. The film depicts a reassuring Forsyteian red-plush world of polished tables, with ponderous officials mulling over the company's welfare: though the image is rather at odds with the goings-on in the House below, where weasly jobbers and brokers chase each other around in the hectic pursuit of quick profits.

The House in fact is only the visible, dramatised centre of a much larger network; nearly all the real stockbroking business is now done in offices in the surrounding buildings, where tele-printers, TV screens and computers can bring the results almost instantly to the brokers. In January 1970 the first part of the new stock exchange skyscraper was opened, which will be finished in 1972 with twenty-six storeys costing £11 million. It will have a telephone system big enough to serve a town of 40,000 people, operating to the 220 members of the stock exchange; it will connect with 1,000 TV receivers, showing price changes of a minimum of 600 stocks, put out on twenty-two channels.

Stockbrokers since Victorian times have been symbols of the obsession with pure money-making, divorced from responsibility, interest or taste; living in stockbrokers' Tudor mansions in the 'stockbroker belt' of Surrey, between Guildford and Epsom, making fortunes simply out of buying and selling shares. They can still, in a good year, make a great deal of money (in 1968 it was reckoned that some of them made £100,000) though in a bad year, like 1970, one or two firms came close to being 'hammered' —proclaiming that they could not meet their debts. Stockbrokers, like other kinds of brokers, are still well-placed to make money, but the 'stockbroker belt' is not quite what it was; a survey in 1965 showed that, out of the 3,509 London brokers, twenty-one per cent lived in Surrey, but thirty-three per cent lived in London itself—most of them in Westminster, Kensington or Chelsea, as the map overleaf (adapted from *The Economist*) shows.

Stockbrokers, like solicitors, have watched since the 1880s the eclipse of rich private clients by the new corporate wealth. They have had gradually to come to terms with the new giants of the city—the 'institutions', the insurance companies and pension funds,[1] with two millions a day demanding to be invested. Stockbrokers' firms have had to become bigger, more concerned with statistics and research, and to try to acquire independent

[1] See Chapter 28.

477

Where stockbrokers live in London

information about industry. The biggest firms have twenty or more partners: de Zoete and Bevan has 40, Lawrence, Prust has 33, Grieveson Grant has 41. Stockbroking has become a more specialised, organised business. The big firms no longer rely wholly on relations and friends to provide their young men, but take on accountants, actuaries or graduates: they even now insist on *examinations* for members (though they still draw the line at having women members). Many firms have their own department of investment analysts (a separate sub-profession) who watch trends in share prices, and visit factories and offices. But how much they can really *find out* about a company's real state is much limited by the effective secrecy of directors, and the weakness of rules about disclosure. Stockbrokers, like journalists, can easily be dazzled by science and optimism, and shortly before the collapse of Rolls-Royce many brokers were still recommending the company to their clients. The small shareholders' role in the stock market has been made much of politically: for all this frenzied buying and selling is often justified as the instrument of people's capitalism or grass-roots capitalism, through which small men become involved in big business. But the mass ownership of shares has progressed far less than in America, and stockbrokers do not present themselves eagerly to the public; the small investor is too much of a nuisance. When the London stock exchange commissioned a survey in 1966, they could claim that twenty-four million people were investing in some way—but nearly all of them through their policies with insurance companies. Only two-and-a-half million of the population, including holders of unit trusts, actually invested personally. Another survey was conducted by Gallup in 1969, which suggested a large increase in unit-trust holders; but the numbers of direct investors may actually have *fallen* in the last few years.[1]

Some of the place of individual shareholders has been filled by the surge of unit trusts (the equivalent of the American 'mutual funds') which swept into Britain in the sixties: and it is here that we feel the full blast of publicity blowing into the musty air of the city. The unit trusts managers are more convincing standard-bearers of people's capitalism than the stockbrokers; they offer more balanced investments, they can cater for very small investors, and above all they advertise themselves directly to the public. In the sixties the business supplements of quality newspapers began to grow fat with huge thick-type advertisements for the big unit trust groups like Save and Prosper and Municipal and General, offering prospects of spectacular gains. A new race of financiers established new fortunes by seeking out small investors—including two prominent Tories, Edward du Cann of Unicorn (now part of Barclays), the former chairman of the Conservative Party, and Peter Walker, now Minister for the Environment.

The managers of the funds compete anxiously in selecting their own mixtures of shares, and their comparative performance is watched as if they were race-horses. They are a rarefied breed of men, like Wasserman of Slater Walker, David Tucker of M and G, James Gammell of Scotbits: they combine extreme numeracy and academic detachment with an intuitive feeling for the market, watching form and judging motivations like bookies. The fund managers have quickened the pace of the stock exchange and

[1] See Michael Blanden in the *Financial Times*, November 26, 1969: 'A decline of grass roots capitalism in the UK.'

may have had some effect on industry; they move in and out of investments more rapidly and ruthlessly than the insurance companies—like submarines compared to battleships—and the emphasis on 'Go Go' funds, promising quick capital gains, made the old stockbrokers look as if they advocated 'Stop Stop'. The fund managers have their own association to defend their interest; but they hardly ever see each other, and some of the most successful, including Ivory and Sime (who run Scotbits) operate from the dour surroundings of Charlotte Square in Edinburgh.

In the mid-sixties the big unit trusts became so successful that they reverberated through the city. Nearly all the big banks belatedly got in on the act—Barclays with Unicorn, Barings with Save and Prosper, Hambros with Allied. Some unit trusts, like Jessel's and Slater Walker (see Chapter 26) developed side-by-side with financiers who bought up slices of industry and established industrial empires. In 1970, with an uncertain stock market, unit trusts have begun to link with building societies, with their more solid attractions for small savers; Save and Prosper are now linked with the Leicester Permanent, M and G with the Bristol and West, and the Target group have formed their own building society. In bad times investors feel much safer with property than with shares.

The unit trusts are the most mercurial and volatile part of the capitalist nerve-centre; they may be the vanguard of people's capitalism, but as such they are the first to come under fire. In the heyday of the stock exchange boom of 1968 and 1969 their claims became bolder and bolder, boasting to customers how they had increased capital by as much as forty per cent in a year; the optimism was sweeping over Western Europe, drummed up more loudly by Bernard Cornfeld, whose Investors Overseas Service based on Geneva was extracting small savings from all over the continent through persistent door-to-door salesmen. But then, in 1970, the slump descended on the stock exchanges of the world. Wall Street faced a crisis of confidence. Cornfeld's company crashed down. All of the British unit trusts survived, partly thanks to the exceptionally strict British regulations; but they showed large losses for their small savers, and new investors were very reluctant to come forward. In the prevailing gloom, the shrewder unit trust managers still managed to avoid the worst falls; but it was difficult to detect any consistent winners, or any rule by which disasters could be predicted or avoided. One rule that was put forward seemed as good as any: that the stock market goes up and down in sympathy with the ups and downs of girls' skirts; the mini coincided with boom, and the maxi with slump.[1]

The neurotic sensitivity of the market might be guessed from the language of stock exchange reports, which describe the movements of share prices with a time-honoured language which seems designed to soften the bad news, as if the shares were the Furies to be propitiated as the Kindly Ones; they do not fall, but ease, sink back, or lose their shine. The language is an odd compound of the sports ground, the turf, the battlefield and the psychiatrist's couch: shares edge forward, score gains, lose ground, rally, advance and put on spurts; like acrobats they take upward or downward turns, jump or soar; like ships they are buoyant, surge forward or sink. It is difficult to remember that they can really only do two things: go up or go down. Often the market appears as a psychiatric patient, taking a turn for the better or for the worse; erratic, unsteady, volatile, liable to suddenly improve, in sympathy with something else, and to put on a brighter appearance. Perhaps the psychiatric language is the real clue, for the capitalist system is very hypochondriac, very psychosomatic. Behind all the calculations, charts and price-earnings ratios, what matters most are the mysterious waves of 'confidence' and 'sentiment', which rule the stock exchange as emotionally as a debutante's heart.

[1] Quoted in the *Stock Trades Almanac, 1971:* The Hirsch Organisation Inc.

26

Bankers

With a group of bankers I always had the feeling that success was
measured by the extent one gave nothing away.

Lord Longford.

OVER the past ten years bankers have slowly emerged into the
public eye, like snails coming out of their shells. A decade ago,
defensive and anxious, they baulked at any kind of public persona.
The tone was set by the Governor of the Bank of England, Lord
Cobbold, who appeared more like a Grand Vizier than a man of
money, and who appropriately moved on to become Lord
Chamberlain. The heads of the big banks lay low, confining themselves to inscrutable annual statements and discouraging 'tomb-
stone' advertisements, announcing that large numbers of shares
were *not* for sale, having already been sold. Industrialists liked to
keep bankers at arm's length, Socialists hated them, and even
many Tories disliked them (Macmillan once referred to them as
'banksters'). Today, it is hard to escape from the confident
pronouncements of merchant bankers; they boom out from the
pages of the bankers' Press, pronouncing their panaceas for the
future of Britain, Western Europe, or the developing world. In
private, they convey the double assurance of men who are not only
getting richer, but are making everyone else richer and happier.

Throughout all the crises of British industry over the past five
years, the shrewdest merchant bankers have done better and
better; and an ambitious young man who might be making

£8,000 a year at the age of thirty-five in a big company, could make £13,000 a year in a merchant bank. Not surprisingly, the cleverer men from public schools have got in on the act, and the merchant banks are full of sons of public servants. Bankers can command both money and apparent power. They merge companies, they organise takeovers or prevent them, they pop up on the boards of companies, newspapers or TV consortia, they reorganise and rationalise industry, they are consulted by the cabinet and shadow cabinet. Applying their universal yardsticks, of balance sheets and profit-and-loss, they have become experts on everything; without even smelling a factory, they can confidently diagnose the trouble, appoint a new manager or close down a plant. They progress from one board to the next: like Mitty-men, becoming a steel-master one day, a brewer the next, an insurance man the next, and a television tycoon the next; 'wearing different hats' (as they like to put it), which gives them a special knowingness, so that they can tell the steelmasters about television, the brewers about insurance, and the government about all of them. More than that, they are international men, always on the move between the capitals of Europe, taking calls from New York, talking about Japan, fixing up deals and contacts with their 'good friends' abroad. They appear as the prophets not only of the new Britain, but of the new Europe—a Europe united not by a common idealism, but by a common interest in money.

JOINT STOCK BANKS

Most banking, of course, is quite different from that. When ordinary people talk about a bank, they mean one of the 'joint stock banks' or 'clearing banks' whose names are to be seen above stone façades in every high street in the country. They have become, like town halls or public libraries, part of the face of town life, and their character seems almost equally institutional, for they exist in a strange limbo between nationalisation and free enterprise. They are among the richest financial institutions in the country, but they are carefully watched and controlled by the Governor of the Bank of England, who prints their banknotes, acts as their master-banker, and keeps an eye on their reserves. The joint stock banks are in the midst of that curious city world, so difficult for the outsider to comprehend, where competition only

exists between small but unwritten limits, where 'it's not done'
lurks behind every counter, with the headmaster, the Governor,
lurking round the corner.

There are now only six joint stock banks in Britain:

	Deposits	Chairmen
National Westminster	£4,021 m.	John Prideaux
Barclays	£3,213 m.	John Thomson
Midland	£2,974 m.	Sir Archibald Forbes
Lloyds	£2,491 m.	Eric Faulkner
National and Commercial Group	£939 m.	James Blair-Cunynghame
Bank of Scotland	£419 m.	Lord Polwarth (Governor)

They are dominated by the 'Big Four', which are still, in spite of
devaluations, among the biggest banks in the western world. In
total deposits (according to *Fortune* magazine) only the Bank of
America, the First National City and the Chase Manhattan came
ahead of the biggest British banks in 1970. The giants first took
shape as the 'Big Five' in the twenties, after a succession of swallow-
ings; after that the Treasury became worried, and let it be known
that they would disapprove of any more amalgamations. So the
position stood for fifty years until, in May 1967, the Prices and Incomes Board made its report on the clearing banks, which revealed
—among its other unsettling remarks—that the Bank of England
and the Treasury had 'made it plain' that they would not prevent
some further amalgamations. In such odd ways is change
heralded in the city. After this unexpected hint, there was a
sudden flurry. The two biggest banks in Scotland, the Royal
and the National Commercial, began walking out together, and
eventually announced a marriage (to use the language of romance,
so favoured in the city). The little English bank with the grass-
hopper sign, Martins, made known its craving for a partner. And
then the two smallest of the Big Five, the Westminster and
National Provincial ('Natpro'), made bold to announce *their*
engagement. Everyone else now panicked at the prospect of being
left on the shelf, and two weeks later came the appalling proposal
by Barclays, Lloyds *and* Martins to set up a *ménage à trois*, between
them worth as much as the rest. This was carrying the hint too
far; the Board of Trade were scared at the thought of two super-
banks, and turned the whole thing over to the Monopolies
Commission. Six months later the Commission, under Mr. Justice
Roskill, produced its judgment, with four of the ten members

dissenting, that the biggest merger should *not* go through. The majority considered that 'such competition as there is among clearing banks is likely to be keener with four large clearing banks than with three banks, with one as large as the other two combined'; they saw 'little prospect of more than marginal benefits resulting from the proposed mergers'. So the Big Five settled into the Big Four.

The clearing banks have their roots not in the city, but in the provincial banking families, most of them Quakers, who grew up in the seventeenth and eighteenth centuries; many old banking names still survive on the boards. The Quakers were a close-knit, persecuted community, who were used to helping each other with money, and they soon became trusted by others as money-keepers. After some early disasters the banks settled down into cautious, conservative businesses with a strong public conscience and an emphasis on trust rather than enterprise: the last bank to get into difficulties was the military bank of Cox and King's in the Haymarket, now absorbed by Lloyds and still with a faint army tradition. The banks are restricted in what they can do with the public's money. They try not to lock up money in long-term commitments: though they have underpinned ailing companies with overdrafts for decades, they do not actually *invest* in industrial companies. Their lending to customers is closely watched by the government, through the Bank of England. The crudest form of control has been by simply setting a ceiling on loans which through the sixties restricted the banks' competition; but in May 1971 the Bank of England published a revolutionary pamphlet, *Competition and Credit Control,* which proposed to link the banks' lendings to the amount they could attract in deposits, and to allow banks to compete in rates of interest (at least in theory).

The banks, like insurance companies, have maintained a rigid division between the board and the managers, which can have a deadening effect on their thinking: as *The Economist* has put it: 'Policy-making in the great British banks goes largely by default. General managers know too much about banking, the directors too little.'[1] A survey in *The Economist* in 1966 showed that, though the clearing banks had changed more than some other institutions (notably discount houses), the gulf was only beginning to be bridged. Of the 221 directors of the clearing banks, a *quarter* were Old Etonians—about the same proportion as in 1935; and only

[1] *The Economist,* June 6, 1964.

nine of the 221 were general managers or retired general managers. There were more industrialists on the boards than in the thirties, but most of them came from old or even expiring industries, like shipping or mining, and hardly any from growth industries like electronics and chemicals; which suggests (commented *The Economist*) that the banks have 'acquired the habit of co-opting their oldest customers on to their boards, where they are then well-placed to help entrench themselves and each other'.[1]

The bank chairmen come from the worlds of hereditary banking and the public service, where fierce competition and publicity do not come easily, and their approach is expressed in their long, ponderous reports every February. The chairman of the biggest, the National Westminster, is John Francis Prideaux, who came from the family merchant bank, Arbuthnot Latham, of which he is still chairman (his mother was an Arbuthnot): he took over in January 1971 from David Robarts, who has been a bank chairman for sixteen years, and whose family were first involved in banking in 1772. Lloyds' chairman, Eric Faulkner, the son of a senior civil servant, went into Glyn Mills bank after Cambridge, and moved from being the chairman of that to being chairman of Lloyds. The Midland, as its name suggests, is more provincial, and less aristocratic in origin than the others; its chairman, Sir Archibald Forbes, is an austere Scots accountant who has moved between the worlds of government and big business for the past thirty-five years.

The most Quaker bank is Barclays—which lends a special poignancy to its current African controversy. Barclays was first formed in 1896 when twenty Quaker banks, mostly in East Anglia, came together, and they maintained some federal character by a system of local directors: there are still old family names on the board, including a Barclay, two Tukes, two Bevans and a Gurney; and the present chairman, John Thomson (not a Quaker), comes also from an old banking family. An important part of Barclays' profits comes from its large subsidiary, called Barclays DCO (Dominion, Colonial and Overseas) which has built up branches all over the commonwealth, and of which Barclays will soon be sole owners; *its* chairman, Frederick Seebohm, comes from another Quaker family, related to Gurneys,

---

[1] 'What Room at the Top?' Survey compiled by Stefan Mendelsohn: *The Economist*, June 18, 1966.

Tukes and Barclays. He went to a Quaker school, and has continued the family tradition of good works, serving on the Rowntree Memorial Trust and chairing a committee on social services. As Chairman of Barclays DCO, Seebohm has prided himself on the bank's contribution to African countries; but in the last few years Barclays' involvement with Black Africa has become compromised by its interest in South Africa, which accounts for more than half of its 1,670 branches. In 1970 it was discovered by the Anti-Apartheid Movement to have lent money, through a client, for the Cabora Bassa Dam in Portuguese East Africa, designed to buttress white settlement in Southern Africa. Barclays' loan was relatively small, less than a million pounds, but what made the bank more vulnerable was its South African branches, which play in with the rules of apartheid; Barclays DCO actively encourages South African investment, and distributes apartheid pamphlets abroad. The campaign against Barclays swept through the universities: students refused to bank with it, and sometimes forced their unions to withdraw their accounts. Barclays anxiously sent round men to argue with the students, without much success, and the campaign deprived the bank both of new accounts and of recruits. At the annual meeting in March 1971 the 'dam busters' conducted a filibuster to delay the approval. For the city it was an alarming precedent for the politicisation of capital.

The joint stock bankers do not take large initiatives, and in their approach to loans they favour the big battalions and the status quo. Rolls-Royce, when they went bankrupt in 1971, had an overdraft of £40 million with Lloyds and the Midland. The British banks do not, as the Americans do, have their own big investigation department to discover which smaller firms deserve credit. Only occasionally do the banks appear in controversial fields (Lloyds lent money to Charles Clore to help him try to take over another of its customers, Watneys, which caused Watneys to take their account elsewhere: the National Commercial Bank of Scotland helped Lord Fraser to take over Harrods).

In their dedication, their lack of greed, and their sense of quiet service, the joint stock bankers provide a placid, safe core to financial Britain. But the banks, like solicitors' offices or department stores, are examples of British institutions stuck in a Victorian pattern, catering primarily for the property-owning middle-classes, and ignoring huge new markets. Only thirty per cent of the British population use the banks—which is hardly surprising since they open when everyone is at work, and close before they come home. In the lunch-hour the 'till closed' notices go up at the counters; and in 1968 the banks unanimously decided to close on Saturdays, the only free day for many potential new customers. This defiant attitude to the public they justify by their chronic shortage of staff, but this, too, is the result of Victorian attitudes to management: the banks have depended on a docile and underpaid work-force of clerks who were thankful for any kind of secure job; and they have been unable to adjust to a situation where they have to compete with more attractive and lucrative employers.

In the last ten years the banks have made some important innovations; Barclays launched their Barclaycard system of credit, copied from America, and thus promulgated the idea that borrowing should actually be *encouraged*. The big banks bought shares in hire-purchase companies and unit trusts, which had grown up outside them. But they have made little attempt to attract the 'great unbanked'; and many potential customers prefer the Post Office Savings Bank or the building societies, which offer much better interest. The post office increased its attractions in October 1968 with the opening of the National Giro, the continental system of cheque-paying invented in Holland which after a bungled launching is gradually increasing its numbers of customers. In April 1970 the post office ventured further into the market-place by announcing a link-up with a hire-purchase company, Mercantile Credit, which would enable them to offer personal loans to their customers.

The oligopoly and secrecy of the banks has been under heavy fire, and in May 1967 they shuddered under a broadside from Aubrey Jones (of the now-defunct Prices and Incomes Board), to whom the Labour government had referred bank charges. Jones (as was his habit) interpreted his brief in the widest terms, and came out with a well-documented indictment. He drew attention to the high profits that the banks were earning, through the prevailing high bank rate; he recommended that the banks should open later, should reduce their work force (by more efficient methods) by twelve per cent in four years, should cut down branches, should absorb their hire-purchase offshoots, should abolish their agreement on common interest rates and publish their profits. There were predictable pained grunts from the banks; the chairman of the clearing banks, Duncan Stirling, said icily that he disliked all the recommendations and could not single out which he disliked most. The unanimity of the reaction seemed to bear out the complaints about their defensive cartel. But three years later they *did* voluntarily publish their assets and profits.

HIRE PURCHASE

Lending money is the main business of the banks, but they only account for a quarter of the total amount borrowed by ordinary consumers. When Lord Crowther produced his report on consumer credit in March 1971 he revealed that the total consumer debt in 1969 had been £12·7 billion pounds, of which £4·2 billion was new credit. Nearly half the new credit was accounted for by money for houses, most of it provided by building societies; a quarter of it came from banks lending to their customers; and most of the rest came from various forms of hire-purchase— whether from shops, mail order houses or the 'finance houses' who are the main hire-purchase dealers. Hire-purchase is essentially an extension of banking, geared to the future: but it was ignored or scorned by the old bankers, and grew up from quite different roots.

Building societies are the most solid form of hire-purchase. They began as poor men's clubs during the early nineteenth century: the first one recorded was in Birmingham in 1781, when subscribers arranged to meet once a month at the Fountain tavern, paying half a guinea a share towards a building scheme. Houses were chosen by ballot, and 'ballot-and-sale societies', often based on pubs, grew up all over the midlands. At the same time the Nonconformist Churches in the midlands and Yorkshire began thrift clubs and sick benefit clubs, which expanded into house-building: and the movement had great support from social reformers, like Bright and Cobden, who saw property as a key to the franchise. The Abbey National Building Society (which now has its ugly headquarters in Baker Street, sometimes thought to be the site of Sherlock Holmes's rooms) represents a merger of chapel and pub—the Abbey Road Baptist Chapel, and the National Society, which met in the London Tavern. Forty-five years ago the combined assets of the two societies were two million pounds: by 1970 they were £1,300 million. The biggest of all is the Halifax, with assets of £1,700 million. It is still based on Halifax, and patronised since 1853—when it was founded—by the Halifax family. It still fancies its Northern independence, and most of its board comes from West Riding.

In spite of their vast expansion, the building societies have kept much of their character of nonconformity and self-help; their chairmen are likely to be earnest, moral men who are proud of their involvement in house-building. Aubrey Jones investigated them, too, and seemed more impressed by them than by the banks. His report felt able to say: 'The building society movement has played a major part in financing the growth of home owner-ship which has taken place over the past fifty years. In 1914 only some ten per cent of the total stock of $8\frac{1}{2}$ million houses was owner-occupied; today there are $17\frac{1}{2}$ million houses, nearly half of which are owner-occupied. The growth and strength of their movement is something about which the societies feel justifiably proud; it has no counterpart in any other country.'[1] But the building societies are not much thanked, either by the people they lend money to, or by the people they don't (a large category, including women and immigrants). The societies' utilitarian attitudes to architecture and their extreme conservatism towards customers are the depressing corollaries of their cautious tradition.

The building societies occupy an odd place in Britain's financial world, competing in a very quiet way, watched carefully by the Bank of England, existing somewhere in that large no-man's-land between the private and the public sector. Like the banks in the nineteenth century, they are gradually merging into bigger units. Already half the total assets of the building societies are held by the 'big six', and amalgamations are proceeding steadily—in the fourteen years to 1968 the number dropped from 900 to 525. In the last few years their sheltered province has been invaded by more aggressive money-men: unit trusts, as we have seen, have made links with them to offset their own loss of custom, and in 1970 the Abbey National, for all its caution, went into partnership with a brand-new company, Property Growth Assurance, to promote the controversial new form of investment—property bonds, without fixed interest, linked to life assurance. This coming-together of three fields from different traditions—building societies, insurance and unit trusts—is part of a new trend in the city, made more rapid by the pace of inflation, to create companies catering for all kinds of investment, and well-placed to deal in all kinds of savings, whatever the current fashion.

Hire-purchase in goods had a more commercial and less moral origin than building societies, and for a long time it was regarded with scepticism. It began with the invention of the sewing-

[1] Command 3136, para 16.

machines in the mid-nineteenth century, which were expensive, long-lasting and productive; the Singer company began selling them by hire-purchase, and their idea was followed by piano-makers and furniture makers. The Civil Service Mutual Furnishing Association was founded in 1877 by a group of senior civil servants (an odd side-line for deputy secretaries) to assist their juniors to furnish their homes. Meanwhile, during the 1860s, 'wagon companies' had been formed in the north of England, to provide hire-purchase for railway trucks (which the railways did not provide) to take coal from the mines to the merchants. From filling this gap, the companies expanded to cars and equipment: the 'North Central Wagon and Finance Company' and the 'British Wagon Company' became two of the biggest hire-purchase concerns.

Hire-purchase, unlike building societies, outraged many non-conformist consciences, and the companies, like the insurance collectors, could be ruthless in enforcing 'snatch-backs' if payments had lapsed. Not until 1938 was a Hire-Purchase Act passed which partly protected the hirer, and effective legislation was not passed until 1962. Much of the prejudice against hire-purchase dissolved in the post-war boom: TV, washing machines, refrigerators and above all cars multiplied under the never-never. Hire-purchase profits depend heavily on making money out of the newly-prosperous masses; and the exploitation of this market, like the market for building societies or insurance, tends to come from outsiders who have grown up outside the city nexus. For a long time hire-purchase was looked at askance by bankers, until in 1958 Barclays took a share in the biggest of them United Dominions Trust (UDT), which had begun in 1919 as an American offshoot, and had grown into a major City institution: their chairman, Sir Alexander Ross, is now the first never-never knight.

Government control of hire-purchase has grown up very gradually and inadequately, as scandals and exploitations have come to light; and shops and companies have been able to disguise their high rates of interests from their customers. When Lord Crowther reported in 1971, he recommended the replacement of the mass of separate acts controlling moneylending with a new act to strengthen the safeguards for consumers, and to insist on the true rate of interest being clearly shown. He also advocated the setting up of a Credit Commissioner to administer a licensing system, to enforce the new Act and to be an Ombudsman for complaints about money-lending.

MERCHANT BANKS

With the merchant banks we come to the traditional heart of the business, with individuals able to take risks, and to make large sums of money for themselves and their clients. The merchant banks stand in relationship to Barclays or the Midland rather as a bookie stands to the Tote. They are controlled by a small number of rich people, dealing largely for other rich people: they do not bother with counters for small customers. Many of them are still hereditary businesses, controlled by the same family over the past century or so. As an institution, merchant banking descends from seventeenth-century merchants, most of them from Germany, who developed into bankers— selling their signatures instead of their goods. They found it more profitable to deal in credit than materials, and they made money both by guaranteeing other people's credit (accepting houses) and by raising loans (issuing houses). In these delicate operations, their integrity and judgment became their chief assets—their main justification for hereditary bias. Ever since the Medicis of Florence, the merchant banks have been dynastic, passing down their know-how, wealth, and sometimes brains.

In the early nineteenth century the London merchant bankers were richer than governments; Rothschilds financed whole armies, and Barings developed South America. But they have never been quite the same since. The great bank of Overend and Gurney collapsed in 1852, and further setback came with the South American slump of 1890, when Barings had to be rescued from ruin by the Governor of the Bank of England (who ordered the other bankers to come to their assistance). A new decline in all banks' foreign business came after the first world war, when nationalism and the rise of Nazi Germany made foreign loans far more risky. Since then the London bankers have turned more to managing other people's money, in pension funds, investment trusts or unit trusts, and to advising industry at home—a connection once considered undesirable, but which now supplies a large part of their profits.

In the meantime the wealth of the merchant banks was being eclipsed by the Treasury, the industrial corporations, and the provincial institutions which were pushing their way up—insurance companies, building societies and joint stock banks. New financiers, working through holding companies, had become more powerful, if less respectable, than the bankers. The city, which can be dazzled by romance, often credits merchant bankers with more influence than they have: many have lived on their names, and clung to old business instead of looking for new. But their connections and knowledge still give big opportunities, and a few banks have had a visible effect on the pattern of trade.

The elite of the banks are the seventeen 'accepting houses', who have the backing of the Bank of England to accept other people's bills—to guarantee payment by one firm to another. The 'acceptance business' is less important today, when many firms are richer than their banks, and can finance themselves; and most banks are more active as 'issuing houses'—floating new issues of shares. But the directors of the acceptance houses, backed by the Bank of England, are regarded as the core of the city establishment. Most are hereditary firms, and only two have been founded since 1900. Families still dominate most of the boards, and most chairmen are hereditary. There were the seventeen banks of the Accepting Houses Committee in January 1971, with their date of foundation, their chairmen or senior partners, and their total assets in 1970:

			£ millions
1763	Baring Brothers	John Baring	141
1804	N. M. Rothschild	Edmund de Rothschild	n.a.
1804	J. Henry Schroder Wagg	Gordon Richardson	410
1805	Wm. Brandt's Sons	W. A. Brandt	110
1808	Antony Gibbs	Sir Giles Gibbs	35
1810	Brown Shipley	I. H. T. Garratt-Orme	70
1830	Kleinwort, Benson	C. H. Kleinwort	326
1831	Hill, Samuel	Sir Kenneth Keith	504
1833	Arbuthnot Latham	Nigel Robson	40
1836	Guinness, Mahon	Charles Villiers	70
1838	Morgan Grenfell	Viscount Harcourt	161
1839	Hambros	Jocelyn Hambro	441
1853	Samuel Montagu	David Montagu	282
1877	Lazards	Lord Poole	193
1880	Charterhouse Japhet	W. R. L. Warnock	37
1919	Rea Brothers	Walter Salomon	41
1946	S. G. Warburg	Sir Siegmund Warburg	141

The old merchant bankers cultivate a formal atmosphere of

Tradition and Dignity, which makes it easier to demoralise clients and to put over tough deals. Their traditional weapon is the Lunch, where guests are ushered into the private dining-room to have their brains picked, to soften them up for a deal, or to provide culture, gossip or prestige. The gentlemanly aura is not quite what it was. In the past ten years the old families have had to recruit more clever men from outside, and to promote some to be partners; but however clever, the newcomers are apt to find themselves left out of the innermost counsels. The main object of merchant banks is, after all, to make the rich richer.

To a remarkable extent, the two oldest banking families, the Barings and Rothschilds, still hold their own; their old rivalry reached a new stage under Ted Heath, who appointed a Baring as Ambassador to Washington, and a Rothschild to run a brains trust in the Cabinet office. The oldest family, the Barings, are descendants of a deaf clothing manufacturer, Sir Francis Baring, who was known as the 'first merchant in Europe' when he died in 1810, leaving seven million pounds. The Barings established themselves as one of the most powerful of the great Whig families: in 1818 it was said that there were six great powers in Europe—England, France, Russia, Austria, Prussia and Baring Brothers. Since the 1890 disaster their financial power has been less spectacular: they are nowadays agents rather than principals: a lot of their business is still in South America. But the influence of the family has remained. Three Barings help to run the bank, and there are no fewer than five separate Baring peerages—Cromer, Northbrook, Revelstoke, Ashburton and Howick. They have provided two Chancellors of the Exchequer, a Governor-General of India (first Lord Northbrook), a novelist (Maurice), a Lord Chamberlain (second Lord Cromer), a Governor of Kenya (Lord Howick) and the present ambassador to Washington and former Governor of the Bank of England (third Earl of Cromer), who, like the first earl (the modernizer of Egypt) could well be called Overbaring.

The second oldest and certainly the most famous of the banking families is the Rothschilds. Their symbol of the five arrows commemorates the five Rothschild brothers who first scattered to London, Paris, Vienna, Naples and Frankfurt. The English house was founded by Nathan, a cotton merchant in Manchester; three of his great-great-grandsons and one of his great-great-great-grandsons are now directors. Rothschilds is now less romantic: no longer does the Rothschild pigeon bring in the news, the Rothschild boat lie waiting off Folkestone, or Rothschild couriers leave daily for the capitals of Europe. Armies (such as Wellington's in Spain) no longer need wait for Rothschild support. They are now, like most banks, much more agents and brokers than entrepreneurs themselves. But in the last few years they have shown some revival in their money-making spirit, founding hire-purchase firms and unit trusts, and making use of 'venture capital'. The most active partner is Jacob Rothschild, son of Lord Rothschild in the cabinet office. Unlike his zoologist father, Jacob shows all his forefathers' zeal and acumen for money; he is a complex character, combining a shy, fastidious manner with a love of competitiveness, whether in back-gammon, big fights or big business deals; and he has brought in ambitious contemporaries, to bring new drive and cunning into the bank.

Other old families still remain in control. Hambros are descended from a remarkable Dane, Carl Joachim Hambro, who set up in London in 1839, and who raised loans for Cavour just before the unification of Italy; they still have important links with Scandinavia. Their chairman is now Jocelyn Hambro, a keen supporter of the Tories who made a great point of increasing his salary to £25,000 a year when the Labour government was trying to freeze wages; he annoys rivals with his public relations and glossy brochures. Samuel Montagu was founded by Lord Swaythling in 1853, and is now run by his great-grandson, David Montagu, another publicist who often appears on television, and is a director of London Weekend Television. The family holding is now comparatively tiny, and Montagu likes to suggest that being a Montagu has nothing to do with his appointment: the large shareholders include the Midland Bank and Pearl Assurance.

In a special position is Lazards, descended from the French-Jewish Lazard Frères, but now emphatically British. Lazards twelve years ago was regarded as the very heart of the English banking establishment, closely linked with Morgan Grenfell; together they typified the 'gentlemen', as opposed to the 'players', preoccupied with hanging on to their money, and stopping things happening. In the 'Great Aluminium War' of 1958 Lazards helped to form the consortium which tried to stop the American intruders Reynolds Metals (helped by Warburg's bank) from taking over British Aluminium. But since then Lazards have become much more like players, and have organised take-overs of the kind they used to deplore. Lazards are part of the huge financial empire of Lord Cowdray, one of the richest men in Britain. Cowdray is the heir to the oil fortune of his great-grand-father, Weetman Pearson, who founded the Mexican Eagle oil company, later merged into Shell-Mex. His main company, S. Pearson and Sons, went public in 1969, valued at £70 million. But Cowdray remains chairman, his cousin-in-law Pat Gibson is deputy chairman, and his twin sister Mrs Campbell Preston remains chairman of the Westminster Press. The Cowdray interests (apart from their large holdings abroad) include a virtual monopoly of the British financial press (with the *Financial Times*, and a half-share of the *Investors' Chronicle* and *The Economist*), the Westminster Press chain of provincial papers, Longmans the publishers and (through them) Penguin Books. The political spectrum, from left-wing Penguin books discussing the revolution to the right-wing *Economist*, is bizarre; but Cowdray has not so far been much given to interfering with political properties, providing they make money. He does not often appear at Lazards (of which he owns two-thirds); leaving it to be run by the bank's chairman, Lord Poole. Poole is very much a city figure in his own right, with a tall, aloof presence and a single intimidating eye. He has mastered both finance and politics; for twelve years he was a key figure in Tory party organisation, and became probably the most effective party chairman since Woolton. He speaks in epigrams, and gives clipped decisive opinions punctuated by 'y' know what I mean?', without much fear of contradiction.

Merchant banks, however much money and prestige they in-herit, tend to depend on the personality and energy of the boss. Two important banks in the last decade have been built up round dominating men. Warburgs was only established in 1946, by a cultivated German refugee, Siegmund Warburg, who came from a Hamburg banking family with old international connections. Warburg quickly perceived new opportunities—particularly in industrial mergers. He advised Associated Television in its forma-tion, Roy Thomson in buying *The Sunday Times* and *The Times*, and the *Daily Mirror* in buying Amalgamated Press and Odhams; he advised Donald Stokes in the merger of BMC and Leyland. He turned to the raising of foreign loans in London, and made links with the advertising agency Masius Wynn Williams, and with Gallup Poll. He brought in a team of clever young men from all kinds of professions. At the time of the Aluminium War he was regarded as the archetypal outsider, always doing 'what's not done'; but now at 69 he is Sir Siegmund, one of the grand old men of the city; like a diva, he is always announcing his retirement from the bank, but never actually retiring.

The biggest of all the merchant banks is a new personal empire. Hill, Samuel was formed in 1965 as a merger of M. Samuel (a family bank then headed by Lord Bearsted, whose grandfather founded Shell) with Philip Hill's, relatively an upstart bank, which had been much enlarged by Kenneth Keith, a brusque number-cruncher who had come into banking from accountancy. The marriage was almost disastrous; Bearsted was supposed to be chairman, Keith chief executive, and another man from Samuel's, Lord Melchett, expected to be number two; but Keith was determined to dominate the big bank, and the Samuel's men were very cross. Eventually an outside dignitary, Lord Sherfield (the ex-ambassador to Washington), had to be brought in to mediate as chairman, and Lord Melchett went off in a huff to become chairman of British Steel. By 1970 Keith had won his full victory, and became chairman. Sir Kenneth, as he now is, is a controversial banker—a relentless fighter, not trying to conceal his ambition and impatience. He has a finger in all kinds of pies; he is a member of Neddy, a director of *The Times*, vice-chairman of BEA, a director of Beechams, of Eagle Star Insurance, of the National Westminster Bank: and his own board at Hill, Samuel's is a careful microcosm of the city, industry and the civil service. He has made some big mistakes; he went into a disastrous property venture with the New York property king, Bill Zeckendorf, and backed Bernard Cornfeld when other banks were sensibly chary. In 1970 Keith tried to merge with the huge property company, MEPC, to form a giant combine of land *and* money (see chapter 29) but the shareholders did not support him, and the deal never went through. His rivals rejoiced.

JIM SLATER

The barriers are breaking down between banking and other money-making activities, and the convention that bankers should remain aloof from industry, as advisers rather than participants, is dissolving. Ambitious men like to have an iron in every fire—industry, property, insurance and banking. Jim Slater, the most phenomenal of all intruders into the city, who only came into the financial field seven years ago, could be classified as financier, unit trust manager, industrialist or banker; and his impact rests on the deployment of all his resources. Slater's astonishing rise— a tempting but misleading model for others—is symptomatic of the British situation in which, while industry as a whole is ailing, great fortunes can be made by buying and selling companies. There are many precedents for Slater's kind of operation; one of them was the late Harley Drayton, who built up the network of investments now known as the '117 Group'[1] which are currently the largest single shareholders in Slater's company. But in recent years Slater has operated with a speed and a capacity to buy in new talent which has eclipsed all rivals.

Still only forty-two, Jim Slater has a sense of command which quickly gives confidence to others; he is a tall, good-looking man, with none of the pale, withdrawn look of so many money-men. He is a salesman as well as a financier, looking you straight in the face as he pronounces his emphatic policies. He operates briskly from his 'nerve-centre', Slater Walker Securities, in a new building next to St Paul's, surrounded by fast-talking young men analysing balance sheets, watching share prices, investigating properties, waiting for opportunities to pounce into companies, to take them over or sell them out. What matters to Slater, he insists, is not making *things*, but making *money*. He is unique in his capacity to analyse situations, to work out his strategy and tactics as if in a war-game, to look at the city manoeuvres from above; he is closer in attitude to the property tycoons (see chapter 29) or to an industrial entrepreneur like Sir Arnold Weinstock than to most bankers in the city.

Unlike most of the entrepreneurs in England, Slater is entirely English. His father, after some time in the army, started a small building-and-decorating business in Kensington (the same kind of business as Heath's father). He wanted his son to have some qualification, and Slater, after school at Preston Manor County School, began an accountancy course. He was not noticeably bright or ambitious; he was called up in the army after the war (he didn't want to be exempted and didn't want a commission) but his experience in the ranks, with men who saw no prospects in their lives, gave him (he says) the urge to push ahead. He came out with new motivation, sailed through his accountancy, and joined a group of metal-finishing companies; he uncovered some

[1] See *Anatomy of Britain* (1962), pp. 394-7.

accountancy mistakes, and was made general manager at twenty-four. He went from there to AEC, the bus-making company, which were soon taken over by Leyland; he became deputy sales director and, without being much interested in buses, much improved their finances.

When he was thirty-two he became ill with a virus and worried about whether he might lose his job; he investigated the stock exchange, and backed a firm called Bernard Wardle, making plastic seat-covers for cars and which had got a big contract from Ford (he knew about it through the motor industry). Slater put his savings of £2,000 into it, with another £8,000 borrowed from the bank. In two years the share value multiplied by seven.

He stayed for a time with Leylands, becoming their financial director, and then went on his own. He met Peter Walker, another city whizz-kid then in insurance, and together they took over a 'shell' company called H. Lotery which owned the old P and O building in the city. They sold it a year later with half-a-million pounds profit; and the company changed its name to Slater Walker, with Slater as chairman. He bought and sold shares on the rising market and supported by the growing value of his own shares he moved into take-overs, culminating in the capture of a major industrial company, Crittall-Hope—a merger of two family-firm window-frame makers. He moved in immediately. He told the directors that he was not there to make windows, but to make money; he fired numbers of workers, and several directors. His principle, he says, is to be ruthless in decision, considerate in execution: and his behaviour at Crittall-Hope (from what I have heard) lived up to the maxim; he was generous and conscientious in compensation. He soon sold off the profitable bits of the company, making more money out of the bits than out of the total: it is a key part of the Slater technique that the sum of the parts is often worth more than the whole.

Slater Walker shares, riding high on the stock market, were being used to buy a whole range of industries—optical shops, rubber manufacturers, building merchants—merging them, rationalising, splitting up, selling off. Slater Walker was well on the way to becoming a 'conglomerate' on the pattern fashionable in America in 1967 and 1968, with huge multi-industry companies like Ling Temco Vought keeping their share prices high by successive acquisitions. Slater perceived more clearly than many

of the American conglomerate-kings the dangers of the dizzy
spiral. By February 1969, before the slump came, he had stopped
issuing 'Slater Walker paper', and moved into banking; he bought
from Isaac Wolfson (an aggressor of an earlier generation) the
merchant bank Ralli Brothers, which Wolfson had not really
exploited. Slater could now proclaim himself an 'investment
banker' which (as he explained in his 1969 report) meant that:
'Slater Walker is now a fully authorised bank able to carry on all
forms of banking business. In many circumstances it acts for
clients in exactly the same way as a merchant bank. In other circumstances, however, it takes a substantial stake in the equity of
the client company as well as acting as its merchant bank.' Slater
was in fact moving towards a formula more common in Germany
and France, of banks being not the agents but the controllers of
industry.

He continued to move in and out of other businesses. He started
his own insurance company. He bought a large share of Hay's
Wharf, on the Thames, and sold it, with a one-and-a-half million
pound profit, to a consortium of Lazards and Max Rayne. He
made another quick half million from his share of Gamages, the
rambling old shop in Holborn, whose site was found to be unexpectedly valuable. He operated not only through his own
company, but through young men whom he had encouraged to go
out on their own—so that they could advance together on a wide
front, with constant surprises.

Slater has survived the heady experience of his seven-year-
wonder with apparent stability. His colleagues and clients watch
his health and psychology, on which so much of their prospects
depend, with obsessive anxiety; but he shows no signs of cracking
up. When the stock market turned sour, he maintains, the experience was 'character-building', and his zeal for money, in the old
Puritan tradition, seems linked with self-denial. He married, quite
late, his former secretary, and lives much as he used to when
with Leylands, in an unpretentious house in Esher—with only a
swimming pool to proclaim his millions. He insists that at home
he can now switch off from his money-mindedness to read Peter
Rabbit instead of balance-sheets; he has bought a farm at
Cranleigh, takes eight weeks' holiday a year and works a four-day
week.

He contemplates his own motivation as if he were talking about
someone else; he sees himself as a chess-player (at which he

excels), extending his skills to the great game of the city, and urged on by a driving desire to prove himself right. Politically, like most self-made men, he supports Heath's views on the need for self-reliance and the dangers of cosseting; he has dined at Downing Street, and he is (like Walker) the very paragon of the new Heath-type Tory—self-made, hard-working, unsentimental, competitive. Certainly in the financial world he has stimulated a new aggressiveness, unleashing energies and money-mindedness: he loves to watch his young protégés discover their money-making potential, as he discovered his ten years before. He also appears more interested in industry and more experienced in it than most city men: he knows something about factories, and prescribes his own rules for the reform of industry (abolish non-voting shares, increase shareholders' powers, relax laws of libel, etc.). But how far can financial re-jigging really cope with Britain's basic industrial problems? There is a quiet irony in the fact that, in the midst of this hectic money-making, Slater was invited to come back to British Leyland—then in serious straits after its merger with BMC[1] —as a non-executive director. The conjunction of Slater and Leyland (whose average profits were by now less than Slater Walker's) highlighted the contrast between the worlds of finance and industry—the one making huge profits out of buying and selling, the other faced with the intractable problems of incompetent management and recalcitrant labour.

Many other financiers have recently made smaller fortunes in the same kind of way as Slater, speculating with shares, buying and selling bits of industry and property; some protégés of Slater, others rivals. Oliver Jessel, born rich from an old city family, was determined to make his own millions, and has built up Jessel Securities with a network of unit trusts and industrial companies. Pat Matthews, the son of a Polish-Jewish immigrant, a cabinet-maker in the East End, began as an aircraft draughtsman, and is now, at fifty, the boss of First National Finance, which combines hire-purchase, merchant banking, unit trusts, and property. Christopher Selmes began speculating in shares at school at fifteen: after school he worked with Jessel and Matthews and then started up his own group, Drakes, which secretly bought control of a company, Franco Signs, with concealed assets which he then sold off at great profit. He is now reckoned to be a millionaire at twenty-six.

[1] See chapter 34.

Financiers often say that shrewd take-overs and exploitation of assets benefit not only them but the whole country, by quickening competition and keeping companies up to the mark. Certainly the raiders have disturbed the somnolence of many boards, and have forced them to pay more attention to their hidden hoards. But the financiers have usually had remarkably little effect on the actual running of the companies. The general public can see *how* little in the case of big department stores, many of which (with their valuable real estate) have in the last decades fallen into the hands of financial operators. The late Lord Fraser took over the Barkers group and then the Harrods group (now run by his son); Charles Clore took over half the shoe shops in Britain, and then the Lewis's group, which includes Selfridges. Many people expected these hard-headed new bosses quickly to transform the leisurely pace of the big stores, with their armies of melancholy assistants, and their fleets of vans ready to deliver a loaf of bread or a tin of sardines. Old customers of Harrods awaited with dread the time when they could no longer leave their bills for a year, and when the acres of grand pianos would be rolled away to make way for quick-selling items. They need not have worried. Even in Clore's shoe shops, the salesgirls still rummage slowly through rows of old shoe boxes.

Can these really be the dynamic, profit-minded empires of ruthless tycoons? The answer is surely that financial skills are very different from management skills, and often opposite in motivation. The financiers like Slater do not usually want to hang on to their industrial companies and are in no position to build up a hierarchy of management, which depends on continuity. The insistence on making money rather than things may generate commercial drive: it does not help to build up the trust and self-respect of workers on which long-term management depends. The very success of many financiers depends on the compactness and flexibility of their own office, and their avoidance of long-term commitments: they are a world away from the kind of efficient management of industry which really benefits the consumers and the country. Between them is the great ravine which separates the city and the factory floor.

27

Accountants

Accountants are the witch-doctors of the modern world and willing
to turn their hands to any kind of magic.

Lord Justice Harman, February 1964.

POPULATING the border-country between shareholders, directors,
lawyers and managers, and often very unsure where they belong,
is the huge and relatively new profession of accountants, whose
status fluctuates erratically between that of a priesthood, a servant-
class and a coven of witches. In the last few years, rather abruptly,
the role of the accountants—and particularly of the auditors who
inspect company accounts—has come to be fiercely questioned;
and facts and figures which before seemed hard-edged appeared
often to conceal areas of very personal guesswork. Whether the
accountants are serving the shareholders or the directors has come
to be a central question of financial democracy.

The more fragmented and diversified a company becomes, the
more important becomes the man who can disentangle the threads
of profitability that hold it together. From the accountants'
knowledge comes his power: the telegraphic address of the
Institute of Chartered Accountants is UNRAVEL. The growth
of the profession has been spectacular. In 1940 there were about
34,000 accountants: by February 1970 there were 80,000—three
times the number of solicitors and more than thirty times the
number of barristers. Their scope has been multiplied by taxation,
which can mould the shape of a modern corporation, and of

which few people except accountants can make sense. The prevailing 'innumeracy' (as Lord Crowther first called it), the ignorance and fear of figures of the average British businessman, has enhanced the accountants' mystique.

Accountants or former accountants have long played a decisive role in British industry. In the slumpish times of the twenties and thirties several large firms were rescued by accountants, as Lever Brothers was rescued by Francis D'Arcy Cooper. Since the war the flow of accountants into industry has become a torrent. Among them are John Davis, the Chairman of the Rank Organisation, and Conservative John Davies, now Minister for Trade and Industry; A. F. McDonald, Chairman of Distillers; Jim Slater of Slater Walker; Lord McFadzean, Chairman of BICC; and Ian Morrow, who moved in to run what was left of Rolls-Royce in 1971—the accountants' victory over the engineers. Probably the most ubiquitous of them is Sir Charles Hardie, one of the pluralists of the city, who in 1970, at the peak of his pluralism, was director of ten companies and chairman of six of them, nearly all of them important: MEPC (£11,750 a year), British Printing Corporation (£9,600), BOAC (£6,500), the White Fish Authority (£4,375), the Vokes Group (£5,187), and Fitch Lovell (£8,500). Hardie is a healthy-looking sixty with a face like a smiling sun, with bright blue eyes piercing out of it. His is a quiet life, he assured me in 1970, never working weekends or evenings. He organises his board meetings for the last two weeks of every month, which each takes only a third of a day. For the rest of the time he sits in his office as a chartered accountant at Dixon, Wilson, Tubbs, Gillett, which analyses his companies' figures for him (he pays his salaries into the firm). He finds much the same problems, he says, in every industry.

The accountants, however powerful, have till recently been a pariah profession. They are a striking example of the British reluctance to accept new occupations; like actuaries or scientists, they have come in through the back door. Their beginnings were squalid. The first accountants, who began practising in the city about 1840, were invariably associated with bankruptcy and liquidations; like undertakers, they had an aura of gloom. With the passing of the Companies' Act of 1862 and the Bankruptcy Act of 1869—which provided for the appointment of an accountant for creditors—the occupation became much more important, but still associated with calamity. Ernest Cooper, a founder of Cooper

Brothers, has described their position when he first went to the city in 1864: 'We could hardly, south of the Tweed, claim to be a profession. There was absolutely no organisation or co-operation, no Institute or Society, no examinations, very few articled clerks, no newspaper, no library, no benevolent fund, and not even a dining club or golf club. Our social position was not enviable . . . I well remember that to be seen talking to, or having your office entered by, an accountant, was to be avoided, particularly in the stressful times of 1866.'

In 1880 'The Institute of Chartered Accountants in England and Wales' (ICA) was founded, which now accounts for more than half the present number, and the job became a profession with its own rules of conduct. Joint stock companies required independent auditors by law, and accountants soon became associated with normality rather than disaster. But they never acquired the dignity of lawyers or doctors. Their education remains stark: there are few university courses, no collegiate spirit, little sense of brotherhood. Most accountants are taught at evening classes or at 'crammers', run by commercial firms for profit—a bleak initiation. They are now gradually beginning to widen the curriculum: but their training like that of actuaries still neglects the social implications of their work. In Scotland their status, like that of teachers and engineers, is higher, partly because the courts made earlier use of accountants: Sir Walter Scott, as early as 1820, recommended that his nephew 'cannot follow a better line than that of an accountant'. Edinburgh had its society of accountants in 1854, twenty-six years before England, and the Scots training is broader, and insists on higher qualifications.

More than half the members of the ICA work in accountants' firms run by partnerships—ranging from single men advising on taxation, to international institutions. Eight firms dominate the profession: one or other of their names can usually be seen above the annual reports of any industrial giant. They are almost the same, remarkably, as the Big Eight in America: these are they, in rough order of importance (they are much too secretive to divulge the size of their staff; 'They'd kill me if I told you,' said one man at Cooper's):

1 Peat, Marwick, Mitchell	5 Arthur Anderson
2 Cooper Brothers	6 Touche Ross
3 Price, Waterhouse	7 Arthur Young
4 Deloitte, Plender, Griffiths	8 McLelland Moores

Their main job is still auditing, and once a year their emissaries arrive at their clients' offices to check through last year's ledgers: nowadays with mechanisation and standardisation, auditors concentrate on checking the systems rather than all the figures. Auditing occupies about eighty per cent of most accountants' time, but as the large partnerships have grown in resources, so they have extended their services to present themselves to their clients (in their phrase) as 'guide, philosopher and friend'. They can know more about a company's workings than most directors; they can advise on taxation problems, systems of costing, pension schemes, capital structure, office organisation. The 'big four' have broader international connections than most bankers and consultants. Travelling from one corporation to another, they can compare their problems—acting as business doctors, putting their stethoscopes near the heart, checking the blood stream, diagnosing intestinal troubles. A large company planning a project a bridge or a take-over will often commission accountants to report on its feasibility, and to introduce what they call 'realism'. After engineers have drawn up plans for a dam, a group of accountants will fly out, peruse the figures, compare them with other projects, cross-examine the engineers, and produce their own gloomier report. The 'special investigation' is being increasingly used by the government and even by the Treasury.

The ICA (the Chartered Accountants in England and Wales) is the biggest group of accountants, but there are five other bodies, including the Scots and Irish Institutes, the Association of Certified and Corporate Accountants (ACCA) with 13,000 members, and the Institute of Costs and Works Accountants (ICWA) with 11,500 members, which was set up in 1919 with the sole object of training accountants for service in industry. In 1970, after four years' protracted negotiations, the six bodies planned to merge, with plans for common education and for a two-tier system to allow for both graduate members and articled students— the traditional 'cheap labour' of accountancy. But the plan was rejected by a large majority of the *younger* members of the ICA who, having just served their time of drudgery, didn't want their numbers diluted by other associations and resented their own council's behaviour. The ICA was left rather shell-shocked by the result, having just built new headquarters in Moorgate at the cost of £2 million to prepare for the merger. As with the engineers, the British passion for autonomy dies hard.

The ICA is much concerned with improving the name of accountancy, particularly in order to attract more graduates. In 1963 only 318 graduates came into the ICA; in 1970 there were 1,095, still less than a quarter of their intake of 4,704. The ICA's propaganda booklet stresses the ancient roots of accountancy, as 'the cornerstone of the business world'; it points out that the earliest surviving records of ancient civilisations—such as the Linear script tablets—as often as not illustrate financial transactions, or are concerned with public finance. A doctor's son, Roger, going into accountancy, explains that it is as creative as any other part of business, a 'fascinating mixture of bloodhound and management consultant'.

The auditor is often represented as the linchpin in the company system—the licensed spy of the shareholders, the independent assessor of a company's performance. The Companies' Act of 1948 demands that at each annual meeting a company shall appoint an auditor. If there is any uncertainty the auditors should say so; but accountants have become accustomed to making only the bare minimum of comments unless the situation is disastrous, so that for Deloitte's or Cooper's to 'qualify their report'—to suggest that sums have not been accounted for—is a terrible indictment of a business. In practice, the auditor is not as unquestionably independent as he appears; though theoretically representing the shareholders, he is in effect appointed by the directors and paid by them; and if he threatens to qualify his accounts, or causes trouble, discreet reasons can be found for not appointing him again. The same auditors, working year after year for the same company, become closely involved in its workings, just as outside directors do, who are likewise supposed to provide independent views. For an auditor to cast public doubt on a company, toppling its share prices and threatening the board, is a brave act; and there are plenty of excuses for not doing it.

The linchpin is very suddenly exposed in a take-over, when the sitting directors are fighting for their lives; and in the late sixties a series of battles brought the auditors painfully into the open. Profit forecasts published by companies like AEI, fighting against take-overs, turned out to be absurdly misleading; Kearton of Courtaulds and Weinstock of GEC both protested against the auditors' judgment. Then in 1969 came the Pergamon affair, (see chapter 30) when Robert Maxwell succeeded in embarrassing the accountants, as he embarrassed so many others. Pergamon, as a publishing firm, showed up very special difficulties; how can anyone value a stock like encyclopaedias, whose worth can fluctuate wildly according to how and when they are sold? By the end of the affair Pergamon's expectation of £2·1 million profits, as audited by one firm, Chalmers Impey, was cut down by another firm, Price Waterhouse, to only half a million.

Soon after the Pergamon rumpus, a Canadian professor of accountancy at Edinburgh, Edward Stamp, delivered a broadside at the English accountants. 'It is extraordinary,' he wrote in *The Times* of September 11, 1969, 'that a profession which believes in "full disclosure" reveals so little about what leads it to its belief in the truth and fairness of its clients' accounts.' He explained that among accountants the word 'principle' lends a 'spurious air of authority and accuracy to a situation which is in fact almost chaotic'. Their approach to principles, he said, may be satisfactory in prescribing the principles of plumbing, wall-papering, or carpentry: 'It is surely not good enough for a profession which believes itself the intellectual equal of the legal and medical professions.' He accused the English Institute of a 'heavy anti-intellectual bias', advised them to launch a full-scale research programme, and proposed a panel of judges to make sure that auditors were in fact independent: though his proposals turned out to be rather woolly. The President of the English Institute, Ronald Leach (the senior partner of Peat Marwick) protested the independence of auditors. But the Institute were sufficiently worried to produce in December 1969 a statement of intent for the seventies, to narrow the differences in accounting standards and to disclose the basis of their calculations; and four months later they published a survey of accounting methods by three hundred major British companies, which revealed how much confusion there was in such questions as stock valuation and research and development. The argument about how properly to present 'a true and fair view' rumbled through the accountancy profession; and Sir Henry Benson, the senior partner of Cooper Brothers and the doyen of the profession, even admitted that the Institute's approach should be firmer. The accountants, however, still dodge the most critical question, of who the auditors are responsible *to*.

It is not simply the issue of independence of accountants that is important to the whole relationship between shareholders and industry: it is the familiar British battle of disclosure against secrecy. All too easily accountants play in with the directors to prevent the true facts about companies coming to light. The Companies Act of 1967 tried to insist on more information being laid bare, by stipulating for instance that sales and profits in separate activities should be separately listed: but giant companies like ICI, supported by their accountants, can make a mockery of the act by giving the broadest possible breakdown of sales, giving no real clue as to the efficiency of different divisions and activities. If shareholders are really to have an influence on how companies are run or valued, then they have to have accountants on their side, as the openers-up of dark places. The battle for disclosure will need more than a new definition of accountants' principles: it may in the end need legislation to allow shareholders to compel the accountants to work in their interests.

TAXMEN

In this world nothing can be said to be certain, except death and taxes.
                                                  Benjamin Franklin, 1789.

Nothing has more boosted the accountants' profession than the growth of taxation, which can turn even a small business into an intricate financial operation. The accountants and tax inspectors have grown accustomed to their intricate embrace, like the interlocking of television all-in wrestlers with their own clinches, throws, grunts and groans. In America the lawyers have taken over much tax work, but in Britain the solicitors funked it, and left it to the new upstart profession (often amazingly ignorant of the law). Company tax brought the accountant into industry, and income-tax and surtax brought him into the home. Tax avoidance (as opposed to evasion) juggling with schedules, covenants, domiciles and discretionary trusts, has made the accountant more important to many families than a solicitor. Avoidance is regarded no longer as a nasty trickery, but as a private duty—a perpetual and inevitable war. 'No man in this country,' said Lord Clyde, former President of the Scottish Court of Session, in a famous judgment, 'is under the smallest obligation, moral or other, so to arrange his legal relations as to enable the Inland Revenue to put the largest shovel into his stores. The Inland Revenue is not slow ... to take every advantage which is open to it under the taxing statutes for the purpose of depleting the tax-payers' pocket. And the tax-payer is, in like manner, entitled to be astute enough to prevent, so far as he honestly can, the depletion of his means by the Revenue.'

Tax inspectors are old bogeys: they were first appointed in the eighteenth century, for all kinds of levies (newspapers were first printed in Fleet Street because it was close to Somerset House, where the papers were stamped for their duty). But the great bureaucracy of the Inland Revenue—still based on Somerset House, spoiling the beautiful riverside building—dates from the gradual extension of income-tax, first introduced by Pitt in 1799. With each new tax it expands further: in 1939 the Revenue had a staff of 25,000; today it has 65,000. The Revenue, not surprisingly, have difficulty with recruitment, and once they have trained a tax inspector (which costs about £8,000) it is not easy to keep him; over half of them leave the service, often to become experts on tax avoidance. The Inspectors' Association told the Fulton Committee that 'the tax inspector is too often the butt of music-hall jokes. He is regarded as the inhuman operator of an anti-social machine cramping the industrialist with high rates of tax and driving many of the best brains out of the country'. Next to the police the taxmen are probably the most unpopular sector of the bureaucracy, and the Ombudsman is bombarded with complaints against them; in the two years of March 1969 he investigated seventy-nine complaints against the Revenue, and recorded 'elements of maladministration' in thirty cases. 'We greatly regret these mistakes,' the Revenue replied, 'but they must be seen in perspective; our tax officers do business with over twenty-five million persons and conduct a vast volume of correspondence. Some half a million "pieces of paper", from taxpayers and from other offices, reach them every day.'

Though income tax has been levied for 170 years, taxation is still talked about as if it were something unnatural and temporary, interfering with some golden age, and distorting the patterns of human life. Industrial managers talk about high British taxation as if it destroyed their incentives and stunted their development. Certainly the impact of the Revenue can be seen in huge areas of daily life and organisation; the oddity of taxation laws explains the spate of weddings in autumn, the rush of dons to lecture in America, the proliferation of private dining-rooms, the fondness of authors for living abroad, and the nomadic existence of stars and pop singers. The future of the public schools, of London clubs or of the Institute of Directors, depends on whether or not they are 'deductible'. But taxation has become as much part of Englishness as the food and the weather: and English dreams of a 'tax haven', sheltered from the gales and squalls of the Revenue, usually turn out to be a chimera. The fiscal exile, living abroad to dodge taxes, unable to set foot in his country for fear of a huge tax bill, is often a forlorn character—a modern Flying Dutchman suffering from loss of identity as well as nationality, and liable to bouts of expatriates' paranoia. The old cry, no taxation without representation, could now also be reversed—no representation without taxation. Tax has become part of nationality, part of the fabric of the British way of life; and only very self-sufficient and cosmopolitan men can break away from it without some sense of diminution.

28

Insurance

The loss lighteth rather easily upon many than heavily upon few.
Act of Elizabeth, 1601.

THE financial giants of the city today are not the bankers or financiers, but the money-managers of the insurance companies and pension funds. In the field of investment it is they, as trustees for millions of individuals, who have taken the place of the magnates, dukes and Rothschilds who dominated the city a century ago. 'The Institutions'—as the insurance companies and pensions funds are enigmatically called—play with about a billion pounds of new money every year, enough to finance a new ICI. Their power has grown up outside the traditional mythology of Britain: there are no good novels about insurance, no fashionable memoirs of forty years with the Pru. Decisions are taken by clerkdoms more remote than the civil service, away from parliamentary questions, and the institutions emerge into the headlines even less than bankers. But their decisions are not only important to the stock exchange and to the millions of policyholders: they are also crucial —or could be crucial—for the climate of industrial competition, and for the character of boardrooms. They represent the largest chunks of capital in the country, and their use of it affects the whole temper of British capitalism.

Insurance is divided into two species. First, insurance against accidents—ships sinking, buildings burning, cars running over people. Secondly, insurance (or technically 'assurance') of a man's life against a *certainty*—death. The first kind is hazardous, based ultimately on a calculated gamble. The second is largely predictable, for the average span of men's lives—when hundreds of thousands are involved—can be quite accurately calculated.

The first kind, gruesomely called 'non-Life' insurance, has the oldest and most romantic origins. Insurance of ships followed Vasco da Gama's voyage, and the first recorded British policy was for the vessel *Santa Cruz*, in 1555. The 'Fire Office' was founded by Nicolas Barbon, son of Praise-God Barebones, in 1680, fourteen years after the Great Fire of London. Insurance followed the path of new inventions—against accidents in ships, trains, cars, aeroplanes, jets, jumbo jets, giant tankers—each invention giving new scope, and new problems. International insurance was a British development, and in the eighteenth century the symbols of British insurance companies—suns, phoenixes or globes—spread over Europe as the marks of trust in British money. In nineteenth-century Germany villagers saw the sun symbol—the face of a man inside a radiant sun—and knelt down to worship it. London no longer dominates insurance in Europe, but it remains its biggest insurance market: another example of Britain excelling at pre-industrial skills.

The traditional heart of 'non-life' insurance has been the collection of rich individuals and their friends known as Lloyd's—the city insurance market. The building of Lloyd's looms like a liner of grey stone, complete with an anchor outside it and a bridge crossing the street. Inside is the famous 'Room', 340 feet long, which contains the city insurance market of Lloyd's. It looks like a cavern in the centre of a streaked Danish Blue cheese. The ground floor is devoted to marine insurance (which accounts for a third of their business), motor and aviation, and the gallery deals with all other insurance from fire and accident to an opera singer's voice. The Room contains sometimes as many as four thousand people, all selling or buying insurance. Unlike most city activities, what is happening is quite clear: Lloyd's, like the stock exchange, is still basically a bazaar, pre-dating the era of office-blocks and telephones and it still keeps its simple seventeenth-century routine, when men gathered in Edward Lloyd's coffee-house to offer insurance for ships. Sitting on school-type benches four-in-a-row, in front of shelves and leather-bound ledgers, are the 'underwriters' of insurance, looking like over-grown schoolboys.

Wandering between the 'boxes' (as the desks are called) are the 'Lloyd's brokers', holding long folded cards, or 'slips', representing a ship, fleet, cargo or pair of legs to be insured.

The Room contains a typical city mixture of new and old devices. In the middle is a raised rostrum containing a man known as the 'caller' in a big red robe with a wide black collar, looking like a town-crier, reciting the names of brokers through a microphone. Above him is the old Lutine Bell, which is rung once for bad news of overdue ships, twice for good news (like the landing of the astronauts); and below it an electronic notice board showing names of brokers. Clerks inscribe the details of premiums and clients in their crowded dog-eared ledgers. The system looks medieval but in its lack of paper-work it is not unlike new ideas of office efficiency. Like most city places, it is very male; even though Lloyd's have now accepted women as members of syndicates, they do not allow them into the Room unaccompanied (though they may use the ante-rooms, and dining-rooms). Men do not seem to miss them, or to react at the sight of a rare girl in their midst: they seem, like civil servants, to enjoy their insulation. The young men are relaxed and self-assured, working, lounging on sofas, or standing chatting as if in a club.

The financial backbone of Lloyd's is made up by over six thousand 'names' grouped in 271 'syndicates', who provide the capital and must pay up for disasters—with unlimited liability. Each of the outside names has to be worth at least £50,000 (£75,000 for foreigners); these two-thirds are sleeping partners or 'backwoodsmen' who never go near the Room. The other quarter, the 'working names', need to put up £12,000 in deposits and about £2,500 in premium trust Funds. To be elected you must be sponsored by six members, and cross-examined by the Committee of Lloyd's; nowadays there are more grammar-school men, but Lloyd's is still a favourite public-school resort, and members include large numbers of old city families. People working at Lloyd's who are not members—known as 'substitutes'—are kept severely separate, and they even have their own substitutes' lavatory.

Lloyd's, like merchant banking, depends on a mixture of trust and daring. They were the first insurers in the world to cover cars, planes or crops, or to insure against earthquakes or twins and triplets. The whole procedure depends upon the 'gentleman's agreement', for the broker's slip is a mere formality, and is not legally binding. Their reputation relies not only upon their reliability, but on their readiness to insure almost *anything*, all in one big room, very quickly: as elsewhere in the city, the speed is the justification of the club. The pride of Lloyd's is its foreign trade: in 1969 nearly three-quarters of their annual premium income of £600 million came from overseas business, in over a hundred different countries. It is the special fascination of Lloyd's that, in spite of its apparent seclusion, it has to be sensitive to all the drama of world affairs: sometimes—as in negotiations over the ships trapped in the Suez Canal—members have to become temporary diplomats in their attempts to save losses. Insurance is critically affected by wars, revolutions, and meteorological disasters.

In the last few years Lloyd's has become very worried about the limitations of its capital in a growing world market—a worry made greater by a succession of diastrous years and escalating risks. After easy profits in the early sixties, Lloyd's men became careless in their underwriting, and signed their names without properly calculating the risks. The building of jumbo jets, giant tankers and vast oil refineries has increased Lloyd's scope, but the risks have been dangerously high to be carried by a group of individuals, each with unlimited liability: a single Boeing 747 costs £10 million to insure, and another £30 for third-party risks. There are now a hundred tankers of over a hundred thousand tons; the premium to ensure them all is £20 million pounds a year, but it costs that to repair three of them (there is now a million tonner on the drawing-board). In one disastrous fortnight in 1969 three giant tankers were lost in a fortnight; in 1970, when the airliners where blown up in Jordan, Lloyd's lost £10 million in three days. To try to expand its financial capacity and to open up into Europe Lloyd's has allowed foreigners—so far about a hundred—as well as women to become members; and in 1968 it appointed a committee, headed by the omnipresent Lord Cromer, to advise on its future capital needs. Cromer went so far as to recommend that the government should give tax concessions —an absurd bonanza (as the *Financial Times* agreed) for what is still one of the richest group of men in Britain. Most of Cromer's other recommendations have been accepted; and Lloyd's has also belatedly expanded into the field of life insurance, the most profitable side of the business. But even with its bigger income, Lloyd's finds itself increasingly overshadowed by the big British insurance companies.

THE COMPANIES

Three-quarters of non-life insurance now comes not from Lloyd's but from 'The Companies'—the big joint-stock insurance companies, which stand to the 'Lloyd's Boys' as a bus to a taxi: they are bureaucracies run not by free-lancers but by salaried managers. Most big companies handle both life and non-life, and are thus called 'composite', although the two businesses are kept separate. These were the biggest non-life companies, based on general business 'premium income' in 1969, and their chairmen:

Royal Group	£372.4 m.	Sir Paul Chambers
Commercial Union Group	£344.7 m.	Ronald C. Brooks
General Accident	£186.0 m.	Lord Polwarth
Guardian Royal Exchange Group	£176.3 m.	Lt.-Col. C. P. Dawnay
Sun Alliance and London Group	£147.6 m.	R. E. Fleming
Phoenix	£86.9 m.	Viscount de L'Isle
Eagle Star Group	£79.4 m.	Sir Brian Mountain
Norwich Union Group	£59.3 m.	Desmond Longe
Prudential	£46.9 m.	Kenneth Usherwood
Mercantile and General	£26.7 m.	Hugh Kenneth Goschen
Co-operative	£23.3 m.	H. A. Toogood
Vehicle and General	£21.3 m.	L. M. Kershaw (see p. 520)

Most insurance companies are old-established city institutions, with head offices within the 'square mile'. Their boards are part of the network of interlocking city directorships, usually with close connections with one or two merchant banks. Like the joint-stock banks, they are made up almost entirely of 'outside directors', the objects of repeated and angry criticism, who meet once a month for discussion and lunch. There was more criticism in 1963 after the Mancroft Affair, when one of the most conservative of the insurance companies, the Norwich Union, sacked a Jewish director on their London advisory board, Lord Mancroft, in response to pressure from Arab states where they had custom. The chairman was an old Norfolk brewer, Sir Robert Bignold, who seemed quite unaware of the repercussions, and soon afterwards resigned; the Mancroft Affair appeared to show the incompetence of outside directors in just the field where they were supposed to excel, and it raised doubts, even in the city, about the recruitment of boards: 'One wonders,' said the *Financial Times*, 'whether this practice can be maintained much longer.'

But it still lingers. The social composition of the insurance boards in 1970 has become slightly less operatic: there are fewer generals and admirals and courtiers. But insurance is still a haven for ancient peers, baronets and dreadnoughts, fortified by a few merchant bankers. Extraordinary backwoodsmen emerge for the monthly meetings from country seats, and retreat back to the shadows: the favourite honour among insurance directors is the Territorial Decoration. The General Accident has seven peers and two baronets among its directors. The Eagle Star has a marquess, an earl, a viscount, a major-general and three baronets, as well as Emile Littler (their link with the showbusiness octopus[1]) and three Mountains, from the family that control it. The Guardian Royal Exchange Group also has a tradition of high-sounding names and long lunches: but recently (a correspondent assures me) 'there has been such a sinking of dreadnoughts there as to make the scuttling of the German Fleet at Scapa Flow in 1919 an event of minor significance.'

The most self-consciously aristocratic is probably the Sun Alliance and London, which includes two of the oldest companies the Sun and the Alliance, which was founded by Nathan Rothschild in 1824. There is still Edmund Rothschild, TD, on the board, alongside a roll-call of the old city names—Lord Howard de Walden, TD, Lord Bearsted, TD (Samuel Properties), Sir Nicholas Cayzer (British and Commonwealth Shipping), Robert Kindersley (Lazards Bank), Lord Aberconway (John Brown), Lord Aldington (National and Grindlay's Bank): their chairman is Richard Fleming, Ian Fleming's most respectable brother, chairman of Robert Fleming's bank. The merchant banks, who set up the insurance companies in the eighteenth century as their creatures, and watched them grow up to dwarf them, still successfully dominate most of them, and prevent them acquiring a very separate character or confidence.

The biggest company for general insurance (where non-life business predominates) is the Royal, with strong roots in Liverpool, whose geography kept it relatively free from bankers' influences. It originated in 1845, when Mersey businessmen decided that London rates were too high; it still has one or two Liverpudlians on the board, including Sir Douglas Crawford the biscuit man, and Sir John Nicholson of Ocean Steamship, and its general manager, Kenneth Bevins, is a Mersey man (brother of

[1] See chapter 24.

an ex-postmaster general) who is one of the most respected of the London insurance managers. It was only in 1960 that the Royal moved its boardroom to London; but it, too, has become part of the nexus of London bankers, with a Baring and a Meinertzhagen (from Lazards) on the board. Their chairman is very much a Londoner—Sir Paul Chambers, the right-wing former chairman of ICI and ex-tax inspector. He is still something of a bull in a china shop, making occasional outbursts about the state of the nation.

The insurance boards have noticeably lacked members who know much about the continent where most of their money comes from —North America. About two-thirds of the insurance companies' non-life income comes from overseas, and the British companies have been well-established across the Atlantic since the end of the civil war. The hazards of America have provided some of the most spectacular losses in the last decade; the riots after the assassination of Martin Luther King cost British insurers £2¼ million (out of total damage of £28 million). The havoc of the American hurricanes with their innocent girls' names reaches the city: Betsy in 1965 cost them ten million pounds, Camille in 1969 four million, and Celia in 1970 about ten million. A single catastrophe can wipe out the year's profits, but disasters also provide the dramatic justification of the whole business. The British Insurance Association (BIA), the lobbyist and co-ordinator of the companies, has a dining-room surrounded by a modern fresco depicting some heroic calamities—the sinking of the *Titanic*, the San Francisco earthquake, the fire at the Crystal Palace. The insurance world has a ghoulish obsession with disaster and death, which emerges in its gruesome advertisements for new policies: 'Are you afraid of life because it makes you think about death?' asks the Phoenix.

Below the board level of insurance companies is the hierarchy of general managers, deputies and branch managers—the non-commissioned officers of the city. Traditionally, insurance has been a field for cautious school-leavers, who go in at sixteen or eighteen and come out at sixty, but in the last few years there has been a large increase, as in most other institutions, in university men; the numbers of graduates entering eighteen major companies went up from 150 in 1967 to 269 in 1969; nearly half went into actuarial jobs, and a quarter were women. But the insurance companies do not pay well enough at the top to get the best men:

among the ten biggest companies in 1969 there were forty-four men earning more than £10,000 a year, and five earning more than £20,000: one, Sir Brian Mountain of Eagle Star, earned £42,000. When salaries were revealed there was much resentment that insurance brokers, regarded by some company people as parasites, earned a good deal more: Ian Bowring Skimming, of the brokers C. T. Bowring, earns £47,800 a year, and Patrick Milligan of Sedgwick Collins earns £43,000; but brokers, whether discount brokers, stockbrokers or job brokers, by operating on the frontiers of business, tend to do better than the men who actually run things.[1]

Below the directors are the managers, the armies of insurance clerks and office workers—about 200,000 of them—and it is here that two intruders are changing the face of the business. The first is the computer, which has more scope in insurance than almost anywhere, spreading its spools, codes and punch cards through the cavernous offices; the computer has cut down the cohorts of badly-paid girls who have made up the basic unskilled labour of insurance, and has divided the offices more firmly into two levels—of cheap labour, still mostly girls, servicing the computer, and more skilled men taking the decisions. The second intruder, more menacing for the bosses, is the arch-organiser of the white collar unions, Clive Jenkins,[2] secretary of the Association of Scientific, Technical and Managerial Staff (ASTMS), who in 1970 began to spread his net towards the city, in the wake of the computers. Jenkins talked in characteristic language about the coolie labour and peasant staffs of the insurance companies, about flabby managements behaving like terrified virgins: 'Every insurance company is going to change the way it works,' he told the *Investors Chronicle* in December 1970: 'Fewer people will work for them and they are going to have to be brighter and sharper . . .' Jenkins joined up with the Union of Insurance Staffs and battled against the companies' own staff associations: the workers balloted, first at the Pru, then at the Royal, and chose Jenkins. 'The staff associations have made up their minds,' he explained, 'that if the management is going to employ experts, accountants, work study men, consultants and computer engineers, then they have to have the same resources on their side.' To many managers, the bargaining tactics were a disruption of the old loyal paternal-

---

[1] For comparison of salaries, see *The Economist*, July 19, 1969.
[2] See chapter 36.

ism of their companies; but others secretly welcomed Jenkins as a goad that would force companies to make more efficient use of their labour.

V AND G

Insurance companies, like all City institutions, dread the thought of government interference, and insist that they can sort out their own problems; but in March 1971 the British Insurance Association faced their moment of truth when one of its biggest members, the Vehicle and General, was suddenly declared bankrupt, leaving all its policy-holders uninsured. The collapse of 'V and G'—coming in the midst of the new Heath philosophy of 'stand (or fall) on your own feet' and just after the bankruptcy of Rolls-Royce—sent shudders, first through the City, and then through the Cabinet. The epic of V and G, not unlike the collapse of John Bloom's washing-machine empire of seven years before, was a story of daring gone wrong: ten years before, three bold intruders, Reg Burr, Lawrence Kershaw and Tony Hunt, had set out to undercut the cartel of old companies which then dominated car insurance. They bought a tiny Liverpool company which insured bicycles, and built it up quickly into a cut-price car-insurance company, working through brokers and offering big no-claim bonuses to good drivers. After seven years they were insuring a million motorists—more than any other company—and making big profits while other companies were struggling. They applied to join the Association, which first thought that their reserves were too small, but by 1966 let them in. The Board of Trade was worried about the reserves of upstart insurance companies, particularly since the crash of Savundra's company in 1966. But the BIA provided the stamp of respectability, and discouraged interference.

The V and G had demonstrated all too clearly (as John Bloom had done) the effectiveness of undercutting, and in early 1969 they forced the cartel to break up—itself a remarkable feat. But they thus faced much fiercer competition, at a time when inflation was pushing up the cost of repairs; they insisted on keeping their rates low, and were soon making huge losses. By mid-1970 the Board of Trade was becoming seriously worried, but were still reluctant to interfere, particularly in the prevailing new Tory mood of leaving the City alone. Eventually in February, the BIA insisted on inspecting the books, with Cooper Brothers; and they quickly pronounced that V and G were insolvent.

The BIA, though it had given its imprimatur to V and G, and had widely advertised the reliability of its companies, at first refused to accept any responsibility for the car-owners left uninsured. There was a public uproar, and one insurer discovered that he would be liable for £44,000 for an injury to a passenger. Eventually the acting chairman of the BIA, Kenneth Bevins of the Royal, announced a special fund to help the uninsured passengers; but they still would not reimburse the policyholders who had lost their premiums. The BIA were reluctantly faced with the fundamental city question: who is responsible for a bankrupt? Either they would have to be responsible for the debts of future bankrupts (as Lloyds since 1923 have been responsible for theirs) or they would have to agree to much sharper supervision and control from the Department. And in the meantime the Department itself was in disgrace; for it was revealed that four months before the crash, there had been a leak of confidential information about the V and G; and the prime minister was forced to set up a judicial commission of enquiry. The idea of insurance standing on its own feet did not look very convincing: for insurers looked to the government as protector of the consumer.

THE LIFE COMPANIES

The most spectacular financial power in insurance lies with the life companies, whose backgrounds are more humble and provincial. The life companies (with relatively small initial capital) receive their money week after week, month after month, and pay back their lump sums only after a lifetime: and so they have funds far bigger than the non-life's. The largest life companies, like building societies, originated in the last century not from the city but from nonconformist movements of lower middle-class men in the provinces: that these poor men's clubs should have become the giants of the city is one of the ironies of twentieth-century finance. These are the twelve biggest life companies (most of which also do non-life business), based on premium income in 1969.

Prudential	£239.5 m.	Kenneth Usherwood
Legal and General	£116.9 m.	Viscount Harcourt
Standard Life	£78.1 m.	T. N. Risk (!)

Guardian Royal Exchange	£73.6 m.	Lt. Col. C. P. Dawnay
Commercial Union	£63.8 m.	Ronald C. Brooks
Norwich Union	£54.2 m.	Desmond Longe
Sun Life	£47.4 m.	C. G. Randolph
Eagle Star	£46.0 m.	Sir Brian Mountain
General Accident	£39.8 m.	Lord Polwarth
Scottish Widows	£37.7 m.	A. I. Mackenzie
Pearl	£23.9 m.	Sir Geoffrey Kitchen
Friends' Provident	£15.4 m.	Edwin Phillips

THE PRU

By far the biggest is still the legendary Prudential, with the motto 'Fortis Qui Prudens'. To the public the Pru is best known for its 11,000 'Men from the Pru', the army of local travellers with their small cars and little books, who collect the weekly and monthly insurance contributions. But to the city of London, the Pru presents a different face, for it is the largest single investor in the country: its *total* assets (a sixth of the assets of all life companies) amounted in 1969 to over two thousand million pounds. Though this is less than the deposits of Barclays Bank, the Pru does not need to keep its money ready, like a bank's, for quick withdrawal: it can invest the whole sum, for a whole generation, without the need to call it back. Every week, the Pru has another two million pounds to invest—pouring it into government stock, industry, or property. Over the last century, Pru and her colleagues, with their massive wealth, have stolen much of the thunder from the bankers.

The Pru is the biggest and oldest of the 'industrial life companies'—those life companies which grew up from the weekly savings of industrial workers. It originated as a company in 1848. In June 1852 a deputation of working men called on the secretary of the new company, and two years later a director appointed agents, to collect weekly savings from the Potteries and the weaving districts of Cheshire and Lancashire. Eager for thrift and self-help, and determined to avoid state aid, the artisans and workers embraced the new security of life insurance; by 1886 the Pru had more than *seven million* policies, with three-quarters of all the industrial life business.[1] The proud Victorian character of the Pru is expressed in its towering pink Gothic castle in Holborn, just on the west edge of the City. (The topography is significant,

[1] Dermot Morrah: *A History of Industrial Life Assurance*, p. 53.

for like its rival, the Pearl up the road, the Pru likes to regard itself as being at arm's length from city influences.) The castle is an astonishing fantasy: outside there is a jumble of pointed windows, pinnacles, gables and steep roofs (in contrast to the plain red glass slab of the *Daily Mirror* across the road). Gothic pillars spring up between stained glass windows, and black-letter notices, like hymn-boards, announce the managers' offices. The great entrance hall was revamped in 1970 with lots of formica, potted plants and blue-patterned carpets, so that it now looks like a cross between a cathedral and a seaside hotel.

On the top floor is the Pru theatre, for amateur theatricals; in the basement are the diesel engines; on the second floor is the ecclesiastical boardroom, with a square throne in the middle. But in spite of the Gothic surroundings, the Pru people are very down-to-earth: their board's lunch is much less pretentious than a merchant bank's, like a hotel rather than a country house: drinks on the sideboard, waitresses instead of butlers, and plain English food. The conversation is matter-of-fact and very professional.

The top men at the Pru are nearly all cautious company men who have spent most of their lives in the building. The old founding families—the Deweys, Harbens, Hornes, Reids and Lancasters—have nearly all retreated (Osbert Lancaster preferred cartooning to insurance), and only the deputy chairman, Desmond Reid, provides a link with the beginnings. The chairman, Kenneth Usherwood, is a dry but genial man whose father first joined the Pru in 1881; he went to Cambridge on a Pru scholarship, and has been in the company ever since, rising to be general manager and finally, in 1970, becoming chairman—which he combines with sitting on the Gaming Board. Usherwood presides unpretentiously over informal meetings of the board twice a week, quietly conscious that his company controls more money than any of the smoother or flashier establishments in the centre of the city.

ACTUARIES

Nearly all the senior managers of the Pru, and of other life companies, carry after their names the initials FIA—Fellows of the Institute of Actuaries—and at this point it is necessary to pause to look at the high-walled profession of actuaries. Like other small professions, they have been intent on remaining beyond the reach of common criticism, laying down their own voluntary codes of behaviour. But actuaries have recently become more sensitive to the charge of narrowness: 'The man who immures himself in his professional castle deprives himself of much,' said Kenneth Usherwood, in his presidential address in 1962; and Ronald Sherman, the President in 1970, quoted Sir Richard Livingstone's definition of a technician: 'A man who understands everything about his job, except its ultimate purpose and its place in the order of the universe.' The institute is anxious to show that its members are not back room boys, but a profession that involves confrontation with the public.

Actuaries are basically highly specialised mathematicians who, after a course lasting on average six years, are versed in the intricate study of probabilities, on which the success of life insurance depends. The name, adopted as an antiquarian whim, is very misleading, and in Germany or Sweden they are more sensibly and prosaically called 'insurance mathematicians'. The profession had its beginnings in 1662 when John Graunt, FRS (who was later falsely charged with being privy to the Great Fire of London), wrote his 'Natural and political observations made upon the bills of mortality', which began the study of expectation of life, and the job was a thoroughly British invention; the stability of life insurance has depended on the actuarial profession ever since. It is still an odd profession, both highly commercial and highly academic. It has grown three-fold since 1925, but it is still very small: in 1970 there were only 814 active actuaries in Britain who were fellows of the institute; 529 of them were in life insurance offices, and the rest were absorbed in specialised fields in government service, pension funds, the stock exchange and consultancy.

Actuaries are the high priests of numeracy, and the more alarmed other people are by complicated sums, the greater the power of the actuaries: their reputation rests on giving 'numerate advice' (as Sherman puts it) or on 'a capacity for analysing a situation and separating the important factors' (as Dr Benjamin, another past president, explained). But the actuaries' confidence is apt to depend on the exclusion of other factors—human, social or psychological—and their own background is not very encouraging. They are highly paid; in the higher reaches of insurance they can earn £15,000 a year. But they emerge from a six-year training which is narrow and barren; most of it is done by correspondence, with a few lectures and classes. As one past president, Charles

Wood, explained: 'It is difficult for the young man to develop his personality if it is essential that he spends a large part of his spare time in study.' They are trying to extend the scope of training with evening courses and sandwich courses, and most new actuaries have degrees: seventy-seven per cent of English entrants in 1970 came from university. But most of the existing actuaries are non-graduates, whose outlook has been bounded by the walls of the city and their profession.

The domination of these cautious mathematicians has helped to hold back life companies from adapting themselves to the public's needs—particularly in providing policies linked to unit trusts and property, which can keep pace with inflation. Much of the new opening-up of life assurance has come from outside the profession, from the unit trust managers, or from enterprising outsiders; perhaps the most remarkable example is Mark Weinberg, the South African lawyer, still only forty, who saw the prospects of linking life assurance with unit trusts and property bonds. In nine years he built up his company, Abbey Life Assurance, to assets of £100 million, before he sold it out in 1970 to the American IT and T, and started a new company with Hambros. The traditional life offices have been slow to see such opportunities. 'The typical life office is like a motor firm dominated by its production side. Men with the most brilliant engineering qualifications and experience are in the driving seats. They design equally brilliant products—which the customer shall have, and which the customer would actually want if he knew what was good for him. By contrast, the job of the much larger, but far less influential, sales side is simply to sell the product'.[1]

INSURANCE AND CAPITALISM

For the city, the important Men from the Pru are not the army of collecting agents, but the small staff in Holborn who look after the colossal investment of two billion pounds; for this sum is far bigger than any investment trust, private shareholding or bank investment. The Pru's chief investment managers, Harry Clark and Angus Murray, are cautious actuaries who are reluctant to consider any issues wider than financial ones; they preserve a modest detachment in their pink castle, and see every company in terms, not of its managers, but of its balance sheet, turnover and

[1] Alan Parker: *Life Assurance: the new deal* (Economist Brief 12), 1969.

price-earnings ratio. But the power of these men, and of the other companies' investment managers, is something which any stock-broker, issuing house or industrial corporation has to come to terms with; a new issue of shares can depend on the raising or falling of an eyebrow, or a twitch of a toothbrush moustache. About half of the voting capital of all companies quoted on the stock exchange is owned by the 'institutions'—including investment trusts and pension funds—and the insurance companies are the giants among them. There are very few big companies where the Pru is not a major shareholder, and there are many where it is the biggest—and therefore in a position if it wishes to sway other votes.

The relationship between the insurance companies and the industrial corporations is one of special political inwardness; for it is the very axle of modern capitalism, and most relevant to the current Conservative belief in the 'questioning role' (as John Davies, the Minister for Trade and Industry, calls it) of private capital in industrial companies. It is part of the Conservative philosophy that by transferring industries from public to private ownership they will be stimulated and spurred on by the pressure of shareholders. But since the biggest blocks of shareholders are usually the insurance companies, the question arises: Do they really *want* to question and stimulate industry?

In the past the insurance companies have been most reluctant to interfere at all. Their basic sanction has been not to invest in incompetent companies: but when they already have a large holding they are always apprehensive of selling it for fear of disturbing the market, and they have frequently hung on to huge investments in very unprofitable companies. The investment managers see themselves primarily not as activators and challengers of the city, but as trustees for their millions of policyholders; they like to talk about their 'fiduciary' role and (like civil servants) about 'those whom we serve'. They have been worried that, if they were to flex their muscles, the Labour Party would begin talking again about the nationalisation of insurance: and in any case they have never known much about industry, who runs it or how it works. The insurance companies, like the clearing banks, have had a built-in inhibition against exercising their financial powers: they feel instinctively that it is excellent to have a giant's strength, but it is tyrannous to use it like a giant. The insurance managers (they insist) do not compare notes about making investments; they normally only come together on the 'investment protection committee' (IPC) which meets once a month.

In the past decade, however, there has been a slow but significant shift in the attitudes of the institutions, which is likely to have far-reaching results. The investment departments have expanded their staff with economists as well as actuaries and—partly to satisfy the ambitions of these young recruits—they have begun to take more interest in the companies they invest in. They have visited factories, cross-examined managers and worried more about how companies are run. The investment managers have found it harder to avoid interfering, not least because men from the companies have come to see them, and have revealed the splits in the boards. The succession of take-overs in the late sixties sometimes forced the insurance companies to make painful choices; in the great bid by Arnold Weinstock of GEC for its rival electrical company AEI in 1967, the position of the institutions was crucial, for they held forty per cent of the AEI shares; they were lobbied by both sides, and most of them opted for Weinstock.

A bolder intervention came to light in May 1970, in the remarkable case of Vickers—the antique shipbuilding and armaments company, the old 'merchants of death', which for the last two decades have been the despair of investors and innovators, and whose board, laden with ex-generals and admirals, has had a legendary somnolence. In 1962 a new managing director arrived, Sir Leslie Rowan, a sophisticated Treasury knight whose attitudes seemed realistic and far-sighted, and who became chairman in 1967; but still Vickers showed little sign of improvement, and no bright hopes appeared on the board. A new chairman, a voluble ex-steelmaster, Niall Macdiarmid, was designated; but the investors had great doubts as to whether he could revive the company. At last the Pru decided to intervene, and together with two other big shareholders, Hill, Samuel and Cables Investment Trust, the Men from the Pru approached Sir Leslie in December 1969 to plead that there should be a new managing-director, who would also be chief executive of the company. Vickers could not risk losing their support, and they agreed; they suggested a man from British Steel, Peter Matthews, and lured him over to Vickers for £19,000 a year. Soon afterwards, Macdiarmid left Vickers, and Lord Robens from the Coal Board became part-time chairman-elect. But the problem of Vickers still worries its shareholders: Matthews is well respected and able but he, too, may be too gentlemanly a man for the appalling task of cleaning up the company.

The case of Vickers showed a rare initiative from institutions, but it also showed their limitations. They were prepared to insist on a new managing-director, but they would not propose their own candidate; and the thought of having themselves to look for managers (as merchant banks do) still alarms them. The idea that they, as the biggest shareholders, should—as Tory policy implies—become the shakers-up of British industry does not appeal to the Men from the Pru. They would not know where to start looking for managers; and they are worried that once they started interfering with the big companies they would frighten away the small companies on which much of their growth depends. So long as they remain thus detached, the notion that shareholders are the questioners of industry remains a fiction. The boards of directors remain self-perpetuating and responsible only to each other, and industrial companies are unlikely to behave very differently whether they are nationalised or not.

PENSION FUNDS

In the last twenty years an even more sudden wealth has emerged in the city—the pension funds, which in March 1971 had funds worth about £7,000 million. Nearly every big company has its own pension scheme; some are administered by insurance companies, but the biggest of them are independent, with huge funds to invest in the market. The Coal Board fund has over £300 million, ICI and Unilever over £200 million each. The pension funds are only gradually becoming aware of their strength and political significance. They have a National Association in an attic in Queen Anne's Gate, which represents seventeen hundred funds, including nearly all the big ones; of the top hundred companies, ninety-seven have their funds in the association, but they do not have much contact with their members. The pension funds had to organise themselves rapidly when threatened by the Labour Government's pension plan; they quickly formed a liaison committee with the CBI and the life insurance companies, and even though the threat has passed, the committee still continues in case of further dangers. To the public, the pension funds are obscure dogsbodies: but to the stock exchange their investment managers are much more important than the chairmen of the companies.

The pension funds have their own Investment Protection Committee, quite separate from the insurance companies' one, which is one of the most arcane centres of financial power. It is made up of the managers of ten of the top pension funds; its current chairman, Ken Parry, is manager of the Iraq Petroleum Fund. In the past the funds have been very reluctant to co-ordinate their policies, or to intervene about management, but in the last two years they have become much more active, and more resentful of the merchant banks; the investment experts are usually self-made men whose whole background is antagonistic to the patrician confidence of the bankers; 'It's really class warfare', said one of the bankers. In 1969 and 1970 the pension funds, under Parry's energetic leadership, began to intervene critically in the boards of several big companies; they were instrumental in appointing A. J. Smith as managing-director of Debenham's; they brought pressure on Burmah Oil to reduce their dependence on British Petroleum; they insisted on the reshaping of the Swan Hunter board. When the National Westminster Bank took over Lombard Banking, they pressed for better terms for Lombard's convertible stock; and they have demanded that merchant banks consult them—like the insurance companies—before their big issues. Ironically, their most spectacular intervention was against *their* Tory government: for the New Tories appalled them by one of their first acts, the withdrawal of government support from the Mersey Docks and Harbours Board, in which they had big investments; the pension funds took the initiative in protesting and briefing MPs, and succeeded in making changes in the Bill. Parry is emphatic that the pension funds will have to involve themselves more in the management of incompetent companies, and that they cannot leave it to the merchant banks, who have failed in their job and anyway have a vested interest: 'We're beginning to tackle management before it gets sour.' But like the people at the Pru, he veers away from actually appointing managers: 'In time we'll probably have to have a pool of company doctors, as the Americans do, who we can put into a company for a time, and then pull back to the pool when the job's done; but that's a long way off.'

CAPITAL AND SOCIETY

The gradual and reluctant emergence of these 'money-managers', the investment experts of the pension funds and insurance companies, as arbiters of industrial policy, is one of the most significant trends of the last two decades. They represent much more than a new class of men challenging the old hold of the bankers; for they raise the whole question of how far the big investors, using other people's money, *should* use their capital to influence companies—and not only in terms of financial efficiency. In America, with the prevailing growth of 'consumerism', and with the concern about industry wrecking the environment and spreading pollution, the debate has already become wider; the institutional investors have been under fire for supporting all kinds of industrial wickedness—from Dow Chemicals' involvement with napalm to Chase Manhattan's support of South Africa—and they have been accused of being totally preoccupied by the financial yield, to the neglect of the 'social yield'. The American protests reached one climax in January 1970, when a group called the Campaign for Corporate Responsibility launched a 'Campaign GM', demanding three extra representatives of the public on the board of General Motors, and a shareholders' committee to monitor the GM management's relations with society. They raised the proposals at the annual meeting, when they gained less than three per cent of the votes. But they have succeeded in getting a black man on the board of GM, and the intensity of the debate, with GM's rather frenzied reactions, caused many big investors (including universities) to state openly their worries about GM's anti-social policies.

The British situation is not yet so open and dramatic. But the big investors—like Barclays Bank over the Cabora Bassa question —are having to face the likelihood that some of their investments will take on a much more political colour; and they will not always be able to shelter behind their role as trustees for their clients. The argument is not a clear-cut one. There is a strong case for shareholders being concerned with their companies' policies—whether financial or social. But the influence of the new money-managers— grey actuaries in grey offices, bound up with dispassionate statistics —is unlikely to be any more enlightened than the influence of the old bankers. And even if a new kind of socially-sensitive money-manager were to emerge, could and should the small investor entrust him with the power to influence the social policies of whole corporations?

29

Property

It's gotta be big.

The late Jack Cotton.

THE most visible part of the wealth of the institutions is the land that they own in the cities; more and more of their capital is being put into real estate. Pension funds are taking over great tracts of the centre of London: the Coal Board fund, one of the first to put money into property, has now spent more than £100 million on it—followed by the other nationalised industries. The *doyen* of the pension funds, Ross Goobey of Imperial Tobacco, known as the preacher of the 'cult of the equity' in the sixties, said in January 1971 that his fund was putting nearly all its money into property. As the future of British industry looks more doubtful, so the future of land looks more attractive: and the centre of London, boosted by the American invasion, the tourist boom and the drift to the South-East, becomes an ever-stronger magnet.

It is here that the role of the institutions impinges on the world of town planning and architecture. In the last two decades many of Britain's city skylines have been transformed from the horizontal to the vertical. The booming value of metropolitan land has turned the centres of London, Birmingham or Manchester into miniature Manhattans. Office space in the middle of London is now more expensive than in New York; it is now up to a general ceiling of £10 per square foot, and in some parts of the city it

fetches as much as £30 per square foot. The land itself in most
cases is owned by the only people who could possibly afford it—
the insurance companies and pension funds, who in property have
found an apparently safe resting place for part of their money-
gusher. But the buying-up of the land, the planning, designing
and leasing of the buildings has been largely put into the hands
of a handful of speculator entrepreneurs—the property developers.
In the last fifteen years there have been few more astonishing
collaborations than those between the cautious insurance bureaucracies, preoccupied with trusteeship and security, and the
adventurous self-made millionaires who, by borrowing huge sums
from the insurance companies, changed the face of the cities, and
made their fortunes. Property is a difficult commodity: it involves
assessing and visualising the potential of sites, patiently bargaining
and buying up clusters of old buildings, negotiating with local
councils and ministers, planning new blocks to cram in the maximum office space. In Manhattan, which was laid out from the
beginning in large criss-cross blocks and where laws are more cut-
and-dried, the operation is easier. But the very jumble and
messiness of London, its zigzags, curves and old buildings, yielded
great prizes for those who could disentangle it.

In London much land is still owned by the old aristocratic
families who first developed it—the Dukes of Bedford and
Westminster in Bloomsbury and Belgravia, the Lords Cadogan and
Howard de Walden in Chelsea and Harley Street—or by other
ancient landlords, the Crown and the Church Commissioners,
Eton College, or Dulwich College. Other bits are still owned by
individuals, departments stores or British Railways. But it is the
property developers—subject to the wayward controls of the
planning authorities—who have taken over much of the role of
master townplanners, which was once the prerogative of dukes,
earls or the monarch himself. Sometimes the developers go into
partnership with the old landowners, sharing their skills in the
exploitation of property in return for a large share of the profits—
as Max Rayne went into partnership with the Church Commissioners in redeveloping bits of Paddington, or with Lord Portman
in redeveloping sites around Portman Square.

The developers visualise how an area of London can be pulled
down and rebuilt, to provide more office space and greater profits.
One of the boldest schemes was that of Joe Levy, now a director of
Stock Conversion, who saw the propsects of transforming a stretch

of the Euston Road, in collaboration with the LCC; he gradually over eleven years bought up the old houses, factories, warehouses and shops, bargaining one by one, while the scale of the redevelopment was kept carefully secret; eventually the plans (designed by Sidney Kaye, the architect of the Hilton) were unveiled to show a row of bleak shiny shoe-boxes without any distinction in what was once a picturesque part of London. Levy's company was reckoned to have made £11 million before tax in that single development.

The office mushrooms produced a new crop of millionaires; according to Oliver Marriott, who has chronicled the boom (now himself a director of a property company, Sterling Guarantees), there were at least 110 people who made a million pounds or more out of property between 1945 and 1965, most of them beginning with not more than a few hundred pounds.[1] Most of the new millionaires were sons or grandsons of Jewish immigrant families; and in the stories of urban development there is often the conflict between two different attitudes to property, the sleepy native view of territory as something to hang on to, as part of the landscape, and the aggressive newcomers' view of land as something to be transformed, bought and sold: the conflict reached a kind of caricature in the two attempts by property tycoons (first Harold Samuel, then Nigel Broackes of Trafalgar House) to take over that Establishment bastion, the Savoy Hotel group.

Some of the beneficiaries of the property bonanza were estate agents, like Harold Samuel or Joe Levy, who quickly saw the way prices were moving (estate agents, though they like to regard themselves as a profession with a disinterested code, like stockbrokers, are not debarred from investing heavily themselves). Others were men, like Charles Clore or Isaac Wolfson, to whom property was part of a larger business; they bought chains of shops, stadiums or factories, with one eye on the real estate. In the course of the fifties giant companies were established, underpinned by the insurance companies; the most celebrated of the new tycoons was Jack Cotton, the flamboyant Birmingham estate agent who built up his wonder-company, City Centre Properties, from his suite in the Dorchester. Cotton was a theatrical, almost lovable man who could not stop himself going too far; he formed subsidiaries with the most prestigious institutions, and then merged his company with Clore's to make the biggest property

[1] For a list of them see Oliver Marriott: *The Property Boom* (Pan Books 1969).

company in the world, with three big insurance companies
—Pearl, Legal and General and the Pru—as major shareholders. But Cotton showed signs of growing megalomania
and ill-health; in 1963 he sold all his shares at an undisclosed price,
some to Isaac Wolfson, and died the next year; the huge company,
with its shares much declined, was then run by a cautious man
from the Legal and General, George Bridge, and some years later
the whole outfit was taken over by Harold Samuel's Land
Securities.

Many of the property tycoons, like Jack Cotton, Bernard
Sunley or Felix Fenston (the son of an impresario), had a passion
for personal publicity, and treated their business as part of show-
business; but others, including many of the wiliest, have preferred
to shroud themselves in mystery. The most secretive and successful
of all is Harry Hyams—one of the two men (Sir Isaac Wolfson was
the other) who refused to see me in the course of writing this book.
He is rumoured to be a handsome, bearded man of forty-four,
with a yacht and a Charles II mansion in Wiltshire; he writes in a
florid hand from an office in St James's on deckled-edged paper
with a crest saying 'Oldham Estates Company Established 1874'.
The son of a bookmaker, he originally worked for Hampton's
estate agency, then collaborated for a time with Felix Fenston;
then started on his own by buying a 'shell', called the Oldham
Estate Company, which owned some old buildings in Lancashire.
With this as his base, he began quickly putting together London
properties in collaboration with Wimpey's construction company,
of which he became a director: in eight years from 1959 the gross
value of the properties of Oldham Estates went up from £22,000 to
£46 million. Hyams' most astonishing monument is the Centre
Point skyscraper at the corner of Tottenham Court Road and
Oxford Street, which for six years has stood empty, patrolled by
guard dogs and with its piazza locked up, in one of the central sites
of London. The story of how Hyams, having been introduced to the
LCC's planning committee by his lawyer, Lord Goodman, made
a bargain which was immensely beneficial to the developers, is
one of the most extraordinary examples of the planners being out-
witted by the developers.[1] Hyams made the very most of the small
site by commissioning a 32-storey skyscraper; it rose up and up,
a building of surprising beauty; but when it was finished, no one
moved in. Year after year it remained empty—together with four

[1] See Oliver Marriott: pp. 134–141.

other of Hyams' new buildings. Yet year after year (much helped by the Labour Government's ban on office building) the value increased with the growing need for office space. In a city with tens of thousands of homeless, Hyams' empty skyscrapers were monuments to the ruthless logic of the developers.

The wildest days of the bonanza are over. Insurance companies have become wise to the profits from development, and make sharper bargains; planning authorities are less gullible, and insist on tenants being found before permission is given. Many of the original one-man companies have been merged or taken over, and now two giant companies dominate the property market. The biggest, Land Securities, employing capital of over £400 million, is headed by Sir Harold Samuel, whose cousin, Basil Samuel, runs another big property company, Great Portland Estates (now much diversified into service industries). Harold bought Land Securities as a tiny company in 1944, soon realised the scope for office development, and spread his empire through London. When he tried to take over the Savoy Hotel group in 1953 he was depicted as the arch-exploiter determined to ruin ancient British institutions; now, in the traditional pattern, he is a respected figure, the first knighted property-man, the benefactor of universities and of the Royal College of Surgeons.

The second biggest company, the Metropolitan Estate and Property Company, was founded by another ex-estate agent, the late Claude Leigh, and is now headed by the pluralist chairman, Sir Charles Hardie, whom we have already encountered (p. 504) as an accountant. In 1970 Sir Charles, after long preliminary talks, announced the breathtaking plan to merge MEPC with the biggest merchant bank, Hill, Samuel, whose insatiable chairman, Sir Kenneth Keith, would then run the whole group. The deal seemed to suit both sides, for MEPC had the cash ready for investment, and Hill, Samuel needed money to expand overseas, and could earn a higher return on capital than property could: 'I thought hard,' said Sir Kenneth, 'and decided it was a natural marriage.' But the shareholders of MEPC, who included many insurance companies led by the Pru, thought it unnatural; they took fright at the size and speculative aspects of the merger, and were wary of Keith's reputation as an aggressive and overbearing boss. In the meantime, another insurance company, Commerical Union, helped by their protégé Nigel Broackes of Trafalgar House, were also wooing the rich giant; they saw it as a useful receptacle for *their* property investments, and two weeks after the Hill Samuel proposal they made a rival take-over bid for MEPC. But that, too, was frustrated by the Pru and by the Take-over Panel. MEPC continued on its own, rather rattled: Sir Charles announced that he would resign the following year.

The terrible ugliness of the new city centres cannot be blamed on the property developers alone: it has much to do with the divorce which now exists between all the parties concerned—the developers, the architects, the occupants, and the freeholders, who are usually insurance companies. The great Georgian squares and terraces were laid out for owners who, whatever their own greed, had some eye for posterity, and some pride in their architecture; the Grosvenors, Bedfords or Portmans could proudly be associated with their squares. But most of the new London developments are planned with no particular occupiers in mind, catering for a vague common denominator, to suit anyone or no one. Architects some-times say that a building is as good as its client; and by this rule non-clients lead to non-buildings. Sometimes even the purpose is changed half-way through—like the Royal Lancaster Hotel, which was first designed as an office building, then as a block of flats, before it turned out as a hotel. The controls of local authori-ties (who have no capital of their own) are essentially negative, and the stricter they are, the more they curb the architects' imagina-tion; sometimes the planning authorities are more to blame than the developers (as when they insisted on lopping off the tops of Castrol House and Bowater House).

In this maze of commercial interests and plot-ratio calculations, the actual look of the building may be the last thing to be con-sidered, and a new kind of architect is increasingly in demand, men like Richard Seifert (of Centre Point fame) or Sidney Kaye, who are experts in the law as much as in architecture. A few developers and insurance companies have shown some concern for good building; Sir Max Rayne, the chairman of London Merchant Securities (now with a large stake in developing the South Bank), has some artistic conscience (he is himself a serious collector of modern paintings). The Commercial Union's enterprise is declared by its own headquarters, designed by Gollins Melvin Ward, one of the few beautiful post-war buildings in the city. The public outcry against architectural horrors had some effect; when planning buildings on 'sensitive sites' the developers now often employ 'prestige' architects, and Sir Harold Samuel's company employs Sir Basil Spence to lend status to its big schemes. But most insurance companies and developers are still content to extract the greatest return with the least trouble. As for the occupants, they usually only come into the scene after the building has been completed. The biggest client of all, the government, sets the worst pattern; government departments, represented by their estate agents, the Department of the Environment, have to find their premises where they can, leasing any old building, and often making very bad deals with the developers. The Department of Employment is overflowing from St James's Square into Mayfair, the Ministry of Education occupies an expensive slum in Curzon Street; while the opportunities for the government to revitalise whole areas of the South Bank and to create imaginative new Whitehalls have been allowed to pass by.

The decline of urban architecture is due of course to much deeper causes than purely commercial ones. The architects and occupants themselves are confused about their purpose and values, and there is no kind of accepted formal style such as gave Georgian London its distinction. British companies do not have the self-confidence, panache or concern for posterity which spurred the American corporations to commission the great buildings of Park Avenue or Chicago. The loss of faith in new British building has generated a powerful reaction of preservationists, led by nostalgic figures like Lady Dartmouth or Sir John Betjeman, who insist that the old is always better than the new, offering no kind of alternative contemporary style. The architecture *malaise* seems to point to a widespread loss of confidence and identity. But so long as new building remains so irresponsible— so subject to exploitation, compromise and cross-purposes—the prospects of recapturing confidence seem remote.

30

Bank of England

Lord Radcliffe: It is very deep in history that bankers have been
regarded with suspicion?
Lord Brand: And always will be by people who cannot get credit.

Minutes of the Radcliffe Report, Question 19739.

In the centre of the city, next door to the Royal Exchange and
facing the Lord Mayor's Mansion House, is the massive quadri-
lateral of the Bank of England whose appearance aptly symbolises
its famous secrecy. Round the whole building at street level is a
blank, windowless façade broken by corinthian pillars, above
which rise six storeys of offices. Inside the Bank has the look of an
eccentric court. Tall men stand in the hall wearing long brown
overcoats and top hats with gold bands; other men, in black
trousers, pink morning coats and red waistcoats, escort visitors
into high-ceilinged rooms perfectly air-conditioned at sixty-seven
degrees Fahrenheit. The Bank is proud of its nickname of the 'Old
Lady of Threadneedle Street': in the exhibition room there is the
original cartoon by Gillray called 'Political Ravishment or The
Old Lady of Threadneedle Street in Danger' in 1797, showing
Pitt as prime minister assaulting an aged hag sitting on a trunk
labelled 'Bank of England', shouting 'Murder! Murder!' (the fear
of financial rape has haunted the Bank ever since). 'The Old Lady'
is the title of the Bank's own house magazine, and the Bank is
fascinated by its own past. In the 'Court Room' there is a weather-
vane so that the directors can see if their sailing ships are in

difficulty. Few people would guess, looking round it, that this was the headquarters of a nationalised industry.

On the ground floor is an interlocking set of rooms reserved for the Governor and directors, decorated in the twenties' Adam style with the splendour and peace of a rich man's country house. A wide carpet leads past the green dining-room, past a pillared hall full of bankers' portraits into the heart of the Bank—the long white room, known as the 'Court Room', flanked with columns and filled with an ornate, hundred-and-fifty coloured carpet. A blue-cloth table stands in the middle, with chairs all round it, and here, every Thursday morning, sit the seventeen members of the 'Court'.

These seventeen are chosen to run the Bank, and to advise the Treasury on financial policy and 'feeling in the city'. Before the war they consisted predominantly of city men—which may have helped to explain the appalling insensitivity of the government to unemployment. Today (partly because of that criticism) they are more diversified. Six are full-time members of the Bank of England; four from banks, seven from industry and commerce; and one from a trade union. When the Select Committee for Nationalised Industries investigated the Bank in 1970, it reported that 'the Court is the only body of men in Great Britain, in either the public or the private sector, which determines the remuneration of its members and then reports it to nobody. Your committee considers this practice inappropriate in a public corporation' (they were perhaps unaware of the similar secrecy of the BBC). They did in the end elicit the salaries of the directors, given overleaf. The part-time directors, in addition to their fees of £500 a year, have the use of a car on Bank business, a big lunch on Thursdays, and can have their own bank account at the Bank of England.

The duties of a director are not arduous: this is how Cecil King, who was appointed a director by Callaghan in 1965 and served for three years, described the experience:[1]

> The directors have been surrounded with an entirely bogus aura of knowledge and power. The Bank is run by the Governor, the Deputy-governor and the Chancellor of the Exchequer. There are four other executive directors, some of whom are and some of whom are not important. The twelve non-executive directors I suppose can theoretically control the Bank, but then the Government of the day can issue a binding instruction. In practice neither happens. The

[1] Cecil King: *Strictly Personal*, Weidenfeld & Nicolson. 1969, p. 142.

Name	Salary	School/University	Position
Sir Leslie O'Brien	£25,000	Wandsworth School	Governor
Jasper Hollom	£18,000	King's School, Bruton	Deputy-governor
Jack Davies	£14,000– £17,500	Tonbridge; Cambridge	Executive director
John Fforde		Rossall; Oxford	Executive director
Kit MacMahon		Australia: Melbourne University; Oxford	Executive director
Jeremy Morse		Winchester; Oxford	Executive director
Adrian Cadbury	£500	Eton; Cambridge	Deputy-chairman, Cadbury-Schweppes
Leopold de Rothschild	£500	Harrow; Cambridge	Director, Rothschilds Bank
Sir Val Duncan	£500	Harrow; Oxford	Chairman, Rio-Tinto Zinc
Sir Sidney Green	£500	Elementary	General Secretary, Union of Railway-men
William Keswick	£500	Winchester; Cambridge	Director, Matheson's
Sir Maurice Laing	£500	St Lawrence College, Ramsgate	Chairman, John Laing Construction
Lord Nelson of Stafford	£500	Oundle; Cambridge	Director, GEC/English Electric
Lord Pilkington	£500	Rugby; Cambridge	Chairman, Pilkington Brothers
Gordon Richardson	£500	Nottingham High; Cambridge	Chairman, Schroder Wagg
Sir Eric Roll	£500	Continent; Birmingham	Ex-civil servant. Director, Warburg's
Sir John Stevens	£500	Winchester	Managing-Director, Morgan Grenfell

Governor and the Chancellor decide what is to be done and the Court concurs. It is not consulted and seldom informed. For two months I was on the Committee of Treasury which is a sort of inner circle of the Court. But as a committee we were told very little and consulted not at all.

At the head of the Court is the Governor of the Bank of England, the headmaster of the city. (The title 'Governor' itself is evocative. There are governors of prisons, schools, the BBC, colonies and the Bank of England: they have a stern affinity.) In the 'square mile' the Governor of the Bank may be known as 'Grandma', 'the little white father' or most mysteriously as 'the Authorities': and it is his job, among many others, to enforce the unwritten laws and codes of city behaviour. His weapons seem mild enough: he will 'drop a hint', 'make observations' or 'frown'; his most potent weapon in controlling monetary policy is—as he explained to the committee —'moral suasion'. But in the closed society of the city, his pressure can be very effective—as was his pressure to set up the Take-over Panel (see p. 549). For bankers and stockbrokers know that he stands between them and government intervention, and anything is preferable to that. The Governor of the Bank occupies the most exposed frontier-post between government and finance; he is expected on the one hand to be a spokesman for the city, and yet to be able to control or persuade the city as if he were outside it— an awkward combination. In 1970 the Governor 'was at pains to make clear', to the Select Committee, 'that close contact with city institutions did not mean that the Bank was unduly infected by city views'. The Governor is appointed by the Crown (that is, the prime minister or chancellor disguised as the Queen) for a period of five years; and he cannot be dismissed—to protect him (as the Governor explained) 'against undue political influence'.

Up till 1966 the Governor was expected to be one of the princes of the city, surrounded with grandeur; since 1920 there had been only four of them—Lord Norman, Lord Catto, Lord Cobbold and Lord Cromer—wealthy and intimidating men, with large outside connections. In 1966 for the first time in the Bank's history a man from inside took over, Leslie O'Brien, with a quite different background. He and his present deputy, Jasper Quintus Hollom, both went into the bank straight from school; both were from un-monied families, and the fact that the Bank has now bought a town house for the Governor for £70,000 suggests (among other things) that they do not expect rich Governors. In a Britain of graduates, the top men at the Bank of England remain interesting exceptions. Bank officials in the past have been non-university men, in sharp distinction to the Treasury; their toiling, nose-to-the-grindstone attitude has been in contrast to the more analytical spirit of Great George Street. But the contrast is fading; the Bank now recruits thirty to forty graduates a year, and among the next generation of Bank of England men there are very academic men from Oxford and Cambridge, including Kit MacMahon, an Australian economist who once wrote a Fabian pamphlet; John Fforde, an Oxford academic who has written a book on the American Federal Reserve Bank; and the Bank's prodigy, Jeremy Morse, Fellow of All Souls and a quintessential product of Winchester, who became director of the Bank in 1965 at the age of only 36.

O'Brien, appointed by Harold Wilson after his stormy relationship with Lord Cromer, was assumed by many to be a more pliable choice; he is an unpretentious man to encounter, like a pixie, still with a mild clerkly look, and slightly deaf. He has something of the same quiet, long-suffering style as Sir William Armstrong—and the two are in fact friends, forming an important alliance between E.C.2 and S.W.1. O'Brien's father was a minor official in the LCC, and his passion is music; he worked his way up through the Bank, and was promoted from Chief Cashier (the man who signs the banknotes) to become a director of the Bank and then to be Governor. His clerical training did not, as it turned out, make him any less independent than Cromer, and foreign central bankers (one of them told me) found him a good deal better informed. He was soon critical of the Labour government's optimism and mounting spending; he introduced more professionalism, brought in McKinsey's the management consultants, and disclosed more information in the Bank's *Quarterly Bulletin*. After the Conservatives came to power he made quite a tough speech at the Lord Mayor's Banquet—the traditional jousting-place for Governors and Chancellors—pressing for an incomes policy against the known policy of his fellow-guest Anthony Barber: 'I do not see how we can expect to maintain a fully employed, fully informed and increasingly well-off democracy in which the development of wages and prices is left to the operation of market forces. The bodies on both sides of the bargaining tables, the unions and employers in both the public and private sectors, are too big and too powerful for such a process to yield us the result most likely to contribute to our general welfare and prosperity.'

In national terms the Governor's position seems a lonely one, caught between financiers and politicians, and resented by successive governments from left and right. But much of his strength comes from his membership of the most formidable of all international clubs, the Basle Club, the group of central bankers who meet each month in Switzerland. The central bankers agree with each other more readily than they agree with their governments: each of them stands to the others as responsible for the stability of his own currency. It is the government's knowledge that if the Governor were to resign the pound would immediately be in danger, that gives Sir Leslie his ultimate deterrent.

MANAGING MONEY

The defence of the pound is the most dominating responsibility of the Bank and the Governor, and it is this, in the past few years, that has brought Governors painfully into the public eye with dramatic interventions, summoning the other central bankers for huge loans. While the pound is in danger the foreign exchange market is the constant worry of both the Bank and the Treasury; Roy Jenkins told the Select Committee that as Chancellor he had sometimes followed the foreign exchange market from hour to hour; and Harold Wilson's memoirs show how far he was preoccupied with the pound (and the Governor) in his first months as premier.

But the operation of the Bank which most closely concerns the rest of the city is the intricate business of managing the 'gilt-edged market' of government stock, which affects the whole supply of money. The gilt-edged market dates back from the invention of the National Debt, which itself brought the Bank into being: William III needed a million pounds quickly, to raise money for his war against Louis XIV, and was ingeniously advised to borrow it from the public. In 1694 the Bank of England was established, with a staff of seventeen clerks, to fix the loan. Since then, the Debt (it is usually given a capital D) has never looked back: governments have gone on using it to raise money quickly without waiting for taxes—particularly in war-time. The Debt multiplied seven times in the first world war, and doubled in the second—by raising such loans as 'Victory Bonds' or 'War Bonds'.

By March 31, 1970, the Debt stood at £33,070,000,000. It is made up of about three million separate accounts, with six million payments a year made to stockholders.

New government loans—known as 'gilt-edged stock' because of their supposed reliability—are floated by the Bank through the extraordinary machinery, half-governmental, half-official, of the Senior Government Broker, who occupies the semi-hereditary post: the families of Daniell and Mullens have been government brokers since 1829, and the current broker, Sir Peter Daniell, an Old Etonian, has been in the firm for thirty years. He is surrounded with ritual—like most gilt-edged people, he wears a top hat in the city—so that it is difficult to remember that he is actually making money. Officially and rather hopefully he is known as 'Broker to the Commissioners for the Reduction of the National Debt': he inhabits the offices of Mullens and Co in Moorgate, only a few yards from the Bank of England, where portraits of Mullenses look down from tall panels. Being privy to the government's plans, Sir Peter is the object of immense interest in the city, and his selling of bonds can generate panic in the stock exchange. His 'tap'— the price at which he will sell one or more key gilt-edged bonds by which the government raises money—sets the pattern of the gilt-edged market.

The government raises short-term loans through 'Treasury Bills' (invented by Bagehot in 1877) which are really IOUs to be repaid (usually) in three months: and here we touch on one of the oddest parts of the fringe between government and private finance. Every Friday afternoon the Treasury announces how much money it will raise by these Bills the following week—usually between £200 and £300 million. These huge sums of money are in effect borrowed largely from the only people who can afford them—the joint-stock bankers. But as go-betweens there exists one of the smallest and oddest professions in Britain—the eighty discount brokers, or 'bill brokers', who borrow large sums from the joint-stock banks and then lend them to the government. Every Friday they lodge their tenders at the Bank of England to buy the Treasury Bills, at a price agreed beforehand by a broker's syndicate, and 'deliberately manipulated' (in the words of the 1959 Radcliffe Report) to exclude outside tenders. The discount brokers nibble their tiny percentage and can grow rich on it. On days when 'money is scarce' the top hats can be seen rushing from bank to bank—just before 2.30 when the Bank of England stops lending—

trying to find a million pounds or so with which to balance their books.

The city's justification for the brokers is partly that they provide a kind of *cushion*—a pet city word—to the money market, making it less volatile and neurotic than Wall Street; and partly that the brokers, by constantly scrabbling around for cheap money, make sure that there are no 'idle lakes' or even 'puddles' of money which are not being drained. But the justification is often questionable. 'If a thunderbolt fell tonight and all the discount houses were wiped out,' asked Ian Mikardo of the Governor, 'what disasters would occur?' 'I will not say that if they disappeared overnight,' replied Sir Leslie, 'it would be beyond the wit of man—or even of the Bank of England—to devise some mechanism which could take their place.'[1]

The Bank can affect the supply of money in three principal ways. It can operate in the gilt-edged market. It can change the liquidity ratios of financial institutions, or it can wield its most controversial and clumsy weapon, Bank Rate—the rate of interest at which it lends money, and hence (by tradition) the interest rate of the joint-stock banks to all their millions of customers. The procedure is still ritualistic. Every Thursday morning the Court considers Bank Rate, and at about 11.45 Sir Peter Daniell, accompanied by a stock exchange waiter, walks in his top hat from the Bank of England to the stock exchange—which takes exactly two and a half minutes—enters the hall, gets up on a chair, and announces Bank Rate. The rigmarole is, in fact, a fraud; it pretends that the Bank of England decides Bank Rate, while in fact it is the Treasury's decision. The Radcliffe Report of 1959 urged that Bank Rate should be announced in the name of the Chancellor, not of the Governor, and the Select Committee of 1970 shared Radcliffe's view: 'It would make the precise relationship between Treasury and Bank rather clearer.' The suggestions were ignored, and Sir Peter still stands on his chair.

In the last decades, several factors have weakened the financial impact of the Bank Rate. The great industrial corporations now largely finance themselves out of their own profits. Government spending has enormously increased so that (as Radcliffe reported in paragraph 49) 'nearly half the total volume of investment is now financed by public authorities'. Hire-purchase business has multiplied, which allows the government to stop

[1] Select Committee: Question 476.

public spending much more quickly by restricting hire-purchase terms, to cut back sales of cars or refrigerators. And the internationalisation of big business has made it harder for the Bank of England, like other central banks, to stop large companies from borrowing money when they want to; as the Select Committee put it: 'As banks and corporations become more internationally-minded and sophisticated in their financial operations, the difficulties of conducting monetary policy in an open economy are not going to diminish.'

The techniques for controlling the spending of money are still, and must always be, a matter of perpetual controversy. The economy is often regarded by chancellors and bankers in homely, mechanical terms, in the language of accelerators and brakes, a touch of the tiller, stop and go, stoking up booms and damping them down, overheating or going off the boil. But the consumers and companies do not react in such straightforward ways; and the bankers' calculations are often defeated by the refusal of housewives or managing directors to react as they are expected to—to stop when they are told to go, or to have an orgy of spending (as happened in the consumers' revolt of 1968) when they are supposed to be tightening their belts or pulling in their reins. It is here that the Bank's self-containment, like that of the Treasury, shows its limitation; their rarefied men can easily forget that their subjects do not behave like boilers, cars, engines and ships, but like people.

BANK AND PARLIAMENT

The task of uncovering the secrets of the Bank of England and scrutinising its policies is one that has baffled successive investigators. When the Bank was nationalised in 1946, and the Treasury became its sole stockholder, Sir Stafford Cripps soon afterwards said half-jokingly 'the Bank is my creature'; Treasury men still like to refer to it as their city arm or 'our East End branch'. But the Act made no provision for the Bank to publish its accounts, and since then, through its smokescreens and its city connections, the Bank has managed to evade close scrutiny by the Treasury, and still more by parliament. It is the most remarkable example of secrecy defeating democracy. A major victory for MPs was achieved when the Select Committee on Nationalised Industries, under the robust chairmanship of Ian Mikardo, the left-wing MP, was allowed to enquire into the Bank; its report of May 1970 is one of the most fascinating of all the reports of that remarkable committee. In brisk dialogue it reveals the habits of thinking and attitudes of the Bank, the Governor and the Chancellor, but it also underlines the extent of parliament's ignorance—and the Treasury's. The committee recalled the experience of Gladstone, when he was Chancellor, who observed that the Bank had, in an earlier age, developed a detached, independent and even hostile attitude towards the government because in those days the government was 'justly in ill odour as a fraudulent bankrupt'. The Bank, Gladstone complained, persisted in this attitude long after governments had manifestly become solvent, responsible and honest, to such an extent that Gladstone had to fight the Bank on those grounds. 'That fight,' the Committee sourly remarked, 'has not been completely resolved even in 1970.'

Time and again the Committee came up against the blank walls of secrecy: 'The Bank could go on operating inefficiently for years,' they soon complained, 'without anyone knowing it.' 'As far as I can see from the evidence,' said Mikardo at one stage, 'every question put in this direction is met with the answer— "Well, we have been here since 1694, so we can't be all that bad, we must know our way around the joint." ' Mikardo was specially shocked by the extravagance of the Bank's new buildings, particularly in Birmingham: they are (as he put it in question 2283) 'at the moment building replicas of the Taj Mahal in a number of provincial English cities'. Above all, the Bank was adamant in its refusal to disclose its reserves: the Governor, Sir Leslie O'Brien, explained that one of the strongest arguments for not revealing them was that the Bank could 'do good by stealth'— that it could rescue companies in distress without spreading alarm. But, said Colonel Lancaster, MP (question 2300) 'as we do not know the size of the reserves, we do not know how stealthy he is being, or to what degree he has been stealthy, so we are back to square one in the argument'.

The question of who is responsible for Britain's monetary policy is a key part of the examination of the British power structure; but here the ordinary citizen, like the Select Committee, comes up (even if he gets through technical complications) against a maze of mystification, with the trail ending somewhere in the confused regions between the Treasury and the Bank. The arguments for an independent central bank are strong ones, both in

Britain and elsewhere; Dr Blessing of the Bundesbank (freely paraphrased by Mikardo in question 2305) told the committee that 'a bank has to be independent because one cannot really trust the politicians—they are all a rotten lot and any of them might seek to get out of a hole by printing money'. The conflict between central bankers and governments is a necessary one, but it need not be fought out in secret; both in Germany and in America it emerges much more openly. What is specially depressing to the outside inquirer is how little either the Bank or the Treasury accepts any need to enlighten parliament or the public: like the mythology of the monarchy, the mystique of the Bank is based on a contempt for the public. The secrecy of the Bank is, of course, bound up with the secrecy of the Treasury. As Anthony Harris of *The Guardian* told the Select Committee: 'I cannot see that it is fair to expect the Bank of England which operates as an arm of the Treasury to be franker than the Treasury itself.' The two entrenched institutions support each other in resisting the suggestion of any permanent select committee for economic affairs (see chapter 14) to inspect them. Mikardo's committee concluded: 'It is in the public interest that the facts should be known about public bodies. Your committee believes that the proper interests of the Bank would in no way suffer if much of the traditional secrecy which has for so long surrounded its activities were to be dispelled.' The Treasury, in a white paper in April 1971, welcomed the report, and promised fuller accounts; it remains to be seen how far they can genuinely enlighten the public.

CITY AND GOVERNMENT

The City's acceptance of the Bank of England, with all its oddities and obscurities, rests on its role as a friendly buffer between the City and the Government; in spite of the rigid exchange controls, it is far less restrictive than continental central banks; and it believes in letting people, wherever possible, get on with it. It is this freedom, City men maintain, which allows them to exploit opportunities more quickly than foreign financiers —as they have done so spectacularly with the Eurodollar business —and at the same time to inspire trust, as responsible individuals who are not subject to governmental direction. The stately style of the old city houses, and the assumptions of the city establishment that there is an unwritten code, reinforce this impression. But from time to time this dignified façade wobbles and for a moment collapses; and the bankers, brokers and entrepreneurs are suddenly revealed outplotting, undercutting and outmanoeuvring each other, in desperate attempts to make or protect money— usually at the expense of the ordinary shareholder. The city suddenly for a few days looks not like a Pall Mall club, but like a Western saloon bar, with bodies all over the place. With each bust-up, there is new talk of the need for a sheriff, or the need for the city to enforce its own rules to prevent the government stepping in.

It is the take-over bid that reveals in full sight of the public the jungle law of the city; for the essence of a take-over is to buy up a company for less than it is worth, and to conceal the bid until the last possible moment; and in the course of the battle many of the intermediaries stand to make quick gains through their inside knowledge. In the sixties a succession of battles revealed to the public how much the shareholders' (and employees') interests were ignored, and in February 1968 the leading city institutions were persuaded that unless they agreed to some form of self-policing to regulate their conduct, they would have to be policed by the government; the dread initials SEC were much muttered (the American Securities and Exchange Commission, imposed on Wall Street after the scandals of the Great Crash). A Take-over Panel was set up, with the backing of the Bank of England, with a special City code, which included a key Article 7 saying that no shareholders, in the company being bid for, should be made an offer that is 'more favourable than a general offer to be made thereafter to the other shareholders'.

Soon afterwards, in July 1968, the panel faced its first test. American Tobacco made a bid for the English cigarette company Gallaher's at well above the market price of the shares, and the Americans' bankers, Morgan Grenfell, together with their stock-brokers Cazenove's, sold £20 million worth of their own clients' Gallaher shares quickly to the Americans, leaving other share-holders in the cold. Morgan's and Cazenove's are two of the most aristocratic firms in the City; both were involved in defending the City Establishment ten years before, in the Aluminium War, and Sir Antony Hornby, chairman of Cazenove's (Winchester and the Guards) and director of the Savoy, defended the Savoy Hotel group in 1953 in a classic battle against the then outsider Sir Harold Samuel. After the American Tobacco deal, the Take-over

Panel quickly issued a statement announcing that 'certain dealings in Gallaher shares' were a breach of the new city code; Morgan's and Cazenove's immediately denied it, and added stiffly that no Press enquiries would be answered by either of them. The next month the Stock Exchange Council (under Sir Martin Wilkinson) produced an ineffectual verdict, which confirmed that Cazenove's had broken the code, but cleared them of blame on the grounds that they did not know they were breaking it 'in the confused and competitive bid situation'.

The Governor, Sir Leslie, then stirred himself and moved into action, writing three menacing letters to the stock exchange, the panel and the issuing houses, warning that unless the code was enforced, there would have to be 'statutory action'—the euphemism for 'the government moves in'. The following year a revised code was issued, and now a full-time panel was set up with a director-general, Ian Fraser, a combative ex-journalist banker brought over from Warburg's; and as chairman, Lord Shawcross, the ex-Labour cabinet minister who had prosecuted at the Nuremberg trials. Their test, too, came very soon, in the elemental form of Robert Maxwell—whose relentless progress showed up in harsh colours like a roving searchlight, the real shape of the scenery. In the chemistry of power, he has precipitated all kinds of by-products. We have already seen (chapter 21) how his attempt to buy the *News of the World* brought about instead the arrival of Rupert Murdoch, and thus the transformation of Fleet Street. Only a few months afterwards he likewise catalysed the city.

This episode began at the beginning of 1969, when Maxwell encountered a man who was his match in ruthlessness—the young American financier Saul Steinberg, who had built up the Leasco data-processing company. Maxwell interested Steinberg in his own Pergamon publishing business, and by dazzling showmanship, including a talk with the prime minister, persuaded him to take it over at the very high price of 37s. a share. Steinberg immediately began buying through his London bankers, Rothschilds, and acquired shares worth £9 million. But by the end of July there were growing rumours that Pergamon's profit forecast—of £2½ million for the next year—was not going to be fulfilled. Steinberg started his own enquiries through his accountants, Touche Ross, who without much co-operation from Pergamon decided that the forecast was much too optimistic. Maxwell, confronted with this, eventually agreed to take only 18s. 6d. for his shares until the profit forecast was reached, though the proposal was not to be made public. The Takeover Panel were now very worried, and tried to press the parties to agreement. Steinberg flew back to London; Rothschilds told the panel that they could not agree to Maxwell's terms; but that evening at a meeting at the flat of (once again) Lord Goodman, Steinberg and Maxwell patched it up. Then a few days later, Rothschilds discovered that one of Maxwell's trusts, in the Bahamas, had sold a large batch of shares. It was the last straw. They finally told the panel that 'all confidence has been dissipated', and Steinberg decided to pull out of the take-over.

Now the panel reacted firmly. They called for a suspension of dealings in Pergamon shares and asked for a Board of Trade enquiry—thus admitting that the solution could not be left to the city alone. But there was deadlock in the meantime: Steinberg had his £9 million in Pergamon shares, but Maxwell insisted on remaining chief executive. The Take-over Panel tried for a new agreement; Lord Shawcross returned dramatically from holiday and warned Maxwell to give up running the company. Maxwell refused. The other big shareholders prepared themselves for battle, and created a 'Third Force' which pressed Steinberg to bid for the rest of the company. In October came the meeting of shareholders, a stormy four hours—the most dramatic meeting since Maxwell was kept out of the *News of the World*. Eventually sixty-one per cent voted against Maxwell, and ousted the Pergamon directors. Steinberg said: 'I've never seen anything like it in the States.' Maxwell said: 'I shall not forget.'

Trench-warfare followed, revealing still more troubles for Pergamon. A new board was appointed, under a staid old MP, Sir Henry d'Avigdor Goldsmith. Steinberg sued Maxwell for £9 million—the cost of his shares. In August 1970 the new auditors, Price, Waterhouse, announced that in the nine months to September 1969, Pergamon had made a loss of £2 million, and decided to wipe off £2½ million from the assets. 'We have saved the patient's life', said Sir Henry 'but at a very high cost indeed.' At the end of 1970 Steinberg announced that he would not bid for the rest of the shares, and in April 1971 the irrepressible Maxwell actually returned as a director, to the board from which he had been sacked eighteen months before.

The Pergamon affair was embarrassing to almost everyone. But it was a victory for the Take-over Panel. They had resisted strong pressure from Maxwell, had insisted on the Board of Trade enquiry and suspended share dealings, and their prestige in the city was high, much due to the acerbic personalities of Fraser and Shawcross: 'I would have thought that they had uplifted the standards of the city by several hundred per cent,' Jim Slater said. 'The knowledge that we can stop the deal concentrates the mind wonderfully,' Ian Fraser told the *Financial Times* in April 1970: 'Part of the game is to persuade one side that the other is not being allowed to cheat; then they will observe our rulings.' The Take-over Panel had succeeded for the time being in patching up the city's own quarrels; but it was a long way from reassuring shareholders outside the 'square mile': the Pergamon affair showed how little the public was normally told about a company's real situation, and how far accounts depended on guesses about the future. As one solicitor, John Francis, complained to the *Solicitors' Journal* (January 9, 1970): 'What the code does undoubtedly do is to elevate still further the status of the merchant banks as advisers rationalising their actions, however inimical to the interest of the shareholders. It fails to impose on them the duties and obligations of professional advisers.'

Most city people seem confident that the city, through the panel, can now regulate its own affairs, and that—in keeping with the Heath philosophy—it will not need to lean on government. But there are many city men, like Lord Poole of Lazards or David Montagu of Samuel Montagu's, who believe that the Take-over Panel cannot cope in the long run with a real burst of aggression, and that the city in the end will have to accept some form of government regulation, on the pattern of the American SEC. The Bank of England, the great monument to British pragmatism and laissez-faire, stands uneasily in the middle of the jungle; and the Governor, the cryptic headmaster of this unruly school, hopes that by reprimands, frowns and 'moral suasion', he will avoid having to call in the police.

PART

SIX

Industry

31

Farmers

Land is about the only thing that can't fly away.
Anthony Trollope.

It is a paradox of British society that although less than four
per cent of the population work on the land—a smaller proportion
than anywhere in Europe—the influence of farmers and landowners penetrates politics quite out of proportion to their
numbers. Many causes are suggested: the wealth of some of the
individual farmers; the importance of marginal agricultural seats;
the lack of an effective anti-farmer lobby; and the lingering fear
that, in a future war as in the last two, agriculture will have an
importance quite separate from its economic contribution. Perhaps the most powerful factor of all is the basic fascination
of town-dwellers with the land, their romantic sympathy with
the farmers' cause, mixed with some fear or guilt in the face of
more extrovert and muscular people. The British, in spite of their
urbanisation, have never come to terms with city life as the
French and Italians have: they have more houses and gardens
(see chapter 23), and still fight against flats. The obsessions of the
urban child with the farmyard and the angry farmer finds its
grown-up equivalent in the government's meekness in the face of
the demands of the National Farmers' Union.

The relationship is complicated by the confusion of town-
dwellers as to what the farmers are *for*. The voters, in subsidising

farmers, are apt to associate them with the splendours of the countryside, the hedgerows, the views of cows and horses in the landscape; the farmer seems to be part of the flora and fauna, a piece of the British heritage. But as farmers are forced to become more efficient and competitive, so the picturesque old farms with patchwork multicoloured fields give way to monotonous prairies; cows are shut up in sheds for 'zero grazing'; horses are forsaken for tractors; hedgerows are ripped up to allow the combine harvesters to thresh across unbroken acres. The voters find that their subsidies, far from protecting the precious countryside, are helping to pay for its dismantling, and for the expansion of an ugly agrobusiness, full of corrugated asbestos. The cross-purposes become more awkward. The townsmen expect the farmers to maintain what they forbiddingly call the 'amenities' of the countryside; the farmers reply that, if they are asked to preserve their hedges or thatched barns, they must be paid to do so. That old romantic picture of the farmer is coming unstuck, and the voter (or the government) may have to choose between supporting a big businessman who has moved into the country, or a kind of park warden who is paid to preserve the countryside for ramblers, picnickers and weekend motorists.

LAND

Nobody's making it any more.
Mark Twain.

Behind these cross-purposes lies the growing importance of the commodity that everyone wants, the land, which in the last decade has loomed much larger in the political consciousness (which has compelled me to include this chapter in the *Anatomy*). Inflation, motorways, motor-cars and greater leisure have played their part in opening up the land and the discussion of the environment (the fashionable word for land) has broken out everywhere. The shortage of land has become much more apparent. The total area of the United Kingdom is only sixty million acres for a population of fifty-two million—just over an acre per head. Britain is one of the most heavily populated countries in the world, and much of the nineteen million acres in Scotland, and the three million in Northern Ireland, are virtually uninhabitable; the huge county of Sutherland has a hundred acres per inhabitant. These are some populations per square mile:

Holland	845
Belgium	775
United Kingdom	559
West Germany	554
Japan	509
Italy	386
France	213
United States	57

The ownership of land has changed a good deal in the last century: in 1883 the biggest landowners were the Duke of Sutherland, with 1,358,000 acres, and the Duke of Buccleuch, with 460,000 acres. Today the biggest landowner, by far, is the Forestry Commission, which owns 2,475,000 acres, on which it plants more than a million trees a year: it owns, in fact, a twentieth of Britain, most of it fairly barren or mountainous. Another huge occupier of land is the Ministry of Defence which shuts off over 600,000 acres—more than one per cent—including some beautiful coastal sites. The other largest landowners are:

The Crown	176,000 acres
Church of England	170,000 acres
National Trust	400,000 acres
Oxford and Cambridge Colleges	275,000 acres

The hereditary landowners still own the biggest private estates; in Scotland some of the largest are the Duke of Buccleuch (220,000 acres), the Countess of Seafield (213,000) and Lord Lovat (160,000); in England there is Lord Leverhulme the soap heir (99,000), the Duke of Northumberland (80,000) and the Earl of Lonsdale (71,000).[1] But there are now far more people who own the land they farm. In 1908 only twelve per cent of agricultural land was farmed by owner-occupiers: but since then death duties have broken up big estates, and rent controls (until 1957) were so uneconomic for landowners that they often sold off their land. Today more than fifty per cent of land is farmed by owner-occupiers. Many hereditary great estates have been broken up, but there have also been amalgamations of small farms which have become increasingly uneconomic; in 1966 there were twice as many farms (933) of more than a thousand acres than there were in 1945. Britain has a much higher proportion of big farms than continental countries—the most important factor in making her farming more efficient—and their numbers will greatly increase in

[1] See Roy Perrott: *The Aristocrats*, Weidenfeld and Nicolson 1968, p. 151 ff. Most of his figures came from the owners themselves.

the next decades; one estimate reckons 2,700 farms of more than a thousand acres by 1985. Many of those farms will often be too expensive to be owned by a single family (a thousand acres can cost half a million pounds) so that they will be controlled by a company or a partnership, and run by a salaried manager.

For nine hundred years or so the value of much of the land remained, in real money terms, about the same as it was in the Domesday survey of 1086.[1] The great agricultural depression in the late nineteenth century had caused the price of land to slump, and by the second world war land was still changing hands for less than it had fetched in the eighteen-eighties. Then, in the late fifties, the price of land began fairly suddenly to rise. Several factors contributed to the change. Agricultural rents had been freed, which made investment in land more profitable; productivity had increased; land attracted lower death duties than other property, so that rich men (like Charles Clore in Herefordshire) bought land for their children. But an important factor was the multiplication of motor-cars, which opened up the spaces to the town-dwellers, and led to a growing desire to escape from the congestion of cities; while at the same time the growth of suburbia and the proliferation of cars made the shortage of space much more evident. The spread of cities uses up another 40,000 acres each year, and in the next ten years (according to Anthony Stodart, parliamentary secretary for Agriculture in 1971) an area the size of Hereford and Leicester would be taken from farming. Land, whether profitable or not, became more and more attractive to businessmen, bankers or financiers. Large investors and pension funds in the city are turning to land as an investment. The desire to own land is a persistent British characteristic; and the new mobility produced by cars and motorways has made it much more possible to be a landowner and a city worker at the same time. Whatever the cause, the increase in land prices over the last decade has been spectacular: these are the figures (from the Ministry of Agriculture) of the average sale prices per acre, for land of ten acres or more:

1959-60	£73
1960-1	£88
1961-2	£98
1962-3	£107
1963-4	£114

[1] Dudley Stamp: *The Land of Britain*, 1946.

1964-5	£148
1965-6	£168
1966-7	£169
1967-8	£178
1968-9	£196
1969-70	£197

INDUSTRY OR AMENITY?

Agriculture is the oldest and biggest industry in Britain, and in the last decades it has become much less of a way of life, and more like other industries. Nowadays farmers can claim to be among the most efficient industrialists: in the last ten years the productivity of agriculture has increased at twice the rate for industry as a whole. The major change came with the last war, when government intervention forced through mechanisation and rationalisation. British farms now supply about half the nation's food, as against 30 per cent before the war (when there were seven million fewer people to feed) and in some foods there is a crisis of overproduction. There are fewer people working on the farms, and more animals: there are now twice as many poultry as people.

Livestock in England and Wales from 1920
(Thousands)

	Cattle	Sheep	Pigs	Poultry
1920	5,547	13,383	1,993	n/a
1945	7,237	12,597	1,732	37,352
1968	8,907	19,189	5,867	104,208

In 1954 the average cow produced 685 gallons of milk a year: in 1969 she produced 840 gallons: she is better fed, better bred, better looked after, with modern comforts like music during milking time. In 1946 the average hen laid 115 eggs for the year while in 1969 she laid 212 eggs: computers are now trying to make hens lay the right coloured eggs at the right time. British farmers now produce all the milk Britain needs, almost all the pork, eggs, barley, oats, potatoes; three-quarters of the beef and veal, and half the wheat. Total sales have been estimated at £2,000 million, or three per cent of national income—equivalent to the combined output of the coal and steel industry. In its transformation, agriculture has become much closer to other industries; farmers can no longer feel proudly detached from the cities. In 1948 only 35 per cent of the total costs of agricultural production came from resources outside agriculture, and by 1963 the proportion was up to 60 per cent; machinery, fertilisers, insecticides and fuel make up a large part of the farmer's costs, while the share of wages or rent has diminished.

Perhaps the most painful interlocking with outside industry has been in frozen foods; the Unilever subsidiary Birds Eye descends on the farmers, making contracts to buy fields-full of peas and beans, to process them into careful uniformity for frozen packets. Processions of pea-picking machines like mechanical dragons each summer roar into the quiet farms of East Anglia, racing from one field to the next, working all night under arc-lights to devour their quota. They work to the minute, talking by radio to the head-quarters, and rushing the peas to the freezing factories in less than ninety minutes. The confrontation between the tough young managers of Birds Eye and the proud farmers of Suffolk and Norfolk is spiky and bitter; they both need each other, but both hate to admit it, and Unilever do not want to take the obvious course—to buy up their own estates—for fear of the political in-volvements. The farmers regard the Birds Eye men as ignorant foreigners, obsessed with the 'Shylock mentality', who treat fields as factories and farmers as hired labour; the Birds Eye men regard themselves as pullers-together of a hopelessly disorganised pro-fession. The dependence of farmers on providing 'convenience foods' for firms like Birds Eye, Marks and Spencer, Findus (Nestlés) or Ross (Imperial Tobacco) has involved them much more closely in the discipline of the supermarket, and made them more conscious of marketing rather than production. They have to produce always the same width of pea, the same fat-content of pork-meat, the same size of apple all over the country, and they cannot defy their suppliers: 'You can farm against the weather, but you can't farm against Birds Eye.' Many farmers dread that they will become so bound to the processers and freezers that they will lose all their in-dependence, like other industrial suppliers of supermarkets. But the food processers have already changed the face of farming, and have made the notion of the independent farmer still more of a myth.

While farmers are being pressed to amalgamate, rationalise and specialise, to build miniature factories in the middle of prairies, the town-dwellers who have subsidised them are streaming into the countryside more than ever before, hoping perhaps to find that story-book landscape they remember from their childhood. For some small farmers tourists can provide a welcome bonanza, paying for their bed and breakfast or camping sites: for many coastal farmers (as the others scornfully put it) 'their best crop is caravans'. But for big industrial farmers, tourists are increasingly a menace.

To guard the public interest, the Labour government set up in 1968 a new Countryside Commission, to replace the old National Parks Commission; its job is to provide parks or camping sites, to build long-distance footpaths, to protect beauty spots, and to supervise the ten national parks (including the Lake District, Snowdonia and the Peak District) which make up nine per cent of the area of Britain. The Commission is run cautiously from Cambridge Gate, in London (the government tried to persuade it to move its headquarters to the countryside when its lease runs out, but it insists on remaining in the city). The members of the Commission are appointed by the Department for the Environment. They are predominantly naturalists and landowners, not exactly your ordinary ramblers; their chairman is J. S. Cripps, son of Sir Stafford and editor of *The Countryman*; and others include Aubrey Buxton, the rich Norfolk bird-shooter and friend of Prince Philip, Sir William Lindsay, a Sussex conservative, and George Howard, the head of the Country Landowners' Association and owner of one of the biggest piles in Britain, Castle Howard.

The Commission surveys with some pessimism the task of reconciling the interests of tourists, farmers and conservationists. One typical bone of contention is the ordinary hedge. The English pattern of hedgerows and quilted landscape only dates back (with Saxon exceptions) to the seventeenth and eighteenth centuries, when the land was enclosed and developed by rapacious landowners; but the hedge has come to be regarded as a special splendour of the British countryside. Now big farmers, with their tractors and combine harvesters, detest the hedges which break up their farming area, harbour vermin and weeds, keep the sun off the crops, and are expensive to maintain; in the last few years farmers have pulled up many miles of hedges, often with a grant to help them. The Ministry of Agriculture argues the hedges are less useful for shelter and soil conservation than used to be imagined, and that 'a well-farmed landscape looks better than a poorly farmed one'.[1] But for bird-watchers, botanists, walkers, or black-berry-pickers, the hedge means nesting-places, shelter and foot-paths.

It is in the hills that the dilemma emerges most plainly—is the taxpayer subsidising the farmer, or subsidising the tourist? Hill farms occupy fourteen million acres—a third of the total agricul-tural area—including some of the most beautiful acres. Most hill farmers, even with eighty per cent subsidies, can only just keep going; a recent survey showed that forty-five per cent of Welsh farmers received less than the average wage of an agricultural worker. Most flocks in Scotland or Wales consist of only one or two hundred sheep, owned by a shepherd and his wife, living in a stone cottage in the hills. Their life is quite uneconomic in urban terms, but it is the life which for the last twenty centuries has been commemorated by poets as the idyllic pastoral existence, and which is still an ideal for hippies in the 'seventies. In purely economic terms it might be more sensible to abolish sheep-subsidies and turn the hill farms into national parks, converting the shepherds into park wardens or tea-room attendants; already the Countryside Commission has begun paying some small farmers in Snowdonia and the Lakes to clear up litter, put up signs and picnic seats and make car parks. Yet the prospect of hills without any real shepherds or sheep is a melancholy one.

The Countryside Commission projects a picture of Britain as a huge park, supplying nature-lovers with well-trodden footpaths, picnic places, litter baskets and lavatories, so that they can admire the view and animals without worrying the farmers. The language of the rural planners—the amenities, visitor-inflow, landscape evaluation, rural traffic control, lavatory bulletins, or recreational routes—is very dispiriting. The taming and cutting-off of nature, which began with the railways, has been taken much farther by the car. The Countryside Commission hopes that tourists will con-fine themselves to 'honeypot' attractions, like the 'casual recreation areas' away from the good farming land; they even suggest that some footpaths that cross over good land might be closed. It is doubtful that the problem will be so easily solved.

As townspeople flock back to the country, they come up against the old simple problem as before the industrial revolution—the ownership of land. The simple craving for open space, not to farm

[1] Speech by Cledwyn Hughes (then Minister of Agriculture) to a conference on 'Agriculture and the Environment', January 21, 1970.

on, but to walk on, breathe on, escape on, will become more passionate as cars and suburbs multiply. The new land-hunger will not be, as it was in the seventeenth century, a question of life and death; but it may be angry. The present generation of walkers and car-owners are easily intimidated by farmers or gamekeepers, and meekly leave the fields when they are told to: the word 'trespasser' still has an awesome sound, even though trespassers are not easily or often prosecuted. But the next generation will certainly become more stroppy. Farmers are the owners of the one commodity, land, that is increasingly in demand; and as their industry becomes more intensive, so they will want to restrict further the public's access and enjoyment. The countryside is the stronghold of most myths about free enterprise, independence, self-reliance, but it may be, in the end, that the wheel will turn full circle—that the common land which was grabbed and enclosed by the landlords in the eighteenth century will be given back to the public, and that the whole land of Britain will come to seem so precious that the public will insist on having it for themselves.

FARMERS AND FARMWORKERS

Many people now maintain that the efficient farmer is simply an industrialist who happens to be geographically separated from the city. The case is over-stated. Farming remains and is likely to remain an occupation like no other, for its business is indissolubly linked with a way of life that embraces the whole family; the house is the office, the fields are the garden, the car is the van, the farm is the shop, and the children can be workers; the family farm remains the most important unit in British agriculture, and even a big farm of a thousand acres can still be operated by a single family with one or two workers. It is the sense of oneness and independence, linked with the separation from cities that still gives farming its unique hold on people. The independence in economic terms is illusory. But in psychological terms it is very real. 'In this business you can still *say* what you think,' said one farmer-tycoon. 'The sugar beet will still go on growing, and that's worth £5,000 a year.'

Farmers still have mixed motives, in which money-making is not necessarily uppermost; and farming can still provide an escape from the world of finance. Industrialists and bankers have been retreating to country houses all through the industrial revolution, and among industrialised countries Britain is unique in the continuity of its 'county' tradition which, however bogus or romanticised, can transform the attitudes of successful city men. It would be rash to equate the possession of a rural retreat with a diminishing interest in money; Charles Clore, Kenneth Keith and Sir Arnold Weinstock all retreat for weekends to big estates; Weinstock applies the same rationalising logic to his farms as he does to General Electric. But farming is not the most sensible or quickest way to make money, and the journey to the countryside usually corresponds to some search for different priorities and values.

It is impossible to generalise usefully about the profession of farmer. At one end are the big farmers who succeed in making fortunes from the land, like Jack Eastwood, the broiler-chicken millionaire with 12,000 acres in Nottinghamshire, who runs one of the few farming companies that have 'gone public'; or Nigel Strutt, the Essex dairy-farmer who runs the Strutt family firms, (Strutt and Parker and Lord Rayleigh's Dairies), which between them own 20,000 acres. At the other end are those thousands of small hill farmers who live below the subsistence level. It is hard, too, to evaluate the standard of living of farmers. Even a farmer near bankruptcy will still have his house, his bacon and eggs and vegetables; and at the top end many businessmen enjoy being farmers because so many perquisites—house, car, gardeners, chauffeur and servants—can be tax-deductible. For small men, farming is still one of the most arduous known ways of making money; there are thousands of small farmers who earn less than £1,300 a year; it is from these that the militants come, who every year process angrily to the towns. Many are forced to sell up their farms and move to the cities: the soaring land-prices have increased the incentive, and a farmer who bought a hundred acres for £6,000 twenty years ago might now sell them for £30,000. But the flight from the land in Britain is less hectic than in the rest of Europe, simply because Britons are already so urbanised. In 1967 there were only 346,000 full-time agricultural workers in Britain—fewer than teachers. But even this number is still falling by about five per cent a year, so that by 1985, at the present rate, there will only be 110,000. Farm workers will be rarer than hairdressers, and the typical farm will consist of a farmer, his wife and a lot of machinery.

NATIONAL FARMERS' UNION

The farmers' champion, representing 85 per cent of them, is the National Farmers' Union, one of the noisiest of all pressure groups. The union is run by 250 people from Agriculture House, a huge and forbidding Georgian block in Knightsbridge (the farmers' most fertile investment: its value has multiplied tenfold since it was built in 1956). Agriculture House does not look much different from other industrial headquarters: no sheep in the corridors, no big men in boots; only a view of Hyde Park as a rural reminder. It conducts its lobbying operation with bureaucratic thoroughness, and remorseless publicity tactics: in one year (it boasts) it issued a hundred press statements to eight hundred journalists and gave fourteen press conferences, rewarded with 100,000 press cuttings, and mentions in twenty radio and television programmes each month. Not surprisingly the initials NFU have a special dread for MPs with farmers in their constituencies.

The NFU is an organisation like no other; neither an employers' federation nor a trade union (though some wild men talk of joining the TUC). It has an uneasy mixture of political and commercial motives, together with sheer defiance: 'I was amazed when I moved in here,' said one official, 'to discover how rude and mean the visiting farmers could be: they think nothing of bawling back at me through the front door as they leave. They insist on having their pound of flesh. Really, they still have pre-industrial ideas.' It was founded in 1908, and in the following sixty years, like nearly everything else, it has been sucked ever closer towards the government. At first it was essentially the spokesman for yeoman farmers; but as the government subsidies piled up, as farms got bigger and more industrialised, so the NFU has moved towards a close and private embrace with the Ministry of Agriculture and the militants regard it (as wild-cat strikers regard the TUC) as the stooge of the government. In the winter, as the annual price negotiations are getting under way, the militants often begin harassing the government and the NFU with demonstrations; tractors block the roads, farmers come up to Westminster with cows or pigs, exploiting their rural mystique.

The headquarters of the NFU presides uneasily over fifty-nine very independent branches. At the top it is run jointly by the (elected) president and the (appointed) director-general—a job which was upgraded in 1970 with the arrival of George Cattell. He is a very urban-looking administrator with a trim moustache, among the swarthy farmers: in spite of his name, he has never been a farmer ('they don't want another ploughman'); he came up through Rootes cars, went into the Department of Employment, and was brought in to reorganise Agriculture House. He believes that the union must represent the whole field of land management if it is to keep its political importance. The president sits on a precarious ejector-seat: he has to be re-elected annually, with 80 per cent of the votes (though there are plans to revise the constitution to allow him a three-year term). If he is noisy enough, like 'Big Jim' Turner, later Lord Netherthorpe, who survived for fifteen years, he can keep the position; but as soon as he is suspected of being too close to the government he is in danger. Sir Harold Woolley was chucked out after six years, to become Lord Woolley. Gwilym Williams was ejected after three years, and became Sir Gwilym. He was succeeded by Henry Plumb, a fresh-faced and polite Warwickshire farmer who has so far managed to take some of the steam out of the protesters by touring the angriest farming areas. He is a persuasive propagandist; he invites urban MPs to try to explain the importance of what he calls 'The National Farm'. But his position is bound to be an uncomfortable one; as one of his officials put it, 'The farmers are always very conscious of We and They, and from the circumference, we look much more like They than We.'

MINISTRY OF AGRICULTURE

Every March the Ministry of Agriculture publishes its Annual Price Review, which doles out about £300 million to British farmers; every preceding winter the officials at Agriculture House embark on elaborate horse-trading with their opposite numbers at the ministry. The clinch between the ministry and the union is an intimate one, kept secret from the public and parliament: the Select Committee on Agriculture complained in 1969 of how little the minister told them: 'The Ministry of Agriculture treats the price review in the same way as the Treasury treats the Budget.' The ministry insists that its relationship with the farmers is detached and critical; 'The Annual Review has in many quarters come to be regarded as the settlement of a pay claim', says the 1970 Review, 'this is not its purpose.' But that is what it is; and the history of the ministry is a classic example of government intervention which begins as a prod, and ends up as a prop. As one ex-Minister of Agriculture put it: 'The trouble is that one moment you put up a support to strengthen the building; the next moment you find the whole building is leaning on the support.'

The government subsidies began in 1916, when German submarines threatened food supplies; Britain then only produced a quarter of her food, and the subsidies were intended to push up production. But even in 1938 the total subsidies of agriculture were only £21 million. Subsidies shot up in the second world war; by the sixties the problem for many foods, like milk, was not how to make more, but to make less. The ministry now insists on 'selective expansion', encouraging some foods—beef, pigmeat, wheat and barley, and discouraging others, like milk, eggs and poultry. The discouragement never goes far enough; British cows, like continental cows, are already producing too much milk; the ministry cannot bring itself to ruin the small dairy farmers, and they are still putting up the milk-price. In the end it will probably have to begin subsidising farmers (as the Americans do) *not* to produce some foods.

There are now about sixteen thousand civil servants in England and Wales looking after about two hundred thousand farmers. The farmer meeting the 'man from Whitehall' is frequently depicted as the archetypal encounter between free enterprise and bureaucracy—the heroic farmer in gumboots and tweeds encountering the bespectacled bureaucrat with pin-stripe and umbrella. The picture is an absurd one, since the farmer is more dependent than anyone on Whitehall, and agriculture has been one of the success-stories of interventionism. The ministry subsidises the farmers, educates them, advises them and trains them: the minister himself is very often a farmer, with a farmyard outspokenness to talk down his cabinet colleagues. The current minister, Jim Prior, belongs to this bucolic tradition; he came straight from his farm in Suffolk to join Heath's cabinet as Minister of Agriculture—his first job in government. He has a comfortably porcine look, red face and white hair, and walks into a room as if it were a field. But he is much more interesting than most of his predecessors; in his narrow-minded constituency of Lowestoft he has been unashamedly anti-hanging, anti-apartheid, pro-European. His rapid rise to the cabinet was partly due to his unwavering support of Edward Heath during the bleakest years of opposition. In the ministry he has moved quickly. He has cut down part of the web of advisory services and committees, and axed about a thousand civil servants. He has taken the first steps to remove food subsidies altogether, and to impose import levies on foreign food—thus breaking the long tradition of agricultural free trade. And he has also shown himself very obliging to the farmers—adding £138 million to price guarantees in the first year. But the most important fact about Prior is that he is a convinced European, and his main job will be to prepare British farmers for the common market.

FARMERS INTO EUROPE

The contrast between the British and continental systems of farming and food is one of the most awkward aspects of Britain's attempt to enter the common market. The British system has ever since the repeal of the Corn Laws in 1846 been based on agricultural free trade, modified by periodic quotas and levies. Cheap food has been allowed to come into Britain from all over the world—New Zealand lamb, Danish bacon, Canadian wheat, French butter—without tariffs. British farmers sell their food to compete with this imported food and are then subsidised by the system of 'deficiency payments' by which the Ministry pays them the difference between the price they get in the shops and the price they are reckoned to need to survive. British housewives have thus had very cheap food in exchange for paying taxes to subsidise the farmers; and even with the new introduction of import levies, food will be much cheaper than the continent's.

The common market system rests on extreme protection; the continental farmers are a much larger proportion of the population, and politically therefore much stronger. The common market guarantees a price to farmers high enough to keep all but the most inefficient in business. All imported food has to pay taxes which bring the price up to the common market price, and the taxes are then used for a special agricultural fund to help the European farmers. The case against the system is a strong one: it pays European farmers extravagantly for stuff which the rest of the world can produce much more cheaply, thus encouraging an 'inward-looking' Europe. Yet the large peasant population on the continent—which has no real parallel in Britain—has to be protected somehow. A still-faster uprooting of farm workers from the land would have dangerous political consequences.

For the British it is specially infuriating. Britain, with bigger farms, greater mechanisation, and fewer land workers, has one of the most efficient farm industries (it is not saying much) in the world. Rain adds to the productivity; continental farmers can expect a drought once every five years or so, but the British drought in 1970 was the first serious one for two decades. In all foods except fruit the British can successfully compete with the continent. But the cost to the British nation of joining this system will be high; food prices will go up by around fifteen per cent; and the levy will have to subsidise the less competent farmers on the continent. This is the paradoxical predicament. The common market requires a free market in other industries where Britain is weak: but it imposes on agriculture—the one industry at which Britain excels—a system of high protection which supports very incompetent farming.

32

Companies

British Leyland has to be good. It's the only motor industry we've got.

Advertisement for British Leyland.
May 1968

In the last decade a hectic succession of mergers and takeovers have turned Britain traditionally a country of small businesses, into a nation of big corporations: next to America, Britain now has many more of the giants than any other western country. To the familiar giants, like Shell, Unilever and ICI, which date back to the twenties and thirties, have been added new ones, like General Electric, British Leyland, Allied Breweries, Bass Charrington. In the mid-sixties the growing competition forced more mergers: weak companies became very vulnerable to takeovers; American and other rivals pressed them to form bigger units. But an important factor was the Labour government, which like other European governments became excited by the idea of the giant corporation, as the engine not only of national competition, but of high technology and higher standards of living. Previous British governments had already become more closely concerned with these big businesses, as they realised that Britain's survival depended on their performances. The coming-together of governments and industries has a long pre-history, going back to the American invasions at the turn of the century and the necessities of two world wars: armaments, aircraft or chemicals long ago became intertwined with government policies.

But in the sixties the connections became more numerous and closer, as one industry after another came into difficulties, and both Conservative and Labour governments felt the need to prop them up, to goad them on, or (difficult) to do both at once. The Labour government felt specially compelled to urge industries to the 'white-hot technological revolution'; government research was stepped up, and the Ministry of Technology was set up as the central agency to stimulate industrial research.

While governments became more concerned, so did the British public; and the captains of industry and managers, who had been for so long ignored or disliked, came to the front of the national stage, smiling and taking applause. I have found a striking scene-change in the ten years since I wrote the first *Anatomy of Britain*. In those days the chairmen of the biggest companies were very little known to the public compared to politicians, ambassadors, governors, or generals fighting colonial wars: their names featured below murky photographs in annual reports, and even George Cole of Unilever or Paul Chambers of ICI, when they first took over as chairmen, seemed remote in the national scene. The best-known chairmen were famous for something else, like Sir Brian Robertson, the wartime general who commanded British Railways, or Lord Chandos, Churchill's wartime minister, who moved from politics into electronics, and gave the impression of having ennobled the whole industry by his dominating presence. Most chairmen (I found) were anxious and defensive in the face of 'gentlemen of the Press', as if they were liable to be depicted as hard-faced capitalists or merchants of death: the mildest questions or hints of criticism would be interpreted as impugning the good name of British industry.

Today the scene is hardly recognisable. Sunday newspapers—even the popular ones—are full of the pronouncements and exploits of industrialists, posing heroically in front of ingenious machinery, or beaming from deep chairs in big offices. On television they tell the *Money Programme* how they manage to be so rich and responsible, and with every new economic crisis they come forward with diagnoses and remedies. In the worst Labour government crisis in 1967 there was even talk of a cabinet of businessmen, including Lord Robens and Cecil King, to take over the management of 'Great Britain Ltd'. The new mythology of big business was promoted by television series like *The Plane-Makers*, *The Power Game* or *The Troubleshooters*, in which those rugged and unscrupulous tycoons Sir John Wilder or Brian Stead, crushing men and women underfoot, turn out to be saving not only their companies but their country from the wicked competition of unscrupulous sheikhs, witch-hunting Americans or corrupt continentals. *The Troubleshooters*, recording the fearless exploits of Mogul, an all-British oil company, showed how far big business could take the place of wars and expeditions as a source of romantic patriotism: the oilmen, who used to be regarded as a kind of shabby third-best to public servants or soldiers, now emerge as the heroic pioneers who show the stuffy men in Whitehall how to get things done. The new tycoons, whether real or fictional, seem to be filling the gap left by the proconsuls or generals, after the retreat from empire and from the military ethos. Fifteen years ago nearly everyone would have known the name of the Chief of the General Staff (Sir Gerald Templer), and hardly anyone would have known who was chairman of Courtaulds (Hanbury-Williams). Nowadays everyone knows about Lord Kearton of Courtaulds, but who has heard of the CGS (Sir Michael Carver)?

In spite of the transformations—the concentration of companies, the stepping-up of research, the sympathy and attentiveness of politicians and the public—the awkward fact remains that the performance of British industry is as bad as, if not worse than, ever. In the last ten years Britain's position, in terms of gross national product per head, has slipped steadily, below all the Common Market countries except Italy, and expected to be overtaken by Italy by 1980: the average British growth-rate in the last five years has been lower than in the previous decade. The great cure-alls of the late sixties are already being called sharply into question. The cult of bigness and concentration is now being demolished by economists and management experts, so that there is already new talk about the 'age of unmerger', of 'effective disorganisation'. The cult of research and the boosting of boffins has been equally disappointing, and science graduates (see Chapter 17) are in serious oversupply. The earlier worries about British industry—that it was not big enough, not professional enough, not prestigious enough—are beginning to be overshadowed by a fundamental worry, that the reason why Britain's growth-rate is so low may be that neither British managers nor the workers *want* to grow faster; and that no amount of tinkering with structures can put right this basic unambition.

The poor performance of British industry is the more remarkable when put alongside the relatively good performance of British banking, farming and retail businesses. While the British buy more and more foreign cars, transistor radios or refrigerators, the continentals come to Britain to raise Euro-dollar loans, to insure their ships, to buy clothes at Marks and Spencer, or to learn how to farm. The contrast raises the question: has Britain, the first industrial nation, become the first to opt out of mass-industry? Have the British lost their old energy and zeal for manufacturing, exhausted and disillusioned in the rubble of Victorian enterprise, and soured by the class conflicts and bitterness that it left behind? Are the British reverting to their pre-industrial values—to their skills in farming, trading, insurance or entertainment—while the era of heavy industry, like the era of empire, fades into history as a long digression?

INDUSTRY AND GOVERNMENT

The mergers and the coming-closer to government in the sixties involved British industries more closely with notions of patriotism and national pride—almost as if they were arms of the fighting forces. As they have merged and faced international competition, so they have—often quite suddenly—found themselves the *only* big British company, in a global battle; and their success has come to be associated with the 'national interest'. Several institutions, formal or informal, have developed to strengthen the ties between government and industry: the Board of Trade has expanded its networks of committees and sub-sections, with ramifications like the Export Credits Guarantee Department and the British National Exports Council. A new national meeting-place came with the formation of Neddy in 1962 (see Chapter 14) which has survived all political changes since. But the most spectacular get-together came with the Industrial Reorganisation Corporation, which in its four-year career became the most controversial of all the Labour government's new institutions. It was set up by an act of parliament in December 1966, after a year's gestation. Its function, as simply defined by the Act, was 'promoting industrial efficiency and profitability and assisting the economy of the United Kingdom', and to this end it was allowed to push forward the reorganisation of any industry, or even to establish a new company, and could draw on up to

£150 million of government money. The chairman of the board was a controversial industrialist, Kearton of Courtaulds (see p. 603), who had close links with the Labour government. The first managing director was Ronald Grierson, a highly polished and fashionable banker from Warburg's. Under Grierson's sophisticated regime, the IRC set up shop with a cluster of clever young men, and not very much seemed to happen. Grierson saw himself more as a catalyst than a driving force; he was also an inveterate internationalist, constantly on the move between New York, Zurich or Tuscany, and the Chauvinist role of the new corporation did not obviously fit with his own instincts. In 1968 Grierson resigned, to become, among other things, vice-chairman to Weinstock in General Electric, and his place was taken by a more provocative figure, Charles Villiers from Schroder Wagg. Villiers came from a very orthodox bankers' ambience—Eton, friend of the Queen, old family, sports a military moustache —but he had a buccaneering approach to his new job. He insisted on a salary of £20,000 a year, whereas Grierson (a rich man) had done it for nothing. He was convinced that Britain's economic situation was desperate, and something had to be done about it very quickly. His conversation and even his published statements had a blood-curdling directness; in describing 'The Urgent Task' in 1969 he outlined Britain's predicament:

> The persistent erosion of our competitive power is underlined in almost every set of international comparisons of productivity and trade performance. It is impossible to continue like this. On present trends in seven years we shall be importing more manufactures than we export. Hence the pressing need to restore our overall industrial competitiveness and to assert it in world markets. It is in this context that board members see IRC's work to bring about improvements in the structure of our industries.

Having made his radical and well-documented diagnosis, Villiers set about using his government backing to reorganise industry, against all the traditions of free enterprise: in this he was enthusiastically supported by the Labour Minister of Technology, Anthony Wedgwood Benn, an ex-left-winger who was now much enjoying the role of tycoon. In the electronics industry, IRC first encouraged the take-over of Associated Electrical Industries by General Electric, and then herded the third big electronic company, English Electric, into the same fold to make one single giant. In cars, they encouraged the merger between Leyland Motors and the British Motor Corporation in January 1969, and agreed to lend £25 million to help with expansion and re-equipment. In smaller mergers their role was more dramatic; when the venerable Cambridge Instrument Company was wooed by the Rank Organisation, who knew very little about precision instruments, the IRC decided that it would be much better linked with another specialist, George Kent, and themselves bought up twenty-five per cent of the Cambridge shares, to support the Kent offer. The most controversial intervention was 'the Great Ball-Bearing Affair' when, in 1969, the Swedish ball-bearings company SKF tried to acquire a British rival, Ransome and Marles. The IRC was determined to stop the Swedes, so they quickly acquired the controlling interest in another ball-bearing company, Hoffmann, and then merged Hoffmann with the two others in the business, Ransome and Marles and Pollard, to make a single British competitor. Here the conflict was painful between the European ambition, to have companies operating on an international scale, and the immediate objects of IRC, to strengthen industry on the national scale and to force mergers in order to keep out foreigners.

Villiers thought that it was part of IRC's job (as he explained to me) to be 'disturbers of the peace'. He liked to bring industrialists into the lunch-room and lecture them briskly about the appalling state of their industry. Like most bankers, he was something of a know-all, and he did have special knowledge which came from being close to the government, and from the expertise of his staff. He presided over a kindergarten of young men with avuncular pride, and he had a board of familiar pluralists, including Lord Stokes of British Leyland, Sir Joseph Lockwood of EMI and the inevitable Lord Goodman.

From the IRC's elegant offices in Pall Mall Britain's industrial problems looked serious, but soluble; what was needed was mergers here, rationalisation there, more capital, better management. Their reports, written in lucid and confident language, had the sure touch of a surgeon who is called in at the last minute but just in time. The young men were constantly going out in the field, to inspect factories or to assess business efficiency. But there was an inevitable aloofness and unreality in their sweeping assessments, and an element of that bankers' arrogance which assumes that money is the solution to everything. The IRC's grand designs stopped short at the point where the real problems

575

begin—the problems of getting managers to manage, or workers to work. 'In the end, it's a frustrating job,' one of the young IRC men said to me, 'because you're not really involved with the human problems of industry—like persuading someone twice your age to do the job differently. We're always on the outside.'

The IRC came up against angry objections from other bankers and businessmen—for providing unfair competition with its bottomless purse, and for using public money where private money was available. But Villiers insisted that it was a prod, not a prop, and that businessmen must face up to their interdependence with government. As he put it:

> The principle of big business and big government is very foreign
> to the nineteenth-century liberal economic teaching on which we
> were brought up, but it is a world which, whether we like it or not, is
> increasingly recognisable by men of affairs in all countries. We have
> been brought up to believe that government should as far as possible
> keep out of business, a principle to be suspended only in time of war
> or in economic crises. But this principle is increasingly 'more honoured
> in the breach than in the observance', and government is itself a
> large buyer and employer. Government is in business in a big way,
> and getting bigger.

IRC paid lip-service to the prevailing European ambition to form trans-national companies to compete with the American giants. Villiers himself (who has a Belgian wife) urged the formation of a kind of European IRC, to restructure industry on a European scale. But the whole trend of the IRC's policy was to prevent European mergers by coalescing British industries in a British context: in their words, 'IRC's client is the national interest.' Villiers argued that British industry simply could not afford to open itself up to European take-overs or mergers; and that companies cannot merge from a position of weakness which would lead (as in the Great Ball-Bearing Affair) to a foreign company having outright control. The difficulty, of course, is that one country or another will always see itself in a position of weakness.

The trend towards state involvement in industry in the sixties marked the end of the long supremacy of the liberal economists who insisted that the government should have as little as possible to do with industry. Their theories were vindicated when Victorian industrialists, like Americans more recently, could dominate the rest of the world without help from governments. *Laissez-faire* was a long time a-dying, through all the years of decline in British industry, through the slump of the pre-war years. But since the last war British industry has been moving towards the pre-Victorian policies of 'mercantilism', in which the state and business enterprises, like the chartered companies, regarded themselves as naturally interdependent.

The change in the relationship involved the beginnings of a transformation of the power structure, with large political implications. Liberal foreigners, particularly Germans, have looked with some envy in the past towards the British separation of centres of power as a kind of democratic safeguard, an assurance that the power of the state could never grow too large. The conflicts between business and government, even if wasteful in economic terms, have been reassuring in democratic terms; the concept of 'the Establishment' may have been born in Britain; but the power of the old ruling class was always limited by its aloofness from the industrial centres, and by the old antagonism between aristocracy and commerce. There are still cross-purposes between British businessmen, civil servants and industry. But in the past ten years Britain has come much closer to the continental concept of the state as the centre of industrial endeavour; and a new breed of businessmen have emerged who—however much they protest publicly about governments—gravitate naturally towards the triangle of industry, Whitehall and Westminster. They hold forth confidently on television or in the press. Most of them will become sirs and a few even lords. They move easily between government committees, they can cope with either Labour or Conservative politicians; they invite cabinet ministers to lunch without worry or elaborate boasting. Their centre of gravity might be found in St. James's Square, where a dozen of the biggest corporations have their headquarters: British Aircraft is opposite Rio Tinto, Distillers round the corner from Allied Breweries; the biggest British advertising agency, Masius Wynne-Williams, is next door: and the Department of Employment is in the midst of them. A chairman, without moving further than a few hundred yeards, could step round for a talk with the secretary for employment, have lunch opposite at *The Economist*; take part in a discussion at Chatham House; could go round to the Reform Club or the Travellers for a drink with a permanent secretary. Ten years ago a keen anarchist with only one bomb might have been seriously worried about where to put it in order to kill off the British power elite. Should it be in the House of Commons, or in the Bank of England, or in the industrial fortresses of

Shell or ICI? Wherever he went, too much would be left unscathed. But suddenly, the decision is easier: the centre of St. James's Square.

The coming together was the latest stage in a process endorsed by both Wilson and Macmillan; but the Conservatives came to power in 1970 committed to its reversal. Ted Heath, particularly after his own experiences at the Board of Trade, was convinced that the state was propping up far too many unprofitable and incompetent industries; and that, far from stimulating competition, it was protecting companies from it. He looked back with admiration to that Victorian liberal economics which Villiers had so specifically rejected. The IRC was one of the first targets of the new Tories, as the chief instrument of state intervention, and soon after the election they resolved to abolish it; Charles Villiers went back to private banking (not to his old bank Schroder Wagg, '*on ne recouche pas*', he explained, but to become chairman of Guinness Mahon). There was some angry debate. 'The abolition of IRC,' said Lord George-Brown, in the Lords in March 1971, 'was caused by political and spiteful motives on the part of some merchant bankers in the city who thought that someone was getting into their act and doing it rather better.' 'What has worried the government,' explained Lord Jellicoe for the government, 'is the clear evidence that the corporation has tended to work not with, but against, the grain of market forces.' But the problem was not so simple, either way.

ROLLS-ROYCE

And in the meantime a crisis was brewing up in the most famous of all British companies, which brought the Conservatives bang up against the complexities of state intervention. The collapse of Rolls-Royce had such huge repercussions that it made almost every part of the British power-structure feel uneasy; engineers, bankers, accountants, pension funds, newspapers, civil servants and even the Bank of England were embarrassed by the crash; everyone tried to point a moral or pin the blame. The Tories could present the story as showing that unprofitable firms must go bankrupt; the Labour Party could gloat that part of it had to be nationalised. But what Rolls-Royce revealed to everyone was the intricate difficulties in the relationship between government and industry—which could not be solved by any kind of dogma. The bankruptcy of Rolls-Royce produced a national trauma without real precedent. Perhaps the closest parallel can be found in the fall of the House of Krupp in Germany in 1967—when the great German industrial empire had to be bailed out by the government. But Rolls fell more thoroughly, and its image had been a more splendid and untarnished one, associated above all with perfection. The phrase 'the Rolls-Royce of . . .' suddenly acquired a grim second meaning: the fact was rubbed home that perfection was very far from being the same as profitability.

Ever since the first world war, when Sir Henry Royce first turned from cars to aero-engines, the pride of Rolls-Royce had been part of the national pride, and very cut off from commercial values. A Rolls-Royce factory has an atmosphere and dedication—almost a wartime spirit—quite different from an ordinary assembly line for cars or chemicals; the great gleaming engines, the test-beds, the white-coated workers, the intricate blueprints, all conspire to impress the visitor that here is an organisation dedicated to some absolute ideal of perfection, like an orchestra; and it was an atmosphere in which only the most hard-bitten and insulated accountant could bring himself to ask nasty questions. Rolls-Royce, alone of the big British companies, was dominated by engineers, and its chief executive since 1957 was one of the heroes of the profession. Sir Denning Pearson was a self-made aristocrat, who began at Cardiff Tech, and joined Rolls-Royce as an apprentice; he is an elegant, courteous man with a high forehead and strong eyes, and total dedication to engineering perfection. He had a short answer when the subject of money came up: 'If you said we're here to make profits,' he said to me back in 1969, 'we'd never be making aero-engines: we'd have gone into property years ago.' The engineers at Rolls, after the two world wars, had grown used to regarding themselves as an essential industry, whose financial problems were for bankers and governments to sort out, and arguments about costing and losses tended to be regarded (I found) as niggling matters in the perspective of their grand enterprises. For years Rolls-Royce had been the special province of Lazards Bank, and their senior partner, Lord Kindersley, one of the grandees of the city, was their chairman until Pearson took over in 1969. The engineers didn't worry about money, and the bankers didn't worry about engineering; they both knew that the government would support them, and Lazards, without saying so, tacitly regarded Rolls as a nationalised industry.

In the fifties and early sixties Rolls produced magnificent new engines which seemed to justify all their confidence; the Dart was designed for the phenomenal Viscount; and the Spey was used in the BAC 111 and eight other kinds of aircraft. But the costs were mounting, and the Spey cost £20 million to develop—which was tactfully written into the accounts as part of the assets. And in the meantime Rolls had to move into the much more expensive field of higher-thrust engines, if it was to keep abreast with its two American rivals, General Electric and Pratt and Whitney. (There are only three major aero-engine companies in the world.) The British market alone was too small for Rolls, and to produce their new engine, the RB 211, they had to have a contract with an American aircraft company. For two years from 1966, Rolls salesmen pursued the third biggest American aircraft company, Lockheed, to sell them the new engine for their projected giant airliner, the Tri-Star; eventually, in March 1968, Rolls won the contract. It was proclaimed by the Labour government and the Press as a stupendous national victory, a great British invasion of America, and the share price reached an all-time peak of 55/- (at which point shrewd investors like Jim Slater sold out). No commentator then pointed out the weaknesses of the contract: its lack of sufficient safeguards against rising costs, its huge penalty clauses, its dependence on a foreign company over which Rolls had no control. The Ministry of Technology, under Wedgwood Benn, had urged Rolls forward; but they had failed to check effectively on Roll's ability to honour the contract.

The development costs of the engine were first estimated at £65 million. But the troubles soon began. The blades were to be made from the new carbon fibre invented in Britain, called Hyfil, which turned out to be damaged when it was hit by a bird; so they had to use Titanium instead. The engine was too heavy, new faults emerged, new modifications had to be made. By the end of 1968 the Ministry of Technology were already worried by the escalation, and by their lack of information from Rolls; but Wedgwood Benn and Pearson were determined to go ahead. From the beginning of 1969, as news of Rolls's difficulties filtered through, the share prices began to fall: they had halved their value by the end of the year. Two banks, Lloyds and the Midland, had by now lent £37 million to Rolls-Royce, and another £17 million had been borrowed through a syndicate of merchant banks, headed by Lazards. By early 1970 still more money was needed, and the IRC were asked to move in; apparently without much investigation, they agreed on a convertible loan of £10 million in July, and another £10 million for the next year. (The fact that the IRC checked so little on the true state of Rolls later confirmed the Tories in their desire to abolish it.) In July 1970 Pearson still felt able to reassure shareholders that the company had ample resources to complete its programme; but at the same time he revealed—an ominous sign—that two new directors were joining the board; one, Lord Beeching, was representing the IRC: the other, Ian Morrow, was a sharp-eyed accountant who was appointed deputy-chairman.

In the course of the summer, while the new government was moving in, Morrow gradually uncovered the true predicament of Rolls: that another £50 million was likely to be needed in the next two years. By the time the Tory ministers came back from holiday the magnitude of the Rolls crisis was beginning to become clear. The cost of developing the RB 211 was to be £135 million—at least twice the original estimate. At first the government thought that, in keeping with its Tory philosophy, the extra money could be raised privately, and the Governor of the Bank of England was asked to try to find £30 million from the city. Then the government decided to put up £42 million, while asking Sir Henry Benson, the accountant of Cooper Brothers, to check the accounts. Whether the money was conditional on a favourable report from Sir Henry was later the subject of angry argument; thinking it was *un*conditional, three big banks—Lloyds, Midland and the Bank of England—agreed to put in another £18 million; and the syndicate headed by Lazards agreed to extend their acceptance credits of £20 million. In return for their new loan the government insisted on a harsh measure: Sir Denning Pearson was demoted to deputy-chairman, and in his place was put the ex-chairman of Unilever, Lord Cole of Blackfriars. Ian Morrow, the accountant, was made chairman of an executive committee, of which Pearson was not even a member.

By January the situation had rapidly worsened. The engineers decided that the new engine would be a year late—incurring huge penalties. Cooper Brothers reckoned that the costs of the further development would be ruinous. And in the meantime there was hardly the money to pay wages. By January 26th the board, with astonishing abruptness, realised that they were insolvent. The news was passed to the Minister of Aviation Supply, Frederick

Corfield, and hence to the prime minister. It was still widely assumed that the government would feel compelled to bail out the company, and that the £42 million would be forthcoming. Heath was determined that the government should not come to the rescue; and the lawyers advised that only by letting Rolls go bankrupt could the government avoid becoming liable for the huge penalties that Lockheed could claim for non-delivery: the extra costs of development and penalties might run into hundreds of millions. The cabinet decided that the parts of Rolls that *had* to keep going—including defence contracts and the work on the Concorde—would be nationalised in a separate company, and a hurried Bill was worked out over the weekend. There was still hope that Lockheed could be persuaded to waive the penalty clauses; but Lockheed too were fighting for their life, and neither Rolls nor the British government could then bring effective pressure on them (though they did later use their influence in Washington). On February 3rd the cabinet had to face its final decision; and, after bitter argument, they agreed, apparently unanimously, on letting Rolls-Royce go bankrupt.

The next evening the posters carried the amazing words: ROLLS-ROYCE GOES BUST. The consequences were immediate and ruthless. The receiver, Rupert Nicholson, moved into the building and a few days later had already announced four thousand sackings. The shares collapsed—many of them owned by Rolls-Royce workers or pensioners who had been encouraged to buy them. The Rolls Pension Fund was wiser, but large blocks of shares were held by the Pru and the pension funds of ICI and BP; they had been caught in the familiar problem of big shareholders in dying companies, that they could not pull out without further depressing the shares. Pearson had evidently kept his faith in the company: he owned two thousand shares: but the financial men were more pessimistic; the deputy-chairman, Whitney Straight, held only 169 shares, and John Smith, a director of Coutts Bank and Rolls, had only 339 shares; just after the crash he set off for the South Pole.

The prime minister was quick to draw the lesson: he told Young Conservatives at Eastbourne that 'for too long much of our apparent prosperity has been based on illusions'. But the lesson was hardly one that he could expect the Rolls workers, the main victims of the crash, to understand; for what had they done to deserve their fate? Dedicated to their work, relatively badly paid, and not prone to strikes, they had invested both their careers and their savings in the company. It was governments, not they, who had fostered the illusions. And the new government was being very equivocal in its approach to illusions; the still more extravagant project of the Concorde (which Heath and other Tory cabinet ministers had approved when it was first conceived in 1962) was allowed to continue without much prospect of recouping its cost; the fact that Concorde was a joint governmental project protected by treaty removed it from awkward commercial questioning.

The Labour Party made play with the Tories' sharp practice, and Wedgwood Benn, addressing a mass meeting of Rolls workers at Derby, called it 'the greatest betrayal in industrial history'. But many Labour MPs were unhappy at their own party's record: and Harold Lever, the former Minister at the Treasury, said in the *New Statesman*: 'It is worth noting that, between Concorde and the RB 211 alone, the nation could well expend £1,000 million of its resources in the areas of its highest skill with little or nothing to show for them. We must topple the uncritical worship of the false gods of size and science. We must abandon irrelevant notions of national prestige. . . .' Perhaps the simplest and most important lesson to be learnt from the Rolls-Royce débâcle was the demonstration that this kind of high technology had outgrown the scope of medium-sized nations, and that projects of such extravagance, if attempted at all, needed both the backing and the market of a whole continent.

MULTI-NATIONAL CORPORATIONS

In the course of the sixties, while governments all over Europe were finding themselves more closely involved with industry, they were also discovering the limitations of that relationship, and in particular the enormous encroachments of organisations which lay largely outside their control—the multi-national corporations. These mysterious organisms, which are now a very fashionable subject for study, were hardly thought about at the beginning of the decade. It can be argued—and often is by their bosses—that there is nothing really new about them, and that their evolution can be traced back to the East India Company. Certainly there are many big companies, including the two Anglo-Dutch giants Shell and Unilever, which have for decades been producing, buying and selling in scores of countries, with international staffs. But the development of complex technologies, and of quick communication by telephone, computer and jet planes, has enormously increased the scope for big companies to operate abroad, and Europeans became aware of it with the massive extension of American companies into Europe during the sixties. What was new about these operations was not so much their internationalism as their control: as one recent historian of the multi-national company, Christopher Tugendhat, puts it 'However large it may be, and however many subsidiaries it may have scattered across the globe, all its operations are co-ordinated from the centre'.[1] It is their remote control, together with their size and resources, which makes them so alarming to national governments; the corporations are able to export products from one subsidiary to another, to link up their factories across the continents, to make losses in one country and profits in another, all in a way that completely outdates the old theories of trade between nations. Yet the national governments are very aware that they cannot do without them—for they bring with them not only technology and employment, but large contributions to exports and the balance of payments. The basic relationship between the multi-national corporation and the nation, in Andrew Shonfield's words, is: 'Anything you can do, we can do better.'

The multi-national company is most often associated with American control, and it was the invasion of companies like IBM, Procter and Gamble, or Esso which brought the phenomenon home to the Europeans, producing a wave of discussion about the 'American Challenge' and the 'European Response'. But the Europeans, too, have been developing their own multi-nationals, and Sweden and Switzerland—two neutral countries very dependent on export and trade—have produced some of the most sophisticated world companies, like SKF, Alfa-Laval, Nestlé or Ciba. The development of those companies has been very independent of the Common Market; but the protective tariffs round the Six encourage outsiders to avoid tariffs by building factories 'inside the wall'; and elsewhere in the world, too, protection has forced the companies thus to internationalise themselves. In the last decades most of the British giants have taken on a more international character: ICI and Courtaulds have expanded into

[1] Christopher Tugendhat: *The Multinationals*. Eyre and Spottiswoode June 1971. p. 12.

the continent and America; Dunlop (see page 604-5) has merged with the Italian Pirelli; Rio Tinto Zinc (see page 605) owns mines throughout the white commonwealth, financed by American and Australian capital; Reeds and Bowaters have paper mills in Scandinavia and North America; Allied Breweries own the second biggest brewery in Holland. These geographical extensions have gradually changed the perspective of the companies: they can begin to think in terms of shifting production from one country to another, of sharing the markets between their different plants. The managers themselves become a new kind of cross-breed, with changeable migratory patterns, very temporary nesting-habits, and special mating-calls. The multi-national managers move round from country to country, inhabiting their own company houses and expatriate society in stateless zones, and looking on each nation's political reactions with tolerant detachment, like explorers noting the oddities of African tribes. Encountering these men in different parts of Europe, I have felt them always to be on the same floating island, like Gulliver's Laputa, watching the eccentricities of the natives below. The fact that the multi-nationals operate from outside existing structures is an important part both of their effectiveness and their unpopularity.

In the British national context, the foreign multi-nationals are likely to emerge as a new kind of bogey—appearing to threaten the economic sovereignty, the security of workers and the bargaining-power of trades unions. A foretaste of their political explosiveness appeared in March 1971, when Henry Ford came to Britain during a prolonged strike at the Dagenham factory, and threatened to take his business elsewhere; he was given a placatory lunch at 10 Downing Street, and there was a backwash of anger at the discovery that British industry was being dictated to from Detroit. Most companies are more tactful, and spend a good deal of time and money in reassuring their host countries: but they are nevertheless in constant conflict with them, trying to force their freedom of action to the limits. And this conflict is inevitable. The multi-nationals are driven by the desire for profits and all that goes with it—change, mobility, innovation. The nations, while wanting the benefits, are preoccupied by different values— by social security, full employment, or safeguarding the environment. There can be no easy compromise between the two.

In the context of these battles the nation-state, having been so much reviled in the post-war years as the engine of aggression and militarism, is beginning to emerge in a more sympathetic role—as the defender of small men and their society against the aggressive instincts of the industrial giants, who tread with clumsy boots and greedy intent across the landscape. However outdated the nation may seem, with its creaking bureaucracies, its chauvinist instincts and its over-centralised structures, it remains the only instrument available for counterbalancing the disruption of international big business; when the national government is weak, as in Italy, the need for that counterweight is most obvious. The formation of Departments of the Environment, both in Britain and France, is one sign of this growing role; and in this respect all nations, whatever their political colour, are having to play a more socialist, or anti-capitalist, role.

This new battle might seem to contradict the expectations of those prophets, like Jean Monnet, who hoped to see the nations gradually withering away in the context of European institutions. But this is too simple a reading. For the multi-national companies will increasingly call for a multi-national response, as well as a national one. Their power to play one country off against another, to exploit cheap labour, to concentrate their research in their home country, can only be effectively countered by inter-governmental cooperation: and their threat to the trades unions can only be met by the formation of international trades unions—which already exist in embryo. The national-state for the time being may provide the only real counter to the corporations; but in the long run these multi-national giants—with their enormous capacity to increase the standard of living on the one hand, to ruin the surroundings and to generate insecurity on the other—are likely to stimulate nations to collaborate with each other to control them.

33

Managers

Managers do not, if they ever did, have a divine right to manage. The process of decision-making will have to be more and more justified and demonstrated to be right in order to command the respect not only of the people working for the company, but the community as a whole.

Campbell Adamson (Director-General, CBI), April 1970

In the course of the sixties the bleak abstract word Management rapidly became a kind of shibboleth, in Britain and all through Europe. Twenty years ago a senior man in an industrial company would be known to his friends as a business man or something in the city; today he is proclaimed with confidence as a *manager*, and the word itself has acquired a heroic and militant ring. Not only industry but other professions—the civil service, the armed forces, the universities and even the Church—cry out for the need for 'management', and subject themselves to enquiries, investigations and reorganisations by management consultants. The concept of the manager, like that of the advertising agent, has been very directly imported from America, and the notion of the manager as a kind of missionary of reason and change has not been better put than by the master-manager of the mid-sixties, Robert McNamara. In this now classic passage he described the manager's mission:[1]

> God—the Communist commentators to the contrary—is clearly democratic. He distributes brain power universally, but He quite justifiably expects us to do something efficient and constructive with that priceless gift. That is what management is all about. Its medium is human capacity, and its most fundamental task is to deal with

[1] Robert McNamara: *The Essence of Security.* Hodder and Stoughton 1967, p. 109.

change. It is the gate through which social, political, economic, technological change, indeed change in every dimension, is rationally spread through society.

Some critics today worry that our democratic, free societies are becoming over managed. I would argue that the opposite is true. As paradoxical as it may sound, the real threat to democracy comes not from over management, but from under management. To under manage reality is not to keep it free. It is simply to let some force other than reason shape reality. That force may be unbridled emotion; it may be greed; it may be aggressiveness; it may be hatred; it may be ignorance; it may be inertia; it may be anything other than reason. But whatever it is, if it is not reason that rules man, then man falls short of his potential.

Like the advertising man, the modern manager sees himself as a benign aggressor into a territory of prejudice and tribal custom. As the district commissioner or the Indian civil servant fifty years ago came to the benighted province of the empire, so his grandson the modern manager turns to his own people, still unthanked for his burden, incurring 'the blame of those ye better, the hate of those ye serve'.

Management is discussed so much as a mystique or panacea that it disguises the fact that what most middle managers are doing is something basically very practical and often deadeningly dull— like housekeeping or shopping, elevated to a life-time career. Between the abstract discussions on the role of the manager and the actual day-to-day problems of men selling kippers or boiling soap, the divide is not easy for the outsider like myself to bridge. But the management mystique must be kept in perspective; not least by remembering that during the decade that the idea of professional management became so thoroughly established, Britain's industrial performance compared to her neighbours' has never been worse. In the despondent words of *Management Today*, the spokesman for the modern British manager (April 1971): 'Chairmen in their annual reports talk of reorganisation, rationalisation, redeployment or re-equipment, yet somehow their businesses plod on from year to year with less visible or measurable change'. The managers, confronted with Britain's poor performance, can blame many other factors—the government, the universities, and above all the workers. But the embarrassing fact remains that American companies in Britain, and some outstanding British ones, can produce far better results with the same kind of workers, the same universities, and the same government.

The shock troops of the management offensive are the consultants, the compact companies of busy, relatively highly-paid men who move round from one company to the next, diagnosing troubles and pronouncing remedies. The consultants, too, are an American idea, and they began in Britain when an American, Charles Bedaux, set up a company in Britain in 1927, mainly to introduce time-and motion-study. Men who had worked for him founded British consultants' groups, who with others began to establish themselves more effectively in the post-war years. In 1956 they formed the Management Consultants' Association, 'to guarantee integrity and quality', with nineteen member firms, the biggest of which are:

> PA Management Consultants
> Associated Industrial Consultants (Inbucon)
> Urwick Orr
> PE Consulting Group
> Cooper Brothers ⎱ branches of accountants
> Peat Marwick ⎰ (see Chapter 27)

Since the idea of consultants is American, it is not surprising that the most successful of them is an American company, McKinsey and Co; to the fury of the British ones. In the last decade the word 'McKinseyised' has acquired a magic meaning. In 1957 Hugh Parker of McKinsey came to London to investigate the organisation of Shell; he then set up an office in London and in the following years moved through an astonishing range of British institutions from Dunlop and British Rail to the BBC and last of all the Bank of England. The Bank was the last straw for British consultants, who protested indignantly; 'What is so bad and so wrong,' said Anthony Frodsham of PE, then Chairman of the Management Consultants' Association, 'is that British firms are patently seen not to be consulted, giving the whole world the impression that only American firms are competent to handle this kind of job.' In fact, McKinsey has become almost as much a British firm as an American, and it is much more successful in Britain than in the States: its managing-director in Britain, Hugh Parker, is one of those ambivalent American expatriates who eloquently analyses British troubles—the amateurism, easy-goingness, insistence on leisure—while preferring to live in Britain because of them. But McKinsey men have the advantage of appearing to be right outside British bumbledom, with their brisk austere manner, like a team of physicians or lawyers. They preach management as a kind of religion, and their bible is a book called *The Will to Manage*.

The psychological relationship between consultants and companies is intricate. The great Professor Parkinson swiftly diagnosed the companies' attitude (*The Director*, January 1960): 'On the one hand they may want scapegoats for the reorganisation upon which they have already decided. On the other they may want to prevent such a reorganisation taking place.' The phenomenal success of McKinsey is a tribute not just to its methods, but to the lack of nerve and the need for reassurance of the men at the top of British institutions. Some of the toughest bosses refuse to have anything to do with consultants, and Sir Arnold Weinstock insists (as he put it to me): 'If you don't know how to run your own business then what do you know?'

BUSINESS SCHOOLS

It will seem strange to the men and women of this country if it is allowed to appear that for industry and commerce, almost alone among the important careers in this country, no form of intelligent preparation is required.

Lord Franks, 1964.

I wonder whether we at home are losing ground through our veneration of the sacred cow of management. If so, we may reach the stage where we have nothing left to manage.

John Tyzack, 1966.

The establishment of management as a profession was marked by the quite sudden appearance of business schools during the sixties, and their birth was accompanied by worries about their legitimacy. There had been plenty of management training colleges, many of them run by individual big companies in stately homes, like The Node in Hertfordshire run by BP, The Vache in Hertfordshire by the Coal Board, or Chewton Place in Gloucestershire by ICI: companies still hanker after the country-house tradition. The Henley Administrative Staff College on the Thames organised (and still does) gentle three-month courses for younger middle-managers to get to know each other. But there had been no serious business schools with university status, and the old universities firmly resisted the idea of management as an academic study which had begun at Pennsylvania University as early as 1881. In 1963 a 'Neddy' report recommended a management school in the interests of productivity, and later in the year the Robbins Report on higher education proposed 'at least two major post-graduate schools associated with a well-established institution'. Lord Franks—the fashionable prophet of that time—was asked to produce a report, which duly advocated one school at Manchester University and one in London, to provide courses for both post-graduates and 'post-experience' students from industry. The establishment of the two big schools coincided with a mushrooming of all kinds of management courses in universities and polytechnics throughout the country; in 1970 it was reckoned that 355,000 students attended 22,000 courses, learning about management somewhere, somehow.

The most favoured of them was the London Graduate School of Business Studies, which was formally opened by the Queen in November 1970, in resplendent new premises in Regent's Park: a Nash Regency façade conceals the elegant modern offices behind—an appropriate symbol for the grafting of a new profession on to old traditions. The expansiveness proclaims that here is a new and self-conscious elite, determined to assert itself against old and sceptical ones; it is like a miniature university, with common rooms, library, lecture rooms and bedrooms. Its governors are the stage army of chairmen—Barran, Duncan, Geddes, Edwards, Partridge and Co. (see next chapter)—augmented by the twin heads of the civil service, Armstrong and Allen. It now takes a hundred students a year, most of whom have already been in industry and who take a two-year post-graduate course for the London degree of MSc; there are other courses for middle and senior executives. There is a faculty of sixty, headed by Dr Arthur Earle, a slow-talking Canadian who used to be managing director of Hoover, and who tries to keep the peace between the carping academics, the impatient students, and the demanding industrial sponsors. Earle himself is emphatic about the main reason for British industrial incompetence—the lack of class mobility, which management education in itself cannot cure. But he also has the authentic missionary approach to business schools as the unacknowledged bringers of enlightenment: 'When you're in the Salvation Army and you go into a pub and someone knocks you on the head, then you're conscious of being a missionary.'

The students themselves are not very obviously a new class. They come from the same kind of background as senior civil servants—seventy per cent from Oxbridge, twenty per cent from

London University, ten per cent from the rest. Most are from direct grant grammar schools, and only two so far have come from Eton. It is the same kind of mixture that goes into the civil service, but Earle maintains that their selection system separates the men with business drive and ambition from the bureaucratic types: they have ten times as many applicants as they can take, and they claim that the London graduates have a higher standard of intelligence than any American school, including Harvard. The London School is determined to be different from the Harvard Business School—more based on disciplines, less on case-studies, and therefore more open to the charge of being 'academic'. But it also likes to see itself as the Harvard of Britain, in terms of prestige. The Manchester School under Grigor McClelland—who used to run a family food firm on Tyneside—is more practical, less university-minded, and more concerned with Europe.

The new sub-profession of 'Business Graduates' coming out of London, Manchester and other schools are a determined trade union, very conscious of being cleverer, more worldly and therefore more expensive than anyone else. They have their own Business Graduates' Association which was set up in 1967: 'The business graduate is here to stay,' says their secretary, Sir David Clutterbuck, a retired vice-Admiral; 'in about five years the critical mass will be reached, as the critical mass of staff college graduates hit the army in the late 'thirties'. They have succeeded well in their main object, money: in 1968 a survey showed that a two-year course could increase earnings by eighty to a hundred and sixty per cent. But they show themselves as a self-centred lobby. 'I think it's on the wrong basis,' says Earle: 'It assumes that it has a separate interest from other businessmen.'

The impact of this confident, self-conscious cavalry on the massed infantry of British industry is fraught with resentments and resistances. Thirty per cent of the London graduates go into merchant banking, consultancies and other finance jobs, where they fit in relatively easily; a third of the rest go into American-owned firms. The big British companies usually prefer to use their own trainees, 'to grow their own timber', in their uninviting phrase: Rio Tinto Zinc is one of the few who have been keen on business graduates. The arrival of a solitary business graduate in a conventional British company, with his equipment of analytical systems, his buzz-words, networks, decision trees and sensitivity training is (as one business professor put it) like landing a solitary missionary in eighteenth-century West Africa. Many of the graduates prefer to go into the safer territory of specialised units, where their bibles and catechisms are more understood and appreciated.

Industrialists are already complaining that the business schools are not quite what they wanted. In 1970, just before the Queen opened the London Business School, the Chairman of the CBI, John Partridge (himself a governor of it), made a speech complaining about the schools being too aloof from manufacturing industry, about teachers being too academic, and about the government not giving enough money. The CBI and the British Institute of Management set up a working party to listen to all the complaints about business schools—that the graduates want too much money, that they cannot be absorbed into the company structures, that they are altogether too arrogant. Dr Earle is not too worried about the criticisms: 'If companies complain that business graduates get too high salaries, then why do they pay them?'

The cross-purposes between industrialists and business schools is, of course, part of a much deeper divide, between the values and purposes of academia and industry, which shows itself all over Europe. European professors have the reputation of being able to make any subject academic and totally unpractical, and businessmen have always suspected academics, not only of teaching useless subjects, but of cultivating such doubts and indecisions, of seeing so many other sides to the questions, that their students emerge with 'analysis paralysis', incapable of making up their minds about anything. A historic broadside was fired in 1964 by Sir Paul Chambers, then chairman of ICI, in a speech to the National Union of Teachers: 'How often have I met men of unblemished character, of high academic achievement, but whose life, sheltered from the harsh need to make important decisions, has left them timid and irresolute, or stubborn because of the fear of making a mistake?'

Even within the American business schools there are growing doubts as to how far management teaching can be divorced from experience. In the sacred pages of the *Harvard Business Review* itself, we find Professor Livingston, one of the recent arrivals from business, saying (February 1971): 'Until managerial aspirants are taught to learn from their own first-hand experience, formal management education will remain second-hand. And its secondhandedness is the real reason why the well-educated manager is a myth.' A more wholesale denunciation has come from Robert Townsend, who built up the Avis car-hire company, in his iconoclastic book *Up the Organisation*; writing about the Harvard Business School graduates, he said:

> This elite, in my opinion, is missing some pretty fundamental requirements for success: humility; respect for people in the firing line; deep understanding of the nature of the business and the kind of people who can enjoy themselves making it prosper; respect for way down the line; a demonstrated record of guts, industry, loyalty down, judgment, fairness and honesty under pressure.[1]

MANAGERS AND MOTIVES

> Managers are not better than or superior to the managed. Just different. And scarce. If there are not enough good managers a country can neither obtain wealth, nor in the end matter much in the world.
>
> *Lord Kearton, November 6, 1970.*

The frontier between universities and industry has never been an easy one to cross—and probably never should be, so long as they present different systems of values; the Warwick University fracas (see Chapter 8) was one sign of the inherent dangers when academia finds itself too indebted to big business. Not surprisingly, the frontier thus requires a painful readjustment for graduates leaving university. In the last decade the numbers of graduates entering industry have risen steadily, keeping pace with the growing output from the universities, and providing jobs for roughly twenty per cent of the total seeking employment and training (compared to about 9 per cent going into commerce). Most companies have lost their prejudice against arts graduates, and accept the fact that with the expansion of universities, they must look there for the cleverest men; the undergraduates (or their parents) have lost much of their distaste for 'trade', and regard big business as being almost as respectable as the public service —perhaps itself a symptom of the return to mercantilism. But the rapprochement was born of necessity, and the industrialists have often (it seems to me) been rather unsure what the arts graduates were *for*; in the recession of 1970 industrial companies cut down their recruitment by about 300, while the graduates went up by

[1] Robert Townsend: *Up the Organisation*, 1970.

about 2,500. Graduates on their side have shown signs of entering industry with increasing reluctance: a survey of a thousand final-year students in 1970, commissioned by British companies, showed that half the undergraduates who opt for industry and commerce change their minds, and half those who actually sign on in one company move elsewhere within a few years; most students look for intellectual challenge above everything, and money at this stage is not an important argument.[1]

The new wave of student radicalism which broke in 1968 produced a new unease among some British companies that they were missing out on a new generation—an unease that was often, no doubt, encouraged by the tycoons' own children. One giant company began to arrange seminars between their senior managers and groups of radical students, at which I was present. The conjunction was quite a painful one. On the one hand were the international managers who had worked their way to the top by way of the bleak outposts of the company, and who looked for recognition and acclaim from the young. They liked to see themselves as a dedicated profession, like doctors; they insisted that they were not in a separate jungle of self-interest, but part of the community linked on all sides with society; that big business was no different from any other kind of life, that they had no sinister power, indeed very little power at all in the face of nationalist governments abroad, and a watchful government at home. The characters of the Planemakers or the Troubleshooters formed no part of *their* self-portraiture. On the other hand were the students, who remained quite unconvinced: they saw the managers, not as public-spirited administrators, nor as heroic Troubleshooters, nor even as exciting villains, but as dull, decent men who had become trapped by a giant system of exploitation; who talked hypocritically about their mission when they were really controlled by profit and material values; who without even realising it, were pressing all governments away from democratic decisions towards the concentration of capitalist wealth.

The question of what really motivates the modern manager has become very political. In the course of the sixties there was a recurrent discussion about the need for 'incentives'—the euphemism for wage claims—on the basis that high salaries for top managers are an essential element in producing greater industrial

[1] 'The Reluctant Graduate': *Management Today*, November 1970.

growth. The comparison was frequently made between the British managers and their less-taxed counterparts on the continent: and to try and make up for it, British companies provided more and more tax-free 'fringe benefits' in the form of company cars, pensions, free or subsidised meals, medical insurance or housing. From time to time directors tried to provide each other with incentives—without consulting their shareholders—by establishing funds to provide capital gains; and in 1966 the chairman (Lord McFadzean) and directors of the cable-making monopoly, British Insulated Callender's Cables, were discovered to be remunerating themselves in this way. After protests, the scheme was abandoned, and McFadzean had to apologise to his shareholders: soon afterwards the Labour government's new Finance Bill knocked such schemes on the head. But the Conservative budget of 1971 gave the incentives lobby what they were asking for—a large tax relief for high incomes, with the top rate of tax reduced to 75 per cent.

But it remains to be seen—if it can ever be proven—how far these incentives will really improve output; for the assumption that money is the driving force for managers is (as one industrial psychologist put it) like arguments about astronomy in the pre-Copernican age. Talking to managers and consultants in Germany I have not been convinced that German senior managers are spurred on by the prospect of higher earnings; they seem to find it quite difficult to spend their existing salaries, and to shy away from the kind of conspicuous consumption (except when abroad) which might draw attention to their high earnings. It is hard to find convincing evidence that senior British managers are craving for bigger houses, more cars or paintings: the weekend page of the *Financial Times*, 'How to Spend it,' suggests a great deal of uncertainty as to what to *do* with the money. A senior executive of Shell or Unilever, eating company meals, driving in company cars, is often too preoccupied with his company battles to have time to think about spending an extra £500 a year; it is hard to visualise how an extra net income would improve his performance. It is the Great Game of business, the love of power and status, which drives the successful managers, and some have more hidden motivations—like keeping away from their wives.

A more sophisticated argument for incentives has been put forward by Ronald Grierson and others: that managers need to be able to save money, to give them the financial security in mid-career, against which to change jobs and take risks. But it is far from certain (it seems to me) that, given the opportunity to save twenty thousand pounds by the age of forty, a successful English manager will use it as a base from which to fly higher. He might equally well decide to go for a very long holiday, to buy a farm or just to retire. 'I know if I earned more money I wouldn't work harder,' said one industrious banker: 'I work as hard as I want to already. I'd go and live in the country.' Even some of the most aggressive British missionaries of management, trained in the stables of multi-national companies, tend to lose part of their faith in middle age, and to come to terms with territorial roots. It is impossible to divorce the question of managers' incentives from the climate of society which surrounds him; the climate of not caring enough about profits, of balancing work and leisure, of lacking the 'will to manage', cannot be altered by a simple switch of the tax system. The early Victorian industrial zeal, to which Ted Heath and the New Conservatives look forward, is not something which can be inculcated in business schools, or infused by legislation.

The task of the modern British manager is not an easy one. He is expected on the one hand to base his whole operation on making profits, on rationalisation, maximisation, cost-effectiveness; for no way other than profits has yet been found to make companies efficient. He has been taught to look towards America as the model for productivity incentives and management philosophy. Yet in their voyage towards America the managers (as so often happens) meet another ship going the other way, full of the rebels against a commercialised society, of the defenders of clean air, pure food, noiseless skies, the prophets of ecological disaster, environmental chaos, pollution, contamination, adulteration, alienation. Their arguments are persuasive, particularly to young managers. But how can a manager be both the aggressor and the defender at the same time? How can he both be single-minded in his pursuit of profit, and yet mindful of all the damage that profits might cause? However much the manager may wish it otherwise, it must be his job to make profits, and the job of others —politicians, civil servants or consumer campaigners—to limit and restrain him.

34

Directors

I wish I knew if I was chairman of this company
It would make a lot of difference at conferences...
D. B. Wyndham Lewis: Lament.

THE question of who is really responsible for Britain's big companies becomes more pressing as their performances become more distressing; but the answer is usually unsatisfactory. The nominal owners, the shareholders, who own the companies and lose money when they do badly, should in theory control them; but over the last forty years it has become increasingly clear, first in America, then in Britain, that ownership has become quite separate from control. The biggest shareholders are in most cases (as we have seen in Chapter 28) the insurance companies and pension funds who have no great wish to involve themselves in the companies' management; the hundreds of thousands of small shareholders cannot effectively mobilise themselves; and the companies' auditors (as we noted in Chapter 27) are instinctively inclined to side with the directors, and to maintain a veil of secrecy round the companies' affairs. Only in moments of extreme crisis, when there is a take-over in the offing or when losses are disastrous, do shareholders sometimes organise themselves to put pressure on management—as they pressed Cunard in 1967, or Woolworth's in 1969, or as the Pru and others pressed Vickers in 1970. But for the rest of the time the shareholders are ineffectual, and the annual meetings are a mockery of financial democracy, with the chairman racing through his business without contradiction.

There have been growing murmurings of shareholders' rebellions, and many politicians believe that shareholders, if properly organised, could induce much better industrial performance; the defence of private enterprise against nationalised industry rests on the assumption that ownership can have a major effect on a company's character. 'The owners could be the most enormous influence for good,' Sir Frederick Catherwood hopefully told the parliament-city liaison group in 1969: 'They could tip the scale between mediocre performance and top-class performance, between three per cent growth and six per cent growth.' 'I'd like to see shareholders more alert,' said Sir Keith Joseph before the 1970 election: 'I think it's beginning. There are beginning to be revolts of shareholders, partly by the force of events.' Sir Brandon Rhys Williams, the Tory MP and former management consultant, put forward a Bill in May 1969 to amend company law to allow a shareholders' committee the right to ask for their own management auditor—which could be a serious threat to the directors. But the idea, he told me, had no support from the biggest shareholders—the insurance companies and pension funds—who prefer to exert their pressure, if at all, on the 'inside track', by talking quietly to the directors out of the glare of publicity. Charles Villiers, the former head of the Industrial Reorganisation Corporation, proposed in May 1971 a rather more practicable scheme, for outside directors to be required to report each year to the shareholders, and for a shareholders' ombudsman to deal with complaints.

In the meantime the big corporations are left, like perpetual clocks, to run themselves; and the effective power resides not with shareholders but with the boards of directors, self-perpetuating oligarchies whose decisions and appointments are very little disturbed by outside forces. In their bastions, it becomes the more important to know what kind of people the boards are. Most directors of big companies are no more and no less than jumped-up managers, and the distinction between the board and the rest is often an artificial one. Sometimes the board is used as a kind of House of Lords, filled with ageing managers who have been pushed upstairs to keep them out of the way, while the operational managers get on with the real business, and a triumvirate a duumvirate or a single dictator decides the real policy. But the directors remain the legal representatives of the shareholders, and it is they who must formally take the responsibility for the company.

How much influence have directors on the performance of their companies? In 1970 the magazine *Management Today* conducted a survey of the directors of the top two hundred companies (by market capitalisation) following up a 1967 survey, and the findings were interpreted by the editor, Robert Heller.[1] He found that:

> ... as then, the average director of a top company is fifty-six. As then, he has one less boardroom colleague; of the total, all but three or four are full time. As then, he has served on the board for nine years, and there is a thirty per cent chance that he had any university education at all. As then, he almost certainly went to a public school: the proportions were seventy-one per cent in both samples. The picture is a conservative one: middle-aged, definitely middle-class, not particularly mobile, although there has been a slight increase in the proportion of top directors with previous experience in other companies, from forty-eight per cent to fifty-two per cent.

A third of the men in the sample, Heller found, held shares in their companies worth £20,000 or more; and he reckoned that four-fifths of non-family directors had no shareholdings in their companies that were significant to them in personal terms. 'From the shareholders' viewpoint, it should be disturbing that most directors' personal fortunes are so little affected by movements in the share price.' This appeared to be confirmed by comparing the statistics of the sample with figures for profitability and growth: 'Companies with directors holding shares worth £20,000 or more in above-average numbers show forty-nine per cent with an above-median profitability and sixty-two per cent with an above-median growth.'

CHAIRMEN

The position and influence of chairmen of big companies varies at least as much as that of prime ministers. There are some chairmen, like Sir Charles Hardie (see page 504), who preside over several big companies, devoting a few hours a month to each, maintaining a deliberate detachment. Others, though full-time in the company, see themselves as holding a balance between strong divisional heads, mediating, compromising, keeping wild horses in check, or sitting back to take a long view ('I'm the only one here who doesn't do any work,' the former chairman of ICI,

[1] 'Britain's Boardroom Anatomy': *Management Today*, September 1970.

Sir Peter Allen, once said). Others are stop-gaps or caretaker chairmen, filling in between two generations, or calming the company down after a too-ruthless predecessor. Others, including the chairman of General Electric and the chairmen of many American-owned companies in Britain, are more like constitutional monarchs who represent the company to the outside world, while the chief executive gets on with the real policy-making and drive. The *Management Today* survey found that, out of the two hundred top companies:

52 per cent have chairmen who are also chief executives.
21 per cent have part-time chairmen.
27 per cent have full-time chairmen who are not chief executives.

The list of the fifty biggest companies inset at page 590 gives some impression of the variety of large corporations, their characters and chairmen (the rating from *The Times 1000*, published in November 1970, is by turnover, which thus includes some freakish companies, including brokers like Czarnikow with huge turnover from commissions and relatively small capital and profits; they are not really industrial companies, but they add variety). At the top of the list are the giant corporations, increasingly with international ramifications, which are the main engines of British technology and exports—as their names suggest, often prefixed by 'British' or even 'Imperial' (though many companies called British, like British Aluminium or British Timken, are American-controlled). These giants all like to 'grow their own timber', recruiting graduate trainees direct from universities; and the chairmen and directors of the biggest of them have spent their careers working up in the company. Most of them nowadays are graduates, though there are still some chairmen like Sir Raymond Brookes of GKN, who left school at 14. Several giant companies have histories going right back to the mid-nineteenth century; Coats, Paton's, Burmah Oil or Cadbury's. In most cases the founding families have lost control, or lost interest; the Samuels who founded Shell, the Levers of Unilever, or the Brunners and Monds of ICI, prefer farming or banking to industry; the old beerage, the whisky barons and the tobacco barons have given way to the new professionalised managers. But there are members of many old families left on the boards; a Cadbury is deputy-chairman of Cadbury-Schweppes, and there are some amazing family-bound companies, like Tate and Lyle, with a Lyle as chairman and a Tate as vice-chairman, and a bevy of Tates and Lyles as directors. In a special category are the American-controlled companies, Esso, Ford, or Gallaher (which was bought by American Tobacco in 1968), where the British board cannot be assumed to be in effective control, and where British operations are part of a global policy. American control is not always dynamic, as Woolworth's makes clear.

The very biggest companies are so complex and diversified that it is impossible for any one man to change their character; but very close to the top of the list are companies which have been built up or merged by single entrepreneurs or families, who keep effective control of their company (often by issuing non-voting shares to other shareholders, who object but are forced to accept for the sake of the profits). They include General Electric (Weinstock), Great Universal Stores (Wolfson), Marks and Spencer (Sieffs and Sachers), Tesco (Sir John Cohen) and Thorn Electrical (Thorn). The fact that so many fast-growing companies were built up by immigrant families confirms the belief that entrepreneurship is always most evident among 'outsiders'. As Professor Barna, the Hungarian-born economist, has put it. ' "the outsider" is likely to be more strongly activated by the profit motive; for him the accumulation of wealth may bring social recognition. He may also see more clearly the unsatisfied wants of consumers and he may be more ready to experiment with new products, new techniques and new forms or organisation.'[1] But what is also evident in these fast-growing companies is that their bosses have a large financial stake in them, and thus associate the companies' fortunes very closely with their own; while in the ordinary big British companies it is rare for directors to hold more than a few thousand pounds worth of shares and (as in the case of Rolls-Royce) they have no great cause for worry when the share price goes down. The detachment and reasoned judgement that makes for the successful administrator is not necessarily what is required in a profit-making company; and the senior civil servants who have moved over from Whitehall to industry have not had a high reputation for increasing their companies' profits.

It is difficult to correlate the chairmen's abilities and characters with their companies' efficiency or profits, because so many boards have inherited hopeless situations from their predecessors which

[1] Tibor Barna: *Investment and Growth Policies in British Industrial Firms* C.U.P., 1962, pp. 56–57.

could take years to put right, and on the other hand many chairmen of profitable companies can bask in the credit for earlier achievements. Some industries, like tobacco, whisky or beer, are so established and circumscribed that there is not very much that any chairman can do about them, except buy up other industries. Often the real achievement of the chairman—like that of ministers in their departments—is impossible to disentangle from the fog of anonymity, or from the glare of public relations. Some of the most effective chairmen can be the men who quietly lay the basis of the future by promoting the right men, reorganising functions, and establishing an atmosphere of confidence. But a few are obviously outstanding. Below are five bosses who have, in very different ways, transformed their companies.

KEARTON AND COURTAULDS

For the past nine years Lord Kearton has been intimately identified with the growth of Courtaulds. He is the most controversial of the tycoons: he loves to venture into politics, and bristles with energy and opinions. Under the Labour government he presented himself as a socialist entrepreneur—to the annoyance of other chairmen—with a different set of values from others. (His critics say that he is just a capitalist *manqué*.) He played a key role in setting up the IRC, and heavily supported Sir Arnold Weinstock (see below) in the electronics take-overs—thus putting more people's backs up; but since then he has retreated into reorganising Courtaulds, which fully occupies his energies. He strides through the offices like a turkeycock, talking always at breakneck speed, interspersing violent views with faint disclaimers—'if I may say so'. He dislikes bankers, hereditary money and high life, and looks back proudly to his own humble beginnings in Staffordshire, and his experiences of other people's poverty in the north-east during the slump.

Kearton is a distinguished scientist and an FRS; he began his career in ICI, then worked on atomic energy in the war, then switched to Courtaulds as a chemical engineer. He emerged suddenly to fame in 1962, when he successfully led the defence of Courtaulds against the take-over bid by ICI, and two years later be became chairman. Since then he has expanded Courtaulds with a succession of take-overs, and had further jousts with ICI; in February 1969 he tried to take over English Calico by organising a consortium round it, which provoked ICI to counter-attack, producing a slanging match between the two chairmen: 'My general attitude now,' said Kearton, 'is one of feeling bored with ICI's neurosis over Courtaulds.' His bid for English Calico was eventually disallowed by the Board of Trade.

Kearton, from his war-work onwards, has been on the government-industry interface, but he likes also to appear as the champion of the independence of big business: 'Today's managerial prayer,' he said in November 1970, 'is: From interference, anarchism, inflation and too much taxation, the Good Lord deliver us. Especially anarchism and inflation.'

GEDDES AND DUNLOP

Sir Reay Geddes has a place in industrial history as the co-architect of the first big trans-national merger since Unilever in 1929—the union of Dunlop and Pirelli. He is a patrician tycoon, tall, handsome and beetle-browed, with a steep head and a fixing stare. His family came from the Orkneys, bursting with imperial ambition; his grandfather built the Bombay docks, and his father and uncle were both Lloyd George politicians, and both through a family connection on the board of P and O shipping. Sir Reay's father was best known for the Geddes Axe, which ruthlessly cut down the armed forces and schools in 1922; he then went on to run Dunlops. His son climbed up through the company, and after an interval under Sir Edward Beharrel (himself the son of a former chairman), the chairmanship went to Reay in 1967. (The dynasty will not be perpetuated: Sir Reay's son is a doctor.)

Sir Reay has been in Neddy, and helped to reorganise ship-building; but he believes now firmly that businessmen should concentrate on their own business, and not get muddled up with government. He sees himself as carrying an inherited respon-sibility, as one of the last of the 'outward-looking generation'. He has a great attachment to the white commonwealth, but like others began to transfer his affections to Europe. It was thus fitting that he was the first chairman to go in, boots and all, into a European merger: in March 1970 he announced a spectacular 'marriage of equals' with the Italian tyre-manufacturers, Pirelli. Both companies had been up against growing competition from the American giants Firestone and Goodyear; and the merger, with a combined turnover óf £940 million, brought them close to their size. The financial and fiscal details were 'a barbed wire entanglement', and the legal complexities required months of work. The merger depended on the patience and mutual trust of the two ambitious personalities. Leopoldo Pirelli is another hereditary chairman, an autocrat who was determined to push the merger through; and the two men—both rather introverted— have a close relationship. The real potential, and the underlying snags, of this marriage will take years to show themselves. As Geddes explained: 'It requires judgment and faith as well as arithmetic.'

DUNCAN AND RIO TINTO ZINC

The most precipitate arrival among the top fifty companies has been the mining company Rio Tinto Zinc, which has spread out in sixteen years from a Spanish mine into an international mining company operating in every continent. The growth of the company is inseparable from the ambitions of its chairman, Sir Val Duncan, who has a stake of about £300,000 in the company. He is a suave, silver-haired old Harrovian, who feels driven to expand and develop the wealth of the world with a Rhodes-type ardour. He was brought into the Rio Tinto company in 1948 (by his banker friend Sir Mark Turner), when its main property was the Spanish mine after which it was named. Six years later Duncan sold off two-thirds of the mine and used the £8 million to develop the company elsewhere, searching for minerals and raising money wherever he could—he uses American money to finance exploration in Australia. In 1962 Rio Tinto merged with Consolidated Zinc to make RTZ, and since then, with luck and judgment, explorations have paid off all over the world.

Sir Val has a global outlook, spends a third of his year travelling, and regards governments as awkward obstacles, to be cajoled, bullied and overcome. He has a straightforward view of countries, as being either stable or unstable, and on this basis he has built up his mining operations on the basis of North America, the white commonwealth and white South Africa. He is impatient of political arguments, and sceptical of black states; in 1969—permitted by the Labour government—he made a large contract with South-West Africa for mining uranium. His Duncan Report of 1969, on the diplomatic service (see Chapter 15), was rather off-hand in its treatment of the third world or 'Outer Area': luckily, it was not implemented.

STOKES AND BRITISH LEYLAND

Lord Stokes, the chairman of British Leyland Motors, is the most vulnerable and exposed of the new industrial patriots. Car companies in every country need a commanding leader—if only because so much depends on the gamble of designing a mass model whose success or failure can settle the firm's future for years. The British car industry since the war has been slow to integrate itself. The over-fat car companies of Lord Nuffield and Lord Austin had grown complacent with their success, and scorned the post-war markets; their merger in 1957, to produce the British Motor Corporation, was never properly consummated, with the factories at Oxford and Birmingham still producing quite separately. By 1967 BMC was in serious trouble, and the next year they merged with Leyland, the rival company based on buses and lorries, which had been built up by Donald Stokes, the wonderman of the industry. At last there was a giant big enough to compete with the foreigners.

Stokes was the hero of the hour—an outgoing and reassuring tycoon who could inspire his workers and knew how to sell abroad; he had worked his way up through the factory floor, and loved buses and cars—he has a row of models in his office. He was (in contrast to his ex-Leyland colleague, Jim Slater) more interested in making things than making money. But this was a doubtful virtue in coping with the great jumble of factories and models; and when he merged with BMC, he did not realise the problems he was taking on—the in-bred management, the poor labour relations, the preoccupation with engineering rather than design and salesmanship, the cross-purposes between Birmingham and Oxford. The merged company, British Leyland, soon found itself facing greater competition from imported foreign cars, and from its American rivals, Vauxhall and Ford; and in 1970 the company made a sensational loss. Stokes sacked some top management, laid off workers, and staked everything on the new popular car, the Marina, which was quite well received on the home market; but the real battle will be on the continental scale, against Renault, Volkswagen and Fiat.

WEINSTOCK AND GENERAL ELECTRIC

The man who has made most mark on British industry is only

the managing-director of his company, General Electric (under the chairman, Lord Nelson) but he is unquestionably the decisive boss. Arnold Weinstock's name—along with Jim Slater's—has become a symbol for ruthless rationalisation. He rose to his power through a succession of mergers in seven years. In 1961, at the age of thirty-seven, he was running the TV business of his father-in-law, Sobell: then the business was taken over by a much bigger, but incompetent, company, General Electric. Two years later Weinstock emerged as GEC's managing-director, and by relentlessly cutting down unprofitable sectors and people, quickly turned it into a spectacular profit-maker: by 1967 it was so successful and its share price so high that it was able to bid for its bigger rival, AEI—now tottering. After a bitter and famous take-over battle Weinstock won (with some help from the IRC) and moved in to cut down the extravagant structure of AEI. Only a year later, the *third* electronic giant, English Electric, became vulnerable. Another company, Plessey, tried to take it over; but once again Weinstock stepped in, again encouraged by the IRC, and at forty-four became boss of the biggest electronic company in Europe. Weinstock's opportunity came partly from the fact that, after fifty years of protection rings and sheltered management, British electronics were having to open up to international competition.

Weinstock likes to present himself as a kind of computer ('A good brain's like a computer; it only makes the wrong decision if you've put in the wrong data'): his own head, rolling around above unmoving shoulders, looks almost like a disembodied brain. He talks non-stop in an emphatic gruff voice, full of tough talk about blokes being in the muck, with a snowball's chance in hell, knocking 'em down and seeing 'em off. He dominates his 182 separate companies by remote control from a Mayfair office, with the help of his mastery of statistics (he specialised in statistics at the LSE). He believes that all problems are basically simple: 'When a problem seems complicated, then it's because you don't know enough about it.' His basic mission, he insists, is to establish the supremacy of the consumer. He can be brutally direct with his colleagues, and lays down that 'the one unforgivable thing in this company is to conceal something if it's gone wrong'. His enemies say that he rules by fear, and that he lacks what his industry most requires—the preparedness to take risks on long-term high technology.

Weinstock is not an inhuman computer; he is driven by a moral purpose and personal integrity that give him a special authority: 'I don't understand what life would be like without a criterion of usefulness; it would be entirely selfish, entirely degrading.' He denies being puritanical—he enjoys racing his own horses, cigars, Bach, farming. But he hates the abuse of privilege, and he lays into the expense accounts and perks of his colleagues. He dislikes organised big business, including the CBI and the Institute of Directors; and he doesn't believe in getting mixed up with other kinds of business. For a time GEC had money in London Weekend Television, where he battled against the producers' extravagance, but he sold out in 1970 to Murdoch. ('It's not our job to be mixed up in a property business,' he explained.) Behind Weinstock's drive there is some sense of melancholy; his parents, both Polish Jews, died when he was young and he was at school during the massacre of the Jews, which gave him as a survivor a sense of special duty. He talks about his job as a burden: 'When things are going right, I feel there must be something wrong, and when things go wrong I feel I've got to put them right.'

Weinstock is very much *sui generis*, a self-contained freak in the British industrial scene. But he has a special relevance to the Britain of the seventies: partly because he is the instrument for sharpening his industry to survive in Europe, after the flabbiness of the fifties and sixties; partly because he shares something of that austere self-reliance of Heath in politics, or Slater in finance— throw-backs to an earlier puritan zeal which equates money-making with self-denial and discipline.

INSTITUTE OF DIRECTORS

The most vocal and publicised organisation of directors is the Institute of Directors, a self-important body which appropriately inhabits three mansions in Belgrave Square. After the war it was moribund, and then was revived by a ginger-group led by Lord Chandos and Sir Edward Spears: it aimed to become a 'Bosses' Trade Union', and to encourage a 'warm family feeling' among directors—a kind of counter-revolution to the Socialists. Since then it has multiplied a hundredfold, and in 1971 had 43,000 members, including 900 women and about 200 members of both houses of parliament who (according to the brochure) 'can be counted upon to see that the views of directors are adequately voiced in parliament and their interests protected whenever occasion demands it'.

For anyone who believes that businessmen nowadays are dispassionate non-partisan men the institute provides a corrective. Once a year in November five thousand directors arrive at the Albert Hall for the annual rally, to celebrate free enterprise, incentives and to condemn taxation and socialism. The rows of five thousand faces include many variations: there are some wide-eyed young men, a few daring styles—side-whiskers, beards, fancy suits; there are some caricatures with huge bellies and tiny eyes, straight from a George Grosz cartoon; there are even a scattering of women, in amazing hats. But most are very uniform—in white shirts, dark ties, dark suits, executive spectacles. After lunch one in ten (I reckoned) have their eyes shut.

Up on the floodlit stage are the bigwigs of the institute who over the years have become a tiny stage army of the right. There is Sir Edward Spears, the octogenarian chairman of Ashanti Goldfields, with his grim circumflex mouth; there is Lord Renwick, the bull-headed co-founder of commercial television, with his rugged face which seems to have grown round his spectacles; there is the director-general of the institute, the immaculate Major Sir Richard Powell (Bart.), whose wavy hair, thin moustache and military movements seem to have come straight from a tailor's advertisement. And there is Sir Paul Chambers, the ex-chairman of ICI and ex-president of the institute, who is a kind of embodiment of their aggressive spirit, a new version of the rugged old tycoon: sometimes his pugnacious mouth breaks into a crocodile laugh; sometimes his jaws fall apart, and he shakes up and down and looks around in amazement or disgust. He speaks with slow emphasis as if every word were worth a few thousand pounds, and takes off his spectacles at the end of each sentence.

The institute encourages a mystique of directorship as opposed to managership, and stays proudly aloof from the British Institute of Management. Sir Richard Powell once explained that 'directors are a kind of aristocracy: they should be men of parts, and they should have interests outside their business . . . you could say we were a gigantic Old Boy network'. The institute encourages the directors to take themselves very seriously: they provide a medical unit (one of the best in the world), language courses, and copious advice on how directors should look after themselves. Their luxuriant magazine *The Director* analyses carefully how much they are paid, how hard they work, why they are fired, whether their sons should take over. The information that emerges is not very reassuring; a survey published in May 1966, for instance, showed that forty per cent of the directors spoke no foreign language, twenty-five per cent took no exercise at all, seventy-five per cent use a company car in their own time, sixty-one per cent take more than one holiday a year.

The institute should not be taken too seriously. To become a 'Fellow', as members are called, requires no more than any kind of directorship, and eight pounds a year. Only a few Fellows are politically active, or take any part in the institute's affairs. But the institute can muster large funds from industry, including a special 'Free Enterprise Fund' for campaigns against nationalisation. 'The idea of a businessmen's lobby isn't altogether attractive,' admitted one former Conservative chairman: 'The institute aren't a particularly *nice* collection of people.'

CBI

The more serious spokesman for directors, and for industry as a whole, is the Confederation of British Industries. The CBI was formed in February 1965—after previous abortive attempts—when three employers' organisations led by the old Federation of British Industries agreed to merge into a single body. The establishment of the CBI was an important climax to the whole coming-together of government and industry over the past decades, outlined in Chapter 32. As one historian of British industry, Professor Stephen Blank of Chicago, has put it:

> The CBI was industry's response to the permanent expansion of government's role in British society ... The CBI was established primarily to provide British industry with a more authoritative voice in what was now seen as a continuous dialogue with government (and of the trade unions) on all of the major economic and industrial issues of the day. It was thus from the beginning a far more politically conscious body than the FBI had been ... The FBI was never quite sure that it was a power in the land—and often it was unsure that it even wanted to be a power. The CBI has never been in doubt. In this, as in other ways, there are certain stronger parallels between the CBI and the TUC than between the CBI and the FBI ... The CBI was committed, moreover, to a far more interventionist policy in the affairs of its member firms and organisations than the FBI. It was determined to urge—and to assist in—the rationalisation and concentration of industrial units[1] ...

[1] Stephen Blank: *Industry and Government in Postwar Britain*, Chapter 8.

Not all businessmen or Conservatives were keen on the merged organisation, particularly at a time when the Labour Party was in power. Enoch Powell attacked the role of the industrial organisations in *The Director*, just before the CBI came into being: 'Remember Caligula, who wished the Roman people had one neck, so that he could cut it off? The Association of These, and the Federation of That, present just that one neck to the Socialist garrotter (and now, not content, these employers seem to be bent on all amalgamating into one great, soft, vulnerable neck!).'

The first director-general of the CBI (at £24,000 a year) was John Davies, the rumbustious Welshman from Shell-Mex who later became Minister for Trade and Industry in Heath's government; the first chairman was Maurice Laing, head of the Laing building companies and a prominent churchman, who at that time was sympathetic to the Labour Party's policies. In the first year or two the CBI seemed quite friendly with the Labour government; it co-operated with George Brown in his 'declaration of intent' about an incomes policy, and showed some confidence in the National Plan. But by the end of 1967, after the collapse of the plan, the economic crises, and devaluation, relations were icy. Davies—partly because much of his fund-raising depended on right-wing businessmen—adopted an increasingly combative approach towards the Wilson government, which he could turn on very easily for television. When Wilson made a peace pact with the trade unions, Davies described it as fit only for use in the lavatory, and Wilson replied 'they might have risen above the level of a suburban Rugby club dinner'. But much of this belligerence was shadow-boxing: Davies already had an eye on Tory politics.

The fact that industry had now one big spokesman (as Powell warned) did not mean that their power was now greater; for their leaders were now, almost inevitably, sucked closer to government. As Professor Blank puts it: 'One could argue that, insofar as the balance of influence between industry and government is concerned, the existence of the confederation has made it possible for the government to exert more influence on industry than industry on the government. The point is, quite simply, that we really cannot assume that the closer relations of interest groups and government in the collectivist environment and even the altered patterns of decision-making characteristic of the new group politics must automatically mean that the balance of influence has swung towards the interest groups.'

The CBI was too cautious for many of its members. In late 1967 a group of its senior members, led by the tireless Sir Paul Chambers and supported by the CBI's own economic director Arthur Shenfield, set up the Industrial Policy Group to express views on 'the fundamental causes of the malaise of the British economy'. The members included many chairmen of big companies, such as Lord Netherthorpe of Fisons, John Partridge of Imperial Tobacco, Lord Boyd of Guinness, Sir Joseph Lockwood of EMI, Lord Cole of Unilever and Sir David Barran, later Chairman of Shell. They quickly achieved fame when James Callaghan, then Chancellor, attacked them in parliament: 'There is a growing view fostered in some quarters that democracy cannot solve our problems. I regard as potentially sinister this new big business organisation which has been set up with some rather dubious people heading it.' ('It sounds as if he has gone off his rocker,' commented Sir Joseph Lockwood.) The group, most of them connected with the Institute of Directors, formed quite a noisy cabal inside the CBI; but Sir Paul was effectively outployed by John Davies, and the group now confines itself to publishing booklets about competition, efficiency, etc. In 1969 John Davies left to take up politics, and was succeeded by a quieter man, Campbell Adamson, who had been in steel companies till he worked for two years in the Department of Economic Affairs. Adamson's style is much more that of an industrial civil servant, and he wanted to de-escalate the confederation's relations with the Labour Party. He kept at arm's length from the 'potentially sinister people', and showed signs of worry about the CBI's links with the South African lobby (whose trading organisation, UKSATA, has an office in the same building but no formal connection).

When the Conservative Party came back to power, the perspective of the CBI immediately changed. There was rejoicing among the right-wing members and delight at the Barber 'businessmen's budget' and the subsequent boom. But some of the new Heath policies soon came as a shock; the collapse of Mersey Docks and Harbours Board and the bankruptcy of Rolls-Royce were not quite what they meant by bringing back free enterprise. The blustering attacks on government intervention, whether from the Industrial Policy Group or from the Institute of Directors, became rather less confident when the new government showed itself actually *wanting* to withdraw.

35

Nationalised Industries

If you keep on pulling up the plant to see how the roots are getting on, it does not grow very well.

Lord Heyworth (Select Committee on Nationalised Industries of 1953)

THE question of who controls or should control industry comes to a head when it reaches the nationalised industries. While the more incompetent private industries, like Vickers or British Leyland, are allowed to decline without much effective complaint from their owners, the shareholders, British Steel or British Rail are subjected to incessant questioning, dogmatising and political point-making. The basis of the political excitement is the old argument as to who should own the means of production, a central dispute between the two parties for decades; but the real problems of control, as with private industry, have little to do with owner-ship. Parliament, as the nominal owner of the public industries, finds itself almost as powerless to control 'its' companies as the private shareholders trying to control the industrial giants. 'The basic fact,' wrote Anthony Crosland in the *Future of Socialism*, 'is the large corporation, facing fundamentally similar problems, and acting in fundamentally the same way whether publicly or privately owned.'[1]

The argument refuses to lie down; it is one of the oddities of Britain that, while the continental countries quietly accept that a

[1] *Future of Socialism*, 1956, p. 480.

large sector of industry has been, and must remain, owned by the state, in Britain the question still produces violent emotional responses. (Is it, as David Marquand suggests, because the nationalisation debate takes the place of the fiercer connected debates about group ideologies?[1]) In the sixties the argument appeared to be simmering down; the Labour Party on their side had dropped their Clause Four—the contentious clause in their policy which required the nationalisation of all the means of production, distribution and exchange; and the renationalisation of steel in 1965, though opposed by the Tories, did not meet very fierce opposition, partly because the steel industry (like coal or railways before it) was becoming unprofitable. The Conservatives appeared to be losing their dogmatic faith in free enterprise, and both sides seeemed to be becoming aware of the complexities of control.

But when the Conservatives returned to power in 1970 the argument flared up again with unexpected violence, and the right wing of the party began again baying for denationalisation. At the crucial ministry, the Department for Trade and Industry, the minister John Davies was himself fairly undogmatic; but under him were two right-wing ministers, both aristocrats from the north-east, who emerged like throwbacks to an earlier industrial era. Sir John Eden, nephew of Lord Avon, comes from a hard-core free-enterprise background; his family's coal mines were nationalised in 1947, and he married the daughter of a right-wing businessman, Sir John Pascoe, who took his son-in-law on to the boards of his companies. In the ministry Sir John, who is responsible for coal, steel, gas and electricity, soon made clear his intentions; 'By and large,' he said in January 1971, 'the public sector should be concerned primarily with those activities which cannot sensibly be done by the private sector.' With Eden is Nicholas Ridley, an outspoken Powellite with boyish good looks: his family owned the Northumberland port of Blyth, and by marriage became connected with the huge midlands company, Guest Keen and Nettlefold; the Ridleys' coal and steel interests, too, were nationalised. Eden and Ridley (with encouragement from Ted Heath) led the new attack on the nationalised industries, succeeding in—if nothing else—demoralising their managers and workers. The real problems of the industries were once again obscured by the political posturing.

[1] *New Society*, February 18, 1971.

In fact, it is not easy to generalise about the nationalised
industries; they include such different bodies as the Bank of
England, the Sugar Corporation, Cable and Wireless Ltd, the
North of Scotland Hydro-Electric Board and now a sector of
Rolls-Royce; the common reason for their state ownership is not so
much political dogma, as the fact that most of them have become
unworkable by anyone else. The core of the state industries is the
great national utilities, which in most European countries are
state-owned—coal, gas, railways, electricity and airways. They all
have exciting histories: they represent the layers of Britain's
industrial revolution. It was on coal that the industrial revolution
was based: the invention of gas (in 1798), of railways (in 1829),
and electricity (in 1881) built up the urban industrial country
which we know. Today they have grown from daring pioneers into
ancient, reviled and unwanted retainers. And as Britain becomes
more involved in affluence, cars and private property, so the
fabric of public services becomes increasingly taken for granted
like rivers, and only noticed and cursed at when strikes interrupt
their flow. The nationalised workers have found to their cost their
difficulty in confronting public opinion. Either they are found to
be indispensable, to the point of danger, as the electricity workers
found in 1970, when public opinion swung fiercely against them; or
they are found to be dispensable, as the postmen found in 1971.

The most obvious characteristic of the nationalised industries is
size: they make the private industrial giants look like midgets.
British Railways in spite of its diminishing numbers, still employs
three times as many people as ICI, and the Electricity Board
has devoured enough capital to build a new ICI every three years.
These are the leading public corporations, with their numbers of
employees, profit, and date of nationalisation:

	Employees 1970-71	Surplus or Deficit £M	Date of Nationalisation
British Railways Board	273,063	+9½ (70)	1947
Post Office Corporation	407,669	?	1969
National Coal Board	285,504	+½ (70-71)	1946
Electricity Council and Boards	196,962	+65 (69-70)	1947
British Steel Corporation	250,000	n.a.	1967
Gas Council and Boards	120,000	+137 (69-70)	1949
BOAC	25,000	+5 (70-71)	1939
BEA	24,868	+11 (69-70)	1946

Their size, as much as their ownership, made them problem children, for when they were nationalised in quick succession, no one had had experience of running huge concerns except generals; and industrial corporations are not at all like armies. In retrospect, perhaps the most surprising fact about the nationalisation was how, in spite of all the theorising and discussion that preceded it, hardly any of the nationalisers had any idea of how large corporations could, or should, be run; it was part of the price of the divorce between parliament and the world of managers. As the problems grew, several of the heads of private firms were called in to advise: they all gave their diagnoses and prognoses, but none had had experience of malaise on such a massive scale. The problems of the big corporations had been compounded of size, old age, service and neglect, for which there was no quick cure.

Though nationalisation is associated with socialism, these industries had been moving steadily towards state control since the nineteen-twenties. The nationalisation of coal was first proposed by the Sankey Commission of 1919. BOAC was created by a Conservative government in 1939. Nationalising electricity was considered by Lord McGowan in 1936, and nationalising gas was recommended by Lord Heyworth in 1948. But it was Herbert Morrison, who created the London Passenger Transport Board before the war, who first eloquently expounded the concept of the public corporation: 'The public corporation must be no mere capitalist business, the be-all and end-all of which is profits and dividends,' wrote Morrison in 1953: 'Its board and officers must regard themselves as the high custodians of the public interest.' He was confident that 'we can combine progressive modern business management with a proper degree of accountability'. But the 'high custodians' became more and more caught between the ideals of service and the demand for profitable running; and in the last two decades one fundamental force had pushed all the corporations in the direction of private industry—competition. When first nationalised, they were indispensable services at a time of shortage, sure of their market, in danger of producing too little rather than too much, and most of them dependent on coal. But the expansion of road transport, natural gas, airways and oil has made each of them, one by one, less secure—setting coal against oil and natural gas; gas against electricity; railways against cars, lorries and airways; airlines against foreign airlines. The outward sign of the competition is the massive advertising: the nationalised industries are among the biggest advertisers in the country, with gas shouting against electricity, BEA against British Rail, and BEA and BOAC both yelling, louder and louder, against their foreign competitors.

It took some time for parliament and the political parties to catch up with the problems of these mysterious new organisms; but as the losses—particularly of British Rail—became more colossal—so the politicians became more worried. The Select Committee on Nationalised Industries inspected them one by one (as Sir Ronald Edwards put it) 'helping to hammer out a general philosophy for running nationalised industries'. And in 1961 an important white paper was published, suitably couched in Treasury language, proclaiming that the nationalised industries 'are not, and ought not to be, regarded as social services absolved from economic and commercial justification'—a knock on the head for Herbert Morrison's high custodians.

The white paper had its effects, paving the way for the Beeching Revolution in British Railways. But the new policy did not, as the chairmen had hoped, put an end to the conflicts between their industries and the 'sponsoring ministries' in Whitehall, which were supposed to be responsible for them; in fact the interference and tension between them has been much greater since. Every minister has his own idea on how to run an airline or a railway, and the definition of running them 'along commercial lines' is still open to many interpretations. The fact that rail fares, electricity charges or the price of steel are basic elements in the cost of living makes them politically always highly sensitive. Most important of all, the nationalised industries are the biggest employers in the country, and their wage increases are a key element in inflation; so that no government can resist pressurising them to stand firm against demands. The fact that the government can keep down the wages in the public sector, while private industry wages leap ahead, adds to their sense of inferiority and dependence.

NATIONALISED CHAIRMEN

If the men are wrong nothing will be right.
Sir Ronald Edwards (*to the select committee, 1968*).

Caught in the cross-winds from parliament, Whitehall and their

own staffs, on lonely and vulnerable peaks, are the chairmen of the
nationalised industries. Their jobs are not very enviable, and
occupants are difficult to find. The chairmen and boards are
chosen by the sponsoring ministries, with advice from the civil
service department, and with occasional interference from the
minister. The patronage involved in these appointments is considerable; in the words of John Morris, a former junior minister
at the old Ministry of Power (now absorbed in the wider-
ranging Department of Trade and Industry): 'At the ministry I
found we had more patronage than Walpole ever possessed. We
had, for instance, to find half a dozen members for one national
and twelve regional boards in the nationalised gas and electricity
industries alone.' The machinery for finding the right men is
miserably inadequate, as nearly everyone who has tried it agrees.
The Treasury's Book of the Great and the Good (see Chapter 12)
is full of 'sound' names; but many of them (as the select committee
of 1968 described them) are 'past the peak of their energy, enterprise and ability'. It is here that the lack of contact between
Whitehall and industry shows itself most seriously; while permanent secretaries often encounter the same stage army of top
industrialists who troop in and out of committee rooms, they see
very little of the men in their mid-forties who might still have the
drive and enterprise to take on the nationalised industries.
Ministers have to fall back on their own acquaintance and gossip
to find the right men; and it is always tempting to find a place on
the board for some deserving but clapped-out politician. Even
when they do find a man who *looks* right, he will probably refuse;
when (for instance) Lord Hall was chosen to run the Post Office
in 1969 he was the fourth or fifth choice on the list.

A new kind of chairman has emerged in the last two decades,
since the nationalised industries came of age. In the first post-war
decade, in keeping with the 'high custodian' idea, the government
appointed war heroes, trade unionists or politicians; Sir Brian
Robertson commanded British Railways, Sir Ian Jacob the BBC,
Lord Douglas the air-marshal was on the flight-deck of British
European Airways; Sir James Bowman of the mineworkers' union
took over the Coal Board. None of them were very interested in
the commercial problems; but the next batch were more competitive and contemporary men. In 1961 Alfred Robens, a former
Socialist Minister of Labour with a trade union background,
moved into the Coal Board: in the following ten years he became,

as Lord Robens, the archetype of the new nationalised tycoon, flying round the mines in his private plane, haranguing the miners, bullying the government, and managing to rationalise and run down the mines without a major revolt from the miners. Towards the end of his time (he is now chairman of Vickers) he showed some signs of egomania, with his attacks on communists and his talk of a businessmen's cabinet to run Great Britain Ltd. But Roben's historical achievement was remarkable: he stamped the Coal Board with his outsize personality, and gave it a dignity and sense of independence which other nationalised industries envied.

The year after Robens took over the coal mines, the Conservative government made their boldest innovation; in 1962 the Minister of Transport, Ernest Marples, brought in Dr Richard Beeching, then a director of ICI, to take over British Railways, with the then unprecedented salary of £24,000. In the following years Dr Beeching, later Lord Beeching, drastically pruned the railway system, so that 'doing a Beeching' came to describe any form of wholesale reorganisation. Beeching's methods, and the commercial climate he generated, survived long afterwards; but after the Labour Party came to power he soon came up against the new Minister of Transport, Barbara Castle, who insisted on a more co-ordinated and controlled transport system; and Beeching left the railways in 1965 to go back to ICI.

The nationalised industries have varied a great deal in their independence. The doyen of their chairmen, Sir Henry Jones of the Gas Board, a silver-haired Welshman, has been in his job since 1960 and has spent his whole career in gas; he has presided over the transformation of his industry from a Victorian hang-over, associated with antique gasworks, smells, and suicides, into a quite glamorous growth industry bringing natural gas from the North Sea, increasingly dissociated from its first maker, coal. At the other extreme have been the successive chairmen of British Overseas Airways which, though one of the smallest in terms of capital and employees, is one of the most politically sensitive—subject not only to the pressures to buy British aircraft and to fly to British areas of influence, but to recurring strikes from pilots, engineers and ground staff. Since 1945 there have been no fewer than *twelve* different chairmen, an average of one every two years, including bankers, industrialists, a scientist (Sir Harold Hartley) an admiral (Sir Matthew Slattery) and an accountant (Sir

Charles Hardie). Most of them have retreated exhausted or
exasperated from the job: 'I think the way it is expected to
operate is bloody crazy,' said Sir Matthew in 1962. Since then
the directions have been less crazy, and chairmen have a letter
authorising them to put commercial considerations above all
others. But it remains one of the most thankless tasks.

In 1971 many chairmen's terms of office expired, and the
Conservative government had to find new men: the table below
shows the principal chairmen in July 1971, with their salaries
and education. The new choices suggested that the nationalised industries were now 'growing their own timber', and were
becoming much more self-perpetuating, more like private
industry. The new chairman of BOAC is Keith Granville, who
had joined Imperial Airways from school in 1929, and had risen

Bank of England	Sir Leslie O'Brien	£25,000	Wandsworth School.
British Steel Corporation	Lord Melchett	£25,000	Eton.
Post Office	William Ryland	£20,000	Gosforth County Grammar.
National Coal Board	Derek Ezra	£20,000	Monmouth School: Cambridge.
British Railways Board	Richard Marsh	£20,000	Woolwich Poly.
Electricity Council	Sir Norman Elliott	£20,000	Privately; Cambridge.
Gas Council	Sir Henry Jones	£20,000	Harrow; Cambridge.
Central Electricity Generating Board	Sir Stanley Brown	£19,000	King Edward's, Birmingham; Birmingham Univ.
National Freight Corporation	Dan Pettit	£17,000	Quarry Bank; Cambridge.
Atomic Energy Authority	Sir John Hill	£17,000	University of London and Cambridge.
British European Airways	Henry Marking	£17,000	Saffron Walden Grammar; London.
British Overseas Airways	Keith Granville	£17,000	Tonbridge School.

up through the hierarchy. He failed to become chairman in 1969,
when he became managing director under the part-time accountant Sir Charles Hardie, but now combines both jobs. In BEA, too,
an airline man, Henry Marking, has taken over; he began as a
solicitor, and moved into BEA as company secretary. In the Coal
Board Lord Robens was succeeded by a much milder and more

intellectual chairman, Derek Ezra: he had worked in the Coal Board since the war, much concerned with European organisations and very committed to the common market; his quiet style and his academic questioning approach could hardly be more in contrast with Robens' rugged tycoonery.

An important exception to the new pattern is the new chairman of British Rail, Richard Marsh. Ever since Beeching left the railways this key job has been an awkward problem; after much havering, it was given successively to two promoted railwaymen—first Sir Stanley Raymond, then Sir Henry Johnson—but it was clear that the railways still needed a ruthless eye from outside. The Conservatives resorted to the Robens formula of ten years before—of bringing in a trade-union politician. Peter Walker, who pressed for the appointment, had come to admire Marsh when he was Minister of Transport, and Walker was his shadow minister: they were both pragmatic men, who had fought their way up. Marsh is still only forty-three, full of drive and ambition. His departure from the House of Commons left a serious gap in the Labour Party, for he was one of the few really able young MPs with a working-class background; but Marsh is a natural tycoon, impatient with waiting about in opposition. He does not regard railways as being very party-political: 'There is an amazing similarity,' he said after his appointment, 'between Labour Party and Conservative Party coal wagons . . . I am confident that it is not the job of nationalised industries to run the social services: that is the job of the government.'

The two most recently-nationalised industries have been not surprisingly the most contentious. The Post Office Corporation was created in 1969 by the Labour government, to free the postal and telephone services from the constrictions of Whitehall. The new corporation was to be run by an independent chairman, and with difficulty a man was found in the shape of Lord Hall—a short, tough nut of a man, a Labour peer, who had been surgeon, fox-hunter, naval officer and tycoon. When the new Bill was debated in the Lords there was some worry that the chairman might be too independent: 'He and his board,' complained Lord Newton, 'will have the same potential as Zeus and the other deities on Mount Olympus . . . in telecommunications he will be able to manufacture and hurl thunderbolts.' Lord Beswick, for the government, assured him that it was inconceivable that the chairman would not comply with directions from the minister.

But Lord Hall did indeed prove too Zeus-like for the incoming Tory government; the new Minister of Posts and Telecommunications, Christopher Chataway, was committed to introducing more competitive methods and more businessmen into the Post Office, and he soon crossed swords with Lord Hall over the new postal charges; eventually Chataway had to resort to his ultimate deterrent—a letter of general direction to the chairman (across this wall between politics and business, formal letters play an important part). Hall's relations became increasingly strained both with Chataway and with his own board; and in November 1970, only fourteen months after his appointment, Lord Hall was dismissed—with much acrimony and angry debate from the opposition. Hall hurled a few thunderbolts, but without causing much damage, and in parliament Chataway made a convincing case that there was no other solution. A few months later Hall was replaced by his deputy, Bill Ryland, who had gone into the GPO from school in 1934, and had been there ever since. The new preference for chairmen from inside the corporations was encouraging to the employees; but it was clear that the Conservatives expected to find them also more malleable to their pressures; and though there was much talk of the corporations being left to themselves once they had been put on to a more business-like footing, the footing was a long way off.

The most exposed position of all, the Windy Ridge of nationalised industries, is occupied by Lord Melchett, the chairman of the British Steel Corporation. For the last forty years steel has been a political shuttlecock, nationalised, denationalised, renationalised and now threatened with redenationalisation at its edges. But in the last decade the whole context of the argument has really changed, for both parties. Steel is no longer a profitable industry; big units have become essential all over Europe; and the Labour Party no longer has dreams of a nationalised industry divorced from the profit motive. It was symbolic of their new attitude that when the BSC was created in 1967 the minister concerned, who was Richard Marsh, should choose the Tory banker Lord Melchett, in the belief that it needed a tough money-man to dominate the old steel barons and their companies. Melchett was in other ways an odd choice; he is the grandson of the co-founder of ICI, Sir Alfred Mond, but his own experience has been much more financial than industrial; with his *mondain* style, his world-weary look and wavy hair, he seems very aloof from the steelmasters. Melchett dealt quite firmly with the steel barons, insisting on centralising the power, and on being himself both chairman and chief executive; after long power-struggles, he effectively controlled the four managing directors, and two of them, Niall Macdiarmid and A. J. Peech, left the corporation in dudgeon. Melchett built up his own team of men, round the triumvirate of himself, the lawyer Mark Littman and the metallurgist Monty Finniston.

But the internal battles of British steel tended to obscure the real problems—the lack of investment plans and of proper costing, the obsolete equipment and methods, the introverted attitudes of the managers, unaccustomed to a buyers' market. When the Conservatives came in the denationalisers, led by Ridley and Eden, were longing to begin the dismantling of British Steel, and the corporation was vulnerable to attack; for after a year of inflation and rising costs, by January 1971 it was losing £2 million a week, and was virtually broke. The Department of Trade and Industry inspected it closely, and insisted on their increasing the price of steel; but when Lord Melchett eventually proclaimed a price rise of fourteen per cent, the cabinet cut it down to seven per cent, insisting that British Steel must make itself more efficient; a few weeks later seven thousand redundancies were announced. In the meantime the argument raged on about denationalisation; the government agreed that bulk-steel producers should remain nationalised—mainly because of the huge integrated plants—but left the way open to denationalise the more profitable lines of the industry, including special steels and chemicals. Thus preoccupied by its political struggles and internal conflicts, the British steel industry was only beginning to face up to the problem of competing with more efficient producers abroad.

All over the world the steel industry has become a national responsibility, whether it is nationalised or not; governments intervene to cut steel prices (as Kennedy dramatically intervened with US Steel), to restrict imports, or to subsidise steelworks. Oil and chemicals have become the basis of multi-national corporations, liberated from governments, trading across the world; but steel, which affects so many other industries, is one of the strongholds of national involvement, regarded as an arm of the economy. British Steel will have to compete increasingly with

German, Japanese or American steel; but the competition will be as much between nations and national policies as between companies: in this context, the argument about public or private ownership looks still less relevant.

36

Workers

Real trade union power has returned to the grass roots from which it came.

Barbara Castle, November 1969.

The trouble is not that the trade unions are too strong. It is that they are too weak.

Edward Heath, October 1967.

AFTER the buffetings and shipwrecks of the sixties it must be hard for any observer to feel confident about the scope of any group of politicians, civil servants or directors to improve the British economy. However neat and convincing their plans look, they are still frustrated by the lack of connection with the people who actually deliver or don't deliver the goods. The gulf separating the rulers and the ruled becomes more painfully obvious as each government promises a new era, only to be followed by more strikes, more wage demands and still no increase in industrial growth. Behind all the depersonalised statistics for low productivity, increased costs and inadequate exports there are certainly great weaknesses of management and investment. But there is also the simple human problem that workers don't want to work harder or to work in new ways (for the British work longer hours, with fewer holidays than most Europeans, but produce less goods). The story of the class divisions in British industry has become depressingly familiar over the past decades; but to the old story has been added a new one—which recurs in other parts of this book, in communications, universities or administration—the general break-up of old patterns of authority, the demands for involvement and self-expression, the resentment of Us against

Them. It is not just Us, the TUC against Them the government
and the CBI: it is Us the shop stewards against Them the TUC:
and Us the individual workers against Them, the shop stewards.
In this dissipation of rivalries, the trades union movement itself has
become much more confused.

TRADES UNION CONGRESS

What are we here for?

George Woodcock, 1962.

The great annual festival of Labour is still the Trades Union
Congress, held every autumn at a seaside resort—a month before
the Labour Party Conference to which it supplies a kind of
menacing curtain-raiser, proclaiming the rougher side of Labour
politics. The TUC is still in many ways a moving and splendid
occasion—the great coming together of the representatives of
workers from all over the country, a procession of trades and
occupations marking every stage of labour history since the industrial revolution and before it, dating back to the medieval crafts and
guilds. Under the domes of the seaside palaces sit the bald ranks of
the great manual unions, the dockers, miners or railwaymen, who
still make up the core of the movement. But they are still inter-
spersed with the more individual craftsmen: in 1971 there were
representatives of 875 Felt Hat Trimmers and Wool Formers, 52
Basket Cane, Wicker and Fibre Furniture Makers, 90 Spring
Trapmakers, 114 Military Orchestral Musical Instrument Makers.
To the old unions have now been added the white collar workers
and professional men, the actors, doctors, teachers, journalists
and the £11,000-a-year airline pilots. Nowadays there are very
few of the old symbols of toil to be seen—not many workers wear
braces or cloth caps, and only about one in ten has an open shirt.
Most delegates have white shirts, dark ties and spectacles: and
several have handlebar moustaches and sideboards.

The style and the idiom of the congress remains strikingly
different from the smooth gatherings of professional politicians,
businessmen or managers, and here the language of power and economics is instinctively suspect; as one delegate explained: 'If
someone says that something is too complicated to understand, it
usually means he doesn't want us to understand'. The TUC still
distils some of the spirit of Us or rather Uz—for its language is predominantly north country. Delegates, without self-consciousness,

626

will talk about the folk, that chappie, brother or comrade. The congress is still a shock reminder, specially to a southerner, of how far Britain remains two nations, with a gulf of cross-purposes between them.

Yet with all its inherent grandeur, to any expectant observer the TUC provides a profound anticlimax. In its 102 years it has accumulated a heavy ritual and formalism, while its first purpose has become lost or disguised. The officials and delegates love to wrangle over the agenda, the points of order, the intricate composite motions which attempt to satisfy several trade unions. The resolutions are recited in a monotone, the chairman is preoccupied with his red light and his bell to stop the relentless speakers. In its century of existence the Congress has become as much an embattled institution—perhaps more so—as the governments or companies it is fighting; and in the process it has walled itself off from the workers and shop stewards at the benches. It has become accustomed to being a bureaucracy, dealing with other bureaucracies, and its public confrontations with governments have become not only formal but often thoroughly bogus. Behind the dramatic headlines about 'TUC slams government', the threats, warnings and cliff-hanging, they share the same worries with the government and the CBI: they have *all* lost touch with the workers.

The organisation of the TUC itself is quite small. The actual council of thirty-four is made up of busy general secretaries who normally meet only once a month round the horseshoe desk in Congress House in Bloomsbury (with a statue outside of one worker pulling up another). Few central union organisations are as weak as Britain's. The TUC cannot order a union to strike or not strike: it can only advise, cajole or bring careful pressure. Each member pays only 8p a year to it: the income in 1969 was £680,000, which had to pay for staff, scholarships, publicity, international affiliation fees, and organising the conference. The most important figure is the general secretary, who is the only full-time member of the council, and thus the hub of the movement (the TUC is still, like the Labour Party, described as a movement, an important distinction from its opposite numbers, the CBI or the Tory Party: it may be unclear quite where they are moving, but they can still move people in the other sense, too). The general secretary can go no further than the council will let him, and the council (as we shall see) are formidable men. But he can speak out in his own right, push them or pull them back, and he has command of the central bureaucracy, with a salary (in 1970) of £5,220 a year. The last three general secretaries have come in orderly progression: George Woodcock for years was deputy to Vincent Tewson; and when Woodcock moved out in 1969, to become chairman of the CIR (see below), *his* deputy Victor Feather took over. Feather in turn, when he retires in three years' time, is likely to be succeeded by his deputy, Len Murray, an economics graduate from Oxford.

Vic Feather, the present secretary, personifies the most attractive side of the movement. He is a genial, extrovert man with a friendly voice and a comedian's nose; and he has a gift for knock-about comedy which can always bring the house down—very unlike his morose philosophical predecessor, Woodcock. He grew up in Bradford, the son of a French-polisher who was victimised for his trade union activities, and who named his son defiantly after Labour heroes—Victor Grayson Keir Hardie Feather. Vic left school at fourteen and a half to work as a flour-lad: he was befriended by Barbara Castle's father, Frank Betts, who then edited the *Bradford Pioneer* and published Vic's essays. He was brought into the TUC in 1937 by Walter Citrine and climbed up through the organisation. His experience made him aware—perhaps too aware—of the limitations of the headquarters: he is adept at the diplomacy of the job, mediating between the union leaders, lowering the temperature with a few jokes, and injecting common sense between hysterical speeches. But he faces a period of exceptional difficulty, when diplomacy will not be enough. In the last two decades, under both Tory and Labour governments, the TUC has been ushered into the central places of the Establishment—to join committees, to sit on Neddy, and above all to discuss prices and incomes. Successive prime ministers have made a point of cultivating the general secretary. But the Heath government's determination to enforce its own incomes policy, and the outright battle over the Industrial Relations Bill (see p. 646) has broken that link. It may be salutary for the TUC to be outside the government's embrace. But the general secretary finds himself in the meantime at the head of a very straggling army.

GENERAL SECRETARIES

It is the general secretaries of the individual trade unions who are the traditional policy-makers of the movement—'barons in a kingless kingdom,' as one of them described them (that recurring metaphor among all kinds of British institutions). Their power *looks* spectacular. Most of them are appointed until retirement, and are almost impossible to dislodge; they can project their own strong views, at the Labour Conference or the TUC or on television, as if they represented hundreds of thousands of members; they can wield the 'block vote', so that three or four of them could (if they agreed) swing the whole TUC. Many of them can dominate the organisation of their own union officials, promoting their favourites and choosing their successors. To the public they appear as the sole representatives of their unions, without much visible opposition.

Certainly, their opportunities to put across their own views and to pressurise politicians are such that industrialists and parliamentarians could envy. But their actual power depends in the end on their ability to control their troops. The big unions were set up at a time when they needed unchallenged leadership, to attain aims on which nearly everyone was agreed. Now the members are much more questioning, the aims less certain, so that many general secretaries, while they talk like confident generals, are preoccupied with trying to prevent mutiny or desertion. And all of them have become more conscious of their vulnerability to public opinion. A show of strength can quickly, in face of a hostile public, turn into a show of weakness.

In the British power structure these men occupy isolated positions at the peak of their union organisations, connecting them up, through a single link in the chain, with the world of high bargaining, planning and politicking. Most of them still are men who left school at fourteen or fifteen, went to work in the bad years of the thirties, and came to power and influence in conditions that were confusingly different: their rhetoric and their militant outlook date from that earlier age. They have worked most of their lives for low wages, and none of them, even as general secretaries, have salaries which allow them much scope. Their own lives are an odd mixture of the homely and the high-powered—of suburban gardening and do-it-yourself, and national conferences and international seminars. They are the only power group in Britain which has not been invaded by graduates, and it is doubtful whether they *will* be invaded: there is a danger that the sortings of the merit-ocracy, creaming-off intelligent boys, will leave the trade union

Union	Head	Members 1970	MPs 1970	Affiliation Fees £
Transport and General Workers (TGWU)	Jack Jones	1,531,607	19	114,870
Amalgamated Union of Engineering Workers (AUEW)	Hugh Scanlon	1,309,097	21	84,844
General and Municipal Workers (NUGMW)	Lord Cooper	803,653	12	60,273
National and Local Government Officers' Association (NALGO)	Walter Anderson	397,069	—	29,780
Union of Electrical, Electronic Tele-communication and Plumbing (EETU)	Frank Chapple	392,401	3	29,430
Shop, Distributive and Allied Workers (USDAW)	Alf Allen	316,387	7	23,729
National Union of Public Employees (NUPE)	Alan Fisher	305,222	6	22,891
National Union of Mineworkers (NUM)	Lawrence Daly	297,108	20	22,283
National Union of Teachers (NUT)	Edward Britton	290,440	—	—
Society of Graphical and Allied Trades (SOGAT)	Richard Briginshaw	235,927	—	17,694

movement with too little brain-power to cope with their future problems. The division into 'eggheads and serfs' (which Sir John Newsom warned of in 1963) will produce its most dangerous gap at the point where trade union leaders uncomprehendingly confront tycoons or civil servants, and vice-versa.

Among the 150 trade unions affiliated to the TUC, the ten shown in the table above account for nearly six million members out of nine and a half million; and of these the biggest two—the Transport and General Workers and the Amalgamated Engineers—account for nearly three million members between them, or a third of the votes. The big unions have got bigger in the last ten years; but it can no longer be assumed—as used to be thought—that larger trade unions would lead to more moderate conservative leadership. In the fifties and early sixties the big unions were dominated by strong right-wing leaders—Deakin, Lawther, Williamson. But since 1968 the two giants have been run by men of the left, Jack Jones and Hugh Scanlon, who are not only more militant than their predecessors but closer to the workers, more interested in the shop floor and notions of workers' control, and more fortified against the blandishments of Whitehall and Downing Street. Both of them, in their style and their policies, are determined to remain 'us', not to become 'them'.

T AND G

The biggest union in Europe is the Transport and General Workers, the 'T and G', with one and a half million members, ranging from North Wales quarrymen to London bus-drivers, with the dockers still as their militant shock troops. It can trace its origin back to the dock strike of 1889, but the present amalgamation was formed by Ernest Bevin from fourteen separate unions in 1922, when wage cuts and unemployment had produced a critical need for workers' unity. After *ten years* of discussions Bevin persuaded them to yield their autonomy, and to impose unity. Bevin framed a constitution to give huge powers to one man, the general secretary—the job he himself filled from 1922 till 1940, when he became Churchill's Minister of Labour. The general secretary presides over a large bureaucracy at the headquarters, Transport House, a plain brick building in Smith Square, Westminster, part of which is used by the Labour Party—an appropriate symbol of the party's indebtedness to the unions. Bevin saw the building opened in May 1928: 'To him it was nothing short of marvellous that a working men's organisation, with a subscription of sixpence a week, could rise from renting a house in a back street to building, at a cost of well over £50,000, an eight-storey office building of its own within a stone's throw of the House of Lords.'[1] The general secretary of the T and G enjoys the same kind of power as the president of the United States:[2] he is the only member of his cabinet who has been directly chosen by the majority of his people. But, unlike the president, he is appointed until retiring age. A dominating general secretary can make sure that officials are

[1] Alan Bullock, *Life and Times of Ernest Bevin*, Vol. 1, p. 406.
[2] V. L. Allen, *Power in the Trade Unions*, p. 207.

sympathetic to him, and his election by the very unsophisticated rank and file encourages demagogy: all the general secretaries of the T and G have been powerful speakers.

Since its foundation the T and G has had only five secretaries— Ernest Bevin, Arthur Deakin, Jock Tiffin (who died a few months after taking office) Frank Cousins and Jack Jones. For twelve years the union was dominated by the electric and prickly personality of Frank Cousins—with an interval of two years while he joined Harold Wilson's cabinet. Cousins had a large say in pushing forward his successor so that when Jack Larkin Jones was elected in 1968 it came as no surprise: he can stay there until he is sixty-five, in 1978. Jones has something of the Cousins electricity, though his presence is less commanding. He has a bullet head and bright eyes behind large glasses; he talks tensely, with nervous movements, pushing up his chin, pulling up his shoulders, slicing the air with anger. His attitudes were forged in the thirties: he came from Liverpool—he was called Larkin after the Dublin dockers' hero— joined the Labour Party when he was fifteen, and was a County Councillor at twenty-two. He fought in Spain, was wounded, and met his wife then. He has from the beginning been on the left of the Labour Party: he has written for *Tribune* and is now a director of it. His committed political position has gone along with evident compassion and sense of decency: he has (like Cousins) championed the rights of coloured immigrants, and he speaks up for the lowest-paid and most disagreeable jobs: 'The dirty, boring manual jobs will need better pay, and more favoured conditions,' he said in November 1970, 'with the dustman and the docker rightly getting more money than the lawyers, the professors and perhaps the pop singers.'

Like other trade unions the TGWU is faced with rebellious shop stewards who have undermined its authority. Jones has been interested in workers' control since the war, when he was involved in workers' councils in the midlands: since he took over the secretaryship, he has spoken a great deal about the need for participation, for democracy with a human face, and he has tried to contradict the image of the autocrat: 'Please don't call me a trade union boss,' he said in a speech to personnel managers in October 1969, 'I am not a boss and don't want to be one. I am working for a system where not a few trade union officials control the situation but a dedicated, well-trained and intelligent body of trades union members is represented by hundreds of thousands of lay representatives.' He has tried to reorganise his own union, to open up better communications with the help of Telex machines between the branches. He wants to get closer to the shop floor, to make officials more accessible to the rank and file, as activators rather than bureaucrats: 'We aim to make the TGWU the most democratic union in the world'. But many people at Transport House are sceptical: 'Democracy is not something which happens naturally,' said one of his officials, 'but bureaucracy is.'

AUEW

The second biggest union, the Amalgamated Union of Engineering Workers, has in theory a much more democratic structure. The biggest component of the amalgamation, which took its present shape in 1971, was the old AEU, which had been formed in 1920, out of ten craft unions: it gave itself an intricate constitution, influenced by the pre-Stalin Soviet unions, with factory workers electing district committees, who elect divisional committees, who elect the national committee: only a small proportion of members bothered to vote, so there was great scope for Communists to elect each other to the top committee. The most important post is not the secretaryship (held by Jim Conway, a right-wing Labour unionist, dedicated to industrial efficiency) but the presidency; and here the change has been dramatic. For eleven years the president was William Carron, who rose to be Lord Carron—a Catholic turner from Hull who was doggedly loyal to the Labour leaders (first Gaitskell, then Wilson) and with difficulty maintained his position as the right-wing head of a left-wing union. Then in 1967, the outward colour changed overnight, when Carron was succeeded by Hugh Scanlon, who was a member of the Communist Party until 1955, and still has quite friendly relations with the Communists. Scanlon began work at fourteen in Manchester at the Metro-Vickers factory, one of the nurseries of trade union militants, where he became a shop steward. His political education came from the Communists, and like Jones he was much influenced by the Spanish Civil War (though he did not fight there). For most of his career he was in Manchester, very close to the shop stewards; he was elected to the executive in 1963, impatient under Carron's respectable rule, waiting for his chance. In the mid-sixties the union was turning more militant; Scanlon's rival on the left was Reg Birch (see

633

Chapter 3), who became increasingly Maoist and was rejected by the orthodox Communists; so that Scanlon had his chance, and got the presidency.

Scanlon is well able to raise the political temperature: he has a predatory look, like a hawk's, with a friendly Lancashire voice which can turn to steel: he speaks with slow-mounting passion, shaking his head with ironies. He seems very self-sufficient: he keeps the politicians at arms' length, and still has the protective layer of the provincial. In negotiating with employers, this makes him very effective—patient, and unyielding. But in politics he is unsubtle; he was intransigent against Wilson's incomes policy, and against the Conservatives' Industrial Relations Bill: he barged ahead with political strikes. But his bark was worse than his bite, and his militant style played into the Tories' hands: 'If the AUEW did not exist,' said the *Guardian*, 'the Tories would have to invent it.' He insists that capital and labour can never find common ground: 'It is hypocritical to think that the fundamental conflict can be resolved at some round table,' he said in 1970 . . . 'There are rules which have to be honoured, but they are the rules of war.'

GENERAL AND MUNICIPAL

The biggest unions show great variety, both in their workers and in their secretaries. The third biggest, the General and Municipal Workers (GMWU) is among the most conservative: it has a large proportion of low-paid workers, including dustmen and road-menders, and half its members work in publicly-owned industries, many of them declining, so that its bargaining positions are often weak. Amazingly it has its headquarters in the stockbroker belt of Surrey, in a white-towered Edwardian mansion called Ruxley Towers. At its head is Lord Cooper, formerly Jack Cooper, who is the son-in-law of an earlier ennobled general secretary, Lord Dukeston (there are a lot of family connections in the GMWU). Cooper is a big, bluff veteran who is what employers would like trade unionists to be like. He sits on Neddy, is a director of the London Business School and Yorkshire Television, admires Sweden's industrial relations (he wrote a pamphlet about it), and remained always loyal to Harold Wilson. But he has not devoted enough time to his union's own ramshackle organisation; and the long strike at Pilkington's glassworks in 1970 showed how little control it could exert.

EETU

The union most rent by political factions has been the former Electrical Trades Union (ETU), now merged with plumbers in the enlarged EETU. It has a long history of radicalism. It began as a small group of telephone engineers in Manchester in 1889; the new trade of electricians soon realised their potential for trouble, with a finger in almost everything from aircraft to television: 'We are in everybody's business.' After the war the ETU was captured by the Communists—partly through the apathy of others, partly by simply rigging the ballot. Eventually, after some television exposures led by Woodrow Wyatt, the unsuccessful candidate for secretary, John Byrne, brought a court case against the executive, including the Communist secretary Frank Haxell, and Mr. Justice Winn found them guilty of 'fraudulent and unlawful devices': Haxell was ordered to resign, and Byrne took his place. The TUC, after agonised conferences, sadly had to eject the ETU from the Congress: soon afterwards it was readmitted with a cleaned-up organisation, and a strong anti-Communist president, Leslie Cannon, who became the most impressive of all the union leaders, before he died in 1970. The leading role was taken over by Frank Chapple, who battles toughly with his militants but faces continuing dissension. In 1970 he led the power-workers on a national strike in which they over-reached themselves, producing an outburst of public anger at the failures in hospitals and essential services.

NUM

The most distinctive union is the National Union of Mine-workers. No miner can work without a union card. There is no 'ten per cent democracy' about them: their self-contained communities have an intense union tradition, and every pit-head has its local office. Because of their local loyalties, they are the most decentralised union; only in 1945 did their forty-one organisations combine, and the branches still control their own large funds. Traditionally the miners have been the militant heart of the trade union movement: they were the precursors of the general strike of 1926, and they continued on strike for six months after it, until they were forced back to work by starvation. But they are no longer dominant in numbers. In 1945 there were over

800,000 miners, in 1970 there were less than 300,000; the running-down of this vast traditional industry has been the greatest single change in post-war employment. Until 1968 the general secretary was a Communist, Will Paynter, a charming and eloquent Welshman, who worked amicably with the Coal Board. In 1968 he was succeeded by Lawrence Daly, a much more belligerent man: his father had been a foundation member of the Communist Party, who was put out of work in 1926 and brought up his family of nine in Penycuik miners' ghetto. Lawrence, the eldest son, also became a Communist ('we were both in the wrong party for the right reasons') and he left the party (like Scanlon) just before Hungary, and later joined the Labour Party. Daly believes in stirring up militancy; and he has advocated the nationalisation of oil and North Sea gas. He came close to a national strike in 1970; but the miners were not united.

WHITE COLLAR

The traditional horny-handed trade unionists have found their ranks depleting, and new kinds of trade unionists arriving in the TUC—paler and quieter men, more articulate and coherent in their talk, but usually flatter in their speeches. The recruitment of office workers and professional people into the trade unions has gathered pace in the last few years. Partly it reflects the simple fact that manual jobs are diminishing, and non-manual ones increasing: in 1970 the total British working population was 26 million, of whom $8\frac{1}{4}$ million came under the broad category of 'white collar' (a higher proportion than any other European country except Sweden). But the 'white collar' union also reflects the new militancy of people who used to regard bargaining over wages and salaries as beneath their dignity, and inappropriate to their class. The pace of inflation and the sense of insecurity have galvanised not only office workers but teachers and doctors, to the point of being prepared to ally themselves with the 'workers': the increase in numbers of the TUC—from $8\frac{1}{4}$ million in 1960 to $9\frac{1}{2}$ million in 1970—is largely due to the white collar unions. The local government workers (NALGO), now with 400,000 workers, joined them in 1964: their smooth-haired secretary Walter Anderson, a former solicitor, has outspokenly advocated sterner TUC action against unofficial strikers (his own union had their first official strike in 1969). The National Union of Teachers (NUT) joined the TUC in 1970; their secretary Edward Britton sees the teachers as the 'spearhead of the movement among professional workers for recognition in a technological society'.

By far the most voluble of the white collar leaders is the Welsh wizard Clive Jenkins, secretary of the Association of Scientific, Technical and Managerial Staffs (ASTMS)—a consciously superior title which embraces a range of jobs from book editors to insurance clerks. Jenkins, still only forty-four, is a phenomenal publicist, who has set himself up as the champion of downtrodden office workers: we have already crossed his turbulent wake in the city. He is a master of the mass media: he used to write a column in the *Daily Mirror*, and on TV he can talk about anything, as one of the stage army of commentators—'the BBC repertory company'. Jenkins has turned upside-down the old image of the trade unionist: he is sleek, well dressed, looking like a very successful boss—which he is. He lives well, has a country house and a cabin cruiser. He is also a brilliant demagogue, quick to exploit any promising issue. He rolls off sly epigrams in his silken sarcastic voice, which bring the house down: he lashes into the common market with unashamed xenophobia, reciting foreign names as if they were all inherently sinister or ridiculous.

The rise of Jenkins was spectacular. He is the son of a Glamorgan railway clerk (his elder brother Tom is also a trade unionist, who may well take over the Transport and Salaried Staffs Association). He began as a lab worker, then became a union officer, where he soon realised the white collar potential, and knew how to stir up new recruits. He became secretary of the union—then called ASSET—in 1961, and has since attracted new recruits faster than he can cope with them—above all from the 'ant-heaps', as he calls them, in the city. Politically, he looks very left-wing: he was a member of the Communist Party for four years, writes for *Tribune*, has visited North Vietnam. But in his union campaigning he shows little interest in equality of pay: he appears to regard senior executives and clerks as equally deserving. In the TUC he is viewed with some distrust: he has not yet been elected to the General Council. 'I love him as much as you do,' Walter Anderson said in 1969, 'but if he makes any more comic speeches from TUC microphones, or does any more acting in front of TV cameras, he might well be advised to seek membership of the British Actors Equity rather than the National Union of Journalists.'

Jenkins is not always as fierce or formidable as he sounds, and he has a powerful rival in George Doughty, the secretary of the draughtsmen's union, DATA, who avoids publicity as much as Jenkins seeks it. DATA, which began on Clydeside in 1913, is the most militant of the white collars: nearly all its executive of nineteen are emphatically left-wing (eight belong to the Communist Party) and DATA people are among the very few Englishmen who are welcome at the Chinese Embassy. Their members are young, and the union is rich enough to afford long strikes. Doughty has clashed several times with Jenkins over recruitment disputes: he wants to have one big union for all engineering workers, and he achieved a big step in 1970, when DATA, together with the Constructional Engineers, formed a federation with Scanlon's engineering union, to form the AUEW: 'I am overjoyed,' said Vic Feather at the wedding, 'this gets rid of the Dickensian image of manual and non-manual as if they were two different worlds.'

Other big unions, including the TGWU, are now looking more keenly for white collar members; and these recruits are already making themselves felt, both in the TUC and inside the individual unions: the AUEW is already being influenced by DATA. They bring with them more effective communications, greater office efficiency, more sophisticated bargaining and very often more militancy (in wages if not in politics) than the manual workers. The white collar expertise may help the more confident and better-paid workers to mobilise themselves; but it does not show much sign of helping the worst-paid. As Jenkins, Doughty or Britton compete in pressing their cases with Scanlon and Jones, so the really underpaid workers—the railwaymen, postmen or farm-workers—tend to bump along at the bottom of the moving staircase.

SHOP STEWARDS

All these general secretaries appear to the public as confident spokesmen for their unions, and they sit on the council of the TUC as the representatives of organised national labour. In the case of publicly owned industries—which employ half the unionised work force—their claim may be justified; for national agreements always have to be negotiated with the national union. But in private industry, while the national union makes agreements with national employers, more and more of the real bargains are made in the factory or plant. The general secretaries have found their power and authority oozing away towards the factories, the local offices, and the men who are closest to the workers and their grievances—the shop stewards.

The shop stewards—now about 200,000 of them—can trace their beginnings to the early industrial revolution; and their equivalents in the printing industry, called 'Fathers of the Chapel', go back to the eighteenth century. Shop stewards were campaigning in 1851 on Clydebank to negotiate piece-rates, which led to the Clydebank lock-out; and it was the spreading of piece-rate—necessarily a local negotiation—which consolidated their power. Before the first world war the shop stewards became much interested in industrial syndicalism and in 1917, encouraged by the shortage of labour and the Russian Revolution, they held their first national conference of shop stewards. They seemed well set to deprive the national unions of their power; but the failure of the general strike helped to discredit them, the depression years and mass unemployment further weakened them, and in the thirties militants spent their energies leading the protests of the un-employed. It was not till the second world war, with full employment again, that the shop stewards reasserted themselves, particularly in the aircraft industry; and in the fifties and sixties, with a shortage of labour in most industries, both workers and managers wanted to bargain locally and quickly, and the shop stewards were the go-betweens. The shop stewards had no wish to emerge again as a national movement: it suited them well enough that the big trade unions should pretend to be making binding agreements, while they held the real levers in relative obscurity. Far less is known about them than about the general secretaries, but the Donovan Commission of 1968, through its surveys by W. E. J. McCarthy, throws some light: it found that 81 per cent of shop stewards had been to secondary modern schools, more than half were not interested in promotion in their firms, only 30 per cent had some kind of training for their job. Most of them had been elected uncontested, by an electorate of about sixty, and spent about six hours a week on their job.

There is no decisive evidence to show that shop stewards have in themselves worsened labour relations or encouraged strikes Donovan's men surveying the motor industry, said (para. 383): 'Our clear impression, reinforced by our surveys of workshop relations, is that shop stewards in the motor industry, like stewards elsewhere, are in general hard-working and responsible people, who are making a sincere attempt to do a difficult job'; they quoted Professor H. A. Turner's findings that 'strikes had been as common in plants where the stewards' organisation was weak and divided as where it was strong.' But shop stewards serve as lightning conductors for all storms and disturbances; and they know that their status depends on their ability to outbid the national unions, and to keep to piece-work rather than productivity agreements. At British Leyland factories the shop stewards have become more organised with the fear of redundancies; they have their own committee of two hundred, and with a life-long Communist Dick Etheridge as a joint chairman:

> Nothing happens at Longbridge,
> without the nod from Etheridge.

In other industries where stoppages can cost millions, the shop stewards have been able to entrench themselves: at Heathrow Airport, where they negotiate with scores of airlines and other employers, the stewards' committee have established themselves as political as well as wages arbiters, opposing any denationalisation of British airlines.

The trade unions have made some attempts to bring the shop stewards closer to them, and to diminish the gap between what Donovan called the 'formal' and 'informal' structures. Jack Jones and Hugh Scanlon have been trying to decentralise their unions' organisation, and to bring their officials closer to the shop floor, and many of the big unions are spending more on training shop stewards; a careful TUC report published in 1968 stressing that 'activities at the workplace are now the springs of union life', proposed detailed courses for shop stewards, and recommended government subsidies. But the rift between the national unions and the factories has deeper causes than lack of co-ordination and training: it is part of the widespread erosion of central authority, and the desire for workers of all kinds to assert their rights on the spot: as Barbara Castle put it in 1969, 'Democracy is breaking out all over.' In the late sixties, the breaking-out became an acute political problem with mounting unofficial strikes over which their leaders had no apparent control.

STRIKES

There is much argument about international comparison of strikes. The International Labour Office in Geneva publishes annual comparisons, which in 1969 showed that Britain was fifth in the list of strike-prone industrial countries: these were the working days lost per thousand workers—in mining, manufacturing, construction and transport:

Italy	4,110
Canada (preliminary figures)	2,550
US (including gas, electricity and sanitation)	1,390
Australia (including gas, electricity)	810
UK	510
France	200
Japan	200
Belgium	100
Denmark (only manufacturing)	80
Sweden (all industry)	30
West Germany	20
Netherlands	10
Norway	less than 5
Switzerland	less than 5

These figures and other comparisons are much disputed—notably by Professor Turner of Cambridge, who wrote a pamphlet contradicting the assertions that Britain is unusually strike-prone[1] and that countries with stronger legal sanctions against unions have fewer strikes. It is impossible accurately to compare the real effects of strikes in lost production and exports, because one stoppage can have long after-effects and can disrupt many other factories, and the French or Italian style of strikes—with sudden ferocious revolts after years of obedience—cannot be equated. But it is clear that the numbers of days lost in Britain have sharply increased in the last few years. Overleaf are the figures for the decade 1960–70, as calculated by the Department of Employment.[2]

There were more strikes in 1970 than in any year since the general strike of 1926: the worst hit industries were coal-mining, engineering, cars and local government, which each showed more than a million working days lost. It can still be argued, as the TUC like to argue, that the number is small compared to days lost

[1] H. A. Turner, *Is Britain Really Strike-Prone?* Cambridge University Press, 1969.
[2] *Department of Employment Gazette,* January 1970.

Year	Number of stoppages beginning in year	Number of workers involved (thousands)	Number of working days lost (thousands)
1960	2,832	819	3,024
1961	2,686	779	3,046
1962	2,449	4,423	5,798
1963	2,068	593	1,755
1964	2,524	883	2,277
1965	2,354	876	2,925
1966	1,937	544	2,398
1967	2,116	734	2,787
1968	2,378	2,258	4,690
1969	3,116	1,665	6,846
1970	3,888	1,784	10,970

by illness (in 1968, 328 million working days were lost through certified sickness, seventy times as many as were lost through strikes). But the huge increase in strikes in recent years does suggest a breakdown in labour relations; and the great majority of the strikes have been unofficial. The Donovan Report of 1968 reckoned that, between 1964 and 1966, 95 per cent of stoppages were unofficial—though usually much shorter-lived than official strikes.

The huge increase in 1969 and 1970 intensified the demands for trade union reform. The unofficial strikes were specially serious because they were so unpredictable, breaking the schedules for delivery, and sometimes throwing thousands out of work in other factories dependent on them. Britain, being so heavily dependent on exports for her economic survival, is uniquely vulnerable to strikes among key workers—like seamen or dockers—who can produce a disruption out of proportion to their numbers. Nowhere is the fragility of a highly industrial democracy more visible than in this ability of so few to affect so many so quickly.

PARTICIPATION

How far are the strikes and discontent in British industry linked to a deep sense of alienation and boredom, both with the work and the way it is managed? The Donovan Commission, in their study of the motor industry as a specially strike-prone industry, said (para. 384):

> It is possible that boredom may be an indirect cause of disputes by affecting workers' attitudes without their being aware of it, but if so, one would expect it to operate in other countries also, and as we have

pointed out motor manufacture is not remarkable for strike-proneness and participation.

As it happened, while those words were being printed they were being disproved: the near-general strike in France in 1968 was set off by the Renault workers who occupied their factory in Paris and locked up their bosses—an eruption that was the more alarming for being quite unforeseen by managers. Not long afterwards the Italian workers in the Fiat factories in Turin struck with greater ferocity, destroying the shining cars that they had been so peacefully making. The lack of comparable disturbances in Germany is fairly easily explained: for German car factories are manned predominantly by immigrant labour, from Yugoslavia, Portugal or Turkey—men who come to Germany for a few years, to save money to send home, and who stay in their own communities, often speaking no word of the language. Having visited car factories in those three countries, I find it hard to believe that there is not some connection between the conditions—the unskilled and deadly monotonous work, rewarded with high wages but low status and small satisfaction—and the special propensity to strike, often with particular bitterness. Working in a car factory is one of the most dehumanising occupations in the world, without even the muscular challenge of coal-mining, and the fact that much of the machinery has been automated only makes the remaining human operations the more mechanical. Most rich countries rely heavily on immigrant labour for this soul-destroying work; but the British midlands workers, well-paid and well-organised, do not want to give up their strongholds.

It must be doubtful whether car-making, like other mass-production industries, could be made much more satisfying or tolerable by reforming their management; for the whole structure of the industry has to be centralised and sectionalised. But the most obvious remedy for the non-communication with workers seemed to be some form of workers' participation: and this old issue is now, once again, coming into the foreground.

The TUC proposed to Donovan (para. 998), though not with very great enthusiasm, that participation should be introduced at three levels: at plant level, with a shop steward involved in running the plant; at regional level; and at board level with trade unionists among the directors. It is at the top level that workers' participation is most obviously practicable, and in Germany it is enforced by law in the coal and steel industries, where *mitbestim-*

mung (co-determination) requires a third of the directors of the supervisory board to be representatives of the workers: the system, ironically enough, was proposed by the TUC, including Vic Feather, who established the basis for German post-war trade unions. The results are far from perfect: the other directors (one has boasted to me) can often conceal the real facts from the workers' men, and the workers' directors tend to get detached from their own people: but co-determination, I suspect, has done something to improve the German industrial atmosphere. The Donovan Commission (with five exceptions) were however very sceptical about it, and thought that workers' directors would find themselves under intolerable strain.

It is on the shop floor that participation has most attraction to radical workers, and is most abhorrent to managers. The agitation for some form of workers' control goes back to the beginnings of the industrial revolution, and reached a peak before the first world war, among the guild socialists and syndicalists. It largely collapsed (as the shop stewards collapsed) after the failure of the general strike, and during the years of unemployment; but it revived in the fifties, and the New Left became much concerned with 'industrial democracy' (though that term has been largely abandoned now that many members of the Institute of Directors call themselves industrial democrats: the militants now prefer 'workers' control'). In 1968 the Institute for Workers' Control was set up, helped with money from the Bertrand Russell Peace Foundation. It is run from Nottingham, largely inspired by Ken Coates, an extra-mural lecturer at the university. It has a small research staff, publishes pamphlets and books, and organises conferences: Jack Jones and Hugh Scanlon are on the committee. In October 1970 the institute held an extraordinary conference to discuss how to defend the unions against the new Tory legislation: the poster showed a worker holding the globe in one arm and jeering at a gross top-hatted capitalist perched on his thumb. The delegates (I was told by an eye-witness) looked odd bed-fellows. There were ordinary-looking workers from docks, mines, chemical or car factories. There were veteran trade unionists, like Ernie Roberts, assistant secretary of the AUEW and Bill Jones of the T and G, who is on the TUC Council. There were delegates ranging from the left wing of the Labour Party to all the sects (see Chapter 3) of the far left—the International Socialists, the Socialist Labour League, or the Communist Party Marxist-

Leninist. There were workers looking like students, and students looking like workers. The cross-purposes were soon evident: *them* sometimes meant the bosses, sometimes the TUC, sometimes the students: 'The right-wing officer is a greater enemy than the gaffer,' said one militant. 'It's him the gaffer sends for, not us.' The students were impatient of the conservatism of even the most radical workers, and the workers resented student interference: 'They have their role, but they should stick to it. They can help us to leaflet, but not tell us what to do.' Among the intellectuals, there was a basic dispute between the fundamentalists, led by Tony Cliff, who believe in total revolution of the workers, and the gradualists, led by Tony Topham, who believe that limited workers' control is possible within the capitalist framework, and is a crucial stage in creating a consciously socialist mass movement: they took the Yugoslav experiment as their model. But all the champions of workers' control reject the schemes for participation put forward by 'enlightened' managements: the British Steel Corporation's worker-directors, they point out, withhold board secrets from the workers' representatives. Workers' control, they insist, cannot be *given* by even the most well-meaning employer: it has to be taken and won.

The demands for workers' control find little response from the mass of British workers, who are accustomed to a straightforward battle with bosses, and would probably be bewildered without it. But the climate may be slowly changing. Take-overs, mergers and closures emphasise the fact that the vital decisions are taken without the men most involved being consulted: as a group of Liberal lawyers wrote to *The Times* after the Pergamon affair: 'It is unacceptable in a democratic society that people should be treated by private individuals and concerns or state enterprises on an equality with, and all too often as of less importance than, the machines they mind.' The militants had great hopes of a take-over on Merseyside in August 1969, when Arnold Weinstock of GEC had announced 5,000 redundancies in three factories as part of the rationalisation following his merger. The workers held a one-day strike and elected an action committee of shop stewards who then boldly decided to occupy and run the factories: 'This we believe has never before been attempted on such a scale by British workers.' The occupation was planned for September 19th, and militants gathered on Merseyside full of expectation. Two days before, the managing director wrote a letter to the *Liverpool*

Echo, pointing out that the occupation was illegal. That evening a meeting was held outside one of the factories, and the workers voted 60–40 *against* the occupation, with women workers swelling the opposition. It was not a total anticlimax—on the nineteenth itself the Minister of Technology, Anthony Wedgwood Benn, came up to inspect the factories, accompanied by Weinstock; the action committee was able to make their case to Benn. But the great occupation had fizzled out; and the Institute for Workers' Control had to console themselves with the dictum of Rosa Luxemburg: 'The mistakes of the working class are more valuable than the wisdom of the most perfect central committee.'[1]

Workers' control is an issue that will not lie down: it still pops up in odd corners of Europe, even nowadays in Sweden. It is most vocal in Britain, not surprisingly, in communications industries, where producers, journalists and printers are all showing an interest in controlling their products; but as other workers become more educated, more bored and resentful, the movement is likely to spread further. The idea of workers' control on the shop floor can still capture the imagination, and it played a role in the French revolt of 1968, where the electronics workers at Brest actually for a time ran their own factory, and made walkie-talkies for other rebels. Politicians nowadays like to refer to the need for participation, and Wedgwood Benn, influenced by his visit to Merseyside, has become a vague champion of it. But how to reconcile the satisfactions of workers' control with the disciplined needs of mass-production, and the intricate requirements of international trade, is a problem that no one has yet been able to solve.

THE BILLS

The controversy is not about law. It's about power.
Lord Devlin, March 1971.

With the mounting strikes in the mid-sixties both political parties worried more about their effects on Britain's exports, and became more impatient of the TUC's unwillingness or inability to do anything about them. In 1965 Harold Wilson set up the Royal Commission under Lord Donovan, a Law Lord who had once been a Labour MP, to consider the role of trade unions, the rela-

[1] See I.W.C.'s pamphlet No. 17—*Weinstock's Take-over*; and Graham Chadwick: *The Big Flame,* Trade Union Register, 1970.

tions between managements and employees, and the possibilities of changing the law. The commission included (at Woodcock's insistence) the then Secretary of the TUC, George Woodcock; and there were also a former general secretary, Lord Collison, and a range of public figures, including Lord Robens of the Coal Board, Lord Tangley the doyen of solicitors, Andrew Shonfield, soon to be director of Chatham House, and Professor Hugh Clegg, the expert on negotiation. The commission sat for three years, and initiated some detailed research; but it did not recommend the kind of bold remedies that Wilson had hoped for. Most of the commissioners were persuaded that any reforms should be voluntary, and that a change in the law would be 'not only useless but harmful'. They did not want to alienate Woodcock; and their main recommendation was the setting up of a new body, the Commission on Industrial Relations (CIR) to conciliate between employers and unions, but purely on a voluntary basis. (The commission was duly set up, with Woodcock as its first chairman, but he resigned after the Tories had changed the commission's function in 1971.) The most effective dissent came from Shonfield, who wrote what was really a total rebuttal of the findings, but was called a 'Note of Reservation', which expounded the social economists' case for a reform of the law: 'All those who have to rely on the output of a particular body of workers for their livelihood are entitled to a clear assurance about the status and purposes of the organisations in whose name the order to use the strike or other weapons of industrial dispute is issued, and about the responsibilities of those in charge of them.'

While Donovan was reporting, Harold Wilson and many of his government were becoming more determined to press through more drastic cures. A succession of damaging strikes had humiliated the government; the seamen's strike of 1966 and the Mersey dock strike the next year helped to precipitate devaluation in November 1967. There was much new talk of the 'bloody-mindedness' of the British workers, the opinion polls showed growing public resentment of the unions, and the Labour government was losing any reputation it had for being specially able to handle the workers. After Barbara Castle moved into the Department of Employment and Productivity in 1968 she put forward a document called 'In Place of Strife' which had the support of Wilson and Jenkins, and which she was confident could be made law. It aimed to make trade unions more responsible, and to safeguard the workers. But it contained three clauses which were anathema to trade unionists—which would enable the minister to enforce a 28-day 'conciliation pause', to impose a settlement in multi-union disputes, and to insist on ballots being held before strikes.

'In Place of Strife' produced more strife within the party than any other Labour Government measure, threatened the whole delicate relationship with the trade unions, and nearly brought down the prime minister. At first Woodcock and the TUC seemed quite calm, and it was among Labour MPs that the real opposition began. In March 1969 the national executive committee of the Labour Party—which has an awkward and ill-defined relationship (see Chapter 3) with any Labour government—rejected the proposals, and Jim Callaghan joined the majority, thus providing a potential split in the cabinet. Wilson was undeterred, and tried to hasten legislation. Roy Jenkins in his budget speech in April proclaimed that the government would soon introduce legislation based on 'In Place of Strife'. Then the left wing of the party really mobilised: Michael Foot exploded in *Tribune* to say that Wilson and the cabinet were heading for the rocks. An action group of Labour MPs was set up, under Eric Moonman, some of whom were determined if necessary to bring down Wilson. Wilson appeared still unworried: 'I know what's going on,' he said, 'I'm going on.'

The opposition was still mounting: Douglas Houghton, chairman of the Parliamentary Labour Party and a union-sponsored MP, warned Wilson that he could not force the Bill through parliament. The TUC had gradually worked itself up to a position of outright opposition, and quickly put forward an alternative policy called 'Programme for Action', which had very little to propose about unconstitutional strikes. A special congress was held at Croydon, which expressed unalterable opposition to any penal sanctions, and with a huge majority supported 'Programme for Action'. Wilson outwardly stood firm, fortified by the opinion polls: but at the same time he had long meetings with the general council of the TUC, trying vainly to persuade them to enforce more effective discipline. At a cabinet on June 17th he still insisted on legislating, if the TUC would not: but the Chief Whip, Robert Mellish, then warned him that the party would not support it.[1] Wilson then knew he was beaten: he was given a face-

[1] Wilson insists that after the meeting several ministers indicated their support for legislation. See Harold Wilson: *The Labour Government 1964–1970.* July 1971. p. 657.

saver from the TUC, in the shape of a 'solemn and binding undertaking' to oblige unions to press strikers back to work when they were considered at fault. Wilson has since insisted that the TUC gave him what he wanted, 'a new and hopeful dimension in industrial relations'. But everyone knew that Wilson had failed in the reforms which he had described as 'essential to the government's continuance in office'. And Heath in the following debate was able to say: 'He knows, you know, the world knows, after last Wednesday, that although they may still wear the trappings of office, the power resides elsewhere.' The melancholy story did not prove that the TUC was able, in itself, to frustrate a Labour government, for the most effective opposition came from the Parliamentary Labour Party. But it showed that only a prime minister in a position much stronger than Wilson's could defeat the combined forces of the left-wing MPs, the unions and their MPs.[1]

A year after Wilson dropped his Bill the Conservatives were returned to power, and Heath picked up *his* Bill, determined to press it through quickly. The Tory Industrial Relations Bill was based on a document called 'Fair Deal at Work' that had been published in 1968, *before* the Donovan Report: the Bill was presented by the new Minister of Employment, Robert Carr, a shrewd and conciliatory man who had spent much time in industry. Its intentions were not very different from the proposed Labour Bill, and in one important respect—the recompense for unfair dismissal—it was notably more generous. But it was more thoroughly worked out and far more detailed. Its most drastic stipulation was in its redefinition of trade unions and their legal rights, dating back to the act of 1891 which first gave them legal status. Under the new Bill a trade union is defined as 'an organisation of workers which is for the time being registered under the Act'; and *registration* becomes the government's main weapon. For the union to be registered, it has to have its rule book approved by the registrar, and the officials must hold themselves responsible for the actions of their members. If it is *not* registered, it loses its legal status, including its right to protection from suits for damages, and exemption from income tax. The Bill introduced an elaborate new structure of reconciliation, including the old

[1] For an effective analysis of the power equations, see Peter Jenkins' witty and well-informed history of the whole affair: *The Battle of Downing Street*, Charles Knight, 1970, especially p. 159–67.

Commission on Industrial Relations now put on a statutory basis, and an Industrial Relations Court at the top of it, with equivalent status to the High Court. But it was through the registration of trade unions that the government sought to increase the discipline and responsibility of the unions, to control their unofficial strikes: and registration became the inflammatory issue.

Faced with the new Bill, with its embarrassing resemblances to her abortive old one, Barbara Castle made an abrupt turnabout, and attacked it fiercely, as if she had never seen anything like it: it was a saddening spectacle, and a misleading one, for it gave the false impression that the Labour shadow cabinet was solidly against the bill, while most of them were fairly half-hearted: they argued against it dutifully in parliament, but were relieved when it was over. The trade unions in the meantime seemed convinced that if they could stop the last Bill, they could stop this one. The two left-wing leaders of the giants, Jack Jones and Hugh Scanlon, set about organising one-day strikes to frighten the government (which probably merely antagonised public opinion); and the militant shop stewards mustered their armies. In January 1971 the TUC held a mass meeting at the Albert Hall, where Wilson spoke and was booed. The next month about 100,000 workers marched to Trafalgar Square, in what Vic Feather claimed was the biggest organised demonstration ever held in Britain. It was certainly a moving display of the emotional roots of the movement, with brass bands, pipes and banners; the Labour Party leaders were advised by Vic Feather to stay away. In the meantime the Bill was passing inexorably through its Commons committee stages, and the polls still recorded the support of public opinion. On March 18th, when the Bill was virtually passed, the TUC held a climactic special congress in Croydon, as they had done for Wilson's Bill two years before. It was full of melodrama. Outside the hall in pouring rain the shop stewards were chanting 'Kill the Bill'; left-wing girls were handing out passionate pamphlets; Welsh miners huddled under their Victorian embroidered banners; Dundee painters, British Leyland workers, *Radio Times* warehousemen held up their scrawled protests:

FEATHER DON'T BE CHICKEN.
THE HUNGRY YEARS ARE COMING.
YANKEE STYLES STOP WORKERS SMILES.

Inside, the general secretaries debated the central questions, whether the TUC should *instruct* unions not to register under the Bill, or simply (as the TUC recommended) *advise* them not to register; and whether unions should continue one-day strikes (as Jones and Scanlon wanted) in protest against the Bill. The general secretaries spoke with magnificent eloquence—they are the last masters of full-blooded rhetoric, making most MPs or barristers seem like whisperers. Vic Feather opened with sad resignation, insisting that one-day strikes would only arouse public hostility. Jack Jones demanded that the council should lead united industrial action. Bob Edwards of the Chemical Workers, in his quavering revivalist voice, invoked the Tolpuddle Martyrs and Peterloo, and appealed for extra-constitutional methods to sweep the Tories into the dust of history. Jack Peel of the Dyers and Bleachers, with long sideburns, green suit and yellow shirt, warned that if the political strikes succeeded 'you'd lose your system of parliamentary democracy'. Clive Jenkins accused the government of re-starting the class war, and demanded a political strategy for the movement. Dan McGarvey of the Boilermakers (whose voice is so huge that it's rumoured he can *spit* the rivets in) asked where the courage of the pioneers of the movement had gone. Hugh Scanlon bitterly attacked the moderates and said there was still a chance of making the government change its mind. But the most forceful argument against unified action came from Walter Anderson, the precise and quiet-spoken secretary of the local government officers: 'Do you really think that my union will be told what to do by the TUC? . . . It took us forty years to decide to come into the TUC, but it won't take anything like that time to decide to get out of it.' It was the white collar unions, like NALGO and the teachers, who insisted on reserving their right to register under the new Bill; because they knew that, competing with other associations, they would lose members by not registering. The rift between the white collars and the blue at that moment yawned very wide.

The radicals were defeated, and that night Jack Jones admitted that his own union might have to register: the next week the Bill passed through the Commons, and there followed (as the government doubtless intended) a massive anticlimax, with no imminent prosecutions, no rigorous enforcements. The object of the Bill, as the Conservatives explained, was not so much to press home legal sanctions as to construct a new *framework*—the phrase was persistent—against which to solve industrial disputes: like the

Race Relations Bill (it was argued) it would create a new atmosphere and new assumptions. But what was clear was that the changes in the law *had* altered the underlying balance of power between employers and employees, to the benefit of the former.

How far the bill can be *made* to work remains very doubtful. It may appear to strengthen the central power of the general secretaries to enforce their own agreements, to bring the shop stewards in line, to bring the 'formal' and 'informal' structures closer together. But it is very doubtful how far most general secretaries really *want* to be more closely responsible for the shop stewards, or to make enforceable agreements. The oozing of power away from the centre, back to the shop floor, reflects much more than the legal weakness of employers and unions; it is part of the deep questioning of authority, the need for self-assertion, the process of 'democracy breaking out all over', which can be full of hope, as well as danger. The control and containment of this new energy, the balancing of local autonomy with the central authority, will be a growing problem of Britain in the seventies, in the trade unions, as in the civil service, in the universities, or in television. It is a problem which the British, with their instinct for decentralisation, should be well qualified to solve. But the real solution depends not on legislation, but on establishing a sense of security, honest communications, and an atmosphere of trust.

Britain and Europe

37

Britain and Europe

Are we not propounding growth and change in a society where don
and docker alike prefer tradition, leisure and stability? This may be.
But many segments of British society have declared for growth, or at
least for the fruits of growth. Their aspirations can be satisfied—
at a price—and they should know the price they must pay.

> *Britain's Economic Prospects: study by the*
> *Brooking Institute of Washington, 1968.*

It is a very difficult country to move, Mr. Hyndman, a very difficult
country indeed, and one in which there is more disappointment to be
looked for than success.

> *Disraeli to H. M. Hyndman, 1881.*

ANY quest for the sources of power must be a frustrating
journey; the politician, the journalist or the ordinary citizen who
sets out to discover the caves of decision-making finds himself led
through a maze which turns out to have no centre, which leads in
the end back to where it began—to the ordinary people, the
workers, the voters, the consumers. The ambitious member of
parliament, climbing up the rungs of government to the cabinet,
still finds that decisions are taken mysteriously somewhere else;
'Power? it's like a dead sea fruit,' said Harold Macmillan when
he was prime minister; 'when you achieve it, there's nothing
there': and Harold Wilson's memoirs are a sad testimony to how
much he felt himself in the control of others—whether fellow-
politicians, bankers, Treasury officials, or foreign speculators. The
shareholder or employee who tries to pursue power through the
financial maze finds himself likewise baffled, following the trail
through the organograms of management, up to the board who
pretend to be responsible to the shareholders, while the shareholders complain about the invulnerability of the board; and at

the top of the pyramid is a man who complains 'I'm only the chairman.'

THE DISPERSAL OF POWER

In any working democracy the notion of a centre of power—except in wartime—is a contradictory one: the sovereignty of the people by definition excludes a concentration of power. Power in Britain today depends on a confederation of interests, which rarely work together. They could be portrayed as in the diagram on the endpapers of this book: the different spheres of institutions and interest-groups connect up with each other and sometimes overlap, but they have no decisive centre. It is in linking one sphere to another that the capacity to influence events lies. The Treasury's power depends on 'making the connections' (see p. 276): the influence of 'establishment' people, whether Lord Goodman, Lord Cromer or Lord Shawcross, depends on their ability to move from one sphere to another.

Yet any portrayal of the British power-structure in mechanical diagrams must be misleading; for the power to influence events depends not just on pulling levers and pressing buttons, but also on changing opinions and attitudes; and contemporary political scientists are inclined to see parliament's essential role not so much as a legislature, but as a means of mobilising consent or a communications centre. In these terms, the capacity of MPs to influence events looks less discouraging. Every sphere turns out to have fuzzy edges, influenced by the pressures and moods of public opinion. And the power of talk, to change people's attitudes and behaviour, can still make itself felt. This might seem to be contradicted by the new Tory government's insistence on 'action, not words': but they still depend on words (however repetitive) to bring about the change of attitudes which is their principal aim.

In the last decade, nearly all institutions have become more sensitive to public criticism and communications. Governments are more concerned with trying to reform them; the press and television have joined in examining and criticising them. At the same time many professions, like the army and accountants, are anxious to recruit better brains, and to compete for the same talents; they all compare more carefully each other's conditions, salaries and prospects. Nearly every occupation nowadays, whether the army, the police, the stock exchange or even advertising, likes to portray itself as a 'social service': they publicise and promote themselves to their customers or potential recruits as being just as public-spirited as anyone else. Behind this self-caricature there is plenty of humbug; but some of the barriers have been genuinely breaking down. The scientists have nervously woken up to a sense of social responsibilities, and the universities— whether undergraduates or dons—know that their high walls have been scaled and breached.

In its zeal to reform institutions, the decade of the sixties might be compared to the third quarter of the nineteenth century, which established or reformed so many of them. The public and grammar schools, the diplomats, the banks, the Bank of England, the trades unions—they have all been picked over and reported on, and civil service reform has been tackled for the first time for a hundred years. Many of the reports—notably those on diplomats and on Oxford—have been defensive, designed to forestall political action; and it is hard to be confident that the Fulton recommendations will in themselves shake up the civil service. What may prove more important is the sensitivity of the civil servants themselves to the needs of society; for they are no longer so sure that 'to be traduced is our peculiar badge of honour' (see p. 238). Socially-sensitive men inside the bureaucracies (like the late Derek Morrell) may turn out to have more influence than all the Fulton Commissioners.

In finance and industry, consumers have emerged as a menacing army, and have begun to throw their weight about. They can still be taken for a ride by a corrupt insurance company or a fraudulent investment trust; but each scandal forces the government, if not the City, to be more watchful. Consumers on the march can turn stony tycoons into jellyfish; and companies like Unilever or British Leyland, whose profits depend on mass consumers, are becoming quite nervous about them. The shareholders, the theoretical owners of industry, are still a pathetically ineffective army; directors can bamboozle them with phoney accounts, and write each other fat service contracts to make sure they are not sacked. But some investors are beginning to stir; major holders like insurance companies and pension funds are intervening in management; protesting shareholders and customers can seriously embarrass a company like Barclays Bank at its annual meeting, with awkward questions and filibusters. There will certainly be a lot more trouble from shareholders in the seventies, in the wake of Ralph Nader in America.

For this general opening-up, the media of communications must, I believe, take some of the credit; it is now hard for institutions, or their controllers (with some notable exceptions like the legal profession, or Harry Hyams of Centre Point) not to explain themselves to society. But much of the opening-up has been illusory; and skilful public relations can provide glittering shop-windows to conceal murky chops behind the façade. The rule of Old Secrecy (as Bernard Crick calls the British system) is still very strong. Ted Heath's promises of 'open government' have already turned sour: there are few men in his cabinet who show interest in educating the public, let alone opening the windows of Whitehall. In the business world, the accountants firmly side with the directors, not with the shareholders, in concealing the true state of the companies. The media can make periodic raids on the secret headquarters, but the battle is unequal; they are too easily nobbled by ministers or advertisers, or deflected into easier and more entertaining pursuits.

In the meantime, from inside the institutions and companies, the authority of those at the top is increasingly questioned. 'Democracy is breaking out all over', not only in the trades unions, but in universities, in communications, among scientists, back-benchers and even civil servants. The clamour for workers' control may often be cooked up or half-baked (for few workers really *want* control); but the rebels often have enough bargaining-power to limit the scope of the men at the top. The vice-chancellors, the editors, the chairmen, the trades union secretaries—they all complain about being King John; they have all had to give in to their barons.

The search for the centres of power leads over the horizon, to the workers on the shop floors, the middle-managers in the bureaucracies, the consumer groups, the customers and shareholders, and perhaps most important, the agitation groups all over the country. Some of them are localised, like the conservation groups, the tenants' associations, the residents groups to stop airports being built almost anywhere; others are nationally organised for a special purpose, like the Child Poverty Action Group or Shelter. This is a major shift in the pattern of power over the last twenty years—the increasing scope of local and specialised lobbies to influence or defy government. It is probably in local mobilisation—particularly in the cities—that the greatest hope lies of building up proper counterweights or antibodies to the massive concentration of power in Whitehall. A young radical who wants to achieve concrete results may find that local agitation holds out more likely prospects than parliament for improving ordinary men's lives.

This dispersal of power and decisions at the roots presents new problems to parliament—and to the para-parliaments, like television, the press, and the institutes, which can help to educate public opinion. The fashionable clamour for 'participation', which crossed over from France after the revolt of 1968, very easily encourages a muddle of jargon about cybernetics, feedback, or data-banks, which leads no one anywhere. The last thing that is required of parliament—it seems to me—is that it should disperse its own remaining power, and abdicate its responsibility in favour of instant participation and computerised voting. But what is clear is that if parliament is really to be the communications centre of the country, it cannot afford to cut itself off from the movements on the ground or from the mass media, and it has to set out to regain the interest of the electors which has been so notably dwindling. It has to show itself able to inspect and criticise the bureaucracies and workings of government—about which a new generation are both more knowledgeable and more sceptical. To do that, parliament has to develop its committees so that they are seen to be the representatives of the public: and to come to terms with television more boldly than it did with the press.

MERITOCRATS AND THE MIDDLE-CLASSES

What is middle-class morality? Just an
excuse for never giving me anything.
Alfred Doolittle, Pygmalion

The questioning and opening-up of institutions over the last decade has shown itself, too, in the social pattern of the elites, and in the inroads that have been made on the old boy nets of ruling families and public schools. In Tory politics, the age of Macmillan now looks like an aristocratic aberration between the pre-war middle-class cabinets of Chamberlain and Baldwin, and the new middle-class Heath men. In 1962 half Macmillan's cabinet, together with bankers, newspaper owners and ambassadors, could be fitted into the same forest of family trees. There are still a few relics of that cousinhood, like Lord Cromer in Washington, Christopher Soames in Paris, or Lord Carrington at the Ministry of Defence, who has great influence in the cabinet. But these men operate in a colder climate than ten years ago, and they know it; Lord Cromer presents himself to Americans not as the latest of a long line of Barings, but as the champion of self-made New Tories. The disdainful style of Macmillan has given way to the harshly professional style of Heath, and to the cult of the self-made meritocrats.

The sixties saw the apotheosis of the clever grammar-school boy. In the civil service, the public schools' hold has been broken; in five years the proportion who came in from LEA schools went up from 29 to 41 per cent. Even in the diplomatic service, the traditional 'outdoor relief' for the aristocrat, only just over half the new entrants are now public schoolboys (see p. 288). The grammar school men may well have brought with them drive and efficiency, and have helped to dispel the aura of amateurism. The heads of the Treasury and the civil service, Sir Douglas Allen and Sir William Armstrong, are encouraging examples. But there is not very much sign that, abstracted as they are from their backgrounds by the educational sorting-machine, grammar-school men are better able to build bridges between the rulers and the ruled. The big grammar schools like to cultivate *noblesse oblige*, but their products are probably more inclined even than public schoolboys to believe in a more ruthless philosophy of self-help. They can easily become obsessed by competitiveness and efficiency without showing any clear idea of what it is all *for*—the Barber-Thatcher syndrome.

The new meritocrats have consolidated themselves most effectively in industry and the city. They lack the casual communications-system of the old aristocrats—the Old Etonian grapevine, bankers' lunches, the country-house circle. But they are better able to build up new communications, with a mastery of publicity and the mass media; and to exploit (for instance) the new sources of wealth from small investors. A New Boy Net has grown up in conscious rivalry to the old; as appears for instance in the growing resentment of the power of merchant bankers by the pension funds and insurance companies—both sides wanting more control over the companies they invest in.

The victory of the meritocrats is not just over the old Tory aristocrats (the recurring cops-and-robbers epic in Tory history). It is also a triumph over the working-class leadership in the Labour Party. The Labour shadow cabinet has nine Oxford graduates, most of them in the top jobs: and Roy Mason stands

out as the solitary authentic worker. It would be wrong to assume
that this necessarily implies an unawareness of workers' problems.
But many of Labour's mistakes, including the misjudgement of
the trades unions in 1969, could be ascribed to their lack of working-
class roots; and some believe that they lost the 1970 election
because of their lack of 'populist' policies. As Anthony Crosland
suggests (see p. 64) the middle-class leaders easily become preoccupied with seeking the esteem of a coterie audience, who share
their own middle-class values.

It is not so much the middle-classes in general who have
come into power, as the graduates; they have in the last decade
emerged as the nation's rulers in nearly every sphere—graduate
soldiers, graduate stockbrokers, even graduate solicitors—though
not graduate trades unionists. In the sixties the annual output of
graduates doubled; and the degree, though it may now lead
on to unemployment, is the most important step on the ladder to
the top, as it was for Ted Heath. The British can claim that their
universities are more democratic than other Western Europeans'
(with 25 per cent from the sons of manual workers, against 5 per
cent in Germany). But British undergraduates, with their colleges
and grants, are also more separated from the rest of the population, more suddenly jolted from their parents' background to
a new one. This can produce quicker social mobility for those
that succeed; but it can also put up a higher fence between the
graduates and the rest: successful climbers are often quick to forget, or romanticise their origins.

A decade ago Michael Young, in *The Rise of the Meritocracy*,
foresaw a nightmare future in which the clever children would be
selected and segregated so effectively that the rest would be
branded all their lives as stupid; and in 1963 the late Sir John
Newsom, in his report on average and below-average children,
warned of the division into 'Eggheads and Serfs'. The comprehensive schools came into being partly to avoid this disastrous
division; but in the meantime there are some hints of the nightmare coming true—particularly on the frontiers between the
trades unions and the Labour Party. The departure of George
Brown, Ray Gunter, Richard Marsh, Frank Cousins from
Wilson's government—all explosive, self-educated individuals—
left a Labour government and shadow government with a much
more well-behaved, like-minded approach; even such a fiery
radical as Michael Foot is an impeccably Oxford man from good

Liberal stock. On both sides of parliament, the professionalisation of MPs threatens to make the House more and more remote from ordinary people, just when they are aware (see p. 11) that the electorate is becoming more unpredictable. The trades union movement, always suspicious of the glib language of power, feels pushed aside by both parties, particularly by the party it invented and financed, and forced into a common market which is itself associated with an elite of bankers and industrialists.

The extent of the class division comes out into the open in the mass media, which increasingly classify their readers, to suit the advertisers into A and B (middle-class) on the one side, and C, D and E (lower-middle and working-class) on the other. The old 'classless' papers like the *Daily Express* or the old *Daily Mail*, have been threatened at one end by mass papers like the *Mirror* or the *Sun*, and at the other end by the heavies like the *Daily Telegraph* or the *Sunday Times*. When serious newspapers attract working-class readers, the advertisers complain that they are reaching the wrong kind of people; the editorial pages are thus made to reflect the advertisers' class-conscious markets. In television terms, the division is perpetuated by the segregation of BBC 2, and by the pushing of serious programmes into late-night slots (for class in Britain is still firmly associated with *lateness*, whether in getting up, eating or going to bed.)

The divisions of class become increasingly associated with divisions of education and information, between those who know how to organise things to their advantage, and those who do not. The middle-classes have learnt how to use the welfare state, and the services and grants that were originally meant to help the poor are quickly applied for by those who are already well-off. State schools in middle-class areas become middle-class schools; grants for extra bathrooms are taken up by owners of bijou houses; the middle-class lobbies concerned with the environment push up the values of middle-class districts, making them too expensive for others, and the cities become more segregated into rich and poor areas. The attempts to break out of this bourgeois enclosure prove abortive: *Which?*, the potential champion of the mass consumer, turns its attention to burglar alarms and making wills; the Arts Council prefers Covent Garden to fun palaces; the Open University recruits forty per cent of its students from the teaching profession.

This continuing class division exacerbates the problem of involving workers and voters in the process of government and administration. In industrial terms, there are many foreign observers who believe (like Dr. Earle of the London Business School: see p. 591) that the social barrier between managers and workers is the main cause of Britain's poor performance. In political terms, the tendency for middle-class parliamentarians to communicate with each other, and not to project themselves to the mass voters, may well be a main cause for the diminishing numbers who vote, and the dwindling interest in parliament itself.

THE NATION-STATE

While at the base power trickles away out of sight, at the top of the pyramid the member of parliament finds that decisions and policies have become interlocked with other countries, internationalised, interdependent, interpenetrating—and will be much more so inside the common market. Industrialists and bankers have to operate in foreign markets with foreign capital. The Treasury and the Bank of England are locked into agreements with the IMF or the Group of Ten. Defence depends on European allies, on NATO and American equipment. Rolls-Royce cannot survive without American support. The two simultaneous tendencies—the moves downwards towards smaller units, and upwards towards bigger ones combine to present the conundrum of contemporary politics: with its power thus dispersing, what happens to the nation-state?

It would be too simple to deduce that the nation, after a thousand years, is slowly withering away. In the early years of the common market, many idealists hoped and believed that national governments would be gradually bypassed or undermined by the new institutions; that nationalism, with its echoes of war and destruction, would become visibly outdated, that men's loyalties would be taken over by the larger unit and that power would ineluctably pass to the triangle of new institutions: the commission in Brussels, in dialogue with the council of ministers, kept in check by the European parliament. The model for Europe in the fifties was America, which seemed so successfully to have resolved the differences of its fifty states. But the dream never happened. In the common market it has been the council of ministers, with each minister representing the interests of his nation, which has been the decisive European body; the pattern has been de Gaulle's *Europe*

663

des Patries, rather than Monnet's United States of Europe. The recrudescence of nationalism has been much blamed on de Gaulle: but the pattern has been endorsed both by Pompidou and Heath (though not by others in the Six). Its acceptance was the French pre-condition for Britain being allowed into the common market; and Heath could not carry his own party into Europe if he were committed to the dilution or dissolution of national sovereignty.

At the same time the flow of European free trade has shown little sign of having broken down national consciousness; and it can be argued that the common market has served to strengthen patriotic attitudes. Each country's industries have reacted to outside competition by merging into larger units within their own country, and by coming closer to their government. Cars, computers or steel have become more than ever the concern of nations, and there have been only a few convincing mergers across frontiers, like the union of cameras and films (Agfa-Gevaert), of rubber people (Dunlop-Pirelli) and a partial get-together of Citroën and Fiat. The hopes that 'European companies' would emerge to compete with the American giants have not yet come true; not just because of the legal and fiscal snags, but because businessmen still distrust foreigners, and look to the support of their own politicians.

Instead there have emerged the multi-national corporations—mysterious and ubiquitous organisms which are nevertheless not as multi-national as they sound. They often have spectacular polyglot staffs; French, Germans and Italians have found themselves having to work together for the greater glory of Badedas or Daz. But their success depends ultimately on having a strong headquarters, which is itself nearly always firmly nationally based. The big multi-nationals will grow bigger and more multi: the resources of some are bigger than those of medium-sized nations. But their powers have not, as some prophets hoped, made the nation-state look hopelessly obsolete. Far from it: the national governments, faced with these giants, see themselves more emphatically as the guardians of social security, of the environment, of orderly planning and of the interests of local communities. They are the mediators between the defensive interests of small societies, and the aggressive interests of international big business. The role of the nation, whichever party has been in power, has become more socialist, in the sense of taking responsibility for long-term planning and the workings of the welfare state: and the impact of these giant free-ranging companies from outside is likely to enlarge that role. The transfer of this fatherly function to a larger federal unity is not something which the citizens are likely to tolerate for a long time.

While the big companies have become more adventurous abroad, at home they have become increasingly buttressed and encouraged by the state: as Charles Villiers simply put it (see p. 576) when head of the Industrial Reorganisation Corporation, 'Government is in business in a big way, and getting bigger.' The expansion of world trade and the lowering of tariffs have internationalised industry in one sense; but in another sense they have made it more national, for governments have decided that industry is too important to be left to the industrialists. On the Continent (even in Germany, which likes to pretend otherwise), the state and industry have always been more intimate; in Britain the coming-together has been slow and reluctant, with much protest and camouflage from the dinosaurs of the Institute of Directors. But the Labour Government moved much closer to industry, as proclaimed by the formation of the Ministry of Technology and the IRC. The spate of mergers in the late sixties produced new giants which were firmly identified with the British patriotism, summed up in that sad advertisement for British Leyland (see p. 570)—'it has to be good; it's the only motor industry we've got'.

The Labour years seemed to mark the final abandonment of the nineteenth-century idea that governments should leave businessmen alone, and a return to the 'mercantilist' assumptions of the early centuries, when chartered companies were regarded as the chosen instruments of the nation's aggrandisement; in this sense at least Sir Arnold Weinstock and Lord Kearton are New Elizabethans, battling for Britain (as well as for booty) as Drake and Raleigh did four hundred years before. The new glory of industry is reflected in its graduate recruitment, in the mythology of the Troubleshooters, or in the alliance with the diplomatic service—which used to hold itself proudly aloof from salesmen and tycoons, but now condescends to help sell reactors or tourism. Ted Heath's talk about industry 'standing on its own feet' will not make much long-term difference to this trend, even if he wanted it to. IRC is disbanded, Rolls-Royce and Upper Clyde Shipbuilders have been bankrupted: but the problem of maintaining employment and exports is still there, and every government, whether it likes it or not, is now interlocked with every big industry. The more fiercely

Britain faces European competition the more closely the government is likely to involve itself. In the big league, *laissez-faire* is suicide.

The old antagonisms between the different centres of power—industry, the government, the aristocracy, the City, the universities—have helped to give Britain her diverse and pluralist character; the spheres kept away from each other by mutual repulsion. But the antipathies are less evident when they are all in different ways dependent on government, and brought together to defend the national interest. Mussolini's old Corporate State—shorn of its fascist philosophy—is now a kind of model in all industrial countries. It is the vision of a close happy consensus of faceless men, united in both commercial and national ambition, which seems so horrible to protesting students in America and elsewhere. In Britain the consensus is still less bland than elsewhere. For instance, the instinct for university autonomy remains stubborn, and the vice-chancellors and the UGC are suitably buffeted between the parsimonious government and the ungrateful recipients. The scientists and engineers still resist the pressure to be practical, which is disastrous for exports and Rolls-Royce, but may have advantages in encouraging freedom of thought. Nevertheless in Britain, too, the students detect an unholy alliance, as they showed at Warwick University. The search for 'alternative societies' (whatever they are) not surprisingly preoccupies the radical generation in Europe and America: for what alternative is there, when government, industry and universities get together? It may be that the capitalist system provides more freedom than any other; that it can become marvellously flexible and tolerant towards any young consumer, providing him with anything so long as it pays. But a commercial system without any alternative values, whether academic, aristocratic, Christian or socialist, can yet provide a kind of hell for future generations.

The British government, as the guardian of the welfare state and the protector of national industry, appears to have gained strength over the last decades. The notion of the United States of Europe, with a genuinely federalist structure, seems further away than it did ten years ago: and the main incentive for bringing it about—the fear of a European war—has diminished so far as to be hardly credible.

Yet there are still long-term forces at work that will (I believe) render the nations not obsolete, but of dwindling importance. It is still hard to escape the fact that the British nation is quite simply the wrong size—too big for some things, too small for others.

Too small to provide its own sophisticated technology; more important, too small to defend itself. As the Americans withdraw from the defence of Europe, so the Europeans will be forced to integrate more seriously their armies and air forces, (for while the Americans have been there, they have never worried too seriously). They will have to standardise their forces and equipment, and to co-ordinate their diplomatic approaches towards the Eastern bloc, and this will limit much further the scope of the nation in traditionally its most important rôle. Joint defence, with its consequences of joint research and joint production, would lead much more decisively towards political integration than the common market has; the British Ministry of Defence, once interlocked with its European counterparts, would have much less prospect of separate adventures, east of Suez or elsewhere, and the scope for an independent foreign policy would gradually diminish.

At the other end, the nation is beginning to look too big: it finds itself increasingly unable to provide the sense of identification, of belonging, or providing a convincing community to which its citizens can feel loyalty. Wars have always been the great centralisers of loyalty, inspiring the outlying provinces with a sense of nationhood. Without war it is much less obvious to ordinary voters in Dundee or Manchester why fifty million people should be ruled from Westminster, by a cabinet of London-based Oxford graduates, living a few hundred miles away.

The real power of the regional separatist movements, in Britain or elsewhere, is very difficult to assess. Between general elections they flare up, but before the election campaigns the national political parties reassert themselves. The special case of Ulster, which requires troops from other parts of Britain and which may end up with direct rule, is hardly a good advertisement for regional autonomy. But whatever the future of the separatist movements, local loyalties are looming larger, and the mobilising of local opinion, with the help of local press and television, can have an increasing effect on national policies. It is not necessarily a progressive force. Many of the most spectacular local victories are of a negative kind—stopping airports or motorways being built, blocking off streets, conserving old buildings without being interested in new ones. Agitations are often closely linked with the defence of property, and where immigrants or the underprivileged are involved the central government is usually more liberal than the local one. But there are also more populist local campaigns in urban areas; campaigns for neighbourhood councils, for play-centres, for tenants' rights. The mass media have given new scope for groups of residents to pit themselves publicly against both local and national governments. The Tory government's decision to build the third London airport on the sea (or perhaps not at all) was a symbolic victory for the power of relatively small communities. The defence of the environment, and the working out of the balance between industry, land and housing, is essentially a local problem, which cannot be resolved at the centre. Most local councils are pitifully unable to deal with it imaginatively, with part-time and often prejudiced councillors: but their quality should improve as local government is reorganised: already in the last decade local government has become a more acceptable occupation for the kind of administrators who in previous generations would have been ruling the empire.

In the European framework, the scope for the regions is likely to increase (as I tried to show in *The New Europeans*[1]) as provincial interests, like the farmers of Brittany, appeal direct to Brussels. Regions on the edge of one country will find common cause with neighbours across the frontier, while old affinities, between the Celts of Brittany and Cornwall, or between Scotland and France, may reassert themselves, by-passing national capitals. There are already practical patterns for regionalism: Germany has a much more federal structure than Britain's; Italy is acquiring one; Belgium is splitting into two or three. In the very long run there might even be a Europe of Regions, reverting to the old medieval pattern.

In the meantime, the interaction of the different units of loyalty —the neighbourhood, the region, the nation, the continent—will become increasingly fascinating and complex. The loyalties of citizens are already at many different levels. One man may look to his neighbourhood for the defence of his environment; to his borough for his housing and services; to his city or country for his hospitals and schools. At the remote level, he may look to Europe for his technology and his defence. And hedged between these pressures and interests, the nation will remain, for the foreseeable

[1] Anthony Sampson: *The New Europeans*, Hodder and Stoughton, 1968, pp. 432-434.

future, the guardian of his social security and human rights—the protector to whom he turns at times of real danger.

INSTITUTIONS AND EUROPE

If Britain goes into Europe, how will the British institutions and their rulers measure up to their continental equivalents? In the most important field—industry—few people can feel optimistic after the setbacks of the last decade. Economists as well as laymen are forced back to the conclusion that the reason why British industrial growth is so slow is that the British simply do not *want* to grow faster than they do now, or have done over the past hundred years; as the Brookings Report suggests: 'both don and docker prefer tradition, leisure, stability'. Comparing the British industrial atmosphere to the continental, it is hard to avoid the impression that the British zeal for industrial organisation has somehow exhausted itself. At the root of the lack of productivity and exports there is often, I suspect, the basic difficulty that both workers and managers are bored with their jobs; in reports of the causes of strikes and absenteeism, the most obvious factor tends to be left out—that the factories and mines are dehumanising places; that conditions of mass-production are increasingly intolerable, except to people who have only recently escaped from abject poverty. The 'English disease' of wild strikes is beginning to infect the continent: the French and Italians respond more emotionally and alarmingly, with sudden and bitter outbreaks. But the British workers, with a longer history of industrial conditioning, respond with a settled pattern of bloody-mindedness which may be politically less dangerous, but is harder to cope with.

The situation of manufacturing industry is the more discouraging when set against other businesses. It has been noticeable in the course of this book how many of the businesses at which the British still excel are those at which they were expert before the industrial revolution. Banking, insurance, farming, entertainment, were activities which the British were envied for in the eighteenth century; it might look as if the industrial revolution has come and gone, leaving Britain back where she was in 1800. This prospect might seem romantically attractive as viewed from the south-western suburbs of London: and it seems to be mirrored in social terms, in the return to dandyism, to pastoral clothes, to boutiques, bazaars, and fringe newspapers—a kind of intellectual Luddism which rejects all mass organisations. Young designers and artists show William-Morrisy hankerings for pre-industrial crafts, and prefer camp sculptures imitating industrial objects to any serious involvement in industrial design. All this may provide an escape-route of fantasy for those that can afford it; but in terms of the industrial centres of the North, and the ten million men who depend on manufacture for their livelihood, the possibility of Britain simply opting out of its industrial past is quite plainly unthinkable.

The thought of British industry, in this half-hearted state of mind, coming up against naked German competition, is not very comforting. But since British industry depends anyway on export for its survival, it cannot avoid the need to compete, whether inside or outside the market. And the common market at least offers a framework within which British industry could gradually be transformed, in a way that by going it alone she has not so far achieved. No one has been able to prove that the common market has itself been responsible for the higher growth among the Six: but the spectacular recovery of Belgium after 1958—a country which had the same antiquated industries as Britain, and a good deal of her industrial somnolence—suggests that the bigger unit has had a mixture of psychological and structural effects which could stimulate Britain, too.

The belief that British industry—and other institutions—*can* be transformed by a new challenge and a new atmosphere, is encouraged by the success of companies in Britain which have been run by un-British managements. Nothing is more striking in looking at British companies than the ease and speed with which outsiders can transform stagnant companies, and produce dynamic results from the same lot of people. The intrusions have their hazards. Some of the wonder-financiers have been only interested in buying and selling properties, which does nothing for industrial efficiency. In the field of television and the Press the application of ruthless profit motives, whether by Lord Thomson, Rupert Murdoch or Lew Grade, shows little concern for the real problems of communication. But in industry and retailing, the energies of a small number of people and families, from outside traditional British attitudes, have had an impact on consumers throughout the country: the price-cutting operations of Marks and Spencers and Tesco, run by Sieffs and Cohens, have revolutionised shop-keeping: Sir Jules Thorn and Sir Arnold Weinstock have helped transform the electrical business: the South African Mark Weinberg has offered cut-price insurance. American companies operating in Britain, in spite of the troubles like Ford's, show on average a much higher rate of productivity than their British-owned rivals. That suggests that British management is at least as much to blame as British workers; and that Britain—at least in her present state—requires invasions from outside the tribe to invigorate her industry.

If so, then entry into Europe should be able to achieve it, if anything can. Whether the British government would allow (for instance) British Leyland to become Leyland-Mercedes, or General Electric to become Siemens Electric, may be doubtful in the current patriotic atmosphere. But the common market can eventually only operate seriously if it allows not only free trade, but free mergers across frontiers; and in some industries, like chemicals, computers or retailing, the British are quite able to counter-attack. As for the problem of the most antiquated and uncompetitive industries, in the North-east or on the Clyde, they will certainly need a special protection; but the common market in Brussels may well in the end prove a more generous benefactor, as it has for the French peasants, than the national government.

Outside the factories, there are many fields in which the British can hold their own. In finance the British—in spite of the troubles of the pound—have a greater international expertise and more freedom of action than the more bureaucratic money-men of Frankfurt, Paris or Milan; the eighteenth-century enterprise which sent insurance companies and bankers all over Europe has left Britain with a tradition of quick operation abroad. British financial skill is not likely to be much help to British industry; but it can tip the balance of payments. In science, Britain continues to have a better record than other Europeans; while still being reluctant to develop her inventions. (That, too, goes a long way back: when in 1857 Sir William Perkin discovered mauve, the first aniline dye, he soon afterwards returned to pure research, leaving the Germans to develop the vast dyestuffs industry.) There is no reason why the marriage of British inventiveness and German marketing zeal should not eventually produce an effective European technology (as the same mixture does translated across the Atlantic): and the challenge of the Japanese, who can both invent *and* develop, may speed the coming-together.

671

In communications, Britain with her nationally-organised Press and television-oriented population is specially sophisticated; the scale of the British industry allows it to export *The Forsyte Saga* or *The Avengers* all over Europe, with no corresponding imports; and the fact that English is becoming the *lingua franca* of Europe (despite a vigorous rear-guard action from the French) gives Britain a unique advantage in all communications.

But it is not for her commercial advantages that the politicians of the Six want Britain in. The dowry has always been more political than economic; and that is still worth a good deal. I have pointed to many faults, as I see them, in the workings of British democracy in this book—the remoteness of parliament, the introversion of the political parties, the ineffective control over the bureaucracy, the lack of counterweights to government. But there are, I believe, underlying factors in the British system which still give it greater stability and tolerance than the rest of Europe enjoys. The instinct for autonomy of institutions, for decentralisation and for balance remains a strong one. The universities—the most important bastions of autonomy—have weathered the storms of the last five years better than those abroad. The brutalities of the British police cannot be compared to those of the French *CRS*. The British talent for muddle, for all its contrariness, can sometimes amount to an inspired instinct for resisting logic and the instruments of centralisation (like identity cards) where they might restrict personal freedom. The British state, in spite of the move towards *étatisme*, remains a much looser kind of entity than the French or German.

And somewhere in the centre of the British system there is still that rarefied talking-shop, parliament. It is demonstrably unable to pull the wires and levers of its bureaucracies; much less equipped, for instance, than the *Bundestag*. Yet it is still able to represent its people more convincingly than the other assemblies. At critical moments parliament can still emerge as the decisive forum, and it is fitting that the common market issue, which passed so suspiciously quickly through the legislatures of the Six, should in Britain convulse both political parties, and bring the individual MP to the forefront as few other issues have done in this century. For it is the rebellious and questioning spirit of parliamentarians that the continent needs most from Britain. The common market question puts the average British MP, caught between the sense of opportunity of Europe and the suspicions of his electorate, between long-term hopes and short-term fears, into an uncomfortable position. It emphasises all the ambiguity about his duty; whether it is to represent, or to lead. But his role is reduced to a cipher if on the most crucial issue he is not free, in the end, to vote as he thinks best for the country.

The British MP, observing the impotence and pomposity of the European parliamentarians at Strasbourg, trying to cross-examine the technocrats from Brussels, is entitled to misgivings about giving up any part of the British parliament's sovereignty: and there are some like Enoch Powell who resort to a semi-mystical view of parliament as the embodiment of the nation's soul. But the fact is that the limits of Westminster's sovereignty have been receding more rapidly than most members care to admit. The election campaign of 1970 showed how restricted the political argument had become, almost to the level of local government issues—with the two parties arguing about the cost of living, taxes and balance of payments, but both carefully ignoring major issues of foreign policy, whether towards America, Russia, Africa or the common market itself. Both parties knew how little room for manoeuvre was left to them; it was that awareness which converted many members of Harold Wilson's government to trying to join the common market: for no alternative viable foreign policy had emerged.

If Parliament is really to be a credible forum for the British problems of the future, it cannot afford to become a gathering of windbags without substance. It needs not only to make much closer contact with the base; but also to grapple with the real sources of economic and foreign policy, which lie outside the frontiers of Britain.

British Universities

and Polytechnics

UNIVERSITIES

Name and date of first foundation (and date of Charter)	Undergraduates 1969–70 (male/female percentage)	Post-graduates 1969–70	Professors 1969–70	Other academic staff
Aberdeen 1495 Ancient Scottish	4,884 (63/37)	383	57	572
Aston 1894 (1965) Technological	2,501 (89/11)	408	30	368
Bath 1856 Technological	1,695 (84/16)	263	23	232
Belfast 1849 Civic	5,304 (70/30)	660	70	592
Birmingham 1880 (1900) Civic	5,037 (65/35)	1,552	127	1,099
Bradford 1882 (1965) Technological	2,861 (83/17)	457	30	349
Bristol 1876 (1909) Civic	5,200 (63/37)	1,007	87	770
Brunel 1957 (1965) Technological	1,523 (85/15)	167	16	201

Percentage of science to arts students	Percentage of all students in residence/ at home	Distinctive subjects	General
46/54	24/30	Soil technology Fish technology	Three-quarter Scots. Rigorous climate, friendly community. Well sited for ski-ing shooting, fishing and sailing.
89/11	15/29	Communication science Environmental health	At Birmingham. Ex-CAT students, anti-binary system. Flats for married students.
86/14	29/11	Horticulture European Studies	Mostly sandwich courses. Involved in Concorde project. Dr. Who buildings, ignoring splendid ones of Bath.
55/45	15/48	Medieval French Scholastic philosophy	92 per cent Irish. Isolated. Womb of the People's Democratic Movement. 'A pub every ten yards.'
58/42	29/11	Brewing Petroleum production and engineering	Centre for contemporary cultural studies. Range of two-subject degrees. Joseph Chamberlain buildings.
74/26	30/15	Applied languages Colour chemistry Textile design	Business studies. Left-wing VC, Edwards: Harold Wilson, Chancellor. Exchange with Russian students. Gloomy precinct.
53/47	38/2	Drama Domestic Science	Fashionable. Stiff competition to get in. Wills cigarette building with neo-perpendicular tower. Commerce and culture.
88/12	18/24	Cybernetics (post-graduate)	Ex-CAT at Uxbridge. VC, Bragg from Rolls Royce. Sandwich courses. Centre of Home Office Community Development project.

Name and date of first foundation (and date of Charter)	Undergraduates 1969–70 (male/female percentage)	Post-graduates 1969–70	Professors 1969–70	Other academic staff
Cambridge 1284 Ancient	8,246 (88/12)	2,121	131	1,081
City 1891 (1965) Technological	2,196 (93/7)	218	20	272
Dundee 1881 (1967) New (by fission)	2,201 (75/25)	223	41	367
Durham 1832 Collegiate	2,780 (65/35)	571	45	351
East Anglia 1963 (1964) New	2,222 (59/41)	229	33	249
Edinburgh 1583 Ancient Scottish	7,963 (60/40)	1,237	130	1,180
Essex 1964 (1965) New	1,372 (70/30)	319	26	279
Exeter 1922 (1955) Small Civic	2,834 (60/40)	445	40	331

Percentage of science to arts students	Percentage of all students in residence/ at home	Distinctive subjects	General
46/54	68/1	Minerology Petrology Land economy	Students can change courses after yearly exams. Women penetrating male preserve of King's and Clare. Post-graduate colleges mushrooming.
93/7	25/37	Ophthalmic optics Air transport engineering	Most applied scientists, fewest women and books. London. Students live in tower block near St. Paul's.
60/40	39/20	TB VD	25 per cent medics. Now freed from St. Andrew's. Town v. Gown feuds. Much Rugger. Rector, Peter Ustinov.
30/70	75/4	Indian civilisation Hittite studies	Prestigious but sleepy. Small library—57,000 books. Ten colleges: students live in castle of Prince-Bishops of Durham. Rowing.
38/62	61/5	East Anglian studies Music with fine arts	Terraced Lasdun buildings near Norwich. Interdisciplinary studies. Student exodus at weekends. Professor Angus Wilson.
45/55	23/30	Astrophysics Linguistics Banking	Scottish National Library. Political files shindy began there. Student pressure forced sale of South African shares. Rector, Kenneth Allsop.
38/62	26/1	Mathematical social sciences Comparative studies	Students live in tower blocks— no wardens. At Colchester. Peter Townsend, Sociology.
33/67	55/5	Social Studies B.Sc. Physical Geology	Public-school atmosphere though few from public schools. Fine arboretum.

Name and date of first foundation (and date of Charter)	Undergraduates 1969–70 (male/female percentage)	Post-graduates 1969–70	Professors 1969–70	Other academic staff
Glasgow 1451 Ancient Scottish	7,142 (68/32)	672	119	1,160
Heriot-Watt 1821 (1966) Technological	2,338 (90/10)	123	20	217
Hull 1927 (1954) Small Civic	3,378 (62/38)	457	37	434
Keele 1949 (1962) New	1,593 (60/40)	224	23	258
Kent 1964 (1965) New	1,946 (61/39)	226	27	242
Lancaster 1964 New	2,004 (65/35)	329	35	282
Leeds 1884 (1904) Civic	7,207 (69/31)	1,607	99	1,140
Leicester 1918 (1957) Small Civic	2,687 (55/45)	569	41	309
Liverpool 1881 (1903) Civic	5,453 (71/29)	1,100	93	813

Percentage of science to arts students	Percentage of all students in residence/ at home	Distinctive subjects	General
52/48	13/66	Naval architecture Urban studies Biology in Loch Lomond	90 per cent Scottish, many live at home. Four-year course, with general first year (like all Scots universities).
82/19	5/45	Environmental studies Interpreting Translating	Plans to move out of Edinburgh city centre. Mostly Scottish but 7 per cent Norwegians. Too few women. Chancellor, Douglas-Home.
31/69	67/6	Swedish Commonwealth studies South-East Asia	Many Africans. Welcomes those who've come up the hard way. Radical students.
23/77	80/3	American studies Social analysis	All four-year degree courses. Bad public relations. Local authority threatened to cut off grants after nude sun-bathing.
43/57	41/4	Language centre	All halls look down on Canterbury Cathedral. Conservative and extravagant: fine theatre.
28/72	63/6	Czech Operational research Systems engineering	Colleges like York. VC, Charles Carter, ambitious rationaliser. Alec Ross runs education.
55/45	31/12	Chinese Leather science African geology	Civic style very central buildings. Cheapest halls of residence. Institute of Dialect and Folk Life Studies. VC, Lord Boyle.
34/66	63/6	Mass communication British archaeology	Home counties students. Victorian studies centre concentrating on the British Empire.
64/36	28/20	Catalan Egyptology Tropical Medicine Gipsy lore	Tidal Institute and Observatory. Beatles played for Union dances in their early days. School of Architecture.

Name and date of first foundation (and date of Charter)	Undergraduates 1969–70 (male/female percentage)	Post-graduates 1969–70	Professors 1969–70	Other academic staff
London 1836 Collegiate	22,859 (70/30)	8,791	807	5,522
Birkbeck 1823 (incorporated 1926)	1,292 (50/50)	1,059	31	145
Imperial College of Science and Technology 1907	2,400 (69/31)	1,600	80	700
King's College 1829	2,017 (63/37)	721	56	237
London School of Economics 1895	1,629 (of total 74/26)	1,414	54	227
University College 1826	3,605 (62/38)	1,760	119	1,100
Dental and Medical Schools St. Thomas's 13th Century to Royal Free 1874	5,500 approx.			
Loughborough 1908 (1966) Technological	2,031 (91/9)	333	26	223

Percentage of science to arts students	Percentage of all students in residence/ at home	Distinctive subjects	General
68/36	28/23	*You name it, they teach it. Largest library (over 4½ million books). Vast federation, of which these are the most important:*	
67/33		Maths or physics and psychology Crystallography	Mature working students. Mainly post-graduate and 70 per cent part-timers. Rugger and riding. Nikolaus Pevsner, Emeritus Professor.
	734 in halls	Mining Transport	Aspires to become University of South Kensington. Glass palaces spreading through museum-land. Nine-story residential block.
50/50	29·2/	Brazilian studies Theology	Formerly Anglican College— lots of theologians, medics, and lawyers. Principal, General Sir John Hackett.
	10/	Industry & Trade Econometrics Medieval economic history	Overcrowded and factory-like. Good library. Asians and Africans. Becoming more post-graduate. Much student trouble.
	30/	Astronomy Italian history	Forty-seven departments. Bentham one of founders. Lord Annan, Provost. Magazine called *Jaundice*.
			Eleven undergraduate ones: Guy's biggest (1,000), St. George's smallest (fewer than 200). Conservative admissions. Jealously guarded identities. Beer-swilling and rugger.
95/5	80/7	Ergonomics Library studies	Takes sport very seriously. Good vacation and summer studies. Very residential.

683

Name and date of first foundation (and date of Charter)	Undergraduates 1969–70 (male/female percentage)	Post-graduates 1969–70	Professors 1969–70	Other academic staff
Manchester 1851 Civic	6,672 (65/35)	1,408	134	1,223
Manchester (Institute of Science and Technology) 1827	2,462 (89/11)	810	32	449
Newcastle 1834 Civic	4,757 (69/31)	855	93	45
Nottingham 1881 (1948) Civic	4,093 (66/34)	978	69	612
Oxford 1249 Ancient	7,801 (81/19)	3,033	118	1,371
Reading 1892 (1926) Civic	4,084 (60/40)	770	73	674
St. Andrews 1410 Ancient Scottish	2,177 (57/43)	201	38	220
Salford 1896 (1967) Technological	2,953 (90/10)	422	21	427

Percentage of science to arts students	Percentage of all students in residence/ at home	Distinctive subjects	General
55/45	31/15	Near Eastern studies Youth work	Huge expanding precinct extends for miles, including the first student village. Echoing circular library.
90/10	25/17	Polymer chemistry Computers Paper Science	Known as UMIST: adjoins university. Shortage of women. Lord Bowden, ex-minister, Principal.
61/37	36/16	Scandinavian studies	Hived off from Durham. Regional concern with redundant miners. VC, Miller —popular with students.
59/41	57/6	Food science Animal production	Comfortable halls of residence. Campus life. Founded by Boots the Chemist. Computer called 'slave'.
36/64	57/2	Armenian studies Assyriology	The most beautiful. Four million books. Expert at intrigue and public relations.
37/63	56/7	Dairying Sedimentology	'University of the M.4' Agricultural—three farms, dairy museum. Pro-Europe. Much revived.
44/56	63/6	Astronomy Marine biology	Only half Scottish: many public-school boys. Easy to get into. Music good. Beautiful surroundings.
84/16	19/25	Business operation and control Gas engineering	Near UMIST. Wants to expand arts. Mobile TV unit.

Name and date of first foundation (and date of Charter)	Undergraduates 1969–70 (male/female percentage)	Post-graduates 1969–70	Professors 1969–70	Other academic staff
Sheffield 1897 (1905) Civic	4,697 (71/29)	932	82	634
Southampton 1862 (1952) Small civic	3,453 (70/30)	868	67	429
Stirling 1964 (1967) New	553 (51/49)	52	15	110
Strathclyde 1796 (1964) Technological	4,465 (79/21)	585	51	641
Surrey 1891 (1966) Technological	1,994 (72/28)	355	23	263
Sussex 1961 New	2,831 (66/34)	851	57	462
Ulster 1965 New	734 (55/45)	63	13	99
Wales	10,093 (68/32)	2,001	167	1,515

686

Percentage of science to arts students	Percentage of all students in residence/ at home	Distinctive subjects	General
61/39	41/9	Japanese Glass technology Ceramics	Vertical buildings on cramped city site, but extending. Halls of residence in what Sir John Betjeman calls 'the prettiest suburb in England'.
52/48	42/3	Aeronautics Astronautics	Good drama in Nuffield theatre like copper armadillo. Institute of Sound and Vibration Research. New Medical School.
18/82	2/20	Finance and investment Industrial science Technological Economics	Two semesters. Chancellor, Lord Robbins. Most women. Exciting buildings. Between Edinburgh and Glasgow.
67/33	11/63	Librarianship Marketing Hotel management	Famous as Glasgow tech. Twenty per cent business administration. 9–5 university. Richard Rose, Prof. of Politics.
88/12	57/10	Home economics Hotel and Catering management	Guildford campus makes splendid conference centre. Lord Robens, Chancellor. Essex on the cheap?
51/49	32/9	African and Asian studies Experimental Psychology	Stiff competition to get in (12:1). Pioneered schools of study and inter-disciplinary courses. Many specialist units and fringe institutes including Collective Psycho-pathology.
55/45	9/8	Czech Serbo-Croat Welsh Human ecology	Mainly in Protestant Coleraine, which vied for university with Catholic Londonderry. First students 1968.
51/49	37/11	*One third Welsh students. Uneasy federation of colleges in their different towns:*	

Name and date of first foundation (and date of Charter)	Undergraduates 1969–70 (male/female percentage)	Post-graduates 1969–70	Professors 1969–70	Other academic staff
Aberystwyth 1872 (1889)	1,984 (62/38)	406	33	301
Bangor 1884 (1884)	1,869 (62/38)	513	36	324
Cardiff 1883 (1884)	2,776 (63/37)	528	42	369
St. David's, Lampeter 1822 (1969)	267 (70/30)	5	6	35
Swansea 1920	2,870 (65/35)	540	36	422
Welsh National School of Medicine 1893 (1931)	327 (83/17)	9	15	63
University of Wales (Institute of Science and Technology) 1866 (1967)	1,629 (83/17)	141	15	212
Warwick 1964 (1965) New	1,497 (61/39)	296	27	212
York 1963 New	1,815 (55/45)	371	24	246

Percentage of science to arts students	Percentage of all students in residence/ at home	Distinctive subjects	General
36/64	51/3	Plant breeding	First college of the university. National library. Half Welsh. Isolated and close-knit.
55/45	44/5	Marine science	Farm with 1,000 ewes and 130 Friesians. Student life good. Only twelve per cent Welsh but paper *Y Dafodyl* first world-wide Welsh student paper.
53/47	28/16	Mineral exploitation Industrial relations	Most resents lack of autonomy. Portland stone buildings.
0/100	97/3	Pastoral theology	'Anglican cuckoo in non-conformist nest.' Residential.
43/57	30/10	Russian and East European studies Oceanography	Prowess in sport. Biggest Welsh college, dividing into two campuses.
100/0	22/23		Magazine called *The Leech*. In Cardiff.
82/18	26/21	Planning and architecture	Called UWIST. Personal tuition. In Cardiff.
38/62	61/7	Computer science	Bureaucratic. Connections with big business. Aimed to be new MIT. Unique maths teaching.
32/68	57/5	Modern Music	Oxbridge college system transplanted. Lord James, VC. Professor Harry Rée runs education.

POLYTECHNICS

Number of students
(1970–1971)

Name and date of designation	Full-time	Sand-wich	Part-time	Constituent colleges, etc.
Brighton 1970	2,024	487	2,086	College of technology, art. Co-operates with Sussex University. High standard.
Bristol 1969	1,700	450	2,506	Technical college, commerce, art. Outside Bristol (students wanted dock site in centre). Building, finance, ceramics.
City of Birmingham 1971	2,930	—	7,078	Two technical colleges. Centres of commerce, art and design. School of music.
City of Leicester 1969	3,250	—	3,400	Technology, art. Boot and shoe-making. Post-graduate courses. Director (R. E. Wood), chairman of polytechnic directors.
City of London 1970	4,100	380	11,400	Incorporates Sir John Cass College, higher work of the King Edward VII Nautical College. Provost, Arthur Suddaby, building up high standard.
Glamorgan 1970	209	694	1,255	Founded by mine-owners. *Academic* registrar. Only poly in Wales. Engineering.
Hatfield 1969	1,608	—	902	Good site, new buildings. Director, Norman Lindop; go-ahead. Aerodynamics, computers, biology. Hot on student welfare.
Huddersfield 1970	893	324	1,436	Incorporates Oastler College of Education. Assistant director, former minister Gerry Fowler. Building, music, catering, textiles.

691

Name and date of designation	Full-time	Sand-wich	Part-time	Constituent colleges, etc.
Kingston 1970	1,678	804	1,467	A lot of engineering, some art. Architecture, three-dimensional design.
Lanchester 1970	1,662	1,581	1,546	Incorporates Lanchester, Rugby and Coventry colleges. Coventry has arts with new buildings, Rugby mainly engineering. Overseas student exchange. High standard.
Leeds 1970	2,500	730	3,700	Art, technology, commerce. Incorporates Yorkshire College of Education and Home Economics. Architect director, Patrick Nuttgens, ex-don. Town Planning. Course for teachers of mentally handicapped.
Liverpool 1970	3,821	—	7,179	Art, building, commerce and technology. Languages in a four-year course with two periods abroad.
Manchester 1970	3,277	398	5,453	Art, design, commerce. John Dalton College of Technology. University of Manchester diplomas and certificates. Post-graduate theatre course.
Newcastle 1969	1,682	801	2,903	Technology, commerce, art, industrial design. Well-linked with the university. Hospital administration. Purposeful director, Dr. Bosworth.
North-East London 1970	n.a.	n.a.	n.a.	Barking, West Ham and Waltham Forest—very dispersed. Independent and ambitious director, Brosan. Centre for institutional studies. (see p. 173).

Name and date of designation	Full-time	Sand-wich	Part-time	Constituent colleges, etc.
North Staffordshire 1970	854	935	3,413	Two colleges of technology and Stoke-on-Trent College of Art. Ceramics. Mining. Food technology. 500 in residence.
Oxford 1970	1,350	200	3,500	Courses in bookbinding, health visiting, hospital administration, fastening and joining.
Polytechnic of North London 1971	4,500	4,000	—	Former North Western Polytechnic, with Northern. Rubber Technology. Strong social work. Courses for shop stewards, industrial relations. Rows about director Miller, from Rhodesia.
Plymouth 1970	1,500	—	2,000	Only polytechnic in the South-West: uncertain academic status. Maritime studies. Plymouth's cultural precinct.
Central London 1970	2,900	9,000	—	First English polytechnic in Regent St. (1838) and Holborn College. 25 modern languages. Fine new concrete blocks in Marylebone. Famous for photography.
South Bank 1970	1,400	1,200	6,500	Borough polytechnic, Brixton School of Building, City of Westminster College, National College for Heating, Ventilating, Refrigeration and Fan Engineering. Degree in secretarial linguistics.
Portsmouth 1969	2,465	1,169	710	Technology, art and design. Wide welfare services, including family planning and careers advice. Naval architecture. Social studies. Strong physics department—work on satellites.

Name and date of designation	Full-time	Sand-wich	Part-time	Constituent colleges, etc.
Sheffield 1969	522	1,328	1,201	Technology and art. Public housing and business admin. Pre-diploma foundation year. Housed in plate-glass box, surrounded by roads. Gemmology, goldsmiths.
Sunderland 1969	1,079	555	772	Technology and art. Accommodation for over 300. Connections with Durham university engineering.
Teesside 1970	313	780	1,841	Constantine College of Technology in Middlesbrough. Private secretaries' course. ICI land. Largest urban area without a university.
Thames 1970	1,344	1,031	1,748	Divided between Woolwich and higher degree work of Hammersmith College of Art and Building. Advanced marketing. Union officials have sabbaticals.
Trent 1970	1,531	1,346	3,257	Nottingham—Technology, Art and Design. Supported by the university and industry. Thermodynamics.
Wolverhampton 1969	1,200	720	2,950	Colleges of Technology, Art. Computers, Radio-chemistry, X-ray crystallography.

Fifty

Chairmen

FIFTY CHAIRMEN

The Biggest Companies in Britain by Turnover,
as compiled by *The Times 1,000*.   (see p. 601).

Company	Turnover	Capital	Character
Shell Transport and Trading (1)	£2,352m.	£1,910m.	British part (40 per cent) of Royal Dutch/Shell the Anglo-Dutch oil giant formed in 1906, with internationalised management.
British Petroleum (2)	£2,243m.	£1,769m.	Part owned by British government, but completely independent of it; like Shell, sells oil throughout the world, but firmly British based. Three hundred million pound stake in the American Sohio Company.
British-American Tobacco (3)	£1,467m.	£659m.	International company, mostly outside Britain; formed in 1902 to sell tobacco abroad, with export business of Imperial Tobacco (see No. 6) which part-owns it. Now also biggest cosmetics group (Yardley, Lentheric).
Imperial Chemical Industries (4)	£1,355m.	£1,581m.	Formed out of four chemical companies in 1926 in defence against the German I.G. Farben. All British board. Expanding into Europe. In 1971 bought Atlas Chemicals in America.
Unilever Limited (5)	£1,145m.	£548m.	Another Anglo-Dutch merger—formed in 1929 from margarine and soap. Still uneasy alliance between London and Rotterdam, with Dutch end getting stronger. Locked in fierce competition with American Procter and Gamble.

696

Chairman	Salary	Remarks
Sir David Barran	£72,809 (1969)	Born 1912. Winchester and Cambridge. Son of Yorkshire baronet; spent whole life in Shell group: made his name negotiating Kuwait oil supplies. Monocled, right-wing —ex-chairman of Economic League.
Sir Eric Drake	£47,118 (1969)	Born 1910; Shrewsbury and Cambridge. Son of doctor. Accountant; joined BP in 1935. Defended Abadan refinery against Iran government in 1951. Negotiated Sohio deal.
Richard Dobson	£26,250 (1970)	Born 1914. Clifton College and Cambridge. Son of Professor of Greek. Classical scholar. Started with BAT in China (recommended by Keynes); interval as Spitfire pilot. Rose up through marketing. Smokes pipe.
Jack Callard	£62,670 (1970)	Born 1913. Queen's College, Taunton, and Cambridge. Engineer. Life time in ICI, mainly selling paint. Successfully started up ICI Europa. Internationally-minded.
Eric Woodroofe	£40,000 (1969)	Born 1912. Cockburn High School; Leeds University. Scientist, worked up through Unilever research, but very market-minded. Unassuming style. Runs three-man special committee.

Company	Turnover	Capital	Character
Imperial Tobacco Group (6)	£1,120m.	£528m.	Formed in 1901, as defence against American tobacco invasion, out of three big family firms— Wills, Player's and Churchman's. Much limited by cancer: now diversified into frozen food (Ross group). Run from Bristol.
Shell-Mex and BP (7)	£1,028m.	£344m.	Sells oil for Shell and BP in Britain in an uneasy partnership, which may dissolve. Includes 63 terminals, 2,600 road tankers and 400 miles of pipeline.
British Leyland Motors (8)	£970m.	£408m.	Merger in 1967 of Leyland and BMC— digesting with difficulty its scattered components.
General Electric (9)	£898m.	£606m.	Result of mergers first with Associated Electrical Industries in 1967 then with English Electric in 1968 to produce the dominant electrical company.
Courtaulds (10)	£627m.	£510m.	Textile company founded by Huguenot refugee in 1816; vastly expanded through man-made fibres and chemicals, but now faced with over-supply.

Chairman	Salary	Remarks
Sir John Partridge	£36,000 (1969)	Born 1908. Queen Elizabeth's Hospital, Bristol. Started with Imps as junior clerk in 1923: worked up through market research and company secretary. Doggedly defends cigarettes against the doctors. Chairman of CBI.
Thomas Grieve (Vice-Chairman and Managing Director)		Born 1909. Cargilfield and Fettes College, Edinburgh. Whole life in oil, with war interval. Chairman of Joint Board is Sir David Barran, see above.
Lord Stokes	£46,060 (1969)	Born 1914. Blundell's School, Devon, and Harris Institute of Technology, Preston. Began as apprentice. Successful salesman and exporter but faced with appalling managerial and labour problems. See p. 606.
Lord Nelson of Stafford	£40,000 (1970)	Born 1917. Oundle and Cambridge. Son of founder of English Electric. Director of Bank of England. Real power resides with the phenomenal managing-director, Sir Arnold Weinstock (see p. 607).
Lord Kearton	£30,025 (1970)	Born 1911. Hanley High School and Oxford. Chemical engineer: joined ICI, worked in war on atomic energy, then switched to Courtaulds: staved off take-over by ICI, then became chairman (see p. 603).

Company	Turnover	Capital	Character
Esso Petroleum (11)	£563m.	£347m.	British subsidiary of Standard Oil of New Jersey—Shell's giant competitor, competing all over the world, with tigers in the tank, golf balls, etc. Strong American influence.
Guest Keen ana Nettlefolds (12)	£512m.	£320m.	Part of the original Chamberlain engineering empire in the Midlands: still based on Smethwick, with huge range of steel products. Biggest customer of British Steel Corporation.
Associated British Foods (13)	£503m.	£148m.	Food company, including Fine Fare supermarkets, Ryvita, Fortnum and Mason, Twining's tea, Sunblest bread, Allied Bakeries. Large Australian and South African subsidiaries.
Dunlop (14)	£495m.	£298m.	Now merged with Pirelli. Founded by John Boyd Dunlop, a vet who invented an inflatable tyre for his son's tricycle. International ramifications, from Malaysian plantations to Midlands factories.
Ford Motor (15)	£488m.	£240m.	Now wholly owned subsidiary of Ford Detroit. Continuing labour problems. Increasingly competing with Ford factories in Germany and Asia. Huge Dagenham complex.

Chairman	Salary	Remarks
Norman Biggs	£26,000 (1969)	Born 1907. John Watson's School, Edinburgh. First twenty years in Bank of England: joined Esso at 45.
Sir Raymond Brookes	£47,000	Born 1909. Right-wing tycoon, fought hard against Labour government; provocative annual reports. He left school at 14. Began as apprentice engineer in Staffordshire. Made big link with Australian steel.
Gary Weston	£20,000 (1970)	Born 1927. Sir William Borlase School, Oxford and Harvard. One of nine children of Canadian founder, Garfield Weston, now President. Anglicised, also runs Australian business.
Sir Reay Geddes	£35,000 (1969)	Born 1912. Rugby and Cambridge. Son of former chairman. Internationalist: family connections with P & O (see p. 604).
Sir Leonard Crossland	£31,741 (1969)	Born 1914. Penistone Grammar School. Worked up through Ford buying department. Strong managing director, William Batty. But real power lies in Detroit.

Company	Turnover	Capital	Character
Gallaher (16)	£447m.	£125m.	Mainly tobacco—Senior Service, Benson and Hedges, Manikin, Ritmeester, Kensitas, etc. Now also own Mono Pumps, Dolland and Aitchison optical group (from Slater, Walker). Controlled by American Tobacco
Dalgety (17)	£413m.	£89m.	International company selling mainly wool from Australia and New Zealand. Includes estates, factories, poultry, etc.
British Insulated Callender's Cables (18)	£404m.	£212m.	Cable-making monopoly and electrical engineers, making power stations, dams, tunnels, masts, etc. Founded in 1870s—huge expansion with electrical boom. Big government contracts.
Hawker Siddeley Group (19)	£402m.	£234m.	Pioneer aircraft company built up by rugged tycoon, Roy Dobson: merged with Siddeley in 1948. Now operates widely on government interface.
Metal Traders (20)	£388m.	£9m.	Dealers in metals, minerals, chemicals.

Chairman	Salary	Remarks
Mark Norman (non-executive)	£5,000 (1970)	Born 1910. Eton and Oxford. Moved between tobacco and banking. Managing-director of Lazards. Gallahers' is run by managing-director, A. W. H. Stewart-Moore, who earns £23,000.
Lt.-Col. C. P. Dawnay	£6,500 (1970)	Winchester, Oxford, Guards. Hereditary banker, first with the family firm of Dawnay Day, now with Lazards. Establishment board. Managing director Withers earns £35,656.
Lord McFadzean	£22,250 (1969)	Born 1903. Stranraer Academy and High School and Glasgow University. Joined BICC as accountant at 29; chairman for last seventeen years. Pluralist director: much concerned with 'incentives'. Involved in conflict with shareholders over tax-avoidance scheme (see p. 596).
Sir Arnold Hall	£41,769 (1969)	Born 1915. Cambridge. Researcher in aeronautics at Cambridge and Farnborough, later Professor of Aviation. Came into Hawker Siddeley at 40, took over in 1957 from Dobson. Solved Comet disasters. Moves easily between academia and business.
Sir John Brown (non-executive)	£2,233 (1970)	Born 1913. Glasgow Academy. Accountant, pluralist chairman. Most of career in India. Managing-director A. F. Baer earns £23,000.

Company	Turnover	Capital	Character
Distillers (DCL) (21)	£382m.	£332m.	Near monopoly of Scotch whisky and both Gordon's and Booth's gin: formed from family distillers in 1877, based on Edinburgh. Moved into petro-chemicals, but wisely sold out to BP. Adam head-quarters in St. James's Square, full of Scotsmen.
Great Universal Stores (22)	£382m.	£218m.	Huge group of shops, including Burberry's, Weaver to Wearer, Easiphit, Woodhouse, Jax and mail-order companies, built up by Sir Isaac Wolfson before takeovers became respectable.
Marks and Spencer (23)	£361m.	£170m.	Legendary chain of shops built up by Simon Marks and his brother-in-law Israel Sieff (now Lord Sieff, president of the company). Through contracts with suppliers has strong hold on many manufacturers.
Rank Hovis-McDougall (24)	£359m.	£158m.	Biggest flour-milling company in Europe: part of Methodist empire of Lord Rank of the Rank Organisation: now includes Mother's Pride, Mr Kipling, Energen, Cerebos Salt.
Consolidated Tin Smelters (25)	£346m.	£49m.	International smelting company, built up by jet-set Portuguese Patino family. Big interests in tin, non-ferrous metals. Malaysia, Bolivia, Nigeria, etc. Patino president. Now controls Amalgamated Metals (q.v.).

704

Chairman	Salary	Remarks
Alexander McDonald	£30,400 (1970)	Born 1911. Hillhead School. and Glasgow University Bland Scots accountant. Came into whisky in 1947, rose to be chairman of White Horse. Commutes between Edinburgh and London.
Sir Isaac Wolfson	£15,000 (1970)	Born 1897. Queen's Park School, Glasgow. Joined 'Gussies' in 1932, and became its chairman in 1946, after which it leapt ahead. Made fortune of about £60m. Wolfson family still retain control. Sir Isaac shares power with his son, Leonard.
Edward Sieff	£28,200 (1970)	Born 1905. Manchester Grammar School and University. Young brother of Lord Sieff, took over as chairman in 1967. His nephew Marcus Sieff is very evident. Sieff and Sacher families control the company, with large personal holdings.
Joseph Rank	£41,700 (1970)	Born 1918. Loretto. Joined father's firm, Mark Mayhew, later bought by Rank's. Took over as chairman in 1969 from his uncle Lord Rank, now life president. Married daughter of Shell tycoon, Lord Southborough. Egg-farmer.
E. R. E. Carter	£6,267 (1969)	Born 1923. Canadian lawyer, operates mainly from Canada where he is also president of the Patino Mining Corp. Managing-director, J. A. McKee.

Company	Turnover	Capital	Character
Allied Breweries (26)	£346m.	£319m.	Biggest beer merger, created in 1961, including Ind Coope, Tetley, Ansells, making Double Diamond, Skol etc.: also second biggest in Holland. Unilever tried to take over. Merged with Harvey's and Babycham.
Rio Tinto Zinc (27)	£338m.	£575m.	Mining company based on white Commonwealth: huge expansion in ten years.
Shipping Industrial Holdings (28)	£331m.	£20m.	Ship-brokers and shipowners. Brokers to Esso. Owns Clarkson's packaged tours. Blue Chip. Maudling was chairman.
Bass Charrington (29)	£315m.	£332m.	Merger in 1967 of Bass, Mitchells and Butlers with Charrington United —all brewers. 10,600 outlets. Created by Canadian E. P. Taylor.
Reed International (30)	£314m.	£259m.	Paper company, including Wallpaper Manufacturers, Polycell and Spicers: big mills in Australia and Canada. Merged with International Publishing Corporation 1970.
F. W. Woolworth (31)	£312m.	£165m.	Original sixpenny store, now much eclipsed by Marks and Spencer and supermarkets. Trying to improve image with new symbol, and brands, 'trading up'. 52 per cent owned by American parent.

Chairman	Salary	Remarks
Joe Thorley	£13,209 (1970)	Born 1913. Ratcliffe College, Leicester. Son of managing-director of Ind Coope. Surveyor, then joined father's company. Japanese prisoner-of-war. Beer man, pushed out wine man (Sir Derek Pritchard) in 1970.
Sir Val Duncan	£45,000 (1969)	Born 1913. Harrow and Oxford. Barrister. Control Commission in Germany, then Coal Board. Brought into RTZ by banker Sir Mark Turner: built it up from one Spanish mine (see p. 605).
J. O. Hambro (non-executive)	£3,000 (1969)	Born 1919. Eton and Cambridge. Chairman of Hambro's Bank. Keen Tory. Company driven by Sir Alexander Glen, crackling with power.
Alan Walker	£32,110 (1970)	Born 1910. Private education. Former managing-director of United Molasses (Tate and Lyle): called in by Mitchells and Butlers; survived all mergers. Ruthlessly shuts down breweries. Gets up at 5.15.
Don Ryder	£30,491 (1970)	Born 1917. Ealing. Editor of *Stock Exchange Gazette*. Became protégé of Cecil King: managing-director of Reed in 1963, under King. Works 18-hour day. See p. 385.
E. L. G. Medcalf	£25,432 (1970)	Born 1912. Secondary education. Joined company as trainee in Liverpool: worked up through Woolworth's branches. Much criticised by ginger-group of shareholders.

Company	Turnover	Capital	Character
Unigate (32)	£301m.	£89m.	Merger of United Dairies with Cow and Gate in 1959. Includes St Ivel, Uniwash Launderettes, Kentucky Fried Chicken and Trufood: biggest supplier of butter and cheese. Seven hundred shops.
Rolls-Royce (33)	£299m.	£223m.	Aero-engines and motor-cars: the tragic failure story of 1971 (see Chapter 32).
Tube Investments (34)	£294m.	£247m.	Midlands engineering group, including Creda cookers, Raleigh bicycles, Debonair spin dryers, Churchills machine tools. British Aluminium.
Union International (35)	£289m.	£73m.	Blue Star Line. Meat combine, owning refrigerated ships, butchers shops (Dewhurst, Eastmans, Hammett, etc.) Headquarters in Smithfield. Controlled by millionaire Vestey family.
C. T. Bowring and Co. (36)	£281m.	£52m.	Insurance brokers and ship-owners, founded in 1811, with world-wide subsidiaries.
Sears Holdings (37)	£277m.	£218m.	Half the shoe shops in Britain, including Dolcis, Saxone, Lilley and Skinner, Manfield, Freeman, Hardy and Willis, Selfridges and other big stores. Knitting machinery. Car sales. Laundries.

Chairman	Salary	Remarks
Sir James Barker	£20,550 (1969)	Born 1914. Colchester Royal Grammar. Began in Rose's Lime Juice—later merged with Schweppes where he became managing-director. Switched to Unigate at 55; first boss from outside Price family.
Lord Cole	£39,616 (1969)	Born 1906. Raffles School, Singapore. Ex-chairman of Unilever: brought out of retirement to salvage Rolls-Royce in 1970.
Lord Plowden	£42,200 (1969)	Born 1907. Switzerland and Cambridge. Donnish; ex-civil servant and postwar planner: became chairman Atomic Energy Authority; Chairman for last ten years, with another ex-civil servant, Sir William Strath, as deputy-chairman.
H. M. Synge (non-executive)	£1,000 (1969)	Born 1921. Shrewsbury School. Liverpool stockbroker: succeeded father as chairman in 1969, presiding over board of Vesteys. Shooting and private flying.
Ian Skimming	£47,549 (1969)	Born 1920. Eton. Joined family firm in 1938: interval in Guards: one of the highest-paid men in the City (see p. 519).
Sir Charles Clore	£3,600 (1970)	Born 1904. Educated London. One of richest men in Britain. Early takeover king: began at 22 by buying Cricklewood Ice Rink. Owns Hampstead Garden Suburb, Lochness and part of Herefordshire. Knighted by Tories.

Company	Turnover	Capital	Character
Coats, Patons (38)	£268m.	£207m.	Old thread and yarn company based on Glasgow—52 mills in 26 countries. Founded by James Coats in Paisley in 1824, producing millionaire dynasties of Coats and Clarks.
Bowater Paper Corporation (39)	£268m.	£296m.	Britain's biggest newsprint producers: most profits come from America, with biggest mill there. Built up to its present size by Sir Eric Bowater, chairman for 35 years until he died in 1962.
Amalgamated Metal Corporation (40)	£268m.	£25m.	Metal and ores. (See No. 25)
Thorn Electrical (41)	£267m.	£146m.	Electronics company built up by Sir Jules Thorn who came from Vienna in the twenties: television, radio, lighting, etc.
Cadbury Schweppes (42)	£262m.	£189m.	Merger in 1969 of chocolate (Cadbury's and Fry's) with fizzy drinks, with drinks leading.

Chairman	Salary	Remarks
Charles Bell	£27,180 (1969)	Born 1907. Chester City Grammar and Cambridge. Joined Coats, Patons in 1930 as graduate trainee: rose through subsidiary companies. Lives in Dunbartonshire.
Martin Ritchie	£33,302 (1970)	Born 1917. Strathallan School, Perthshire. Joined Glasgow family firm Andrew Ritchie, eventually merged with Bowaters. Large personal fortune. Took over in 1969.
Sir Paul Benthall	£3,000 (1969)	Born 1902. Eton and Oxford. Like Sir John Brown, began in Bengal. Highest-paid director earns £27,007.
Jack Strowger (Chairman-elect)	£10,000 (1970)	Born 1916. Lowestoft Grammar. Suffolk-born accountant, still has (amazing) affection for Lowestoft. Joined Thorn in 1943: prepared Thorn's takeovers. Groomed as heir-apparent by Sir Jules, but with many conflicts.
Lord Watkinson	£24,992 (1969)	Born 1910. Queen's College, Taunton, and London University. Minister of Defence under Macmillan government: began in family engineering business. Deputy is Adrian Cadbury.

Company	Turnover	Capital	Character
Burmah Oil (43)	£253m.	£765m.	Oldest oil company, founded in 1886: discovered oil in Iran and founded BP: still has 23 per cent holding in it. Much criticised by shareholders for lack of diversification. Explores in North America and Asia. Includes Castrol, Rawlplug, etc.
Joseph Lucas (44)	£251m.	£116m.	Midlands company making car and aircraft electrical equipment. Virtual monopoly. Bad labour relations—e.g. Girling Strike of 1969.
Allied Suppliers (45)	£251m.	£61m.	Grocers—retail and wholesale. Includes Home and Colonial Stores and Lipton's. Unilever owns 40%.
C. Czarnikow (46)	£245m.	£7m.	Commodity brokers: biggest sugar-dealers. Agents for Australian government. Connected with Barings and Flemings.
Tesco Stores (47)	£238m.	£42m.	Biggest supermarket chain built up by Sir Jack Cohen the son of a small Whitechapel tailor, who began selling tins of beans in Hammersmith Market. Now has 800 shops.
Rank Organisation (48)	£237m.	£179m.	Originally based on Odeon Cinemas, now extended into Xerox, television, bowling, dance halls, bingo, hotels, etc.

Chairman	Salary	Remarks
James Lumsden (non-executive)		Born 1915. Rugby and Cambridge. Glasgow solicitor, expert on company law. Deputy-Lieutenant of Dunbartonshire. Chief Executive is Nicholas Williams, also solicitor from Rugby, who began in Anglo-Indian family law firm.
K. S. F. Corley	£38,000 (1970)	Born 1908. St Bees School, Cumberland. Joined Lucas at 19, worked his way up. Keeps bees, walks on fells.
Malcolm Cooper	£20,000 (1968)	Born 1907. Joined as lawyer at 24; worked up through management.
R. E. Liddiard	(Private Company)	Born 1917. Oundle and Oxford. Married chairman's daughter. Polish military medal.
Hyman Kreitman	£15,200 (1970)	Worked in family shoe business, married Cohen's daughter and moved into Tesco: took over from father-in-law in 1968 but Cohen still in evidence as President. Runs it from modest office in Cheshunt. Large holding.
John Davis	£64,000 (1970)	Born 1906. City of London School. Domineering accountant. Took over chairmanship in 1962 from Lord Rank, now president. Millionaire in Rank and Xerox shares—richest of 'hired hands'. Supports Conservative Party.

713

Company	Turnover	Capital	Character
Tate and Lyle (49)	£228m.	£163m.	Sugar refiners: United Molasses, etc. Near monopoly. Founder Sir Henry Tate, financed Tate Gallery.
Boots Pure Drug (50)	£224m.	£110m.	Chain of chemists, now including Timothy White's, founded by Jesse Boot, later Lord Trent. Firmly based on Nottingham.

Chairman	Salary	Remarks
John O. Lyle	£20,246 (1970)	Born 1918. Uppingham, and Cambridge. Joined family firm in 1945: took over from Sir Ian Lyle, now president. Family militantly Tory since attempted nationalisation in 1948. Gives £9,000 a year to free-enterprise organisations.
Willoughby Norman	£18,000 (1970)	Born 1909. Eton and Oxford. Married the boss's daughter. Son of baronet. Managing director Dr Hobday is research biochemist —also from Nottingham.

Index

Index

Index

Index

Index

Lord Chancellor, 355, 357–60 (*see also* Hailsham, Lord)
  as reformer, 358–9
  balance of legal and political power, 358
  functions of, 358
  Gardiner as, 359
  protocol, 359
  salary and privileges, 358
Lord Mayor of London, 472, 538
  banquet, 542
  dinners, 474
Lord Rayleigh's Dairies, 564
Lords, 474
Lords, House of, 3, 578
  appointment of deputy speakers, 360
  atmosphere and procedures, 22–3, 26
  attempts at further reform, 24, 25–6
  clubbiness of, 22, 24
  Communist Party representation in, 24, 59
  debate on appointment of judges, 352
  debate on Post Office Corporation, 621
  Law Lords in politics, 356
  life peers (*see separate entry*)
  limitation of powers of, 23–4
  members:
    expense allowance, 23, 202
    analysis of professions, 25
    political balance and Tory top-heaviness, 24, 25
  renunciation of titles, 24
  Rhodesian sanctions, rejection of, 25
Lotery, H., 499
Loughborough University, 242
  Institute of Consumer Ergonomics, 422
Louis XIV, 543
Lovat family, 204
Lovat, Lord
  large private estate, 557
LSE (London School of Economics), 51, 164, 262, 607
  cosmopolitan atmosphere, 180
  Court of Governors, 180
  foundation and background, 180
  student revolt, 180, 182, 185
Lubbock, Eric, 63
Lufthansa, 414
Lugard, Lord, 277
Lumsden, James, Chairman Burmah Oil (*see inset* 50 Chairmen)
Lustgarten, Edgar, 163
Lusty, Sir Robert, 272
Lutine Bell, 514
Lux, 411
Luxembourg,
  leisure habits, 427
Luxemburg, Rosa, 646
Lyle, Sir Ian, 118
Lyle, John, Chairman, Tate and Lyle (*see inset* 50 Chairmen)
Lyons Corner House, 413
Lyons, William, 181

McCann, Erickson, 411
McCarthy, W. E. J., 639
Macaulay, Lord, 236, 237
McClelland, Professor, 284
McClelland, Grigor, 592
  principal Manchester Business School, 592
McCrum, M. W., 133, 134, 138
MacDiarmid, Niall, 527, 623
McDonald, Alexander F., 504
  Chairman Distillers Company (*see inset* 50 Chairmen)
MacDonald, Gus
  Free Communications Group, 467
MacDonald, Ramsey, 70
MacDougall, Sir Donald, 279, 280
McFadzean, Lord, Chairman of BICC (*see inset* 50 Chairmen), 504
  BICC incentive affair, 596
McGarvey, Dan, 651
McGibbon and Kee, 460
McGowan, Lord, 16,
McGowan, Peter, 61
Mackenzie, A. I., Chairman of Scottish Widows, 522
Mackenzie, Kenneth
  The English Parliament, 217
McKenzie, Robert, 15
Mackenzie, W. J. M., translations from Plowden Report, 245–6
McKinsey and Co., 450, 540
  analysis of Bank of England, 542
  penetration of British institutions, 589
Mackintosh, J. P.
  The British Cabinet, 7, 32, 57, 77, 373
  MPs and job satisfaction, 21
McLelland Moores, 505
Macleod, Iain, 87, 89, 90, 91, 92, 93, 98, 178, 278
  death of, 103
  on attractions of cabinet membership, 69
  on ministers and civil servants, 257
Macleod, Lady, of Borve, 463
  ITA member, 463
McLuhan, Marshall, 198
Maclure, Stuart, 168
MacMahon, Kit
  Executive Director Bank of England, salary and education, 540, 542
Macmillan, Harold, 18, 33, 76, 80, 82, 87, 100, 104, 106, 108, 119, 134, 135, 160, 162, 163, 201, 205, 317, 320, 359, 447, 453, 655, 659
  adroitness of, 102–3, 115
  contrast with Heath, 96–7, 98
  crypto-Socialist?, 114
  interdependence of industry and government, 477
  political philosophy, 104
  PR image of unflappability, 416
  purges of, 13, 91, 96
  relationship with Heath, 89–90, 96
  resignation, 218, 360, 482

749

Index

759

Index